The Children of Sánchez

✳

The Children of Sánchez

AUTOBIOGRAPHY OF A MEXICAN FAMILY

OSCAR LEWIS

VINTAGE BOOKS

A Division of Random House

NEW YORK

VINTAGE EDITION, AUGUST, 1963

VINTAGE BOOKS
are published by ALFRED A. KNOPF, INC.
and RANDOM HOUSE, INC.

Manufactured in the United States of America
79C8

I DEDICATE THIS BOOK

WITH PROFOUND AFFECTION AND GRATITUDE

TO THE SÁNCHEZ FAMILY,

WHOSE IDENTITY MUST REMAIN ANONYMOUS

ACKNOWLEDGMENTS

IN THE COURSE OF WRITING THIS BOOK I HAVE ASKED A number of my friends and colleagues to read and comment on the manuscript. I am especially grateful to Professor Conrad Arensberg and Professor Frank Tannenbaum of Columbia University, to Professor William F. Whyte of Cornell University, and to Professor Sherman Paul of the University of Illinois, for reading the final version. I should also like to thank Margaret Shedd, Kay Barrington, Dr. Zelig Skolnik, Professor Zella Luria, Professor Charles Shattuck and Professor George Gerbner for reading an early version of the Consuelo story; Professor Richard Eells for reading part of the Manuel story, and Professor Ralph W. England for reading the Roberto story. For their critical reading of the Introduction I am grateful to Professor Irving Goldman, Professor Joseph B. Casagrande, Professor Louis Schneider, Professor Joseph D. Phillips, and my son Gene L. Lewis.

I am grateful to Dr. Mark Letson and Mrs. Caroline Lujan, of Mexico City, for analyzing the Rorschach and Thematic Apperception tests and for their many helpful insights on the character structure of the members of the Sánchez family. The test protocols, the analyses and my own evaluation of them will be published at a later date. To Gerald Markley, I am grateful for his assistance in translating some of the materials which appear in the Marta story. To my wife, Ruth M. Lewis, companion and collaborator in my Mexican studies, I give thanks for her invaluable assistance in organizing and editing my field materials.

I am indebted to the Guggenheim Foundation for a fellowship in 1956; to the Wenner-Gren Foundation for Anthropological Research and to the Social Science Research Council for grants-in-aid in 1958, and to the National Science Foundation for a research grant in 1959. Finally, at the University of Illinois, I should like to thank the University Research Board for financial assistance, the Center For Advanced Studies for a fourteen-month research assignment in Mexico, and the Department of Anthropology for a leave of absence to carry on this research.

CONTENTS

INTRODUCTION

THIS BOOK IS ABOUT A POOR FAMILY IN MEXICO CITY, Jesús Sánchez, the father, age fifty, and his four children: Manuel, age thirty-two; Roberto, twenty-nine; Consuelo, twenty-seven; and Marta, twenty-five. My purpose is to give the reader an inside view of family life and of what it means to grow up in a one-room home in a slum tenement in the heart of a great Latin American city which is undergoing a process of rapid social and economic change.

In my research in Mexico since 1943, I have attempted to develop a number of approaches to family studies. In *Five Families*, I tried to give the reader some glimpses of daily life in five ordinary Mexican families, on five perfectly ordinary days. In this volume I offer the reader a deeper look into the lives of one of these families by the use of a new technique whereby each member of the family tells his own life story in his own words. This approach gives us a cumulative, multifaceted, panoramic view of each individual, of the family as a whole, and of many aspects of lower-class Mexican life. The independent versions of the same incidents given by the various family members provide a built-in check upon the reliability and validity of much of the data and thereby partially offset the subjectivity inherent in a single autobiography. At the same time it reveals the discrepancies in the way events are recalled by each member of the family.

This method of multiple autobiographies also tends to reduce the element of investigator bias because the accounts are not put through the sieve of a middle-class North American mind but are given in the words of the subjects themselves. In this way, I believe I have avoided the two most common hazards in the study of the poor, namely, oversentimentalization and brutalization. Finally, I hope that this method preserves for the reader the emotional satisfaction and understanding which the anthropologist experiences in working directly with his subjects but which is only rarely conveyed in the formal jargon of anthropological monographs.

There are very few studies in depth of the psychology of the poor in the less well-developed countries or even in our own country. The people who live at the level of poverty described in this volume, although by no means the lowest level, have not been studied intensively by psychologists or psychiatrists. Nor have the novelists given us an adequate portrayal of the inner lives of the poor in the contemporary world. The slums have produced very few great writers, and by the time they have become great writers, they generally look back over their early lives through middle-class lenses and write within traditional literary forms, so that the retrospective work lacks the immediacy of the original experience.

The tape recorder, used in taking down the life stories in this book, has made possible the beginning of a new kind of literature of social realism. With the aid of the tape recorder, unskilled, uneducated, and even illiterate persons can talk about themselves and relate their observations and experiences in an uninhibited, spontaneous, and natural manner. The stories of Manuel, Roberto, Consuelo, and Marta have a simplicity, sincerity, and directness which is characteristic of the spoken word, of oral literature in contrast to written literature. Despite their lack of formal training, these young people express themselves remarkably well, particularly Consuelo, who sometimes reaches poetic heights. Still in the midst of their unresolved problems and confusions, they have been able to convey enough of themselves to give us insight into their lives and to make us aware of their potentialities and wasted talents.

Certainly the lives of the poor are not dull. The stories in this volume reveal a world of violence and death, of suffering and deprivation, of infidelity and broken homes, of delinquency, corruption, and police brutality, and of the cruelty of the poor to the poor. These stories also reveal an intensity of feeling and human warmth, a strong sense of individuality, a capacity for gaiety, a hope for a better life, a desire for understanding and love, a readiness to share the little they possess, and the courage to carry on in the face of many unresolved problems.

The setting for these life stories is the Casa Grande *vecindad,* a large one-story slum tenement, in the heart of Mexico City. The Casa Grande is one of a hundred *vecindades* which I came to know in 1951 when I studied the urbanization of peasants who had moved to Mexico City from village Azteca. I had begun my study of Azteca many years before, in 1943. Later, with the help of the villagers, I was able to locate Aztecans in various parts of the city and found two families in the Casa Grande. After completing my study of village migrants, I broadened my research design and began to study entire *vecindades*, including all the residents irrespective of their place of origin.

In October, 1956, in the course of my study of the Casa Grande, I met Jesús Sánchez and his children. Jesús had been a tenant there for over twenty years and although his children had moved in and out during this time, the one-room home in the Casa Grande was a major point of stability in their lives. Lenore, their mother and the first wife of Jesús, had died in 1936, only a few years before they moved into the Casa Grande. Lenore's elder sister, Guadalupe, age sixty, lived in the smaller Panaderos *vecindad* on the Street of the Bakers, only a few blocks away. Aunt Guadalupe was a mother substitute for each of the children; they visited her often and used her home as a refuge in time of need. The action of the life stories, therefore, moves back and forth between the Casa Grande and the Panaderos *vecindad*.

Both *vecindades* are near the center of the city, only a ten-minute walk from the main plaza or Zócalo with its great Cathedral and Presidential Palace. Only a half-hour away is the national shrine to the Virgin of Guadalupe, the patron saint of Mexico, to which pilgrims flock from all parts of the nation. Both Casa Grande and Panaderos are in the Tepito section, a poor area with a few small factories and warehouses, public baths, run-down third-class movie theatres, over-crowded schools, saloons, *pulquerías* (taverns where *pulque*, a native alcoholic drink, is sold), and many small shops. Tepito, the largest second-hand market in Mexico City, also known as the Thieves' Market, is only a few blocks away; other large markets, La Merced and Lagunilla, which have recently been rebuilt and modernized, are within easy walking distance. This area ranks high in the incidence of homicide, drunkenness, and delinquency. It is a densely populated neighborhood; during the day and well after dark, the streets and doorways are filled with people coming and going or crowding around

shop entrances. Women sell *tacos* or soup at little sidewalk
kitchens. The streets and sidewalks are broad and paved but are
without trees, grass, or gardens. Most of the people live in rows of
one-room dwellings in inside courtyards shut off from view of the
street by shops or *vecindad* walls.

The Casa Grande stands between the Street of the Barbers and the
Street of the Tinsmiths. Spread out over an entire square block and
housing seven hundred people, the Casa Grande is a little world of
its own, enclosed by high cement walls on the north and south and
by rows of shops on the other two sides. These shops—food stores,
a dry cleaner, a glazier, a carpenter, a beauty parlor, together with
the neighborhood market and public baths—supply the basic needs
of the *vecindad*, so that many of the tenants seldom leave the im-
mediate neighborhood and are almost strangers to the rest of Mexico
City. This section of the city was once the home of the underworld,
and even today people fear to walk in it late at night. But most of
the criminal element has moved away and the majority of the residents are poor tradesmen, artisans, and workers.

Two narrow, inconspicuous entrances, each with a high gate, open
during the day but locked every night at ten o'clock, lead into the
vecindad on the east and west sides. Anyone coming or going after
hours must ring for the janitor and pay to have the gate opened.
The *vecindad* is also protected by its two patron saints, the Virgin
of Guadalupe and the Virgin of Zapopan, whose statues stand in glass
cases, one at each entrance. Offerings of flowers and candles surround
the images and on their skirts are fastened small shiny medals, each
a testimonial of a miracle performed for someone in the *vecindad*.
Few residents pass the Virgins without some gesture of recognition,
be it only a glance or a hurried sign of the cross.

Within the *vecindad* stretch four long, concrete-paved patios or
courtyards, about fifteen feet wide. Opening on to the courtyards at
regular intervals of about twelve feet, are 157 one-room windowless
apartments, each with a barn-red door. In the daytime, besides most
of the doors, stand rough wooden ladders leading to low flat roofs
over the kitchen portion of each apartment. These roofs serve many
uses and are crowded with lines of laundry, chicken coops, dove-
cotes, pots of flowers or medicinal herbs, tanks of gas for cooking,
and occasional TV antenna.

In the daytime the courtyards are crowded with people and animals, dogs, turkeys, chickens, and a few pigs. Children play here because it is safer than the streets. Women queue up for water or shout to each other as they hang up clothes, and street vendors come in to sell their wares. Every morning a garbage man wheels a large can through the courtyards to collect each family's refuse. In the afternoon, gangs of older boys often take over a courtyard to play a rough game of soccer. On Sunday nights there is usually an outdoor dance. Within the west entrance is the public bathhouse and a small garden whose few trees and patch of grass serve as a meeting place for young people and a relatively quiet spot where the older men sit and talk or read the newspapers. Here also is a one-room shack marked "administration office," where a bulletin lists the names of families who are delinquent in paying their rent.

The tenants of the Casa Grande come from twenty-four of the thirty-two states of the Mexican nation. Some come from as far south as Oaxaca and Yucatán and some from the northern states of Chihuahua and Sinaloa. Most of the families have lived in the *vecindad* for from fifteen to twenty years, some as long as thirty years. Over a third of the households have blood relatives within the *vecindad* and about a fourth are related by marriage and *compadrazgo* (a ritual relationship between parents, godparents, and godchildren). These ties, plus the low fixed rental and the housing shortage in the city, make for stability. Some families with higher incomes, their small apartments jammed with good furniture and electrical equipment, are waiting for a chance to move to better quarters, but the majority are content with, indeed proud of, living in the Casa Grande.

The sense of community is quite strong in the *vecindad*, particularly among the young people who belong to the same gangs, form lifelong friendships, attend the same schools, meet at the same dances held in the courtyards, and frequently marry within the *vecindad*. Adults also have friends whom they visit, go out with, and borrow from. Groups of neighbors organize raffles and *tandas*, participate in religious pilgrimages together, and together celebrate the festivals of the *vecindad* patron saints and the Christmas *posadas* as well as other holidays.

But these group efforts are occasional; for the most part adults "mind their own business" and try to maintain family privacy. Most doors are kept shut and it is customary to knock and wait for permission to enter when visiting. Some people visit only relatives or *compadres* and actually have entered very few apartments. It is not common to invite friends or neighbors in to eat except on formal occasions such as birthdays or religious celebrations. Although some neighborly help occurs, especially during emergencies, it is kept at a minimum. Quarrels between families over the mischief of children, street fights between gangs, and personal feuds between boys are not uncommon in the Casa Grande.

The people of the Casa Grande earn their living in a large miscellany of occupations, some of which are carried on within the *vecindad*. Women take in washing and sewing, men are shoemakers, hat cleaners, or vendors of fruit and candy. Some go outside to work in factories or shops or as chauffeurs and small tradesmen. Living standards are low but by no means the lowest in Mexico City, and the people of the neighborhood look upon the Casa Grande as an elegant place.

The Casa Grande and the Panaderos *vecindades* represent sharp contrasts within the culture of poverty. Panaderos is a small *vecindad* consisting of a single row of twelve windowless one-room apartments which lie exposed to the view of passers-by, with no enclosing walls, no gate, and only a dirt yard. Here, unlike the Casa Grande, there are no inside toilets and no piped water. Two public washbasins and two dilapidated toilets of crumbling brick and adobe, curtained by pieces of torn burlap, serve the eighty-six inhabitants.

As one moves from the Panaderos to the Casa Grande, one finds more beds per capita and fewer people who sleep on the floor, more who cook with gas rather than with kerosene or charcoal, more who regularly eat three meals a day, use knives and forks for eating in addition to *tortillas* and spoons, drink beer instead of *pulque*, buy new rather than second-hand furniture and clothing, and celebrate the Day of the Dead by attending Mass at church rather than by leaving the traditional offerings of incense, candles, food, and water in their homes. The trend is from adobe to cement, from clay pots to aluminum, from herbal remedies to antibiotics, and from local curers to doctors.

In 1956, 79 percent of the tenants of the Casa Grande had radios, 55 percent gas stoves, 54 percent wrist watches, 49 percent used knives and forks, 46 percent had sewing machines, 41 percent aluminum pots, 22 percent electric blenders, 21 percent television. In

Panaderos most of these luxury items were absent. Only one household had TV and two owned wrist watches.

In Casa Grande the monthly income per capita ranged from 23 to 500 *pesos* ($3 to $40 at the current rate of exchange). Sixty-eight percent showed per capita incomes of 200 *pesos* or less per month, ($16), 22 percent between 201 and 300 *pesos* ($24), and ten percent between 301 and 500 *pesos*. In Panaderos over 85 percent of the households had an average monthly income of less than 200 *pesos*, or $16, none had over 200 *pesos* and 41 percent had less than 100 *pesos*.

Monthly rent for a one-room apartment in Casa Grande ranged from 30 to 50 *pesos* ($2.40 to $4); in Panaderos from 15 to 30 *pesos*, ($1.20 to $2.40). Many families consisting of husband, wife and four small children managed to live on from 8 to 10 *pesos* a day (64¢ to 80¢) for food. Their diet consisted of black coffee, *tortillas*, beans and chile.

In Casa Grande there was a wide range of level of education, varying from twelve adults who had never attended school to one woman who had attended for eleven years. The average number of years of school attendance was 4.7. Only 8 percent of the residents were illiterate, and 20 percent of the marriages were of the free-union type.

In Panaderos, the level of school attendance was 2.1 years; there was not a single primary-school graduate; 40 percent of the population was illiterate; and 46 percent of the marriages were free unions. In Casa Grande only about a third of the families were related by blood ties and about a fourth by marriages and *compadrazgo*. In Panaderos half the families were related by blood and all were bound by ties of *compradzgo*.

The Sánchez family was one of a random sample of seventy-one families selected for study in the Casa Grande. Jesús Sánchez was in the middle-income group in the *vecindad*, earning a wage of 12.50 *pesos*, or one dollar a day, as a food buyer in the La Gloria restaurant. He could hardly support even himself on this amount and supplemented his income by selling lottery tickets, by raising and selling pigs, pigeons, chickens, and singing birds, and, in all probability, by receiving "commissions" in the markets. Jesús was secretive about these extra sources of income, but with them he managed to support, on a very modest scale, three different households located in widely separated parts of the city. At the time of my investigation, he lived with his younger, favorite wife, Delila, in a room on the Street of the Lost Child, where he supported her, his two children by her, her son by her first husband, her mother, and the four children of his son Manuel. Jesús' older wife, Lupita, their two daughters, and two grandchildren, all of whom he supported, lived in a small house he had built in the El Dorado Colony on the outskirts of the city. Jesús also maintained the room in the Casa Grande for his daughter Marta and her children, his daughter Consuelo, and his son Roberto.

Except for an old radio, there were no luxury items in the Sánchez home in the Casa Grande, but there was usually enough to eat and the family could boast of having had more education than most of their neighbors. Jesús had had only one year of schooling, but Manuel, his eldest son, had completed the six grades of primary school. Consuelo had also graduated from primary school and had completed two years of commercial school as well. Roberto left school in the third grade; Marta completed the fourth.

The Sánchez family differed from some of their neighbors by having a servant, who came during the day to clean, do the laundry, and prepare the meals. This was after the death of Jesús' first wife, Lenore, and while the children were young. The servant was a neighbor or relative, usually a widow or a deserted wife who was willing to work for very little pay. Although this gave the family some prestige, it was not a sign of wealth and was not unusual in the *vecindad*.

I was introduced to the Sánchez household by one of my *vecindad* friends. On my first visit I found the door ajar, and as I waited for someone to answer my knock, I could see the rather dreary, run-down interior. The little vestibule which housed the kitchen and the toilet was badly in need of painting and was furnished with only a two-burner kerosene stove, a table, and two unpainted wooden chairs. Neither the kitchen nor the larger bedroom beyond the inner doorway had any of the air of self-conscious prosperity I had seen in some of the better-to-do Casa Grande rooms.

Consuelo came to the door. She looked thin and pale and explained that she had just recovered from a serious illness. Marta, her younger sister, carrying an infant wrapped in a shawl, joined her but said nothing. I explained that I was a North American professor and anthropologist and had spent a number of years living in a Mexican village studying its customs. I was now comparing the life of city *vecindad* families with that of the village and was looking for people in the Casa Grande who would be willing to help me.

To get things started, I asked where they thought people were better off, in the country or in the city. After a few questions of this nature, which I had used to advantage in previous interviews, I began at once with some of the items on my first questionnaire. These called for the sex, age, place of birth, education, occupation, and work history of each family member.

I was almost finished with these questions when the father, Jesús Sánchez, walked in brusquely, carrying a sack of food supplies over his shoulder. He was a short, stocky, energetic man, with Indian features, dressed in blue denim overalls and a straw hat, a cross between a peasant and a factory worker. He left the sack with Marta, spoke a few words of greeting to Marta and Consuelo, and turned suspiciously to ask what I wanted. He answered my questions in short order, stating that country life was far superior to city life because the young became corrupt in the city, especially when they did not know how to take advantage of what the city offered. He then said he was in a hurry and left as abruptly as he had entered.

At my next interview in the Sánchez household, I met Roberto, the second son. He was taller and a shade darker than the other members of the family and had the physique of a trained athlete. He was pleasant and soft-spoken and gave me the impression of being unusually polite and respectful. He was always polite to me, even when he was drunk. I did not meet Manuel, the elder brother, until many months later because he was out of the country at the time.

In the weeks and months that followed, I continued my work with the other sample families in the *vecindad*. I had completed the data I needed on the Sánchez family after four interviews, but I would frequently stop at the Sánchez house to chat casually with Consuelo or Marta or Roberto, all of whom were friendly and offered useful information on *vecindad* life. As I began to learn something about each member of the family, I became aware that this single family seemed to illustrate many of the social and psychological problems of lower-class Mexican life. At this point I decided to try a study in depth. First Consuelo, then Roberto and Marta agreed to tell me their life stories, stories which were taped with their knowledge and permission. When Manuel returned, he also co-operated. My work with Jesús began after I had been studying his children for six months. It was difficult to gain his confidence, but when he finally agreed to allow me to record his life story, this further enhanced my relationship with his children.

Because of the need for privacy in obtaining an independent version of each life history, most of the recording was done in my office and home. Most of the sessions were recorded individually, but on my return visits to Mexico in 1957, 1958, and 1959, I managed to have group discussions with two or three family members at a time. Occasionally, I recorded at their home in the Casa Grande. However, they talked more freely when they were away from their *vecindad*. I also found it helpful to keep the microphone out of their sight by attaching it to their clothing; in this way we could carry on our conversations as if it weren't there.

In obtaining the detailed and intimate data of these life stories, I used no secret techniques, no truth drugs, no psychoanalytic couch. The most effective tools of the anthropologist are sympathy and compassion for the people he studies. What began as a professional interest in their lives turned into warm and lasting friendships. I became deeply involved in their problems and often felt as though I had two families to look after, the Sánchez family and my own. I have spent hundreds of hours with members of the family; I have eaten in their homes, have attended their dances and festive occasions, have accompanied them to their places of work, have met their relatives and friends, have gone with them on pilgrimages, to church, to the movies, and to sports events.

The Sánchez family learned to trust and confide in me. They would call upon me and my wife in times of need or crisis, and we helped them through illness, drunkenness, trouble with the police, unemployment and family quarrels. I did not follow the common anthropological practice of paying them as informants (not informers!), and I was struck by the absence of monetary motivation in their relationship with me. Basically, it was their sense of friendship that led them to tell me their life stories. The reader should not underestimate their courage in bringing forth as they did the many painful memories and experiences of their lives. To some extent this served as a catharsis and relieved their anxieties. They were moved by my sustained interest in them, and my return to Mexico year after year was a crucial factor in increasing their confidence. Their positive image of the

United States as a "superior" country undoubtedly enhanced my status with them and placed me in the role of a benevolent authority figure rather than the punishing one they were so accustomed to in their own father. Their identification with my work and their sense of participation in a scientific research project, however vaguely they conceived of its ultimate objectives, gave them a sense of satisfaction and of importance which carried them beyond the more limited horizons of their daily lives. They have often told me that if their stories would help human beings anywhere, they would feel a sense of accomplishment.

In the course of our interviews I asked hundreds of questions of Manuel, Roberto, Consuelo, Marta, and Jesús Sánchez. Naturally, my training as an anthropologist, my years of familiarity with Mexican culture, my own values, and my personality influenced the final outcome of this study. While I used a directive approach in the interviews, I encouraged free association, and I was a good listener. I attempted to cover systematically a wide range of subjects: their earliest memories, their dreams, their hopes, fears, joys and sufferings; their jobs; their relationship with friends, relatives, employers; their sex life; their concepts of justice, religion, and politics; their knowledge of geography and history; in short, their total view of the world. Many of my questions stimulated them to express themselves on subjects which they might otherwise never have thought of or volunteered information about. However, the answers were their own.

In preparing the interviews for publication, I have eliminated my questions and have selected, arranged, and organized their materials into coherent life stories. If one agrees with Henry James that life is all inclusion and confusion while art is all discrimination and selection, then these life histories have something of both art and life. I believe this in no way reduces the authenticity of the data or their usefulness for science. For those of my colleagues who are interested in the raw materials, I have the taped interviews available.

The editing has been more extensive in some cases than in others. Manuel, by far the most fluent and dramatic storyteller in the family, needed relatively little editing. His story reflects much of its original structure. The Manuel story perhaps more than the others, however, loses a great deal in transcription and translation because he is a born actor with a great gift for nuance, timing, and intonation. A single question would often elicit an uninterrupted monologue of forty minutes. Roberto spoke readily, though less dramatically and more simply, about his adventures, but he was more constrained and reticent about his inner feelings and his sex life. In the case of Consuelo, a great deal of editing was necessary because of the super-abundance of material. In addition to the taped interviews, she also wrote extensively on various incidents about which I had questioned her. Marta showed the least facility for extended monologue and for organization of ideas. For a long time she would answer most of my questions with a single sentence or phrase. In this respect she was like her father. With time and encouragement, however, both of them became more fluent and had their moments of eloquence.

Manuel was the least inhibited in using typical slum slang, with its profanity and strong sexual metaphor. Roberto, too, spoke quite naturally but he would often preface some rough expression with a polite "By your kind permission, Doctor." Marta, too, spoke her natural idiom. Consuelo and her father were the most formal and "correct" and rarely used vulgar terms during the recording sessions.

The translation of lower-class Mexican Spanish has presented for-midable and in some ways insoluble problems, particularly in attempting to find equivalents for slang expressions, idioms, and jokes with sexual innuendo. I have tried to capture the essential meaning and flavor of the language rather than to render a literal translation. Inevitably, some of the unique quality and charm of the original as well as the personal style of each individual has been lost. The English translation gives a surprisingly high level of language and vocabulary to relatively unlettered people. The fluency of language and the vocabulary of Mexicans, be they peasants or slum dwellers, have always impressed me. On the whole, the language of Manuel and Consuelo is somwhat richer than that of Roberto and Marta, per-haps because the former have had more schooling. Manuel's use of such sophisticated terms as "subconscious," "luminaries," and "por-tentous opulence" may be surprising, but Manuel reads the Spanish version of the *Reader's Digest* and has a flair for intellectuality. More-over, in this day and age, even illiterate slum dwellers pick up ad-vanced ideas and terminology from TV, radio and movies.

It will become apparent to the reader that there is a marked con-trast between Jesús Sánchez and his children. This contrast reflects not only the difference in rural and urban backgrounds but also the difference between pre-Revolutionary and post-Revolutionary Mexico.

Jesús was born in a small village in the state of Veracruz in 1910, the very year which marked the beginning of the Mexican Revolution. His children were born between 1928 and 1935 in the slums of Mexico City. Jesús was brought up in a Mexico without cars, movies, radios or TV, without free universal education, without free elections, and without the hope of upward mobility and the possibility of getting rich quick. He was raised in the tradition of authoritarianism, with its emphasis upon knowing one's place, hard work, and self-abnegation. The children of Sánchez, although subject to his domineering and authoritarian character, were also exposed to post-Revolutionary values, with their greater emphasis upon individualism and social mobility. It is all the more striking, therefore, that the father who never aspired to be more than a simple worker managed to raise himself out of the lower depths of poverty, whereas the children have remained at that level.

In the nineteenth century, when the social sciences were still in their infancy, the job of recording the effects of the process of industrialization and urbanization on personal and family life was left to novelists, playwrights, journalists, and social reformers. Today, a similar process of culture change is going on among the peoples of the less-developed countries but we find no comparable outpouring of a universal literature which would help us to improve our understanding of the process and the people. And yet the need for such an understanding has never been more urgent, now that the less-developed countries have become a major force on the world scene.

In the case of the new African nations that are emerging from a tribal, nonliterate cultural tradition, the paucity of a great native literature on the lower class is not surprising. In Mexico and in other Latin American countries where there has been a middle class, from which most writers come, this class has been very small. Moreover, the hierarchical nature of Mexican society has inhibited any profound communication across class lines. An additional factor in Mexico has been the preoccupation of both writers and anthropologists with their Indian problem, to the neglect of the urban poor.

This situation presents a unique opportunity to the social sciences and particularly to anthropology to step into the gap and develop a literature of its own. Sociologists, who have pioneered in studying urban slums, are now concentrating their attention on suburbia to the relative neglect of the poor. Today, even most novelists are so busy probing the middle-class soul that they have lost touch with the problems of poverty and the realities of a changing world. As C. P. Snow has recently stated: "Sometimes I am afraid that people in rich countries . . . have so completely forgotten what it is like to be poor that we can no longer feel or talk with the less lucky. This we must learn to do."

It is the anthropologists, traditionally the spokesmen for primitive people in the remote corners of the world, who are increasingly turning their energies to the great peasant and urban masses of the less-developed countries. These masses are still desperately poor in spite of the social and economic progress of the world in the past century. Over a billion people in seventy-five nations of Asia, Africa, Latin America, and the Near East have an average per capita income of less than $200 a year as compared with over $2,000 a year for the United States. The anthropologist who studies the way of life in these countries has become, in effect, the student and spokesman of what I call the culture of poverty.

To those who think that the poor have no culture, the concept of a culture of poverty may seem like a contradiction in terms. It would also seem to give to poverty a certain dignity and status. This is not my intention. In anthropological usage the term culture implies, essentially, a design for living which is passed down from generation to generation. In applying this concept of culture to the understanding of poverty, I want to draw attention to the fact that poverty in modern nations is not only a state of economic deprivation, of disorganization, or of the absence of something. It is also something positive in the sense that it has a structure, a rationale, and defense mechanisms without which the poor could hardly carry on. In short, it is a way of life, remarkably stable and persistent, passed down from generation to generation along family lines. The culture of poverty has its own modalities and distinctive social and psychological consequences for its members. It is a dynamic factor which affects participation in the larger national culture and becomes a subculture of its own.

The culture of poverty, as here defined, does not include primitive peoples whose backwardness is the result of their isolation and undeveloped technology and whose society for the most part is not class stratified. Such peoples have a relatively integrated, satisfying, and self-sufficient culture. Nor is the culture of poverty synonymous with the working class, the proletariat, or the peasantry, all three of which vary a good deal in economic status throughout the world. In the United States, for example, the working class lives like an elite compared to the lower class of the less developed countries. The culture of poverty would apply only to those people who are at the very bottom of the socio-economic scale, the poorest workers, the poorest peasants, plantation laborers, and that large heterogenous mass of small artisans and tradesmen usually referred to as the lumpen proletariat.

The culture or subculture of poverty comes into being in a variety of historical contexts. Most commonly it develops when a stratified social and economic system is breaking down or is being replaced by another, as in the case of the transition from feudalism to capitalism or during the industrial revolution. Sometimes it results from imperial conquest in which the conquered are maintained in a servile status which may continue for many generations. It can also occur in the process of detribalization such as is now going on in Africa where, for example, the tribal migrants to the cities are developing "courtyard cultures" remarkably similar to the Mexico City *vecindades*. We are prone to view such slum conditions as transitional or temporary phases of drastic culture change. But this is not necessarily the case, for the culture of poverty is often a persisting condition even in stable social systems. Certainly in Mexico it has been a more or less permanent phenomenon since the Spanish conquest of 1519, when the process of detribalization and the movement of peasants to the cities began. Only the size, location, and composition of the slums have been in flux. I suspect that similar processes have been going on in many other countries of the world.

It seems to me that the culture of poverty has some universal characteristics which transcend regional, rural-urban, and even national differences. In my earlier book, *Five Families* (Basic Books, 1959), I suggested that there were remarkable similarities in family structure, interpersonal relations, time orientations, value systems, spending patterns, and the sense of community in lower-class settlements in London, Glasgow, Paris, Harlem, and Mexico City. Although this is not the place for an extensive comparative analysis of the culture of poverty, I should like to elaborate upon some of these and other traits in order to present a provisional conceptual model of this culture based mainly upon my Mexican materials.

In Mexico, the culture of poverty includes at least the lower third of the rural and urban population. This population is characterized by a relatively higher leath rate, a lower life expectancy, a higher proportion of individuals in the younger age groups, and, because of child labor and working women, a higher proportion of gainfully employed. Some of these indices are higher in the poor *colonias* or sections of Mexico City than in rural Mexico as a whole.

The culture of poverty in Mexico is a provincial and locally oriented culture. Its members are only partially integrated into national institutions and are marginal people even when they live in the heart of a great city. In Mexico City, for example, most of the poor have a very low level of education and literacy, do not belong to labor unions, are not members of a political party, do not participate in the medical care, maternity, and old-age benefits of the national welfare agency known as *Seguro Social*, and make very little use of the city's banks, hospitals, department stores, museums, art galleries and airports.

The economic traits which are most characteristic of the culture of poverty include the constant struggle for survival, unemployment and underemployment, low wages, a miscellany of unskilled occupations, child labor, the absence of savings, a chronic shortage of cash, the absence of food reserves in the home, the pattern of frequent buying of small quantities of food many times a day as the need arises, the pawning of personal goods, borrowing from local money lenders at usurious rates of interest, spontaneous informal credit devices (*tandas*) organized by neighbors, and the use of second-hand clothing and furniture.

Some of the social and psychological characteristics include living in crowded quarters, a lack of privacy, gregariousness, a high incidence of alcoholism, frequent resort to violence in the settlement of quarrels, frequent use of physical violence in the training of children, wife beating, early initiation into sex, free unions or consensual marriages, a relatively high incidence of the abandonment of mothers and children, a trend toward mother-centered families and a much greater knowledge of maternal relatives, the predominance of the nuclear family, a strong predisposition to authoritarianism, and a great emphasis upon family solidarity—an ideal only rarely achieved. Other traits include a strong present time orientation with relatively little ability to defer gratification and plan for the future, a sense of resignation and fatalism based upon the realities of their difficult life situation, a belief in male superiority which reaches its crystallization in *machismo* or the cult of masculinity, a corresponding martyr complex among women, and finally, a high tolerance for psychological pathology of all sorts.

Some of the above traits are not limited to the culture of poverty in Mexico but are also found in the middle and upper classes. However, it is the peculiar patterning of these traits which defines the culture of poverty. For example, in the middle class, *machismo* is expressed in terms of sexual exploits and the Don Juan complex whereas in the lower class it is expressed in terms of heroism and lack of physical fear. Similarly, drinking in the middle class is a social amenity whereas in the lower class getting drunk has different and multiple functions—to forget one's troubles, to prove one's ability to drink, and to build up sufficient confidence to meet difficult life situations.

Many of the traits of the subculture of poverty can be viewed as attempts at local solutions for problems not met by existing institutions and agencies because the people are not eligible for them, cannot afford them, or are suspicious of them. For example, unable to obtain credit from banks, they are thrown upon their own resources and organize informal credit devices without interest. Unable to afford doctors, who are used only in dire emergencies, and suspicious of hospitals "where one goes only to die," they rely upon herbs or other home remedies and upon local curers and midwives. Critical of priests "who are human and therefore sinners like all of us," they rarely go to confession or Mass and rely upon prayer to the images of saints in their own homes and upon pilgrimages to popular shrines.

A critical attitude toward some of the values and institutions of the dominant classes, hatred of the police, mistrust of government and those in high position, and a cynicism which extends even to the church gives the culture of poverty a counter quality and a potential for being used in political movements aimed against the existing social order. Finally, the sub-culture of poverty also has a residual quality in the sense that its members are attempting to utilize and integrate into a workable way of life the remnants of beliefs and customs of diverse origins.

I should like to emphasize that the Sánchez family is by no means at the lowest level of poverty in Mexico. About a million and a half people out of a total population of approximately four million in Mexico City live in similar or worse conditions. The persistence of poverty in the first city of the nation fifty years after the great Mexican Revolution raises serious questions about the extent to which the Revolution has achieved its social objectives. Judging from the Sánchez family, their friends, neighbors, and relatives, the essential promise of the Revolution has yet to be fulfilled.

This assertion is made in the full knowledge of the impressive and far-reaching changes which have been brought about by the Mexican Revolution—the transformation of a semifeudal economy, the distribution of land to the peasants, the emancipation of the Indian, the strengthening of labor's position, the spread of public education, the nationalization of oil and the railroads, and the emergence of a new middle class. Since 1940 the economy has been expanding and the country has become acutely production conscious. Leading newspapers report daily in their headlines record-breaking achievements in agriculture and industry and proudly announce huge gold reserves in the national treasury. A boom spirit has been created which is reminiscent of the great expansion in the United States at the turn of the century. Since 1940 the population has increased by over thirteen million, to reach a high of thirty-four million in 1960. The growth of Mexico City has been phenomenal, from one and a half million in 1940 to over four million in 1960. Mexico City is now the largest city in Latin America and the third or fourth largest city on the American continent.

One of the most significant trends in Mexico since 1940 has been the increasing influence of the United States on Mexican life. Never before in the long history of U.S.-Mexican relations has there been such a varied and intense interaction between the two countries. The close co-operation during World War II, the rapid tempo of U.S. investment, which has reached almost a billion dollars as of 1960, the remarkable influx of U.S. tourists into Mexico and of Mexican visitors to the United States, the annual migration of several hundred thousand Mexican agricultural workers to the United States, the exchange of students, technicians and professors, and the increasing number of Mexicans who are becoming U.S. citizens have made for a new type of relationship between the two countries.

The major television programs are sponsored by foreign controlled companies like Nestlé, General Motors, Ford, Procter & Gamble and

Colgate. Only the use of the Spanish language and Mexican artists distinguish the commercials from those in the United States. American department-store retail practices have been made popular in most of the large cities by stores like Woolworth's and Sears Roebuck and Co., and self-service supermarkets now package many American brand foods for the growing middle class. English has replaced French as a second language in the schools, and the French tradition in medicine is slowly but surely being replaced by U.S. medicine.

Despite the increased production and the apparent prosperity, the uneven distribution of the growing national wealth has made the disparity between the incomes of the rich and the poor more striking than ever before. And despite some rise in the standard of living for the general population, in 1956 over 60 percent of the population were still ill fed, ill housed, and ill clothed, 40 percent were illiterate, and 46 percent of the nation's children were not going to school. A chronic inflation since 1940 has squeezed the real income of the poor, and the cost of living for workers in Mexico City has risen over five times since 1939. According to the census of 1950 (published in 1955), 89 percent of all Mexican families reporting income earned less than 600 *pesos* a month, or $69 at the 1950 rate of exchange and $48 at the 1960 rate. (There are 12.50 *pesos* to the dollar.) A study published in 1960 by a competent Mexican economist, Ifigenia M. de Navarrete, showed that between 1950 and 1957 approximately the lower third of the national population suffered a decrease in real income.

It is common knowledge that the Mexican economy cannot give jobs to all of its people. From 1942 to 1955 about a million and a half Mexicans came to the United States as *braceros* or temporary agricultural laborers, and this figure does not include "wetbacks" or other illegal immigrants. Were the United States suddenly to close its borders to the *braceros,* a major crisis would probably occur in Mexico. Mexico also has become increasingly dependent upon the U.S. tourist trade to stabilize its economy. In 1957 over 700,000 tourists from the United States spent almost six hundred million dollars in Mexico, to make tourism the single largest industry in the country. The income from the tourist trade is about equal to the total Mexican federal budget.

One aspect of the standard of living which has improved very little since 1940 is housing. With the rapidly rising population and urbanization, the crowding and slum conditions in the large cities are actually getting worse. Of the 5.2 million dwellings reported in the Mexican census of 1950, 60 percent had only one room and 25 percent two rooms; 70 percent of all houses were made of adobe, wood, poles and rods, or rubble, and only 18 percent of brick and masonry. Only 17 percent had private, piped water.

In Mexico City conditions are no better. The city is made more beautiful each year for U.S. tourists by building new fountains, planting flowers along the principal streets, building new hygienic markets, and driving the beggars and vendors off the streets. But over a third of the city's population lives in slumlike housing settlements known as *vecindades* where they suffer from a chronic water shortage and lacking elementary sanitary facilities. Usually, *vecindades* consist of one or more rows of single-story dwellings with one or two rooms, facing a common courtyard. The dwellings are constructed of cement, brick, or adobe and form a well-defined unit that has some of the characteristics of a small community. The size and types of the *vecindades* vary enormously. Some consist of only a few dwellings, others of a few hundred. Some are found in the commercial heart of the city, in run-down sixteenth- and seventeenth-century two- and three-story Spanish colonial buildings, while others, on the outskirts of the city, consist of wooden shacks or *jacales* and look like semitropical Hoovervilles.

It seems to me that the material in this book has important implications for our thinking and our policy in regard to the underdeveloped countries of the world and particularly Latin America. It highlights the social, economic, and psychological complexities which have to be faced in any effort to transform and eliminate the culture of poverty from the world. It suggests that basic changes in the attitudes and value systems of the poor must go hand in hand with improvements in the material conditions of living.

Even the best-intentioned governments of the underdeveloped countries face difficult obstacles because of what poverty has done to the poor. Certainly most of the characters in this volume are badly damaged human beings. Yet with all of their inglorious defects and weaknesses, it is the poor who emerge as the true heroes of contemporary Mexico, for they are paying the cost of the industrial progress of the nation. Indeed, the political stability of Mexico is grim testimony to the great capacity for misery and suffering of the ordinary Mexican. But even the Mexican capacity for suffering has its limits, and unless ways are found to achieve a more equitable distribution of the growing national wealth and a greater equality of sacrifice during the difficult period of industrialization, we may expect social upheavals, sooner or later.

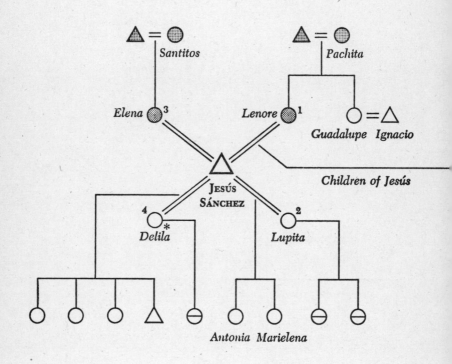

Santitos

Pachita

Elena ⊙³

Lenore ⊙¹

Guadalupe Ignacio

Children of Jesús

JESÚS
SÁNCHEZ

⁴○* Delila

Lupita ²

Antonia Marielena

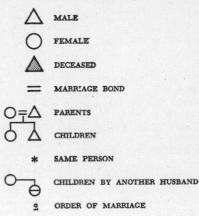

MALE

FEMALE

DECEASED

MARRIAGE BOND

PARENTS

CHILDREN

SAME PERSON

CHILDREN BY ANOTHER HUSBAND

ORDER OF MARRIAGE

and Lenore

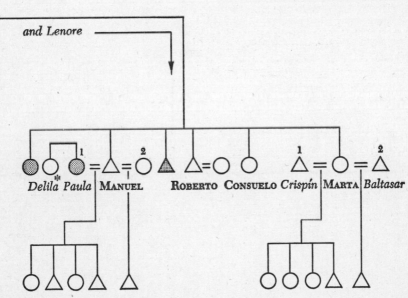

Delila Paula MANUEL   ROBERTO CONSUELO *Crispín* MARTA *Baltasar*

Prologue

Jesús Sánchez

I CAN SAY I HAD NO CHILDHOOD. I WAS BORN IN A POOR LITTLE VILLAGE
in the state of Veracruz. Very lonely and sad is what it was. In
the provinces a child does not have the same opportunities children
have in the capital. My father didn't allow us to play with anybody,
he never bought us toys, we were always alone. I went to school
for only one year when I was about eight or nine years old.

We always lived in one room, like the one I live in today, just one
room. We all slept there, each on his little bed made of boards and
boxes. In the morning, I would get up and make the sign of the cross.
I washed my face and my mouth and went to haul the water. After
breakfast, if they didn't send me for wood, I would sit in the shade.
Usually, I would take a *machete* and rope and would go into the
countryside to look for dry wood. I came back carrying a huge bundle
on my back. That was my work when I lived at home. I worked since
I was very small. I knew nothing of games.

My father was a mule driver in his youth. He would buy goods and
transport them to distant towns for sale. He was completely illiterate.
Later he set up a tiny stand on a road near the village where we were
born. Then we moved to another village where my father opened a
small general store. He had only twenty-five *pesos* in his pocket when
he arrived there, but with that capital he began to work up his business. He had a *compadre* who sold him a large sow for twenty *pesos*
and that sow gave him eleven pigs in each litter. At that time, a two-
month-old pig was worth ten *pesos*. One was a gentleman with ten
pesos then! *Pesos* were really worth something! And that was how my
father began over again, with much perseverance and saving he lifted

[3]

his head again. He began to learn to reckon, to add figures for his accounts and, all by himself, he even learned to read a little. Much later he opened a really big store with a lot of goods, in the village of Huachinango.

I follow my father's example and keep little notes of what I spend. I write down the birthdays of my children, the numbers of my lottery tickets, and what I spend on the pigs and what I earn from their sale.

My father told me very little about himself and his family. All I know about him is that I knew his mother, my grandmother, and a man who was my father's half-brother. We didn't know his father. I never knew my mother's side of the family because my father didn't get along with them.

My father had no one to help him. You know how it is, in some families they don't get along well with one another, like, for example, my daughter Consuelo and her brothers. Some little disagreement comes between them and each one goes his own way. And that's how it was with my father and his people. They lived apart.

In my own family we were more united, but my brothers grew up and left home, each one going his separate way. Because I was the youngest, I stayed at home. My oldest brother joined the army and was killed in an accident. His rifle went off and he killed himself. Then there was Mauricio, the next oldest, he had that store in Huachinango, the second store, because the first one closed up when the Revolution came. My brother Mauricio was in the second store when four men came to rob it. He grabbed one of them and disarmed him. But another one struck my brother from behind and killed him. He died quickly, his belly was ripped open. That's two. Another one was my sister Eutakia. She died over there in Huachinango, when she was still young, about twenty years old. Then there was a brother of mine, Leopoldo, who died here in Mexico City in the General Hospital. So out of the five brothers and sisters—there were six, except one died very young; I was a twin—so there were five of us, and of these five I'm the only one left in the family.

My father was not a loving or affectionate man. Naturally, like the majority of heads of families, he was very economical. He never noticed exactly when I needed something, and in the provinces there wasn't much to spend money on. There were no theatres, no movies, no football, no anything. Now life is fuller but at that time there was nothing. So every Sunday my father gave us only a few *centavos* to spend.

There are all kinds in this world and not all fathers spoil their children. My father believed that too much attention to a child would ruin him. I believe that too. If one spoils a child, he won't grow and develop and become independent. He will be fearful.

My mother was born in a small town, I barely remember the name of it. She was a person who didn't talk much and because I was the youngest, she never told me anything. My mother was a quiet person, a woman with a great heart and she gave me much affection. My father was harder, stricter, more energetic. My mother was a decent and upright woman, conscientious about everything, including her married life. But my parents had their quarrels because my father had another woman and my mother was jealous.

I was about seven years old when my parents separated. The Revolutionaries had already sacked the store . . . the business was finished, the family was finished, our home was broken up, and naturally, I went with my mother and with my brother, who worked as a *peón* on a sugar *hacienda*. I, too, worked in the fields. Two years later my mother got sick and my father came on a *burro* to see us. We were living in a very poor little house. It had a roof only on one side of it; the other side was uncovered. We borrowed corn because we really had nothing to eat. We were very, very poor! There were no medicines of any kind for my mother, no doctors, no anything, and she went to my father's house to die. So their reconciliation took place at the very end.

Well, when my mother died, my tragedy began. I was about ten when I went to live with my father. I stayed there for two years and then left home to work. We had no stepmother until much later, at the very end. I had already left home when this happened. My father married a woman there, a woman who robbed him, took everything away from him and threw him out into the street, she and her brothers. They were about to kill him one night, for his money, but some neighbors stopped them, and then the woman left him. They had had a legal wedding. The woman, together with the people there, took the house and everything from my father.

Then he bought another little house on the other side of town, the same town, and he went into business again. But there he got deathly ill. Yes, at times we men want to be very strong and very *macho*, but at bottom we aren't. When it is about a question of morality or a family thing that touches the very fibers of the heart, it hurts and a

man cries when he is alone. You must have noticed that many people
drown themselves in drink and others grab a pistol and shoot themselves, because they cannot bear what they feel inside. They have no
way to express themselves or anyone to tell their troubles to, so they
grab a gun and that's all. They're finished! And at times those who
believe themselves to be *machos* are really not so when they are alone
with their conscience. They are only braggarts of the moment.

When my father died, he left a little house over there with some
goods, which I took over. I was the only one of his children left. I was
already here in Mexico City, working in the restaurant. Some people
down there sent me a telegram.

When I came, my father was still alive, and I saw him die. He told
me, "I'm not leaving you anything, but I will give you a piece of
advice. Don't get mixed up with friends. It's better to go your way
alone." And that's what I've done all my life.

What he left me was very little. This half-brother of his, together
with the people there, had me thrown in jail. I gave him what my
father left for him in a written will, I was supposed to give him 50 percent. But he was a very lazy man, good for nothing and didn't like to
work. Well, I followed the will to the letter, and according to the law.
Why, I even gave him an old Singer Sewing Machine that was in the
house. I said to him, "You can take this uncle." I, being good-hearted
and sincere, said to him, "Look, this is what goes to you and take this
machine for your wife." Well, even after all of that, he had me thrown
in jail. For a hundred *pesos*! I told him, "You're a miserable so-and-so."
I gave him the hundred *pesos*, the others divided it up and left him
with ten. You see how it was? Even among your own relatives you
can't trust anybody when it comes to money. People want to grab all
they can.

Ever since I was little I liked to work. I was ambitious to earn money
for clothes. I saw my father make money with his little business, and I
wanted to have something of my own, not on a very large scale but
I wanted to earn it with these, with my hands, not with my father's
money. I was never greedy for the inheritance from my father, not at
all. I used to think, "If some day I have some money in my pocket,
I want it to be through my own work, not because somebody gives it
to me, a neighbor, relative, uncle or my father, no, sir. I want to earn
it with these hands of mine." And another thing, when I left home I
knew that if I didn't work, I wouldn't eat.

I was about twelve when I left my father's home. I ran away without telling anyone. First, I worked at a grain mill, then as a field hand on a sugar plantation, and then as a cane cutter. It was hard in the fields and I worked with a hoe all day long in the sun. They paid one and a half *pesos* per thousand canes but I could barely cut half of that and so I earned only seventy-five *centavos* a day, not even enough for food. I was very hungry and passed whole days without food or with only one meal a day. That's why I say, I had no childhood. I worked this way for about four years.

Then I met a Spaniard who owned a corn mill. He knew I had some experience with scales and weighing and one day he said to me, "I am going to Mexico City. If you want to come, I can give you work."

"Yes, sir, I'm ready." All my baggage consisted of a little box that held my clothes. I wanted to know Mexico City as I had never been anywhere before. We took the train the next morning and arrived in Tacuba, where we stayed. After working for him for a while, he threw me out. We had a quarrel over the weights of a scale. He was looking for an excuse to throw me out. You know how people are when they see someone more ignorant and illiterate than themselves! They do what they want, no? At that time I had just come from an *hacienda* and I didn't know anything! My eyes were blindfolded. I didn't know a single street! I had already used up the little money I had. There I was without a *centavo* and not knowing a soul.

Well, as some people say, "Where everything else is wanting, God steps in." There was a man who worked in a mill nearby. He used to pass by every day. One day he saw me and told me his boss wanted me to work for his mill. That night I was standing on the street corner with my little box of clothes under my arm, without a *centavo*, without any idea of what to do. If I had had money, I would have gone back to my homeland. At that moment this man passed by as if he had fallen from the sky. He said to me, "What are you doing here?" I told him. He said, "Don't you worry. Let's go to my house and I'll find you a job." But there was that union business. The next day we went to see his boss. He told me I had to be in the union to work in his mill. I didn't even have a *centavo*. We had come from La Tlaxpana and I walked nearly to Tepito. The millers' union was there. They asked me how much money I had on me. When they found out, they said nothing could be done. So I went all the way back on foot, without a bit of food in my stomach. There I was back in the same situation, going hungry. That's why I sometimes scold my children, because I've always given them food and a roof over their heads.

So I started going to the grocery stores to see if anyone was looking for an errand boy or helper. I knew something about the grocery business and could wait on customers rapidly. I went from store to store with no luck. There was bread everywhere and me so hungry, you have no idea how it feels. After a few days I met a man in La Tlaxpana, a block from where I was staying. He had a grocery store. He asked me, "Do you want a job?"

"Yes, sir."

"Do you have references?"

"No, sir. I just arrived from Veracruz." I was praying to God that he give me work or something. I explained that the only man I knew had a mill nearby. He went to speak to the man and then said he would take me on trial for two weeks. The pay was fifty *centavos* a day and food. There I was the next day with my package of clothes, for I had no place to leave it. I went to work at once. I was quick, I went around as if I were on wheels. I needed work, I had to eat. Two weeks went by, then a month, then three. I was very happy. I worked from six in the morning to nine at night without rest. I ate my breakfast cold in the store, there was no time to warm it. There were many customers. I delivered orders and lugged boxes I could barely lift, cases of beer, sacks of salt.

One morning my boss brought another boy from a village and he said to me, "Hey, Jesús, come over here. This boy is going to take your place. You're no damned good, get out." With those sweet and comforting words he fired me. That's all there was to it. There was nothing to be said. The next morning I was out on the street again.

But these difficulties help one to become a man, to appreciate the true value of things. One learns what it means to earn a living with the sweat of one's brow. To grow up away from your parents helps you to become mature.

When I was at the store, I had met a boy who had a relative who was a janitor in a building downtown. I asked for a note to this man and went to see him. I showed him the note. "Sure, why not? The building is empty," he said. "Pick out any place you like and put your box there." I stayed there without a *centavo* and once more I began to look for work.

That's when I found a job in the La Gloria restaurant. They paid me twelve *pesos* a month and three meals. I went in with my package of clothes and began to do everything they asked me. I was eager to work and while lifting a heavy package I got a hernia. I went to the toilet and saw a little lump here in my groin. I pressed on it and it hurt. I went to a doctor and he told me I had a hernia. I was lucky because the doctor belonged to the General Hospital and had me admitted. Now what about my job? I spoke to the owner, a Spaniard, a decent man, a real human being. I asked permission to go and be operated. They operated on me quickly but then I did a stupid thing. After the operation it hurt near the stitches and so I lifted the bandage and touched it and infected myself. Instead of being in the hospital for two weeks, I was there for five weeks.

When I got out I went to the restaurant and found someone at my job. But the owner took me back. Yes, I've worked there for over thirty years, and I've rarely missed a day. For the first fifteen years, I worked on the inside as a general helper and learned to bake bread and make ice cream. I worked fourteen to fifteen hours a day. Later, I began to do the shopping for the restaurant and I became their food buyer. When I began to work I earned eighty *centavos* a day. Now after thirty years, I earn the minimum wage of eleven *pesos* a day. But I could never live on this wage alone.

In thirty years I've rarely missed a day of work. Even when I'm sick I go. It seems that work is medicine for me. It makes me forget my troubles. And I like my work. I like all the walking I have to do and I enjoy speaking to the market vendors. I know them all after these many years of buying fruits, vegetables, cheese, butter and meats. I look for the best buys and all that. One has to know about buying, because each fruit has its season, no? Like melons. They're getting good at this time and I can buy them. The early melons were bad. They come from different places, from Morelos, from Michoacán, Cortazar. The ones from Guanajuato are very good; also the yellow ones from Durango. The same with oranges, they come from all over the Republic. Vegetables, too. The best avocados come from Atlixco and Silao, but they send most of those to the United States. The same with tomatoes. One must observe much to learn to know fruits and to be able to buy.

I buy six hundred *pesos'* worth of food for the restaurant each day. They give me the money in the morning and I pay cash for each purchase. There are no bills or receipts. I keep my own accounts and hand in a list of expenses each day.

I get to the restaurant each morning at seven to open the iron shutters. Then I work inside for a while, have breakfast and leave for the market at nine-thirty. Two boys assist me and they cart the purchases back to the restaurant. I get back at about one-thirty and usually there is something missing, so I run to the market again. I go back to the restaurant at three o'clock, have lunch and leave about four to look after my pigs, to sell lottery tickets and to visit my daughter Marta and the children.

My work companions at the restaurant think well of me and appreciate me because I am the oldest employee in the establishment. We joke and tease a lot and this, too, is a distraction. I've always behaved myself and gotten on well with my boss. A lot of workers hate their boss and don't feel loyal, but in that respect I am well off because I know my boss holds me in high esteem. To show his appreciation he allows me to work seven days a week and all holidays, so I can increase my earnings. For years I've worked on Wednesdays, my day off. I respect my boss and I do my best. He is like a father to me.

All I do is work and take care of my family. I never go to *fiestas*. Only once, when we lived in Cuba Street, some people in my *vecindad* made a *fiesta* and I danced a little. I didn't drink much and went right home to bed. For me there are no outings, no parties, no nothing . . . only work and family.

And I have no *compadres* where I work. I consider *compadrazgo* a serious thing, a matter of mutual respect. When I needed *compadres*, I chose older people, not youths or my fellow workers. Before you know it, young people invite you to drink with them and do things together. Some even kill each other, and that is bad. When I am invited anywhere, I don't go.

It was at La Gloria restaurant that I met the mother of my children, Lenore. I fell in love with her. She was short but broad-shouldered and dark-complexioned. I was about sixteen and she must have been two or three years older. She had been in Mexico City longer than I, and had had a husband in free union. I accepted her with a child of ten months. I was very happy to do it. It seemed perfectly natural to me, but the child got sick and died soon after. I was earning only eighty *centavos* a day and couldn't afford to pay ten or fifteen *pesos* a month for a place of our own, so I went to live with her family. I was young, very poor and very foolish in those days. I was stupid, like a piece of wood. But at fifteen, what experience did I have? All I knew was that I wanted to sleep with her.

But, as we say here, after twenty-four hours, a corpse and a house guest begin to stink. Her brothers drank a lot and came home and beat their wives and we had difficulties. I tried hard to find our own place to live in and finally found a room that rented for ten *pesos*. I didn't even own a bed. My wife sold bread crumbs and leftover cake and earned more than I did. Sometimes she earned eight *pesos* a day. Yes, selling pays well and there I was buried like a potato in that restaurant.

Lenore had a strong personality and that is why I couldn't live very peacefully with her. She wanted me to marry her but that made me angry. I thought she wanted to tie me up for life! It was wrong of me, but that's the way I was.

Lenore was the first woman I had ever had. We lost our first child, a little girl named María. She died a few days after birth, of pneumonia. Some say her little abdomen burst. Manuel was born next and I was happy to have my first son. I was even proud to be a father. I looked at him as though he was some strange person. Being so young, I lacked experience. One doesn't feel love right away, but my children always gave me pleasure. But at that time, we lived in misery. I earned only eighty *centavos* a day, and it didn't go far. Naturally, when Lenore was having a baby, she couldn't work and without her ten or twelve *pesos* a day, we lacked everything. She usually helped with the house expenses.

After Manuel, there was another boy who died in a few months. He died because of lack of money and because of ignorance. We had no experience and didn't struggle to save the baby. Lenore was a good person but she had a terrible temper and would get bad attacks of the heart and the bile. She always had trouble with her milk. She was not one of those affectionate mothers who pampered their children. She didn't beat them, that I remember, she was about average there, although she would get very angry and use strong words with the children. She didn't kiss or hug them, but they were not badly treated by her. She went out all day selling cake.

I wasn't very affectionate with the children either. I don't know whether it was because I didn't get much affection in my childhood, or because I was left to take care of them alone, or because I was always worrying about money. I had to work very hard to get them food. I didn't have time for them. I think in most homes, arguments and tragedies have an economic base because if you have fifty *pesos* a day expenses and you don't have the money, it bothers you and you worry and quarrel with your wife. I think that's what happens in most poor homes.

When Lenore was pregnant with Manuel, I began to see Lupita on the side. Lupita also worked in the La Gloria restaurant. Lenore and I had a lot of arguments and every time we did, she wanted to tear the house down. She was terribly jealous and really made a scene. When I'd come home from work I would often find her in an angry mood, any little thing upset her. She would fly into a rage and get sick. Her pulse would almost stop and she would seem to be dead. The doctor didn't know what caused these attacks. I couldn't take it. I wanted affection. After working all day I wanted someone to speak to, someone who would understand me, someone to whom I could pour out my troubles. You know, there are many types of people and when a poor man doesn't get any affection at home he finds it outside the home. The doctor once said to me, "To be content, a woman needs a husband who keeps her well dressed, well fed and well screwed, and for that, he must be strong and remember her often. Do this and you will see how things are."

Lenore had a strong temperament in that way, and I believe it was one of the reasons . . . well, she might have lived . . . but, well, a woman who is always quarreling makes her husband forget her. It's not the right sort of thing to do, I know, but that's when I propositioned Lupita at the restaurant. I'm not a very strong fellow but I've always been a little hot-blooded. That's my nature. Before Lupita, I had gone to a whore house on Rosario Street, but I got an infection there. It was because I wasn't careful, lack of experience, nothing else. Since that time I never went to one of those places. Today, I wouldn't go there even if it's free!

But in spite of my bad conduct, I have had the good luck to never have heard that any of the women who have lived with me weren't true to me. They were all dark women and of very passionate temperament . . . here in Mexico we believe that blondes are less strong sexually . . . but even if I didn't make use of them for a time, they didn't go out looking for another man. An honest woman, especially if she has children, must control herself and wait. I have had five wives . . . there was one with whom I had a son but she married someone else. That son of mine is twenty-two years old now and I think it is time I went to gather him up and claim him. Yes, I had five women, and a few on the side, and luck still favors me, all in all. You cannot tell me it wasn't luck when a nobody like me, an illiterate without schooling, without capital, not tall, not young, not anything, is lucky on all sides, with women.

Another man would be in jail by now! But I value my freedom and never looked for unmarried girls. No! All my women had already been married before I lived with them. Otherwise, there would be complications. If they had been virgins, I would probably have had to marry one of them in church or by civil law or I would be in jail for twenty years!

Anyway, when I began to have relations with Lupita, I didn't go into it with the idea of having a family with her. But she became pregnant very soon. I would meet her at her room on Rosario Street where she lived with her two small daughters. They were so little they didn't know what was going on. But later they always respected me and even called me *papá*. At that time I was earning very little so I couldn't support Lupita, who continued to work at the restaurant. But for the past fifteen years I've paid her rent.

Here in Mexico, when a woman with a child is accepted by a man, as I accepted Lenore, she usually doesn't feel she has a right to protest if her husband goes out. She knows she has blundered. It is different if the wife were a virgin and married by civil and church law. She would have every right to complain. But Lenore was difficult. Well, I suffered a lot with her but I never abandoned her. I was faithful to my banners. I only left the house for a few days each time we quarreled. I always came back because I loved the children.

Then one night she died, and what a blow it was. It was about seven o'clock at night, we were drinking *atole* and eating *gorditos* when she says to me very sadly, "Ay, Jesús, I'm going to die this year." She was always complaining of headaches. Then at one o'clock in the morning she said, "Ay, ay, I'm dying, take good care of my children." And the death rattle began. What time did I have to do anything? The doctor came and gave her an injection but it did no good. She was pregnant but the doctor said she died from the bursting of a blood vessel in her head. What I suffered during those days! I walked the street like a somnambulist. It was a good thing the grandmother was in the house. She took care of the children.

Part I

Manuel

I was eight years old when my mother died. I was asleep on a mat on the floor next to my brother Roberto. My little sisters, Consuelo and Marta, slept on the bed with my *mamá* and *papá*. As though in a dream I heard my father calling. He called to us when he saw my mother slipping away from him, when he had a feeling she was going to die. I was always a sound sleeper and my father had to shout. This time he really yelled. "Get up, you bastards! Get up, you sons-of-bitches. *Hijos de la chingada!* Your mother is dying and you lying there. On your feet, *cabrones*." Then I got up, very scared.

I remember my mother's eyes and how she looked at us. She was frothing at the mouth and couldn't speak. They sent for a doctor who lived only a block away but my mother didn't last long. Her face became dark and she died that night. My mother died carrying inside her another brother of mine, well on his way, because I remember that *mamá* had a big belly. Another woman was nursing my sister, that's why Marta remained so small.

Whether it was on account of the pregnancy or really a "congestion of the liver with the heart," like they told me, I don't know. But when my mother was laid out, the thing she had in her stomach, my brother, was heaving inside. It was still heaving and my father had a desperate look on his face. He did not know what to do, whether to let them cut her open and pull it out or let it stay there. My father cried a lot; he cried and went to tell all his *compadres*.

Her death came as a shock to everyone. She was only twenty-eight years old and oh, she was healthy, so healthy. People had seen her washing the courtyard and doing her housework in the morning. Why, that very afternoon she was still delousing my *papá*. My mother was sitting in the doorway and my father at her feet.

At that time we were living in a *vecindad* on Tenochtitlán Street. In the evening my *mamá* said to me, "Go out and buy some fried *tortillas* and corn gruel." I went around the corner and bought the food from a woman who had a stand. I'm certain it was on a Monday because the day before was Sunday and we had been on an excursion to the Basilica with my father and mother.

That Sunday we all ate avocados and chitlings and *chirimoyas*, things that are very bad for the bile if you eat them before or after a fit of anger. Well, on Monday morning my mother had a real fit of anger on account of my brother Roberto. She had had a bad quarrel with a woman next door.

The whole day passed. My father came home from work and both of them were in a good mood. They were still having their supper when we children went to bed. That night my mother had her attack and there wasn't even time for my father to call a priest to marry her before she died.

A lot of people came to the funeral, people from the tenement and from the market place. I don't know how long you are supposed to keep a body in the house but my father didn't want them to take her away and people began to complain because the body was already decomposing. At the cemetery, when they lowered my mother's casket into the ground, my *papá* tried to jump into the grave with her. He cried as though his heart were breaking. My father cried day and night on account of her.

After she was buried, *papá* told us we were all he had left and we should try to be good children because he was going to be both father and mother to us. He kept his word exactly as he promised. He loved my mother a lot because it took him six years before he married again, before he married Elena.

I believe my father loved my mother very much, in spite of their many quarrels. My father was very stern and a man of action. He used to quarrel with my mother because he was always a stickler for having things very clean. If he found something where it shouldn't be or anything that wasn't right, he'd start a fight with her. And when I saw them in a big argument, I'd get terribly scared. Once my parents were having a hot argument and my father got excited and tried to strike my mother with a knife. I don't know if he did it just to scare

her, but anyway I stepped in between them. I didn't even reach up
to their waists. I stepped in and my father calmed down right away.
I began to cry and he said, "No, son, no, we're not fighting. Don't
get frightened."

My *papá* was dead set against alcohol—he didn't even like to smell
it. Once my *mamá* went to celebrate the Saint's Day of my aunt
Guadalupe and they gave her quite a few drinks. So they had a big
argument and I remember vaguely that my parents separated. I must
have been three or four years old. At that time we lived at No. 14
on the Street of the Bakers in a *vecindad*—just one room with a
kitchen. My mother went to live at my aunt Guadalupe's on the
same street. They asked me whether I wanted to stay with my *papá*
or my *mamá*. I guess I felt more fond of my mother at that time for
I decided to go with her. They were separated about two weeks.

My mother's nature was just the opposite of my father's. She had
a happy disposition and liked to talk and chat with everybody. In the
mornings, I remember, she sang while she lighted the charcoal fire
and made our breakfast, she never stopped singing. She loved animals
and that was the only time we had a dog. "Yoyo" used to take great
care of Roberto and me. My *mamá* wanted lots of singing birds and
plants in the house but in those days my *papá* was against spending
money on things like that.

Mamá loved parties and did things in a big way. When she made
a *fiesta* on my father's Saint's Day, or even a small celebration on
our birthdays, she prepared huge casseroles of food and invited all
her relatives, friends, and *compadres*. She even liked to take a drink
or two, but only at a party. She was the type of person who would
give away her own meal to anyone who needed it, and she was always
letting some homeless couple sleep on the floor of our kitchen.

We were a happy family while she was alive. After she died, there
were no more parties at our house and no one ever came to visit us.
I never knew my father to have friends; he had *compadres*, but we
never saw them. And as to visiting, the only homes my father ever
entered were his own.

Most of the time my mother worked to help my father. He paid
the rent and gave her money for food, but my aunt told me he never
gave my mother money for clothing or other things. For about five
years she sold cake crumbs in the neighborhood where we lived. She
would buy cake trimmings and crumbs from El Granero bakery and

sell little piles for five and ten *centavos*. After that, she got in with some people who bought and sold second-hand clothes. She used to take me to the Roma district when she bought clothes for her market stall.

It was there that something very sad occurred, about which I am the only one who knows. There was another man in my mother's life. I don't know, but I believe that my mother had married my father for love. They had met in the La Gloria restaurant where they both worked. But there was another woman, Lupita, who also worked there, and my mother was jealous of her. She told me once that this woman was my father's sweetheart. Perhaps that is why my *mamá* began to see the second-hand-clothes man on the sly. She used to take me along, maybe to protect herself or to avoid getting intimate with him. I don't know if they ever saw each other alone.

I was very mad about this, except that the man, like men do with children, gave me spending money when we went to the movies, or he'd buy me something. But in spite of that, I wouldn't let go of my mother. I'd put my arms around her and wouldn't let her talk to him. Once I threatened to tell my father. She said, "Go ahead and tell him. He'll kill me and then you'll see how you'll get along without me." Well, after that I no longer had the courage to do it. My father was always very jealous.

I don't know how long this thing with that man lasted but we went to the movies only three times and then my mother died. He must have really loved her because he even came to the wake. When I saw him come into the house and stand there, I had a feeling of hatred for him. My father was there, how did he dare come? Later, that man took to drinking and went completely to the dogs. Within a year, he also died. Now I can excuse him, because he honestly loved my mother. I couldn't understand things then.

My *mamá* was very fond of going on religious pilgrimages. Once she took Roberto and me with her to the shrine at Chalma. Chalma is the popular shrine for the poor, who, with much faith and love, walk the sixty kilometers through the hills. It is really a hard trip, a sacrifice, to go loaded with blankets and food and clothing. When we went, there were many people. It took us four days to get there and we slept in the hills or in towns at night, right outdoors on our straw mats. Roberto and I were afraid at night because we heard the women talking about the witches that sucked children's blood. One *señora* said to my mother, "Be careful with your children because the witches are very active at this time. Just think, they found three children yesterday with not a drop of blood left in their bodies."

Roberto said, "Do you hear that, brother?" And we both were filled with fear. I said, "Do you know what? We will cover up our heads with the blankets at night and they won't know that we are children."

Along the road were crosses which marked the spot where someone had died, and all the women believed that the spirit of the dead one was waiting to possess the children that passed by. The women, those carrying children, shouted out the name of their child every time they passed a cross, so the child's soul would not remain there.

In the hills, we saw balls of fire going from one peak to another and people would say, "It's a witch! A witch!" And everyone would kneel and start to pray. The mothers began covering up their children. My *mamá* put her arms around us under the blanket so the witch wouldn't get us. They said the best way to catch a witch was to kneel before a pair of scissors, opened to form a cross, and pray the Magnificat. With each Our Father you must make a knot in a *rebozo*. When the last knot was made, the witch was supposed to fall at your feet and then be burned in a fire made with green wood.

As we walked through the mountain passes, my *mamá* told us some of the legends about Chalma. She showed us "The Pack Driver," a rock which looked like a man in Indian dress, leading a *burro* and a dog. This teamster, they say, had killed his partner up there in the mountain, and had turned to stone. Later, we passed "The Compadres," some rocks in the middle of a river. These were *compadres* who had sinned by fornicating right there in the river, and they, too, were turned to stone. And there was another curious rock formation that looked just like a priest, with *sombrero* and cape, his hand on his cheek, as though he was thinking. Who knows what sin he committed, but he too had been punished by heaven. The old people believe that these rocks turn toward the Church, once a year, and when they finally reach the Church, they will be disenchanted and transformed to their original selves.

We saw the Penitents, people who had vowed to walk the rocky road to the shrine on their knees, or with their ankles tightly tied. They moved slowly, helped along by *compadres*, and arrived bleeding, with their skin worn off, and sometimes with their bones showing. That sight impressed me most.

My *mamá* and all her family went to Chalma regularly. They were also very devoted to the Virgin of San Juan de los Lagos, but that pilgrimage took longer; we went with my mother every year. My *papá* accompanied her only once; but he never went to Chalma. He didn't like religious pilgrimages and that was another thing they quarreled about. My *papá* has always said about my *mamá's* family, "They are very saintly, but they drink all the way to the shrine."

It was true that my mother's brothers, José and Alfredo and Lucio, drank a lot, in fact, they all died of drink. My aunt Guadalupe also liked to drink her daily *copita*. But I do not recall that my mother's mother, my grandmother, drank. She was the kind of sprightly old lady who always walked erect, and was very, very clean. She never wore anything dirty, even her shoes were kept polished, and she dressed very severely, in a black silk blouse and long black skirt.

My grandma used to live with my aunt Guadalupe, in a room on the Street of the Painters. Grandma would come to our house every day at breakfast time, after my *papá* had left for work. She helped my *mamá* by washing our faces and necks and hands. She scrubbed us so hard with the *zacate* I felt like screaming. She'd say, "You grimy rascals, why do you get so filthy?"

My grandmother was steeped in religion, even more than my *mamá*, and she was like a godmother to us, teaching us to cross ourselves and to pray. She was devoted to the Archangel San Miguel, and taught us his prayer, and the Magnificat, which she said was the best medicine against all ills. She had an hour for prayer on all the festival days, the *fiesta* of the Palms, the Pentecost, the Day of the Dead . . . all of them. On the Day of the Dead she lit the candles, put out the glass of water, the bread of the dead, the flowers, the fruit. After she and my mother died, no one ever did that in our house. My grandmother was the only one who was rich in tradition and who tried to pass it on to us.

My father's family lived in a small town in Veracruz and we knew almost nothing about them. When Roberto and I were very small, my *papá's papá* sent for us. My grandpa was alone because my grandma and uncles had died, I don't know exactly how. My grandpa had the biggest grocery store in Huachinango and many people in the village owed him money. He said the store was ours and my father finally sold it. But an uncle of mine, my grandfather's half-brother, had my father put in jail to get the money away from him. I think they wanted to kill him or something but at night my mother sneaked out and went to the jail. It was only a country jail, and she hit the guard with a club. I'm not sure what she did but she got *papá* out of jail and we beat it as fast as we could, back to Mexico City. As a result, my father didn't get a single penny out of my grandpa's store.

I was six years old when Consuelo was born. Roberto and I saw the midwife come in and there was a lot of movement going on but we didn't understand anything then. We were put out of the room and then we heard a baby's cry. I always liked to hear a baby crying and for me it was a very nice thing to have a sister. But she slept in the bed with my parents, and when my mother carried her around all the time, nursing her, and calling her "my pretty little daughter," I began to have an ugly feeling. My mother noticed that I was jealous and said, "No, no, son, you know you are my favorite. Don't believe anything else." It was true, because when she went out selling she always, always, took me with her. We left Roberto with my grandma and I went with *mamá*. Knowing how much she loved me, I would ask for everything I saw and would go into a temper if she didn't buy it. She used to say, "*Ay*, son, I love you very much but you are very demanding. I wonder what you will be like when you are big."

One day my *mamá* and I were going to the Granero bakery for cake crumbs. She was talking to her *comadre*, Consuelo's godmother, when I noticed blood running down *mamá's* leg. I asked her if she had cut herself and she looked down and saw the blood and said, "I guess I really did cut myself." She went home to bed and sent for my father.

Later, the same lady who had brought Consuelo arrived, and again we heard a baby cry. My brother and I must have looked like a pair of scared rabbits for my *papá* came out and told us not to be frightened, that the lady had brought us a new sister in her suitcase. When I saw Marta for the first time I thought she was very ugly. I said, "*Ay, mamá,* you should have better asked the lady for a whiter, prettier one."

My father was very, very happy when his daughters were born. He really would have preferred to have had only girls. He was always more affectionate to my sisters but I didn't notice it so much then because while my mother was alive my *papá* still loved me. As for Roberto, I don't remember exactly. My *papá* never did like very dark people and it was probably on account of Roberto's dark skin that my father disliked him. But when we were little he was not so severe with us. He spoke to us with a different tone of voice. I guess the worst thing that happened to me and my brother was to grow up, because I was very happy until I was eight.

It was at about that time that I became aware of sexual intercourse. It happened that my *mamá* was lighting the charcoal fire and had sent me next door to borrow the fan blower. I ran off to our neighbor's house and went in without knocking. There was Pepita in bed with her husband, with her legs up and he with his pants down and everything. I felt embarrassed, I couldn't tell exactly of what, but I felt that I had surprised them doing something bad. Pepita looked upset, they stopped moving but didn't change their position. She said, "Yes, take it, it's over there on the brazier." Then I went home and it occurred to me to talk about it to my mother. *Ay!* what a spanking she gave me!

After that, I wanted to experience it for myself and tried to get the girls of the *vecindad* to play "*papá* and *mamá*" with me. My mother had a girl to help her in the house, and I played that game with her, whenever we were alone. One day she went to the roof to hang up clothes and I followed her. "Come on," I said, "let's do it." I tried to raise her dress and pull down her pants, and just as she was about to give in, I heard someone tapping at a window. Our house, at that time, faced a stocking factory, and when I turned around to see who was tapping, there were all the factory workers, men and women, at the windows, pointing at us and laughing. Someone shouted, "*Cabrón muchacho*, just look at the little bastard." Did I leave that roof quickly!

The first day my mother brought me to school I was frightened and burst out crying. When the teacher wasn't looking, I ran right back home. *Señorita* Lupe, my first teacher, was strict and would throw the eraser at anyone who was out of order. Once she gave me such a blow with a ruler that it broke on my wrist.

That year I met my friend Santiago. He was my guardian angel in school, and used to protect me. When bigger boys hit me, right away I'd tell Santiago, and he would go after them. But he wouldn't help me against younger boys. He'd say, "Aren't you ashamed to cry? If he's smaller than you, beat him up!" Santiago taught me to defend myself, to swear and use dirty words, and he told me all about what you do to women.

I stayed in that school until the fourth grade. It was there that I got my nickname, *Chino*, because of my slanty eyes. Roberto entered the first grade when I was in the third and from then on I got into lots of fights because of him. Poor kid! Even when he was little he had a hard time! He was always getting into trouble. At recess I would see them dragging him, crying, to the principal's office to punish him for something, and I would get angry and interfere.

My brother once came to my classroom crying and with his nose bleeding. He said, "Francisco, the Pig, hit me, for nothing at all." Without a word I went to the Pig's room and said to him, "Francisco, why did you hit my brother?"

"Because I wanted to, and so what?"

"Well, hit me," I said, and he hit me. I went at him and gave him a very hard punch. He lunged at me with a knife and if I hadn't ducked he would surely have cut my face.

They sent for my father; unfortunately it was a Wednesday, his day off, and he was at home. That afternoon I was afraid to go into the house, and stood looking through a crack in the door to see what mood my father was in. But he didn't hit me that time. He only told me to avoid fights as much as possible.

One Mother's Day, I came home singing a song we had been re-hearsing in school. "Forgive me, dear Mother, because I can't give you anything but love." My father was at home and he seemed very proud and happy about something.

"No, son, we can give her something else, because just look at what I bought." I saw a little radio standing on the wardrobe.

"How nice, *papá*," I said. "Is it for *mamá?*"

"Yes, son, it's for *mamá* and for you, too."

That's how my father spoke to me then. He had won on his lottery ticket and bought it with the prize money. Afterwards, I came to hate the radio because it caused arguments in the house. My father got angry with my mother for playing it so much. He said it would get out of order and, "Nobody pays for anything around here except me!" He wanted the radio on only when he was at home.

After my mother's death, my grandmother took care of us for a while. I loved her and, after my mother was gone, she was the only person who really, truly loved me. She was the only one I went to for advice, the only one who cried if I didn't eat. Once she said, "Manuelito, you are very willful and you worry me. The day I die you will see that no one else will cry to make you eat."

My grandmother never hit us, though she sometimes pulled my hair or my ears if I refused to go with her on an errand. My *mamá* had hit us more, especially Roberto, who was very mischievous. Why, once, when my brother wouldn't come out from under the bed when she called, my mother grabbed the iron and shoved it at him. It hit him right on the head and raised a big bump. Compared to my mother, my grandma was a symbol of tenderness.

My father got along well with my grandma; that is, they never had differences. She taught us to respect him because he fed and supported us. She was always saying that we should appreciate having the kind of father we had, for there were few like him in the world. She gave us good advice about everything and taught us to respect the memory of our mother.

Sometimes my aunt Guadalupe took care of us. One evening my *papá* sent us out to buy candy. I think he expected us to take long, but I came back prematurely and saw my father trying to put his arms around my aunt, by force, right? I believe he was making love to her, and I had surprised them. I don't think I liked it, but, well, he was my father, no? and I didn't judge him.

Then my father began to hire women to take care of us. I don't remember the first servant's name; she smoked a lot and her teeth were all yellow. Once she was washing and I went and put my hands up under her dress. "No, be quiet, let me alone, go away, or you'll see what you get, you bloody little bastard." The old girl didn't want me to, but I lifted her dress and saw her tail. *Ay!* she had a lot of hair and was ugly.

We moved from the Street of the Painters to a *vecindad* on Cuba Street. Our room was small and dark and very dilapidated, and seemed like a poor place to live. That was where my father met Elena.

I don't remember the exact numbers of our doors, but let's suppose we lived in Room No. 1, and Elena lived with her husband, in No. 2. All my *papá* did was to move her from No. 2 to No. 1, and she became his wife. Before that, I almost considered her a playmate. She was very young and pretty, and often asked me to read the comics to her because she couldn't read. She was our friend, no? So we felt betrayed when she and my father fell in love. She came to our house as a servant, to cover up the affair, and ended up as our mistress!

One night, her husband sent word that he wanted to see my father. Now, my father is a pretty small fellow, but he went. I saw him grab a knife and put it under his belt before he left. They locked themselves in and I was very worried. I told Roberto, "Let's go up to the roof. If we see that fellow start something we'll both jump him." We were only kids but we were on the roof, watching. We couldn't see them, though, because they had even closed the inside door. I was really scared. I thought maybe that fellow was going to kill my father. Then my *papá* came out and after that Elena stayed in our house.

The people in the tenement were scandalized at what happened— Elena walking out of one room and into another one. And what guts my father had! But because of the scandal *papá* had to move and we went to live on Orlando Street.

On the day we moved, my father came home early from work, at 1:00 P.M. on the dot, and since he always liked to have things done quickly, he said, "All right, take down the bed and roll up the mattress."

So we rolled it up and, to hide the spots and stains, he covered it with a bedspread. Then, right away my father wanted us to move the furniture and gather up all our pots and pans. Elena took them off the hooks and put them in the tubs, so she could carry them with her. We had lots of tubs to store water, because there has always been a problem of water shortage in the *vecindades*. We didn't rent a cart; we carried the things ourselves. *Papá* paid a porter to carry the wardrobe, since our new house was over a block and a half away.

It was a bigger, prettier *vecindad*, and for the first time we lived in a place with two rooms. It made me feel as if we were rich and I was very happy about it. Our rooms were on the third story and there was only a tiny railing on the landing that faced the courtyard, so my father had a real fence put up to keep us from falling.

But my father wasn't satisfied with our rooms on Orlando and we moved back to Cuba Street, where he knew two women who worked in the restaurant. One of them had a daughter, Julia, whom I was very fond of. It was my ambition to make Julia my *"novia,"* but her family was better off than we were and I felt sort of inferior. When I saw how nicely her house was furnished I decided I'd never ask her to be my girl friend.

At first Elena tried to be nice to us. She had never had any children and was very affectionate with all of us. I don't know why, but after we moved to Cuba Street she didn't treat us so well. That's when my father's attitude toward us began to change. She would fight with Roberto at the slightest provocation and my father beat my poor little brother more than ever. The only time I had the impression that my father cared for Roberto was when a dog in this *vecindad* tore a piece of flesh from my brother's arm. My father was very upset and turned pale; he got completely confused and didn't know what to do—some neighbors had to help.

But it is true that Roberto had always been very difficult, you might say, impossible. He was very stubborn and put up a fight about any little thing. Elena would say, "Wash the floor," and Roberto would answer, "Why should we wash it? You're the housewife." And so there was a big argument and when my father came home Elena would pretend that she was crying. He would grab his belt and give it to both of us. He made us wash the floor and the dishes and Elena would sit on the bed and laugh to make us madder.

We were once seated at the table, having supper—my stepmother, my sisters, Roberto, my father and I. I was about to take a gulp of coffee when I turned to look at my father. He was staring at me and Roberto and he said, as though he really hated us, "Just to see you bastards swallow gives me a pain, yes, just to see you swallow, you filthy sons-of-bitches." We hadn't done a thing, yet that's the way he spoke to us. Since then I've never sat at the table with my father.

Having lost our mother, we children should have been closer; we should have backed each other up. But we could never be like that because my father always stepped in between us boys and the girls. He stood in the way and wouldn't let me do my duty as the older brother. If my mother had lived, things might have been different. She was a great believer in the tradition that minors should respect their elders. If she had lived, maybe my sisters would have respected Roberto and me and we wouldn't have had to abuse our authority.

Here in Mexico, the idea is that the oldest child should look after the younger ones, sort of keep them in line. But my father didn't allow me to and I never felt as if I had sisters because I couldn't correct them. He'd say, "Who are you, you son-of-a-bitch, who are you to

hit them? I'm the only one around here who is working his ass off
and none of you bastards has a right to put a hand on them."

My sisters, especially Consuelo, tried to create bad blood between us
and my father. She knew just what to do to make him beat us and
pull our ears. Since the beginning, my father never let us play with
her, or let her run, because she was so puny and that's why, well, I
didn't take her much into account. Consuelo was always a whiny kid,
really, no one could whine like my sister. I'd give her a little slap, and
she'd burst out bawling. When my father came home she'd begin to
rub her eyes to make them red and he would say, "What's the matter,
child? What's wrong, daughter?" Then she would blow up any little
thing into something big. For a light slap, she'd sound off like an
ambulance siren. "Look, *papá*, he hit me on the lung!" She always said
that because she knew it was the part of the body that would worry
my *papá*. He fussed a lot over her because she was so skinny, and, of
course, he whacked us hard.

"Skinny"—that's what we called Consuelo—always put on a humble
face for my father, like Sister Juana Inés de la Cruz at the Crucifixion.
All suffering and resignation, but she had small, sharp nails inside, you
know what I mean? She was always self-centered, that sister of mine,
and man! did she make Roberto and me mad.

I don't know why my father was so harsh with us and so fond of the
girls. He had one tone of voice for them and another for Roberto and
me. It's probably because he was brought up the old-fashioned way.
He told us, on the two or three times he ever reminisced about his
life, that my grandfather was very strict with him and used to beat him
a lot. And that's why he must have decided that for us to respect him
he must be, first, a he-man, and then a father. We never talked back
to him, we always respected him, in fact we worshiped him, so why did
he treat us that way?

My father beat us, not out of cruelty, but for deeper reasons, because of his love for Elena. Naturally his wife meant more to him than
his children and he beat us to make up to her, to please her. Deep
down he loved us too, but he wanted us to amount to something and
when he saw that we didn't do the right thing he felt cheated, disappointed. He used to say that Elena was a saint and that we were
riffraff, that we had evil hearts and never wanted to understand her
or allow her to be happy. But, to my way of thinking, his love for
Elena was a mixture of affection and gratitude, and my father is, well,

very loyal. I don't think he loved Elena as much as my mother, because my mother was his first love, a real, true love.

When it came to my stepmother, I tried to keep my mouth shut, because I knew it wouldn't turn out good for me. I always advised Roberto to keep quiet but he'd say there was no reason for him to shut up because that woman was not his mother. Elena treated my sisters better, because they were girls and were too small to resist her. But we boys were big enough to figure things out.

Once, we were having a chat about family things, and I happened to tell Elena that my mother sometimes affectionately called my father "Old Tomcat." Then Elena called my mother a dirty name. I really got mad. My mother had her own way of loving my father and giving him nicknames and Elena had no right to insult her. We had a big argument and when my father came home he beat me. But usually I kept quiet when she said something to hurt me. I was, well, careful, but Roberto was like a volcano; you just touched him and he exploded.

If anything wrong took place, if something was missing, whatever it was, Roberto was blamed. Once he was punished for something I did and I felt bad about that ever since. It was the only time I did such a thing. My friend Santiago had said to me, "Take something from your house so we can go to the movies." The first thing I saw was a crucifix my father had gotten from my grandpa, so I took it and we sold it.

That evening they looked and looked for the Christ and couldn't find it. Then they beat Roberto for stealing it. I wanted to confess, but when I saw my father so angry I got scared and kept quiet. I never told anyone about this incident. That's the way it was, when anything went wrong it was Roberto who always, always got the blame.

It was after *mamá* died that Roberto first began to filch things from the house. Most of the time when things were missing, he was the one who took them. After the Christ, I never took anything from the house. Roberto's stealing, when he was young, was petty thievery, something his friends told him to do. For example, *papá* would send home a dozen eggs and Roberto would grab one or two and go out and sell them. That's how he got spending money. My poor *papá* had a hard time making ends meet. He always bought shoes and clothes when we needed them, and he provided us with the best school supplies, but there were days when neither my brother nor I had five *centavos* between us. I used to envy my schoolmates who could buy lollipops or tidbits. Well, you always feel bad then. But *papá* couldn't make enough for so many of us. I understand this now.

By the time I was in the fifth grade I had my first girl friend. She was Elisa, the sister of my friend Adán. I used to go to Adán's house to sing because he played the guitar. Elisa's parents watched her very carefully, but they accepted me as a friend of her brother. I took advantage of the situation and asked her straight out to be my girl friend. She was older and taller than I; I was about thirteen and I had to stand on something to kiss her. I took her to the movies where we could kiss and embrace. But that was all you did with a *novia*. If you go to bed with your *novia* you are practically married.

Because of my friends I began to neglect my studies, but my teacher, Professor Everardo, was a decent fellow and you might say that, man to man, I was a friend of his. When I was still a new boy in that school, something happened which gave me pleasant memories later in life. There was a boy named Bustos in my class. He was the school champion because he could lick all the runts in fist fighting. The first day there was a teachers' meeting and Bustos was left in charge of our room. He called me to order, but not in a polite way, and so I said to him, "No, you shrimp, you can't yell at me."

"I can't?" he said. "So you're a tough guy, well, well."

So I said, "I'm not so tough but if you think you've got as much guts as I just because you're a big shot here, you're making a mistake, pal. I'm from Tepito, and we don't take any crap from anybody."

Well, I punched him in the nose, right there in the classroom, a hard sock and his nose and mouth were covered with blood. Then the boys all said, "Bustos, *ay!* that's some wallop the kid gave you." After that they nicknamed me "No. 20" because that was my number when they called the roll. Since I had licked the biggest kid in the school I became famous and everybody kept saying that No. 20, No. 20, won the fight. After that none of the boys ever bothered me because, even though I was very short, I was strong and had powerful arms.

Josefa Ríos was the first girl I really fell in love with, a blond, with white skin and very pretty. There was a boy, Pancho, whose parents were, well, sort of better off, and he sure was handsome. Well, I was madly in love with Josefa and she was in love with Pancho, and Pancho paid no attention to her. I became so jealous that I tried to provoke Pancho to fight, so Josefa would see I was better than he. But Pancho never wanted to, because he knew I had licked Bustos.

Then one time the principal's Saint's Day was coming up, and all classes had prepared something to perform in her honor. Our room had nothing prepared. I got to school early one day and nobody was there and, as I always do when I'm sad or happy, I started to sing. I didn't notice that Professor Everardo was listening. He came in and said, "Look, Manuel, you have a good voice; now we have something to perform on the principal's Saint's Day." But I really didn't know why he said that until several days later when the affair took place. The first grade put on a dance number, the second a declamation, the third something else and so on until they reached the fifth grade, and then they announced, "Fifth grade, Section A, a song dedicated to the principal, sung by pupil Manuel Sánchez Vélez." Holy Mary! I hadn't known anything about it, and I was scared to death, and there was Josefa in the first row.

I hid under the benches, and didn't want to come out. Everybody looked and looked until Bustos saw me and dragged me out. They took me as if I was a prisoner. Well, I got up on the platform and sang a song which was popular at the time, "Amor, Amor, Amor" . . . "Love . . . love . . . love . . . created by you, by me, by hope . . ." At that time, my voice was clearer, it really was, and I could sing much higher. I sang through my tension and fear, and kept looking at Josefa. Then, just like awaking from a dream, I heard applause, a lot of applause, very loud, really. Ah, then I felt very proud, Josefa was applauding me more than anybody, and I said, "Oh, God Almighty, can it be that she will notice me?" Well, after that I wanted them to let me keep on singing.

That same afternoon I said to Josefa, "I have something to tell you. Will you allow me to see you from now on?" I remember how happy I was when she said, "I'll be waiting for you at six on the corner near my house." I was very happy, naturally, and I came at six on the dot, but she didn't show up. Pancho had spoken to her that very day, so, of course, she went out with him and left me "whistling on the hilltop," as they say here.

Well, school continued and I played hooky at least one day a week. That's when I started smoking with my friends. We'd be going along and one of the fellows would say, "How about taking 'three drags'?"

He'd hand me his cigarette and I'd take three puffs, and pass it to the next guy.

I had to hide my smoking from my father. I have even popped burning cigarettes into my mouth when he came home unexpectedly. He caught me once, when I was twelve, smoking in the courtyard with my friends, and right in front of them he said, "Aha, you bastard, so you already know how to smoke? Now you have to work to keep yourself in cigarettes. Just wait until you get into the house, you'll see, you little son-of-a-bitch." After that, my friends kidded me when I asked for a cigarette. "No, kid, why should we, if your *papá* is going to hit you!"

It wasn't until I was twenty-nine that I first smoked in my father's presence. It was a kind of small rebellion against him, no? I am still uneasy when I do it, but I want him to see that I am a man now.

In looking back, I seemed not to have had any homelife. I didn't have much to do with my family and spent so little time at home I can't even remember what we did there. Besides, I have no memory for everyday things. I have an aversion for routine and only the very good or very bad things, the exciting things, stick in my memory.

I don't want to sound ungrateful, but about my father . . . the truth is, he always mistreated my brother and me. What I mean is that he made us pay for the piece of floor we slept on, and the bread we ate, by humiliating us. True, he was very loyal and responsible, but he imposed his strict personality upon us, and never permitted us to express our opinions, or to approach him. If we asked him something, he'd say, "Slobs! what do you know? Shut your snouts." He would squelch us every time.

In a way, it was his fault that I didn't come home. I never had the feeling that I had a true home because I wasn't free to bring my friends there. In the afternoons and evenings, when my father liked to read, he chased us into the courtyard. "Get out of here, you mules. A man works hard all day and he can't even read in peace. Get out!" If we stayed inside, we had to be absolutely quiet.

Maybe I am hypersensitive, but my father's lack of feeling for us made me think we were a burden to him. He would have been happier with Elena if he didn't have us; we were like those heavy loads that one carried only because one must. I will never forget the look of hatred he gave Roberto and me, while we were having supper that day. I went into the kitchen to cry, and couldn't eat because of the lump in my throat.

Many times I wanted to say, "Look, Father, what have I ever done to you? Why do you have the worst opinion of us? Why do you treat us like criminals? Don't you realize that there are sons who are addicts, who abuse their families right in their own house? Or who even kill their own fathers?" Someday, if I dare, I would like to say this to him, in a nice way, of course.

But whenever I tried to speak out to my father, something stopped me. With others, I had more than enough words, eh? But with him, something formed in my throat and didn't let me speak. I don't know whether it was the profound respect I felt for him, or whether it was fear. Perhaps that is why I preferred to live my life apart from my father, and from the rest of my family, too. There was a gulf between us, a disunity, and although I respected them, and was hurt to see what was happening to them, I shut myself off. A selfish attitude, yes, but I believe I hurt them and myself less that way.

I used to go out with my friends all the time. I practically lived in the street. I went to school in the afternoon; in the mornings I sometimes went with my friends to work in a tannery, to make engravings on leather. I only went home to pick up my books. I still ate at home, but I ducked out as soon as I finished. I really did it to avoid getting into difficulties with my stepmother, to avoid getting beatings. My father didn't say anything to me about it because, I guess, it was better for him that way.

I liked to work when I was a boy. I must have worked since I was very small because the first job I had my father used to call for me and when I got my money I handed it right over to him. I remember how good I felt when my father hugged me, and said, "Now I have someone to help me." I was a shoemaker's assistant in a workshop a few blocks from our house. I used to work until late at night; there were times when we worked all night long. I don't think I was over nine years old then.

My second job was making belts, then I sold lottery tickets in the street, and for a while I worked with Elena's younger brother, as an assistant to my grandmother's cousin's son, who was a mason. While I was still in school I was night watchman in a bakery shop. My uncle Alfredo worked there and he taught me how to make biscuits. As I look back, almost my entire life has been spent working—even though the work wasn't very productive—so why do they say I am a lazy bastard and a son-of-a- this or that?

At the end of the school year they handed me my flunk notice. Professor Everardo was very fond of me but he failed me anyway. It hurt me on account of my father, and I thought my teacher had been unfair. After that, I lost interest in my studies. I was stupid when it came to grammar, to conjugating verbs, and only average in arithmetic, but I was outstanding in world history and geography. These studies fascinated me.

When it came to sports, to physical strength, I was first in my class. I have always been a good runner and in the sixth grade I came in first in the 100 and 200 meter races. I also liked anything that had to do with motors and once in a while I dreamed of becoming a mechanical engineer, of having a career. But I've left all that behind.

We still lived on Cuba Street, near my grandmother. She kept coming to visit, bringing us little cakes and sweets or clothing, and asking how our stepmother was treating us. Once I ran to her house because my father had hit me. I wanted to live with her, but that night my *papá* came and made me go home.

I have a poor memory for dates, but I remember the day we moved to the Casa Grande because it was my father's Saint's Day and it was the day my grandmother died. When my uncle sent word of her death my father had said, "What a nice little present for me!"

The day before, she had sent for us and I was impressed because she knew she was dying; she died with all her five senses intact and she had a word for everyone. To me she said, "Kneel down, child, I'm going to sleep. Now take good care of your brother and sisters. Behave well in life so that life treats you well. Son, don't be wicked, otherwise your mother's spirit and mine won't rest in peace." She asked us always to pray an Our Father in her name because it would be like food to her. Then she blessed us. There was a knot in my throat but by that time I felt like a man and tried hard not to cry. My uncle José was drunk as usual and was dancing outside her room.

My aunt Guadalupe and my uncles washed and dressed my grandma for the funeral. They put a clean sheet on the bed that day and laid her out while they went to buy the coffin. The four of them lifted her into the coffin and put under it a tray of vinegar and onion to absorb the *cáncer* that leaves the body of a dead person. There were two candles at her head and two at her feet, when we arrived for the wake. All night people sat around drinking black coffee and eating bread and telling off-color stories which made me very angry. My father sat on one side, talking to my uncles. I heard him say, "You see, Alfredo, look at our case. What is the use of all the rivalry and disagreements, when this is the end, the reality of things?" They had always had conflicts, but anyway my father helped them with the funeral expenses.

Well, then we began life in the Casa Grande. The boys there, the Casa Grande gang, tried to provoke me to fight. I had not lost a single fight at school and so, when the gang surrounded me, with the strongest of them egging me on, I just said, "Well, come on, brother, you're done for."

What a fight we had! We were covered with blood but he got the worst of it. There was only one of them that dared fight me after that, a fellow nicknamed the Donkey, because he had a very big penis. One day he knocked a tooth out of my brother's mouth and that was when I took him on. The Donkey and I had a wonderful fight. I gave him a sock that made him cry, but when he saw that he couldn't manage with his fists, he bit me. I still have the scar on my shoulder where his teeth dug into me. After that we became close friends, closer than I was with my own brother, because we kept nothing secret from each other. The Donkey was none other than my present *compadre* and best friend, Alberto Hernández.

From our first fight, I was attracted to Alberto. I liked him a lot, although I usually had opinions contrary to his. I don't know why, but no sooner did he come out with an idea, than I said the opposite. But in the things that counted, like if someone picked a fight with one of us, we always stood together. We saw each other every day; wherever Alberto was, there I was too. In a word, we were inseparable. We confided in each other, all our joys and troubles, our conquests and secrets. And he always treated me, because he worked and had more money to spend.

Alberto was a year or two older than I, but he had had a lot more experience, especially with women. He had wavy hair and big eyes and the girls liked him, even though he was a country boy and talked like an Indian. I was impressed by the things he knew. While I was still a schoolboy, he had worked in a mine in Pachuca, had washed cars, waited on tables, and had traveled the highways. He had never gone to school because from the beginning he had to support himself. His

life was harder than mine, because his mother had died when he was
a baby, and his father had abandoned him. First, his mother's mother
took care of him, then his mother's sister. He was living in the Casa
Grande with this aunt and her husband.

Even though I was younger than he, Alberto talked to me about
matters of the bedroom. He told me of different positions, about women
with "dog," and things like that. What a *cabrón* he was when it came
to women! To this day he is a great one with the ladies. We nicknamed him Three Daily, because he was so *puñetero*, so hot. Why,
once when we went out selling newspapers, he stood next to a car and
saw the woman driver with her dress up and her knees showing, and
right then and there, he put his hand into his pocket and began mastur-
bating.

We kids used to go to the bathhouse and peek through holes in the
walls to see the girls bathing. Once Alberto came running to tell us
that a pretty girl, Clotilde, was taking a bath, so four of us hired the
bath next to hers and watched her. We saw her naked and she
sure had everything! There we were peeking, with our hands in our
pockets, rubbing away, racing to see who would come first.

Alberto and I were members of the Casa Grande gang. There were
about forty of us then; we played games, like *burro*, or told dirty jokes
together, and we were always very proud of keeping up the name of the
Casa Grande. The guys from the streets of the Barbers, the Painters, or
the Tinsmiths could never get the better of us. At dances we kept our
eyes peeled to see that they didn't hang around trying to make the
girls of the Casa Grande.

Every sixteenth of September a certain gang would come with sticks
to make war against us. We would let them come in through one of
the gates and, meanwhile, the janitor's son, who was a member of our
gang, would lock the other gate. When all of the gang was inside, he
would run and lock the first gate. Then we would let them have it in
all the courtyards, with stones, pails of water, and sticks.

We never let anyone get the better of us, Alberto and I were the
first to take on any others . . . we were known as good fighters and
were always put up front against other gangs. We fought so much
in those days, I began to dream about it. I dreamed that Alberto
and I were surrounded by five or six guys and I jumped to escape
them and went up and up until I reached the electric cables, out of
everyone's reach. I said, "*Ay!* I can fly! I can fly!" Then I made myself

go down by putting my feet vertical, toward the ground, and I said to Alberto, "*Compadre,* get on." And he got on my back and I began to fly again. "You see? They can't do anything to us now!" I kept flying until we passed the cables. Then suddenly I lost the power and I felt myself fall. I kept dreaming this for many years.

The thing is, growing up in our environment here, we see the realities of life so close that we must learn to have a lot of self-control. Sometimes I had an intense desire to cry because of something my father said, but instead, because life, cynicism, had taught me to put on a mask, I laughed. For him, I did not suffer, I felt nothing, I was a shameless cynic, I had no soul . . . because of the mask I showed. But inside, I felt every word he said.

I have learned to hide my fear and to show only courage because from what I have observed, a person is treated according to the impression he makes. That's why when I am really very afraid inside, outwardly I am calm. It has helped me too, because I didn't suffer as much as some of my friends who trembled when they were grabbed by the police. If a guy shows weakness and has tears in his eyes, and begs for mercy, that is when the others pile on him. In my neighborhood, you are either a *picudo,* a tough guy, or a *pendejo,* a fool.

Mexicans, and I think everyone in the world, admire the person "with balls," as we say. The character who throws punches and kicks, without stopping to think, is the one who comes out on top. The one who has guts enough to stand up against an older, stronger guy, is more respected. If someone shouts, you've got to shout louder. If any so-and-so comes to me and says, "Fuck your mother," I answer, "Fuck your mother a thousand times." And if he gives one step forward and I take one step back, I lose prestige. But if I go forward too, and pile on and make a fool out of him, then the others will treat me with respect. In a fight, I would never give up or say, "Enough," even though the other was killing me. I would try to go to my death, smiling. That is what we mean by being "*macho,*" by being manly.

Life around here is raw, it is more real, than among people with money. Here, a boy of ten isn't scared off at the sight of the female sexual organ. Nor is he shocked when he sees a guy lifting someone's wallet, or using a knife on a man. Just having seen so much evil at close range makes him face reality. After a while, even death itself doesn't frighten us. We get our bruises in the struggle against life at a very early age, see? And a scab begins to form. It never disappears, like a blood scab, but remains permanently on our spirit. Then, there comes another blow and another scab, until it gets to be like a kind of armor which makes us indifferent to everything.

People with more means can afford the luxury of allowing their sons to live in a world of fantasy, of only seeing the good side of life, of protecting them from bad companions and obscene language, of not hurting their sensibilities by witnessing scenes of brutality, of having all their expenses paid for them. But they live with their eyes closed and are naïve in every sense of the word.

All during my boyhood, and even afterward, I spent a lot of time with my gang. We had no chief or leader . . . he would have to be too good at everything . . . but some boys were outstanding in one way or another. We didn't have bad characters like some gangs. There was one bunch in our neighborhood that was known for stealing money from drunks, and for taking marijuana. Only one boy in my gang took to the needle and went bad. In my day, we never did anything worse than grab the girls by their behinds . . . things like that . . .

At that time I very much admired my older cousin, Salvador, the only child of my aunt Guadalupe. He was the terror of the gang of the Street of the Bakers, a really tough gang; of all the members he was the one that was most feared. But I admired him only because he was a good fighter. Otherwise, I didn't think much of him because of the nasty way in which he spoke to my aunt, especially when he was drunk. He took to the bottle and went to the dogs quickly because of a woman he was in love with. He had a son with her but then she went off with another man, the one who finally killed my cousin with an ice pick.

When I was about thirteen, some of the older fellows in the gang wanted to take me to a whore house on Tintero Street. "Not me, brother, to Tintero Street I don't go. My father is liable to kill me. No!" But they said, "What about this guy? Are you a queer or what? It's about time you went. We're going to pay for a broad for you and you are going to screw her." I didn't want to go because I was afraid of getting an infection.

I was, and still am, terribly afraid of getting venereal disease. I was very young when this fear of mine began. Once, in the steam room of the bathhouse, I saw a man with a penis that was half-decayed and full of pus, and that scared me just to see it. Then, someone took me to a museum where I saw pictures of the children of syphilitics . . .

and one of the boys in the Casa Grande had had gonorrhea four or five times. He cried when he urinated and I heard him scream with pain when a doctor treated him.

Once my father also scared me. When I was about twelve, I had arthritic pains in my heels and he saw me walking on my toes, to avoid the pain. He thought it might be from something else, and one day he locked me in the bedroom with him. "Pull down your pants, I want to see. *Cabrón,* how many women have you been with in Tintero Street? I don't want grandchildren that are going to be one-eyed, crippled idiots! Pull down your pants and let me take a look."

"No, *papá* I don't have anything, no!" I was terribly embarrassed to let my father see me . . . I already had hair there and . . . well, I turned my face away because I was so ashamed. But he wasn't satisfied to just look. He took me to a doctor and the faker gave me pills, although nothing was wrong with me.

That's why I did and didn't want to go to Tintero Street with the boys. But they told me that if I squeezed lemon juice on my member afterwards, I wouldn't catch anything, and so we went. Alberto and I and another guy went with the same *señora.* I was so nervous it wouldn't even stand up. My legs were trembling. One of the boys got on top of her and went to work. When he got finished he said, "Now you go."

"O.K.," I said, "but if I catch a disease, you bastard, are you going to give me the money to get treated?"

"This trembling idiot doesn't seem to be a man," they said, and I had to go through with it. I got on top of the *señora.* She moved in a very exaggerated way and it wasn't a bit pleasant. I was thinking that the old girl had had lots of experience, that with her anyone who wanted to could get his end in. I didn't like it at all. But the boys were satisfied with me and so that was over with.

After that, the fever, this sex business, got hold of me in such a way that all I did was to go around thinking about it. At night, my dreams were full of girls and sex. I wanted every woman I saw. And when I couldn't make some girl, I would resort to masturbation.

It was at about that time, I think, that Enoé was working for us. She was a woman who lived in our courtyard and came to the house every day to clean and to cook. Her son was one of my friends. Well, I went after her because I knew that Elena's brother, Raimundo, had laid her. I thought, "*Chirrión,* why only Raimundo? Others also like a *'taco,'* no?" But she said, "Ah! *jodido* . . . you'll have to answer to your *papá*." It seemed that my father was also sighing for her!

I didn't have luck with our servants because my *papá* always got them first. The same thing happened with La Chata. She was very fat and I didn't like her. She made me angry by trying to force me to eat after school. If I said no, she would say, "You're not going to eat? Good, that means more for me." And she would sit right down on her double-sized behind and eat my food.

But she was a woman, and once I spoke to her about . . . this thing. "No," she said, "you are too little, what could *you* do?" But I insisted.

"Well," I said, "maybe you won't feel anything, but I will. Let me! Come on!"

"Well, why not?" she finally said. "Come to see me at my house." So I went to her house, but she had changed her mind. "No! You're just a kid, what do you know about such things? Go on home." And then she told me about my *papá*.

Up to that time I had fooled around with a couple of girls in the *vecindad* and in school . . . Julita, my cousin, the three sisters who lived in the middle courtyard, María . . . about eight in all. But it was just play . . . *papá* and *mamá*, because I was too young to do anything with them.

Then I met Pachita at a dance and she was different altogether. She was a champion dancer and we liked each other. She would press up close to me and would get very flushed when we danced. One night I took her to a hotel.

Well, when we got to the room, I began to kiss her on the neck and on the arms, and she returned my caresses. I took off her shoes and stockings . . . that is the most exciting thing for me . . . the one who struggles a little, who shows a little shyness, excites me more. She was that type. If I wanted to put my hand in a certain place, she wouldn't let me. Well, little by little, I made my way in, and then I felt a completely new sensation in my life because this girl had what we call "dog." You feel something absorbing, sucking . . . well she was the only woman I climbed eight or nine times, while I was going with her. As a matter of fact she was an expert and taught me a lot . . . different positions and how to hold back. That's when I learned that women enjoy it too. But she wasn't for me because I wasn't the one who had dishonored her. Women who have screwed others were not to my liking.

There was a fellow named the Rat . . . he was finally killed . . . well, he wanted to teach me how to be a pimp. He would say to me, "Don't be a jerk, brother. Get hold of a broad and dance with her and get her to fall in love with you. Then you dishonor her and put her to work in a cabaret." He was a good dancer and that was how he got so many girls. I kept saying no because I didn't like the idea. Then he showed Alberto and me one of his girls and he planned for us each to dance with her and treat her to beers until she was so drunk we could all screw her.

So we went to work on that girl. We shoved beer into her, three to our one, until we couldn't any more. We got two nembutals into her and that girl got the three of us drunk! She stood the three of us off and came out walking straight. The Rat couldn't believe it. He said, "I'll be a son-of-a-bitch! How can that fucking broad take all that?" She was one girl who gave us the slip.

Alberto and I were pretty low, really, we were a pair of rascals. He had dishonored a *señorita*, a virgin, and as a result of that, somewhere, there is now a son of his. But he wasn't serious about the affair and wanted to get rid of her. "*Compadre*," he said to me, "there is nothing to do but for you to take her. Make love to her, sleep with her, so I can say, 'You have betrayed me with my best friend.'" I, out of loyalty to my friend, didn't even realize what a dirty trick it was, so I helped him out.

At that time Alberto was in charge of his uncle's second-hand-clothes stall in the outdoor market. The stalls were lined up on both sides of the street, just outside the big market. This stall specialized in "white clothing," that is, underwear, and I helped Alberto sell when I was not in school. He juggled the accounts and didn't turn over all the money, so we went to the movies every day. For more than a year, we went to the movies every single day.

Sometimes we stayed to see the picture three or four times, so we'd buy a couple of big rolls and fill one with beans, another with rice, another with cream or avocado, and we'd take a pile of food with us. We drank two or three sodas apiece, ate oranges, squash seeds, candy, nuts . . . well, we left a huge pile of garbage behind every time. And Alberto paid for everything. He would spend about twenty-five *pesos* a day, of his uncle's money.

Seeing that his business was going down, Alberto's uncle sold the clothing stall, and we didn't have easy money any more. The person

who took care of the stall after that was a girl, Modesta, whom we used
to chat with. She liked us and treated us to *tacos* and sodas. She was
not attractive . . . her face was full of pimples and she had a cataract
in one eye . . . but she had a very provocative body, a nice little
behind and a pretty bust. So when we didn't have money for the
movies, Alberto and I would go to see her.

One time we went with a plan in mind. The stall had a counter
and a back wall, and she sat between. I jumped over the counter and
said, "Hi, Modesta. How goes it? *Caray!* You look more delicious every
day."

"Aha, you bloody bastard. Are you beginning?" she retorted.

"No, really, you've got everything. You're all there." And so we
talked, to heat her up, no?

Finally, she said, "Listen, Manuel, and what does it feel like when
you do it?" She was a virgin then, right?

"*Ay*, don't be foolish. I can't tell you that. We have to do it, to
know." She was sitting on a bench, with her legs apart. "Look, I'll give
you an idea, more or less." And I put my hand between her legs . . .
"And then you just do this, see?"

Alberto signaled to me, to get her on the floor. It was just about
noon and there were lots of people around. But before she knew it I
had her down, under the counter, and Alberto threw a sheet over us. I
unbuttoned her blouse and grabbed her breasts, kissing and biting
them, and went to it.

People were passing by and the sheet was going up and down, up
and down. Alberto told me later that people could see the sheet moving
and he kept pinching me and telling me to stop, but I didn't feel or
hear him. While I was entertaining her that time, Alberto grabbed two
or three children's drawers from her stand, so that we could sell them
and get enough money to go to the movies.

I visited Modesta a few times after that. Once I pulled down her
panties and was stopped short by the sight of blood. I got scared because I thought she had a bad disease or was rotting or something.
That's when I learned about women having "*la regla*."

Menstruation has always seemed like a dirty thing to me, perhaps
because so many of the women I have had were unclean in their habits.
Qué brutas! If there is something I cannot stand, it is the smelly odor
of women. More than once I was in bed, kissing here and biting there,
with all going along well, until the moment came to part her legs . . .

well, sometimes the stink was so bad all my desire fell, and I had to ask her to get up and wash. I have always been allergic to a dirty woman.

At home, Elena kept getting sicker and sicker. She was pale and looked queer; *papá* took her to the doctor and it turned out to be tuberculosis. *Papá* beat us more than ever if we upset Elena. Once he claimed Roberto pushed her and made her much worse. She fell and struck the edge of the washbasin, right over the lung, but I don't think that could have been the cause of her illness. What happened was that she and Roberto had quarreled and she fainted and fell. Later, my father claimed it was our fault that Elena died.

My father was always an extremely jealous man. Once, I believe, Elena was thinking of leaving my father for a butcher, a little runt of a guy. My father found out and one day he came home from work earlier than usual. He grabbed a knife and went toward the butcher shop. Roberto and I followed with rocks and sticks in case he needed help. We saw him go into the shop and talk to the butcher but nothing happened. He went home and bawled out Elena, but not with the same strong, dirty words he used with my mother.

He almost lost faith in Elena another time, because of his nephew. My father had lost track of his family and found this nephew by accident. By chance, my father saw a notice in *El Pepín*, the comic magazine; "Sr. David Sánchez is looking for Sr. Jesús Sánchez, who left Huachinango plantation in the year 1922." My father wrote to him, and David came from Veracruz to live with us. He was the son of my father's brother. I don't even know the names of my uncles! David and his mother were the only ones left and they thought my father must have died too. Every All Saint's Day they had been putting up a candle and food offering for my father's spirit.

Well, my father got David a job in the La Gloria restaurant and we all got along fine. But one day, my *papá* came home and found Elena sitting on David's knee. Now David had always impressed me as being a person completely without malice or evil. Of all my relatives, he was the one I liked best. He had retained the purity of the country and was not rotten like the people of the city. He had a clean soul. That's why I say he wanted nothing from Elena. It was she who had gone after him, and as a result, David went back to Veracruz.

May God forgive me, but I even believe that my father was jealous of Elena and me. I really believe it, because when a person is angry, he looks at you in a particular way, and that is how my father used to look at me. I didn't realize it then but today I can see he was suspicious of Elena and me.

To avoid all the quarrels between Roberto and Elena, my father rented another room in the Casa Grande. We children lived in No. 64 and Elena and her mother, Santitos, lived in No. 103. Elena's two younger brothers and her sister, Soledad, also lived in No. 64 for a while. We got along well with all of them. Santitos was very nice, very reasonable. She always treated us well, and still does to this day. And, strange thing, she never blamed us for Elena's death, like my father did.

I was no longer sore at Elena; I began to feel a certain affection and pity for her. I went with her to the tuberculosis dispensary and saw how they gave her the *numo* (pneumothorax). They pushed a kind of tube with air right into her ribs. My father, poor fellow, was terribly worried and he took her to the best doctors he could find. He put her into the General Hospital and quite often sent me there with fruit and food for her.

I believe it was while Elena was in the hospital that my father came home with a cage full of birds. I thought, "How strange that my father bought birds." I remembered the arguments he had had with my mother because she had wanted him to buy birds for the house. The next day he bought more birds; he kept buying more until the walls of our room were hung with cages. And what a noise when all those birds began to sing at once. It sounded nice, it made me think I was in the country or in a forest.

But my father made Roberto and me get up at six o'clock in the morning to feed them, and I hated the birds for that. I always had trouble getting up early and when I heard my father say, "Manuel! Roberto! Up!" it was terrible for me.

The first few days when my father called, I'd say "*Ay, papá,* my legs hurt. Let Roberto feed the birds." But Roberto soon caught on and I had to get up too. We had to chop several kilos of bananas with a large *machete,* and mix the fruit with flour and some greens. Then we put the food in each cage, changed the water and cleaned up the bird's mess.

One day my father said, "Manuel, you are going to the market to sell birds." It felt good to help my father, I was glad he thought me worthy. But at bottom I was ashamed of the work. I carried the cages, one on top of the other, and walked through the market trying to sell the birds.

One Wednesday, along came my father, to see how I was doing. While we were standing there, an agent of the Forestry Department came up and asked my father to show him the permit to sell animals. My *papá* didn't have any permit and since he had never been involved in these things, he got very nervous. I think the bribe he gave the police was larger than the fine.

After that he sold birds only to neighbors and to his fellow workers; he got a lot of customers when he became the *compadre* of a big bird-dealer who lived on the Street of the Potters. I think my father went into selling birds and then pigeons, turkeys, chickens and pigs because, after being a worker for so many years, he discovered that he had a taste for business. It came late to him, but he realized he could make more money that way.

I began to get wind of the existence of my half-sisters, Antonia and Marielena, when I was about fourteen. Before that I had no idea my father had another wife and other children. But I do remember that once, when I was ten years old, my father took me to help him in La Gloria restaurant. On the way home, we came to Rosario Street and my *papá* said, "You wait here on the corner." He left me and walked into a tenement. I wondered, "What's my *papá* doing there, whom is he going to see?" I got a feeling something like jealousy. I even wondered whether my mother had been right in believing that my father had another woman.

Now I realize that he had been visiting Lupita. She is the mother of my half-sisters. As a child I never knew her and even later I scarcely exchanged three words with her.

Once I came home after midnight and noticed that an extra person was sleeping in my sisters' bed. Roberto was in his usual place on the floor and my father was in his bed. I tiptoed to the girls' bed and leaned over to see who was there. My father, who must have been watching me in the dark, said suddenly, "It's your sister."

"My sister?"

"Yes, your sister Antonia."

Well, after that I didn't say anything; I just went to bed. Nobody had ever told me about her before. I wondered, "Where does this sister

come from?" I was anxious for the morning to come so I could see my
new sister.

She was not attractive as a girl although likeable and pleasant in
the way she chatted. But she always had a kind of unfriendly feeling
toward us, something like a grudge. From the very beginning, she
hated my father and gave him trouble. She'd use swear words and
talked back to him in such a way that I wanted to slap her across the
mouth. Why, once my father was telling her she shouldn't do something, and she said, "I can do as I damned well please, and what's it
to you anyway . . . who's getting the raw deal, who?" That's the way
she screamed at my *papá*.

I never liked Antonia after that. I stayed away from her as much
as possible, partly because I was afraid I'd see her as a woman, not
as a sister. We hardly spoke to each other even though we lived in
the same house.

But my brother Roberto was very much in love with her. I do not
know how my father got wind of it, but he found out. I can't tell
whether Roberto loved her as a sister, or like a woman, but the fact
is he was terribly fond of her.

Meanwhile, Elena wasn't getting better in the hospital and she
came home. When her condition became serious, my father sent us
to my aunt Guadalupe to get the priest. The priest asked whether my
father had been married before and we said no. Then he went ahead
and married Elena and my father, so that her soul could rest in peace.
I believe my *papá* still has the marriage ring.

One afternoon, when I got home, Marta said, "Go to Elena's room."
I went in and she was dead. My father had been quite hopeful a few
days before, because she had been gaining weight. He thought this
was a sign she was getting better, and then she died. I remember the
scene very well. The coffin was in the middle of the room, a lighted
candle at each corner. Some people were there, and my father was
standing in the doorway. When he noticed me, he said, "Look at what
you've done, you bastards, you, you are the ones who killed her, you
sons-of-bitches."

I understood it was because of his grief, a burst of despair, but that's
the way my father has always been. I don't know why, but no matter
what happened he always said, "It'll go bad for you and wherever you
go, they'll shut the door in your face." He was always wishing me bad
luck. That day my father made me so ashamed I hid behind the door,

and inside of me I said, "Forgive me, forgive me if I did you any harm, Elena; forgive me for any wrong I may have done you," and that's all I could say.

Roberto was there crying, crying over her; Consuelo was also there, and my father, grief-stricken, blaming us for her death. She was laid out just two days—not like my mother—and then we buried her in the same cemetery. My father bought a little piece of ground "in perpetuity," and had a little brick fence put up around it. He paid a man to take care of the grave.

Well, after we buried her, my father's attitude toward us became more bitter and gruff. His grudge against us grew bigger, he always blamed us that he couldn't live happily with her. Life at home became worse and I spent more and more time out of the house.

Just opposite the clothing stall, where we hung out, was a restaurant, Lin's Café, owned by a Chinese. A pretty girl, Graciela, came to work there as a waitress. She had dark curly hair and light skin. I liked her right away. "*Ay, ojón!* Really, *compadre*," I said to Alberto, "that one has everything! *A todo dar!* Look how pretty that girl is. How much do you bet that I'll tie her up?" I said it just like that, without meaning it seriously.

"Yeah? What do you mean, tie her up? She won't even notice you. You don't find bugs like that on your *petate!* That dame goes out with guys who dress well and who have *centavos*."

In the evening we had supper there, and I saw Graciela in passing. I was a little embarrassed because I still couldn't use a knife and fork very well . . . at home we never used them, we ate with *tortillas* . . . but I soon became expert, because from then on, I ate all my meals there, day after day. It became a big habit with me . . . in fact, I misspent fourteen or fifteen years of my life in that place and in other cafés.

I asked Lin for a job, but there was nothing doing for me there. He taught me how to bake bread and later he sometimes let me pay for my meals by baking for him.

Anyway, I had bet Alberto that I could get Graciela to be my sweetheart, my *novia*, and I set out to do it. It took money, so I said to my father, "Listen, *papá*, I'd like to earn a few *centavos*. I'm in school but I can work at the same time." I spoke to Ignacio, my aunt's husband. He said, "Well, why not come and sell newspapers with me, what's wrong with that?"

The next day I went out selling newspapers with Ignacio. We went over to Bucareli Street where we waited for the *Ultimas Noticias* and the *Gráfico*. Papers sold for ten or fifteen *centavos* and we would make about four and a half *centavos* a paper. I got my papers and my uncle said, "Now start running."

I said, "Where?"

"Well, any street you want, just run and shout *Gráfico, Noticias!*" I started running, running, from the Caballito de Troya down Francisco I. Madero, then I went up Brasil all the way to Peralvillo and from there I returned, running all the way, past my house. I sold my papers and was back again in the Zócalo. As soon as I returned, I gave Ignacio the money. "That's fine, look you made yourself two *pesos*." I went home, washed my face, combed my hair and went to school.

At first, Graciela didn't take to me at all, not at all. I know this because once I was eating supper in one of the booths in back and she didn't see me. She was talking with Alberto and told him, "Don't bring that heel, Manuel, if we go to the movies, because I don't like him."

That really hit me hard, "Why in hell did she say that? I never did anything to her." So I said to myself, "Just for spite I'm going to make you my *novia*." She told one of the other waitresses, "He's all right but he doesn't work, he doesn't do a thing, wasting his time like a fool with his little books. I bet he does not even go to school. He doesn't go to school or to work, so what good would it do me to go with him?" Ah, well, I was pleased to hear that and decided to look for a job.

The sixth-grade final exams were coming up and I was afraid I was going to fail. My teachers didn't have a good opinion of me and wanted to expel me, but my father asked them to give me another chance and they did. I passed the exams and graduated. I was a little disappointed because no one in my family came to my graduation. I expected my father to congratulate me or give me an embrace, but he didn't. He didn't even do it on my fifteenth birthday, or my twenty-first, when a boy really becomes a man. He didn't even change his tone of voice with me!

After my graduation, I told my father I was through with studying and wanted to go to work. It was the biggest mistake of my life, but I didn't know it then. I was determined to make Graciela my *novia* and all I wanted was to get a job and earn money. My father was pretty sore because I didn't want to study for a career. I think if he had talked it over with me like a good friend, I might have continued school. But instead, he said, "So you think you want to work? Do you think it's so nice to have someone boss you around all your life? I'm ready to give you a chance and you throw it away. O.K., go be an idiot. If that's what you want, go to it."

Alberto had already gone to work in a shop where they made glass lamp fixtures. He didn't know how to read or write, but he was smart and was making good money, anyway. Since we wanted to be together, I went to look for a job in his shop. I told the *maestro* that I knew how to work the machines and the drills, and he accepted me.

But I kept breaking the glass pieces and my finger tips were skinned and bleeding from the emery. They burned horribly and I finally confessed that I had never worked the machines before. So they set me to polishing glass, instead. Polishing was easy, but very dirty work since glass is polished with soot. Later they taught me how to shape *"cocolitos,"* pendants, on the machines. You grab a piece of glass with three fingers and told it tightly against the wheel to cut it down. I caught on to this work quickly and they kept me. Raimundo, Elena's brother, was living with us then, and I even got him into the shop. We worked the machine together and between us, we knocked out two or three thousand *"cocolitos"* a week.

The *maestro* treated us well; on Fridays, he gave us tickets to the fights, and on the days we worked late, he blew us to our supper. But he knew how to stick us, too, the bastard. He really was sharp, and we were the suckers. He'd say to me, "*Ay! Chino,* Raimundo says he can work faster than you on the machine."

"What? The dumb ox!" I'd say. "How can he work faster if I was the one who taught him?"

Then the *maestro* would go to Raimundo and say, so that I did not hear, "So *Chino* can do two to your one, eh? He says he can beat you without trying." So we two fools began competing with each other, going at a fast pace and producing more for the *maestro.* That's how he got double work out of us.

The pay was very little and because I ate at a lunch counter with the boys during the week, by Saturday I had only seven *pesos* left. When I got home that night, I said, "Look, *papá,* all I have left from my wages are five *pesos,* take them." At that time, my father was pretty sore at me on account of Elena's death. Anyway, he was standing by the table and I put down the five *pesos*. He stood there, looking hard at me, picked up the five-*peso* bill and threw it in my face.

"I don't collect alms from you, you bastard. Go and spend your few pennies with your fucking friends. I'm not asking you for anything. I'm still strong and can work." That hurt me a lot, because God knows that was all I had. The next time I tried to give him money, he did the same thing. After that I never gave him a single *centavo!*

Later, another *maestro* offered me a job drilling holes in glass. He paid by the piece and offered me three and a half *centavos* a piece. Other places paid less, so I took the job thinking I'd make more money. Well, I worked fast and hard all week. The thousands of holes I drilled there! On Saturday, when the week was up, the *maestro* said, "Come on, boys, let's see how much pay you get." The old man couldn't read or write and he had one of the boys figure up the wages. "Let's see how many pieces *Chinito* made." The old man's eyes stood out, he really opened them, when my pay totaled 385 *pesos*.

"No, no young man, no! How am I going to pay a kid of his age three hundred eighty-five *pesos!* Better keep the whole lousy shop! I don't get a thing out of this place, I just keep it up to entertain you fellows. I'm the owner and so help me God, I don't make more than fifty *pesos* a week on it. No! I can't give you that much money. The trouble is that you work too quickly."

"But, *maestro*, if you pay me by the piece, I have to hurry, no? And you promised three and a half *centavos*, didn't you?"

"Yes, but I didn't think you would earn so much! All I can give you is a hundred *pesos*, take it or leave it!" Well, I had to take the money, but that is when I began to hate to work for a boss.

Graciela became my *novia*, all right, just as soon as I started to work. Every night, after the job, I went to the café to see her and I didn't get home until past twelve o'clock. We went to the movies several times and I began to feel I loved her a lot, with a real passion.

It was about that time that I learned to play cards, to gamble. The first time I played was one Saturday, when I came home to the Casa Grande after work. There, near the water tank were some friends of mine, Domingo, Santiago, the fellow who is now in jail for killing a guy, and a couple of others. Santiago said, "Look, look, here comes the hard worker, the bastard turned out to be a worker."

"Sure, you stupid ass! *pinche guey!* You just pound the pavement all day. Do you think everyone is a pimp?" That's how we kidded around with each other. Then Domingo, knowing I had my week's pay in my pocket, said, "Come on, *compadre,* let's play a little game of poker."

"But I don't even know how to eat this crap, brother! What a joke! Do you think I'm a sucker, a *pendejo?*"

"I'll show you, I'll tell you when you win! Come on, we'll only play for five *centavos,* go on, sit down."

Well, they knew I never said no, so we all kneeled in a circle behind the tank, where we could see by the courtyard light. Naturally, I lost that time, but I learned the rules of the game. I made a real study of it, going around asking questions all week. I had the great advantage, or perhaps disadvantage, of learning it quickly, and in a week I was a good player. I always had unusual luck when it came to playing poker, a luck that seemed boundless, even excessive.

Without noticing it, I was caught up in a whirlwind of card playing. If a day passed without a game, I was desperate. I looked for boys to play a round or two. I began betting at five *centavos* but soon I was betting my whole week's pay. I always felt certain I would win. Even if I had been losing and was down to my last five *pesos,* I would say, "Let's see if with these five, God wishes me to rise again!" Fine, as if by magic, always, well, nine out of ten times, with my last five *pesos,* up I'd go!

The fellows would say; "What happened? You bum, someone is passing you cards on the sly! Keep it on the up and up . . . none of this 'sucker' stuff . . . don't go hiding little cards under the table . . . you bastard, if there were no thieves there would be no distrust!"

And that's how it went. Once I lost seventy *pesos,* but that was because the winner, a man named Delfino, left without giving us a chance to win back. He owned a few trucks and had lots of *centavos* but when he saw he was winning he got up and said, "I've got to go boys. I have something to attend to . . . man, I forgot all about that lousy appointment."

When he left I was shaking with anger, because I hadn't won a single game. "The bastard," I said. "He made a sucker out of me."

The next day was Sunday, the day we usually played soccer in the courtyards. I went to the bathhouse for a shower and as I came out, holding my bundle of clothes, I bumped into Delfino.

"What's up, *Chino?*" he said. "Do you want revenge, you bastard? All you need to play is money and balls."

"Sure, do you think I'm a cripple or something, you'll see."

He went to call Domingo and the Bird, two compatriots from his homeland, Chiapas, and we sat down to play. First we played *"conquián"* but when I won, Delfino wanted to switch to poker.

"O.K.," I said, "any ass hole is good enough for me—*cualquier culo me raspa el chile.* No matter what, this time you'll sweat to take my money away from me."

And so we started a round of poker. Well, that was a game to remember! I started out by betting two *pesos.* When it went up to thirty *pesos,* the Bird dropped out. Then Delfino bet fifty . . . he must have had a good hand . . . whenever he got a card, he blew on it and rubbed it between his legs, on his testicles, for luck.

"You've got to heat it up to have it come," he said, "make it curdle . . . It got me three sevens already, imagine!" He said that without showing his cards, see? But I had him killed from there on because I had three kings and a knight. I bet fifty more, very calmly.

"*Puta madre!* Slut of a mother!" he said, "now you're really offering yourself up. Damn it, you're pretty sure of yourself, you son-of-a-*guayaba!*"

"Yes, I'm up against the wall, but I know how to defend myself. I get along. Don't tremble, you runt. Get hold of your cigarette, your hand is shaking!"

Again he rubbed his cards between his legs, but I had the guy licked, because I drew another king.

"You're doing all the rubbing and blowing, but I'm the one who is going to suck the tit!"

When he saw that I had four kings he said, "Whoring mother! How do you expect me to believe that? No, this isn't luck, this must be dirty tricks!"

"Look, you did the dealing, not I. I have only my little tail to help me. If there were no God for suckers well, brother of my soul . . ."

I picked up over a thousand *pesos* in that game. Then I stood up. "I'm going, fellows . . . I didn't remember that I had an appointment . . . dammit, man, I forgot all about it."

I tell you, I was famous in the Casa Grande for being, well, a little less than a wizard at cards. Everybody watched my hands when I dealt, but I swear I never used tricks. It is just that I had extraordinary luck, luck without limit! I won so often that some of the boys swore they would never play with me again. They advised me to go to the elegant casinos to gamble, but there the cards are all marked. There they would take me over. I told my friends, "No, I'll go along here with my little luck. I'm satisfied to make enough for my little expenses, right?"

My luck led me into more and more gambling; the bad thing was that I never benefited by it, because after the game I went out with my friends and their girls and threw it all away. I never did anything practical with my winnings.

When my father learned about my gambling, naturally, he was very angry. But no one in my family knew how much money I won nor how I spent it.

Every night I went to the café to see Graciela. She was busy waiting on tables and I used to spend most of my time in the kitchen, talking to her friend, Paula, who worked there too. The curious thing is that although I loved Graciela desperately, I preferred talking to "Shorty," that is, Paula. I found her more understanding, and I got her to "light up" Graciela by putting in a good word for me. When Paula saw me jealous of some guy or depressed because of a quarrel with Graciela, she would say, "Don't worry, Manuel. Don't pay any attention to the way she is, because I know that at bottom she really loves you. She told me so." That's the way she talked, always making me feel better.

The truth was, that my relations with Graciela were insecure. I was always afraid of losing her. I had bad dreams in which she betrayed me in some ugly way; I felt anxious because of her. She was so pretty, men were always after her—she was lucky that way. Some of her customers left her fifty-*peso* tips. But she seemed to love me, and, on more than one occasion, she was jealous of me too. We finally broke up because I insisted on going to Chalma with Shorty.

Paula had told me that she was going to Chalma with her mother and sister Delila. I was planning to go too, so I said, "Just you three women? What the hell, maybe we'll go together." When I told Graciela she said, "Oh, yes? Well, you're not going."

Now, when we had a disagreement, I always made it a point to tell her off. I had to have it my own way, and I also made it clear that I wasn't stuck on her, though I really loved her very much. I'd say, "I don't understand why some men fight over a woman. If you ever cheat on me, I won't fight for you."

About two months before I went to Chalma, a chap from Puebla,

Andrés, came to the café and I noticed him give Graciela the eye. It seemed to me she also looked at him in an interested way. The day I was supposed to leave for Chalma, I spoke up.

"Look, Andrés, I've noticed there's something between you and Graciela, and if you're a friend of mine you have to be straight with me. Tell me the truth and I promise I won't lift a hand, I won't do anything to you."

"No, Manuel, how do you expect Graciela to go out with me if she is your *novia?*" he said. "You're the one she likes, and I'm not the type to play a dirty trick on you."

Meanwhile Shorty and her mother were preparing *tortillas* and hard-boiled eggs for the trip, grub for the road, as we say here. We carried the suitcases on our backs, and took the bus to Santiago Temistengo. That year, my friend Alberto went with us. We were very happy together, Shorty, Alberto and I, praying and singing on the way. We passed through the woods and it was beautiful at dawn. The smell of the pine trees and the country was fine and sometimes from the top of a hill we could see a little village way off, and the little Indian women making *tortillas.*

An hour before arriving at the Sanctuary, there is a gigantic *ahuehuete* tree at which the pilgrims usually stop. This tree is the nicest thing about going to Chalma. It is hung with women's braids and children's shoes and other testimonials of the pilgrims' faith, and it is so wide I think it would take ten men to encircle it. The tree stands between two hills, and a little river flows out from under it. Well, we pilgrims arrived tired from the road, and with much faith in our hearts, bathed our feet in the healing waters and all our tiredness and ills left us.

The entrance to Chalma is down a winding road that leads right to the Sanctuary. It always gave me the greatest satisfaction to enter the Church and kneel in the cool darkness and see the figure of the Sainted Christ of Chalma. He seemed to be receiving me alone, and that gave me a wonderful feeling, because I had much faith at that time. I asked the Saint to give me strength, to show me the way to earn enough money to marry Graciela, and not to let her betray me.

Absolutely nothing happened between Shorty and me on that trip. On the contrary, I wanted Alberto and Paula to become *novios* so all four of us could go out together. I talked with Paula about my problems with Graciela all during the trip, all the seven days. Then I noticed that Paula looked at me in a special sort of way. Once I pretended that a poisonous scorpion had bitten me. I fainted and everything, and she was scared, poor thing, really scared, more than you get for just a friend. So I said to myself, "God! could it be possible? She's probably in love with me." But I had no idea of getting involved with her.

My prayer to the Lord of Chalma went back on me because as soon as we returned Andrés told me that Graciela was his *novia*. I was very angry, I felt like busting his bones, but I tried to keep my word not to hit him. "O.K., Andrés, except that she'll have to come and tell me herself."

"Well," he said, "that won't be possible because from now on I don't want you to have anything to do with her."

"Oh, no?" I said. "So now it's not a matter between friends. Now it's a question of man to man, and I'm going to show you I'm more of a man than you are," and then bang! I gave him such a sock he fell down head over heels. I lifted him up and leaned him against the wall, and bang, bang, I walloped him in the stomach.

I went to speak to Graciela. "Good evening," I said. "I was bringing you a gift, a compact I bought at Chalma . . . but when Andrés told me about you two I stomped on it and broke it." I came close to her and asked, "Graciela, is it true Andrés is your *novio*? Answer me, don't be afraid."

She stood there looking at me very sadly. She just nodded her head, and did not speak. My first reaction was to slap her face. But I'd never fight over a woman; it would show her I loved her a lot. I controlled myself. "Ah, how nice! Let me congratulate you, Graciela, look I'm a gambler and I play it straight, win or lose. This time I lost, right? It doesn't matter, Graciela, here is my hand, let's remain friends, no hard feelings."

She stood there, very angry by now, and burst out crying. "What the hell," I said, and I turned around and left.

Well, I was very unhappy about all this. I changed my job, and went to work for some Spaniards. I started at eight *pesos* a day. They paid me for Sunday too, and so I made fifty-six *pesos* a week. Now I had a little more money and I didn't have to turn any of it over to my father either.

About Graciela, I thought, "If she did this to me, I'll pay her back in kind, with someone she's close to so it'll be real hard on her. I've

got to make her suffer." Right away I decided on Shorty, and I began
to court her. After that I went to the café every day to see Paula. I
asked her to be my *novia*.

"But it's not right, because you are in love with Graciela. How is it
that you are talking to me this way?"

"No, really, I told you that so you'd tell her and make her think I
really loved her. But I'm not in love with her. After all, didn't I always
chat with you when I came here?"

I don't know where I got all the arguments, but the fact is it was
a hard job courting Paula.

It lasted over a month and she always said, "I'll think about it,
I'll think about it." Finally, she said, "Well, all right." By then she
wanted to be my *novia*.

Paula had a big quarrel with Graciela on account of this. Paula said,
"So what are you complaining about? You pulled the same dirty trick
with Andrés, who was his friend. Besides, he wasn't your husband,
only your *novio*. Now he's *my novio* and I love him."

Then Graciela said, "The trouble is, Andrés really wasn't my *novio*.
I said this only to see if Manuel loved me, because Andrés told me that
Manuel was just trying to make a fool of me."

Andrés had convinced Graciela to test me; they had put on an act
which I fell for. After that, I didn't feel I loved Paula, but because of
the eternal vanity, the *pendejo machismo* of the Mexican, I couldn't
humiliate myself by going back to Graciela. I loved her with all my
soul and deep down I really wanted to say, "Come back to me . . .
let's go together seriously . . ." But I set my pride and my vanity
above everything else. My heart told me to tell her the truth, but I
was afraid that she would make fun of my sentiments. It was a play
of tactics between us, and little by little, without either of us wishing
it, we took different roads.

So I continued to see Paula and to take her out. I got her to quit
her job at the café, and she found another, weaving children's coats.

I once caught Paula in a lie and thought she was deceiving me.
She had told me she was going to Querétaro to see her sister who was
ill, but while she was away, Delila blurted out that Paula was in
Veracruz, with a man and a girl friend. When Paula returned, I said,
"How were things in Querétaro, Paula?"

"Well, fine."

"And how's your sister?"

"Well, she wasn't very ill, but you know how people exaggerate these things."

When she said that I slapped her in the face. "Look, don't give me any of that crap; you didn't go to Querétaro. Don't pull anything on me. You took yourself a little trip to Veracruz."

"Who told you?"

"Somebody, as you can see," I said. "So you did go to Veracruz?" and bang! I slapped her again. I was really very angry with her and I beat her.

She began to cry, "Yes, Manuel, but I swear to you by my mother, by all I cherish most, may my mother drop dead, if I did anything bad. What happened is that my girl friend was going with this fellow and she asked me to go along to protect her."

I was pretty sure Paula had cheated on me. "No, sir," I told her, "I'm not taking any of that stuff from you, and if you're that easy to get, you come with me now, we'll go to the hotel."

"No, Manuel."

"No?" I said to her. "But you did go off with the other fellow, didn't you? So if you're a street walker come on with me and tell me how much you're going to charge. You can't be worth more than fifty *centavos*, not for me anyway."

She was crying and crying. "Look, Manuel, please come with me, do me a favor, I beg you." Well, deep down I hoped she hadn't done anything bad. We went to her friend's house, and the girl backed up Paula's story.

I wasn't entirely convinced and, whether she liked it or not, I made Paula go with me to a hotel that night.

I should explain that in Mexico, at least in my case, even if I believe that my *novia* loves me, there is always a doubt, a jealousy, no? And one day the man says, "Give me proof of your love. If you love me you will go with me." I had never thought of going through either a civil or a church wedding, it simply never occurred to me, and that is true of most of the men and women I know. I always assumed that if the woman loves me and I love her and we wish to live together, then the legal papers and things like that are not important. If my *novia* were to demand that I marry her and set up a house for her, I would immediately act offended and would say, "Then it isn't true that you love me! Where is your love if you set up conditions to love me?"

There is also the matter of being poor. If one begins to examine what a marriage comes to, a poor man realizes he doesn't have enough money for a wedding. Then he decides to live this way, without it, see? He just takes the woman, the way I did with Paula. Besides, a poor man has nothing to leave to his children so there is no need to protect them legally. If I had a million *pesos*, or a house, or a bank account or some material goods, I would have a civil marriage right away to legalize my children as my legitimate heirs. But people in my class have nothing. That is why I say, "As long as *I* know these are my children, I don't care what the world thinks."

A civil marriage is not costly like a church wedding, but then one rejects the legal responsibilities too. We have a saying, "The illusions of matrimony end in bed." I couldn't commit myself to all the legal responsibilities at the risk of suffering a failure later. We didn't know each other profoundly and how could we know how we would react to intimacy? And the majority of women here don't expect weddings; even they believe that the sweetheart leads a better life than the wife. What usually happens is that the woman goes with the man and it isn't until after a honeymoon of about six months that she begins to protest and wants him to marry her. But that is just the conventionalism of women. They want to tie a man up in chains!

We have a firm belief that it is one thing to be lovers, and it is another to be man and wife. And if I ask a woman to be my wife, I feel as much responsibility toward her as I would if we were married. Marriage wouldn't change a thing! That is the way it was with Paula and me.

We continued to go to hotels on the sly for a few months, but I was not satisfied. I think that at bottom I was looking for a way to escape my father, for a way to leave my home, once and for all, and to become a man. So one evening I said, "Take your choice, Paula. Look, I'm going this way, your house is the opposite way. From now on I don't want you to go to your house. What do you say to that?"

"No, Manuel," she said. "What about my mother and brothers and sisters?"

"Oh, well, then you don't love me. Choose either of these two roads, except that if you go home, we won't see each other any more. If you go with me, you'll be my wife, you'll live with me."

Well, she made up her mind, and instead of going home, she came with me. That's how we got married: I had just turned fifteen and she was nineteen.

Roberto

I STARTED STEALING THINGS FROM MY OWN HOUSE WHEN I WAS SMALL.
I saw something I liked and swiped it without asking anybody's
permission. Just like that. I began by stealing an egg. It wasn't
that I was starving, see? because my mother fed us well. It was just
for the fun of filching it, and sharing it with my friends in the courtyard, and feeling important.

I stole twenty *centavos* from my mother when I was just a little
fellow, five or six, more or less. Twenty *centavos* at that time was like
ten *pesos* today. My father gave us five *centavos* every day, but all
my life I've always wanted more, and when I saw a twenty *centavo*
piece on the cupboard, well, there wasn't anybody around and I
thought I might as well take it. I bought some candy and it was my
bad luck that they gave me a lot of change, all single *centavos*.

So I had a lot of money in my pocket, right? When I got home in
the evening, they began to ask about the missing coin. I thought,
"*Caramba!* as soon as they get the idea of fishing me they'll find the
money and I'll get a licking I won't forget for ten years. I'd better
go to the toilet."

The toilet, which was right inside the house, had only a half-door,
so when I threw the *centavos* into the toilet bowl it made a hell of
a big noise and they knew what I did. Even though I flushed the coins
away forever, they knew. Now, wasn't that something? Like I said,
I was a bad egg from the time I was born. So I got a real thrashing
that day. My mother, my father, and my mother's mother, may she rest
in peace, gave me my punishment so I wouldn't do it again.

My mother took good care of us. She was loving to me, but she

loved Manuel the most. She rarely hit me, and I know she loved me
a lot because she always took me with her wherever she went, me
more than the others. She used to say, "Roberto, let's go and get the
cake trimmings."

"All right, *mamá*, sure, let's go."

My mother and father usually got along well, except for one terrible
quarrel which left a lasting impression on me. My father was holler-
ing at my mother, may she rest in peace, and, well, he was pretty mad.
My mother's mother and my aunt Guadalupe kept him from hitting
her. His key ring fell on the floor during the fight and I grabbed it and
ran out. It had a razor blade on it and since my father was very
quick-tempered, I thought he might want to use it on my mother.

My aunt, my granny Pachita, and the servant, Sofía, all jumped in
and held him off. When I came back to the house, the fight was over.
My father took me with him to the Villa where he prayed to the Virgin.
I saw him cry and I cried with him. Then he quieted down and bought
me a *taco*.

Every year the Three Kings came on the sixth of January and left
us toys in the flowerpot stand where my mother kept her favorite
plants. But one sixth of January the Three Kings were unable to come
to our poor house, and I felt I was the unluckiest child in the world.
We children got up early, like all children do on that day, to look for
our toys. We went looking in the flowerpot stand, then we looked in
the brazier to see if the Kings left something for us in the ashes and
charcoal. Unfortunately they didn't, so all that was left for us to do
was to go out to the courtyard and watch our friends play with their
toys. When they asked, "What did the Kings bring you?" Manuel and
I said, "They didn't bring us anything."

It was the last sixth of January my mother spent with us before she
died. After that I cried for years.

We were living in one room on Tenochtitlán Street. My father and
mother slept in one bed, Manuel, Consuelo and I slept in the other.
When Marta was older she slept with us too. We slept crosswise, first
Manuel, then Consuelo, then Marta, then me, always in that order.

I had a real problem. I always wet the bed, right up to the age of
nine or ten. They called me the champion bed-wetter in the house. I
wasn't the only bed-wetter, because Manuel and Consuelo also did
it sometimes. On account of this habit of mine, my father and mother
gave me several whalings and threatened to bathe me in cold water

in the morning. Once my mother actually did. Of course, I'm not blaming her; she did it to break me of the habit, but it stayed with me for a long time.

I was about six when my mother died in my father's arms early one morning. Her death was a shock and a torment to me all my life, because I feel I was to blame. The day before she died, we all had gone to the Basilica with my aunt and my uncles, Alfredo and José. We were very happy. My blessed mother was always celebrating our Saint's Day and we ate pork and stuff like that, which you know are not good for you. They bring on attacks, and my mother came down with an attack on account of me.

Actually, what happened was that later that day she asked me to bring the bird cages down from the roof. My mother was very fond of birds, understand? She kept the walls covered with bird cages, just because she loved the little creatures. So I climbed on the roof and some dirt dropped over to our neighbor's side and the woman there began to throw water on me.

"You brat, why don't you watch what you're doing?"

My mother ran out to defend me and had an argument with the neighbor. If she hadn't had the argument, my *mamá* would not have died. Anyway, whether I feel guilty or not, that's what happened.

They woke us up at about 2:00 A.M. I didn't want to get up because I had wet the bed and was afraid they would punish me. But we saw my father crying and we got up frightened. I knew something bad was happening because my father had my mother in his arms. We were all crying at the head of the bed when the doctor came. Our relatives tried to get us out of the house but I fought to stay.

I didn't want to believe that my mother was dead. They laid her out and that night I secretly got into bed with her. They were looking for me, and I was sleeping next to my mother under the sheet they had covered her with. At that age I already knew that dying meant the person left this world forever, though I told my brother and sister, "Don't cry, *mamá* is just sleeping." And I went close to my mother and said, "*Mamá, mamá,* you're sleeping, aren't you?" I touched her face, but I knew she would never wake up again.

I missed my mother then, and I still miss her. Since her death I felt I could never be happy again. Some people feel relieved when they talk about their troubles, but I've told this to many people and it has never helped. I feel calm only when I run away, when I go off as a vagabond, when I am alone in the country or up in the mountains. I believe if my mother were still alive I'd be very different. Or perhaps I'd be worse.

When my mother died, my grandmother was a second mother to me. I followed her around all the time. I called her little grandmother with the same love that I had called my mother, *mamá*. She was always good to us, but was very strict and stern in character. After all, she was old and had been brought up in the old style. They were more upright in everything.

She came to live with us and took good care of us. She sold cake crumbs in the plaza and I used to visit her all the time. I felt an urge to be with her because she understood me and used to give me lots of advice. The rest of the family, even my aunt Guadalupe who was closest to us, used to call me *"negro cambujo"* and "devil face." I never knew what "black *cambujo*" meant but it hurt me just the same. So I always stuck close to my grandmother.

Manuel never wanted to go with her to buy the cake crumbs or the bread. I was the one who liked to go with her. I don't know why, I was only a kid, but I felt that if I went along with her early in the morning, nothing could possibly happen to her, and thank God, we never came to any harm. One time Manuel went with us and he made my grandmother very angry. A vendor was selling sugared crab apples on a stick, shouting, *"Tejocotes, tejocotes* one *centavo."* Manuel, who was always teasing my grandmother, began to yell, "Grandmothers, one *centavo* . . . a *centavo* a grandmother . . ." Well, she scolded him and tried to grab him, but, of course, she could never catch him. He was a fast runner. He was only fooling, but he made her cry that time, and it hurt me very much.

We were living on Cuba Street at the time, yes, on Cuba Street, because my *papá* had just gotten to know Elena, and my grandmother left our house and went to live with my aunt Guadalupe. I felt even more lonely and really missed my mother then, because as long as my grandmother was there, I didn't feel as though my mother was gone.

When Elena came to be my stepmother I went to my granny Pachita to complain, telling her Elena this and Elena that. My grandmother was my crying towel in those days. I really unburdened myself with her. I even stole the plants and, well, I didn't steal them, they were my mother's and I didn't want Elena to touch them, so I would bring them to my grandmother or to my aunt. But I lost my poor little grandmother too, for she died soon after.

From the beginning, my stepmother didn't like me and I didn't like her. We did not get along very well, my young stepmother and I. For me there was only one mother in all the world, and even though a hundred others came along and wanted to act like my mother, it was not the same thing. Besides, I had learned from my friends that stepmothers were bad.

Elena was about eighteen years old, I think, or less. Anyway, she was too young and lacked experience to take care of a widower with four children. She didn't know how to get us to obey her, especially me, for I was the wildest. If she had spoken to me nicely, I would have been putty in her hands, but she always wanted to control me, to order me around, to dominate my life. Ever since I was small, I didn't like to have anyone but my mother or father order me around. If Elena laid a hand on me I would fight back. I always defended myself physically, I never knew how to defend myself with words.

One of the reasons I fought so much with Elena was because on account of her Manuel and I had to sleep on the floor. Once I heard my *papá* and Elena talking. She was saying that we had had the bed long enough and that the girls were growing up. So my father ordered Manuel and me to sleep on the floor—not exactly on the floor, because my *papá* bought straw mats for us. I guess at that time he couldn't buy a bed.

I cried a few times but never said a word to my father. It hurt and I had a feeling of anguish around my heart. I felt sad, like a dog, sleeping on the floor. I missed my *mamá* very much then. When she was alive we slept on beds and were better off. Even after she died . . . before Elena came . . . we slept in a bed, with my *papá*, in the place that Elena took.

I was very happy sleeping next to my father. What fights Manuel and I had when he took my place next to my *papá!* We would argue until my *papá* said, "Everybody shut up and go to sleep." Wham! Out would go the light, off would come his shoes, his pants would be put on the chair, and then everything was quiet.

From the beginning, one of the things that I didn't like was that Elena had been living with another man. I was very much afraid for my father, because her ex-husband might take revenge or something.

My father gave me many scoldings and beatings on account of the ideas my stepmother put into his head. She was not entirely wrong but she embroidered the truth and twisted things. And many times she provoked me into being bad. If I jumped on the bed and got it dirty, she said, "Get off, *negro cambujo!*" That would hurt me and I answered, "You filthy old bag, why do you call me black? If I am black it is because God made me that way." Then she would hit me and I would hit her back and make her cry.

When my father came home, instead of saying "hello," she heaped it all up on him. So my father, who was all worn out from the day's work, would become exasperated and wouldn't even listen to me. He just beat me. The next day I tangled with Elena again.

My poor father! How much money my quarrels with that woman cost him! How many fifty's, hundred's, three hundred's of *pesos*, how many coats, shoes and dresses, to content the *señora*. How mad it made me! She saved the money and I sometimes stole it from her because of the way she got it from my *papá*.

Although I haven't been able to show it, I not only love my father, I idolize him. I used to be his pride and joy when I was a kid. He liked me more than my brother, because when he'd go anywhere, he took me first. Many times just the two of us would go to the Basilica or to the movies or just take a walk in the evening. He still loves me with the same deep love, except that he doesn't show it any more because I don't deserve it.

My father was always very dry with us; he didn't talk much and we could never discuss our problems with him. I tried to be close to him. I wanted him to treat us in a special way, like other *papás*, to talk with us, to fuss over us. I liked so much the way we used to kiss his hand when he came home, or hug him. I felt my father understood me better in those days, although even then I missed a sign of affection, a word of encouragement.

Only twice in my life did my father speak intimately to me. He asked me, "Son, what troubles you? What is the matter? Tell me your troubles." I felt the most important and happy person in the world to hear him call me "son" so affectionately. Usually he called me Roberto or "you," and scolded me with bad words.

I have always disliked it when a son raises his voice to his father. Whenever my father scolded us or even just talked to us, it was impossible to look him in the eye, because he had a fierce expression. When I wanted to explain myself or at least clear up the truth a bit, he would not let me speak. "You, shut your mouth," and, "The only thing you are good for is this or that." I have never answered him back when he bawled me out. Instead I reproached myself. I told my brother and sisters that if my father was not good with us it was our fault. A father is sacred, especially mine. He is a good, fine person. There isn't another like him.

My father never beat us unless there was a good reason. He hit us with a broad belt he still wears. It was double thick and he'd hit us hard, especially me. He whacked us so much we sort of got hardened and didn't feel it any more, even though when he was angry he laid it on. Unfortunately for me, I had the damndest habit. When I was being whipped, I'd knock my head against the wall or the wardrobe or something else. I kept whacking myself on the head, without knowing why.

Then, when I was about ten years old, my father took to using an electric cord, a very thick one, two meters long. He folded it in four parts and tied a knot in it. Wow! then we could feel the punishment. Every time he gave us a lash, it raised a welt. And my father wasn't the type who stopped with the one who did it, he went after both of us alike. He was impartial that way.

My father always urged me to go to school. How stupid I was not to have listened to him! I could never explain to myself why I didn't like school. When my classmates were sent to the blackboard they did their exercises quickly and were sure of themselves, but when I was called up, I felt a weight on my back because I knew everybody's eyes were on me. I thought they were whispering about me. I wanted to be way ahead of them and because of this I couldn't concentrate and it took me longer.

My mother, my aunt, or my grandmother would take me to school; sometimes they had to drag me there. I had a feeling of desperation about them leaving me alone with all those boys and girls. I felt inferior compared to so many people.

I was in the first grade for four years, not because I was stupid but because I played hooky. I did second grade in one year but when I passed to the third grade I attended only two or three months and never returned. Because of my friends and perhaps because I had so little liberty in my home, I enjoyed playing hooky and often went to Chapultepec Park. My father was notified when I missed school and would be waiting for me with the strap when I got home.

When we were children, my brother and I were closer to each other. He always protected me; for years Manuel was the handkerchief I dried my tears on. I used to be quite a coward and a crybaby, very *rajón*, as we say in Mexico, because if somebody would just shout at me, I'd start crying. I was afraid of the older boys. They'd threaten me and I'd cry; if anyone touched me, I'd scream. Right off I'd go running to my brother and he, poor fellow, had a lot of fighting to do on account of me.

I was in the third grade when Manuel graduated. I didn't have the courage to face all those boys without him and that is why I quit school.

I don't know why but I have always felt less than a nobody. Never in my whole life did I feel that there was anyone who paid attention to me. I have always been sneered at . . . belittled. I always wanted to be something in life, to do whatever I felt like and not have to take orders from anyone. I wanted to make a kite of my life and fly it in any field.

I wanted to be somebody in athletics, to be a great automobile driver or motorcyclist and compete in races. I have always wanted to be an aviator. One day my *papá* took me to the Lagunilla Market to buy me a cap. He said, "Which cap do you want?" I immediately asked for one with goggles, the kind aviators use.

When I played with my friends, the game was always aviation. To make it more real, I would lower my goggles and go up on the roof to run there like a plane. Or I would go running around the courtyard. I'd tie ropes to the water pipes and make a swing. That was my airplane and I really felt as if I were flying. That was one of my dreams. Whenever a plane flew by, even to this day, I keep watching it, longing to fly one some day.

My head was cracked open because I wanted to fly. My cousin Salvador, my aunt Guadalupe's son, may he rest in peace, was very playful and liked to fool around with us. One time I asked him to give me an airplane ride, that is, to swing me around and around. He always did whatever we wanted and so he took hold of my wrist and ankle and began to whirl me around. He suddenly lost control, and wham! I was dashed against the wall. My head was opened and when I came to, my *mamá* and *papá* and everybody were very alarmed. I was covered with blood but I didn't get scared. Actually, I enjoyed the fact that I was bleeding. It left a scar here on my head.

I am full of scars. I was always getting banged up. My head was opened other times, by falling off the roof or getting hit in stone fights, in wars, with my friends. Once I nearly lost an eye and I bled so much I thought I was going to die. I was running and fell on a sharp little toy shovel I was carrying. It went right into my left eye, but they took me to a doctor and I can still see out of it pretty well. The worst scar and one of the worst frights of my life was when I was bitten on the arm by a dog.

I learned to swim before my brother did even though he had gone often with his friends. I sort of hung around them hoping they would take me. I used to play hooky to go swimming in a pool not far from my house. There was an attendant there, Josué, whom I admired very much because he was a good swimmer and a nice guy. He was tall, strong and very husky. I don't mind telling you, he had some body. I wanted to be like him, nice, big, strong, and able to get some recognition. He used to talk to us about how he had been all over the Republic.

Once, when I was eight years old, I didn't have money for a ticket to the pool. Manuel, his friend Alberto, the Donkey, and I were standing outside the gate trying to scrape together money, when a drunk came by. This man gave Manuel and the Donkey the money they needed. So I said, "What about me? Aren't you going to give me some, too?" He just started off, and I said, "Listen, *señor,* won't you give me what I need for a ticket?"

"Who are you?" he says.

"I'm the brother of one of the boys you just gave some money to." And I told him how many *centavos* I needed to get in.

"No, you little son-of-a-bitch. Get out of here. You're too black."

That hurt me very much. My brother and Alberto went in without me, leaving me feeling desperate and humiliated.

When I played hooky, or when my father sent me to the Lagunilla Market to carry home the things he bought, I got into the habit of taking my little sister Marta with me. I have always liked her better than the others. I don't know whether it was because she had never known our mother or because she followed me wherever I went.

I taught Marta how to hitch rides by jumping on to the bumper of the trolley and holding tight. I used to take a little white dog from the Casa Grande too, because he followed me everywhere. There we would be, comfortable and happy, sticking like flies to the back of the trolley, with the dog running after us. Everybody would stop to look at us, people would put their heads out of the cars and buses to see the spectacle. I thought they were admiring us and I enjoyed it.

I liked to jump while the trolley went at full speed. Marta was very brave and learned to do it too. I not only risked my life, I risked hers, but she enjoyed it so much that it made quite an impression on me. I believe that's why I preferred her to Consuelo and Manuel.

I used to take her with me to Chapultepec Park and to the Villa where we would climb the steepest hills. I would braid three cords together to make a strong rope and I tied one end around my waist and the other around hers. I picked out the most dangerous cliffs and would climb up first, and pull her after me. She loved it and never complained.

I want to make it clear that I always respected Marta as a sister. Contact with a woman aroused my natural feelings, right? But it's very different with my sisters. It pained me that sometimes my father would act suspicious when he found out we went here or there. He would ask, "And why did you go? And what did you do?" and he would question Marta to see if we had done anything bad. I had worked once in a bakery at the Military Hospital where they paid me with bread and rolls. Later, it occurred to me to take Marta there to see if they would give us some rolls to eat. The hospital was very far out and when my father learned that I took her there, he gave me a terrific beating.

There was a big difference between Marta and Consuelo. Consuelo was more intelligent and persistent and liked to study. When she decided to do something she stuck to it. She never played with boys like Marta and was very reserved even with girls. She was nice and quiet, and very thin and frightened-looking.

When we were little, I got along well with Consuelo. Later, I was surprised at how my sister changed. She blew up at practically nothing and would create a tempest in a glass of water. She had an uneven temperament and seemed to me to be unsociable, secretive and irritable. She was very dry and didn't have much to do with people. But apart from that, she was good, all good.

The trouble between Consuelo and me began after my stepmother came to live with my father. I ate breakfast late, after the others, because, I don't know why but ever since I was little, I was ashamed to sit at the table without doing some chore. I always did work around the house, like lighting the charcoal fire, putting up the coffee, cleaning the bird cages and feeding the birds. No one told me to, but it pained me not to do something before I ate.

After the family had eaten, I'd hunt around the kitchen for food. Many times, right in front of me, Consuelo or Elena would pour the leftover coffee down the drain, or crush up my bread. I would say, "Ha, ha! you make me laugh! I'm not even hungry." I would grab one of the bananas we fed the birds and would go out. I'd send them to the devil, not out of anger but out of hurt feelings. The truth is that when they destroyed my breakfast like that, I felt great anxiety in my heart and a lump in my throat. I would cry, not in front of them, but in one of the little shower rooms in the courtyard. I tried to keep quiet about these things because I knew if I told my father, he'd scold them and maybe even punish them with the strap. He did scold Consuelo at times, but she didn't change.

But I have always been a brother to my sisters. I have never punished them without a reason, like if they didn't obey me, or because they talked back to my *papá*, or called me "lousy black." I am heartbroken at the thought of how many times I have beaten them. I want to ask their pardon, but when I see them I lose my courage. It makes me suffer, because a man shouldn't beat a woman. But I only slapped them with the palm or the back of my hand. And when I slapped, it was only on the arm or the back, or the head.

But when my father came home Consuelo would tell him that I had kicked her or hit her on the lung. *Ay!* my God! Those weren't caresses my father gave me because of those lies! On my word! I speak from the heart, that I never hit her like that. She was a little liar then, and it was Elena's fault that, well, the blessed woman is now at peace, God has her in heaven, but when she and my sister accused me and exaggerated, my *papá* thrashed me with that doubled electric cable that had a copper wire inside and a knot on the end.

How difficult Consuelo and Elena made life for me! I felt that they were against me and that I constantly had to be on guard. And my father favored the women. He had always taken better care of them and it seemed to me that he loved my sisters more. Rather, he loved us all equally, but only they had the privilege of having him demonstrate it to them. He had always preferred women. I never paid attention to it, it never bothered me. On the contrary, I liked it because that way I was more sure of my sisters, that is, the way I see it, they could never say as an excuse that they had missed their father's love . . .

I'll tell you why I hit my sisters. It wasn't because I felt any hatred or bitterness toward them. It was that I never liked my sisters to play with boys. But they didn't pay any attention to me and it's logical, isn't it? because, well, little girls naturally have to play with little boys.

I had this feeling because ever since I was small I've been very mean toward little girls, as mean as they make them. I was full of malice. Sometimes I would take a little girl to the toilet when nobody was home. I always tried to find a way so that we wouldn't be seen, and then I'd begin to feel her up, with her consent, of course. I was only about five or six, and even after my mother died, when I was eight or nine, I still did it. That's why I didn't want my sisters to play with boys, because I figured the boys could do the same thing to them. Just feel them up, as we say, that's all I ever did to the little girls.

When we were older, Manuel, my cousin Matilde, my cousin Julia, and I began to play. My brother went off with Julia in one direction, and I went off in another with Matilde. She was the stepdaughter of my uncle Alfredo, so she was not actually related to me. Unfortunately, ever since I was little and even now that I am grown-up just the slightest contact with a woman, if I would just touch a woman or shake hands with her, stimulates my natural feelings so that I cannot control myself. It's the same with all men, I suppose.

So I had the idea of going to the bathroom with Matilde. There were no inside toilets in the *vecindad* where she lived; they were out in the courtyard, so it was convenient for what I wanted to do.

I convinced her and we went. I told her to lie down in the corner. I lifted up her dress and pulled down her panties, and at that time I couldn't call what I had a member, it was just barely sprouting, but I put it between her legs. I really couldn't do anything and I didn't even know where it should go, but with her consent, there were the two of us, trying to do it this way and that, playing *papá* and *mamá*.

So I did this shameful thing with my cousin and that's why I was always trying to watch over my sisters.

When we moved to the Casa Grande I was still quite small. Our first room there was very tiny and in terrible condition. The floor was full of holes, out of which came large rats. We would lose lots of things down those holes, money, marbles, combs. There was no electricity there then, until my father paid to have them connect it up. I liked being in the dark, or having only candlelight, but my father has always insisted on modern comforts. He liked a place to be roomy and very clean, and that is why we moved into a larger room.

Elena liked to keep the house nice, too. Man, she was always wanting this and wanting that for the house, and moving around the furniture. I never liked all that changing about, but say what you will about Elena, she made our house a place to be proud of, an example to the neighbors, because it was always clean and orderly. Our house has changed a lot since then and is no longer respected. Before, it was so well thought of that people passing by even took off their hats. And all the time my father lived with us, he never fell behind in the rent. On the contrary, he paid one month in advance and, as a reward, the landlord gave him a free ticket to the bathhouse.

The law in the Casa Grande was . . . new tenant . . . new fight. To get into the gang, I had to pass through a number of tests. They put their best *gallos* or fighters on the new boy, to see if he was acceptable as a friend. Before, families moved in and out wholesale and there were lots of free-for-alls. Anyone who saw me in the courtyard would hit, pinch, or throw stones at me. If I was carrying something from the store, they would knock it down, and then I would get punished again at home. And so, as the amount of pain the human body can stand has its limit, so patience has its limits, and you find yourself obliged to fight.

One day I was walking by and there in the courtyard, waiting for me, were my brother and the four Ramírez boys. They were waiting for that decisive bout. Manuel had felt obligated to propose me as a member of the gang. But I wasn't going to be their butt just because I was new. My brother said, "Come on, fight." Daniel was going to be the one to test me. I called out to Manuel, but it made him mad that I should be such a coward. "Don't be a slacker. Defend yourself. I won't be fighting for you all your life."

Then they threw Jorge Ramírez at me, and they said, "Mix it up with him or we'll beat the hell out of you." So, whether I wanted to or not, because I was so damned afraid of those guys, Jorge lasted two or three punches and went away crying. I drew blood. After that I fought Hermilio and Daniel . . . all good friends . . . as these were friendly fights, even though they seemed very real. I fought everyone of them until I got to the main *gallo,* and beat him. I figured that was it, but neighbors kept moving in and I had to test them, to make them come into our circle. If they didn't, they were led a miserable life.

I began to like fighting. I didn't go complaining when they hit me, but would tangle with anybody immediately. Thus, I relieved my brother of the responsibility of having to fight for me. Actually, I never wanted to fight with anybody, but they kept looking for it. I had to defend myself and continued to do so all my life.

The top *gallos,* the ones who fought best, became part of the group of leaders. They were ranked like the army: Wilfredo, Captain; Ignacio, Lieutenant; Hermilio, Second Lieutenant; Manuel, Sergeant; I, Roberto, Second Sergeant; and so on. When we measured our strength with the captain, we were the ones who decided what we would do when we played. One after another of us began to dominate.

There is a game, "follow the leader," in which ten or fifteen of the gang would get together and follow "the hand," the leader. If he jumps over a sewer, all the others have to do it. If they don't, we gang up on them. When I was "the hand," there were quite a number of complaints brought to my *papá.* I got into trouble because I jumped the fence around the little garden here in the *vecindad.* I could jump it easily, but there were boys who couldn't and they began to destroy it. Also, there were my escapades with the water and sewer pipes. They were all the way up at the top and I used to climb to the roof that way. As a result, I pulled down or loosened a few pipes.

I liked to walk around the rooftops, too, and fell more than once. Most of the time, I fell feet first, standing up, and that's why the boys called me the "Orangutang." When we played soccer and would lose the ball on the roof, the "Orangutang," to make a good impression, would climb up to look for it. The neighbors would tell Elena, or complain to my father and he would send Manuel to look for me. He was always sensitive about the neighbors' complaints. Later, when I got home, I relaxed my body and waited to receive the blows.

When Elena asked my father for permission to visit her mother, who lived in a village in Jalisco, I begged her to take me. Consuelo, whom Elena loved the most, thought she should be the one to go but my *papá* sent me along, to look after Elena, or perhaps to spy on her. Anyway, the two of us left on the train. It was my first long trip and my memories of it are pleasant.

To me, to recall is to live again! I liked the way of life there. The village was picturesque, with unpaved streets and adobe houses. I liked the village church the most. I got to know Elena's family, her mother, Santitos, her brothers, Raimundo and Arturo, her two sisters, Soledad and Concha, who later died. *Señora* Santitos was a fine person, very decent. Like Elena, she had no schooling and didn't know how to read and write. I liked them all.

They taught me how to milk the cows, and I even drank the milk straight from the teats. I would push aside the calves or the baby goats and lie down and drink! We spent about a month there, a happy month for me.

Another time I got along well with Elena was when I was ill, with *espanto* or fright, according to her. I was sleepy all the time. I didn't eat, I was pale and thin and had rings under my eyes. I never knew what illness I had. Only Elena and her mother knew ... they said it was *espanto* and they tried to cure me with all kinds of herb concoctions. My father always looked out for us and sent me to a doctor. Elena took care of me that time, as there was a truce between us on account of me being sick. If she had always treated me the way she did then, maybe she would still be alive, or at least we would have gotten along better.

When I was about eleven years old and still in the first grade, I ran away for the first time. I went to Veracruz with no more than the clothes on my back. I had no money to start out with. In those days, I never got to have a whole *peso* in my pocket all at once. I was limited to the five *centavos* my father would put under our pillows each morning before he went to work. On Sundays, we got twenty *centavos* each. But I usually spent my money right away and never had any in my pocket. On the road all the money I had was what one driver gave me.

My excuse for running away was that my father scolded me, but in reality, he always scolded me. The main reason was that I heard the boys talking about their adventures and I wanted to find out for myself. So I went to Veracruz. I chose that place because I had been to Veracruz once with my father and mother, Manuel and Consuelo, who was a nursing baby then. My grandfather had died and some uncles of mine had put my father in jail and had taken away his inheritance. Just to think of it made my blood boil! Imagine, my uncles had done this to my father! Such shameless, materialistic people! Money was everything to them! But my uncles were dead and I didn't know about my other relatives until later.

Right off the bat, I walked about twenty-three kilometers on the Mexico-Puebla highway. I have always liked the road; walking is my life. I've walked from Maltrata all the way along the railroad tracks as far as Orizaba (about seventy kilometers), just to see the vegetation and the fantastic view. The train would pass by and I could have jumped it (I don't have the old-fashioned bad habit of paying fares) but I preferred to walk along, admiring the scenery. I like to walk day and night, until I fall down with exhaustion. Then I go to sleep at the side of the highway. I can find grass anywhere and I'd cut a pile of it for my bed.

On the highway I felt happy and carefree. The problem of food didn't worry me. It was easy for me to go up to a shack and ask for work to do in exchange for a *taco*. Everybody gave me something to do, draw water from the well, chop wood, or any simple thing like that, and then they'd give me something to eat. Lots of people would tell me to sit down to eat first, and then they wouldn't let me do anything for them. They would fix up a pack of *tortillas* and salt and off I'd go.

I had laid out a route and went as I had planned. From Los Reyes, I walked as far as the crossroads, where the highways to Texcoco, Puebla, and Veracruz meet. No damned car would stop for me, even though they saw I was a kid. A bus picked me up and they asked where I was from. If I had known that saying you are from Mexico City closed doors to you, I would have said I was from somewhere else. People from the capital have a very bad reputation. At the carnivals and *fiestas*, whenever they catch anybody stealing or doing something wrong, he turns out to be from there. During Holy Week and the Carnival on July 24, lots of dope addicts and homosexuals from Mexico City go to Veracruz. I saw some there, dressed up like women. Who knows why they do this? It is nauseating.

I traveled alone. I never wanted to take along friends because I have always preferred to go on my own. It is easier for me to get around by myself. I would ask people the way. By asking, you can get to Rome.

When I left home, I felt as though a great weight was lifted off me. To live with other people is hard. I never wanted to be tied to the family again. Sometimes I would ask for lodging for a night and I would stay with a family for a few days. But I wasn't comfortable because what I was looking for was to be free. And so I went, like the air, without difficulty, without direction, free . . . People would ask, "Why did you leave home?"

"Because my father scolded me. I have a stepmother." How I used Elena as an excuse! I think that was why I was always making her mad, so that I could use her as a pretext for my lies. I had the luck of a canaille, for I achieved my ends for the moment. I call myself canaille, because I used another person to cover up my lies. What I have gone through is nothing, compared to what I deserve.

Like all adventurers, when I arrived in Veracruz, I asked the way to the sea. I reached it and sat on a navy dock all day looking at its vastness. The sea was beautiful, overpowering. I was there all day and saw how the tourists and the watchmen, who guard the docks and the cargoes, had nothing else to do but fish. When it was nightfall I wondered where I was going to sleep. That is the least problem there, because it is very hot. I decided to stay on one of the beaches, the best and softest one. At night the tide rises, so I stayed some distance from the sea.

The next day I felt like eating. I hadn't eaten anything the day before. I was so entranced, watching the sea and the fishing. I went over to the docks, because of the cargo boats anchored there. I saw a lot of people walking back and forth. They were a rough bunch, dark-skinned guys, huskier than hell, the bastards. I approached the boat cook and asked if he didn't have any work for me in exchange for a *taco*. He felt sorry for me and it was because of that cook that I worked as a longshoreman for the first time in my life. I carried any little stuff and they would give me meals in return. We started work at eight and stopped at twelve, then began at twelve-thirty and quit at four-thirty. That was the way I got my food and lodging, for they gave me permission to sleep on the boat.

After a while, it didn't look like such a good setup for me. A boat would come in and I would stick to it like a leech. But the next day it would pull out and I would be homeless and without food again. I was always having to look for a place to eat and sleep. But I knew that if anybody died of hunger it was because he was lazy. If you helped the fishermen on the free beaches pull in their nets, you wouldn't get money but they'd give you a few fish. In one casting, they get all kinds of things, from sharks to turtles. I sold the fish, keeping one or two which I'd ask the fisherman's wives to cook for me.

I was willing to work at whatever came along, so I could eat. I never earned a copper working, they just gave me fruit, for the most part. I even ate wild greens and there were times when I didn't taste bread for two weeks. When I had nothing to eat, I would ask the watchmen to let me take a few pieces of coconut. When ships came in from Tabasco, or from places where they grew fruit, I had a feast day!

I began to have worries about a place to sleep because I heard that the police van was going around the beaches, where all the riffraff of Veracruz gathered. Anyone found sleeping on the sand would be taken off to jail. Nothing happened to me, but I slept with less calm, and went further away from the beach, toward the mountains. I didn't dare go away from the docks in the daytime—they were the source of life for me.

About three months passed like this. The time came when I felt like going home. I thought of the family only once in a while, but when I did, I felt like getting back home as fast as I could. There were moments when I felt brave enough to leave, then I would lose heart. I never wrote home, because I didn't know how to write a letter and I didn't want them to know where I was. I imagined that if my *papá* found out he would come and beat me to death. That is what I thought, but I went home anyway.

The return trip was hard because I had to walk from Veracruz to Puebla. It took me eight or nine days. I walked day and night, as no damned truck would pick me up. I took the Córdoba road and came to the police booth at the entrance of the city of Puebla. My shoes were all worn out, strong miner's boots that my father always bought for us. I asked the truck drivers for a lift, but they refused. Some of them made fun of me. I paid no attention to them but I felt lonely for the first time, alone as a feather flying through the air. I sat at the side of the road, crying.

Finally, the police stopped a truck and said, "Take care of this kid adventurer. He is headed for Mexico City." I got on and we arrived late at night, at the Merced Market, near the Zócalo, the central square of Mexico City. Imagine, it was my first time there. I had been to Veracruz but had never seen the Zócalo! When I crossed in front of the National Palace, I saw the great big clock in the Cathedral as it struck three. There I was, all alone in the plaza. I hurried home, knocked at the *vecindad* gate and the *portera* let me in.

Outside our door I sat, wondering whether or not to go in. I expected a terrific beating. I started to knock, but sat down again. Then something strange occurred. I am not superstitious, but if you had seen what I have, you would consider me a superior being. Sitting there, at that hour, I saw someone dressed like a *charro*, a cowboy, come down from the roof near the water tank. He lit something, a cigar, I think, because the fire was so big. I kept staring and wondering what the man was looking for. Then the cigar fell to the ground and the man disappeared . . . just like that. I figured he must have been kidding around . . . but where did he go?

I have always liked danger and strong emotions and when there is something unfamiliar, I want to know more about it. So I climbed up to the water tank, way up to the top. I went to the little garden and to the bathhouse. Rumors had gone around the *vecindad* that these places were haunted. Well, if I were superstitious, I would be dead now, because as I went to the bathhouse I heard a tremendous noise, a crash, as though something had broken. I got panicky and ran back to our door and knocked. They called out, "Who is it?" and I said, "Me, *papá*."

My father opened the door immediately. "So you finally got back, son. Well, come on in." He was very nice. I thought he would meet me with a belt in his hand and give me the hiding of the ages. But he said to me, "Did you have any supper?" We had no kerosene stove then, just a charcoal brazier, so he got himself to work and lit a fire. He heated the beans and coffee and said, "Eat. When you are finished turn out the light." Then he went back to bed. As I knew he left for work early and that he was a light sleeper, I turned out the light and there I was eating in the dark. Then I went to sleep . . . and he hadn't scolded me or hit me or anything.

The next day, before he left, my father gave me a terrible bawling out, which I well deserved. Then I noticed Saint Anthony, in the wardrobe, upside down, with my shirt wrapped around him. Elena took him out and said, "Well Señor San Antonio, now that you have brought him back to us, return to your place." And she put him back on his feet. I don't really know whether I am a good Catholic or not . . . I don't like to talk much about religion, but it made me laugh when she did that. At the same time, I wondered whether it really had a deep meaning.

That afternoon the storm broke loose, and I got what I had expected the night before . . . but good. After that, the common ordinary days followed, one after another, here in the *vecindad*. My friends tormented me to tell them about my adventures and I felt like a big shot because all they knew was Chapultepec Park. I felt very proud talking about what I had done, about not having money or anything to eat or a place to sleep.

I also told a bunch of lies about the women I had had in Veracruz. I did it because my friends, boys younger than I, talked about how good so-and-so was, and that they did such-and-such with her. They topped me and so as not to be left behind, I told them that in Veracruz I too had had good "linings," as we say.

I was working in the bathhouse, when a woman, the wife of a tailor I knew, came in and asked for an individual bathtub. She was with a man who ran a shell game in the streets, a con man, and right there he asked her . . . well, what he asked her. She said, "No! How can you think of such a thing. If my husband found out he would kill me." So he says, "Yes, but you are not going to tell him."

The fellows who worked in the baths with me heard this dialogue. Well, he convinced her and they went into tub No. 1 together. One of the attendants, an older man, climbed to the roof to watch. After a while, he came down and said, "Man! He put her through all the positions." So I climbed up too and saw them doing this sexual business and it excited me very much. All the rest of the day I kept thinking, "I wonder how you do it? I wonder what it feels like?"

So I started talking about it with the boys and we decided to go to Tintero Street that night. I wanted to do it, but didn't like the idea of going with a woman, least of all where you could get a disease. But the boys said, "Go, *Negro*, and knock off one small piece. What can it amount to? So you know what it feels like to be a man." I said to myself, "Oh, so that's what you have to do to be a man. Well, then I've got to do it." So I went.

The woman I drew said, "Come on over, kiddo, don't be afraid." I really felt like running out, but she said, "Come on, climb on. Don't be scared. Is this your first time?"

"Yes, lady, I'd better go."

"Don't be afraid. You'll see how nice it feels." She took me by the

hand and the next thing I knew I was on the bed and we began to do
. . . what we did. I liked it and after that I kept going on my own . . .
only a few times . . . but I kept going.

I worked in the bathhouse all this time, watching the lockers, hand-
ing out towels and soap, even giving massages for extra tips, but then
the other boy who worked there began complaining that we weren't
being paid enough . . . only two *pesos* fifty *centavos* a week, so, to even
things up, we took fifty *pesos* out of the cash box but that bastard of a
boss went and told my father we took more and my father made good
for it. So I lost that job and got a beating besides.

Then Miguel, a friend of mine, asked me if I wanted to work in a
glass shop. I had to enter as an apprentice at two *pesos* fifty a week,
but I did it to learn the trade. About two months later I went to work
in José Pinto's glass shop. It was just a small shop then, but now that
man has a big place, a house of his own, a bank account and a car. He
was one man I knew who could get ahead. He paid for piecework and
I made about thirty to thirty-five *pesos* a week.

All that time, I gave my father every *centavo* I earned. I was happy
and proud to do it. My father used to tell my brother, "Manuel, you
should learn from Roberto. He's younger than you and he's setting
you a good example. He turns over everything he earns. How about
you?"

Naturally, when I heard him say that I felt wonderful. I was satisfied
with what my father gave me, bus fare and one *peso* a day for expenses. I didn't drink or smoke then and I liked to work. All my life I
liked to work, and when I do I don't talk or fool around. I shut myself
off and pay no attention to anything else.

After six months, I got tired of cutting glass and my uncle Alfredo
took me into the bakery to teach me baking. I went because I loved to
eat the bread hot from the oven, but baking itself didn't appeal to me.
My cousin Tomás, my great-aunt Catarina's son, was a mason and he
offered to teach me his trade. I liked that because I had to work on tall
buildings. I always liked being way up high . . . that's why I climbed
trees and poles and played on roofs . . . but I lost that job because I
stole a steel nameplate right off the side of the building. It was so
pretty and shiny that I chipped it off the wall. Unfortunately, someone
saw me. So I went back to work in a glass shop. There things worked
out badly because on Saturday, our payday, the boss never had enough

to pay us. He spent his money all week on drink and on Saturdays he would hide.

By the time I was thirteen, I had been a stevedore, a locker boy, a glass worker, a baker and a mason. The next thing I tried was varnishing furniture. When I took that job everyone warned me that the *maestro* was very tricky, especially on payday. And it was true. I really had to chase that man down the street on Saturdays, or look behind the furniture or in all the wardrobes, to get him to pay me the lousy eighteen *pesos* I earned for the week. I ran after him like he was a thief. I followed him to his house and saw him go in and then the *señora* would have the face to tell me he wasn't home. And when I caught him, he would never give me my full pay. I got tired of that game after a few weeks and quit. I didn't look for work any more and just bummed around.

Once I was in the courtyard talking with the boys about my adventures. I got myself worked up, talking about Veracruz and how there was so much fruit along the highway. I was so worked up I felt like going back again and, without stopping to think about it, I went home, grabbed a pair of pants and a T-shirt and a paper bag, and took off. I don't think there was as much as twenty *centavos* in my pocket, and that's how I took to the road a second time.

I got to know Veracruz real well. Because of the experience I had the first time, I more or less knew the ropes and it was easier for me to get food. I don't remember anything particularly impressive about that second trip except that I saw a hurricane. I liked the way the wind pushed me but at the same time it frightened me, especially when I saw palm trees loaded with coconuts kiss the pavement. I saw the sea enraged . . . it wiped away a large part of the wall at the entrance of the bay, carrying it off like a piece of paper.

I didn't get to know my father's relatives that trip. They lived in Córdoba, but I didn't know that until I returned home, until we read David's advertisement in *El Pepín*.

My father had always bought copies of the comic magazines for Elena and for us kids. What quarrels and races we ran waiting for him to arrive with the "comics." Consuelo and Marta were always given preference and read them first. I don't know who saw the ad, but someone showed it to my *papá*. My father had never spoken of his family . . . this time he sat down and wrote a letter. It was a rare thing, something new for us, to see him write a letter.

I remember David's arrival very well, for I took my father to the bus terminal. One morning, very early, at about five o'clock, my father said, "Roberto."

"At your service, *papá*," I answered.

"Let us see if you, who has bummed around so much, knows where the buses from Córdoba arrive." So I took him, and we knew my cousin by the flower he wore in his lapel. He was big, a giant, and when he shook hands, what a grip he had! We took a taxi home and spent the whole day talking to him. He told us about the village he lived in, and about his mother, Olivia, who had married my father's brother, who was deceased. She was now living with her second husband, who was a peasant.

David lived with us and my *papá* got him a job as night watchman in La Gloria restaurant. David always behaved well and we all liked him. Years later, after her death, he told me about an incident with Elena. He told me in confidence, I don't believe Manuel or my sisters know about it. David happened to be lying on the bed one day, and Elena sat down on his legs, on his lap. He jumped up like a spring and said, "No, Elena. I may be poor and very Indian, but to do such a thing, no. You are my uncle's wife and we must respect each other, so please behave in a different way." Elena was very angry with him after that. Ah! how furious it made me. If he had told me when she was alive, who knows how it would have gone for Elena. *Caray!* without doubt women are the biggest tramps!

David went back to Córdoba on some pretext, but later he returned with his mother. They took me to Córdoba with them. I liked it very much there. I stayed with them for a month, and I didn't want to leave. I didn't have the comforts my father supplied, but I was healthy and happy. I prefer country life. It is calmer and quieter, one can breathe tranquilly. You feel the honesty even in your elbows! They are a different type of people, more respectful and upright, a different manner of being. Here in the city I have always to be alert, ready for anything from anybody.

I wanted to be a farmer, and I learned the work while I was there. Olivia's husband taught me everything, how to plow, to cultivate, to hoe, to plant, to weed, to harvest, everything. He held little classes for me there in the fields and I learned to plant sugar cane, corn, beans and rice. It was useful to me later, because when I traveled about, I worked in the fields. There are parts of the Republic where there is no other way of life. I would go to work anywhere that had the same vegetation as Córdoba or Veracruz, because I loved it so. The third and fourth times I ran away from home, I went straight to Córdoba.

After the fifth time I left home, I didn't go because I wanted to but because my father threw me out. He had good reason to. I didn't help him at all; I didn't even behave myself well enough to deserve being in the house, and so he would throw me out on the street all the time. As Elena helped pour fuel on the flame, he would hit me and bawl me out. For me, a bawling out has always hurt more than a beating; I prefer a bad beating to a little scolding. Blows hurt more physically, but when he called me a bum, a good-for-nothing, and a pig, it hurt me morally. He would say I wasn't a decent person, and the only thing I was good for was to cause him headaches or shame. Really, I preferred him to beat me.

Anything Roberto did wrong, Manuel and his sisters would feel too, because my father would yell at all of us. He was letting me have it all the time. When he was in a bad mood not even the flies dared fly. None of us could go near him. It wasn't until after Elena died that I rested up from the scoldings and beatings she had caused my father to give me.

I was right at the foot of the bed when Elena died and I can still see the look in her eyes. I don't know whether she was cursing me or forgiving me. I never knew. Her eyes were already glassy and she kept looking at me. Inside me, I was asking her to forgive me for all I had done to her, for all my offenses. I asked that God forgive her and take her away quickly, or make her well. I have always prayed that when somebody is very ill. She kept staring at me, and I will never forget the look. Then, she just moved her arms, and that was the end.

She died, and my father felt like dying too, at that moment. Everyone was shocked and there was a lot of activity then. I think they told me to take her blankets and pillows to No. 64, to make room to lay her out. I nearly fainted when I got to the water tank and some boys there held me up so I didn't fall.

I don't know what it was, but something scared me that time. My *papá* kept looking at me . . . I felt he was accusing me with his eyes, as if he were telling me that I was to blame. He always said that we were to blame for Elena's illness, particularly me, because I was the one who got her into rages more than anyone.

When Elena was still alive but very ill, I learned about my half-sister Antonia. One day my father came home early, which surprised us because he had never done that before. He called Manuel and me to him and pulled out a photograph.

"This is your sister."

"Good Lord, how can she be our sister?" I said to myself. I thought she looked pretty, with her two braids. "How can she be my sister if she is already grown up?"

Then he said, "We've got to find this girl."

"All right, *papá*."

"Wherever you see her, bring her here." That was the order my father gave us. Then he got the help of private detectives and they found Antonia, I don't know where.

She had run away from her mother's house; this Antonia and I certainly seemed to be chips off the same block. One night my father said, "Roberto, go to bed. Wait here, I'm going to bring your sister." I was on pins and needles to see her. Consuelo and Marta were asleep, my brother was out, so I was the only one guarding the house and my sisters.

They arrived at about midnight, and from the time she entered the courtyard, the girl cried. She kept crying and crying and I didn't get to see her face. All night long I was tempted to go over and see how she looked and to hear her speak, to see whether she had a pleasant voice or not. And all night long, Antonia cried, there in my sisters' bed.

The next day my father went off to work and immediately Manuel and I spoke to her and asked her all kinds of questions. It turned out that she and her mother Lupita lived on Rosario Street which was only one block from the school we went to. I remembered having seen Antonia in the street, and having liked her, without knowing she was my sister.

My father had another daughter with Lupita, Marielena, who was also my half-sister. I never got to know her well or to love her, but she had a strong, noble character and was very religious. You had to be careful what you said to her, and I always treated her with special respect. Lupita had two other daughters, Elida and Isabel, who were

Antonia's half-sisters. I respected them too, but they always seemed dry and unpleasant to me.

From the first moment Antonia came to live with us, I began to like her . . . to be completely frank, she became the great love of my life. Before that I had had *novias*, but of the three I only seriously liked Rufelia, a girl who lived in our courtyard. But Rufelia was light-skinned and superior to me, and I hadn't declared myself to her. I just loved her from a distance. My first *novia*, a short pretty girl, turned out bad and played me for a sucker. I liked her but was too ashamed to ask for a kiss. Once I kissed her and ran home because I was so embarrassed. We were sweethearts for a few months, but it turned out that she was knocked up by some tramp, and that was the end of our courtship.

My other *novia* was a servant of a neighbor. She took a great liking to me and she'd use my sisters to arrange a date with me. She asked me to be her boy friend, but that wasn't a real courtship, just kid stuff. The great love affair of my life, to my torment, and despair, was my half-sister Antonia.

We were about the same age, thirteen or fourteen. I didn't tell Tonia how I felt about her. I just watched her and kept quiet. She made the beds, swept, made coffee, served breakfast, and, of course, my brother and I were feeling good at having a new sister. Consuelo and Marta did too. So it was Antonia here and Tonia there, and from the beginning when she sat down at the table I felt I had to sit beside her and eat. When Consuelo or Marta sat in my place next to her, I'd get into a squabble with them.

The more time went by, the more I liked her. I don't mean as a brother, for I had other feelings toward her, but during all the years she lived with us, I never spoke or hinted to her about my feelings. Without her wanting to, she caused that feeling to grow stronger day by day.

I used to go to work in a glass-fixture place. I'd start work at nine in the morning and quit at six, but it took the bus an hour to get me home, so I would return at about seven in the evening. Everyone would be eating supper except Antonia. She always waited for me. She knew I was fond of refried mashed beans, so when I got home she would say, "Do you want some juicy fried beans, Roberto?" And the two of us would sit down and eat out of the same plate.

Antonia slept in the bed with Consuelo and Marta, and my father slept in the other bed. Manuel and I usually slept on the floor outside in the little kitchen, but sometimes we also slept in the bedroom. In the morning, I always got up when my *papá* did, and I would heat his orange-leaf tea and give him a little bread with it, before he went off to work. Then I would go into the bedroom to light the *veladora*, the votive candle for the Virgin. Antonia would wake up and say, "Oh, what a pest you are."

"Ah, come on, get up you loafers . . . it's late," I'd say.

"No, no, we don't feel like getting up yet."

Consuelo wouldn't even answer. As usual, Manuel was dead to the world. Antonia and I were the only ones who talked. Lots of times she would say to me, "Don't go. Lie down here for a little while and let me sleep." And she would make room for me in the bed. She would move over and I would lie on the edge of the bed, she covered with her blanket and I with mine. She would move over to me, and would fall asleep nestled against my ribs or back.

It disturbs me to talk about these things . . . but, anyway, I never entertained an evil thought about her . . . never! It pleased me that she told me to lie down. I could have lain down any other place but she made room for me. I felt as though I were in heaven . . . to have someone you shouldn't love, so close. That's the way it was and that's why sometimes I thought of taking my life.

As a result of all this attention and affection she showed me, in a sisterly way, my love grew day by day. I more than loved her, I worshiped her, and for many years I suffered. My suffering began from the time she came to our house. I realized it wasn't logical, it wasn't reasonable for me to have this feeling toward her, but I couldn't control it. I couldn't tell her I loved her and not exactly in a brotherly way, for she had the same blood I did. So far as I know, my father never noticed my suffering, nor did my brother or sisters.

Well, it came to the point where I tried to keep her from having *novios*, and of course I had more than one reason for doing so. I didn't want her to look at absolutely anybody, I just wanted her to look at me. And I suffered on that account, because she liked the boys.

So, because of Antonia, I began to stay away from home. It was one of the main reasons I started to go on the bum, looking for trouble. When I felt I couldn't stand it any longer, I'd pick up with just the money and clothes I had on me, many times with only five lousy *centavos* in my pocket, and just go off.

There isn't a state in Mexico I haven't set foot in. And I've been across the border twice . . . a wetback at fourteen! I feel as though I've traveled the world. I would go with the idea of not returning or at least of staying away long enough to forget. The thing was to get away so as not to tell her anything. I didn't want to be close to temptation.

When Antonia had her sickness, I could tell from the very beginning that there was something wrong with her. But I never did know who was the rat who made her pregnant. I have never found out and that has always bothered me. Yolanda, our neighbor, tried to get me into a fight with my best friend, Ruperto, by telling me he was the one. He denied that he had ever been her boy friend when I threw it up to him, but since they stuck the thorn into my heart, the doubt in my mind has remained ever since.

I knew that it was Luz, the policeman Fulgencio's wife, who made Antonia abort. As a matter of fact, I was even in the house when it happened because they took out a bunch of bloody rags in a paper bag. After that, Antonia was sick and sort of nervous and had some very nasty attacks. She'd scratch on the sheets and pull out her hair and bite herself. We'd hold her down, because she really bit herself hard, like she meant it. She would kick out and it was tough on anyone who tried to grab her because she'd scratch his skin off. She went so far as to strike my father. She also gave me a couple of kicks in the chest which knocked me over, but that was when she was having a crazy fit and didn't recognize absolutely anybody.

Then they sent her to a sanatorium for treatment and I didn't get to see her. I suffered a lot in those days, and later too, because I saw that other boys had their girl friends and they embraced and kissed them, and talked with them, but me . . . sometimes I asked myself why I had to go and fall in love with my sister.

Then I joined the army, first because I wanted to be a soldier, but most of all, because it was getting impossible for me at home.

Consuelo

I HAD NOTHING BUT BITTERNESS ALL THROUGH MY CHILDHOOD AND A feeling of being alone. We lost our mother when all of us were little: Manuel was barely eight years old, Roberto was six, I was four, and my sister Marta was two. I hardly remember anything about that time. When my mother died, I saw her stretched out, partly covered by a sheet. She looked very serious. Someone lifted us up to kiss her and then they covered her face. That was all.

I felt alone partly because of losing my mother and partly because of the way my brothers and sister treated me. I was never as close to them as they were to each other. They would share candy and toys while I had to beg them for things. Manuel defended Roberto from the other kids in school and even though he would clout him on the head, Manuel would help my brother with his homework.

If I just raised my voice to Marta, I would be beaten by my brothers, especially Roberto. My body hurt from these vicious beatings but it was nothing in comparison with the pain, strong and sharp, that I felt when I saw how they hated me. While my stepmother, Elena, was still alive she defended me, even though they made her cry too. Either she or I would complain to my father, who handed out rough treatment to my brothers. But the next day my brothers would punish me.

I felt hounded by my brothers. I wasn't afraid of them really, but rather felt a deep emotion that I relieved by crying secretly in the corner between the bed and the wardrobe. I would cry until I was tired or until La Chata, the woman who worked for us, returned from the market. She would comfort me and call me "daughter," which I didn't like but didn't dare complain about.

On a few occasions I felt happy because my brothers would tell me a story or describe a Nativity scene or give me a little present. It was generally Roberto, because Manuel never gave us anything. Once in a while he would buy us *tepache,* a drink made of pineapple, vinegar, sugar and water, to have with our dinner. Manuel was in charge of correcting us at the table when we ate and he made us miserable by trying to act like the older brother.

He would come in at mealtime and start ordering us around with his sergeant's voice. "Skinny, go call Chubby!" But Marta almost always refused to come . . . we had to pull her in by the hair or by the arm. Then she would flop down on the box which served as her chair, making a show of her bad humor. I would say, "Go wash your hands, you pig."

"What business is it of yours? Damned skinny brat! Always butting in where she shouldn't."

"Shut your snout and go wash," Manuel would order.

"Oh, I'm terribly afraid of you! Shut me up if you can, you cursed *Chino.*"

Manuel would start to take off his belt to hit her and Marta would then get up, quickly dip her hands in the white enamel washbasin, wipe her hands on her dress, and fall back into her chair, making faces at him.

Manuel would then send me to buy the *tepache.* I would object. "Not me! It is always me! You're not a king here. You don't even let a person eat." But I would go.

Roberto usually came running in while we were eating. If the janitor or someone was chasing him, he would enter through the roof, yelling insults at whoever was after him. Then he could say, "Have you finished eating? Is there anything for me?" And La Chata or Santitos, or whoever was serving us, would give him some food too. He would grab the jar of *tepache* and take a long gulp, without bothering to get a glass. This would get Manuel angry.

"You bastard! Why are you such a pig? Can't you drink like other people? You are always being a slob."

Roberto would smile. "Each of us swallows in our own way, no?" The he would begin eating his toasted *tortillas.* At the first sound of noisy chewing, Manuel would throw a spoon or *tortilla* at him and a fight would start. That was the way the meals went . . . Manuel scolding and hitting and the rest of us fighting back. The meals usually ended with Roberto going to eat in the kitchen, Marta running out crying, without finishing, me sitting quietly for fear of being hit, and only our big brother enjoying the food.

Things like this happened when we were alone, because on Wednesdays, my father's day off, nobody dared speak at dinner. The first one he heard open his mouth he would send to eat in the kitchen. This was more apt to happen to the two boys; Marta and I were only scolded, with: "Shut your mouth," "Learn to eat right," "What's going on? Is an animal eating, or what?" He would turn to us with a cold look which made me, at least, feel afraid.

Wednesday was the day when I got even with my brothers for everything they did to me during the week. The thing that annoyed my brothers more than anything else was for my father to send them on errands. I would tell my father I felt like having chocolate, a fried egg, or a *torta* to take to school. Immediately, my father would send Manuel or Roberto to the store to buy the tablet to make chocolate. If it was an egg I wanted, they would have to fry it for me. At night it was the same; I would begin to pester for things. It made me happy inside to see my brothers' angry faces and I would take advantage of the situation to get them into trouble. "Look, *papá,* he says he's not going to. He's hunching up his shoulders at you. He's giving me dirt looks." These were the lies I told to get my brothers punished.

The next day the blows from my brothers would begin. I would fight back but in the end it was I whose body was black and blue, or whose nose or mouth was bloody. My brother Roberto must have thought he was fighting with another boy, for once we were on the floor, he would kick me or I would be forced to go under the bed. Nearly always I had to call for help from a neighbor, *Señora* Yolanda, or I used to run crying to *Señor* Fulgencio, a policeman who lived with his wife in No. 68, and ask him to punish my brother.

I have always been the sickly one of the family and my nickname, which I detested, was "Skinny." My father used to worry a lot about my health, for I kept catching colds or getting intestinal infections. Once I lost a whole year of school because I was sick. My father took me to a homeopathic doctor who gave me tiny pills to take every half-hour. His favorite remedy was enemas of boiled senna leaves and my father plied me with them. I spent a lot of time alone in bed. My father never allowed visitors in the house, and my brothers and sister would play outside all day.

My *papá* had taught us to always keep our mouths shut. We were not supposed to answer back a single word to anybody if we were scolded about our behavior. Always, always, whatever grownups did was right. "Respect grownups"—those were the words I would hear when I wanted to talk back to La Chata or to complain about school.

Toward my father I did feel respect, as well as fear and much love. When I was a little girl, they would say to me, "Here comes your *papá*," and this would be enough to set me trembling and make my heart beat hard. In the Casa Grande he almost never let us go out into the courtyard, and those were his orders to La Chata. So when my sister and I would go out I was afraid we wouldn't get back to the house before my father arrived. Our playmates knew my father's rules and when they would see him appear at the entrance to the tenement they would warn us, shouting: "Here comes your father." The distance between me and the house seemed like endless kilometers.

If my father caught us in the courtyard he would push against the back of our necks and say to us: "Where did I leave you? *Zas!* Into the house! There is no reason to go out, you have everything in the house!" This scolding also carried over to the person who was taking care of us. When he scolded her with: "Why are the children outdoors, *señora?* What are you here for?" La Chata would only say, "*Ay, señor,* but they go out, they don't obey me." Then my father would square accounts with us.

But I do not remember that he hit us girls like he did my brothers when someone complained about them. He would beat them hard and this frightened me very much. He hit them with the electric-light cable or with the kind of leather strap that had a flexible end. The next day I could see how their flesh stood up and turned black and blue. Thank God, I never was given a real beating like my brothers were.

When my father came home from his work at the restaurant, he would wash his feet, change his socks and sit down to read his newspaper. I used to look at what he was reading, but I didn't dare ask about it, because he never liked us to interrupt him. The only one who could interrupt my father was Marta. He would hold her on his knees or seat her on the table so that she could play with the unlit cigarette he always held between his lips. Then he would give her five *centavos* and send her out to play.

When he came home in a good mood, my father would sit in the kitchen in a little chair and delouse us, comb us, or fasten our shoes. When he took care of us like that, I felt an enormous pleasure, since I always noticed that his ordinary manner was to have a hard expression on his face, with his cigarette in his mouth, his hand on his forehead, and his feet tapping at a fast rhythm under the table. This kept me from seeking his caresses, his affection, particularly when I would try to talk to him and before finishing the word *"papá,"* I was shut up. "Go on, go on and play somewhere. Stop bothering me. What a nuisance, *hombre!* You don't let a person read in peace."

There were very few times that I came near my father. I almost always preferred to do my sewing, or my homework, or to be playing with my dishes on the floor near the kitchen door. I would tell my sister: "Ask my father for money to buy candy," "Tell him to give you milk." Sometimes my sister succeeded in making herself heard and sometimes she was also shut up. So then I would ask Elena or La Chata to ask him for a bit of sugar or food to play with.

One of the things I remember clearly was that we moved many times when I was young. This annoyed me very much because my father would give us no warning. He would come home from work, order the boys to roll up the mattresses with whatever happened to be on the beds, dump clothing and kitchen things in boxes, and start carrying pieces of furniture to the new house. If something was cooking on the stove, whoever was taking care of us at the time would have to carry the pots, hot charcoals and all. I used to think, "What a nuisance, back and forth, moving from one place to another," but I never protested aloud.

The first move, after my mother's death, was to the *vecindad* on Cuba Street, where we met Elena. She later became our stepmother. Elena lived with her husband, a few doors away. She had no children, and she let Marta and me come and play with some little yellow ducks she was raising. One day my father invited Elena to eat with us. This was odd because my father never liked to have strangers in the house. We children didn't ask any questions but just ate quietly, watching. My *papá* was very nice to her. After that she stayed in our house and lived with us.

Then we moved to another *vecindad* on Paraguay Street. I remember there were many mice in that house. In the mornings Roberto and Manuel would chase them and kill them with a broom. We didn't

live there long because Elena began to get dizzy spells and would sit
with her back to the sun whenever she could. My father thought our
room was too dark and damp for her so we moved to a two-story
tenement on Orlando Street. Of all the houses I have lived in, that was
the only one I liked.

I was delighted that it had windows. It looked pretty to me. We
had many plants. In the little dining place were two Carolina plants
that my father took great care of. When he came home and sat
down to read, he would keep getting up to clean the leaves with
his handkerchief, and would tell Elena that she ought to wash them
with soapy water. I liked the odor of damp earth and when my
father would empty the big flowerpots onto newspaper to clean
out the worms I liked to put my hands in the dirt. But my *papá* always
sent me away: "Go on away. Don't get yourself dirty. Get out of here."

Elena tried hard to take good care of us but things happened which
made my father want to move again. Once Roberto was almost run
over by a truck and later the same thing happened to me. Then Marta
fell off the roof but luckily she was caught by the clotheslines and
electric cables. My father was very much upset and hit Elena and my
brothers for not taking better care of her. The very next day we moved
to the Casa Grande.

I didn't like this new *vecindad* at all. It had no stairs or windows
and the courtyards were long and narrow. We lived in only one room.
The electric light almost always had to be on.

In the Casa Grande we moved three times until my father found a
room which satisfied him. He was very fussy about cleanliness. Whenever we moved to a new place he set my brothers scraping the walls
and scrubbing the floors. Room No. 64, the one in which we still live,
was terribly dirty and my father had the walls painted pink and the
door blue. In his enthusiasm, he had a shelf made in the little space
between the washtub and the water closet and on this he kept the
plants Elena loved.

When Elena lived with us I never felt that we were poor because
our room always looked nicer than our neighbors'. I was proud of
our house. It was clean and had curtains in the doorway. The two
metal beds had yellow bedspreads and the wardrobe was kept polished.
The big table on which we ate was covered with a checked tablecloth,
which had its matching napkins. These, of course were never used
except when we children grabbed them as handkerchiefs. We ate from

clay bowls with wooden spoons but Elena had some nice white cups and saucers and platters which she kept for company.

Our four chairs stood at the foot of the beds. There was another, smaller chair made of colored straw, that my father liked to sit in when he read the newspaper. As long as I can remember, we had a radio, a little RCA Victor, that stood on a shelf made especially for it. Odds and ends, such as tools, old magazines, shoes, boxes, a wash-basin, the burlap bags my brothers slept on, were always kept under the bed or wardrobe, carefully out of sight.

When my father had finished paying for the table and the wardrobe, he bought the chiffonier. It was shiny and had three large drawers and two small ones. My father was very happy when it was delivered and he kept rubbing it with a rag to make it shine more. He let Elena decide where it was to go, and the next day he bought a flower vase for the top of it. He began to send flowers every few days from the market—gladiolas, dahlias and beautiful, beautiful roses. Then he made a little shelf for the votive light, under the picture of the Virgin of Guadalupe. Later, he bought Elena a dressing table. Our room was full of furniture then.

The kitchen was in a tiny, inner courtyard that had no roof. When the rainy season came it was very inconvenient to cook there. My father didn't want to shut out the light and the air, and he tried to roof half of it. But when he began to raise birds, he had the whole thing roofed to keep them dry. The last thing my father did to improve the house was to buy some metal spoons and two glass shades for the electric-light bulbs in the bedroom and in the kitchen. After that, Elena got sick and he didn't take care of the house any more.

My father hired La Chata to help Elena because my stepmother was not strong enough to work hard. La Chata did all the heavy work in our house for five years. She would arrive at 7:00 A.M., the time my father left for work, go for the milk and light the charcoal stove. While the milk and water for the coffee came to a boil, she washed the supper dishes from the night before. Manuel and Roberto would ask for their coffee and go off to school. Marta and I stayed in bed until the room warmed up or, if we had to go to the toilet, we would run barefoot to the toilet in the kitchen, shivering in our underwear. After breakfast, Elena would take her basket and go to the market while La Chata piled the furniture onto the beds so that she could wash the floor. If she were in a good humor she would let me sit on the bed and watch her through the chair legs, but usually she chased everyone out of the house when she cleaned.

We ate lunch at three o'clock, crowded around the little table in the kitchen. After the meal, we would have to go to the movies with Elena, whether we wanted to or not. She loved the movies and went almost every day. She would leave a note for my father telling him in which theatre he could find us and sometimes he would join us there. It would be dark when we arrived home and we children would have our coffee and bread and go right to bed. Marta and I slept in one of the beds, my father and Elena in the other, and my brothers on burlap bags on the floor. By nine o'clock, the front door would be locked and the light turned out.

On Saturdays and Sundays, we would get up at different times, long after my father had left for work. Manuel was the laziest one in the family and was usually the last one to get up. His habit of sleeping late interfered with the housecleaning, for no one could sweep while he lay on the floor, wrapped from head to foot in his blanket. What a sleepyhead he was! When he finally did wake up he would stretch himself with great effort, rubbing his eyes and yawning desperately, his hair falling in his face. He didn't like to go for haircuts or to wash himself.

One morning Elena and Roberto decided to light a firecracker and toss it under his covers. We waited in the doorway to see what would happen. When it exploded Manuel jumped up violently and ran around the room, his head still wrapped in the blanket. We all laughed to see how frightened and angry he was.

Sometimes on Sundays, Elena would take us on outings to Chapultepec Park, to Xochimilco or elsewhere. Once in a while she would take us to see my grandmother and my aunt Guadalupe. Roberto and Manuel would carry Marta and me on their shoulders all the way there. My grandmother made candies which she sold in the street and she always gave us some. After she died, we continued to visit my aunt.

But these visits to my mother's family had to be kept secret because my father would punish anyone who took us there. He didn't like my mother's family because they drank a lot and criticized him for marrying Elena. My stepmother was very nice about it and never told him we went there. She was always seeing to it that nothing happened to us.

I don't know why but I have always preferred the company of

older women. While my brothers and sister played outside with their gangs of friends, I would sit in the doorway, sewing and chatting with La Chata. She would tell me how happy she used to be before her husband left her, and how *Señora* Chucha, who lived in Room No. 27 in the Casa Grande, had stolen him away. I rarely had friends but La Chata encouraged me to make friends with Candelaria, Chucha's daughter, so that she could spy on the family. Candelaria was very ugly but she had a little blue crib I liked to lie in, pretending to be her baby. Every time I came home from Candelaria's, La Chata would question me about the family. She hated *Señora* Chucha and often complained to my father that Chucha had insulted her and was mean; especially when Chucha was drunk.

One day La Chata went for the milk, came back hurriedly and ran out again. Usually it was hard for her to get past the narrow door because she was so stout, but this time she went in and out easily. My father was reading to Elena, I was playing with some toy furniture Elena had bought for me, and Marta was playing marbles on the floor. We heard shouts and screams and we ran out to the courtyard. My father would not let Marta and me see what was happening but Elena climbed the ladder to the roof and could see La Chata fighting with Chucha. Soon my father came back with La Chata. Her hair was disarranged and she was very agitated, explaining to him what had happened.

When she had gone home, my father and Elena laughed at the quarrel and commented on how funny the two women had looked rolling around on the ground. The next day La Chata came to work as though nothing had happened. But Candelaria never spoke to me again and I didn't go to her house any more.

Another one of my "friends" was *Señora* Andrea, who lived in No. 28. She was a motherly-looking woman with big breasts. She was an expert housekeeper and taught me how to sew. I helped her by taking care of her children. I spent whole days in her house and often Marta or Roberto was sent there to look for me. My friendship with her came to an end when she accused Roberto of stealing a razor. My father gave him a beating and had to buy a new razor for Andrea's husband.

Roberto had become very stubborn and rebellious and was quite unbearable at home. He had never been able to get along with Elena and it made him mad to see me around her a lot. He would say to

me, "Dumb kid. She's not even our mother. Stay away from her." He
insulted Elena to her face and she would spank him or pull his hair.
Later he would be punished by my father; he got a beating almost
daily. He fought with Manuel, too, and always got the worst of it.

Roberto often disappeared for one or two days and we thought
nothing of it, but once five days passed and my father became worried.
Someone advised him to wrap Saint Anthony in my brother's clothing,
put it upside down inside the wardrobe under lock and key and, he
said, Roberto would be back in a week. My father did it and Roberto
was back on the seventh day. He had gone to Veracruz to look for my
father's family. He had gone without money or extra clothing, knowing
only that they lived near a *hacienda*. After that, running away became
a habit with him.

It was my stepmother who took me to school for the first time. She
told me: "You stay here. In a little while, I'll come and bring your
coffee." I expected her to come back in a short time. When I saw that
she wasn't coming, my face must have been all twisted, because the
teacher patted my chin and said, "Don't cry, little girl. Look, you
have lots of little friends here. Your mother will be here in a little
while."

The morning I entered the second year of primary school it was
very cold as we stood in line to register. Almost all the mothers were
waiting but Elena wasn't there yet and I became alarmed. I saw the
girls file in one by one and the mothers step up to give their names.
Elena arrived exactly at the moment when they were asking me my
second family name, that is, my mother's name. When Elena saw that
I didn't know, she whispered to me, "Look, I'm going to give you the
same name as mine. You won't be mad?" I answered that I wouldn't
be, and that's how it was that I was registered as Consuelo Sánchez
Martínez. When my brothers and my aunt found out, they all said
that Elena wasn't my mother, that I was a fool, that I should go with
her if I loved her so much.

In this grade, I was robbed for the first time. This was very upsetting
and my brothers made fun of me. A lady had tricked me into letting
her hold my new cape and box of school supplies and then she had
disappeared with them. From that day on, under the threat of getting
a beating, one of my brothers had to take me up to the gate of the
school, where he would repeat: "If any dame talks to you . . ." All I

had to do was to tell my father that Manuel or Roberto didn't take me to school and it was enough for him to beat them.

How important I felt toward the middle of that year in school when the *señorita* said that we were going to learn to use ink. I remember going through the doorway with my books under my arm and my hands empty so that people could see my ink-stained fingers. Every time she told us that we were going to use ink, I would ask my father for a new penholder. And I always got everything I wanted. All I had to do was to show my father the list of school supplies and the next day I had everything I needed. It was the same with clothing; as long as it was for school, we had it almost before we asked him for it.

Elena was the first one to teach us to pray. At night she made the four of us kneel down and repeat the words she said. The most balky were Roberto and Manuel, who poked each other with their elbows and laughed until they got themselves put into the kitchen. As for me, at first I too didn't like to be kneeling with my arms crossed, without blinking an eye. I remember how, when I was four or five years old, my father would take my sister's hand and mine at night and make us cross ourselves. My father and Roberto crossed themselves every morning before going to work; they were always more strict about this than the rest of us.

When I was six or seven, Elena would tell us the Examples, which she had learned from the priest in her village. A miracle always took place in these stories, and Our Lord would appear to the person who had been good. In one Example a daughter who disobeyed her mother and was lacking in respect, was punished by Him. She went to confession and the priest told her that if a flower grew out of a nail she would be forgiven.

When I heard this story I thought, "How wonderful it would be if such a day should come for me." Often under cover of the darkness of the room, I would cry because I had been bad during the day, and I even felt glad at the thought of the punishment I would suffer. I would beg forgiveness and would promise faithfully not to get angry or shout at my brother. The Examples we heard Elena tell was my first real religious instruction. While she lived with us we went to hear Mass (my father never took us) and we learned how to celebrate the religious *fiestas,* like the Day of the Dead and Holy Week.

The first time I attended catechism was after we moved to the Casa Grande. One afternoon, while Elena and I were having coffee and were looking at a comic book, I heard a little bell ring. I looked out and saw some children running, each carrying a little stool. I asked no questions but suddenly a heavy figure appeared dressed in black, her hair combed in a bun and a rosary on her breast. She passed close by me ringing a little bell. "Aren't you coming to catechism?" I smiled and nodded.

I asked my father's permission. He agreed and sent all four of us. How glad I was to go! There I was, running through the courtyard with a little chair in my arm. My sister and two brothers also carried their stools. The *señorita* was speaking to the seated children. I had never before heard anything like what she was saying. Elena had taught us Our Father and the Ave, besides a prayer to the Angel, but it wasn't the same thing.

They always gave us candies as we went out. That first day, we all tore off at a run to show my *papá* what they had given us. I really felt happy. All by myself I began to take on the obligation of going to catechism. It made me very angry that Roberto and Manuel didn't come. I told on them to my *papá*.

One time I saw the *señorita* with a group of older girls around her, answering in chorus. When the *señorita* had finished, I asked a girl, "What was that?" She answered, "You mean you don't know! Those were God's Commandments." I was embarrassed and didn't say anything. Besides, I was afraid that the girl was going to hit me.

When catechism was over I told the *señorita* that I wanted to learn the Commandments. "But they are preparing for the first communion," she said. It was like a ray of light breaking over my head. I said nothing, but from that time all I wished for was to make my first communion and to die. I don't know why this desire came over me. I didn't even know the meaning of the first communion and I didn't ask.

Then the *señoritas* didn't come to teach us any more. We waited in vain with our little stools. I went back home angry. My *papá* asked me, "What's wrong, daughter?"

"Nothing, nothing is wrong with me." But I felt as though nobody remembered me any more. We were left quite a long time without catechism but I memorized all that I had learned.

Santitos, Elena's mother, and her three youngest children came to live with us. They all slept on the floor. Santitos was very religious. She was always dressed in black and prayed every night, which seemed unusual to me at that time. When I saw Santitos praying with her rosary in her hands and her face so serious, I thought it must be because she was going to die. One afternoon when Santitos was praying with her rosary, I asked her what my Lord Jesus Christ was like. With all the good will in the world, she set herself to teach me. How difficult it turned out to be. And how I respected Santitos! She taught me the *Señor Jesucristo* and the *Yo Pecador*. I asked my *papá* to buy the book with which to make my first communion. He agreed and in it I read how you were supposed to act before the priest.

The only bad memory I have of Elena is that she was the one who disillusioned me about who the *Santos Reyes* (Three Kings) were. When I was about eight years old I still believed in the Three Holy Kings who came bearing presents to children on January 6. I resisted believing the truth for some time. Even my brothers had told me a lot about the *Reyes*. During the Christmas *Posada* season, as evening would begin to fall, Roberto or Manuel would sit with Marta and me in the doorway, and would show us the three most brilliant stars in the Big Bear constellation. "Look, little sister, do you see those stars there? Those little stars are the Three Kings." I remember how every year a little before falling asleep I would look at the sky and it would really seem to me that the stars were coming closer. In my imagination I surrounded them with an intense light that dazzled me even after I was asleep. On the next day I would find the toys.

This year I decided to spy on my father, to see if Elena was right. At night Marta and I made believe we were asleep. Finally my father was satisfied that we were sleeping and I saw him put some toys in our shoes. It was true! My dream was over and I felt sad. The next day when my father got up to go to work, he said the same as every year. "Hurry, daughter, go and see what the *Reyes* brought you! Go on!" I looked at my presents but I no longer saw that magic thing that had surrounded my toys. This was the only time I did not like Elena.

The strongest impression remaining with me of that period was of a night when we came home from the movies. Generally my *papá* would carry Marta, while Elena took me. On this particular night everything was very dark, and suddenly the grownups were absolutely silent. As he opened the lock, my father told Elena to hold on to me. My head was pressed very tight against her skirts. They told me to close my eyes and Elena carried me. I didn't hear a sound, not my father talking nor the key in the lock—nothing. When I could open my eyes, I was already in bed. I asked why they had made me

close my eyes, but my father only said, "Go to sleep. It's late now."
I went to sleep, very curious; the next day, Roberto told me that they
had seen ghosts, nuns walking on the wall with a priest in front of
them. I don't know whether it was true or not. My father never told
me anything.

I always seemed more afraid of things than my brothers and sister.
Once, when I was eight or nine, Roberto gave me a terrible fright by
throwing a sackful of mice at me. The shock was so great I fainted.
After that I had a horror of mice and rats, more than anything else in
the world. Every time I saw one of them, dead or alive, I would scream
and run.

I remember one morning in the Casa Grande an ugly old rat came
out of his hole. I was asleep but pretty soon I woke up enough to
hear something gnawing under the bed. I opened my eyes wide and
hardly breathed, expecting the animal to climb up on the bed. As the
sound got closer and closer I began to call to my father, at first softly,
then a little louder. When I actually heard the animal at the head
of my bed I gave a wild scream. My father got up like a flash and
put on the light. The animal started to run. I kept screaming, "The rat!
the rat!" My brothers jumped up from their bed on the floor and
chased the rat with sticks. But this animal was hard to catch; he kept
escaping and they couldn't kill him. When finally they succeeded in
hitting him (I still get goose pimples all over when I think of it) the
animal squealed and I screamed. I kept hearing his horrible, piercing
cries. Every time they hit him, I would jump. After that, my father
had a new floor laid.

I couldn't imagine, when I first took a disliking to the Casa Grande,
how much more I was going to hate it and to suffer there. I thought
that Elena would always be with me, but it wasn't like that. There in
the Casa Grande she died, and after her death came the disorganization of the family, the gradual hardening of my father from day to
day, the growing hostility of my brothers toward me, and a series
of sufferings, brought on perhaps by my own lack of character.

Before Elena died, my troubles were not so great. I felt that I had
everything, my father's love and Elena's. Though my brothers hit me,
they did not do it all the time, and besides, their blows were not
always hard. I had never even minded the fact that my own real
mother was not alive. For instance, when I was in the third year of
school, the teacher taught us a hymn to mothers and there were

grand preparations to entertain the mothers with dances, recitations, and drawings. It hurt me. At that time, for me there was nothing so sublime as *father*. I thought: "Mothers, mothers . . . why do they make so many *fiestas* for mothers if fathers count for so much more? My *papá* buys us everything and never abandoned us. They should make a celebration for fathers and then I would go out dressed up in an Indian costume or in anything else."

But then Elena began to get sick. Later we learned that she had tuberculosis. She would stay seated for hours in the sun so that it would strike her back. Her hair in the sun looked reddish-blond. She had gotten thin and had fainting spells even though she took lots of medicines and went from one doctor to another.

My father was very worried and pampered her more and more. He had always bought her nice dresses and shoes with high heels, even a little fur jacket, and he took her wherever she wanted to go, but now he brought her presents every day.

As Elena got sicker and sicker, she took the advice of her doctors and went to the hospital for a long stay. My father was very sad. Every afternoon, now, he was a little later in getting home because he went to visit her. He would pat my head and say, "Do you miss Elena, *madre*? There, there, she'll be back." And I saw how a tear would appear. On Wednesday, La Chata's day off, my *papá* would bathe us, give us our breakfast, wash our socks and have the boys do the housework.

But the house was no longer the same; little by little it began to decline. I regretted particularly that our plants were dying. My father complained a good deal about this. Sometimes I would hear him shout: "*Caray*! We can't keep anything here! It's a shame! It doesn't seem possible that there isn't anyone to take care of things." La Chata kept quiet; Santitos also.

La Chata tried to keep the house clean but we children jumped on the beds and on the table and messed them up. When we had quarrels or just in fun we would grab chunks of charcoal from the carton under the sink and would throw them at each other, making black smudges on the walls and floor. La Chata grumbled and scolded us in coarse language and put us out into the courtyard. We, in turn, would complain to our father that all she served us was stale bread and potatoes with eggs. When Elena had been with us we all ate well, but La Chata hid the milk and fruit and made special dishes only for herself and for

my father. She wasn't nice to us at all but when we told my father he
would shut us up.

Perhaps because he needed money to take care of Elena or because
he liked to be in business, my father began to sell animals. He started
out with fifty birds, which he kept in wooden cages of all sizes. My
brothers cleaned the cages twice a day but in spite of that the house
began to smell and to look dirty. The walls and floor were always
spotted with birdfood and droppings. At first my father had only
small birds, like parakeets and thrushes, but later he bought parrots,
pigeons, pheasants, and once a large, ugly bird that ate only raw meat.
We had turkeys and even a badger tied to the legs of our chiffonier.
Almost all the wall space in the bedroom and the kitchen was hung
with cages. My father got rid of the plants to make room for boxes of
chickens. He put in another shelf for some very fine cocks. We children
had to collect the eggs and put them in the dish closet.

When Elena finally was to come home from the hospital my father
had the rooms whitewashed and bought a few plants once more. But
she was still very ill and went to live in Room No. 103 in the last courtyard of the Casa Grande. With her went the dressing table, the bed
and bedspread, the curtains, the flower vase, the remaining lamp shade,
any many of the nicest things in the house. We were not allowed to
enter Elena's room but once in a while Santitos would open the door
and let us see her from the courtyard. When she felt well, Elena would
go up to the roof and I would talk to her from below and show her
my sewing.

After Elena had moved into her room, Antonia, my older half-sister,
arrived. I was asleep the night my father brought her. The next day I
found a new face in the house. She was lying next to me in my bed.
"Why don't you greet your sister?" my father said. My brothers talked
to her but not I. I didn't say a word to her. I watched from afar. I was
extremely jealous. I never before had seen my father with anybody.
How was it possible that Antonia existed? But I didn't dare ask my
father and he gave me no explanation.

Several days before he brought her, my father had told us just this
much: "I am going to bring your sister. She is a *señorita* already. She
has finished the sixth grade." At that time, the word "*señorita*" meant
to me a young woman with long wavy hair and eyeglasses, dressed in
a dark tailored suit, someone to be respected, so I was really eager to

meet my sister. But when I saw her she was very different. Antonia's face was thin and her eyes somewhat pop-eyed; her straight hair was tied with a ribbon and she wore an ordinary dress. I was partly disappointed and partly satisfied because she made me feel less discontented with my own appearance.

At first Antonia was very kind, and little by little, began to win our confidence. She fixed up the house and made it look nice again, with curtains in the doorway and flowers on the altar. But later she made the four of us suffer very much. What made me begin to hate her was the distinction my father made between her and the rest of us. He seemed to change completely.

The first sign of this came one afternoon when he arrived home angry. He came in, saw a bench in the middle of the kitchen, kicked it to one side with his foot, and shouted at me: "Stupid, imbecile! You see things and just leave them there. Get that bench out of here, quick!" For a moment I didn't know what to do. I had no idea where to put the bench. Finally I shoved it under the sink. I was shocked. My father had never before used words like that to me. To my brothers, yes, but never directly to me.

That night I refused to eat my supper, thinking that it would bring the results it had on many other occasions. If I refused to eat, my father would lovingly talk to me and ask me what it was I wanted and would send for delicacies. This time it wasn't that way. I went to bed without eating anything and my father paid no attention to me. He began to read the paper to Antonia. I was under the covers holding back my tears. I was ashamed to cry before this new person who was my sister.

On countless occasions the taste of tears was part of my coffee. "Stop clowning and eat," was what my father would say. It no longer mattered to him if I cried. The first time I heard Antonia answer him back I couldn't believe my father's reaction in not saying anything at all about her ill-mannered behavior. In our case we didn't even raise our eyes when he scolded us, not even Manuel, who was the oldest, while she could shout at him freely. Whenever he bought a dress for Antonia, it always had to be better quality than ours. My father almost always gave things to her to dish out. All this made me feel like I was nobody in the house.

One thing my father had strictly forbidden us to do was to touch the radio. It always had to be set for the station that he had been listening to the night before. Also, the furniture could not be moved unless he had given permission, or he would yell, "Who shifted things out of their place? Don't I count for anything in this house? Let's put everything back." So when I saw Antonia turning on the radio one morning, I told her not to or my father would get angry. She paid no attention and turned it to another station. This frightened the four of us but when my father learned about it he didn't say a word.

One day my father gave Antonia a box of Max Factor face powder which she had heard advertised on the radio. She had told him to bring a box for each of us and when I saw him come home with one box and give it to her, it hurt me. Antonia took it and said, "Look, Consuelo, you take from here too." But I said contemptuously, "No. What do I want it for? You use it." Tonia was offended and went out.

I was serving myself some coffee when I heard the door slam and my father suddenly stood right in front of me with an expression on his face that made me tremble from head to foot. "What did you do to Antonia?" he demanded.

"Nothing, *papá*," I answered. "I just told her that I didn't want any powder."

"Imbecile! Stupid, nasty girl! The next time you do a thing like that, I'll slap you in the mouth. You'll pick up your teeth halfway across the courtyard," he said, clenching his fists. I only lowered my head and went to sit in the doorway. That night I went to bed without eating and in the darkness I cried and lamented that Elena wasn't living with us any more.

The continual lying to us also began. In the afternoons when my father came home, Antonia was all dressed up and they would go out. They would say that they were going to the doctor but they went to the movies. I would see my father and Tonia walking across the courtyard. She would take his arm and the two of them would walk away together. When *papá* went out with us he always held us tightly by the arm and when we arrived home my arm hurt. As for my brothers, he never even let them come near him. Almost always they walked in front or in back, but never next to him.

I had a bad opinion of Antonia on other counts too. She put postcards of half-naked women and follies dancers around the mirror of her dresser. We were all worried about them, even Manuel who at that time stayed away from home all day and never took an interest in what was going on there. I finally complained to my father, demanding that he take away the pictures. He didn't say anything then but two days later the pictures were replaced by portraits of Pedro Infante and other actors which Antonia showed to her friends.

That was another thing that seemed unfair to the four of us. My father would never permit our friends to come into the house. If he ever happened to come home and find them there, he would chase them out: "Outside, little girl. Go play with your mother. It is too late for visiting now." But he never did this to Antonia's friends and would converse and laugh with them.

We had never noticed our birthdays or saint's days until Tonia insisted on celebrating my father's Saint's Day. It was his first party and for the first time, too, we had special glasses in the house for serving "Cubas." On Antonia's birthday, my father bought her everything, a dress, shoes, stockings, and even a cake. We had the pleasure only of seeing the cake, because my father and Antonia would take it to her mother Lupita's house, where they made the party and cut the cake.

Perhaps because of pride or to avoid being scolded or to hold back our tears, we never asked for a piece of the cake. But it bothered us a lot. Marta would look at it from the bed and whisper to me, "They only buy a cake for her. Let them take their dirty old cake. It isn't even good." I once dared ask my father who bought Antonia's cake and he said her mother did. I didn't believe this because Lupita had hurt her hand at the restaurant and was not working at that time.

We all wanted birthday cakes after that but my father said, "What do you think I do? Sweep up money with the broom? I have to pay for the rent, the light and food. Where am I going to get it all?" It was that way every time I asked him for something that wasn't for school.

There was something inside me that screamed, that wept, when my requests were rejected, especially when I saw how my half-sister was humored. I thought to myself "How can you make my *papacito* spend so much money. Poor little thing, he works so hard! Doesn't it hurt you?" I would go to Yolanda's house and tell her what I was thinking. I looked for consolation from her and she would tell me to bear it, not to say anything, that my father would have to notice how unfair Antonia was. But I waited and waited and he never noticed anything. On the contrary, I felt that my father was cutting himself off more and more from the rest of us.

At first Marta didn't seem to mind the change in my father. But later, when she was wild and wouldn't go to school, he began to scold her and beat her with a strap. Then, she too began to blame Antonia, and to damn her. Marta's words were music to my ears and I encouraged her. But most of the time there was a heaviness in my heart and my cheeks burned with shame when my father yelled at us and called us lazy bums.

Naturally, I asked myself a lot of questions. At night my head went round and round and I would get lost in the darkness of my room. Sometimes when I would cry, Antonia would try to console me, but I always rejected her. I wouldn't accept her words or her caresses. "What's wrong, Consuelo? Why are you crying? Did my father scold you?" This last question seemed so cruel to me that if I could I would have slapped her. At night when my sister would try to read us some story or the paper, I didn't like the idea. I thought that she did it only to win over my father more, and so when she began to read, I would turn my back and make believe I was asleep.

I couldn't understand that it was because Antonia was older that she was treated differently. I only knew that my father loved her more. I began to doubt that I was really his daughter. That is what I felt when I would see his indifference, not only toward me, but toward Marta, who used to be his pet. Now he hit her whenever he got a complaint from Antonia. He never hit me, but the words he said to me were worse than whiplashes. I never answered back. I couldn't; the words wouldn't come out of my mouth. They only went to my head and made me want to get out of the place and not see anybody.

It was about this time that I had a nightmare which caused me to wake up sweating and crying. In it I saw my father in his faded overalls and trousers, with his *sombrero* on. He was beating and chasing the whole family without mercy. He hadn't yet struck me, and I kept yelling to the rest, "Get out! Get out! *Papá* has gone mad! He's going to kill us!" Everybody ran out. Chairs were knocked over, dishes broken. From the kitchen doorway I saw that my father had tied my sister Marta with a rope to the legs of the bed and was beating her with no concern for where the blows landed. He stood over her, watching the pleading look on her face, and even when she began to bleed he kept on beating her. Suddenly, one of the blows hit the brass spittoon which was always kept in the house, it overturned, and his feet got wet. I yelled at him. "*Papá, papá.* You've gone mad! Let her alone! You're going to kill her!" But he paid no attention to me and kept on whipping her. While I was shouting I woke up. I went back to sleep, only to go on dreaming the same nightmare.

But this time in my dream my father had moved the bed and the shelf of the saints to a different wall. Manuel and Roberto were in the bedroom, Marta and I in the kitchen. One of the panels of the bedroom door was only half-closed and I looked in. I saw my father leaning over the bed, holding in his hands a heart, the heart he had torn from the body of a young painter, Otón, who lived in the same tenement. Otón was lying on the bed, face upward. I could see the cavity from which his heart had been torn. My father was holding the heart high and offering it to somebody. I had a terrible fright and awoke with the same cry that I always make when I dream. I have never been able to get rid of the sight of my father holding that bloody heart in his hands.

The day Elena died, Marta, Tonia and I were at home. My father came in and with tears in his eyes told us to go and bid her good-bye. The three of us ran to her room. On the way I kept saying to myself, "*Ay*, dear little God, it isn't true, it isn't true." When we entered, Santitos was there holding her rosary. Elena was very pale, her lips purple, her hair spread over the pillow. Roberto was there crying; Marta and Tonia cried too. I had a big lump in my throat. Santitos took Elena's hand and we received her benediction. Then my father sent Marta and me home, where we cried like two lone coyotes.

At the funeral the next day we all cried, especially my father. He put his arms around me and said, "She has left us, daughter, she has left us forever." Elena was buried under a *pirú* tree in the Dolores cemetery. When we arrived home my father immediately went to her room to dispose of her things. Most of them went to her mother, some were sold. Tonia followed my father and asked for Elena's dressing table and her good coat, which he gave her. Later, I asked him for some remembrance of Elena and he gave me a little porcelain doll.

After that I began to feel horror toward my home. My father would turn out the light and make us go to bed right after supper. He would spend the evening out of the house with Tonia or would sit in the kitchen until very late. Roberto and I hated each other more and more. If he were in the courtyard, I would go into the house; if he were in the house, I would go into the courtyard. In the morning I would pray to all my saints that he would still be asleep so that he wouldn't hit me. Sometimes I left for school without breakfast to avoid him, and I dreaded going home again.

To be sure, I was no angel. Knowing that it annoyed Roberto for the door to be open, I would open it. If he closed it, I would open it

again and again, until we would fight. Roberto hated me so much that
he would have killed me if he could. Once he tried to strangle me, banging my head against the headboard of the bed.

Another time, I'll never forget as long as I live, I had my back
to him as he was standing in the doorway and I felt a little breeze pass
my left side. When I turned around to see what had caused it, I felt
a kind of fogginess and a bitter taste in my mouth, for only a few
centimeters from me, stuck in the wall, was a knife with a very sharp
blade. All I could do was to turn around, look at my brother, and then
continue searching for what I needed.

Roberto kept watching me from the door. I didn't show that I was
afraid or angry. He came over, giving me a shove that knocked me
down, and pulled out the knife. At that moment I felt as though the
delicate tissues of my heart were coming away little by little, causing
a bitter liquid to drip down and kill me. But I got up off the ground,
realizing that if I provoked him, he would finish what he wanted to do.
So I left and went to Yolanda's house.

In spite of everything, I had to admit that after we fought, Roberto
would come over to me and say, "Little sister, did it hurt? Forgive me,
yes? Please, little sister." To which I would yell, "Get out of here, you
damn black one. I wish you'd die! Beat it . . . you just wait until my
papá comes!" And there I would be, rubbing my eyes, squealing with
pain and rage.

After my father came home and Roberto got his beating, he would
go to cry in the dark kitchen, sitting between the brazier and the dish
closet, his hair hanging over his forehead, his nose filthy, one suspender
of his overalls hanging down over his shoulder. He would sob for a long
time, with nobody to comfort him. We wouldn't notice when he left,
but in a few minutes, people would start coming around to complain
that Roberto had beaten a child or had done some other nasty thing.

Yet, in his own way, Roberto kept on trying to win the affection of
everyone in the family. I remember one time when he came home with
his windbreaker and pants pockets full of nuts. Two days before, he
had gotten a terrific beating from my father "to pay" for something he
had done. Everyone in the house was disgusted with him. I can still
see him as he came home . . . in his gray overalls, his "miner's" shoes
scuffed, one shirt sleeve torn, his hair covered with dust. At that time,
he seemed hateful to me, but now, as I think of it, how beautiful my
brother was as he came in, holding out his jacket to Marta, Tonia and

me, offering us the nuts. He divided them into piles, one for each of us, and even helped me shell mine. But I wasn't taken in . . . I knew he would soon hit me again for one reason or another.

I remember one night very well, when Roberto was about fourteen. The room was dark, not even the votive light was lit, and I was lying in bed with my hands under my neck, thinking . . . wondering why my father had changed toward us. Roberto came in, spread out his sack and pillow on the floor at the foot of my father's bed and lay down.

There was a dance going on in the courtyard and we could hear the words of a popular song. It went more or less like this: "The soul of my drum, because my drum does have a soul, says it lost its peace because it is black. And even though you don't like people who are dark, they have white souls and their hearts are white."

I don't know whether Roberto was dreaming or was just drunk, but the lines aroused such emotion in him that he began to sob, louder and louder. He said reproachfully, "Yes, *papacito,* you don't love me because I am dark, because my hide is black. That's why none of you love me . . . but my soul is white!"

It hurt me to hear what he said. Actually, I had never paid attention to my brother's color. I hated him for hitting me, but not because he was dark. I believe that Roberto very much wanted my father to comfort him, to embrace him, at that moment. My father reacted to his words, because he spoke gently and said, "Shhh . . . be quiet and go to sleep . . . go to sleep now, hear?"

One evening my father was sitting at the table, reading. It was past eight o'clock and he had already taken off the overalls which he wore over his trousers and shirt. He often kept large sums of money in his trouser pockets because he was a food buyer for the La Gloria restaurant. He wore the overalls to protect the money from the thieves that abound in the city markets. Marta was playing on the bedroom floor; Antonia and I were listening to a radio drama. We heard a knock on the door and Antonia opened it.

There was my brother, Manuel, holding the arm of a rather fat girl, who was wearing a purple dress and a blue sweater. She was not pretty for her features were dark and irregular, but her black hair was nicely curled. My brother was trying to get her to go in, pushing her ahead of him. Finally they entered and my father stood up to receive them. Manuel presented Paula and my father told her to sit down. She was nervous and sat down on what must have seemed to her "the bench of judgment." Manuel remained standing while my father eyed him up and down.

"*Papá*, I spoke to you about Paula . . ."

My father said, "Yes." Then he said to Paula, "What are you thinking of, girl? Do you believe that this tramp is going to take you out of your difficulties?" She didn't answer. "Yes, girl, he is a bum who knows only how to play pool with his friends."

My father then told Marta and me to go out to the courtyard. We obeyed like little lambs. The truth is that I was embarrassed by my father's severity. He should not be scolding her like that. As we left I heard him say, "You are going to regret this a thousand and one times, girl, because this one is not a man."

Outside in the courtyard I leaned against the wall. I felt sorry for Paula. I went to *Señora* Yolanda's house and told her, "Imagine, Manuel brought home his *novia*." She said, "So he is married already, eh?" I sat down. "Married?" I hadn't understood. I began to feel proud, for now I could say I had a sister-in-law. That's how my brother got "married."

In school, I liked to be alone all the time. I used to think my classmates were either stuck-up or quarrelsome. I would stay in the classroom, drawing, sewing, or simply looking at the blackboard with the *señorita* sitting at her desk. If I went outside for recreation, I would sit off to one side where there weren't so many girls to take a bite of my roll; or I would go up to the roof to look at my reflection in the water tanks.

I did not think I could ever be pretty. I felt inferior because I was small and thin. My skin was too dark, my eyes slightly slanted, my mouth too large, my teeth too crowded. I searched for some good feature. My nose was straight but big, my hair very thick and dark but would not take a curl. I wished I were lighter-skinned and plump like Marta, with dimples like hers. I dreamed of being blond. Staring at myself in the water I thought, "Consuelo, Consuelo, what a strange name. It doesn't even sound like the name of a person. It sounds very thin, as though it were breaking."

The caretaker usually brought me out of my dreams, taking me by the shoulder and saying, "What are you doing here? Don't you know you can't come up to the roof? Go play or I'll take you to the principal." Blushing with shame, I would go down and sit in the sun in the little garden. When the first bell rang for us to go back to our classrooms, I would wait for the others to get lined up, because otherwise they almost always pushed me. I let them push without protesting; I was afraid of them.

My sister Marta wasn't afraid, of either girls *or* boys. She played with both. It made me furious to see her surrounded by boys, squatting with her legs apart, leaning on the ground with one hand, holding a marble in the other, calculating the distance. I used to embarrass her by making scenes when she was with her friends. Also, I didn't like her wandering around with Roberto. They would both play hooky and come home with their clothes dirty and torn. Sometimes when I went out looking for her I would see her hanging on the rear bumper of a bus, taking a free ride.

There always was trouble between Marta and me, especially when I wanted to delouse her, or have her wash the dishes, or make her clean her face with a damp rag. And I could never, never, get her to sew. Trying to do this was the cause of big quarrels in which she would throw the iron at me or scratch my hands all over. Later, she would accuse me of having hit her and pulled her hair, and in a way she was right, though I don't remember having dragged her "across the whole room and the courtyard," as she told my father.

As soon as she felt the first blow from me, Marta would answer with kicks, bites, pinches, scratches, and whatever else she could. When I saw her like that, I laughed so much I lost my strength. I would feel my stomach stretch like a rubber band, and then all I could do was hold her hands so she couldn't scratch me. When she didn't succeed in hurting me or if I had locked her in, she would throw herself on the floor and bang her head on the boards or against the wall. She would cry so much her face would get red and if one of my brothers saw her he would take it out on me without asking any questions.

La Chata, probably because she was tired of these scenes, did not mix in. She would begin to sing or simply go on making *tortillas*. I couldn't do anything with Marta except complain to my father, and never with the result I expected. Instead of scolding her for stealing rides or playing only with boys, he would say to me, "Who are you to hit her?" Or, "Let her play with whomever she wants," or, "The day I find out that you hit her, I'll smash your face." In spite of this I always wanted to correct my sister, and even more when she grew up.

As a matter of fact, I really didn't know how to treat Marta. I saw her as a candy doll, dressed in blue, on a white cake, but in reality there was no sugar in her. Instead of being sweet, she was spoiled and selfish. I looked upon her tantrums as the caprices of a five-year-old, which she would get over when she grew up. I would think, "She doesn't want to lend her doll, but she will when she is a little older . . . She doesn't want to share her candy now, but later on she will."

I remember once, during the days when my father would give us five or ten *centavos* for sweets, that Marta came back from the store holding a lot of candy in her skirt. I was standing in the doorway watching the others playing and she went into the room. When I turned to look for her, there was no one inside. I peeked under the bed and there she was eating the candy.

"*Ay*, just look at this one! Selfish! You hid so you wouldn't have to share. Miser!"

Her mouth was so full of sweets she was hardly able to talk. "It's none of your business. They're mine!"

I laughed and let her finish the candy. But she did the same thing many other times. I tried to help her with her homework . . . once I spent a whole afternoon making a painting she needed for her teacher . . . another time, she had to hand in some sewing and I loaned her mine. Each time, she took it and acted as though she had done it herself. "Oh, well," I said, "it doesn't matter." And I let it pass.

One afternoon when I was almost thirteen, I was in bed with terrible cramps. We had no help in the house at that time. When Roberto and Marta came in, laughing and playing, I asked my sister to make me some tea. She looked at me scornfully. "No! What for? Get up and do it yourself. All you do is lie around and want everything handed to you."

"Damn kid," I thought. "All right then, I'll ask Roberto."

"What about you, little brother? Won't you make me some tea? My stomach hurts me so!"

"Me? No! What are you talking about?" They went out again and left me there, crying and holding my stomach. I waited a long time for my sister to grow out of her "caprice age," but it got worse with time.

My half-sister Antonia annoyed me in the same way as Marta, because of her tomboyish games. I watched her and the others from Yolanda's house, with my sewing or my notebook in my hand, or standing in our doorway because I didn't want to leave my father alone. When they passed near me, I told them they looked like runaway horses or like men. Tonia only laughed, which would make me angry and I would complain to my father: "Look, *papá*, Tonia goes running through all the courtyards and her dress goes way up. Talk to her." Sometimes my father would make her go in. Other times, without even lifting his eyes from the paper, he would say to me, "Yes, go on and play. I'll talk to her right away."

Tonia and her friends invited me to play, but I never would. Yolanda, too, encouraged me to play: "Go on, Consuelo, go and play. You act like an eighty-year-old woman, not a youngster of thirteen. You'll be getting old right away, *hombre!*" But I thought of how their bodies moved as they ran, and thinking of my own body, I felt ashamed, afraid that my dress would fly up. Only once in a while, when I felt really gay, seeing everybody laughing, would I go out to play "eighteen." When I began to run, I did it too stiffly and was almost always caught.

Many of the fights with Roberto were because I didn't like to do anything in my house. "Wash the dishes, kid," he would order me, and I would answer, "Wash them yourself, dope. Who are you to order me around!" But in the neighbors' houses I would do all kinds of housework and take care of their children. I went home at dinner time or just before my father arrived. Then La Chata would say to me, "Light of the street, darkness of your own house," because I helped others.

By that time I was in my sixth year at school and had a lot of homework. When I wanted to study, my brothers and sister would put on the radio or yell. Sometimes I went up on the roof to read, sitting on a box and using a rag for a sunshade. But even this didn't work; La Chata or Antonia would come to hang clothes or Roberto would come up with a mouse tied by the tail and chase the animal from one roof to the other. This made me fly down.

Later that year Roberto ran away and joined the army and I had more peace. Until then, I would ask my friend, *Señora* Dolores, for permission to study in her house. Sometimes I would go to the library outside the Casa Grande or to one of the shops of the tenement. In a strange house, they wouldn't bother me and I could study, which was really the thing I liked best. Then I would go home and refuse to do something they asked me to, and again I would hear, "Light of the street, darkness of your house."

I liked school better than home too. I always got the good-conduct badge, and I almost always had first place (first row, first seat) in all grades. Sometimes I would lose this place and be put back three or five seats, but afterwards I would win it again. How proud I used to be when the teacher asked a question about something and I was one of those who raised their hands!

As for my teachers, I admired them, but I thought so little of myself that I never aspired to be like them. For me everything was impossible then. How could I ever become so pretty and well educated as they? How could I become worthy to get up before a group of girls and have them sit or stand at my command? No! Undoubtedly, this was not for me.

One of my teachers, *Señorita* Gloria, once told us something I never forgot. In sewing class a girl asked her if she had ever thought of getting married. The teacher blushed and said, "Yes, of course. All of us have to get married someday." Felipa López, who was most daring, said, "Haven't you ever been in love?" *Señorita* Gloria tried to smile and answered, "Love is a wonderful thing, but I'm not gullible. Love is like a star, it starts out brilliant and dies down. You should never believe young men who say, 'I love you.' You must be careful and not venture into the unknown. Many men lie and one shouldn't believe them." I never forgot what she said. I think this is why I never let my boy friends deceive me, for when they say, "I love you," within me I laugh at them and repeat, "Don't believe it, don't believe it."

That year, when I was thirteen, I began to menstruate. It happened one day in school, frightening and embarrassing me terribly. My head ached and I had cramps all morning. María, a girl who sat next to me, told the teacher and we were both allowed to go to the bathroom. There I saw blood stains on my dress and underwear. María told me not to worry because it happened to all women and that it meant I was now a *señorita*. I was disappointed because I had always thought that when I became a *señorita* I would wear high heels, nice dresses and eyeglasses and would use lipstick. But there I was still in socks and school uniform! And later I noticed that everyone treated me the same as before, not even noticing that I was different.

The teacher sent me home, where I tried secretly to wash the stains from my clothing. My cramps were so bad I cried and had to tell Antonia. She was very nice to me and gave me camomile tea and lots of advice. I was worried that my brothers would find out but Antonia showed me how to take care of that too. When La Chata came back from the market, Tonia told her and she seemed happy about it, saying, "*Ay*, now we have a *señorita* in the house." She was the one who told my father but he never said anything to me about it. Whenever I complained of cramps he had someone make me tea or he would send me to the doctor for an injection.

I don't believe my father came to school a single time in all the years I spent in primary school. He knew nothing of the things that happened in school and he never asked. He signed my report cards and that was all. If there was a parents' meeting he would say he couldn't leave work to attend but he would give me the money or do whatever it was they wanted. When I completed the sixth grade I asked for a white dress for graduation. At first he refused but I finally got it. As usual, he bought it without me and I didn't like it. It had a round collar and little embroidered roses. My schoolmates thought it was nice but it made me feel like an insignificant child on the day that meant so much to me.

I had begged my father to come to the graduation exercises, but he never appeared. I kept sticking my head over the balcony to see if he had come. Even when all the sixth graders and their parents were sitting at the table in the mess hall for the luncheon, I kept turning round to look for him. How awful I felt to see my classmates with their parents. Some of the fathers came in their work clothes but they were there anyway with their daughters. How much I wanted my father to appear by magic and be with me!

Before putting away my graduation papers, I showed them to my father. As always, he only glanced at them and said nothing. In the *vecindad* they asked, "Did you pass, Consuelo?" and, "What are you going to do now?" I could only say, "Who knows? I don't know what my father wants me to study next." But all my pride in my schoolwork had been dashed to the ground by my father.

And that was my life as a little girl—ignored when I would do well in school or when I would ask questions at home, or answered sharply by my family. This made me feel stupid or it made me think that they didn't love me. But I never knew why.

A whole year passed before I went to school again. I spent this year working, first sewing and then in a shoe factory downtown. A friend of Marta's had told me that a dressmaker, *Señora* Federica, was looking for an assistant. "I don't know how much she will pay, see, but she is very nice." That was enough for me to go and take the job. The *señora* said she would put some money aside for me each week but she never paid me.

Actually, the pay did not matter to me. What interested me most was not being hit or scolded and not having to watch my father's actions. I thought, "What do I want to be in the house for? If my father doesn't like the way I serve him, let Antonia wait on him." Tonia and I took turns serving my father his supper. Unfortunately—I don't know whether it was my fault or not—my father never liked what I gave him. If it was cold, he would say it was dog food. If it was hot, he said I never paid any attention to anything. If there were lumps of milk in the coffee, or if there weren't, it was swill. He would say, "You're good for nothing, useless! The day you go to some other house they'll slam the door in your face. You can't do anything."

I think Tonia also felt mortified. She would say to me, "Wait, Consuelo, I'll give him supper." But my father wouldn't accept this. It had to be her one day and me the other. He would say, "Dope! Learn from your sister. She's clean. She knows how to do things. But you? What do you know?" That is why I preferred to be working without pay.

Señora Federica first taught me to turn the cloth tapes. Afterwards, I learned the jobs of making hems, pressing, and sewing on buttons. She was also going to teach me to sew on the machine and she did give me opportunities to use it when she went to deliver a dress, thinking perhaps I would begin to sew. But I never dared. When she wasn't there, I wouldn't touch the machine for anything. I was afraid of it. I thought that if I stepped on the treadle, I might sew my fingers to the material and not be able to stop the machine.

She had a young nephew who hid, from the first day, whenever he saw me come in. He was very shy, which seemed unusual to me because the young men of the Casa Grande were very brazen. When they saw girls, they would call them their "flowers." I felt very homely, and when this boy ran from me, I thought I really was.

I would go home from the *señora's* at eight or nine at night. When there were blackouts, her brother, Gabriel, or her sister and their nieces would take me home and once in a while I asked them in. The first time I did this, I walked through the door praying that my father would not be rude, and I think it helped. My father just lifted his eyes from the newspaper and invited them in. I served coffee and we had supper. It was the first time I had ever brought visitors to the house.

During this year (when I was fourteen years old), I visited my aunt more often, but I didn't seek her out as much as I did *Señora* Yolanda, who was the one who knew my troubles as well as I knew hers. She taught me to crochet and to knit with needles, to make *panecillo* and *polvorones* and to make use of old *tortillas*. I was the person she trusted most at that time. But this friendship broke up later, leaving only a feeling of resentment on my part, because Yolanda became good friends with Tonia and changed toward me, little by little. Tonia would give her sugar, coffee, and dead flies or bananas for the birds. *Papá* had never allowed us four to help ourselves to the fruit he brought daily. If we did, there were big blowups in our house. But Tonia could take whatever she wanted.

The change in my father toward us was not unnoticed by Yolanda, who warned me on various occasions, "Don't be foolish. Keep an eye on your father or Antonia will take him away from you completely." I would try to follow her advice, but how could I make my father take any notice of us? When I tried to converse with him, even about the same things Antonia did, he would only say, "I'm not interested in other people's affairs, just my own, and that's all."

As for caressing him or doing things for him, neither Marta nor I could. But Tonia got into the habit of washing his feet when he came home from work and cutting his calluses. If she hurt him, he would just laugh. When he came from the bathhouse where he would go every third day, she would insist on combing his hair and putting on the brilliantine. Once in a while she would find a gray hair and pull it out and my father would joke about it. "A gray hair? And I so young?" and they would laugh together. But everything he asked *us* for had to be brought to him on the run and then he would take it almost angrily.

Then my father gave instructions that neither my clothes or Marta's should be sent out for washing any more. It seemed to me that he was beginning to treat us like strangers. La Chata taught me to wash. Later I also had to wash his heavy work clothes. It was all the harder for me because my *papá* had never before permitted me to do any housework. He had said, "Don't scrub floor, it's harmful to the lungs," "Don't sew, it's bad for your lungs," or, "Don't hit her on the back." My *papá* was always afraid that I would get Elena's disease.

The first time I washed his clothes I cried into the tub, partly because my back burned and the bones in my hands hurt, and partly because I was afraid that the clothes would not come out clean. When

I finally got to wring out the clothes, I felt as though my strength was gone. I ended up soaked from head to foot.

And the floor! The first time I washed the floor my father had to take me to the doctor. My legs, from my knees to my ankles, were swollen, and the hand with which I held the brush was bleeding. Not very much, but it bled. This was the end for me. Now I really felt outside the family. I began to make faces behind my father's back when he scolded me. Only once did I tell him what was happening to me, but he paid no attention, so after that, never again.

One night, while I was still working for *Señora* Federica, my father said to me, "Antonia's sister, Elida, is coming to take you to a woman who is going to teach you to work. She is coming for you at seven in the morning. Be ready." Tonia's half-sisters, Elida and Isabel, had begun to come to the house to visit and I knew them well. I liked Elida and was glad to go with her the next morning.

We took the bus downtown and got off at the Alameda. It was the first time I had ever been in the center of the city. As we walked past the park, I hardly listened to what Elida was saying. I saw trees, the monuments, the passing automobiles, the men wearing suits (instead of work clothes) hurrying along. It was the other end of the world for me. I felt so skinny, so badly dressed in spite of being clean, that I imagined everybody was watching me. I stumbled. I felt upset.

When we arrived, Elida said, "Look, go up to the top floor. Ask for Sofía, the *maestra*. Tell her I sent you." Upstairs, the *señora* greeted me pleasantly. I began by painting the edges of the shoes. She showed me how to hold the shoe so I wouldn't dirty my dress. She knew a lot about shoes and leather and had taught Elida and Isabel. That's why they called her *maestra*. Before that, *maestra* had meant to me only a school-teacher.

At one o'clock everybody put down the tools and went out. The *señora* said we were going to eat up on the roof where there was a woman who cooked for the "boys." "Boys?" I said. "But they are men. They don't look like boys." We began to go up the stairs. It was the first time I had ever gone up so many steps. I felt as though I were in a high swing. I was afraid to go up fast and kept looking down. I thought that if I stepped while I was looking up I would fall down the stairs. When I got out on the roof, I felt saved and sighed with relief.

There was a rule that the men must not bother the women. The men

ate on one side and we on the other. When the *señora* and I appeared
at the door, all the boys looked at me, which made me lower my eyes
and put on a very serious face. Naturally, somebody started kidding,
"Sofía, don't be rude. Introduce us to your little sister." The *señora*
smiled and said, "Why not, boys? Step up and I'll introduce you to the
child."

But they didn't consider me a child. They all called me *señorita*.
I felt like calling them idiots. They offended me with the word. When
they said it, I thought there was some hidden meaning behind their
words. Afterwards I got used to it. Everybody respected me there,
except a boy named José. He continually came over to speak to Sofía.
While I stood there with my eyes cast down, he would pucker up his
mouth and throw me a kiss. I would keep myself from laughing and
would not look at him. I didn't believe that such a handsome young
man would pay any attention to me.

Once, when I came to work early, José grabbed my arm and began
to make declarations of love. I listened without believing him. I just
let him talk, and when he finished I told him that I was too young
for him. It made me laugh to hear him say he wanted to marry me.
I couldn't even imagine what the word meant. José was the first one
to ask me if anybody had ever kissed me. "Kiss?" How could I have
done anything like that? It was a dirty thing, I told him.

But once I was in the darkness of my house, when everybody was
asleep, I would dream with my eyes open. I could see myself in a
beautiful evening gown, in a luxurious room, dancing to soft music
with José. Or him in a dark suit, smoking nervously, waiting for me
in the street. I would think, "Good. Let all those girls in the courtyards
see what it is to have a boy friend."

José kept on trying with me. One time I went down to get water
for Sofía, and José, who was hiding on the stairs, took me by the arm.
"Consuelo, I want to talk to you." We spoke in low voices. "I have
nothing to discuss with you, José," I said, trembling to see his strained
expression. I was afraid of him. For several days I had been hiding
so as not to see him. When he was convinced I meant it, he didn't
bother me again. He would just shake his head when he saw me.

Fermín came to live in the tenement six or seven months before I
celebrated my fifteenth birthday. He was a relative of my stepmother,
Elena. This young man was a shoe finisher, and was very handsome,
even though his hair and face were usually covered with the dust of

the shoe shop, and he wore old overalls without a shirt. He would follow me when he saw me on the street and say, "Consuelo, Consuelo, don't be so proud. Just turn around and look at me. Don't be mean. Look at me, or else I'll throw myself under a bus—while it's parked." I wouldn't say a word but I would smile and, with him behind me, walk faster, frightened to death that we might meet Roberto. If my brother were to see me, he would knock me down.

When I paid no attention to him, Fermín tried to win Antonia's confidence. One night my father sent Tonia and me for the bread. I don't know whether they were in cahoots or not, but I saw Fermín standing in the entrance to the tenement, very clean and his hair combed. Antonia said to me, "You stay here while I go for the bread," and walked on. I felt as though a bucket of ice water had been poured over me. I was afraid because of all the insults I had given him, like, "Take a bath first," "Pachuco," "You're *loco*." I also thought of the gossip if I were to be seen in the street with a man at this hour.

But he said, "Consuelo, I love you, honest to God, I want to marry you. But don't call me *Pachuco* just because I work." He seemed so ridiculous talking to me like that, looking at me so sadly. I felt like laughing. He went on, "When I see you pass by, I feel like yelling, you are so pretty. Tell me when I can see you and you'll make me the happiest man on earth. Tell me what you want me to do. I'll do the impossible for you. Tell me!" I noticed that he had very nice features. To be talking in this way seemed stupid but on seeing how tender his eyes were, I stopped smiling. Tonia was coming back with the bread, so I hurriedly told him. "Yes, yes, wait for me in a little while in the corner of my courtyard."

On the way back Antonia asked me what he had said. Disinterested outside but very excited inside, I said, "Nothing, he just wants me to be his girl." Tonia said, "Do what he says. He's very handsome. You see how he keeps after you." But I didn't get out that night. At supper time my father was right opposite me. When I heard a whistle that seemed to say my name, I almost spilled my coffee. Tonia made signals to me with her eyes. I finished my coffee quickly and asked my father for permission to show *Señora* Yolanda my sewing. It didn't work.

A few days later I met Fermín as I was coming home from work. I explained that my father was very strict and didn't let me go out alone at night. He accepted my explanation on the condition that I come out that night; if I didn't, he was going to knock on my door. Holy Virgin! Knock on the door! The house would fall in on me! "Yes, this time I'll come out. Honest, Fermín. Wait for me."

At eight sharp I heard the first whistle, and it made me jump. "What's wrong with you, clown?" my father immediately yelled at me. "Nothing, *papá*, I think I was falling asleep." That was very good, because then he didn't let us go to sleep immediately. I took advantage of the opportunity to ask him to let me go out for a little walk. He agreed.

I went to Irela's house—a friend of Marta's. I remember the advice she gave me: "Go on, don't be a fool. Now that they've let you go out, give them something to hit you for."

"All right, but tell me if anyone comes, eh, Irela?"

I shot across the courtyard like a skyrocket and was still trembling when I got there. Fermín greeted me, "Good evening, my love, I've been waiting for you and at last you're here." Then he kissed me. I held my breath and felt as though I was smothering. I pressed my lips together and with my eyes wide open looked at his eyes, which were closed. It lasted only a moment. When Fermín felt that I wasn't kissing him back, he moved away and said he knew I didn't love him but that later on I would. Meanwhile he thanked me for having given him that kiss. "I gave him a kiss!" I sighed with relief. Now I knew what a kiss was.

But then I remembered how dirty he looked during work and it disgusted me. I said good-bye to him and went back to Irela's house. "You're terrific," she said, and kept laughing to see me scrubbing at my mouth with my hand and making faces. I felt like throwing up. She asked me, "And you didn't like it?" I told her I didn't, thinking that I would set her a good example. But as she kept talking I realized that she could teach me things.

The next night at eight sharp, there was Fermín's whistle. I managed to get out. As soon as he saw me, he kissed me. There was another kiss on leaving. Meanwhile he talked to me, "When I get the money together, we'll get married, little one. You'll just see what a pretty house I'll fix up for you. Or I'll take you to my homeland, my village in Jalisco." I listened to all of this leaning on his shoulder or watching his eyes, which was what I liked best about him. But to manage to be with him was a triumph, as I would hardly ever get permission from my father. Fermín trusted me and waited hours for me to come out, sometimes with luck, other times not. Even if it rained, he was there. My father didn't suspect me.

But I was happy only when I was at work. Once I got home it seemed unbearable to watch my father do nothing but read—or get mad if we made noise. How enraged I became when he beat Marta or Roberto with a belt. But I was not able even to speak. I couldn't move from the spot. In those moments I wished I were made of smoke so I could just drift away.

While she did the house work, Antonia would turn on the radio and listen to Cuban music all day long. She liked the *danzón, huaracha,* and swing. She usually danced when my brothers were away. I must confess that when I saw her dance for the first time I was embarrassed. I was about twelve years old at the time and had never seen that kind of dancing. I suppose I was too strait-laced. She would listen to a *huaracha,* then begin to move her whole body from one side to the other. *Híjole,* how ugly it looked! Every once in a while she would clap her hands together to feel the music better. In spite of everything, I liked the rhythm, but I didn't dare confess it even to myself. How I criticized my sister! I considered her indecent. When she stuck out her belly or sucked it in, it made me feel like turning away my face, but I kept looking.

Little by little, without really noticing it, I began to dance too. This would happen while we were sweeping or washing the dishes, to the music of the radio. Tonia would dance with my brother and I would watch them from the kitchen, seated on a stool, or on top of the head-board of one of the beds. One day I saw Tonia shake her shoulders while she danced. I jumped right off the stool where I was sitting and clamored, "How do you do it? Teach me! Teach me!" She good-naturedly explained it to me, but as hard as I tried, all I could manage was a ridiculous movement that made her laugh. I finally learned it after days of practice.

There were almost always dances going on in one of the *vecindad* courtyards. But of course my *papá* wouldn't let us out. I had to dance in the house while Tonia was doing the housework. But at that time I didn't know what a real taste for dancing was. I was still satisfied with dreaming. I would see myself going to a dance, wearing a blue dress, well groomed, everybody turning around to look at me. I was the center of attraction. A very serious, good-looking young man would be escorting me. Nobody dared say anything coarse around me; there would be nothing but respect! I would dance in a reserved, dignified way to a slow, smooth tune. I wouldn't be like Tonia who smiled at this one and made eyes at that one. My God, that wasn't nice! She was a terrible flirt and had no shame.

One time my father bought new dresses for Tonia and me. Mine was gold-colored, with a branch on it picked out in tiny glass beads. It was the most elegant one I ever had and I put it on right away. The noise of a dance in progress was very loud and I began to move my feet and make signs to Tonia that she should ask permission. She shrugged her shoulders and wouldn't. A pang of anxiety seized me. I would have to ask him myself! Tense all over, I asked my father for permission. "*Papá*, won't you let me go to the dance? Please." My father's curt tone didn't stop me. "Let the boys go with me, *papá*. Let Manuel and Roberto come with me. Please." This time it worked. I got permission.

The dance was in the courtyard of No. 80. I went with my two brothers, one on either side of me. I didn't put on my sweater so I could show off my dress. The courtyard was filled with people. I began to tremble all over. My brothers and I stood in a corner. Manuel, of course, found himself a partner and left us. Roberto stayed close to me. I kept my arms crossed tightly so as to hide my bosom and my excitement.

The piece finished and nobody had invited me to dance. There I was, wanting to dance so badly I could hardly stand it! I kept thinking I wouldn't get to dance and pressed my arms together tighter. It was becoming very serious when a young man came over and asked my brother's permission to dance with me. I found myself in the arms of Sergio, a boy who lived in the middle courtyard of the Casa Grande. At the touch of that young man's arms, I felt bothered and I wasn't able to follow his steps. My whole body trembled. I was stiff as a stick. He did his best to lead me but my feet were clumsy.

The piece was over and I thought, "What a fool! I couldn't even move. I guess nobody will ask me to dance now." I held on to my brother's arm. Another piece began. It was a very fast and rhythmic tune in vogue then, "*Chinito, chinito, toca la malaca*," etc. I was happy when I saw the same boy coming to ask me to dance again. The steps he took were new to me but I warmed up a little. My stiff muscles relaxed and I began to dance with spirit. All the boys watched me. I was new there. I saw some of them go over to my brother, then turn to look at me with a serious expression on their faces. At the third piece, my brother Manuel came over and took me out to dance

Nereidas, the *danzón.* I managed to dance it with a lot of self-confidence. I relaxed my body and let the music take it. I danced eight or nine numbers with my brother and that boy.

There were dances continually after that and I fought for permission to go out, but with no luck. My father wouldn't allow it. "No sir! Begin going to dances? Nothing doing!" I would get angry and refuse to go to bed. They would turn out the lights and I would sit there against the door frame in the dark kitchen crying, until my legs got numb. When I heard a piece I liked, what a fit I would have! It would make my head ache. But there was nothing to be done.

The fact that my father and Antonia went to her mother's house every week made things easier for me. Roberto was almost always home at that hour, but I would sneak out to the dance. Manuel hardly ever came to the house, so I didn't worry about him. But I had a real hatred for Roberto. He would come over while I was dancing and say, "Get home, brat." I obeyed him because I was afraid and ashamed of making a scene in the courtyard. I was also afraid he would tell my father.

Sometimes my father didn't go out at night and so I had to become tricky. First, I asked permission. Then I begged, cried, had tantrums. But I couldn't get him to give his permission. One night I was sitting in the doorway of the dark kitchen, with my elbows on my knees and my face in my hands, feeling desperate. I wanted to dance so badly, I decided to sneak out. With a little effort, the wall pegs on which pails were hung could be used as a ladder to the opening in the ceiling. From there it was only a question of one step to the roof.

When I heard my father snore, I pulled over a chair with great caution, and holding my breath and carrying my shoes in my hand, I climbed up the pegs. I put on my shoes and there I was! Now, who would lend me a ladder to get down? Fortunately, *Señora* Yolanda appeared at that moment. I made a sign to her to keep quiet and asked for a ladder. Yolanda smiled when I came down the steps. "What are you doing, girl?"

"Shhh, be quiet, or my *papá* will hear us." She took me to her house where I washed my face and combed my hair. I was ready for the dance and I wasn't running any risk. Roberto was already asleep and so was my father.

I arrived at the dance and as usual it was full of boys. Some girls were sitting down and others standing up leaning against the wall with their arms interlocked. You could tell from their faces a mile away how much they wanted to dance. The boys of the older gang were all together in a rough circle. Some were moving their feet, some clapping their hands, while others were just watching and picking out their next partners. A group of younger boys were practicing steps. A bulb of about 100 watts lit up the spot were the phonograph was.

It was the custom to make a circle around the best dancers and clap hands to encourage them to keep on dancing. This was when the boys would cast glances and smile crookedly out of the evil thoughts in their minds. If the girl was a good dancer, those in the circle would send in another boy to show off what he could do. There really was atmosphere. Everybody tried to make himself stand out among the rest.

When I arrived at the dance, I stayed in a corner away from the light, in case my brother was around. This would give me time to get away. Besides, I didn't like to go to the center where the best dancers were. Roberto's friends were my partners: Hermilio, the Gorilla; Gustavo, the Night-Smell; Angel, the Dim Light, and Tomás, the Duck.

I returned by way of the roof with the same care that I had left. My father had not awakened. I did this whenever my father wouldn't give me permission, or didn't leave the house. But one night I began to climb up the pegs, as usual. Suddenly, I felt a smack on the legs. That whack was followed by two more. I turned around and saw my *papá* and I felt my blood run cold. "Get down off there, fast!" When I came down, I expected to be hit some more. But fortunately, no.

Then I had my fifteenth birthday. How many things my friend Angélica Rivera and I dreamed about! Sometimes, sitting in the courtyard, we told each other what we wanted for that day. She imagined, just as I did, the courtyard all decorated and clean, with a canopy over it in case of rain, a gate that permitted only guests to enter, and chairs all around. I saw my father and brothers in dark suits, and, above all, me in a long blue dress, with spangles to make it shine. My little sister would have a long dress, too. And finally, a small orchestra would be playing. How pretty I would look to Fermín. What a couple he and I would make as we danced the waltz, with everybody's eyes on us—my father watching me from the table and thinking that his daughter was now a *señorita*. Those were the dreams Angélica and I used to have. She would always say, "God willing." But I would say that it had to be, that my father couldn't let that day pass by unnoticed.

Unfortunately, it wasn't like my dreams. The day I was fifteen I didn't even realize myself what day it was at first. I went to work; later it seemed to me that there was something I had to do that day. What a bitter taste to remember that it was my fifteenth birthday, the most important one in a girl's life! I sat on my bench, with an apron on, my hands all stained from the shoe dye, in the dust that flew from the machine where I had been planing the soles. I was cleaning some white satin shoes. I just sat there caressing them. I felt like crying, but held back. "Some day I'll have the money to buy the things I want. Some day my father will have to realize that I am not as bad as he says. Some day—" I finished cleaning the shoes, but when I saw the white sheen of the satin and the elegant workmanship, I couldn't control myself any longer and went out to the toilet to cry. My soul ached to think that nobody cared about me.

I left work very late, with almost no desire to get home. I took the bus all alone. On the way I wondered why I should have such luck. Maybe I wasn't even the daughter of my father. Maybe that was why he didn't pay any attention to me. As I entered the tenement, I met Roberto who said, "Come on, we're waiting for you to cut the cake."

I brightened up and regretted all the things I had been thinking. I hurried to the house. Sure enough, there was a cake on the table, and it had an ear of corn on it made of cream. But it looked so poor to me in comparison with Antonia's that I was at the point of feeling humiliated. Antonia, smiling, said, "Go on, there's your cake."

I didn't answer. My father told me to cut it. "I don't feel like it now. I'm tired. Put it away." Roberto gave me a dirty look; Marta and he told me again to cut it. Roberto handed me the knife, put the little candles on it and lit them. When I saw how happy Roberto was, I relented and blew out the candles. My wish was that I should be able to study later on. The next day I went to work and who wanted ever again to think of the night before?

I was a *señorita* now and I didn't want to play in the courtyard any more. It didn't look right for me to be running about outdoors and I didn't want to leave my father alone. Besides, Tonia and her friends almost always were in the courtyard talking about things that embarrassed me. She liked to play rough games like *burro*, and the one night I did play, I jumped on Tonia, who was the *burro*, and it was the embarrassment of my life when she stood up unexpectedly and I remained hanging by one foot from her shoulder. I wanted to weep with rage, but I took it quietly and planned to get even. Several days later, Tonia and I began to argue and when she took a kick at me, I caught her foot and lifted it up so high I made her lose her balance. She fell and covered her face to hide her tears, because it had hurt her very much. She took it, too, and said nothing to my father. And so we were even.

On another occasion we were eating, and I was going to sit down. Whether intentionally or not I don't know, but Tonia pulled the chair from under me and I fell. My soup went all over me, burning my stomach. Tonia laughed, but then from the bottom of her heart begged me to forgive her. I said nothing, just turned and looked at her with my face very serious, making everybody laugh. Later I got even when I pushed her cup quite hard just as she was bringing it to her mouth. I chipped her tooth and the edge of the cup bruised her nose. It made me laugh just as much as she had. Tonia, however, got mad. "*Ay,* how rough you are!" she said.

About this time Tonia ran away from home. I don't know if she had tried to do it before or not, but Roberto had had orders to keep an eye on her wherever she went. On this particular morning, Antonia told me that we were going to the baths and that she would pay for my ticket. I noticed she was putting a lot of clothes into a bag, and asked about it. She said she was going to have them fixed. We started for the Florencia baths, which were far away, but Antonia explained that the *señora* who was going to fix her dresses lived around there.

The bathhouse was very crowded because it was the day of the week when prices were lowered. We had to wait in line for our compartments. I undressed in the tiny enclosed space, hung my clothes on the hook, wrapped my self in a sheet and went into the hallway to look for Tonia. She wasn't there, nor in the shower room where lines of naked women and children were waiting their turn. The smell was bad there and children were crying, so I went into the steam room, walking carefully over the slippery floor. I had fallen several times in the bath house . . . Marta had too . . . and was afraid of being hurt again. There were only some very fat women in the steam room, and an argument was going on because one lady wanted to lower the heat and another wanted to raise it. Tonia wasn't in the swimming pool either, so I finished bathing and dressing and waited for her in the entrance hall.

A long time passed and Tonia didn't come for me. I got bored and asked the man in charge if he had seen her. He told me she had already gone. Angry, I ran home, thinking she had played a dirty trick on me. When I asked for Antonia, Roberto got so scared he jumped up from his chair. "No, she hasn't come." He immediately left his breakfast and went to look for her. She wasn't at her mother's house or in the streets. Roberto looked everywhere. I guess someone let my father know because he came home early. Roberto paid for his carelessness; my father hit him very hard.

It was night before they found her at the railroad station with some other women. My father dragged her home. She didn't seem to be scared, but I was. I was afraid she would be beaten to within an inch of her life, and as a matter of fact, she was. After the beating, my father locked her into the room where Elena had died. We had been forbidden to enter that room before and the ban was all the more strict now. My father ordered her food to be brought to her. She was not to be allowed out for any reason. Sometimes, when my brothers and La Chata weren't looking, I went to see her. I felt sorry for her. All she could do was poke her head out of the little opening above the door. She told me what had happened. "When I left the baths, I met two *señoras*. I told them I needed work and went with them." What none of us knew until much later was that these women ran a house of prostitution.

That night my father had cried a lot, when he thought we were all asleep. It hurt me very much to hear him cry. I would never have given him such pain, no matter how much he shouted at me. After all, if he was mad at somebody he had to work off his anger. I wouldn't mind if he took it out on me, so long as he didn't get sick. Anyway, my father was right about everything. I was very foolish and inept. I wanted to wait on him always but I could never do anything well. I would just get dazed and go round and round. And it was bad that Antonia had run away, because people would look down on her. I was never going to let anyone have a bad opinion of me! How far I was then, in my imagining, from what was actually going to happen years later.

Antonia was finally permitted to come back to live with us. In spite of the fact that I would talk to her and we kidded around every once in a while, I couldn't get to like her. She spent a lot of time with *Señora* Yolanda, who would tell me everything Antonia told her. Once Yolanda said, "Look after your father. Antonia has said she hates him and all of you and that she is going to make you pay for everything she suffered when she was a child." She wanted vengeance and planned to take our father away from us by getting him to move to her mother's house.

Yolanda also told me that when we were all out of the house (Roberto and Manuel at the glass factory where they had jobs and Marta and I at school), Antonia would do witchcraft with a neighbor, *Señora* Luz. Barefoot, Antonia would put the chairs up on the bed and sweep the floor very carefully with the twig broom. Then she went to Luz, who was of a different religion, Evangelist or Spiritualist, and both of them would come back to our house carrying bottles of water, herbs and flowers under their aprons. They would lock the door and stay inside for about a half-hour.

Yolanda spied on them through a hole in her door across the way, and later, pretending to be hanging clothes, went to the roof where she could see down into our kitchen. She said she saw Antonia lighting a fire in the brazier and Luz sprinkling water from the bottles onto the walls and the floor, muttering something. When the fire was going well, Luz burned the herbs and flowers. She and Antonia stood by the blaze, watching it and saying something. When the ashes were cool, Luz scattered them about the room while Antonia made her evil wish.

Yolanda said that Luz would come out soon after that, with her paraphernalia covered up, and Antonia would lock the door after her to wait for the smoke to disappear and the water to evaporate. Later she would open the door and do her housework as though nothing had happened. I do not know whether or not this was true, but it was what Yolanda told me. Afterwards, Roberto also told me that Antonia was a sorceress and I do believe this about Antonia, because she really hated us and tried to do us harm.

I am not sure it had a connection with what Antonia did, but a little later, every week for three or four months my father went to Pachuca and returned with bottles of yellowish liquid with herbs in them. Sometimes the water was green, other times white or colorless. He put the bottles in the left corner of the kitchen and gave strict orders that no one should touch them. I never saw him drink the water or sprinkle it or anything like that, and however much I remained at home, I never knew what it was for. Perhaps he was using it as medicine to counteract the work of Antonia. Only Heaven knows. I did not understand it.

After that nothing was ever right for my father. He began saying harsher things to us: "I'm fed up with you bums! I am tired of working day after day and you lying around here like pigs, just eating and sleeping!" For me these words were like blows. I felt like running away, but I couldn't. I just would lower my head and cry. This went on daily. Roberto very often didn't come home for days. Just Marta, Antonia, and I remained at home.

The first time I talked back to my father (not saying anything rude, just denying something) was one afternoon when he accused me of taking chickens to give to "that witch," my aunt. I answered, "It's not true, *papá*. I never take anything." I felt a smack full in the face, and I crouched in the corner of the brazier and the dish closet. Antonia was there and I was ashamed that he treated my family like that. How different it was with her family! When Elida or Isabel came, he would say, "Tonia, serve your sister coffee. Sit down, Elida, let's have a talk. Here's change for the bus."

Then Antonia began to get sick. She had been having trouble with her *novio*, a boy in the Casa Grande, whom she was crazy about. He had left her for another girl because, I think, Tonia had told him she was pregnant. I say this because she became ill with a bad hemorrhage and someone later told me that she had taken some strong herbs to get rid of a baby. Tonia nearly went out of her mind when she lost her sweetheart. The doctor told my father she was the kind of girl who must have a man or else she would get sick. A little later she began to have terrible attacks.

One day I came home from work and found the house very upset. I had gotten used to seeing the house messy and sad-looking but this day it was dead! Soiled dishes and casseroles on the table and in the sink, the floor unswept, the stove very dirty. The door to the bedroom was shut and my father and brothers were sitting despondently in the dark kitchen. Chairs and things from the bedroom were piled up on the floor. I started to speak and my father shut me up. "Sh, idiot! You will wake her up!" Tonia had had her first attack, breaking and throwing things, jumping almost to the ceiling, pulling her hair, making horrible noises. She woke and did the same thing until a nurse came and injected her with something to put her to sleep. This went on for days. Then she was sent to a sanatorium, where she stayed several months.

Later, things happened as Yolanda had told me they would. When

Antonia got out of the sanatorium, she and my father went to live at Lupita's house, leaving us alone in the Casa Grande. One afternoon my father said unexpectedly, "I'm moving to Rosario Street. That's where I'll be. I'll come to see you every day. Do you want to come or stay?" I said I didn't want to go. My pride prevented me from telling him that I would go wherever he went, that I wanted to be where he was. When I saw him carrying his blue box on his shoulder and heard him say to Roberto, "Open the door," I felt as if I were going to fall and I supported myself on a chair. When he was gone, my brother and I looked at each other. We didn't know what to say. Roberto went into the toilet to cry and I felt a bitter liquid rise in my throat and eyes, but not a word or a sob left my lips.

The next day my father came with Antonia and her sisters and took away the dressing table, the bedspreads, sheets, pillow cases, table-cloths, the flower vase, the curtains and even our new kerosene stove. Once again the house was stripped and left bare. We never again had curtains or pillow cases or flowers. If Marta and I attempted to fix up the house my father would tear down what we put up and order us to leave things as they were.

Nevertheless he lived up to what he had said. He came to see us every afternoon to leave expense money. But when he was offered supper, he would say, "I don't want anything," in a cutting tone of voice. I didn't insist.

After my father left, I felt I needed my mother. I couldn't control myself any more and began to cry as if my heart was going to break and until my eyes ached, turning to look at the picture of the Virgin and asking why my father was like this toward us.

He had never left us before. We were used to living with him, to seeing him every day sitting in his chair reading, washing his feet, or examining the chickens and giving orders that they be washed or their coop changed. My father's presence was everything; it filled the house. With him there, I felt my home complete. Now I began to have a feeling that was unbearable. "Am I not my father's daughter? Is it a sin to be an orphan, my Lord?" I kept asking. I cried for my mother and waited and waited for an answer. How horrible I felt doing this. I had never called her before with such desperation. I shouted, shouted to my mother. I wanted to be answered from the unknown, anything. But only silence followed my words.

Marta

MY CHILDHOOD WAS THE HAPPIEST ANY GIRL COULD HAVE. I FELT FREE
. . . Nothing tied me down, absolutely nothing. I could do what I
wanted and hardly ever got punished. If I cried, my *papá* petted
me and gave me money. When he locked me indoors I escaped through
the roof. I was rude and talked back to everyone because I felt that I
was my father's favorite. I gave my stepmothers and the women who
worked for us a hard time. Most of them didn't stay long; only Enoé
and La Chata stuck it out for four or five years. But I made them cry,
and Elena, my first stepmother, cried too.

My friends looked up to me and made me feel like their chief. When
we played baseball I decided where everyone was to go; no matter what
we did, they had to get my agreement first. They saw that my father
gave me the best of everything, and that I had money and fruit to
give out. That's why they were always coming by for me and asking
me to play. I never lacked friends and I felt "big" in my circle.

From the start, I didn't like school and went only to please my *papá*.
I couldn't stand being shut up in a room and I cared nothing about
learning to read or write or do sums. I spent three years in the first
grade and another two in the second. At the end of the fifth grade,
when I was fourteen years old, I quit. I never planned to be anything
in life, like a nurse or a dressmaker: Tarzan was my favorite and I
wanted only to be his companion.

I was a tomboy and played boys' games . . . *burro,* marbles, tops and
dice, depending on the season. Those were the only toys for me and
I broke the dishes and doll furniture Consuelo kept so neatly in a

box under the bed. I never played with girls, but was delighted with dressing and undressing dolls.

My *papá* treated us girls like royalty. He fed us, bought us clothes, sent us to school, and didn't let our brothers mistreat us. He hardly paid attention to them, except when we complained. Then he would grab them and beat them without mercy.

But I was not like Consuelo. She led a quiet life and had almost no friends. She couldn't go out like I did, because my father was always taking care of her. We argued a lot: when I came back from the bakery with an assortment of rolls, she'd always grab the kind I liked. When my father brought home fruit, I'd take the ones she wanted. She would hide the little boxes full of my things and if I knew which toy was her favorite I'd go and break it. I was always after her in a mean way. I'd tell my father when she went out, so that he would hit her. She did the same, because she didn't want me to run around like a tomboy.

Consuelo was sad and didn't like to go out and play. She made things worse for herself because she was always at home. When Roberto came he would pull her braids, and then Manuel would order her about and she had to obey or get hit.

It's a funny thing, but I confided more in my half-sister Antonia, and my sister-in-law Paula, than in Consuelo. It was because she acted superior and saw things in a bad light. She didn't know how to give positive advice. And I always thought she was stingy and selfish.

When I was little I liked Roberto best, because he gave me things and took me with him. But he was always very touchy and bossy and lied a lot. Manuel lived in a different world from ours. Perhaps because he was the oldest, he had always been distant and reserved. It seemed to me he was more hypocritical than the rest of us and said things he didn't feel. He walked around with a lie ready on his lips. But neither of my brothers hit me when I was little; they began to show their temper when I was old enough to have *novios*.

Manuel and Consuelo spent most of their childhood in school. They were a pair . . . serious, resigned, quiet. But I was more like Roberto, the rascal. We were really wild. He didn't like school any more than I did and would escape by climbing out of the classroom windows. He showed me how to hide my books in the bathhouse and, instead of going to school, he'd take me to Chapultepec Park. We would climb in all the forbidden places and get chased by the Presidential Guards. If he had money, my brother would rent a boat and take me rowing. He stuffed me with sweets and chewing gum to keep me from getting hungry and when it was time to return from school, we'd hop a bus, get my books, and go home.

Roberto taught me how to hitch onto buses and trolleys; we traveled all over the city that way. He got spending money by stopping kids in the park and scaring them into giving him things—pencils, pens, coins, whatever they had. Later when he joined the army and was in uniform, it was even easier because he threatened to arrest them. Roberto would also grab ladies' purses and then we had more money; I had a big collection of lipsticks, compacts and wallets.

I was so happy when I was young! Once, Roberto and his gang took me with them to the park. I was the only girl among ten boys. We went to one of those open-air restaurants near the Amusement Park and ordered *tortas* and orange drinks. Then I noticed that one by one, the boys got up and went off, some for cigarettes, some to the toilet, until only Roberto and I and two boys were left. One boy said to my brother, "Go on, *Negro*, disappear with your sister." We went on one of the rides and they went elsewhere. We stayed on that ride three times around while the waiters were hunting for us. We made our escape and took the bus home. That's how we got food without paying.

When Roberto went to the Lagunilla Market to carry home the fruit, cheese and meat my father bought, he would take me along. He spent the fare on candy (we were always hungry and always eating) and we would hitch on to the back of the bus. A little dog, named the Rat, would follow us, and Roberto taught him how to carry a piece of fruit or a package of meat. The Rat followed Roberto everywhere and my brother took as good care of him as he did of me. But later someone poisoned the dog and killed him.

I was about eight years old when my *papá* went into the bird business. One day he brought home a big cage that had a cardboard roof and bars made of cane. He had bought young *centzontles* and it was Roberto's and Manuel's job to whistle at them until they learned to sing. But the birds picked at the cane and made an opening through which a dozen and a half escaped. Elena was very worried, thinking that my father would get mad.

When my *papá* got home, Elena told him the birds had died. She looked so scared that he couldn't help laughing. He already knew the birds had flown away because the janitor's wife, who was the biggest gossip in the *vecindad,* had told him. He didn't get mad that time.

Of my three stepmothers, I guess Elena was the best. She was the first woman, other than my aunt, whom I remember letting me sit on her lap, combing my hair and fondling me. But I never called her *mamá* like Consuelo did. The thing I liked most about Elena was that she covered up my misdeeds and never hit me; even when I was nasty to her, she didn't complain to my father.

My aunt says Elena was about seventeen years old when my father married her. I remember that she played jump rope with us in the courtyard before she came to live in our house. She had been married to a man who beat her so much he damaged her lungs. She was already sick when she came to us and that's why my *papá* hired help for her. He never liked his women to work too hard in the house.

Consuelo was the one who was most fond of Elena and always sticking up for her. When I was fresh to my stepmother Consuelo would hit me, but Elena would say, "Let her alone, Skinny. After all, she is little and doesn't know what she's saying."

Elena fixed a swing for me in the kitchen, which was in a little inner courtyard. There was no roof over it then, only boards to keep the rain from coming in. She tied a rope around one of the boards and put a small piece of wood at the bottom for me to sit on. One day I was swinging and Consuelo tried to get me down. I fought and cried until Elena said, "Come here, Chubby." They always called me that, never by my name. But I kicked and shouted that I didn't want her to touch me. Consuelo slapped me but Elena came to my defense. She really was good to me, but I was so little, I hardly remember her.

I was ten years old when Elena died. My *papá* said Manuel and Roberto killed her. He may have been right, but I believe it was mostly the operation that killed her, because when they took out her ribs she kept losing weight until she died. They say she died of tuberculosis but I don't think so because my father is very fussy about contagious diseases. I think she had a tumor or something.

Elena looked very pretty when she was laid out. My *papá*, or maybe her mother, bought a white dress and a blue veil and dressed her like the *Purísima Concepción*. The night of the wake my *papá* was angry because there was a dance going full blast in the courtyard. They didn't even turn down the music.

I met my stepmother Lupita before Elena died. My half-sister Antonia came to live with us and she took me secretly to Rosario Street to meet her mother and sisters. Lupita received me well, but not my half-sister Marielena. She got mad every time I came there. I think she was jealous of us and angry at my *papá*. But Lupita was always nice to me and gave me bus fare and little presents.

My *papá* used to take Antonia to see her *mamá* every Wednesday. He didn't know that Antonia and I went there during the week. One Wednesday, I wanted to go with them and began to cry. So my *papá* took me, telling me to greet the *señora* politely and to behave myself. That's all he said. He never once mentioned that the *señora* was his wife. Nor did any of us tell him that I already knew her.

Before Antonia came to live with us, my *papá* slept in the same bed with Consuelo and me. The other bed had been moved to Elena's room and after she died it was given to Santitos, her mother. So when Antonia took my father's place in our bed, he slept on the floor. Later, when Antonia went wild and ran away with some boys, my *papá* locked her up in Elena's empty room, and he slept with us again. When he bought another bed, it was for Antonia. He slept with us until we were quite big.

My father was so good to Antonia, that people in the *vecindad* began to gossip about it. They thought she wasn't just his daughter, but also his mistress . . . or at least, that there was something between them. Everyone noticed that my father gave Antonia all his attention and bought her the best of everything. He would make us go to bed early and the two of them would get dressed up and go out for supper and a movie.

My friend Angélica, who lived opposite us in the same courtyard, told me what the neighbors were saying. But I didn't do a thing. When it came to my father, I never interfered. I was a spectator, just listening and watching, and keeping my mouth shut. I never felt free to say to my father, "Just think, so and so says that . . ." I was afraid that he would get angry and hit me. In his presence, I always trembled a bit and was careful how I spoke.

Roberto and Consuelo were very jealous of Antonia and would throw a fit every time she had her way. Roberto and Antonia fought like cats and dogs. I would take Antonia's side and Consuelo would help Roberto. When my *papá* came home in the afternoon, he would settle the fight in her favor.

Once, on the Day of the Three Kings, Consuelo had a big fight because Antonia received nicer presents. They had both asked for dolls, and Antonia got a pretty blond one, while Consuelo's was dark and had a face like a death head. Antonia also got a watch. Consuelo was so angry she cried and refused to take the doll; it made her sick to realize that my *papá* loved Antonia more. Those two girls each had a crisis. After that they changed and got along better.

I didn't really miss my mother until I went to school, On Mother's Day when all the children made presents to give to their mothers, I was left with my gift in my hand. Mother's Day was the saddest day in the year for me. The older I grew the more I needed my mother.

The only things I knew about my mother were what people told me. I had been deceived into thinking that she had died of a cerebral congestion brought on by overeating, but my aunt Piedad, the second wife of my uncle Alfredo, told me recently that a doctor had warned my mother that if she didn't get rid of the baby she was carrying, she would not live to see it born. She was ill with each pregnancy because she had a bad heart and liver, and sick kidneys. She did not accept the doctor's advice and died. The doctor wanted to save the baby but my *papá* said, "Better let her take it with her."

My aunt Guadalupe insists that my mother died from a bad disease she caught from my *papá* . . . because he had gone with other women. But La Chata, the woman who worked in our house, said my *mamá* died of anger, because of my brother. According to her, my grandma also died because of us, but my aunt said no, she died of a tumor. La Chata thought we were so bad we were capable of killing anyone. She claimed that her health was ruined in our house, because of the way we upset her bile, and that had it not been for my father, she never would have worked for us. We didn't like her and often chased her out. My *papá* used to beat my brothers and then go to her house to beg her to come back. He'd give her money for the movies and that would calm her.

La Chata used to wash clothes for my mother, and knew the whole family. She was my aunt Guadalupe's *comadre* but they didn't get along well. La Chata said that I looked like my *mamá* . . . short and fat, like a little barrel, and that is why my *papá* preferred me to my brothers and sister. According to La Chata, my *mamá* and *papá* had many quarrels because they were both jealous types. When my *mamá* worked in the Baratillo Market with her three brothers, she had to speak to a lot of men, and though she was serious and stern with them, it worried my *papá*. When Roberto was born dark, my *papá* didn't like him because he thought my brother was not his son. And as for my father, he went with so many women that La Chata said he must have put Cupid in the pawnshop and forgotten to get him out!

La Chata thought my *mamá* loved us a lot because she kept us dressed like little dolls. My *mamá* was away all day, selling cake crumbs in the morning and second-hand clothing in the afternoon. I was suckled by my aunt Piedad, because my mother had no milk for me. She had puerperal fever when I was born. But my mother did not neglect us because we were left in the care of her mother or her sister.

My aunt Guadalupe, who helped bring me up, told me a lot about my *mamá* and her family. I would bother her with questions and she would answer like this:

"Holy Mother! How can I remember when I was a little girl? I suppose you'll be asking where I was born? Well, I was born on a lousy straw *petate* in Guanajuato. I was the oldest girl and I alone . . . alone as the corn on the stalk . . . took care of my brothers and sisters while my *papá* and *mamá* went to sell sugared fruit in the street.

"I suppose you think they let us play with other children like you kids did? Oh, no! From the time I was small I struggled with my brothers. My mother had so many children . . . there would have been eighteen, but some were miscarriages and others died. Only seven of us grew up, Pablo, I, Bernardo, Lucio, Alfredo, your mother Lenore, and José. There was a half-sister, too, because my *papá* 'slipped' a little outside."

My aunt Guadalupe had always been jealous of my *mamá*, who had the good luck to be favored by my granny Pachita. My granny never liked Guadalupe's sons, but when my *mamá* took a misstep with a railroad worker and had a baby girl when she was fifteen, my granny took care of her and the infant. My *mamá* was abandoned by the father of her child and the baby died of pneumonia after a few months. That was when my mother got a job as a dishwasher in the La Gloria restaurant and met my *papá*.

My mother and father first set up house on Tintero Street, where there were all those bad women. My *papá* didn't like it and they went to live in a room with my grandmother. Later they found a room of their own. At first they had no bed and slept on the floor. After Manuel and Roberto were born, my *papá* won on his lottery ticket and bought the big metal bed we still have. Later, he won the lottery again and bought the radio. My aunt said that radio caused a big quarrel in the house, because one day my *papá* came home and found my *mamá* listening to it. He said, "Who told you to turn on the radio? You're such an Indian, such an imbecile, you don't know how to take care of anything. Turn it off before you break it!"

My mother was angry and said, "Look, Jesús, I will never again touch your radio!" And she didn't; she died without turning it on again. My aunt is still angry at my father for that. She said he only understood food and rent, and never thought a person needed more. He shouted at people, but underneath he was a coward and didn't even have the heart to kill a bedbug . . . that his heart was made of cardboard. My aunt never got along well with my *papá*. That's why she talks like that.

There is a woman, Julia, who lives in my aunt's *vecindad*. Julia was the wife of my uncle Lucio, and she knew my mother well. She and my uncle and Julia's two children, Yolanda and Maclovio, lived in my mother's house for three years. Julia would help my *mamá* in the house and Yolanda was the one who carried me around and cleaned my tail. They all slept on our kitchen floor and left when my uncle Lucio died.

My uncle couldn't stand his stepchildren and hit them a lot. He drank and didn't provide for them. At mealtime, he made the kids sit under the table, so he could kick them while he ate. My *mamá* took pity on them and gave them food; otherwise those poor kids would have starved. They had always worked as servants and never had a single toy.

Yolanda told me that the most enjoyment she got out of childhood was when she lived with my *mamá*. Yolanda used to grab the five-*centavo* pieces my *papá* left under our pillows each morning. She also snitched cake crumbs from my *mamá* and would sneak into the toilet to eat it. When we caught her, we told my uncle Lucio and he would give her a good beating on the head. But Yolanda was not so badly off then . . . she had food and shelter . . . my *mamá* gave her everything.

According to Julia, my *papá* was very happy with my *mamá*. He never hit her and though he didn't like fiestas, he took her when she wanted to go. He gave her expense money but she worked because she wanted to have extra *centavos*. She liked nice clothes and earrings, and when she went out she always took a bus or a taxi. She never walked. Even to go to the market, she would take a bus. She helped her mother and her sister with money and didn't want my father to think he was supporting her family.

The trouble between my uncle Lucio and Julia started when she went out to sell. She met a railroad man and began to live with him while she was still living with my uncle. My aunt says that Julia bewitched my uncle, because he suddenly changed. Instead of beating his wife, he gave in and begged her for things.

She must have given him "coconut water," because when we see a wife bossing the husband and flirting with others, we know she has him all tied up. The woman washes her behind in this "coconut water" and gives it to her husband to drink. Sometimes women make a tea of an herb called *toloache*, and if she gives it to her husband, he gets weak in the brain.

Julia must have prayed to the Dark Saint and measured my uncle with a black ribbon, because one morning he got sick with dropsy and died. My mother blamed Julia and ran her out of the house.

Julia was also known to have cast a spell on her first husband, the father of her children, because he had died suddenly too. She blamed it on the fact that he had led a life of sin and drank too much. He would hit her all the time. In fact almost everybody hit that woman. She had three husbands . . . because after my uncle died, she left her kids and went off with that railroad worker. All three men drank and beat her and all three died at her side. Now she is living a good life with Guillermo Gutiérrez, because even though he doesn't give her expense money, he never hits her.

People tell me that my little mother knew about my *papá* and Lupita from the very beginning. Here there is always some gossip who runs and tells the wife. A man hardly gets out of another woman's bed, and his wife already knows. Once my *mamá* and my aunt Guadalupe went to a *fiesta* on Rosario Street and they discovered where Lupita lived. My *mamá* took a pair of scissors and stood with it outside Lupita's door, shouting insults and daring her to come out. But Lupita didn't, and my aunt dragged my *mamá* away by the hair, so nothing happened.

According to my aunt, my *papá* also went with Lupita's niece, who worked at the same restaurant. My aunt said my *papá* "swept" that restaurant clean, and if the boss hadn't been a man, he would have fallen to my father too. *Papá* had a son with Lupita's niece, but never helped her because she married a man who accepted the child. I have never seen this half-brother of mine and only Lupita knows the name of his stepfather. My grandma tried to find out who he was because she was afraid that some day, when we grew up, this half-brother might make love to Consuelo or me. All we know is that his name is Pedro and that he looks just like my *papá*.

Lupita was on the night shift in the restaurant and my *papá* was on the day shift for a long time, until they met. She already had her daughters, Elida and Isabel. She told me that all the rest of her children were my father's. The girl born between Antonia and Marielena died. She said that with each pregnancy my *papá* disappeared and forgot his obligations, and that she didn't see him again until after the baby was born. Once, he left her for two years. She said my *papá* never helped her . . . yes, once in a while he got around to giving her a *centavo*, but to pay regular expenses or to pay the rent, no. He didn't give her a thing, and to have her children she had to look for someone to take her in.

According to Lupita, she suffered a lot, right? She worked hard to support herself and her girls. Then she cut her hand and had to stop working. But it makes me angry, because knowing my father, I doubt that he didn't give her a *centavo* and that he didn't attend her, the way she says. I never had a discussion with her about it and only she really knows, but how am I going to believe her when she says that about my father? I just let her talk!

To this day, I cannot forgive Lupita for going with my *papá* while my mother was alive. But it is not for me to question my father's affairs, and I make it my business to get along with my stepmother. She was neither mean nor affectionate toward us; if she had been loving and had tried to kiss or caress us, it would have offended me. I have no complaint about her, but there will always be a barrier between us.

They say that when my mother died, my *papá* went crazy. He jumped into her grave and wanted to die too. From that day to this, he has been very serious. I never see him laughing or happy. He is always sad and thoughtful, alone with his problems and his expenses.

By the time I was out of school, most of my mother's family had died. There were left only my aunt Guadalupe; her husband, Ignacio; my aunt Piedad, my uncle Alfredo, and their two sons; my great-aunt Catarina and her son and daughter and all their children; and a few other cousins. On my father's side I knew only my cousin David and his mother Olivia.

My uncle Alfredo died a little while ago. He caught pneumonia because when he came home drunk his sons were angry and let him lay on the damp floor all night. The next day he went to Guadalupe's house to borrow her pail and soap for a bath. He said his chest hurt and he was going into the steam room. In a few days he was dead. My poor aunt suffered a lot of grief because she had buried her whole family, her parents, her five brothers, her only sister, and her two sons. She was the only one left, except for Ignacio and us.

When I was about twelve, I began to take account of things and stopped playing with boys. I liked to dress up and I changed my clothes every day. Consuelo was doing my washing and ironing then and was annoyed. So I had to learn to halfway wash my things myself. I spent my pennies on ribbons and adornments and pasted beauty marks on my face. For a long time, I wore an artificial carnation in my hair, thinking it made me look pretty, even though it was torn and spotted and the stem wire showed. My father seemed to enjoy seeing me fix myself up like that.

Once I got into a fight with a girl who pulled off my beauty mark. I was so mad I tore her dress from top to bottom, as though it had been cut with a scissors. I was always getting into fights because some girls are vipers; they get jealous, tell lies about each other, and start trouble.

I fought with boys too. If they said or did anything to me, I never let them get away with it. One fellow who was bigger than I, tripped me when I was running around the courtyard. I fell and cracked my head. I wasn't scared, just very angry, and when my head was better, I went after him for revenge. I hit him so much, his mother complained to my *papá*. But my father didn't pay any attention to her.

My best friends were Irela and Ema, the daughter of Enoé. Chita was also my friend, but not so much as the others. We had all grown up together and defended each other tooth and nail. If one was treated badly by her family, the others invited her to go home with them. If one ate, the others ate, even if it were only beans. I placed all my confidence in these girls and we did everything together.

La Chata had the habit of sending me to the *pulquería* every day, for a bottle of *pulque* to drink with her dinner. She did it secretly, because my *papá* had forbidden us to go into such places. One day, I had the idea of buying an extra bottle for me and my friends. We went up to the roof where no one could see us drink it. After that, we bought a small bottle of *tequila* every Sunday and finished it off together on the roof. There were times when we were so drunk, we couldn't climb down the ladder. If I didn't know how to control myself, I would have gotten the drinking habit, like Irela and Ema.

We smoked on the roof too, and told dirty stories. Then we would go and buy chewing gum to take away the odor of the nicotine. Irela and Ema would steal—once they stole money from the school bank— but I never joined them. I just didn't have that desire for extra money or things. I had enough spending money because during school vacations my father let me work in an ice-cream factory near my house. They paid me two or three *pesos* a day and I spent it all on myself. My father never asked me for the money I earned. With it I bought what I pleased, socks, sweets, clothing . . . but most of the money went to rent a bicycle or to go to the swimming pool with my friends.

I liked having money of my own and I enjoyed working better than going to school. When I was in the third grade, I found a job decorating shoes; I worked from ten in the morning to eight at night, and earned more money. Lilia, a friend who lived on the Street of the Potters, told me of a better job cutting out stamped wooden figurines. I took it but lasted only two days, because of an incident with the boss.

Lilia and two other girls and I worked in a little shop in front of the room in which the boss slept. He was fat and ugly, the kind of man who nauseated me because, in spite of being old, he still looked at girls. I think the bastard had evil intentions from the moment I arrived, the way he leered at me and smiled. I couldn't stand the sight of him.

On the second day, the boss told me to make his bed. While I was in his room, he entered and started to hug and kiss me. Then he took out his "bird" and made me put my hands on it. I began to shout for Lilia, but she didn't hear me. I was very frightened, right? But I didn't let him, and he got angry and said, "When I find out that you are going to get married, I'll intervene. I'll tell everyone that you can't marry because I've already had you."

That was at about six o'clock in the evening. Lilia and I left at seven. I cried and cried and told her what had happened. That night we both got drunk and we never went back there to work. Instead, I took my old job at the ice-cream factory, where the boss was a woman.

Irela, Ema, Chita and I joined a *palomilla,* a gang of about twelve girls who lived in the Casa Grande. When you enter a gang, if you do not defend yourself, you can only cry. In any gang there is at least one girl who has a reputation for being mean, for fighting rough. The others begin to be afraid of her and give in or run away. But if you find out the last her shoe is made on, if you stand up to her, the fury often turns out to be a phony, nothing but a mirror, reflecting the weakness or strength of the others. I never liked to see anyone take advantage of timid girls, so I often stuck up for them.

We girls had many fights over *novios,* and our talk was mostly about boys. One would say, "Look, so-and-so is slipping with her *novio,* so you have a chance with him." Or, "She's a pig and a gossip and doesn't deserve him." If a girl had a boy friend she'd tell the others how he hugged and kissed her and when he asked her to go stand in dark places with him. We found out that the favorite line of the boys was to say, "If you really like me, come to bed with me and prove it." And we knew they would leave a girl who didn't. The girls who were truly in love with their *novios* usually went. Having the proof of their love within reach, there was nothing else for them to do.

The year I joined my gang, there was a heat wave among the girls, and one by one they were shelled, like corn. It started with the older girls and ended with the younger ones. Tina was the first to go and the others didn't want to be left behind. It got so, we asked each other, "Well, where did you lose it, on a bed or on a *petate?*" Most of the boys took their girls to a hotel, for an hour or so or, if they could, for a whole night. Some did it in an aunt's house or at a married sister's, or anywhere they could.

I had my first *novio* when I was twelve. Donato was the son of Enoé who worked for us. They lived in No. 32 in the Casa Grande. He was a good boy, but very ugly. I looked down at him a little because his mother was our servant. I imagined myself her mistress! My *papá* and my brothers were very strict and were always keeping an eye on my sister and me, so I never once had a chance to go out with him. If I had been a little older, I could have managed it, but at that time I had to be home by six-thirty and in bed by eight. At ten o'clock the courtyard lights were turned off and almost no one went out. It is different now because of TV. Neighbours go in and out of each other's houses to see the late shows and the courtyard lights are on until midnight.

A few years back, people were afraid to go out at night because this section was known for its criminals, pickpockets and dope addicts. It wasn't so crowded then and there were big ditches in which they often found the bodies of people who had been drowned or strangled. This *vecindad* was a real robber's nest. Men and women would disappear mysteriously and it is believed that lots of them were buried under the floors. That's why so many families had cement poured over the flooring.

Every day someone was robbed, or murdered or violated. There is a story about a girl in Tepito who had a boy friend. He was one of the worst kind. Once he invited her to the movies. He had pre-arranged with some other boys to take her home through the market, and there they grabbed her, dragged her into one of the stalls and they all raped her. They say that there were so many that her anus came out, and then they killed her.

Sometimes there were real waves of terror and no one dared go out or complain. The law isn't very strict about assault cases and they almost don't even take notice. Little by little, a better class of people came to live here and the situation changed.

But people are still afraid at night because they say there are ghosts here, lost souls wandering around. The older residents claim money is buried near the watertanks and that sometimes a hen, or a man dressed like a *charro,* appears there. Roberto once saw him and other strange things happened to my brother when he slept on the roof. Once he went to sleep above and woke up down below. Another time, he felt someone pulling him by the feet.

Consuelo was in the toilet once when a ghost called her by name and scared her. Another time, it happened to Manuel. He was coming home very late one night and saw an old woman pulling a cart loaded with furniture. He noticed that she went into one of the courtyard shower-rooms and heard all the furniture falling. He ran to help her . . . but there was nothing there. He came home looking white.

My *papá* and I once passed by a funeral and we heard the people cursing the dead man all along the way. My *papá* told me they had to curse the soul of a good man to put it at rest, otherwise it would haunt people. My stepmother Lupita was haunted by the dead. They followed her so much, she had to curse them to keep them away.

There are still some terrible *vecindades* around here. They are called "Lost Cities" and are made up of wooden shacks with dirt floors. The Casa Grande looks like a queen alongside them. On the Street of the Bakers, near my aunt's house, is a "Lost City" half a block long. It is the worst *vecindad* in our *barrio.* If you walk in there halfway well-dressed, everyone looks at you. The way they treat you depends on how you are dressed. Outsiders are afraid to go in but my sister-in-law

Paula's family has always lived in places like that, so I am used to them.

I knew the gang of girls who lived in the "Lost City" near my aunt's, and there wasn't a virgin among them. The boys there even took advantage of the little girls. When I was young, a fellow named "Guts," who was the terror of the neighborhood, lived there. He was a *"teporocho,"* which means he drank straight alcohol, and was unbelievably fast with a knife. When he went to the movies with his gang, they sat up on the balcony and smoked marijuana. You could smell it all over the theatre, and if the movie were a daring one, you could hear them saying dirty things.

My *barrio* has everything, even prostitutes. We girls used to go down to Tintero Street just to look around. It's a street full of prostitutes; on the first block you find girls of fifteen or sixteen, on the next are older women, who are ugly and fat, with fallen breasts. They charged three or five *pesos,* and even then the men bargained. On Orlando Street, where we once lived, the women were nicer but they charged more.

Rosario Street was the worst. I used to pass by on my way to Lupita's house. There the women lived in little stores that were open to the street. There weren't as many stores as women, so two or more lived together. They each had a bed and a bureau and a mirror, with a curtain dividing off their space. They'd put up pictures of saints, movie actors and naked women. They'd sit in the doorway, with their legs apart and their dresses pulled way up. They didn't wear slips so you could see their brassières through their nylon blouses. When the women finished with a client, they washed themselves (they always had a jug of water ready on their charcoal burners) and emptied the washbasins into the street, splashing anyone passing by.

In the morning, when these women fixed up their rooms or went to the market, we couldn't tell them apart from other women. But in the afternoon, when they were made up, we could spot them right away. They all worked for the same madam and had to turn in a certain daily quota to her. If they couldn't make the quota, they'd accept any amount offered.

We'd always see a lot of men hanging around those streets, waiting, or just watching attentively. Those with little money were looking for a woman they could afford. I've seen married men and boys from the Casa Grande there, and other men I knew . . . bums, drunks, cripples, and kids from the neighborhood. Many boys don't know what it's all about and have to go there to learn. Afterwards they are ready to do it with other girls.

I knew only two girls from around here who went to work on Tintero Street. If any girl from the Casa Grande lived that kind of life, she did it far away where we wouldn't see her. Those two girls went bad because they ran away with boy friends who later made them work in cabarets and dives. A girl who falls in love with that kind of man is really a lost soul.

My second *novio* was Mario, the Soldier, the fellow my sister ran off with later. He was called the Soldier because of the way he walked. I saw him for the first time at a dance in the Casa Grande. Every week, the boys rented a record player, and anyone who wanted to, could dance in the courtyard. I was going to school at the time, and was still in braids and anklets. It was just seven o'clock and the dance was about to begin. I had to get my dancing done before my *papá* came out and whistled for me.

My friends and I were leaning against the wall, waiting for someone to take us out to dance. We were making bets on who would catch the most boys. One of the girls said, "Here comes Mario, the Soldier." He was wearing a red sweater and didn't look as rough as the other boys. I liked him right away. He came over and took me out to dance. From that moment he didn't let me go. He danced only with me and wanted to know my name. I never told my real name at those dances, so I said it was Alicia. He wanted to see me the next day and though I told him I couldn't, he said he'd wait for me on the corner. We both went home early.

The next evening when I went for bread, there he was at the corner. I saw him several times but it never reached the point of going out together or hugging and kissing. He didn't learn my real name until much later.

Alberto Gómez of this *vecindad* was the *novio* of Chita, my friend. Then he began speaking to me and Chita said I had taken away her boy friend. I danced with Alberto and he tried to kiss me now and then. But it didn't last long because right after he became my *novio* I met Crispín.

I went for milk every afternoon and my friends usually went with me because I bought candy at this time. If I didn't have spending money I bought less milk and mixed it with water. With the money I saved, I always had enough for a treat. Crispín worked as a polisher in a furniture shop on the same street. One day, when I was alone, he came out and asked me to be his *novia*. He told me his name and I told him mine and we went out that night.

We just walked and talked; he didn't kiss me or touch me or anything. But on the way back, we bumped into Consuelo with her *novio*, Pedro. She yelled at me and gave me a sock and insulted Crispín. I was afraid she would tell my father. But Crispín spoke to her later and she gave him permission to go with me. She said she didn't want me running around coquetting, but that if I promised to be serious about him, it would be all right.

I was thirteen when I began to go with Crispín. From that time on, my fears, scares, chases and beatings began. My brothers, especially Roberto, were always watching me. My *papá*, who had never before hit me, beat me three times, once with a whip and twice with a strap, because he saw me talking to Crispín.

Crispín and I would go for walks, but he never came near my house. Consuelo helped me keep our meetings a secret from my father and brothers. She allowed me to go to the movies with him. I would say, "I'm going to Mass," and the two of us would go to the matinée. The people in the *vecindad* were getting accustomed to seeing girls go to the movies with their *novios*, but if my *papá* had known he would have hit me.

Crispín was the first one to really kiss and embrace me and that's why I liked him a lot. Once in the movies he kissed me so much that he "heated my ears." Inside me, I felt something discharge. It was the first time I wanted to be with him. Right away he asked me to go to a hotel. But by the time we left the movie I was more in control and I said he'd have to wait until I was fifteen. He kept on trying but I always managed to put him off.

Once he invited me to the movies and I said I couldn't go. Later that day, Manuel and Paula went to the movies and took me with them. I happened to sit next to a boy, Miguel, who once had spoken to me about being his *novia*. I never responded because I was Crispín's *novia* by then. But all through the movie we kept looking at each other.

Someone must have told Crispín because a week later he brought it up. He asked me if I had met anyone when I went to the movies with my brother. I said no and he slapped me hard, saying I was cheating. That was the first big quarrel we had. We didn't speak to each other for a week.

We had other quarrels over dancing. I liked to dance but he was jealous and didn't want me to go alone. He learned to dance so that I would have no reason to dance with others, but whenever I heard of a dance somewhere, I'd go secretly with the girls. At that time Crispín lived just across the street from the Casa Grande and his shop was near the ice-cream factory where I was working, so he could easily spy on me. His friends helped him and when one of them saw me at a dance, he would tell. Crispín would go after me and pull me away. Even though I danced in a decent way, not shaking and moving around like my sisters Consuelo and Antonia, he would get very angry.

Twice I caught him with another girl, but he told me he wasn't at all serious about her, that it was nothing more than a passing whim and that I was the only girl he cared about.

Meanwhile, my friend Irela began to go with Ema's brother, my ex-*novio*, Donato. Irela's mother was one of those excessively respectable, careful women, who would shout insults at a girl if she just saw her walking with a boy. Yet all her children turned out bad. Her sons were known thieves and Irela got into trouble too.

Irela didn't get pregnant but anyway she went to live in Donato's mother's house. He worked in a bakery and spent the little he earned on shoes and dresses for Irela. She was pretty and he was ugly and the truth was, they didn't make a nice couple. She didn't pay attention to him at all. She didn't care whether he had anything to eat or wear, and let her mother-in-law do all the work. Donato was one of those men who had the habit of bringing his friends home and Irela didn't like to stay there. So she came over to talk to me for hours. I was going with Crispín and wanted to know as much as possible about what men do, so I asked her lots of questions.

Then Donato caught her in the movies with another boy. In revenge, that night he took her to his friend's house and right there, on the bare floor, they both "blew" her. Then he threw her out.

She began to live with this one and that one, because she liked nice clothes and movies. She had the good luck not to get pregnant with all those boys. Then she fell in love with a tramp named Pancho. She had so many to choose from and she picked the worst! She left a good boy like Donato for a lazy bum, a pig, a calamity, who didn't work and who beat her. She loved that barbarous creature and believed that when he hit her, he was showing his affection for her.

She lived in a corner of her mother-in-law's house and didn't even complain. We all said as a joke that Pancho had better aim than the others because after all her experience without getting pregnant, his bullet hit the mark. He was the one who gave her a baby.

The next one to fall was Ema. Her mother, Enoé, worked in a hospital and was away from home a lot, so Ema found it easy to go to a hotel with her *novio*. The next day she came and confided to me what had happened. "Just think," she said, "he couldn't do a thing and the dunce came out of the hotel very angry."

When I heard that, I said, "If he didn't dishonor you, better break off with him now. Why continue? He has already tried you out and the next time he will get straight to where he has to go."

But she adored him and two days later she told me that the worst had happened. She kept going with him but had the misfortune to get pregnant right away. Then her "adoration" abandoned her, and left her to her family.

Many times one's friends are more helpful than one's parents, or sisters or aunts. Unfortunately, Mexican mothers do not tell their daughters about life and that is why they have to bear the cross of disillusionment. Even if a mother took note of what was going on, she wouldn't have the courage to ask about it. She couldn't find the words to get the truth out of her daughter. She would let it go until the damage had been done. Then, when the daughter was pregnant and the boy had already abandoned her, the mother would not accept the painful truth, the dishonor.

That is why girls do not confide in their mothers. If girls say they have a *novio*, they get a beating; if they ask for permission to go to the movies, they get screamed at and called sluts, prostitutes, shameless hussies. These words hurt and that's why, when a boy makes an offer, they accept. Many girls go off, not because they are hot, but to spite their fathers, mothers and brothers. The girls are like holy-water fonts, everyone lays hands on them. He who doesn't hit them for one thing, hits them for another. Mexican daughters are really mistreated at home. That's why there are so many unmarried mothers.

Nowadays there are few girls who are worth anything; they have pretty faces and well-formed bodies, but the truth is they are not virgins. It is sad for the man who really loves them; he loses the chance of real happiness in marriage. Many girls know how to fool men into thinking they are virgins, but sooner or later the husband finds out. Some wives even tell them, because instead of having more affection for the man who accepts them, they look down upon him for having been taken in.

The Mexican daughter suffers because she doesn't trust her parents. She prefers to confide her secret, intimate problems to her friends. For example, menstruation. Most girls find out about this outside the home . . . Mine began when I was thirteen and I was very frightened. No one had prepared me for it. I knew from my friends that when you go with a man for the first time you bleed, so that day I couldn't explain why I bled. My sister-in-law Paula was living with us then, and I asked her, "Why am I bleeding?" I didn't go with any boy but, just look, I am bleeding."

She scared me more because she said it wasn't ever going to stop. I let loose and began to cry. I thought it was going to be that way forever. All Paula said was, "Go and change yourself."

I was afraid that my dress and slip would get spotted so I put newspaper between my legs. Later, Irela told me about using rags. We didn't know about napkins then.

Crispín and I were *novios* for about a year and a half. I liked him a lot and we had good times together, but he was too interested in other girls. One night, four months before my fifteenth birthday, we had a fight. I had seen him walking with a girl and it made me so angry I wanted to break with him. He said if I left him I would be responsible for what would happen to him. I was afraid he might kill himself or do something crazy and then they would blame me. He kept begging me to go to a hotel with him. He said, "If you really love me, you'll go with me."

It had always been my golden illusion to be married in white in church, and to have a home of my own. I wanted to bring up my children without a mother-in-law or relatives to bother me. I knew that if one ran off, it didn't usually turn out that way. Besides, one's parents suffer, and people say things. But when I told my friends of my dream, they laughed and said, "Look who thinks she is going to marry!" Most of them did not get married and are living in free union.

Now that I think of it, someone should have warned me about men, especially because I played with boys so much. But no one ever explained things clearly to me about the dangers and the temptations. So when Crispín said he would ask my father for permission to marry me, on condition that I sleep with him first, it seemed reasonable. I suppose I was weak, but I was afraid I would lose him forever if I didn't. The result was, that same night we ended being *novios* in order to continue as lovers.

First, I had to go home for a sweater. My father was not living there then, because he was taking care of Antonia, who was sick at her mother's house. Only Consuelo was at home when I came in. My friend Ema was with me, to help me get away. She carried a jacket on her arm and I slipped my sweater under it, so my sister wouldn't take notice. I said I was going to borrow the comics from a friend and got out of the house without trouble. I met Crispín, and no one, not even Ema, knew where we went.

He took me to a transient hotel near the Penitentiary. Now that I have seen other hotels, I realize that place was one of the worst. The night went badly. He undressed without shame, but I had never undressed in front of a man and was very embarrassed. I didn't sleep at all because I was afraid of my father. I had always been afraid of him and now I thought he would be looking for me in fury. When we heard the Red Cross ambulance sirens, I was sure the police were after me.

The next morning, at five o'clock, Crispín took me to his mother's house. He left me waiting outside. I felt ashamed and thought everyone was looking at me as though they knew what I had done. I was full of fear that Crispín would not marry me after all. He kept me waiting for an hour and I was beginning to think he had abandoned me, when he came out. He had spoken to his parents about me and they were not in agreement that I should stay there. So he took me home.

Roberto met us in the courtyard and made a big fuss. He threatened Crispín with a knife and called him every name in the book, until Crispín promised that his parents would come to ask my father for me.

There was a scandal in my house when my family learned the truth. Everybody wanted to hit me. Consuelo managed to give me two lashes, but I scratched her arms until she bled. Manuel raised a hand to me, but Paula intervened. Paula was the only one I confided in and she cried as though I had been her sister or her daughter. She said I did a very foolish thing. I had never been close to Paula . . . she was reserved and serious and had a temper . . . but I shall never forget that no one, not even my sister, cried for me the way she did.

When my *papá* came home from work, I stayed outside in the courtyard. I was afraid to face him, but he didn't say a word, nor did he hit me. I had already "slipped" and he acted like he wasn't interested in me any more. When Manuel told him Crispín's parents were coming he said he didn't want to know anything about me and that I should arrange my own affairs. When they came, it was Manuel who spoke to them. He warned them that I knew nothing about housekeeping, that I hadn't had my first communion until I was thirteen, that I was at a disadvantage because I didn't have a mother. They said that it would be all right, that they would teach me everything, little by little. My *papá* told Manuel to ask for a two-year waiting period, because I was so young.

My father didn't speak to me for a month, and treated me badly. I felt terrible and was ashamed to look him in the face. I had been his favorite and I couldn't take my punishment. I was so upset that one night I began to cry very hard. I couldn't stop crying, until my *papá* spoke to me. I asked him to forgive me and he said, "Don't be a fool. I am your father and will never abandon you." After that I felt better.

Crispín came to the house every day, or took me to his house, or to the park. Once in a while, very secretly, we went to a hotel. On my fifteenth birthday, my friends came to my house with a record player and made a *fiesta* for me. My *papá* had planned to give me a big fifteenth birthday party, with a new dress and everything, but since I was no longer a virgin and didn't count for much any more, the only thing he gave me was a pair of shoes.

A week later, I went to live with Crispín in his mother's house, once and for all. He no longer spoke of us getting married but I was terribly afraid of becoming pregnant while I was still living at home. Again, my poor *papacito* had to run around looking for me, because I was afraid to tell him where I was.

Part I I

Manuel

I DIDN'T HAVE A HOME OR FURNITURE OR ANYTHING FOR MY WIFE. ALL I had were my wages. So I took Paula to my aunt Guadalupe's house. She and my uncle Ignacio lived alone in a little room on the Street of the Bakers. When I told my aunt we had come to stay, she said, "What do you mean, you've come to stay? What the devil sort of kid are you?" She turned to Paula and asked, "What do you think? Are you in love with him?"

Paula blushed and bent her head. So I said, "O.K., are you going to let us stay or not?"

"Why sure, son," she said, "I'll be glad to. You know you're always welcome. Here's a blanket. Spread it out on a cardboard so as not to get it dirty." My aunt didn't have a bed then and we all slept on the floor. That's where Paula and I had our honeymoon, on the floor.

My aunt and uncle slept with the votive candle burning, so we had to wait until they were fast asleep before we undressed and went to bed. We spent a terrible night because we were afraid they would hear us. Paula said, "Don't make so much noise." I answered, "Shut your mouth. You're the one making all the noise. You're the one causing a scandal here tonight." We kept scrapping all that night.

And so our married life began. We paid no rent but I gave my wife five *pesos* a day for food. My aunt was a good person but had always been poor, much poorer than my mother and father. She worked for others, washing laundry or helping in a restaurant, and my uncle sold newspapers, but between them they didn't make enough to eat more than one meal a day. If they ate more often, it would be just beans and chile. But they never complained about being poor; they were satisfied with the way they lived. Ignacio was proud to be a member of the newsboys' union and never thought of doing anything else. It wasn't that he lacked intelligence, but that he didn't know how to focus it to improve himself. More than anything, he and my aunt remained poor because they liked to drink.

Paula and I were afraid of what her mother and brother would say when they found us. I had betrayed their trust and thought they would make an awful fuss. But I was wrong. From the beginning, my mother-in-law was reasonable. I bumped into her on my way to work a few days after Paula had gone off with me. "Holy Mother of God!" I said to myself, "here it comes!"

"Good morning, Manuel," she said.

"Good morning, Cuquita."

"And Paula?"

"Well, she's all right, Cuquita."

"Good! So you got what you wanted, eh?"

I was ashamed and kept looking down. "Forgive me. I don't know what came over me, but that is the way it was. But don't worry, I'll provide for her and we'll go on living as man and wife."

"Fine! Why don't you come up to the house this evening?"

"Sure thing, Cuquita."

I still had to square up with my father because I had just walked out of the house without asking or telling anybody. On the day I ran into my mother-in-law, just as though he had been reading my thoughts, my father sent Roberto for me. "And *papá* said to bring your wife."

"Holy Mary!" I thought, "the cat's out of the bag."

When we got there, Paula didn't want to go into the house. I was pushing her, when my father opened the door. "Come in," he said. His face had the expression of a judge, and I felt as if I was in front of a jury. *Madre Santísima!* I was scared, because I always had a lot of respect for my father.

He sat down at one side of the table and we sat on the other side. "So now you're married, eh? you little bastard."

"Why, yes, *papá*."

"And how much are you making?"

"Fifty-six *pesos, papá*."

"Fifty-six *pesos*? Why, you bloody idiot, are you stupid enough to think you can support a wife on bird seed? At your age, and you've got yourself such a responsibility! Now you've really screwed yourself."

He said that right in front of my wife. Sometimes my father is too frank, no?

Then he turned to Paula. "How old are you, girl?" She was holding my hand and the poor thing was trembling. My father's face was very stern, and even though he was short, he had a loud voice.

"Well, I'm sixteen, *señor*." She made herself out to be three years younger.

"So now what? Where do you live? How does this *cabrón* treat you?" Finally, my *papá* turned to me and said, "O.K., now get to work and behave like a decent human being. You've got to take care of her; you've taken on an obligation."

The worst was over. I don't remember who was cooking in the house at the time, but my father said, "Give them some supper. They probably haven't eaten all day." We ate, but poor Paula was very ill at ease because my father didn't like her at first.

We lived with my aunt for over a year. I got to know my mother's brothers, Alfredo, the baker, and José, because they came over every evening. I had once worked for my uncle Alfredo, but I scarcely knew my other uncle. I met him in the street once in a while and he would give me my "Sunday" money, to buy a treat. At Guadalupe's, they would sit around drinking and talking for hours, and I spent a lot of time with them.

My uncle José gave me some interesting advice. He said, "Son, now that you are married I will tell you something that you should heed all the days of your life. Look here, son, the first move a woman makes is to go for your knees. Very good. Up to there you may permit her. The second move will be to your waist. When she does that, screw her in any way you can, because if you let her get to your throat you will never in all your life get her off you."

My uncle was always complaining that his wife had bewitched him and at that time he was going to a *curandero* to fight the evil. "That *cabrona*," he said, "she has me by the middle, the old witch. Every time I get home she is puttering about with her herbs, with her filthy sorcerizings. She has me enchanted and I don't know how to get rid of it." He said she had him bewitched, but the fact is that my uncle, may he rest in peace, kept his poor wife with her eyes blackened and her body bruised.

When my uncle José hit his old lady I defended her because I didn't like to see a woman being beaten. Once, when I saw my aunt

Guadalupe with a bruise, I said to her husband, "Why is my aunt going around with a black eye? Look, you lousy half-pint, if you are hitting my aunt, you'll have to settle with me, see?" I don't think he laid a hand on her after that.

But my uncle José's advice was good. A wife needs to be watched. If you don't act that way toward a Mexican woman she begins to take the reins in her own hands and runs wild. I have heard women say, "My husband is very good, I have everything I need in the house, but I want a man who dominates me, not one who lets me dominate him." So I have always dominated my women, in order to feel more manly and to make them feel it too.

Time passed, and then I had a little trouble with my uncle Ignacio. He was a bit drunk one evening and asked my wife when she was going to pay him. Paula, not understanding, said she didn't owe him anything. He told her to stop pretending, that she knew very well what he meant. When I came home from work she told me about it and I had a big argument with him. I wanted to beat him up, then and there, but because of my aunt we left that same night and went to live with my mother-in-law.

My mother-in-law and her husband lived in one room and a kitchen on Piedad Street, No. 30. At that time all four of her children, with their families, were living with her: Delila and her baby, Faustino and his wife, Socorrito and her husband and their three children, and Paula and me. The room was not large, and the rough wooden floor, on which we slept, was uneven and full of holes. All over the walls you could see finger marks and spots where they had killed bedbugs. There were great quantities of bedbugs in that house, something I was not used to . . . because of my father, right? Because he was extremely clean, and in our house we hardly had animals or insects. Here there was only a common outside toilet, which was always in a disastrous state.

The room had one bed, in which Faustino and his wife slept. The rest of us slept on pieces of cardboard and blankets or rags spread on the floor. The only other furniture was a broken-down wardrobe, without doors, and a table which had to be put into the kitchen at night to make more room. Socorrito slept with her husband and children in the small area between the bed and the wall. Paula and I spread our bedding at the foot of the bed. My sister-in-law Delila and her son slept on the other side of Paula, and my mother-in-law and her husband slept in the corner, near the kitchen, where the table stood during the day. That is the way the thirteen of us, five families, arranged ourselves in that little room.

When so many people live together in a single room, naturally there is a brake, a restraint, on one's liberty, right? As a boy in my father's house I didn't notice it so much, except when I wanted to talk to my friends or look at dirty pictures. But as a married man, I had more bitter experiences. Living together like that, never, never can there be harmony. There are always difficulties, like the time my brother-in-law insisted on removing the light bulbs whenever he left the house, because he had paid the electricity bill.

There the conditions were terrible for me. All my life I have kept late hours, going to bed late and getting up late. So there I was stretched out, while they got up early, running, jumping, shouting and disturbing me. I would wake up with terrible headaches from so much noise.

Living together like that in a single room also affected our sex life. The family was always there and one could not satisfy the appetite of the moment, because it was a matter of having witnesses, no? When we had the opportunity of being alone and were enjoying ourselves a bit, someone always came suddenly to knock at the door and stopped us short in the act. That was when one felt cheated and disillusioned.

It was also embarrassing, even laughable. Pancho spent the night spying on me, and I spent the night with one eye shut, waiting for him and his wife to go to sleep. That's the way we would all pass the night, waiting for an opportunity, and fearing that we might hear each other.

Once something very funny happened. Pancho had returned from a trip and he had desires, eh? We all went to bed and when they thought we were asleep they began to kiss and kiss. When the two of them must have been feeling good, Socorrito got up quietly, on tiptoe, and unscrewed the light bulb a little so no one could turn it on suddenly. She got back into bed and they were saying nice things to each other, and kissing. When Pancho got to the point of getting on top of her, the cursed bulb unexpectedly went on, all by itself, and he quickly jumped off. They both giggled and I had all I could do to keep from laughing.

Once I had a little trouble with my sister-in-law Delila. One night when I had worked late, I was very, very sleepy and went to bed next to Paula. In my sleep, it seemed to me that Geofredo, Delila's son, was crying, it sounded like he was suffocating, so I reached over and nudged Delila. The next day she told my mother-in-law and my wife that I had grabbed one of her breasts. Paula and I had an argument that time.

I had been working, but I had a fight with my boss and quit, thinking I would find another job right away. I had experience working in a lamp shop, in a leather-goods factory, in a bakery, and I could even paint a house. We had the idea that if a man knew a little about a lot of different things, he would never die of hunger. But no matter where I looked, there was no work. We really had it rough for a long time. Even when I found a temporary job, we were very poor, because I earned only a miserably low wage, and I had to wait a week to get paid.

My poor old woman never complained. She never asked me for anything or said, "Why do you treat me like this? Why should it be like this?" Because of the poverty in which we lived, I even went so far as to tell her, "Look, old girl, I feel like leaving you. You have a right to live a better life. I'm no good. I can't give you anything at all. I don't deserve you."

But Paula loved me—it was more than love—she worshiped me, all her life she worshiped me. And I loved her too. Every day, before going to look for work, I would say, "Here, take these three *pesos* and get yourself something to eat. That's all I have."

"And you, aren't you going to have breakfast?" she would say.

"No, old girl, the *señora* who has the stand in the market will give me credit." I told her this because I knew two people couldn't eat on three *pesos*. My thought was, at that time, to go to my friend Alberto and ask him to treat me to coffee and something. He always had some *centavos* to help me out.

From time to time, because I wasn't working, my mother-in-law looked hard at me and my brother-in-law Faustino snubbed me. Before that, when Paula and I were *novios*, Faustino, Pancho, Alberto and I often went out together. We used to go to dance halls to pick up a couple of little "cats," servant girls, and take them to a hotel for some fun, or we'd all go to the movies with our women, or we'd play cards. But when I was out of work, Faustino and Pancho didn't treat me so well.

All that time I swear I put my whole heart into looking for work. I had a friend, Juan, a big strong fellow, who had some trucks for hauling construction materials. When I was very desperate I went to him and said, "Look, Juan, do me a favor, brother, I beg you, find me a job, no matter what or how much, but just get me a job. I haven't been able to give my old woman any money for days and we're eating off my mother-in-law and I'm ashamed."

"All right," he said, "I'll come by for you at five in the morning."

Sure enough, he got me a job splitting rocks in the Pedregal. They gave me a hammer and a chisel, and told me they paid four *pesos* a load of rock. "Well," I thought, "if I do two loads, it'll be eight *pesos*." But I sure was disappointed; from five-thirty in the morning to six at night, I barely did half a load. The hammer handle had scorched my hands, my blisters had broken, and the whole damned day I made only two *pesos*.

When Paula saw my hands she burst out crying. She was so sorry for me that I cried too. I was touched, and said, "Come now, don't cry, old girl, because it makes me feel bad. Better go and buy black coffee and beans. I'll bet you haven't had anything to eat." She was proud and sometimes days would go by without her eating so that she wouldn't have to take food from her mother.

The next day, Juan came for me. I had a fever from the work I did, but I got up to go. In the truck, Juan said, "You know, Manuel, this is very hard work for you. I'd better take you along on the truck to help me with deliveries." He'd give me five, eight or ten *pesos*, depending on the trips he made. I was very grateful to him.

Well, so time passed. Paula and I had lived together for almost three years and we didn't have any children. I wasn't pleased and said, "Looks like I'm living with a man; you don't seem to be a woman. When are we going to have a child?" At that time I didn't know what it cost one to bring up children, or how bad one felt not to be able to provide for them. I didn't think of such things.

I kept fighting with Paula. I had a certain distrust of her because she had not been a virgin when I first slept with her. It made me mad that she had deceived me, but then I thought, after all, those who had gone before me didn't matter. What I wouldn't stand for, would be any who came after me. But I didn't trust her completely, and when she didn't become pregnant I thought she had taken something to cure herself. I kept accusing her, and she kept praying to God to give her a child. Today I understand that I was the one to blame because I was too young; my semen was too thin to produce a child.

Then, one day, my wife told me I was going to be a father. "Man alive!" I said, "really? You're not fooling me, old girl?"

"No," she said. "It's true."

"Thank God!" I told her. "Lets see if this doesn't change our luck. Come on, old girl, let's go to the movies." All I had was eight *pesos*. "It doesn't matter, we'll spend two *pesos* in the movies, but we have to celebrate this. Come on, *mamá*, let's go."

Well, I took her to the movies and we were very happy. I was more affectionate toward her than usual, and told her that I didn't want her to bend over or lift anything heavy.

I kept making the rounds with Juan. Then he began to have very little work. I thought, "Well, I'm a rotten egg, I bring bad luck, just as soon as I hook up with somebody, things begin to go bad with him, too."

One time, when we hadn't eaten all day, I went to my father to see whether he could help me. He looked hard at me when I came in. I was very skinny then, very skinny. I weighed only fifty-two kilos; now I weigh seventy. My wife had also lost a lot of weight after she began to live with me, although she was still quite buxom.

"You don't look very good. What have you been doing?"

"Well, working, *papá*."

"Just look, your shoes are torn, your pants are all patched up; I don't remember seeing you like this before."

"Well, no, *papá*, things haven't been so good with me."

"It's obvious, you don't have to tell me, you bastard. Now you know it's not the same thing having to go out and break your frigging back getting things for yourself."

"You're right, *papá*."

"I think you're coming down with tuberculosis. What's the matter with you, aren't you eating, or what's wrong?"

"Well, no, *papá*, I do eat, how do you expect me to go without eating?" But actually he wasn't fooled.

"O.K., sit down and have supper." The truth was that I was awfully hungry, I felt as if I had a great big hole in my stomach. There were fried bananas on the table . . . and good things I had been longing for. I really had myself a fantastic supper. Then I didn't know how to

ask my father to lend me five *pesos*. Five *pesos*, and I couldn't find
the words to ask him! But he understood what was on my mind.

"Here, take these ten *pesos*, you'll find some use for them."

I almost felt like crying because I felt I wasn't man enough to make
a living. At that moment, I began to hate humanity because I felt I
was incapable. I thought, "I work hard like others, but it doesn't pay
off. I'm just not man enough." That's what I thought when I left my
father's house.

I practically flew home to see my wife. It was a long time since I
had given her ten *pesos* in a lump sum. I came home and the first
thing I saw were her dry lips, dry from hunger and thirst. I felt like
a heel and I wept. My stomach was full, I had eaten a lot . . . I was
a bum for filling up when my wife hadn't eaten. I shouldn't have
eaten either and so I cried.

"Why are you crying, Manuel?"

"Nothing, go on and buy yourself something for supper."

I gave her the whole ten *pesos* and all I said was, "Buy me five
centavos' worth of cigarettes and in the morning give me my bus fare
so I can go out and see what I can find." I used to do this every
morning.

When Paula was five-months pregnant, Raúl Álvarez asked me to
come to work in his lamp shop. He had gotten an order for 18,000
pieces and had promised delivery in two weeks. My job was to take
ordinary sheets of glass and cut them up into various shapes for
lamps. I worked day and night to fill the order.

The first week I drew two hundred *pesos*, just like that.

"Holy Mother of God!" I said. "Praised be the Lord." I came home
and said to my wife, "Look, *mamá*, this is what I earned. I'm only
going to take out twenty-five *pesos* to buy myself some shoes. Right
now you need more things than I do. Buy yourself a tonic; get
something so the kid will be healthy. We don't want him to be born
puny."

I worked there for about a month, when my brother-in-law Faustino, the one who treated me like dirt when I wasn't working, became
sick. He was paralyzed from the waist down. He said to me, "*Compadre*," (I'm the godfather of baptism of his two children) "be a
good fellow, go and help out in the café, brother, won't you? If I
don't go to work I'll lose my job. Take my job for two or three days,
until I get better."

"Man alive, *compadre*," I said, "you can see I'm just barely getting on my feet. I've just gotten this job with *Señor* Raúl. How am I going to ask him to let me off for a couple of days?"

"Aw, come on, be a good fellow," and he looked at me so sadly that my conscience got the better of me.

"O.K., I'll go; but only for two days; here's hoping you get well soon!"

I went to work in the restaurant. But Faustino recovered slowly and the two days stretched out and became a week, then two weeks. I earned fifteen *pesos* a day and of this I gave my wife only five. The rest I turned over to my *compadre* to pay for the doctor, medicine, rent and food. I thought, "Well, I'm lending him the money; it's like a saving. He'll give me back the whole amount in a lump sum and I'll be able to pay my wife's hospital bill."

Well, it didn't turn out that way. One time, while my *compadre* was still sick, my godson Daniel became ill and at night I had to go every two hours to get a woman to give him penicillin injections. After that my *comadre* Eufemia got sick, and so there I was taking care of all three of them and paying for everything. But I would think, well, I'm actually saving my money. I imagined I was saving. The situation dragged on like that for more than a month and a half. And so I lost the job with *Señor* Raúl.

Then one morning I went to work in the restaurant and was surprised when the boss stopped me and said, "You can't work now, because Faustino is back." He had gone back to work without telling me! Three days later Faustino burned himself very badly at the restaurant and had to quit anyway. Even then he didn't tell me, so that I could have gone back again. He knew I didn't have a job and that Paula's delivery date was getting close. I went to all the shops looking for work and sometimes they'd give me a few pieces to do. I even went peddling. I'd make ten *pesos*, five *pesos*, no more.

My wife's older brother, Avelino, who drank a lot, came home to his mother's house. He was in bad shape and in two weeks was dead. We all chipped in for the burial, my brother-in-law hocked his watch and one way or another we got enough together to bury him. Two days later my wife began to have labor pains. My brother-in-law had died on Thursday and on Saturday my child was born in the same room. I was very worried because they said that Paula might get *cáncer* or something, on account of the dead body having been there.

On Saturday morning I ran to get the midwife. She told me to buy cotton, gauze, umbilical thread and a basin. We raised Paula from the floor to the bed and fed her white corn gruel while she was in labor because it's supposed to have a lot of calcium. I wasn't in the house when my child came because that same week, as though God took pity on me, I was offered a job cutting glass at twelve *pesos* a day.

I asked my boss to pay me and let me have the day off so that I could be at home with my wife. But he said, "What do you want to be fucking around there for? Are you going to help her push, or what? Are you going to give birth or is she? We've got lots to do, so get to work." Well, I needed the money to pay the midwife, so I stayed.

It seemed like the longest day of my life, no? We had to clean up the whole shop and I was very filthy when I got out. That work is as dirty as a charcoal burner's. I went to the market to buy some clothes for the child. I was running between the stalls when I met my brother. He yelled after me, "Stop running, she's already given birth."

"What did she have?" I called, still running.

"A girl," he said.

"Oh, well, it doesn't matter." Then I got home and there were my mother-in-law, Socorrito, Pancho, and everybody, looking at me, to see how I would take the news. I stood there like a jerk and just said, "I'm back, old girl." She looked tired after her ordeal. I kissed her forehead and she showed me the baby. "Is this my baby?"

"Yes, don't you like her?"

"Yes, she is pretty." I must have made a funny face or gotten red because everyone burst out laughing. Pancho said, "What a face you made, brother-in-law! It is your first daughter, that is why you came running home. I'll ask you how you feel when you have a few more."

That was how my daughter Mariquita was born. I was especially happy that day because my father, who had never set foot inside my house, came to see his granddaughter. Neither Consuelo nor Marta had come to see us, but Roberto had been to our house once or twice.

When the baby was about three months old, we went to visit my father. I had met him on the street and he had said, "When are you coming over? When are you going to bring over the baby? You're acting as though you don't have a father or a family. I don't know why you bastards are like that." So we visited him for supper one evening. Afterwards I said, "We're going now, *papá*, good night."

"You're going already? Where are you going? The baby is not leaving, so scram if you want to, but the baby stays."

"What do you mean she's not going, *papá*?"

"No," he said, "the baby stays here with me. Come on now, Paula, grab some space in the bed and lie down there with the girls, and, you, roll out your bed things on the floor, you bastard, and go to sleep."

"Are we going to stay on with you, *papá*?"

"Sure you're staying here; don't think I'm going to let my baby leave." So that's how we began to live with my father.

I was partly glad and partly angry at my father's decision. Glad, because it was nicer and cleaner in my father's house, and I thought my old woman would be better off. I really hated to live at my mother-in-law's house. My heart still shrinks up when I recall the condition it was in! I took our things out of there little by little so that Cuquita would not be offended.

But I was angry at my father for one thing. From the very first day, he separated me from my wife and would not let me sleep with her. She slept on the bed with my two sisters, and I was ordered to sleep on a burlap bag on the kitchen floor. As though there had been no change in our lives, my father made me sleep alone! Now that I have sons, if God permits me to see them married, isn't it logical that I should let them sleep with their wives? So that they feel like men?

My memory is so poor that I cannot remember exactly who lived in the Casa Grande at the time. There was a servant there, but I don't remember who it was. I know Roberto was in the army because I remember a telegram from him, telling me he was in some kind of trouble. Only Marta and Consuelo were living at home. My *papá* might have been staying at Lupita's house at that time.

I began by giving my father fifty *pesos* a week to help with the household expenses. I kept this up for a few months, then one week my boss didn't pay us, and so I didn't give anything to my father. No one at home said anything. The same thing happened the next week, and then another. My boss paid me five and ten *pesos* at a time and before I knew it I had spent them. That way, I soon forgot my obligation at home.

I even thought, well, my father has enough money to go around. He had always paid the rent and brought home lots of food. I also began to think that, after all, Paula kept the house clean and washed my father's clothes and cooked, so the food he provided her was like the pay you give to a servant. And so I stopped giving Paula money, too. I didn't have another woman at the time, but I was already neglecting my wife.

Once again, I began to go out with my old gang in the Casa Grande. Alberto and I were working in the same shop, and we were always together. In a way he wanted to imitate me, because six months after I married, he took this girl, Juanita, to live with him. But she became jealous of the fact that Alberto preferred to go out with me instead of staying at home with her. She couldn't stand me and was always putting ideas into his head. Later, because of her, we began to grow apart, little by little, although we were still an open book to each other.

The only trouble with Alberto (because even though he was illiterate, he was very intelligent) was that he liked to drink. Once a week for sure he'd go on a drunk. He'd say, "Come on, *compadre*, let's have a few." I never really liked to drink. I had gotten drunk twice and it made me sick. That was one big difference between us.

Another difference was that he was satisfied to be a worker and I wasn't. Even at that time, I didn't like having a boss over me, but Alberto didn't mind, so long as he could steal a little on the job. He would say, "If my *maestro* gets rich on the fruit of my labor, it is only fair that I take something from him, to equalize things." To Alberto, the only kind of boss who wasn't good was one you couldn't rob.

Alberto quit the job at the glass shop to become a bus driver. The pay was low but drivers make up for it by keeping back some of the fares. I didn't like working in the shop without my *compadre*, so when Santos, my daughter's godfather, suggested that I open up a shoe shop, I took to the idea. Santos said, "Get hold of two hundred *pesos*. You can make shoes and sell them at a profit of five *pesos* a pair." I thought, "Suppose I make five-dozen pairs of shoes a week. That makes sixty pairs . . . that makes three hundred *pesos* profit a week. Why that's wonderful!"

Santos loaned me the lasts and a stitching machine, and I borrowed the two hundred *pesos* from my father. My *papá* was impressed when I told him about the profits I could make. I heard him say to another man, "Just think, the time one wastes working, when there are such good businesses. Look at what Manuel says, and here am I stuck in the La Gloria, working like an animal all these years! Maybe he will really get up in the world and accomplish something!"

So I went into business. Santos went with me to buy the leather, and we started making shoes. But I knew nothing about shoes or business then, I worked only by God's good will. I never made a budget, to know what my costs were. I never noticed whether my capital was growing, or going down. I never even took the precaution of figuring out how many pairs of shoes I could cut from one skin. And Santos did not do right by me, because he let me use second-grade material and some orders were canceled. For the soles, he told me to buy rubber tires, but he never mentioned that I should buy flattened out tires, so that the shoes should be presentable.

I had a lot of expenses. I rented a little shop in the Casa Grande, and I had one man working at the machine and three men finishing. It was the custom to give a shoemaker his *"chivo,"* that is, ten *pesos* a day as an advance on his wages. Shoemakers here work all night on Fridays, and on that day I had Paula send supper for all of us.

My father had asked me several times why I didn't chip in something for household expenses, so I had to give him money too. I did that four or five times, but then I said, "Look, *papacito,* right now I don't want to take five *centavos* out of the shop. I want to expand it, by God!" He agreed, and didn't bother me for money for a while.

I don't remember exactly what happened . . . one of my finishers, Chucho, went on a binge for two or three weeks, getting drunk every day. He later died in the street, abandoned and drunk, poor thing. But I took pity on him, thinking that the workers kill themselves to earn so little, so I raised the finishers twenty *centavos* for each shoe, and the machinist ten *centavos*. I wanted to show others how a boss should treat workers. I didn't want to exploit them the way my bosses exploited me. They were all satisfied, and no one complained of me as a boss. They were happy, but unfortunately, I was completely incompetent.

Instead of making a profit, without knowing it, I was actually losing on each pair of shoes. Then I sent someone, I don't remember who, to deliver twenty-five pairs of shoes, and he took off with the money. To make a long story short, my business went broke and all I had left was about two hundred *pesos* worth of materials. I sold it to Santos for sixty *pesos*. It wasn't the first time anybody lost money in business, but I took it pretty hard.

After my business failed, I gave up trying to plan my life and get ahead. I lost the little confidence I had in myself and lived just from day to day, like an animal. I really was ashamed to make plans because I didn't have the will power to, well, to carry them out. I couldn't stick to things or follow them up. I understood others better than myself, and even dared to offer suggestions to my friends about how to improve their lives. I have helped others, but I couldn't analyze my own problems. Concerning myself, I felt null and void.

To me, one's destiny is controlled by a mysterious hand that moves all things. Only for the select, do things turn out as planned; to those of us who are born to be *tamale* eaters, heaven sends only *tamales*. We plan and plan and some little thing happens to wash it all away. Like once, I decided to try to save and I said to Paula, "Old girl, put away this money so that some day we'll have a little pile." When we had ninety *pesos* laid away, *pum!* my father got sick and I had to give all to him for doctors and medicines. It was the only time I had helped him, and the only time I had tried to save. I said to Paula, "There you are! why should we save if someone gets sick and we have to spend it all!" Sometimes I even think that saving brings on illness! That's why I firmly believe that some of us are born to be poor and remain that way no matter how hard we struggle and pull this way and that. God gives us just enough to go on vegetating, no?

Well, after my failure, I didn't care about shoes any more, so I went back to job hunting. I worked on lamp fixtures again, and after work, the only thing I did was play cards, go to the movies and to baseball and soccer games with my friends. I was hardly ever at home. When my second child, my son Alanes, was born, my father paid for the midwife and everything.

My half-sister Antonia had come back to live with us in the Casa Grande. She and Paula became close friends, closer than my sisters. Why, Antonia even confided to my wife that I looked like a man she was in love with. She said it was too bad I was her brother, because she liked me very much! Then Paula told me that Tonia had "pulled a bad one," because she was pregnant. I couldn't call the father to account because Antonia wouldn't tell us his name.

Then Tonia took some herbs to cause an abortion and got very sick.

She went crazy, really crazy. She had fits and when she saw my face she got worse. She screamed, "His face, his face!" My father looked at me suspiciously after that, which hurt me a lot, because I never had evil thoughts about Antonia. She said that only because I looked like the man she had loved.

Finally, the doctors sent Tonia to an insane asylum and, little by little, she got better. The doctor told my father that Tonia was the type of woman who couldn't stay well mentally without a man. That's why later, when she began to have children with Francisco, we didn't say anything.

Antonia must have been mentally ill, because she tried to put a hex on my father. Julia, the wife of Marta's godfather of the first communion, warned us that Tonia was watching my father and was taking his measurements. The older people here, the common people, believe that through sorcery, or by invoking a saint, or by measuring someone with a tape, or scattering salt or dust in the house, a devil or evil spirit will get control of a person's body and will kill him.

I don't believe witchcraft really exists, but when I was living at my aunt's house, I saw a woman curing a man who had cataracts in both eyes. She took a fresh egg laid by one of her own chickens, rubbed his eyes with it and then broke it open. It was black inside so she told the man that his blindness was caused by sorcery, by his his own wife! And she gave him a counterremedy.

I guess my father believed in these superstitions because he would scold us if we spilled salt while anyone was eating, and once he was very angry with me for bringing home a belt made of snake skin. He made me get rid of it before something bad happened to one of us. When he found out about Antonia, he went to see a witch too. She gave him water to sprinkle in the room, so that the spell would not take effect.

But Antonia continued to be my father's favorite. He bought her whatever she wanted, and no matter what she did or said, he'd comment, "That's fine, that's fine." It always struck me as strange that my father could be so sweet, so very sweet, to others, and so hard to us. In the case of Antonia he was trying to compensate for his neglect of her and Lupita all those years. Also, because she helped at home. Marta and Consuelo had no mother to teach them and they were useless around the house.

One thing that had always bothered me, was that no one in my family ever treated me like an older brother. It was my duty and right, for example, to have stopped Marta when I saw her keeping company with Crispín. I really wanted to speak to that fellow, man to man, but I was afraid that Marta or my father would put me in a ridiculous position by not backing me up. Once I asked Marta to hold my daughter Mariquita, and Crispín told her not to, just as though she were his servant or something. I got mad at that and spoke up.

"Listen, Crispín, why do you tell my sister not to hold my child? I want you to understand that I know you have struck Marta on more than one occasion. Well, let me tell you that the next time you put a hand on her you won't be seeing her any more."

The logical thing to expect was for Marta to support her big brother, isn't that so? Well, she did just the opposite. She said, "What are you mixing into my affairs for?" That's what she came out with.

"Look, Marta," I said, "never, never again will I mix in, even if I see you dying. Even if you are being dragged on the floor I won't do a thing."

Later, when she ran off with Crispín, my father blamed Roberto and me. He never allowed us to meddle in her affairs and then he blamed us. The same thing happened with Consuelo. From the beginning I was wise to that fellow she went with. Why shouldn't I be, since I was the same type!

Twice I had to fight with my brother, to teach him how to respect his elders. The first time, he called me "*pinche guey*," for no reason at all. "Watch what you're saying, you son-of-a-bitch. You are insinuating you went to bed with my wife and that you have made a fool of me. You're offending her, and me too, imbecile!" While I was speaking, *pas!* he punched me in the face. He was strong, but I beat him up, right there in the courtyard.

The next fight we had was when Consuelo came in crying because he had hit her. He said she had been flirting at a dance, acting like a little whore. So I said, "Roberto, it's none of your business what she does. What do you give her anyway? Besides, she works . . ." Again, while I was talking, he socked me. I got him on the floor and beat him so hard he had to get the fellows to pull me off. That time I even bit his nose. When the boys intervened, I got up, saying, "This kid has got to learn some respect for me." I think he did, too, because he told the boys, "*Ay!* my brother is short, but how strong he hits. You have to be careful with that guy."

Roberto was always watching his sisters. Just like my father, he was against decent women going to dance halls. After all the things Roberto got himself into, it turned out that he was the one who was following my father's morality. The thing was, that for Roberto, a woman . . . well, he had such a narrow, abstract notion of what female chastity should be, that he thought a girl should be absolutely pure. And that is something difficult to find these days.

Today, if you invite a girl to the movies and act like a gentleman, she says later that you are a jerk. But the man who comes along and starts using his hands . . . even though she resists, because a woman is always saying no . . . well, that's the man for them. My brother was so retiring that I didn't think he would ever get married.

Roberto suffered from a lot of complexes. So far as women were concerned, there were a lot of undercurrents there. It wasn't that he was not able to take a woman and go to bed with her. He was just as capable as anybody. I knew because of some information I got from a woman who had gone with him. It was that Roberto believed he was ugly, so dark and ugly, that he thought that the woman who married him would deceive him at the first opportunity. He knew that if anyone made a fool of him he wouldn't be able to control himself and there would be very serious consequences.

The thing about Roberto was that he was too violent. He was capable of grabbing a guy at any moment and giving him a bath in blood, of caving in his ribs, or of sticking a knife into him. It's not that he was a criminal . . . just very bad-tempered. But when his rage cooled down and he remembered the shape he left the guy in, he might cry with remorse and ask for forgiveness. My poor brother was a tangle of contradictions.

Roberto was really very noble, the most noble in the family. If he were surrounded by people of culture and understanding, he would be a happy person. He really liked nice things. He liked to talk to people more educated than he, and he was always alert to learn new words and to express himself correctly. If he had contact with people in a higher social sphere, he would straighten out. He really hated the nauseating atmosphere we lived in . . . all that we had to rub shoulders with every day.

I attribute a lot of his trouble to the mistaken idea we have that it is a matter of self-respect or pride to show no fear. Roberto really didn't know what fear was; he was incapable of running away from trouble. If somebody pulled a knife, he pulled one, and used it too. And he was worse when he drank. I have said to him, "I don't know what you are after. Can't you get drunk decently and sleep it off, like other people do? What does it cost you? But no, you have to go out and look for someone who will pick a fight and beat you up! If you have so much anger in you, why don't you let me make a boxer out of you?"

He would have made a good boxer, but he didn't want to be one. He said he hated fighting. He was good at sports . . . if he had the support of a sports club, he might have been a champion swimmer or bicycle racer. He would have been a real luminary. But that business of going around hitting people and stealing just couldn't go on. The day he killed someone, who would the guy's family take it out on? Me, of course! But he never thought of the consequences of his actions. He was like a runaway horse. Nothing could stop him, not blows, not advice, scoldings, jail . . . nothing. He was not satisfied with ordinary emotions, like me, but he needed more action, an outlet for the fire that was inside him.

At bottom, I believe he was afraid of something. In my poor judgment, it was his subconscious at work, trying to defend itself from something indeterminate. Perhaps he felt the lack of love too strongly. His life was really sad, sadder than mine and our sisters, because he had never known real love.

During all this time I had kept myself informed about Graciela, and then I began to hang out at the café where she worked. She had married a man named León, but had left him after three months because he was a thief and sold marijuana. He was one of the worst, a real murderer! His body had so many scars, it looked like a map! I used to see Graciela in the street every once in a while, and each time felt something stir inside me. She gave birth to a son at the time my first daughter was born.

When I had the shoe shop, friends who knew I had been in love with her, would say, "You know what? Graciela is working in a café on Cuba Street," or, "I saw Graciela working on Constantino Street."

One time I went to deliver some shoes, and I had two hundred *pesos* on me, a pretty large roll, no? I was passing Constantino Street and saw Graciela waiting on tables there. I thought, "I'm going in so she can see that I'm well off now."

A long time had passed since we had last spoken to each other. We were polite and had a chat while she served me supper. I managed to take out a fistful of *pesos,* and I could see she was impressed. I wondered whether she still cared for me, so I went back to the café about three times. Then she disappeared and I didn't know where she was working. I thought, "Well, maybe it's better this way." I had been with Paula five years, and I hadn't had relations with any other woman during that time.

One day as my friends and I were going to the Florida movie theatre, we passed by a café and there was Graciela, working. So I thought, "Good! Now I know where you are."

Then I really went after her. I ate at the café every day and made it my hangout. I began to get close to her, pretending to just renew an old friendship. Little by little, the affection she had for me came back. As for me, I kept fanning the spark in my heart, until I felt my old love again. I began to get somewhere with her, but it cost me a lot of work.

One evening, she agreed to go out with me and another couple. We went to a cabaret and had a few beers. While we danced, we kept looking at each other. We kissed and she looked a bit dazed. Then she said, with a lot of passion, "Kiss me, kiss me." I knew I was making headway and I said, "Graciela, Graciela, when will you be mine?"

"One of these days, tomorrow, the day after . . . one of these days," she said. The next day at the café, I reminded her of what she had said. "If it's all right for tomorrow, why not now?"

"So you believe me?" she said. "I was just talking. I didn't mean it. After all, you are married, you have your two children and I know your wife. So how do you think we can do this?"

I waited for the café to close and invited her out for *tacos.*

"Fine," she said, "I'm hungry. I can't eat this stuff in the café any more." Trying to be clever, I took her down Orégano Street and then turned the corner at Colombia, where there was a hotel. Well, she caught on and about fifteen yards before reaching the hotel she stopped.

"Let's keep walking, Graciela, please."

"No," she said, "I know what you're up to, nothing doing."

"No, look, believe me, I don't want a thing from you." But I finally came clean with her. "All right, Graciela, it's true I want you to be

mine tonight." No and no and no, we were arguing out there in front
of the hotel for three hours, she and I. I argued this way and that,
but she absolutely refused to come with me.

I finally got mad, grabbed her arm in a tight grip, and kicked
the door open, forcing her in. I asked for a room. The manager went
ahead of us, opened the door and I pushed her in. I tried to undress
her but she wouldn't let me. Actually, deep down she did want to,
but her mind told her she shouldn't. "Leave me alone, Manuel,
please leave me alone. By all that you love most in this world, leave
me alone, because if I do this I won't be able to live. You are married,
you have children, have pity on me and leave me alone."

But I was obsessed. All I wanted was to have her.

Well, then I had to urinate and since the toilet was outside, I
went out. She locked the door and wouldn't open it when I knocked.
I went to the manager and said, "Please unlock my door. I think my
wife must have fallen asleep."

"Why, of course," and he opened the door with his key. She was in
bed and I got in.

After a long hard battle, it was then about four-thirty in the
morning, after struggling with her for an hour and a half, she gave in.
But by that time, either because I had used up so much energy or
I don't know what, I found I couldn't function . . .

Holy Mother of God, was I in a sweat! Was I ashamed! I said:
"Dear God, how can this happen to me? No, no, it can't be." Well, I
was in a frightful stew and terribly embarrassed. There she was
ready for me and I said, "*Madre Santísima*, now what am I going to
do?" So I said, "*Mi amor*, I know that you are now willing, but I'm
going to punish you. I'm going to make you suffer the way you made
me suffer." I was lying, the reason was I just couldn't. So I lit a
cigarette and prayed to all the saints: "Please, St. Peter, St. Paul and
St. Gabriel, help me recover so I can go on with it." Well, after some
time I felt my strength coming back, and I said to myself, before it
changes its mind and goes soft on me again, I'd better hop to it.

Well, I think it was the most wonderful night I ever had in my
whole life. We just let go completely. It was as if the whole stream
of love within us two overflowed, broke the dike and overflowed.
She was as insatiable as I. One, two, three, five, six, seven times we
had each other, and when dawn came we were still making love.

At daylight we had to get up for work. She was afraid of what her mother would think. But I said, "You've got nothing to be afraid of. You're a full-grown woman. If you were a young, unmarried girl it would be different." When we got outside everything seemed to be yellow, cars, houses, men, women. Both of us looked pale and tired. She went to her job, only two blocks from there, and I to mine. That is, I went to the shop, but I was like a milkman's horse sleeping on the job.

We two continued making love. We'd always go to a hotel. My wife didn't think it unusual for me to come home at twelve, one, or two in the morning because I'd been doing it for years. I don't know to this day if she ever found out that I was going with Graciela. We never had any trouble about this. My brother and sisters didn't know anything about it either. The only one who always knew everything was Alberto. I told him all my problems, all the things that were troubling me.

I realized that my love affair with Graciela was harmful to me in every respect. If my wife found out she might go so far as to leave me and I didn't want that for I loved her too. I loved her a great deal, but with a different kind of love. Paula was passive, anything I wanted to do was all right, but she didn't respond with much passion. Perhaps that was her nature; she had other ways of showing me her love. But she didn't excite me as much. Graciela responded in a way that satisfied me and my vanity. She worshiped me. With Graciela, every time I touched her it felt like the first time, as though she were a different woman. I loved her passionately, madly, I couldn't think of living without her. And I didn't have to worry about her becoming pregnant because she couldn't have any more children.

My life became a living hell, because I couldn't imagine going on without both of them. I wanted to have them both without either of them feeling bad about it. I was always thinking of Graciela and of my wife. I couldn't sleep any more. All night long I kept turning and twisting, I suffered from a terrible restlessness. Once I even said to Graciela, "Look, I can't live without you. Let's set up house, leave your mother and let's move into a room. We'll manage one way or another, but I'm going to stay with you."

But when I got home and saw my wife sleeping with my children, I felt ashamed. I hated myself. I said, "How can I be such a good-for-nothing? I've got to leave that other woman. Here is my poor little wife with my children; they don't deserve this kind of treatment."

It got to the point where I was hoping my wife would give me an excuse to leave her. I was short-tempered with her; once I beat her hard, very hard. You see, I was used to absolute obedience on her part, not forcing her with blows, but on the basis of yelling at her. Alberto had come to see me one morning, and I asked Shorty for something, I forget what. She was in the kitchen and she shouted back, "I'm busy right now! Stop bothering me."

She had never talked back to me before. "Here is Alberto and look at the way you answer me! Will you give it to me or must I make you give it to me?"

"No, man!" she said. "You just give orders around here! How are you going to make me? Get it yourself." I got up, not very angry yet, saying, "I'm telling you . . . Shorty . . ." and *pum!* she gave me a slap. Right in front of Alberto!

I don't know, I was so angry that I went blind. I felt a red band over my eyes. I was so ashamed in the presence of my friend that I went after her and really beat her up. Later, Alberto said, "What a brute you are! Brother, how strong you are when you're angry!" because with one blow, I made her fly, just as though she were a doll. He tried to stop me, but couldn't. Her mother was there too, washing clothes. She didn't interfere at first, but when she saw me kicking Paula, she said, "Don't kick her, can't you see she's pregnant again?"

Another time I hit Shorty, was when she beat up Mariquita and left the child black and blue all over her little body. Shorty had a very strong temper, a strong spirit . . . she was very active and quick . . . and she hit the children hard. That day I got mad and said, "Look, never again! Don't think I'm going to let you do this to my daughter. If you as her mother can do that, then you show no human qualities. You are not worth anything, and from here on our relations will end, if you hit her like that again. I'll take her away and you'll never see her. If she needs discipline, spank her on her behind and no place else!"

That's how I spoke to her, see? She didn't know any other way to bring up children, because her mother had always beaten her and her sisters that way.

I had some trouble with Graciela on account of Domingo, my third child. I had told her I didn't get along with my wife and no longer slept with her. I had to fool her so she would keep seeing me. But Graciela saw Paula in the street and noticed that she was pregnant.

"So you don't sleep with her, eh? I just saw her and she's in the family way again."

"Ah," I said, "so you saw her? So what do you want me to do? I just touched her once and it stuck."

Actually, I had contact with my wife almost every day. I often did it because I felt guilty. I thought, "I can't neglect my wife to that extent. I've got to do my duty toward her because if I don't provide her with satisfaction, who will?" And many times I did it without wanting to, just to do my duty. I couldn't see Graciela every day, just every three or four days; sometimes a week went by before we slept together. I explained to her the best I could, and it seemed reasonable to her that I just couldn't help having relations with my wife.

I acted like a real canaille to Paula. When Roberto was in jail in Córdoba, my father sent me to see him. Instead of going alone, I took Graciela with me. I had only 150 *pesos* in my pocket . . . not enough to take her to a hotel or to good restaurants . . . so I took her to my cousin David's house and sponged on my aunt. I presented Graciela as a friend I worked with, but my aunt wasn't fooled. She was annoyed with me, and when she saw me getting into Graciela's hammock, she made me sleep on the floor with David. That whole week, Graciela and I had to get together in the sugar-cane field.

Back in Mexico City, I spent every evening in the café. I almost never ate at home. I got so I couldn't enjoy a meal except in the café. Once, as I was sitting there, my mother-in-law came hurrying in. "Manuel, Manuel," she said, "Paula needs you." Graciela was standing right by.

"What does she want me for?"

"Hurry," she said, "she's dying." I got up as if a spring had been released and ran home. Paula had had a bad hemorrhage, the whole house was full of blood. I became terribly alarmed and ran for the doctor. I did what he asked me to and went and bought the medicine. That time my wife was annoyed with me for not being around when she most needed me.

But once Paula was taken care of, I returned to the café. I realized I was a heel for acting that way. I struggled against it with all my strength. I struggled as hard as I could to leave Graciela, but I couldn't, I couldn't. So I went back to the café. The next day Paula had another hemorrhage and the doctor told me, "If she has one more, don't spend money for medicine, buy a coffin."

"Holy Mother," I said. "Dear God, it's not possible." I don't know what the cause was, maybe it was from a fit of anger. The child was pretty far along, about seven months. My wife got well and my son Domingo was born normal.

Once Paula said to me, "I'm going to get myself cured."

I said to her, "Why? What are you going to cure? So you don't want to bear my children any more? I don't want to have a murderer for a wife. You have no right to take the life of a being that can't even defend itself. It's a bigger crime and more despicable to kill a being that can't defend itself than to kill a man in cold blood." And we never lost a child.

The only ideas I had about women and childbirth I learned from my married friends. My wife didn't know much either. Neither her mother nor my father ever told us anything about such matters. Paula always nursed each of the children about a year or until she got pregnant. There were two years between Marquita and Alanes and Domingo and only one year between Domingo and our last child, Conchita. We always had sexual relations up to the day the child was born but after the birth we waited a month or so, never the required forty days.

It was close to a year after Domingo was born, that there was an incident with Consuelo, which made us leave my father's house. Consuelo had never liked my wife and, to humiliate her, she spit on the floor just after Paula had cleaned it. It bothered my wife, and all I did was to whack Consuelo a couple of times on the arm. Then Marta grabbed the scale weight and tried to hit me with it. So I took them both by the hair and held them down on the bed, to keep them from moving, right?

But Consuelo has an enormous imagination, no? She and Marta should have been actresses. They blew it up big. Consuelo said I beat her on the lungs and whipped her like a horse, and as a result Paula and I had to leave the house where our two sons were born.

I rented a room in the Matamoros section. I bought my wife a bed, my father gave us a wardrobe, a table and a kerosene stove. Then Delila and my mother-in-law asked whether I would like us all to live together in a room in a private house. Ana, the sister of my mother-in-law's husband, who had her own little house, was willing to rent to us. It was a humble home, but the first private house, with a garden, I had ever lived in, and it was something very nice for me.

When I saw how other people lived . . . the nice homes in the movies, and magazines, and in rich neighborhoods, the luxuries that exist, I felt . . . well, degraded, to live the way I did. I felt unfortunate, but at the same time, it should give me incentive, no? That is when I say, "I have to rise . . . I must reach that level." Because, in reality, it is humiliating, saddening, not to have a nice home and to have to live with other people all the time.

The only time in my life that I have felt fully happy, was when we lived in Ana's house. Paula and I and the babies shared one room with Delila and her son, and my mother-in-law and her husband. We got along well together. It was the only time I can say I felt like a man, in the sense that I fulfilled my duties at home. On more than one Sunday, I stayed home and painted the table, or the chairs, and saw that my wife was comfortable.

When Alanes suffered from earaches and couldn't sleep I cured him, the way my mother had cured me. I made a paper cone and put the point in his ear. Then I lit the paper with a match and let it burn as long as he could stand it. I did this two or three times, until the *aire* left his ear and he was able to sleep.

At that time, I did what I had always wanted to do on Sundays. I took my wife and children first to the market to buy *tortillas*, cheese, avocados and cooked pork and then to the park to eat our *tacos*. I was working again and giving my wife sixty *pesos* a week for expenses, although I was making one hundred and fifty. The rest I kept for going out with Graciela. Life was pleasant for me. I had the love of my wife and of Graciela; I needed both of them to be happy.

Ana's house was in a *colonia* far from the center. Few people lived there at that time, and it was frightening for me to go home at two or three in the morning. There were lots of assaults and robberies, and in the morning they'd often find dead bodies in the river or in some field. But scared or not, I'd still get home very late every night.

A year later, Ana needed the room for some relative, and asked us to move. So Delila and her mother found a place for themselves and Paula and I again lived alone. Paula found a room with an outside entrance in the same section, because rents were low there. I was earning less and we were not eating well. Our fourth child, Conchita, was born soon after we moved in.

Graciela was working and would never accept money or anything from me. She said her conscience hurt when I spent the money my children needed. We'd go to a restaurant for supper, and instead of being like other women and ordering a good meal, she'd just ask for coffee and milk. I got sore on account of this, but she always said, "No, I'm not hungry." If I wanted to buy her a skirt or some little thing, she always said she didn't need one. Why, I even bought two pairs of pants for her son, but I had to work hard to make her accept them.

Graciela told me, one day, that a certain *Señor* Rodolfo kept coming to her house and that her mother was trying to get her to hook up with this man. "What shall I do, Manuel?"

"*Mi vida*, what do you want me to say? What can I tell you? Unfortunately, you have to solve this problem alone." Then she disappeared from the café for three days. I kept going there, as I always did. On the fourth day she returned. I was very angry but pretended to be calm.

All evening she busied herself with little things and didn't come back to sit with me. I was convinced that something special was up. When the café closed I said, "You're hiding something, and you're going to come clean right now." I grabbed her arm and took her to a hotel.

In the room, I said, "Look, *mi vida*, I want you to understand completely my love for you. For me you are God on earth, and therefore you have an obligation to be frank with me. Tell me what's come between you and me. I love you more than anything else and I have faith in you. I know you didn't do anything wrong. Tell me, but be frank about it." Well, that's the way I kept talking to her for a long time.

Graciela was sitting on the edge of the bed. She lifted her head and said, "I'm going to get married."

I felt as if I were hit by an electric shock; everything turned black all around me. She burst into tears. "I swear to you by the life of my child, which is the most sacred thing I have in the world, that the only one I love is you. I know I'm going to suffer, but give me a chance to find a future for my son. You have your wife, unfortunately, you have your wife. Let me live, Manuel, don't stop me."

I felt a terrible sorrow inside me. I understood that she was absolutely right. She said, "Answer me, say something, strike me, beat me, but don't remain silent," and she fell to her knees and put her arms around my legs, crying bitterly.

"Graciela, you know something, get out of here . . . but get out of here right now, while I have the strength to see you go. Because I swear to you if you don't, later I won't be able to let you go. You are absolutely right, you have a right to be happy, and all you've had with me is suffering, beatings at home and the contempt of people for keeping company with a good-for-nothing like myself. Get out of here, Graciela."

"No, Manuel, don't chase me out; I don't want to leave you this way, Manuel, for the love of God. Look, even though this is the last night we'll spend together in our whole lives, Manuel, I want to say good-bye to you in a different way."

She didn't want to leave, so we spent the night together. In the morning she said, "I'm not getting married. I won't marry anybody. I was going to do it for my mother because I don't want to hurt her, but I don't care about my mother, I don't care about anything in the world, you're the one I love. I'm not marrying anybody." So that's the way it stood.

After that, I went to visit Graciela's mother. I had always had the power to persuade people, at least those in my class, and that is why they called me "Golden Beak." It must be true, because I was able to convince Graciela's mother to accept me. I told her, "Look, Soledad, I can control everything in life but my feeling for your daughter. I have the blindest passion for her and she is the most beautiful thing in my life. I am poor and cannot offer her anything, but do not deprive me of her company. True, our situation is ambiguous, but I swear that your daughter is and will be the only great love of my life." The *señora* was very sentimental, she even cried, and I won her over to my side.

It was at about that time that my wife told me she was not well. She had not yet lost weight and I swear that I never believed she was seriously ill. I told her to go to Public Health and see what the doctors thought. That night she said they wanted to hospitalize her, because they didn't know what was wrong. But she didn't want to go because she was afraid of hospitals. Besides, she was nursing Conchita and had no one to take care of the children.

I didn't pay much attention to her. All I could think about was the problem I had with the two women. I went about in a state of terrible confusion, like a crazy person. I didn't notice that Paula was getting thin, that she urinated a great deal and was thirsty all the time. She never told me that her health was getting worse.

One day my father came to visit us. He had become fond of Paula, as if she were his own daughter. He liked her more than me. He realized that she was self-sacrificing, hard-working and clean. She never complained about anything. When he saw her, he said, "Listen, child, what's wrong with you?" He insisted that she go back to his house so he could take her to a doctor.

I was so blind, so stupid, so unobserving that I hadn't seen how ill she was. I thought it was something simple, like a cold. I said to her, "Old girl, get well; you must get well. We must go to Chalma this year."

"Yes," she said, "I'm going to get well." She made a vow to walk there on her knees if she recovered. But to my mother-in-law she said, "*Mamá*, I know if I go to my father-in-law's house and lie down, I won't get up. Please take care of my children."

She was so anxious to spare me pain that she told me she was going to get well. She had a feeling she was going to die and kept it from me, a good-for-nothing who didn't deserve to have anybody care about him.

She went to my father's house and that night I moved our furniture to my mother-in-law's. I saw her in the morning: "*Mi vida*, here I am, but I've got to leave for work."

"Fine," she said, "and may God bless you."

When I got back from work in the evening, my father met me at the door. "Come in, you good-for-nothing, you god-damned son-of-a-bitch, see what you've done, *pinche cabrón*, you're the one who's responsible. It's your fault if she dies." I don't know why but I had a feeling it was the truth. While he was talking to me I couldn't look at him.

Paula heard him bawling me out. She looked at me with eyes full of love . . . and he said that in front of her! My answer? Nothing! I wanted to shout that he was wrong but, as always, I swallowed my words, because he was my father, no? But that time, more than others, I felt mortified.

I got down on my knees by the bed. "Here I am, old girl." She put out her hand and held me. I can still feel her fingers. She caressed

my head and pulled at my ear. She smiled at me, then she lay there
as if she were sleeping.

The baby began to cry, and I was very much upset because she
woke up Paula, who then had to nurse her. In those days, when I
saw how ill my wife was, I had an aversion toward the baby. It
seemed to me as she nursed at the nipple, that she was sucking away
Paula's life. And when she cried at night, disturbing my wife, it
made me angry. I felt this rancor toward my youngest child for a
long time.

The next day Paula was worse and when I came back from work,
my father again greeted me with, "*Hijo de la chingada!* Son-of-a-bitch!
You see, you didn't give her enough to eat. Why do you bastards
marry if you cannot see to things. Now what? If this woman dies, what
will you do with your children?" I wanted to hold my ears and tell
him, for the first time in my life, "Shut up! Shut up!"

Someone, Delila I believe, sent for a priest to give Paula the last
rites. Seeing him there scared me, and I said, "Father, I want to
marry this woman." He turned to look at me.

"Hmmm, now that she is dying you want to marry her. And you
had all those years to do it!" He didn't marry us! I was going to pay
him . . . they usually ask if you have money to pay before they
come . . . but I didn't, because he had refused to marry Shorty and
me. He went out angry. But I was angry too. He was a servant of
God; if God saw one of his children . . . no matter who . . . suffering,
he wouldn't go and give him another blow, the way that priest did
to me.

After that, my father told me to run for the doctor because Paula
was failing. "Yes, *papá*," and I ran, forgetting to take bus fare with
me. It was past midnight and I hurried all the way to Rosario Street
on foot. Dr. Ramón lived in the same house as Lupita. Antonia greeted
me and told me that the doctor had been drinking. She went upstairs to see him, because I was so tired, and soon came down with a
prescription.

"He said to inject this immediately."

I had to walk back to the Casa Grande. I had been on my feet all
day at the shop, and they swelled up on me. When I got to the house,
my father gave me money for the medicine and I had to walk again,
looking for a drugstore that was open, "*de turno.*" After that, back
at the Casa Grande, I began knocking on doors to find someone to

give the injection. It was about 4:30 A.M. and no one opened his door.

At five o'clock Paula was in a coma, and I desperately went to try again. This time a woman woke up and agreed to give the injection. Damn her for waking up, damn her for giving the injection! I have always cursed that moment, but now I believe my wife's time had come, that possibly it was her turn to die, because a little while . . . a few minutes . . . after the injection, Antonia came running yelling, "Don't give the injection! Don't give it or she'll die!"

My wife began to move her arms frantically. We could see her heart palpitating hard. Then the doctor came running in. "Did they give the injection?" He told us that the medicine had to be mixed with blood first, or it would bring on a heart attack. Then, what he did, was to take blood from my brother (he had the universal type) and inject it into her. She began to move, then, little by little, she opened her eyes. And then she died. She died.

"*Papá*, she's dead, my wife is dead!" I shouted with desperation, with rage, with all the anxiety of life. He ran in and embraced her and cried. I banged my head against the wall, I tried to break it with my hands. And I shouted with all my soul, "It isn't possible! There is no God! God cannot exist!" It pains me now, but that is what I blasphemed. I had so much faith that she would get better! Not for a moment did I believe that she would die. I remembered that God had said faith can do anything. So when she died, I blasphemed.

I believe that the good-for-nothing, worthless doctor killed her. The bum was dead drunk, and without seeing the patient, he prescribed the medicine. A few days before he had analyzed her urine and said she had diabetes. We had called in Dr. Valdés, a high-priced doctor, who said it was not diabetes. But seeing how ill she was, he washed his hands of the case. Later the doctor told me she was intoxicated, or perhaps had tuberculosis of the stomach. My father latched on to that to say that I had killed her, I had starved her to death.

It is true that I didn't spend enough time with my wife and children. I should have come home early every day. Yes, I neglected her, but I swear that never, never did I leave my wife without money for food. I could have given her more, but she had at least enough to eat. It was the medicine that killed her!

Consuelo says that I didn't love Paula, that I never showed her affection. But it is that I followed my father's school, because even when he was living happily with Elena he never permitted himself to show affection for her in our presence. I was the same way with Shorty. The only time I loved her up was in bed, in the dark. In front of my father and brother and sisters, I was tyrannical with her. I was very strict in my way of speaking, but she must have felt affection on my part because she continued to love me all those years.

My father kept throwing it into my face that it was my fault . . . that I wasn't man enough . . . that I had neglected her . . . that I didn't take her to a doctor in time. He lowered me to the level of assassin. I wanted to shout, "Isn't my suffering enough? I lost part of my life, part of my heart has left me! It isn't true, what you are saying." But he said it in anger. Right or wrong, he was my father and had worked to support me and, at one time, had had illusions of love for me. So I wasn't able to answer him, though I knew he was lying. He was my father. As far as I am concerned, my father can do anything with me he wishes. Even if he tried to kill me, I wouldn't defend myself.

I kept my wife laid out two days . . . a day and a half . . . I don't know how long I kept her. When I saw her lying cold and stiff, I wanted to die. I even grabbed a knife to kill myself, but my son came in and asked me for five *centavos*. I burst out crying and thought, "How can I kill myself? My poor children!" I was going crazy, so crazy that I didn't even know how much the funeral cost. My friend Alberto and my father, took care of everything. Lots of people came to the wake . . . they came from the cafés Paula had worked in, from the cafés I ate in, from the market, from the *vecindad*. I wanted to tell them all to go away and leave me alone with the corpse.

She was buried in the Dolores cemetery, in the same grave as my mother and cousin, for after seven years they remove the bones and bury someone else on that spot. I have a horror of funerals. They say that just before the coffin is lowered, the corpse breaks out in goose pimples, because it is aware that it is about to be buried. The coffin gets heavier and heavier, because the body doesn't want to be buried. That is what happened to Paula's coffin, even though she had lost so much weight and was all bones.

I hope that when my turn comes, when I get the final kick from "*el coco*," that they leave me on top of a hill, in the open air, or that they wrap me up like a mummy the way the Pharaohs did, or at least, that a surgeon removes my brain, so that I won't suffer in my grave.

I don't know why, but I have a horror of being buried. I'd prefer to be devoured by coyotes on a hill, than by worms under the earth. Yes, I am more afraid of worms than of wild animals.

I've never gone to the cemetery since. I don't go because I believe that my wife will feel my presence and that instead of bringing her peace, I will bring her torment. She would get restless in her grave because she had loved me so. Feeling my presence, she would want to get out to speak to me, to embrace me, and she wouldn't be able to.

I believe that crying over the dead is sheer hypocricy, because I noticed that I cried a lot for Paula, showing, after her death,. the love I should have shown while she was alive. It is not love that makes a person cry like that, but a feeling of guilt. That is why I say I will never go to the cemetery again, not until my own funeral.

The day I buried my wife, in the midst of my despair, in the middle of my great sorrow, I thought, "I still have Graciela. I still have her." I clung to the thought like a drowning man to a raft. But when Graciela heard about Paula's death, the deep remorse and the whole combination of passions she felt, made her do the last thing she should have done. The day I buried Shorty, Graciela went off with *Señor* Rodolfo, the man her mother had always been trying to get her to live with. She loved me with all her soul, she adored me, right? But she wanted to punish herself, and her first reaction was to go off with him, a man she didn't love.

So I lost both of them at one stroke, the mother of my children and the love of my life. Graciela should have waited, if only to console me. We should have helped each other, because in a way we were both to blame.

After that I walked the streets. I was surrounded by people, but I felt myself completely alone. Nobody cared for me, nobody noticed my sorrow. I felt I was the only one who was suffering, and as the time passed, as the days went by, I hoped to stop feeling the emptiness my wife left at home. But it got worse and worse and worse. I loved my wife even more after she was dead, just as my father loved my mother more. I believe my life is a repetition of my father's, except that he took care of his four children, and I didn't.

For three days and nights, I stood on the corner where Graciela lived, waiting for her to come out. I didn't eat or sleep or anything. I just stood there. I was hoping she'd come out so I could kill her, because I felt she had betrayed what was most sacred to us.

When Alberto saw the state I was in, he said, "*Compadre*, listen, I think we'd better get out of here. You're going to end up bad. We'd better go be *braceros*. Let's go to work across the border." He kept talking that way until he convinced me.

I just stopped by the house to ask my father for his blessing, and to put on an extra pair of overalls and my new windbreaker. At first, my father didn't want me to go, but he finally gave me his blessing. We went to say good-bye to my brother-in-law and *compadre* Faustino, and the first thing we knew, he latched on to us and came along. I said, "Okay, then, here go the three of us."

I had eight *pesos* in my pocket when we set out for California.

Roberto

I JOINED THE ARMY BECAUSE I ALWAYS LIKED GUNS, AND I HAD A YEN
for adventure, or at least for seeing new places, right? Well, when
this fellow Truman came here, on March 3, 1947, to meet with
the President of Mexico, I went to see the great man arrive. It
was the first time in history, if I'm not mistaken, that a president of
the United States had come to visit our country. So a lot of people
went to the airport to see him, and I went too.

I was standing in the front row, right opposite the reviewing stand,
by the Air Force headquarters, and they had a sign there which
said, "Join the Air Force." So just like that, without giving it a second
thought, I signed up.

I was still very much of a child, sixteen at the most, and very short,
so the first thing the captain said was "Kid, you have to get permission from your parents."

"Sure thing, I've already got it." I was lying, because I didn't even
know myself I was going to enlist, see? Well, at any rate I passed all
the tests and signed a contract with the Mexican army for three years.

When I went home I told Manuel, "You know what, brother? I've
joined the army. I'm a soldier now."

"What'd you go and do that for? You're crazier than a she-goat."

"Sure, man, I've joined up; you'll see me in my uniform very soon,
and you'll be jealous." Well, he didn't believe me because I'd never
before taken such a drastic step.

I didn't tell my father a thing until I got my uniform. That day I
went back to town and I barely got through the front gate of the
Casa Grande when the fellows started saying, "Well, well, well, look
what the Blackout is wearing!"

"How do you like it, fellows?"

"How did you get in? and in the Air Force at that? Are you going to be a pilot? Are you a cadet, or what?"

"No, I'm just in the Air Force, that's all," and I wouldn't tell them any more, just to make them sore. When my good friend Daniel Ramírez saw my uniform, he wanted to enlist. I didn't urge him because his brothers were tough guys and might get sore at me, but I finally promised to take him with me to join up.

In the evening I didn't have to tell my father a thing because he saw my uniform.

"So now what have you done?"

"Nothing, *papá*, I've joined the army."

"But how and when and who gave you permission?"

"Well, a few days ago."

He stood there looking at me, then he said, "Well, let's see how this turns out. Behave yourself like a gentleman, be honest and work hard, and if you do this you'll get along all right." This was the advice he always gave me.

Three months went by and we trained every single day. I slept at home and went to the military airfield each morning at six for roll-call and training till five in the afternoon, when we were free. One morning we were lined up at reveille, when Captain Madero said, "Anybody who wants to volunteer to go to Guadalajara, step forward."

We no sooner heard the word "Guadalajara," which meant traveling, when all of us, there were about forty or fifty of us recruits, stepped forward. But when the captain explained the conditions, only six stuck it out; among them me and my friend Daniel.

They gave us leave at six-thirty in the evening so I went to say good-bye to my family. My father was reading when I went in. I stayed a while, then said, "*Papá*, I'm going to leave." He didn't answer me and I waited. Finally he raised his eyes and saw me.

"Fine, what time are you leaving?"

"Well, I'm going to Guadalajara."

"What do you mean, Guadalajara?" Then he really took a good look at me, understand? When he heard the news he was surprised.

I said, "Yes, they're sending us to Guadalajara; I've got to go." It wasn't true, because I had volunteered. Well, my father cried and embraced me like he rarely did, and well, I felt as if I were in heaven. I don't know what it's like in heaven but that's the way I

felt. When my father talks to me like that and embraces me, I sort
of choke up and tears of joy come to my eyes. And he even gave me
fifty *pesos*.

He said, "Take this; buy yourself something on the road."

"Sure, *papá*, thanks. Well, I'm going. Give me your blessing." So
my father gave me his blessing and I said good-bye to my brother and
my sisters.

That evening I had a date with a girl named Elvira, who had been
tipped off in advance that I was going to ask her to be my *novia*. I
knew she would say yes, because Daniel's *novia*, Lola, who later
became his wife, had arranged the whole thing. I had never seen
Elvira before, understand? And when she came, I didn't care much
for her but I felt obliged to ask her to be my girl friend. We kissed
right off, there in front of Lola and Daniel. Then we sat on the grass
and I put my head on her lap. I thought I'd better make hay while
the sun shines and show that girl I know what to do. I may be ugly
but I'm not a dope! That was all that happened and we left for
Guadalajara the same night.

We had all been paid off that day, so everyone bought something
for the road. One fellow bought a bottle of Bacardi, another some
tequila. Most of the fellows liked to drink. As for me, being somewhat of a kid and innocent, I bought a can of Nestlé's milk, a loaf of
Bimbo bread and a few peaches. I drank milk until it came out of my
ears and I invited the fellows to have some. They offered me what
they had too, but I said, "No, fellows, my stomach is not in good shape
and I'm not drinking now." By the time we got to Guadalajara, most
of the fellows were half-stewed.

The second lieutenant, who was in charge, became confused and
put us on the wrong bus from Guadalajara to the airfield to which we
had been assigned. So we had to hike twelve kilometers on a dirt
road. We arrived worn out and covered with dust. We were well
received by the captain and all the ranchers there, for the barracks
were actually on an *hacienda*. They let us rest a week, then we got
our assignments; in the hangar, on the airfield or in the groves.

I was assigned to guard the fields, so the ranchers wouldn't steal
the crops. The major was pretty mean to us fellows working in the
garden. He wouldn't let us pick any fruit from the trees; we could
eat only the stuff that fell to the ground. That's how I got malaria.
You wouldn't expect it in that temperate climate but still I got it,

because I ate oranges which lay on the ground, in the sun, for several days, see? We ate a lot of fruit like that, then drank it down with water.

The first few weeks at the camp I was sick with melancholy, thinking about Antonia. I didn't eat or sleep. I did my duties mechanically. I would borrow a horse and go off into the mountains alone . . . thinking of nothing else but my half-sister. Little by little, I got over it.

It was there in Guadalajara that I got roaring drunk for the first time. We were celebrating Army Day and a corporal and I were sent to Jalisco to buy *tequila.* When we reached the distillery the fellows working there called me over.

"Hey, soldier, come here. Look, wouldn't you like to have a little horn?"

"What's that?"

"Well, it's a goat's horn filled with *tequila.*"

"No, I can't right now. I'm on an errand and can't drink."

"Man alive, one little horn won't hurt you."

Well, they insisted and I sat down to drink. The *tequila* was warm, right from the still, and tasted nice and sweet. I had three altogether. When the corporal finished buying the *tequila,* he said, "O.K., Private Roberto, let's go."

When I stood up I was so dizzy I almost fell. Outside, the fresh air felt like a punch right in the face. Imagine, the first time in my life I took a drink and they played the dirty trick of giving me warm *tequila!* My corporal said, "Young fellow, now look what you've gone and done."

"Please excuse me, Corporal, but what happened is they gave me three little horns to drink and I didn't know what was in it."

So there I was, making a complete fool of myself because the liquor was beginning to have a terrific effect on me. The driver wouldn't let me on the bus. I don't know whether they like soldiers or hate them in that part of the country, but what I do know is they have lots of respect for them. So when the corporal insisted, I was allowed on, but instead of riding inside the bus I had to climb on top and sit in the baggage rack, to sober up a bit. They put me up there like a lousy piece of baggage. The corporal went along with me to take care of me, and I was really stewed, singing, "Hurrah for Jalisco," like I was a native of those parts.

We got off the bus and had to walk to the airfield. Well, I really kicked up the dust that time because I kept zigzagging from one side of the road to the other. I was stewed good and proper. When we got back I said to myself, "I'll never take another drop." Well I never told a bigger lie in my whole life.

When we got back, the festivities were in full swing. The ranchers had roasted a couple of young bulls, a calf, some pigs and turkeys. It was a big party, with lots of soldiers and people from the village. There was a rodeo, horse racing, and a little of everything. When we arrived, everybody said, "Sit down, Corporal, and you, too, Roberto," and they offered us more drinks. Well, I just gulped *tequila* by the glass and bucket. They called the drink *"changuirongos"—tequila* mixed with soda pop, any flavor you like, and with ice and fresh limes, and they have a kick like a mule.

That was the first time I felt my life was in danger. There was a fellow there, a private first-class, whose name was Raúl, only we called him the Gorilla. He and another fellow, Cascos, were drunk and were dancing and having a good time. I don't know what happened but for some reason the Gorilla got sore at me. So he says to me, just like this: "Come here, Private Roberto."

"Sure, Corporal." Because he was a private first-class, he was like a corporal, and a corporal was considered like a sergeant, and so on up the ranks.

So I said to him, "What can I do for you, Corporal?"

He said, "You know what? You can go and fuck your mother."

Words like those usually start a fight here in Mexico, but I said only, "What's wrong, Corporal? Has the liquor gone to your head so soon?"

"Not at all, I'm not drunk," he says, "I'm cold sober."

I thought to myself, "This looks bad." So I said, "All right, if you say so, it's all right with me, and we'll let it go at that."

"Oh, you will? Well, I want you to go ahead and say something to me, because I'm going to knock the shit out of you. I just don't like you, that's all, so we're going to have us a scrap."

"Well, I can't fight with you, you're my superior." By this time he pulled the bayonet out of his rifle—he had sharpened it up to a fine point—and went at me. Just then the second lieutenant came by and slugged him with the butt of his pistol, and quieted him down. After that I carried around a bit of a grudge against this fellow.

The Gorilla became gentle when he was doped up with marijuana and he'd start talking about philosophy, literature and theology. Well, stuff I didn't know anything about, so I didn't understand what he said. I'd just stand there listening. Why, even the second lieutenant himself, and the major would listen to him. Of course, the major was an educated man and could answer the questions the Gorilla put to him. They had a regular session together and, hell, this made quite an impression on me. It was one of the pleasant moments I had in the service.

Later, he, Cascos and I became good friends, but that god-damned Gorilla kept giving me trouble. He made me grow marijuana out there in the garden because he and Cascos both liked to smoke it. I grew the weed for the simple reason that the Gorilla ordered me to. Of course, it wasn't allowed, but the army doesn't go around watching the fellows.

They planted the marijuana out of sight in the back section of the garden, about five hundred meters from the barracks. The seeds came in the package with the marijuana, and it is amazing how the plants grow and spread. They taught me how to cultivate it and I had to keep the ground spaded and watered. I took care of the garden until it was harvested.

The fellows offered me marijuana many times, but I never accepted. They knew perfectly well that I didn't smoke the weed, yet, once when I asked them for a cigarette, they tricked me by giving me my favorite brand mixed with the drug. I took three puffs and got dizzy. My head felt hollow and I looked at everyone in a strange way. When I walked, I felt I was not on the ground but on something soft. My body floated and my nerves didn't obey me.

I felt a call of nature and went behind a cactus. When I tried to get up, I fell backwards and got full of thorns. It made me laugh to find myself in such a condition. I tried to spit and no saliva came out. The fellows were laughing at me . . . I wanted to take it out on them, but I was weak, my whole body felt loose. Then I fell asleep and missed my duty in the hangar. That smoke had such a terrible effect on me that I ended up in the hospital. I think that might have been how I developed malaria. I never smoked marijuana again.

I was almost court-martialed because Cascos, the Gorilla and I were caught in the marijuana plot and arrested. And you know what? I wasn't the least bit worried because I felt I wasn't to blame and that justice would be done. I would have been court-martialed along with the other two but Cascos saved me. This was the first and only time I got a square deal.

When the hoof-and-mouth disease came to Mexico, another important thing happened to me, perhaps the most important thing in my life. The disease was so bad they placed the whole territory around Guadalajara in quarantine. Not a chicken or an egg could come in or out and we had to kill the sick cattle. If two or three out of ten cattle were sick, we had to kill the whole herd to prevent the disease from spreading. For this reason the peasants hated us like poison.

The government paid the peasants for killing their cattle, but they weren't paid what the animals were worth. Suppose a team of oxen were worth two thousand *pesos;* they wouldn't even get fifteen hundred. The peasants were awfully mad about this and they took revenge on us soldiers because we were the ones who shot the animals. But we were just obeying orders, right?

One time Daniel Ramírez, Francisco, Crispín somebody, and I went out on horseback. There were four or five of us. We had gotten leave and they loaned us horses to go to Zapopan for soda pop or *tequila.* We had to be back for rollcall at 6:00 P.M.

Well, it was getting dark so we galloped along on our horses at a good pace and came to a grove of trees called Devil's Gully. As we went by, a fusillade broke out, but I mean a hot one—the first time in my life this had happened to me. They were shooting at us with 30-30 rifles and 7-millimeter Mausers. Anyway, we galloped out of range, but two of our boys fell. They wasted a bullet on me because it only scraped my leg. We couldn't see who was shooting; all we could see were the gun flashes, understand? We had to run for it.

Daniel and I went back for the boys who were shot. One of them was dead. He was well skinned, as they say in Veracruz. So we went to headquarters and made our report and the second lieutenant said, "Get your weapons and form a platoon." And though I was wounded, I asked the second lieutenant to let me go with him, but he said, "No, you have that taken care of."

"No, I tell you, Lieutenant, it's nothing, I'd like to go along with the rest of you. Just a little tourniquet and that's all that's necessary." He agreed and I went along with them. When we got there the attackers were gone, and we did a little exploring around. Four months later, we caught them.

Some of the ranchers had hundreds of heads of cattle, see? If any of the animals got sick, they took their cattle off their land at night and drove them up into the hills to keep them from getting killed. Well, once I was on night duty, from twelve midnight to six in the morning, and I had to walk over the whole airfield to see that no cattle were wandering around on the landing strips. This field was, without exaggeration, about three kilometers wide and four deep.

I was at one of the control points when I heard a noise, like the lowing of cattle, and a pounding of hooves. I went to report to the corporal but he had gone out to eat. I turned on a large searchlight for a moment and saw a hell of a cloud of dust. I ran toward it as fast as I could, yelling, "Halt! Who goes there?"

"It's me, soldier, don't shoot."

"How about stopping the cattle!"

"I can't, almost all the cattle have already moved out." There was really a tremendous herd of cattle.

"All right," I said, "I can't seize the cattle but I can detain you, so come along with me."

"Now look, soldier, don't."

"Well, where are you taking these cattle? Are you a rustler or are they yours, or what?" So he tells me they're his but I'm not going to believe him because if they were he wouldn't be out with them this time of the night.

He said, "No, really, look, they're mine but I have a couple of sick cattle on my ranch, and of course I'm going to kill them, but the others are healthy and I don't want them to be killed because the government doesn't pay what it should."

So we stood there discussing back and forth. Finally he offered me a hundred *pesos*.

"No, sir, I can't accept a single *centavo* of your hundred *pesos*. If you want to give them away, you can pay a fine with them and they'll let you out of jail."

"Well, I'll give you three hundred."

"No, sir." So at last he got up to five hundred. It was the first time in my life that I had such a big sum of money. Well, that was over, the cattle had gone and so had the rancher and I went back to the field post.

Then the corporal arrived with a buck private.

"What's new soldier?"

"Well, everything is quiet corporal."

"What do you mean? Didn't you come here a little while ago looking for me?"

"Well, yes, I was going to report some cattle. I tried to stop them but some one scared them off."

"Don't give me any of that stuff. Come over here."

Well, the corporal was no fool, right? After all, he'd been in the army a long time and knew all the angles, so how was I going to trick him? He took me aside and said, "Now tell me what it's about." Well, I understood there was no point in my telling him lies.

"Well, you see, Corporal, this is what happened: a guy was moving his cattle. I let them go."

"What do you mean you let them go? Don't you know what your orders are?"

I said, "Sure, Corporal, but he gave me a more sensible order. He gave me a hundred *pesos*."

"Don't screw me," he says. "What do you mean, a hundred *pesos*? You may be just an innocent babe but you're not going to risk a court-martial for a hundred *pesos*."

So I said to him, "No, you're right; to be frank with you, he gave me two hundred *pesos*." Well, he now sort of half believed me, but he kept on lecturing me and bawling me out because I failed in my duty. Finally he said to me, "All right; give me a hundred *pesos* and fifty to this fellow and mum's the word between you and me."

I say this was the most important event in my life because if I hadn't let that rancher go and hadn't accepted the money, I wouldn't have turned into the bad egg I became. This sort of thing happened a couple of times more. The third time they gave me two thousand *pesos*. But I didn't know how to take advantage of all this money. It was for doing something bad, so I should have at least tried to be careful and cover up a bit, and invest the money wisely. Instead, I blew it all. I wasted it on my friends, on running around with women and on drinking. I got into the habit of throwing away my money.

I liked it a lot in the army. I became a corporal, but I didn't stay out my full time. I don't know why, but I rub people the wrong way, maybe on account of my dark complexion or because I have bad blood. Anyhow, this corporal had it in for me, he really did. Five or six times he tried to have me arrested for no reason at all. I would immediately put in a request to speak to the major. We both appeared before him, and the corporal gave his side of the case and I gave mine. The major saw I was getting a raw deal, and tore up the notice. "Go back to your detail," he told me. The corporal could never get me arrested and always had it in for me.

Well, it happened that we were getting training in hand-to-hand combat, and it was my hard luck to have this corporal as my partner. We were simulating combat, but this fellow wasn't simulating at all. He said, "On guard!" I put myself on guard, grabbed my rifle and got ready to parry his thrusts; he was just supposed to go through the motions, right?

But he didn't do it that way. At first he made two or three simulated thrusts, then he aimed a real "*fondazo*" at me. Well, it was lucky we had already had some bayonet drill and I was able to deflect his thrust to the left with my rifle; I parried it so his shoulder came up against my chest, and we stood like that.

I said to him, "What happened, Corporal? You went too far that time."

"You son-of-a-whore, you're not watching! Step lively or I'll kill you."

Well, when I heard him swear at me I grabbed my rifle and gave him a half-swing, socking him on the chin with my rifle butt. I really wanted to kill him right then and there. When I hit him he spun around, because I gave him such a terrific whack. I wanted to stick the bayonet in his back, but by the grace of God I was able to hold back. I came to my senses right off. If I'd stuck the bayonet in the corporal, I'd have pinned him like a butterfly. But all I did was to give him a light poke in his rear end.

The second lieutenant saw this and right away blew the whistle. This was the signal to stop, see? Everybody stops right where he is, without moving. The second lieutenant came up to me and said, "What did you do, you damned fool?"

"You see, Lieutenant, he made me do it. If I didn't do this to him, he would have done it to me, and a lot worse."

He said, "Shut up! You don't even seem to know what you've got yourself in for; anyway, you're in real trouble. Put down your gear!" I took off my belt and helmet and put my rifle on the ground. I thought, "Well, now, *Negro*, you're going to die in jail."

What a fuss they made over the corporal! They called out the medical corps. They bandaged up his wound. It actually wasn't anything serious, just a scratch.

I went along with the second lieutenant. He said, "Look, my boy.

if I hold you now and you go to trial, you'll get at least eight or ten years in jail, on account of insubordination and the thing you've just done."

So I said to him, "All right, Lieutenant, I'm ready to take my punishment, which I deserve, but I also ask that I be allowed to tell my story."

"No matter what you say, you were insubordinate to an officer. You get the hell out of here as fast as you can." Then he stuck his hand in his jacket, took out twenty *pesos*, and gave it to me. "Scram, and may God be with you, because I haven't got the heart to . . ." According to the rules, he was supposed to turn me in, to arrest me right then and there. Only God knows if he got away with it. This was such a tremendous thing he did for me that I'll never be able to thank him enough, because I'd still be in jail right now.

So I left the army without papers or anything, and I lacked five months to complete my three-year enlistment. The army is not that happy-go-lucky, because you sign a contract and you can't get out before you finish your three years. So I didn't have the right to leave the way I did. It's a crime, and I was a fugitive. I felt pretty bad about getting out this way, understand? because I wanted to have an honorable discharge.

In Guadalajara I had a *novia* who really loved me, and when I deserted, I went to say good-bye to her. I shouldn't have done it, because she insisted I take her with me. It didn't matter to her how we would live, all she wanted was to be with me. At first I told her I was being transferred to Mexico City, but when she kept on insisting, I had to tell her that I was going to desert and couldn't offer her any kind of a future at all. Despite this, she said to me, "I don't care, I want to be with you." But of course I had to leave her. My love life has been a failure, except for her. She really loved me.

Manuel and his wife, Paula, may she rest in peace, were living in the Casa Grande with my sisters when I got back. My father was staying at Lupita's house because Antonia was still not well. I went to see her on a few occasions, but then my *papá* told me not to bother her any more. He wanted to know what business I had there and why I should be hanging around the house making a nuisance of myself. I found out Lupita had complained that I kept looking at her daughters in a peculiar way. I was offended and I rarely went after that.

Sometimes I borrowed a bicycle and rode over to a bar near Lupita's house. I would sip beer and peek out of the door to see if Antonia had gone to buy *tortillas* or bread. I knew what time she usually came out and just seeing her was a consolation. Once, I was riding by on my bicycle when she came out of the *vecindad* to get some matches. I had cigarettes and two boxes of matches in my pocket, but I couldn't think of any better pretext to get close to her than to go into the same shop for cigarettes.

I rode in the wrong direction on a one-way street and when I came up to her I swerved the wheel and made an eagle stop. She was coming out of the shop and she kept looking at me out of the corner of her eye. I stared right at her and went in for my cigarettes. Then I went back to the bar just so she could see me. I ordered another beer and there I stayed.

She got me into trouble with my father by lying about me. She said I tried to run her down with my bike and that all I did was hang around spying on her. I didn't see her much after that, until she moved back to the Casa Grande.

Meanwhile I got to know my sister-in-law Paula better. I had met Paula when my brother first presented her to my father. That was when my father warned Paula that my brother was a canaille, a bum, a man without balls . . . he was so hard on Manuel that even I felt small listening. Paula felt bad about it and thought my father's character was too strong. But by the time little Mariquita was born, Paula and my father were joking together.

I was happy when I learned I was going to become an uncle and when Mariquita was born with white skin and blue eyes, what pleasure I felt! I said, "At least one person in the family will have blue eyes." My *papá* joked about it, "Listen, Paula," he said, "might there have been a little cheating in this matter?" I, too, am sorry to say, teased my sister-in-law by saying that a blue-eyed baby in our family must be contraband. Poor Paula! She turned red, green, yellow and all colors. But in a short while Mariquita's eyes turned as brown as Manuel's.

Anyway, my *papá* took on the responsibility of Paula and the babies that were born one after another. My brother began to fail in his work and didn't give his wife expense money. When I had money I gave it to Paula for medicines or shoes for the children. I gave her "Sunday money" every week, and it didn't bother me at all to do it. My brother kept on playing cards and dominoes and became less and less responsi-

ble. I gambled too (though I never played with Manuel because I felt
we were competing), but then I had no one depending on me.

I never understood why my brother had two women at one time.
I once saw Manuel with his great love, Graciela, and I asked if she
was his sweetheart. "Yes," he said. "I mean no, she is just a friend."
"What do you mean, just a friend? Poor Paula! How you are deceiving her." I don't know if Paula ever found out, but I believe she
must have because there is always someone who runs to tell the wife
her husband is fooling around.

I was getting over my appendix operation when Manuel laid his
hand on Paula and beat her up. *Ay*, how that hurt me . . . I cried and
limped over to stop him, but he even hit me. And Paula was so good!
That woman cried for me when she learned I was going around fighting
with knives and razors and guns and when she saw me after I had
been stoned or kicked. She kept giving me advice and told me that I
could have a good future if I gave up being a tramp. She made me
promise to stop fighting, but that was impossible in my neighborhood.

I was still wearing my uniform and it gave me a bad reputation and
got me into fights. It was well known that the army was full of vice
and soldiers were not liked. On the second day I was home, I got into
a brawl when I went with Consuelo to buy bread. As it never failed,
there was a wise guy who passed a remark at my sister. I don't mind
them throwing compliments such as "Good-bye, good-looking," or,
"What a doll!" or, "What a pretty little body you have," or any reason-
ably decent thing, right? But when they say, "Good-bye, hot mama,
what a delicious little piece you are," or when they say to me, "How
goes it, brother-in-law?" I cannot overlook it.

So I threw a dirty look and insulted his mother and the attack began.
With the "look" you can say as much as a Huastecan swearing parrot
and it is one of the things that has gotten me into fights. Well, I was
a boxer in the army, but when I got home, they considered me a professional. I was so quick with my fists, they called me Attila. Then I
began to use a knife and wounded a few guys. If it was up to me, I
wouldn't fight at all, but I have to get even with all those damned
people.

I often got into trouble because of my sisters. As usual, I took charge
of them when I lived at home. Twice, I caught Marta in the street with
this guy Crispín and I had to punish her. She was still very young
and he didn't look good to me. He was older and more mature and I

knew the type. Consuelo also caused me a lot of headaches because of the way she danced and flirted.

One evening, Marta didn't come home and I looked everywhere for her, asking around discreetly if anyone had seen her. I felt desperate, thinking an accident had happened to her, when it suddenly occurred to me that she might have gone off with someone. I felt it was my fault for not having watched her better and I ran up and down all night looking. That night was pure martyrdom for me!

In the morning, I met her with Crispín. How furious I was to see that cursed character with his mocking face. I still cannot explain why I let him go without doing a thing to him. But I hit my sister because I understood that she was no longer a virgin. I told her that now she was a woman of the world, that she must get married and be respectful and faithful to her husband. She said they would marry, but they never did.

That miserable wretch! He was always jealous and gave my sister a rough time. He was even jealous of me! Why, once, when they had their apartment, I went to visit Marta and his sister came in. Marta and I were sitting on the bed and my sports shirt happened to be hanging loose outside of my trousers. I don't know what that woman told Crispín but she insinuated something that would have been pure infamy. I have done terrible things in my life, but she was degrading me to the level of a beast.

When I saw her again I said, "Look, *señora,* be grateful that we are in my sister's home and that you are a woman, because if you continue your insinuations I will have to bust you right where it hurts."

Then Crispín piped up, "Don't you speak to my sister that way!"

"You go frig your mother! And as for you, if you take it out on Marta, if you touch a hair on her head, you are a dead man, your days are numbered." That's what I said and I meant it from the heart.

I really couldn't stand the guy because he deceived my sister. It hurt me very much to see what had happened to her. If it were in my hands, and I'm going to sound like an irrational beast, I could kill him as easily as I am saying it, because he is not a man. I think the midwife made a mistake when she said he was a man.

When Antonia came to live at the Casa Grande I had more headaches. I was working as a varnisher at the time. I went in at seven o'clock and at ten they gave us a half-hour to go home to eat something. I liked that fine because it gave me a chance to check up on Antonia.

One day I came in and discreetly asked Enoé where Antonia was. Enoé said that my sister had gotten dressed up and had gone out. That made me very angry and at the same time I had a presentiment of something.

A few days before, I had persuaded Antonia to have her picture taken at a studio. I thought she might have gone to take out the photos, so I decided to walk over there. I grabbed a knife and stuck it into my belt, because the studio was located in a street where the flower of the underworld lived.

Sure enough, there was Antonia walking arm in arm with Otón, a boy I had seen her with before. The moment I saw her with her *novio,* my eyes clouded over and I felt completely blinded. My blood went down to my feet and my body got chilled. I felt very bad, but continued walking automatically until I caught up with them. Antonia pushed Otón away from her side and he looked plenty worried when he saw me. I had warned him the last time to keep away from my sister.

I had said, "Look, I know you're crooked. You are just like me and worse and I don't want you to go with her. She deserves someone better than you. I'm telling you nicely now, but the second time it won't be so nice, see?" I was sincere when I said that because I knew she could never be mine and I wanted someone better for her. I was right about Otón because now he is a first-class drug addict.

Antonia, who was also short-tempered, was furious with me. "What business is it of yours?" But she was smart enough to start for home when I told her to get going. Then I asked Otón if he was armed, because I was, and that he should get ready to defend himself. But he didn't want to fight.

"Wait, no, Roberto. Calm down and listen . . . your sister and I are *novios.* I spoke to her and she corresponded."

"Don't be a jerk, Otón," I said, "you grab at anyone . . . you've been around, and that's why I want you to leave her alone. Get on guard." And I opened my jacket to show him my knife.

"Look, I too am carrying something to fight with, but one shouldn't fight for a woman. It is not worth the trouble."

When I heard that, I punched him in the face. It made me mad to hear him say my sister was not worth the trouble. She was worth more than trouble! I wanted to fight with this guy, but he wouldn't, so I went home.

I scolded her and told her Otón was one of the worst . . . that he smoked marijuana and took morphine, that he robbed and was a vagabond and an adventurer. It wasn't true then, but, well, I was trying to discourage her. Then I said more than I wanted to say. "You are right, Tonia, it is none of my business. I see clearly that what I feel in my heart for you is impossible."

She must have realized my sentiments because she said, "Well, now you understand things better."

"Yes, now I see that nothing is possible for me here." I asked her to sign her photos for me and to forget what I had said. I put four pictures of her in my wallet.

That night I had such a feeling of desperation that I wanted to die. I thought Tonia would tell my father and I wanted to do away with myself. I put some strong medicine in a glass of water and planned to drink it. I wasn't afraid to die, but God illuminated my thoughts and I repented. I spilled out the medicine and broke the glass. The next day I walked around in a daze. Even the sun didn't warm me.

After I lost Antonia's love, because that was the way I understood it, I decided to ask Rufelia to be my *novia*. She knew how I felt about Tonia, because the day my sister moved back to Rosario Street, I cried bitterly. Rufelia came in and heard me wailing because Antonia was gone. She understood and told me not to cry, because after all, it was not a good thing. So I declared myself to Rufelia, and told her I said those things about Tonia only to attract Rufelia's attention. She didn't know what to think or say and asked me to give her time to answer.

She kept putting me off, but finally promised to tell me on Sunday. I was waiting impatiently at the gate of the Casa Grande, when Otón, Antonia's ex-*novio*, came along and said: "Come, Attila, come and play cards." Well, I was feeling very manly and I wanted to show him that I knew as much as he, so we sat down right there and started a game. Rufelia saw me and I think that was what influenced her to reject me.

She said I was a poor man, and what could I offer her anyway? Her *novios* gave her things and fulfilled their obligations, but it didn't look as though I could give her anything. It wasn't love she wanted, but money, I thought. It so happened that I had about a thousand *pesos* in my pocket because the day before, out at the race track, I had snatched a purse from a high-society lady with a fancy hairdo. I was tempted to show the money to Rufelia, but I thought that if she was so materialistic she was not for me.

Rufelia's family had been just like the rest of us when they had first moved into the Casa Grande. They were as poor as we and we were all good friends. More than once, Rufelia's mother came to borrow one or two or even ten *pesos* from us, and we did the same. But later, Rufelia's father managed to learn something about mechanics and quit his job as a driver's helper to take one servicing refrigerators. From then on, that family went up. Rufelia's brothers attended high school and her parents began to fix their home. First, it was a gas stove, then a dining set, a radio, a *"tele,"* a balcony for the boys to sleep on . . . until they became the Rockefellers of the courtyard.

As they went up economically, they stopped speaking to their neighbors. I don't say that just because I once did them favors they were obliged to speak to me, but I could not see why they had to insult and offend me, or ignore me completely. I couldn't explain why some people change so radically. It seemed like I was no longer good enough for them. No wonder Rufelia turned me down.

At about the time I was courting Rufelia, strange things were happening in the Casa Grande and I was blamed. Someone threw salt in the doorway of Rufelia's house, and then in Angélica Rivera's and a few others, and everyone said I was doing it to punish Rufelia for refusing me and to create discord in the *vecindad*. Of course, it was only talk, because I never did anything like that.

One morning Rufelia and her mother and the butcher woman surprised *Señora* Chole of No. 93 picking up salt and garlic from her doorway and rubbing it on the door of my house. They heard her saying, "You black son-of-a-whore," and, "You mother-fucking bastard, I hope your ass end rots," and other stuff like that. *Caray!* I still don't know why she did it. That family in No. 93 never spoke to anyone, and from the beginning I noticed that *Señora* Chole had something against me.

I never believed in witchcraft, even though I have been places where it is practiced to this day. And I never used love potions or any of that nonsense some suckers buy. Here in the capital, the boys say things about witches and potions, but they are only joking. In my gang, we don't believe it.

But I do know of some cases of people getting sick because someone had done them harm. My *papá*, for example, or a man I knew in Córdoba, whose wife made an idiot out of him by sticking pins in his photograph and burying it on their piece of land. He was a rough character, a man who had hair on his chest. He and I shot at each other one time, over something that came up between us. But later, he wouldn't eat or drink, and would just sit in his doorway. He never left his wife's side, until he went completely mad.

I knew another man who was dominated by his wife. She yelled at him and even hit him and it was well known that she had put him under a spell. How could you explain it any other way? When I was in Chiapas, they told me to be careful because, there, women do harm to a man by giving him "coconut milk" to drink. They wash the vagina when menstruating and use the water to make the man's coffee. Once he drinks it, they say he is completely under the woman's power.

When I heard that, I wouldn't take food or liquid in the house I was staying at, absolutely none, because there was a girl from Tehuantepec who was in love with me. They say that when a *Tehuana* wants a man, she does something to make him go to her, even if he is in China. As a matter of fact, they succeeded in putting the bug in my ear, and I went around with a piece of gold in my mouth to protect me.

When I wasn't working, I would usually go home to eat at about two o'clock. This time Enoé was in the house, washing clothes. I never like a servant to dish out my food, so I helped myself to rice, beans and stew. I sat down to eat and my attention was caught by the movement of Enoé's buttocks as she washed. I got up very quietly and bent down behind her to look up her dress. She noticed this. "*Ay!* you damned black one. Get out of here! *Vaya!*" and she threw water on me.

"What, wouldn't you like a dark little fellow like me? A bit ugly, yes, but with more luck than money!"

"*Ay,* go to hell, you!"

Later, I was lying on the bed, watching her iron. We started to talk and I don't know how we got to it, but she asked me for twenty *pesos*. I didn't have a *centavo* but I offered her ten, and she said, "Very well, we'll do it, but don't tell anyone, do you hear?"

"No, Enoé, don't worry." I was very excited because she had accepted me. She closed both doors and got ready, when she repented and made fun of me. She said, "How could you believe . . .? Well, you are just like your father. He too comes around touching me!"

When she said my father was after her, my desire for her turned to hate. Why hadn't she told me right away instead of leading me on? I wanted to die of shame . . . I was disgusted with myself, but really, I hadn't known . . . that imbecile of a woman never dared mention it to me again. As for my father, he was in a privileged position and I was not the one to judge him.

Once, when I was still out of work, I went to Chapultepec Park. All I had in my pocket was twenty *centavos*. It wasn't the first time I had no money on me, but it was my bad luck that a chance to swipe some money came up and I didn't want to let the chance go.

It happened there was a half-drunken fellow on the terrace of Chapultepec Castle. He was pretty wobbly and the bottom of his jacket was raised up so that his billfold was sticking out of his pants pocket, in full view. It would have been easy for me to leave him alone and just walk away. It shouldn't have made any difference to me that he would have been robbed by another person anyway, right? But the temptation was too great, I couldn't control myself, and without thinking twice, I lifted the billfold and went off. It contained five hundred *pesos* and for a fellow like myself, without a *centavo*, it was a lot.

I don't know what made me do it. It was not to get pleasure out of it, but ever since I was a kid I always had a yen for what belonged to someone else. I didn't steal to buy luxuries or to accumulate a pile; I wasted it all on a big drunk. I did it for excitement, and to have facts to back up my tales to the fellows.

I've never given my father hot money. For me my father was sacred and I just couldn't give him bad money. I have given him only what I earned honestly, although not as much as I should.

I admit openly that the first time I landed in the Penitentiary it was my own fault. I had had troubles before, but never anything like this. I was working in a place where they made fancy light fixtures. What happened was, we were celebrating the foreman's Saint's Day, and I went to the boss's shop with two other boys who worked there—Pedro Ríos, alias the Tiger, and Hermilio. We had a few beers and *pulques*, and were already a little wobbly when we left.

We got on a bus with only two or three passengers and we sat down in the back. I felt like smoking, like I always do when I drink; I'm like a chimney, I just smoke and smoke and smoke. Well, I asked the Tiger and Hermilio for a cigarette. They didn't have one, and I didn't mind getting up and asking those in the bus if they wouldn't do me a favor and sell me a cigarette. The first one said to me, "Look, I don't have any. If I did, I wouldn't sell you one, I'd give it to you."

"Thank you very much," and I left him. And that's the way it was,

I left and didn't say a thing, nor did I have any reason to insult him. When I got back to my friends, the Tiger said, "Those god-damned sons-of-whores." And I said, "Yes, they don't care if a fellow is dying. Let's get off here and buy some cigarettes."

But when we began swearing, a passenger got insulted and said to me, "Who are you swearing at, you bastard? After coming around like a bunch of deadbeats, you have the nerve to swear at us!"

"No, sir, I didn't swear at anybody at all. Actually I was just talking with my friends, but if you felt you were insulted then go ahead and feel insulted."

"No you don't, you son-of-a-whore," and he started toward me. When I saw him coming I tried to stand up, but he knocked me back on the seat with a punch. When he hit me in the face I got angry and hit him back. Hermilio and the Tiger tried to separate us, but the man became even more stubborn. So I knocked him down. His glasses smashed to smithereens and, it seems, I broke his nose.

Well, the bus stopped and all the other passengers got off. The driver got up and said, "O.K., you so-and-so's, the three of you ganging up on this man!" The driver's son was sitting right next to him. So he said to his boy, "Open up the tool box and hand me the gun in there."

Just hearing somebody mention a weapon when I'm in a fight makes me mad, awfully mad. I just go crazy. So I said to him, "Go ahead, you bloody son-of-a-whore! If you take out that thing I'll kill you right on the spot," and I pretended I was going to pull out a knife. I didn't have any, I just wanted to see what he'd do. A lot of them talk big but if you pull out a knife or pistol, they back up.

But he called my bluff and took us to the Police Station No. 5 and they locked us up. It was then about ten or eleven at night. The judge called us in, one at a time, to get our story. They took down our statements, but locked up Hermilio and me. I was glad the Tiger got out, but it seemed strange to me that they should only let him go free. We told him to notify our boss to come and pay the fine, but he went home to sleep.

The next day some people came over, with pencil and paper, shouting and asking whether anyone wanted a message taken to his house. If a person is arrested and doesn't have time to notify his family, these people do it, but they take advantage when they get to the house and ask for any amount they want. When our boss finally arrived at the Precinct, we were already going to be sent to El Carmen. It was impossible for him to pay the fine immediately and we ended up in the Penitentiary.

Never in my life had I been in jail . . . not even to visit a friend. They accused me of bodily injury, on account of the bloody nose, and property damage, on account of the glasses. That's why they sent Hermilio and me up for three days. Well, it was tough in prison. You have to be a real jailbird, a brave man, not to be cowed by that place. Every prisoner is fingerprinted and an information sheet on him is filled out. That's the first step; the second is when they search you for marijuana, cocaine, a knife or something like that. They make you take all your clothes off in the courtyard.

As soon as they shoved us in, they immediately began to rob us, beginning with the guards. You can't imagine the expressions of greed on their faces as they look you over. One of them shouted as we came in, "The lioness just gave birth!" which meant a new batch of suckers had arrived. Unfortunately, we had put on our best clothes for the party.

The guard told us to undress, he insisted that we had to be searched . . . that we were in a court of justice . . . justice! As we began to dress, one of them said, "Let's see that shirt." Then, "I like this undershirt. Hand it over."

"No, *amigo!*"

"Hand it over!"

And whether I was willing or not, they took my shirt and trousers, and gave me some old rags to put on.

The third step is when you go into the bull pen, where all those accused of a crime stay for seventy-two hours, until it is decided whether they have to serve a term or whether they can go free or out on bail.

The cells are small, three by two meters, steel walls and cement floors, a solid steel door with a little opening in it. The personnel there is all militarized, from the guards down to the last prisoner. Everyone here has some special rank. Military discipline is enforced and that is why they use the titles: majors, which is the highest rank, captains, and all the ranks there are in the army. They ask, "Are you going to pay for the *talacha?*" which means the cleanup, as there are brigades going around constantly, cleaning up. Either "you enter by the door," that is, you pay right away, or if you have no money, they say, "We can wait until some visitor comes to see you." If later you don't give the money, they make life very difficult for you.

If, from the beginning, you are not going to pay, you go right to the baths and they fumigate your clothes and make you go under the ice-cold water. After that, they put you in the steam-room. We went through it, but we didn't do the *talacha* after all as our families later paid ten *pesos* for us.

On the third day, they called us to the court to give us our cards as permanent prisoners. Hermilio wanted to throw himself over the railing to kill himself. I felt like doing the same thing but lacked the courage. I had to keep an eye on him constantly because if I didn't he would have thrown himself overboard.

We were plenty scared. I felt I was absolutely lost. I was not very religious but I had faith in the grace of God and the Virgin of Guadalupe. I vowed that if I got out, I would walk barefoot all the way from the "peni" to the Villa of Guadalupe; I promised to give away my shoes to one of the prisoners as a sacrifice. I also vowed to go to Chalma.

Well, at the very last minute, just before we were to go into the cell block, Consuelo arrived with some papers to sign. I didn't even read them, you know what I mean? She worked for lawyers and got them to take care of our case. At six o'clock, they set us free, provisionally, under bond. We had to sign in every week.

I gave away my shoes and went out barefoot. Hermilio's family was outside waiting for him. Nobody came for me, but that didn't matter. I walked all the way to the Villa, begging alms to give to the priest. I didn't collect much but it was a great satisfaction to turn it all in.

When I enter a church, I feel I'm carrying a heavy load, especially on my conscience. I always stay in the last row, just inside the door, and although it is crowded with worshipers, I feel alone with my thoughts and prayers. As far as I am concerned, only God and I are in the church. And when I leave, I feel relieved. Even my clothes weigh less. That's why if I don't go to Mass every week, I don't feel right.

Back home, I was ashamed to go out into the courtyard. The whole *vecindad* knew what had happened. I may have been a hero to some, but to most I was a disgrace. One evening, I stood outside our door for a breath of fresh air. *Señor* Teobaldo, the butcher who lived in No. 67, came by. He and all the other butchers and their wives were fighters and most of us kept out of their way. Teobaldo's brother-in-law, who lived in the third court, was a real criminal with a long prison record. One look from him and he made people's hair stand on end. He even frightened me!

But I wasn't scared of Teobaldo, although he fancied himself a scrapper. He had once shot at me and the boys with grapeshot, and whenever he was drunk he made a big scandal, kicking at doors and cursing. If anyone threw him a dirty look, that person was as good as dead.

The evening he passed by me, he was drunk.

"Good evening, *Negro*," he said.

"Good evening, *Señor* Teobaldo."

"What crooked thing are you doing now?"

"Nothing. Just taking some air."

"Fuck you! You have something crooked up your sleeve, but let me tell you, you bum, if you ever have anything to do with my family, or if you ever enter my house, you will die on the spot."

"Look, *Señor* Teobaldo, I have always respected your family and you have respected mine. You're a bit drunk, otherwise you wouldn't dare speak to me like this. You better go lie down. If you want to insult me when you are sober, go ahead, but then I will be able to answer you."

"I don't give a damn. You may be the boss of this courtyard, but I'm going to let you have it. You may be one of the worst, you have been to the 'peni' and may have killed two or three guys, but that doesn't mean a thing to me. For me, you are worth a pure and celestial fuck, you filthy ass-lover!"

Then he pulled a knife on me. That, and his offensive words, were too much and I took out the automatic .38 I happened to be carrying. If his wife hadn't appeared I don't believe I would have stood any more from him. From behind his back she signaled to me that he was crazy, so I let her grab him and pull him inside.

He was the only neighbor in our courtyard who ever tried to provoke me into a fight. And a fight with him meant death for one of us. He did it a few times and even went so far as to accuse me of stealing some hens from his sister-in-law, but I managed to avoid getting involved.

I did not forget my vow to go to Chalma and made preparations for the pilgrimage. I finally went with Manuel; Paula and her two babies; Delila and her son, Geofredo; Paula's mother Cuquita; Cuquita's husband; Paula's brother Faustino; and I don't remember who else. Something strange happened on that trip. We were walking with other pilgrims at night. It was very dark and the only one who had a lamp was a man at the head of the line. We kept following him because he was the only one who could see. We listened to the "voice of the people," telling us which way to turn, what to watch out for, and so on.

We took a detour and found ourselves in a bean field. "No, this is not the way," some people said, and they decided to stop. Then we noticed that the man with the lamp had disappeared. He was gone. So, the people began crossing themselves and saying it was a very bad sign, that he must have really been a witch who was trying to mislead us, because children had come along on the pilgrimage. The parents were very scared and a circle was formed and the women with children were put in the middle to protect them.

I was still in uniform and a lot of people began to turn to me for advice. So we began to take over the leadership, my brother and I. We said no one should move until dawn, so that we could explore a bit. The truth of the matter was, I did not remember the road at all because I hadn't gone to Chalma since my mother died. She used to drag all of us kids with her each year, but I couldn't remember much.

As it got lighter, Manuel and I collected firewood to make a fire because it was very cold for the women and children. Then I noticed that there was a cliff just fifty meters ahead of us and if we had kept walking during the night we would have gone over it. The people were more convinced than ever that a witch had been guiding us.

I remember one time, when I went with my mother, they really got hold of a witch. The people caught her and yelled, "Burn her! Burn her!" They said she had sucked the blood of two children who had been found dead next to the river. They accused this woman and burned her with green wood, right there in the plaza in Chalma. I saw the big bonfire but then they wouldn't let me look any more. I heard cries, terrible screams, and they told me it was because they were burning a witch. There was a lot of savagery in those days. Maybe she was innocent, but that was the way they did justice.

Another bad thing happened on that trip. When we got to Chalma, we couldn't find a place to sleep. There, you even have to pay to sleep around the outside walls, where there are a lot of poisonous scorpions. My brother and I made a kind of lean-to with a sheet, up against the wall of a house, and we all went to sleep. I don't know why it happened, there was no reason for it, but a scorpion came and stung my brother Manuel. We were all scared because within a matter of five minutes, if a man is not treated quickly, he is dead. Manuel was already beginning to clench his jaws.

Paula, who was pregnant, put some saliva on the sting because it is believed that the saliva of a pregnant woman is more poisonous than a scorpion and would counteract it. But I kept saying, "What do I do now? My God!" I was afraid he would die on me.

Someone said, "Make him run. Run him to the mill." It was the only place they sold medicine against scorpion stings. The miller mixes this potion and only he knows what it is made of. The people drink it and get well and aren't even curious enough to ask what goes in it. Well, I wouldn't let Manuel run, because the poison would spread faster, so Faustino and I carried him to the mill. He said the potion was as bitter as gall, but he drank it and got well, though he still felt dizzy.

We were all happy when he was able to speak again and his jaws were not sticking together any more. Lots of people have died of scorpion bites because they couldn't get to the mill in time. We had plenty to give thanks for when we got to the Sanctuary.

I walked from the outer door to the altar on my knees. At first I felt tired and burdened down, depressed, but as I walked on my knees, praying with all my heart, I felt a great sense of relief. At the end of each prayer I felt like crying. When I reached the altar, the foot of the altar of the Lord, I bent my head and cried. I wasn't tired or sad any more. I lighted a candle, left a little silver heart and a few *centavos* there and I was happy to have kept my promise. I don't believe it is God who needs those *centavos*, but it was a very big satisfaction for me to leave them for some mortal who needed them more than I.

Well, on the way back we were caught in a terrific storm. Did we get wet! The women, the babies, everyone . . . wet to the bone. We were chilled and hungry and tired when we got back to Mexico City and everyone went right to bed.

The next day I had more strength and vigor and was less backward about going out. I didn't feel ashamed any more about talking to people about the jail. My friends had a morbid curiosity about it and asked me a lot of questions. Whether I felt like it or not, I gave them the details, with the intention of influencing them to stop fighting and stealing.

I went back to life with the gang . . . there was always something going on. During Holy Week, on Holy Saturday, we had fun throwing water and raising Cain. Two or three gangs would get together, so it was fifty to a hundred fellows doing it, instead of just a few. It is a tradition here, but they go too far on that day. Instead of throwing water, a lot of people throw stones at the buses and autos and shop windows. Some of us get mad and it leads to fights, right?

Once, on Holy Saturday, there was a big battle over on the Street of the Miners. Over a hundred people got into a brawl and a jeep with three policemen came along and tried to calm them down. The cops wanted to arrest one of them, but the people here are pretty tough. They don't scare easily. Well, boom! down came the first bucket of water from a roof and landed on the jeep, see? Well, that was the beginning of the end for the cops because after that the people started throwing oranges, tomatoes and limes. One threw a stone and broke the windshield. The cops chased him and the people turned over the jeep. They blocked the cops and the boy got away.

Four more jeeps came as reinforcements. The cops were sore, damn them, but everybody put on an innocent look, like they were saints with halos. No one had done a thing, so of course there were no arrests.

Another holiday I like to celebrate is the twenty-fourth of June, the day of St. John the Baptist. They open the baths and swimming pools at two in the morning and lots of people go swimming, no matter how cold it is. It's a matter of tradition. We begin to swim at that hour and it goes on all day long. At the Casa Grande baths, they give us corn gruel, *tamales,* and they throw pears and carnations into the pool. There's a lot of commotion and the girls look mighty tempting. It's so crowded that even if you don't want to, when you swim you're likely to touch some lady's breast. Even in the big pools, the same goings-on take place. There are women that go on that day especially to get themselves fingered. They say they like the sport, though the rest of the year they never go swimming. But on June 24, there they are!

Man alive, what I've always liked best, what I've enjoyed more than anything else, are sports. The happiest moments of my life were when I was swimming, or bicycling or hunting, because, how shall I put it?

I feel that I'm somebody, that I amount to something. I've always had the feeling that nobody had any use for me, that nobody paid attention to me. And of course that's the way it should be, for who am I for anybody to pay attention to?

I've had a lot of opportunities to go hunting with my uncle in Veracruz. We've hunted jaguar, wild boar, deer. I was once chased by a boar and if it hadn't been for some big boulders, this little black boy would now be saying his prayers with St. Peter . . . if I were lucky enough to be up in heaven.

Another time, I was invited by a friend to hunt alligators in Putla. To get to this place you have to walk through the mountains for three days and no one speaks a word of Spanish there, only *Popoloca*. The people there go around covered with nothing but a loin cloth and nobody thinks bad of it. I don't expect to be believed just because I say so, but it was like that. Those people don't know what the word fear means. They catch alligators all the time because of the damage they do to the cattle. I didn't stay long but I was really happy hunting alligators in Putla.

Each time I went off on an adventure, I made sure to get back in time to sign in at the Station House. I signed in regularly for four months . . . I was still signing in when I was thrown into jail again.

My second time in jail was terrible, and it was all a case of mistaken identity. I was picked up in September, 1951, at about midday, when I was at Chapultepec Castle shooting at birds with a slingshot. I was killing *tórtolas,* for I enjoyed eating them. This time, by bad luck, two guards saw me. I could not say that I wasn't doing anything wrong, as it is punishable to shoot at the birds. I went up to them and said, "Don't get me into trouble, because if it is on account of this slingshot, I'll throw it away." I had about two *pesos* on me, and I offered them this money, but they didn't accept it.

One of them said, "Listen, he looks like the one we have been looking for." I didn't give this any importance, but since I was in the army, I know the tricks they use to throw people off. They said to me, "Come with us." One of them had his gun in my back and the other his bayonet in his hand. This made me very mad . . . especially when they pull a gun on me . . . maybe it is from fear . . . I wanted to throw myself on them in rage, but I said, "I'll go, but because I want to."

If I had known what was waiting for me, what it was going to cost me, I wouldn't have gone. But I thought it would be easy. When we arrived before the superintendent, he said to me, "So, my friend, we see each other once more. Don't you remember the time you ran away from me?"

I said, "You've got me mixed up with someone else."

"Don't you remember?" he said. "And you sure are like a deer. Tie him up." A soldier brought a rope and they tied my wrists.

"Take him to the tower." The tower was in the Castle itself, and they tied me to a railing of a spiral staircase. They tied the rope around my body and then passed it under my knees, so that I couldn't walk. I was very mad, but the guards just laughed—they were real brave with a lone, tied-up man.

They accused me of having been the author of many robberies; of stealing hoses, wire, lamps, and many other things. They wanted to make me say I was guilty, and asked me a thousand times for the things that were missing . . . how I had gotten them out, where I had sold them, endless questions which always got the same negative answer. The same soldier who tied me, put the rope around my neck and pulled it hard, supporting himself against the railing. All I could manage to say was, "You son of a . . ." and I lost consciousness but did not fall. My head just dropped over to one side.

At nine o'clock at night I was still tied up like any ordinary criminal and swearing a blue streak at everybody. One of the guards said to me, "Say, pal, they are really giving you the business. I don't think they put special guards even on the worst criminals." I asked him to loosen the rope around my hands a little. He said, "Well, I will but I shouldn't do it." I think that the guard himself realized his error.

He asked me if I was hungry, and sent out for some *tortas* and coffee. I thought, "At least they are going to untie me while I eat my food." But no, the soldier fed me, that's how I ate my *tortas*.

The patrol arrived a little later. They untied me and took me to the office. I said, "*Ay, chirrión,* it's a good thing you guys got here. They've made me take a lot of punishment and I don't even know why."

"That's a lie," said the guard.

"How can it be a lie if I just got through untying him and his hands and wrists are all marked and numb?" the patrolman answered.

The police patrol took me in the paddy wagon to Station No. 6, where they drew up the charges against me, without asking me any questions, understand? They just banged away at the typewriter and I have no idea what they wrote, and when they finished they wanted to make me sign the document. According to them it was supposed to be my statement, but actually I hadn't opened my mouth except to give them personal data, my name, where I was born, my father's name and stuff like that.

I asked them to let me read what I was going to sign and they wouldn't. And so I didn't want to sign, because I know if you're going to sign something you have to read it first. They said: "Sign, you son-of-a-whore, or we're going to give you a warming over."

"Well, do anything you want with me, but first let me see what I'm going to sign." That was the end of that, and they put me in the *separo*.

The *separo* is what they call a room, about four meters by six, where the toilet is. Of course you can't even call it a toilet, it's just a dung-heap. A prisoner came up to me. He was one of those fellows they appoint as head man because he's the most cocky with his fists or a knife, understand? the toughest fellow. He came up to me and said, "What's the matter with you? What are you sore about?" I tell him, "Nothing, they claim I robbed some things." He says, "Look, you, don't be a boob; here you talk and talk straight; here you're up against straight 'brosa.'"

He was talking *caló* to me, see?—a special dialect of the underworld. I had learned *caló* a long time back, and so as not to appear queer I started answering him in *caló* because that was the right thing to do. If I had answered him in ordinary Spanish it would have turned out worse for me. Well, he said, "Here you talk 'derecho,' you're among pure 'brosa' and nobody 'se chivea.'" This is a home for the innocent because none of us have done anything wrong; however, we're all here.

"Look, man, I really didn't steal a thing."

"O.K., that's the end of that. And now how about shelling out for a candle?"

So I tell him, "Sure thing, man."

You see, there's a custom that when you're locked up you have to give a *peso* or few *centavos*, according to your means, to buy a candle for the Virgin. Because they always have a little altar made by the prisoners themselves, some of them hardened criminals and others serving their first rap. In the Penitentiary, there is a special cell con-verted into a little church, with an altar and candles burning day and night. A priest comes once a week to say Mass. One of the prisoners is given the job of taking care of the Virgin's altar.

Then this guy, the head man, says, "Out with your wallet!"

"All I have is twenty *centavos.*"

"Let's see," he said to his lieutenant. "Put him on the scale," which means they searched me from head to foot. I hated this and protested but there was nothing I could do. They just took the twenty *centavos* and didn't bother me any more.

The food in Station No. 6 is terrible. They give you coffee with what they call milk, but it's just colored water and there's nobody to dish it out. Each one serves himself from the big milk jug. The first one to dip in gets clean coffee, while the last fellow gets it after everybody's hand has been in it, full of dirt and everything, see? because some of them don't have a cup to dip with, so they stick in a pop bottle with their hands.

I had to do some fighting in there for the simple reason that, although we all slept on the floor, one on top of the other, still one fellow or another would have a spot he preferred, see? his own special place. And the Lord help anyone who lies down there without asking his permission, because they always chose the best places, the ones that aren't close to the toilet. Somebody will have to sleep sitting right on the toilet bowl.

I didn't think I could sleep a wink, because the smell is foul, something you can't stand. Well, you can stand it but God only knows how you suffer. And the man is lucky who has the luxury of having a bed made of newspapers, or the superluxury of a sheet of cardboard to lie on. So it happened I went and sat down next to one of those special places that belonged to one of the toughest guys there and he gave me a kick and said, "Hey, you, '*vato*,' scram."

So I tell him, "What makes you think I'm going to scram?"

"Oh no? Well you scram or we're going to cook up a '*sopa de chuladas.*'" I stood up and we began to fight with our fists. They all began to holler and make a racket, and the trusty, the guy that asked me for money for a candle, says, "Quiet, '*brosa*,' otherwise you're going to get a '*berga.*'" He meant that if we didn't calm down, he was going to step in and somebody would get his face smashed. Well, then someone said, "Let them fight it out in a fair fight. All right, so everybody shut up," and they calmed down, and we went on socking each other.

To make a long story short, I can't say I won or lost, because the trusty stopped the fight, saying, "Look, this boy showed he's a straight shooter and has guts, so if anyone tries to take him on, they're going to take me on too." Well, nobody bothered me any more, right? So I said to myself, "Fine, that's over, I've had a rough time, but nobody's going to bother me any more."

But how wrong I was! They bothered me again, but this time it wasn't the prisoners, it was the prison officials. I spent six days incommunicado in Police Station No. 6, here in Mexico City, in the Federal District; and, just the words Station No. 6 mean torture, understand, it's brutal punishment that very few can take. They took it out on me for six days, three beatings a day, see? a beating for breakfast, another one for dinner and another for supper, and for dessert, another beating in the middle of the night.

The reason they did this was to make me tell where I sold the things they claimed I'd stolen from Chapultepec Castle. It was not true, understand? But the police here use these methods to make anybody confess he's guilty. Not somebody who *is* guilty, but anybody they want to make confess. Because they really give you a tough beating, see? They hit me very hard in the stomach and that's why I believe I've had a delicate stomach ever since.

The first time it happened, there was a banging on the cell door: "Roberto Sánchez Vélez, step up front!" It was my tough luck to be thrown in with the top criminals in the city, and they all knew what happens when you get called out this way. You get warmed over, that's the expression in *caló,* and even the prison officials use it. It means you're going to get beat up. So nobody says anything; they just look at you and wait to hear you screaming.

The cops grabbed hold of me; the convicts call them the lamb, the hangman and the shepherd. The lamb is the fellow who talks to you in a sort of deep and friendly voice, with a big smile on his face, so you'll confess the easy way. And the shepherd, well, you might say he's just waiting to see what happens. As for the hangman, well, his name tells you what his business is.

So the first cop, I mean the lamb, said to me, "Look, boy, don't be a fool, you're already in, and it can go bad for you here, worse than that, we can beat you to death. But it's up to you, it depends on whether you let go and sing. So let's see, we want you to sing and cough up a few saints." This thing of the saints meant he wanted me to tell him if I knew about other robberies and that sort of stuff, understand? You get the point; they began to handle me like I was one of the worst criminals, asking me about a whole bunch of robberies I didn't commit.

The honest truth is that they caught me shooting at birds with a slingshot. That's what I told them.

When they saw that they weren't getting anything out of me, the hangman grabbed hold of me and said, "Don't be a shit-heel, you son-of-a-whore." And he punched me in the pit of my stomach, so all I could do was bend over and put my hands on my belly.

"Oh, so you're trying to defend yourself. Don't try that stuff here." And he makes out like he was going to hit me down there again, and I put my hands down there to protect myself, then he socks me up between my jaw and my ear, and that's the way it went from then on.

"Oh, my God, how am I going to get out of this?" I thought. "If this keeps up, I don't know if I can take it. It's worth confessing to get them to stop." This is what went through my mind, right? But I still kept hoping I'd have the strength to hold out and take the punishment. I thought, maybe they'll try it this once or again tomorrow. Well no, it lasted six days, three beatings a day, or rather four beatings, like I told you. But they couldn't make me say what they wanted.

More or less, that's the way the "warm-ups" went. You get called by your name and all the rest begin the kidding and shouting, "Let's go, *compadre*. They are going to warm you up a little on account of it's getting cold in here." The toughest of them trembled when they knew that a good beating was waiting for them. During those six days everyone they took out cried, and lots of them looked husky and like a hundred percent men. There is always a morbid curiosity about these things. In the cell block there was a little window that unfortunately opened on the corridor and we would climb up to watch our companions in misfortune being tortured.

They gave me the torture called *"del ahogadito"*—the little drowning. They make you strip off every stitch of clothing down to your undershorts, then they distract your attention and when you are least expecting it, you get a punch in the stomach or in the liver and before you can catch your breath, they grab you by the hair and push you headfirst into a barrel of water. They keep you under for a few seconds, but it seems like centuries and then they say, "Now you'll sing." I couldn't even talk, no less sing, but they don't give you time to breathe before they do it again.

I cursed at the cops and at everybody. I took in their whole genealogical tree. They tortured me anyway. There are some who put up their fists when they are being tortured and these get it worse. Besides

"the little drowning" there were other tortures, like "the little monkey."
In this one, they strip the prisoner and put him up on a pole that goes
across the room under the ceiling, making him hang head down by his
knees. Then they take a live wire and shock his testicles with it. They
say that there are lots who can't take this one and die. There is another
torture which consists in turning on an electric grill, and putting your
hands, palms up, on it. I am not exaggerating when I tell you these
things, because even if one wanted to exaggerate, it still wouldn't come
near what is really the truth. There are no words to describe the things
that go on in that place.

After Station No. 6 they took me to the Penitentiary and I passed into
the hands of the courts. A criminal is always sent first to Headquarters
and to Station No. 6 for investigation. Their method of investigating
is to beat up people and make them confess to crimes they never
committed. They didn't get anywhere with me, thank God, because I
guess they didn't torture me as much as they do other poor people.

The faces of those three cops really are engraved in my mind. One
of them was killed. If the others fell into my hands, I would give them
time to defend themselves before I attacked, not like they did to me.
But I hate all police, whether they wear uniform or not. All I have to
know is that they represent the so-and-so justice and if it were in my
power, I'd wipe them off the map . . . I'd wipe them off!

On the second day in the Penitentiary, they took me to court. They
had me slated for a federal court because I was accused of robbing the
nation, that is, federal robbery. So they put me in the wagon, which is
called the Julia. It had a big cage in it, and they took me along with
other prisoners to the Santo Domingo court on Cuba and Brasil streets.

I didn't have any shoes on, see? I was still wearing pants, though
they were practically worn out, like my shirt; it was a shirt in name
only. My own clothes had been stolen right away by a tough prisoner
who sold them to get his "mota" or marijuana. They sell marijuana,
cocaine, heroin, opium, all kinds of dope right inside the prison. That's
the kind of perfect inspection they have there. You can imagine how
perfect it is when the guards themselves smuggle in the stuff.

I was still hopeful and kept saying to myself, "Dear God, dear God."
If there is anything good in me, it's because at least I have a blind
faith in Christ, Our Lord. I hoped that God would send my thoughts
to my brother and sisters, or to some friend who would show up there
in time. And sure enough, I was leaning against the bars of the door

in the room we were locked in, when I saw Manuel walking up the stairs.

I shouted and whistled and he turned around. He started toward me but the police stopped him. I spoke to the head guard who was in charge of us. "Chief, please let me talk with my brother. Look, I've been incommunicado for so many days. It's the first time I've seen him; nobody knew where I was."

"All right," he said, "O.K., just for a minute, no more."

So I spoke to Manuel. He gave me a bag of bananas and a sweater. I naturally perked right up, because I thought, "Well, at least they know I'm alive, and if I die, they will know where to find me."

Manuel began to bawl me out. "So you see, that's what you get for being a bum; for not working, like my father says. You're always getting into trouble."

"All right, brother," I said. "Why don't you lay off . . . at least listen to me for a moment." And I started giving him the details, but time was limited. He asked me when I was getting out. I said, "I don't know when I got in and I know less about when I'm getting out." .

Then they took us back to the cell block. Me they put in Section "A," where the worst criminals are kept, see? They always figured me among the worst, although I'm proud to say I'm like the birds that cross the swamps and don't get their feathers dirty.

I was put in a cell way back in the section where there was more danger of getting into fights; either I'd get killed or I'd kill someone. To prevent this, I paid the major a few *centavos* to be moved to a cell that was closer to the gate. I was pretty lucky, because there were only eight of us in it. We slept on the lousy concrete floor, with no cover except the clothes on our backs.

My sisters, Manuel and my father came to visit me, one at a time, and my father got busy trying to get me out. He sent a lawyer, who strung me along for seven months. "We've got the release now, tomorrow you leave, young fellow." Another time he'd tell me, "This time it's sure, you're leaving this afternoon." Or, "You're leaving at midnight. Your family is coming after you. They're bringing you clothes and shoes and you'll go right off with them to the Basilica to give thanks to the Virgin." I waited anxiously for the moment to come. Again I promised the Lord of Chalma I would pay Him a visit if He would make them see I was innocent. Day after day, I kept asking Him this . . . every minute, each beat of my heart was a plea to the Lord. Well, this went on for seven months.

There are hold-up men operating right in the prison. Some of the fellows made it a regular practice of robbing. They are fellows whom nobody comes to visit, see? They haven't any family, or if they have, the relatives don't come to see them because they are criminals. Well, these fellows make a practice of going to the courtyard during visiting hours to see who gets something they'd like to have, so they can take it away from him later.

One time, Consuelo, my aunt Guadalupe, Marta and my uncle Alfredo, may he rest in peace, came to see me, and they left me five *pesos*. Inside that place, it was fabulous amount of money. A dope fiend is capable of committing murder for that sum. When you come back from visiting, a cell door would open and a hand would pop out and they'd jump on you, screaming and swearing. Like they say in the pen, they were "taking the boy down," they were taking away the money, food, and things your family had left.

When I was given the five *pesos*, I went back to the empty cell. The floor there was broken up in places where the concrete was gone and the dirt was showing. That's where I put my money, shoving it under the dirt, and I went out again, to get my food ration. I was walking along, carrying my food, when a fellow named Aurelio began to stare at me. I realized what could happen to me, because a dope fiend is born full of marijuana. I think if you open up his head, instead of brains you'll find marijuana smoke. This dope fiend had been smoking for years. I know because he told me once when we were, well, not exactly friends, but companions in adversity, understand?

Aurelio said, "Give me some money for a '*mota*.'"

"*Caramba!* Why didn't you tell me before, I'd have given you the money for a fag. Look, you can fish me, I'm all out, I've just divided it with the boys, and when I went downstairs just now, I bought a candle from the prisoner who owns the store and spent my last *centavo*.

"Nothing doing," and he grabbed me by the shoulder and shook me. "No, you don't, and don't get stubborn."

Well, I got mad and said, "You're not going to fish me, you'll get no money for a fag, and you're not going to do anything about it, either."

So then he pulled out his knife and made a pass at me. Luckily for me, instead of sticking me with the point, he swung at me with the side of the blade, get me? We call this stroke a "*planazo.*" I managed to put my hand up and block him with my candle. He wasn't on the level with me; he didn't give me a chance to get my knife. Well, this got me even madder. He came at me again, and I defended myself as

best I could and thanks to God, I came out ahead. He didn't take anything away from me, but he sure did scare the hell out of me, right?
That was the first time.

But the second time I really got it. It was after visiting hours and I
was walking to my cell to leave the food my family had given me when
one of them pulled me into a cell, and then a fellow puts a knife up
against my throat and another one holds a knife up against my ribs.
There were four of them. Well, anybody with just a little common
sense, at a time like this, wises up, right? so the best thing for me was
not to move and do like they told me.

So one of them says, "We need money for a 'jab.'" You see, these
fellows took morphine by injection.

"Fine, O.K., just leave me something to buy myself a candle or a
bit of bread."

"How much change do you have on you?" I believe I had four or
five *pesos*. He said, "Well let you keep a '*baro*'" (a *peso*).

Now these fellows are very dangerous, believe me. Though I really
pity them because when they don't have their dope they get into a
terrible state. They suffer a whole lot . . . they roll on the floor, they
twist and they say their whole body hurts them, see? Inside of them,
they feel like they're burning up. You know, you can tell a dope fiend
by his face, a mile away, understand? If he denies it, all you have to
do is look at his forearm.

Well, that was the end of that, and I left feeling madder than a
bull. But there was no other way out for me. If I had lost my head
and fought back, I'd have been worse off.

Such things are not allowed, understand? but unfortunately, when
the guards see these goings-on, they just turn the other way. Every
corridor has a sentry box with a telephone, and a guard armed with
a Thompson machine gun. But when there's a fight, the guard just
looks on and does absolutely nothing to stop it. He could easily call
up the front office and ask them to send somebody to separate the
men, because when two prisoners start a fight, it spreads to the rest
in the cell, and a lot get hurt.

The day in prison begins with reveille at six in the morning. Four
squads, one for each of four rows of cells, come banging away with
their clubs to wake up everybody. The guards yell, "Up now, you
sons-of-whores, you're off the gravy train. Line up for your gruel
and Glory be, you'll never get out of the pen." The way those guys

talk! As far as I am concerned they can blow up the pen and all those so-and-so's with it.

Then we go downstairs and line up for rollcall. I became a corporal after a while and it was my job to call the roll in the morning. I called out the first names and they'd answer with their last names. We reported to the major when all were accounted for.

The bugles then play "*rancho*," mess call, and we all lined up for breakfast. They'd give us corn gruel and milk, a roll and beans and a jar of water. Then we'd go down for drill which lasted about three hours. I didn't go to this military training because in a very short time I became an "*influyente*," see? That means I paid one *peso* every week to the major of the cell block to be marked present. The major was a prisoner like the rest of us, except that he was in charge of keeping order, of handling complaints, and stuff like that. When you give him your *peso*, you don't have to get up at six in the morning and do drill. The reason I didn't want to go was that I had no shoes.

After drill, anyone who wanted to could go to his cell. Or you could go to the courtyard and walk up and down like a caged lion, just back and forth. I was one of those lions.

At noon, they blow assembly for another rollcall. After that, you got your ration, usually beans, rice, stew and bread. I believe the stew was made of horse meat, though they said it was beef. Anyway, the noon meal was a little better. They blew assembly again for work or three more hours of drill. Then back to the cell blocks.

At six in the evening they blow another assembly to take down the flag. After that comes mess call. Evening rations consisted of coffee with milk, or corn gruel and bread. Back to the cell blocks, later, a bolt came down and all the cells were locked.

Taps were sounded at nine o'clock, but before that the "oil workers" get busy, though actually they operate all day long. They are the dope pushers. They walk around on the sly, like they were selling cigarettes or candy. "Get your fag for a *peso*," or maybe two *pesos*. The men say, "Pssst!" just like they call any ordinary peddler. "Let's have one. What kind is it?"

"Pure goat."

"Sure it's goat?"

"Sure thing. It's a lamb's tail."

While they're still lined up, even in the daytime, the prisoners start delousing the marijuana, that is, taking out the seeds. And they roll their cigarettes with wrapping paper and smoke like it's the most natural thing in the world. Well, not too openly, just a bit under cover, on account of the guards.

It was pretty bad; it's hard to describe. No matter how much I try, I fall short. You have to go through it yourself or at least see it to know what it's like. The gangs operating inside the prison are the worst I've ever seen, because they are made up of people who don't care any more if they are free or in jail, whether they murder or get murdered, see? To join one of these gangs, you have to have two or three scalps under your belt. These gangs are organized inside the prison, but even when the members are released they get together on the outside, to commit all sorts of crimes.

The leader of the gang doesn't take just anybody, and no one can go up and ask him. He does the picking to suit himself, quietly. He'll talk with one fellow and then another; and even though the prisoners won't tell the police anything, because they'd get killed if they did, they talk freely among themselves about what each fellow did. In this way, the leader gets a line on everybody, and when he decides to ask someone to join, you can be sure he's the meanest in the bunch.

There was no gang in my cell, but I found out about them because I used to be a "*chícharo,*" a sweeper in the prison barber shop. And then I worked in the bakery. The worst types worked in the bakery. The fellow who was my boss was one of the biggest gang leaders, see? although he never bothered anybody, because that's the way these gang leaders are—a leader through and through, never says anything, except when he's doped up and his mind gets weak. That's when he begins to do damage.

I used to hear them talking about the gangs, understand? One time the boys said to my boss, "Listen, send this kid out."

"No, you can speak openly in front of him, he's on the level. He handled himself O.K. when Aurelio tried to knife him." This conversation took place when he was first considering me for the job, understand? So they said, "All right, kid, you keep mum about anything you hear in this place."

"Sure, O.K." Actually, I don't think I heard anything important. The boys used such high-powered *caló* that sometimes I couldn't make out the words, understand? At that time they were planning a break, but it never came off.

The gangs were the bosses not only of the prisoners, but even of the guards and the guard captain. Why, one of them controlled the head warden. That's going pretty far, isn't it? A prisoner actually did, and his name was the Frog. He's a fellow who killed 132 or 134 people. He was a soldier in the infantry, as I remember, and once when he was on duty there was some kind of a student riot. People still don't know exactly how it happened but he started firing his machine gun on the crowd of students. He killed students like you strike down flies, sweeping the students with his machine gun. He was responsible for over a hundred deaths, in addition to which he killed a crook and a guard in prison.

It wasn't just a rumor, about the Frog controlling the head warden, understand? He walked about freely throughout the prison and if the head warden came by, the Frog was the one who walked in front. And if the Frog didn't like something—well, suppose he figured something should be done for the prisoners, he'd say, "This has to be fixed." He'd say it as if he were thinking out loud, so the head warden could hear him, and carry out the orders.

I had various dealings with the Frog. I used to steal for him when I worked in the bakery. I stole lard, brushes and, well, I didn't steal the warden's mother because she never came, right? Of course, I delivered the stuff to him, and he always paid me something. I don't say I'm proud of it, but the way things were I had to do it, if I didn't they'd treat me like I was the biggest "*primo*" there, understand? "*Primo*" means shit-heel in swear language.

So I turned it over to the Frog, because he had a shop right inside the prison. He sold cigarettes and other things. Even if a prisoner didn't have drag with the head warden, if he had money he could set up his own little shop, understand? Although you have to pay through the nose to do it, you can get permission. There's two brothers with plenty of money who run the Juana restaurant right inside the prison. They say it's the best restaurant in Mexico.

As for the sex life, I tell you it's the lowest kind of promiscuity, even though the homosexuals are separated from the men. The homosexuals have their section in the back part of the prison, see? These men, I don't know what else to call them, have their section made up of wooden shacks, understand? And there'd be a fellow putting on lipstick in broad daylight, some would be washing, others sewing, others cooking, others making *tortillas*, others flirting.

Unfortunately, many fellows in prison are so corrupted, they've fallen so low, that when the desire comes over them and there's no woman to relieve them, they bribe the guards with fifty *centavos* or a *peso*, to let them go to the "*jota*," the homosexuals' section. When he gets inside, well, you can imagine what happens. He picks the "girl" he likes best. They all go dressed like women, though whenever there's an inspection, they dress like men. Those are the rules, see?

This homosexual business made a big impression on me. One day, the news released over the prison microphone was that one of the prisoners had been sent to Tres Marías for raping another prisoner, a boy of eighteen. There used to be women in the Penitentiary, in a section apart. No one could go there. Well, I shouldn't say no one because a bribe goes a long way in prison. If you want to bribe a guard or two, you can get through. But this is at least more acceptable because you were going to have relations with a woman, right?

I never got to visit any woman in jail because I always ran into difficulties. Besides, it was a big risk; if they caught you bribing a guard and leaving your section they put you in solitary confinement in Tres Marías. Tres Marías is a round prison, with just one floor, so that the cells are in the form of a triangle. Only half the cell is covered by a roof. When it rains, well, you can imagine how terribly wet and cold it gets there, especially at night. During the day you can be in the sun, or in the shade, but you don't have the right to smoke, or to have a blanket or anything.

When I had been in for a few months, I saw Ramón Galindo there in jail. I knew Ramón and his brothers since I was a kid, although he was older than I. They used to sell charcoal over on the Street of the Gardeners and were as poor as the rest of us. Then Ramón got hold of a bicycle and started a renting agency. I don't know by what art he did it, though I can well imagine, but he built up his agency to quite a big thing. He was able to build a decent house and become a money lender. He loaned money at 20 percent interest a month, bought a car and was well set up.

I learned later that he had dealings with a lot of people from the underworld, whom he met in the local saloons. He used to be quite a drinker; they would often find him stretched out dead drunk in the street, until one day he swore never to touch another drop. He kept his word and things went well with him from then on. He began

to buy "hot" articles very discreetly from his safer friends and over-
night he became one of the richest men in the neighborhood.

He was in jail for having killed a taxi driver in a street fight. When
I met him he had already become a prison instructor in personal
defense. I don't know how he managed it, but later he became the
head of all the prisoner personnel and ended up closely tied to the
head of the Secret Service. In fact, when he got out he became a
Secret Service agent and his sons are now policemen. It was pretty
neat, because he continued to be a buyer of stolen goods. I know
this very well, for I became his right arm.

Well, that's the way things went in prison for the seven months I
was there. I learned something concerning friends during that time.
Those on the outside who claimed to be my friends when I had money
and who followed me wherever I went, didn't take the trouble to
visit me, understand? When I had hard luck, I don't remember a
single one who even sent regards with my family. I found out there
are very few real friends in this world.

When I least expected it, they released me. They had taken me to
court in the *Julia* many times, and finally confronted me with the
two park guards. The day I was set free, I was in court, still barefoot,
wearing a suit which was a real insult, a suit with stripes so you look
like a zebra. My father and Marta were there. The lawyer told me
that I was going to be set free because they had grabbed the guilty
fellow. "So please excuse us," said the judge.

I told him, "Sir, do you think that by saying 'excuse me' you are
going to wipe out the seven months of suffering I've gone through
here? And the moral suffering of my family, and the fact that I'm
branded for the rest of my life?"

He said, "Now, don't take it that way, because if you do, then
you'll stay." So there was nothing for me to do but keep quiet. If I
had gone on, I would have had a lot to tell the authorities. So I was
free, with only an "excuse me" to send me on my way. "Excuse us,
we've caught the guilty one."

It cost my poor father 1,200 *pesos* to get me free. He was robbed
because my case was an easy one and the lawyer didn't earn his fee.
There was no material evidence against me and two of the "witnesses"
contradicted the other three. I agree that when one commits a mis-
demeanor he should be punished, but I was falsely accused. Before

they committed this injustice to me, I believed in the law, but after that I didn't. If this is justice, then what is injustice!

Seven months they stole from my life! It is not that I'm bitter, but I hate everything that represents the law. The police and the Secret Service are just thieves with a license. For any little thing, they beat you. I'm always ready to face up to them, to tell them off. That's why, when there is a strike or a riot, I join in, without asking what the demonstration is about, just to get a chance to beat the police. And when a policeman is killed, I'm not exactly happy but I feel he deserved what he got.

There is no law here, just fists and money, which is what counts most. It is the law of the jungle, the law of the strongest. The one who is economically strong can just laugh. He commits the worst crimes and is an innocent dove before the judges and the police because he has money to give out. But how differently it goes with a poor man who commits a minor offense! What happened to me isn't a thousandth of what has happened and is still happening to others. I really don't know what justice is because I've never seen it.

If there is a Hell, it is right there in the Penitentiary. I don't wish my worst enemy to be in a place like that. Six boys from the Casa Grande spent time in jail, but only one of them was a real criminal. The others, like me, got into trouble through fighting and bad luck. I don't mean to say that I didn't deserve to be taught a lesson, because if I didn't do what they accused me of, I have done other bad things. I've been a bad son, a bad brother, a bad drinker . . . I'm convinced I needed punishment, but I never stop complaining that they locked me up unjustly.

Mexico is my country, right? And I have a special, profound love for it, especially for the capital. We have a freedom of expression and above all, a freedom to do whatever we please, that I haven't found elsewhere. I have always been able to earn my living better here . . . you can support yourself even by selling squash seeds. But regarding the Mexicans, well, I don't have a good impression of them. I don't know whether it is because I myself have behaved badly, but it seems to me that there is a lack of good will among them.

The law of the strongest operates here. No one helps the ones who fall; on the contrary, if they can injure them more, they will. If one is drowning, they push him under. And if one is winning out, they will pull him down. I'm not an intelligent person but at my work I always came out on top . . . I earned more than my fellow workers. When they noticed it, they got me into trouble with the boss and pushed me out. And there is always someone who tells who robbed, who killed, who said what, or who was going bad.

Could it be for the lack of education? There are so many people who cannot even sign their names! They talk about constitutionalism . . . it is a pretty, resounding word, but I don't even know what it means. For me, we live by violence . . . homicide, theft, assault. We live quickly and must be constantly on guard.

They let me out of prison at about two-thirty in the afternoon. I went straight to the Villa to thank the Virgin. I told my family of my vow to go to Chalma. It was not the time of the year for the Lord's celebration and no one wanted to go. My aunt Guadalupe told me to keep my vow, so I went absolutely alone. This time I walked barefoot all the way from Santiago to Chalma, about thirty or thirty-five kilometers. I walked without stopping. The going was tough. The road was so muddy it felt like chewing gum and my feet sank and were scraped by the stones.

I paid no attention to the pain. I kept my mind on fulfilling my vow and not backtracking. The rougher the road, the better for me, because the more I suffered physical pain, the more satisfied I was. For me, that was the purpose of the pilgrimage, to suffer and make a sacrifice. I felt beaten down and in despair going there, but on the way back I felt only a great sense of relief.

A short time later, I was picked up by the police and put into jail for not signing in for my first offense during the seven months I was in jail. When you don't sign in three consecutive times, the bonding company informs the Secret Service and the police start to look for you. I think that is unconstitutional, because the bonding companies should have their own private police, not the ones from the judiciary. Anyway, I got out right away. I hung around for a while and then took off for Veracruz.

Consuelo

THE NIGHT MARTA WAS MISSING, I WORRIED MORE ABOUT WHAT MY father would say than about Marta. Roberto looked for her everywhere, while Paula and I waited at home. Finally, we heard my father's key in the door. I made believe I was sewing; Paula and the baby were asleep. My father immediately asked, "Where is Marta?" His voice sounded dry and punishing. I didn't dare answer. Roberto jumped up as he always did when my father came in, and said, "She hasn't come home." We waited for a deluge of strong words and curses, but my father knew how to surprise us. He said, "Ay, ay, let's go look for her." They both went out.

A little later I heard Manuel whistle and I opened the door for him. He never asked questions about the family and this time was no exception. I didn't tell him anything and watched him spread his "bed" on the floor. He was lying down when my father walked in. "What happened? Did she come back?" Manuel jumped up without understanding.

My father turned on him. "Go look for your sister, cabrón, bastard! Here you lie while she is out there! Let's go." Generally, Manuel was slow to carry out an order, but this time he became light as a feather.

The three returned very late. My father's face was hard and bitter, Roberto hung his head, Manuel was sleepy-eyed. My father ordered us to go to sleep and turned out the light. I could see his short form, unmoving, standing in the kitchen, as though rooted to the cement floor. He was smoking, and the red tip of the cigarette burned in the dark. I did not comprehend the significance of my sister's act. I knew only that my father was sad and worried. I fell asleep, waiting, waiting.

My father awakened the boys very early and made them go out to look for Marta. He left me the telephone number of the café and went to work. At about three o'clock in the afternoon, Marta walked in. She looked so young with her braids and socks! But she seemed to expect a fight and I gave it to her. I took my role of older sister seriously. "Where were you last night?" She turned and gave me a look of scorn which made me furious. She began to insult me and I grabbed a belt which was hanging behind the door. I managed to hit her a few times, but she defended herself, screaming and scratching. The fight ended when Roberto came home.

I went to the water tank in the courtyard to wash the blood from my arms and it was there that I learned from Irela that Marta had spent the night with Crispín, the one who later became her husband. I understood then and began to cry inconsolably. Crispín's parents came to talk with my father, but I didn't hear them because I was sent out of the house.

When Marta went to live with Crispín I was very angry. I had dreamed of her studying and going to school, neatly dressed and with eyeglasses. I had imagined her at her fifteenth birthday party and her wedding, with my father leading her to the altar! In place of my dream I began to see a nightmare, my little sister living in free union, carrying her child, going to the plaza in a torn apron, uncombed hair, and flapping shoes. Thus was another of my illusions destroyed.

When I first visited the room Crispín set up for Marta, I was impressed because it had everything they needed, a bed, a table and chairs, a little kerosene stove and enough dishes and pots. But later they quarreled a lot and when Marta told me that Crispín had hit her, how angry I became. I saw him as a brutal, jealous husband, who didn't fulfill his obligations. I mixed into their arguments, always defending my sister. But later, when I heard Crispín's side of the story, I realized that it was Marta's fault. She insisted on going out with my brother Roberto and with her gang of friends, exactly as she had before her marriage. When Crispín objected, she threatened to get Roberto after him. Roberto backed up Marta in everything and, as a result, Crispín didn't want any of us to visit them. When I criticized Marta for not keeping her house clean, or for not obeying her husband, she would turn on me and accuse me of liking Crispín. After that, I kept out of their affairs, but I still believe that if Marta had behaved better, she and Crispín might have had a good life together.

At home, Paula was expecting her second child. My father had a wire strung across the room to curtain off her bed and behind it Alanes was born. Over a year later, Domingo came into the world. My nieces and nephews were well received when they arrived, but the first one, Mariquita, was always the favorite. She brightened up the house and I fell in love with her.

I also learned to love Paula, who seemed like a saint. She lived for her children, although she punished them in a way that infuriated me. My Mariquita was only eleven months old when she tasted the back of her mother's hand. For some reason, Paula held that little girl responsible for everything her brothers did. If they wet the bed, or fell, or knocked something over, it was Mariquita who had her hair pulled or her bottom spanked. I never dared interfere but usually left the house, slamming the door behind me.

Paula loved Manuel no matter how wretchedly he behaved to her. She covered up his faults and never complained to us or to my father. She spent all day sewing and mending, and caring for the children. She rarely saw a movie or went out or had an extra dress. Manuel was always out of the house, coming home after midnight or at dawn. Paula was ready to serve him at any hour, turning on the light, waking up everyone in order to give him his meal. Or sometimes at three or four o'clock in the morning he would turn on the light to read. This made me very angry because I had to get up early to go to work, but Paula never said a word about it.

I don't remember ever seeing my brother treat his wife with affection. He spoke brusquely to her or not at all, burying himself in a magazine or newspaper story. I don't believe he really loved her. He even preferred to sleep on the floor rather than crowd into bed with her and the children, but, in any case, their marital life was handicapped because they had no privacy. Once in a while they would tell us they were going to a movie but I think they went to a hotel instead.

As I grew older, I became more aware of the restrictions one had to put up with when a whole family lived in a single room. In my case, because I lived in fantasy and liked to daydream, I was especially annoyed by having my dreams interrupted. My brothers would bring me back to reality with, "Hey, what's the matter with you! You look dopey." Or I'd hear my father's voice, "Wake up, you. Always in the clouds! Get moving, fast!"

Coming back to earth, I had to forget the pretty home I was imagining and I looked at our room with more critical eyes. The crude dark wardrobe, so narrow it reminded me of a coffin, was crowded with the clothing of five, seven or nine people, depending upon how many were living there at the time. The chiffonier, too, had to serve the entire family. Dressing and undressing without being seen was a problem. At night, we had to wait until the light was out or undress under the blanket or go to sleep in our clothing. Antonia cared least about being seen in her slip, but Paula, Marta and I were very modest. Roberto, too, would get up in the morning wrapped in his blanket and go into the kitchen to dress. We women wouldn't dress until the men and children went out so we could close the door. But there was always someone wanting to get in, impatiently banging and telling us to hurry. We could never dawdle.

It would have been a great luxury to be able to linger at the mirror to fix my hair or to put on make-up; I never could because of the sarcasm and ridicule of those in the room. My friends in the Casa Grande complained of their families in the same way. To this day, I look into the mirror hastily, as though I were doing something wrong. I also had to put up with remarks when I wanted to sing, or lie in a certain comfortable position or do anything that was not acceptable to my family.

Living in one room, one must go at the same rhythm as the others, willingly or unwillingly—there is no way except to follow the wishes of the strongest ones. After my father, Antonia had her way, then La Chata, then my brothers. The weaker ones could approve or disapprove, get angry or disgusted but could never express their opinions. For example, we all had to go to bed at the same time, when my father told us to. Even when we were grown up, he would say, "To bed! Tomorrow is a work day." This might be as early as eight or nine o'clock, when we weren't at all sleepy, but because my father had to get up early the next morning, the light had to be put out. Many times I wanted to draw or to read in the evening, but no sooner did I get started when, "To bed! Lights out!" and I was left with my drawing in my head or the story unfinished.

During the day it was Antonia who chose the radio programs we all had to listen to; in the evenings it was my father. We especially hated the Quiz Kids (*los niños Catedráticos*) because my father would say, "A child of eight and he knows so much . . . and you donkeys, you don't want to study. Later you'll be sorry." When my father or Antonia were not at home, how we would fight over the radio!

If La Chata was in charge of the house, she lorded it over us in her own way. She made us wait in the courtyard until she finished cleaning and sometimes, due to the cold, I would have to go to the toilet. She would refuse to open the door and I would jump up and down yelling, for all the neighbors to hear, "Ay, La Chata, let me in. I have to go. I can't stand it any longer." Then she would get even by leaving the front door open so that the passers-by in the courtyard could see my feet under the door of the toilet. I would try to hide my feet and would beg her to please shut the front door. But she'd say, "Oh, who's going to notice a kid."

The toilet, with its half-door, gave us almost no privacy. It was so narrow that La Chata had to go in sidewise and leave the shutter ajar in order to sit down. Antonia would always crack some joke about the person using the toilet. If Manuel stayed in too long, as he usually did, she would say, "Cut it short or shall I bring you the scissors?" To me she'd say, "Are you still there? I thought you were already in San Lazaro." San Lazaro is the exit of the city sewage system and she meant that I had fallen into the drainpipe. Other times I was the one who gave trouble. I would tease Roberto when he was in the toilet by opening the front door, saying the smell was too strong. He would shout angrily, "Close that door or you'll see what happens." But I would escape into the courtyard before he came out. Or when someone was in the toilet I would begin dancing in front of the door and yelling that I had to go in. I remember Manuel coming out holding his magazine or comics between his teeth, pulling up his pants, looking daggers at me. Antonia never came out until she was ready, no matter how much of a scandal was made, and often were the times when I had to chase everyone out of the room so that I could use the chamber pot.

Sometimes the jokes were rude. Antonia was constipated and suffered very much from gas. She tried to hold it but often she just laughed and said, "Why should I hold it in if it gives me stomach aches." But if any of us went to the toilet for that reason she would joke about it, "How hoarse you are . . . you have a cough, pal." And we might say, "And when you go on like a machine gun at night we can even see your blanket rising." When we were little and someone made a noise my father would laugh and say, "Ay, who was that? It must have been a rat." But later he would scold harshly and send the guilty one to the toilet. When he was not present, Manuel and Roberto would carry on by calling each other names like "slob" or "pig" and making each other blush for shame. If no one commented, we usually passed over a slip and paid no attention to it.

But these annoyances were insignificant compared to that of being scolded in the presence of everyone else. I often thought that if my father had berated me in private, I would not have minded so much. But everyone heard the awful things he said to me, even though they pretended not to, and it hurt and shamed me more. My sisters and brothers felt the same way. When one of us was scolded, the others felt equally punished. My father's words would build up little by little, until they covered us and made us fall in a crisis of tears.

I began to stay away from my home as much as I could. While my father did not live with us I went to all the dances I wanted to, even against Roberto's wishes. Manuel did not care very much what I did, but Roberto still watched me like a hawk. If I danced two or three consecutive dances with the same boy, he would say, "Don't dance with him any more. I can't stand him!" He would look at the boy fit to kill; they could tell just by looking at him that he was keeping an eye on me. If I didn't obey, he would yank me out of my partner's arms and drag me home. I would go back to the dance if I could, just to show him that he couldn't order me around. But he would tell my father and I would be scolded. Even when I cried and promised not to go any more, as soon as the music began I couldn't hold back. I would leave my coffee on the table and run to the dance.

Roberto's friend, Pedro Ríos, who lived in the Casa Grande, had become my *novio* even before my father left us. Pedro was very nice and let pass all the bad times I gave him. One of the things he disliked most was for me to go to dances. But I went anyway, to get even with him for getting drunk. He would watch me, then take me out on the floor to talk to me while we danced.

"You're just making a fool of me," he said. "You do it because you know I love you, but if you keep it up we are going to have a real fight."

"I'll break up with you, before I quit dancing," I'd say, and that was what finally happened.

At that time, the boys of the *vecindad* used to say, "The girls from Casa Grande are for us only," and it was true. The stranger who tried to find a girl in the Casa Grande was to be pitied because the boys would fight him or give him trouble. Pedro and others from the gang said we girls should not dance nor talk to strangers, but I did not pay any attention. I would dance with any stranger as long as I liked him. That is how I met Diego Toral.

Diego was a fair-skinned young man, half reserved and half a joker. He dressed well. I had to find an excuse to stop going with Pedro to become Diego's sweetheart, but Pedro did not give me any reason to break up. Since I liked Diego very much, I was the sweetheart of both of them. I used to see Diego only when I went dancing. If Pedro and Diego were both at a dance, I would leave. One day Diego asked me to meet him at a nearby school building. I had already told Pedro to wait for me at the same hour at the arcade on the side of the Street of the Tinsmiths. The building had two exits and Pedro was waiting for me at one while I, running, went to the garden at the other side to meet Diego. My heart was pounding furiously. "I came for just a few minutes, you know how my brothers are." Diego was satisfied.

I returned to the arcade to see Pedro. He insisted that we walk toward the garden. I didn't want to because Diego might still be there but, I do not know how to explain this, instead of being afraid I felt comfortable. I was laughing to myself at both of them.

I did not go very long with Diego, but he proposed to me. At that time marriage meant nothing to me; it did not even seem real. Diego said, "Wouldn't you like to have a beautiful house with upholstered furniture?"

"Upholstered?" I did not know what that meant. He would describe his work to me, but while he talked I thought, "You think I believe you, huh? No, Sharpy. You can't fool me! Don't believe him, Consuelo, don't believe him." But then going back to sweetness, I would say, "Yes, I'd like it. It would be nice." But inside, I was laughing. I was distrustful of all of them. I do not know why. Probably because love was never my ideal.

My brother Roberto's friends were my friends. But always, thanks to his influence and to the fact that I never liked mean, practical jokes, all of them respected me. Other gangs feared the boys from Casa Grande because they were bullies and trouble makers. I often heard about the Casa Grande gang having a fight with the gang from the Casa Verde or from the Street of the Potters. Those from Casa Grande used to get together at the arcade in such a large group that they interfered with traffic. They would sing or play, tell jokes, and fool around.

When there was a moon or stars, the "loafers" or the "lazy bastards,"
as my father would call them, came together at the door of our house.
They used to sing love songs if Pedro and I were on good terms; if
not, songs of defiance or despair. For example, once when Pedro and I
were extremely angry, they sang, "Hypocrite, simply a hypocrite.
Perverse one, you deceived me; with your fatal line you poisoned me.
And because you don't love me, I'm going to die." From my bed I
delighted in listening to their wonderful voices and felt lullabyed,
knowing that Pedro was there. I felt that all the songs were meant for
me. But the neighbor women insulted them: "Lazy bums! Aren't you
ashamed of yourselves? Why don't you take your noise some place
else?"

Some time later, a family with a record player for rent, moved into
Room No. 53. On the tenth of May, Mother's Day, they played the
mañanitas (birthday songs) for the mothers. It also became a custom
to sing the *mañanitas* to the Virgin of Guadalupe at about four or five
in the morning and to bring the priest to consecrate her every year.
We girls and some of the neighbor women used to get up, well
wrapped, because it is cold at that time of the day. Before beginning
the *mañanitas*, the janitor would set off rockets.

The day that made me angry was St. John's Day, June 24. At exactly
two in the morning, the whistle from the public bathhouse blew. It
was deafening. Everyone awoke. The older boys from the gang would
go to swim at that hour; some of the girls would go swimming too,
but I never went. Marta used to tell me that they gave away corn
gruel, *tamales*, sweets and flowers and that they had swimming
matches, in which my brother Roberto participated. The record player
at the swimming pool played all day. They told me that they really
lived it up, but I wondered how they looked, dancing in bathing suits.
That was the reason I never went.

Later on, a new custom appeared. On the Saturday before Easter,
they would throw water at each other, until they were soaked. It
probably started with burning the effigies of Judas. That day, I was
watching from the main roof, and saw some boys throw brick powder
in a paper sack on the people below. The gang from the Street of the
Potters was going around in a big circle in the street and suddenly
someone threw a can of water at them. Others quickly came with cans
and buckets of water and that's how the custom started.

But the water throwing got out of hand and I hated it. They no longer
had respect for anyone. In the Casa Grande, the boys began to soak

the girls, too. Men and women chased each other with pails of water. Everyone was showered, even if they were dressed up and ready to go out, for that day is generally a day off. The girls were a horrid spectacle, their hair dripping water and their dresses stuck to their bodies. One could almost say they were nude. I looked on from the roof or from behind the door, half enjoying it and half angry.

I liked the Christmas celebration better and I did take part in that. On Christmas Eve all of us cleaned and adorned the courtyard. We watched to see that the kids from other courtyards did not pull down the decorations. Some brought wood from the roofs for the luminaries at night; a luminary is a small bonfire on the sidewalks, celebrating the coming of a holy day.

But after all that work, my father would not let me go out. I usually spent those nights crying. At midnight, the bath house whistle blew, the kids hit the telephone poles (these are made of iron and produce a sound similar to that of a bell), horns were blown insistently, bells tolled, and everyone hugged each other and said, "Merry Christmas!" I wanted to have a good time like the others, but by that hour our lights were out, we were all in bed and my father was watching to make sure that we did not go out.

I loved all things religious and never stopped attending the religious obligations I had taken on with such conformity and delight. I deposited my faith, my hope, in Him, in Him whose permission I asked for everything. To Him I offered all the sufferings and pleasures that fell to me in school, at work, or outside during the day. All through the afternoons and nights when I was left alone, I would offer Him everything and talk to Him and make Him promises. I have always fulfilled the First Commandment, Love God above all things, but I have never managed to fulfill the Second, Do not take the name of the Lord in vain. Unfortunately, I have found need to lie.

The first time I went into a church, it seemed to me as though I was entering the sacred precinct, that is, as if the doors of peace illuminated by pale rays of light were opening for me. My prayers always were that my brothers should not turn out bad, that He should make them change and pardon them, that He give me strength to go on. I had to help them develop, to study, to be very capable. In church, I felt insignificantly tiny. He represented everything there was for me, there at the altar. I almost always went alone to church and to the cemetery, always promising to be good and humble. "Do not permit pride to enter me," was what I asked for myself. I wanted to be as humble and good as St. Francis of Assisi, but it didn't turn out that way.

For years I didn't stop asking my father to put me into a school for nuns. I tried for a long time, even up to the time I was eighteen years old. But what a disillusion it was when Yolanda and *Señor* Alfredo, her husband, told me that one had to pay a dowry in order to become a nun. They also told me about the sufferings one had to go through, but that didn't make any difference to me. To sleep on a hard bed seemed to me to be a meritorious thing, a sacrifice, yes, but it was to serve Him who had suffered so much. I saw a movie at that time which showed the entire Passion of Christ, and I cried and cried and felt like shouting. If I had been there to be allowed to embrace the Lord and help Him with His cross! That memory will never be erased. The humility with which He suffered! My love for Him was greater than ever. When my brothers made me cry or my father scolded me or I was going through a bad moment of any kind, I would think, "If He who was divine suffered so much, why shouldn't a poor human like me suffer? What does my suffering mean compared to His!" And I would feel resigned.

I didn't learn the meaning of Mass until I was seventeen or eighteen years old. One afternoon I left the office with Lupe, a girl who worked with me. I was working for an accountant then. Lupe had received much more religious instruction than I and always went to Mass. She asked me if I did, and at first I said yes, but because she seemed like such a simple person, I dared ask her, "Listen, and what does the Mass mean?"

"Haven't they told you?"

"No, never. When I go, I kneel when everybody kneels and get up when everybody gets up, and say what they say. But I don't know why. Why do you have to get up or kneel with the bell?"

"Look, when they ring the bell—" And then I learned the grand significance of the Mass. When I least expected it, I had that deciphered for me.

I took part in my first religious pilgrimage when my uncle Ignacio and my aunt went on the newsboys' union pilgrimage. We marched four abreast. Some carried flowers. Although they were very poor people, they kept in order. Some sang hallelujahs. I just kept looking straight ahead toward that distant point I was soon to feel so near. I was very happy to be there. The second time was much later when I graduated from commercial school, and all of us, dressed in cap and gown, set off for the Basilica to give thanks. Never, never did I lose hope that I would see Him.

Once, on Roberto's Saint's Day, Crispín paid for the rental of a record player to celebrate. At one point, Crispín and Marta pulled the chair out from under me as I was about to sit down. Of course, there were people present and they laughed when I fell. I felt like dying of embarrassment and fury, but went right into the house without saying a word. There I was safe from the laughter because my father didn't permit the doors to be open. He just gave the electric current to run the music.

A few minutes later I got even with Marta and Crispín. I emptied a pan of water on them from the roof while they were dancing. Marta couldn't take the harmless joke and went in to tell my father, shouting, "*Papá,* look at what that Skinny did! Tell her not to start up with Crispín."

I came down the stepladder, laughing, but once I saw my father my laughter was cut short. Before all the people, I got a slap and a scolding from him. "I'm sick and tired of supporting people who don't deserve it." My father hurt me very deeply, and I began thinking of how I would run away the following day. And that's what I did. I got together the few clothes I had and went to Santitos' house

Santitos lived in a small stand built of scrap wood and heavy cardboard, in the little market of the Martínez *Colonia.* Her merchandise consisted of a few vegetables, candies and herbs which she kept on a board. At her place I was glad to eat plain nopal leaves roasted on the clay griddle, and to sleep on a dirt floor with just a piece of straw mat under me and some strips of bedspread covering me. The colony was on the outskirts of the city and we went to sleep to a kind of lullaby made by the croaking of toads and frogs. I would wake up with my whole back eaten by fleas, and I slept wrapped from head to foot for fear of the rats.

At night, by the light of the little candle Santitos bought when the kerosene gave out, the two of us would sit on a low bench, she talking to me about religious things or drowsing, and I with my hand on my chin and my eyes half closed, listening to her sweet, kind voice which made me sense the thing I was always seeking—a home and a mother.

I really was happy during the week I stayed with her. I felt like her daughter. I didn't have a single quarrel, there was no rush about any-thing. She never scolded me or made me realize how miserable I was. If my father hadn't come for me, I would have stayed there. But he came with his harsh voice and said, "You must come home or I will have you locked up in the reformatory."

"I don't want to go. I am very happy here," I said to my father. But it didn't mean a thing. He remained standing in the doorway waiting for me. Crying, I said good-bye to Santitos. She cried too, but I went back to my house.

A short while later, I moved to Lupita's on Rosario Street. My brother Roberto did not trouble me there, for he was not allowed into the house. I had a superficial friendship with my half-sisters, Antonia and Mari-elena, but down deep I guessed they didn't care about me. On several occasions when Tonia introduced me to her friends, she said I was an acquaintance; she almost never introduced me as her sister. This offended me, but I didn't fight with her about it because I didn't like to say that she was my sister, either. I considered her very crude, her vocabulary and her jokes made one blush and laugh. My father's younger daughter, Marielena, was very fickle. I couldn't care for her because she was nasty to my father and talked back to him in a common and demanding way.

The ones who were nice to me were Lupita and her older daughters, Elida and Isabel. They were her daughters by another man, whom she had left when she discovered that he was married. My father had also deceived her by concealing that he was married and I don't think she ever forgave him for it. At any rate, she never asked him for anything, even when her children were small and she really needed help. You might say he practically abandoned her until Antonia was eight years old, though he and Lupita both worked in the La Gloria restaurant. When Antonia got very sick and begged to see her father he began to visit them every three days and to bring food and presents. Because he was so good to Antonia, Lupita took up with him again. But even after Marielena was born, Lupita didn't make any demands on my father.

At first, I felt no affection for Lupita. When she was nice to me, I thought she was being hypocritical. To me, she was my father's "other *señora*," the one who had made my mother suffer. But when I saw how good she was to her own daughters and to my brothers and sisters, I began to doubt that she was capable of being mean. Besides, when I saw that her room was smaller and poorer than ours, I was convinced that my father had preferred my mother and us.

My father never paid as much attention to Lupita as he did to his other wives, perhaps because Lupita was stout and older than he. Lupita had a low opinion of men; they were all irresponsible and romantic. When I asked for her advice about marrying Pedro Ríos, saying he was a serious type of person, her answer was, "God protect you from the serious ones, and you protect yourself from the clowns!" There was no man good enough for a woman to marry, in her opinion. But her bitterness and distrust never hurt anyone, for she was good and kind to all. She made every sacrifice for her children and never abandoned them. Her daughters were her world and to me she was the ideal mother.

Elida and Isabel never started up with me like my half-sisters. Once I confided to them that I felt left out, and Elida consoled me, saying, "No, Consuelo, don't pay attention to them. After all, you are here with your *papá* and this is your house." I appreciated her words but went on feeling bad about my half-sisters and the difference in my father's treatment of us.

One day, the money arrangements were changed. I stopped giving my father money the day he threw my wages at me. That day I had given him fifty *pesos* and kept nothing for myself, as usual. In the evening, I had asked him for money for stockings and he wouldn't give it to me. The next day I asked him again, but with more assurance: "*Papá*, give me money for stockings. I have only these and they are all torn. Just nine *pesos*."

I guess my father was in a bad mood because he threw the fifty *pesos* in my face. "Here! Here is your money! I don't want anything from any of you any more. I still have enough strength to work."

As usual, I said nothing and went outside to lean on the railing and cry. Lupita came over and told me to pay no attention to my father. I didn't answer her because my tears kept me from talking. But I thought, "I promise myself that from now on I will never give him anything again. I'll find things to do with my money." And so it was. It consoled me to keep my money to buy the things I needed. I had my job and could get loans whenever I wanted. I never gave my father money again, nor did he ask me for any. Only one time did I venture to ask him how the little pig was that he bought with the first fifty *pesos* I gave him. He answered that he was going to sell it because it was very fat. That was all.

My world existed outside the house. I got up, drank a little coffee after cleaning up or going to the baths, put my things together, and left for work. Once I was there, I was happy. I hardly ever had any work in the afternoons. I had no fits of temper during the day—quite the contrary. I had presents and words of flattery. It is hard to believe, but words like "*niña* with the green eyes" or "Miss Consuelo" lifted my spirits. I was given orders politely and if I made some mistake (I almost always did) the only rebuke was "*niña* with the green eyes."

I hardly went to the Casa Grande any more, only once a week to see Paula and the children. Manuel had borrowed money from my father to set up a little shoe factory and for a while had worked with a will. He attended his business and seemed to enjoy it. I remember seeing him, with a cigarette in his mouth, holding some shoe soles, going back and forth between No. 64 and his shop. I could always tell when things were going well for him because he walked quickly with a firm sure step as though he was more in touch with the earth. He sat at the table and ate and spoke with more assurance. This meant that he had money in his pocket. Whenever he had a sizable roll, he was sure to take it out and wave it in our faces.

One day, the father of Manuel's *compadre*, who was also a shoemaker, stopped me in the courtyard and said, "You are Manuel's younger sister, aren't you? Well, tell your father that if Manuel doesn't mend his ways, his business will go broke. Your brother plays cards a lot, my son too, with their little circle of friends, and they will both go down if they keep on. They locked themselves in the shop and have been playing a game for the past three days and three nights."

I listened to the man but I didn't tell my father. My brother must have lost a lot of money, because the workers would come to our house to collect their wages. Manuel would hide behind the door, saying, "Tell them I'm not here." Once I yelled, "Manuel, someone is looking for you," and he came out, whether he wanted to or not, muttering, "Damn gossip! May your snout burn for sticking it into what is not your business."

The following week my brother's shop was empty . . . he had sold everything, and my father was shouting at Manuel, who just stood there with his hands in his pockets and his head to one side. When he tried to say something, my father would shut him up. Not only did Manuel lose the business, but he lost my father's confidence.

Later, Tonia went against me when she saw that her mother was treating me well and I left the house on Rosario Street because of a violent quarrel. Roberto had come to see my father, I don't know for what. Antonia worked in a cabaret and had come home drunk that morning. When she saw my brother, she ran him out of the house. I felt my blood boil; in spite of everything, Roberto was my brother and it hurt to see him humiliated like that.

I was willing to face Antonia and stop her nonsense. Since her illness, everyone was afraid of her and she was the boss of the situation. She had told me once, "I use the fact that I was sick, to fight with everybody. I just yell at them and they fold up. It pays me." It was true, but that night I thought I would unmask her. I would prove that she could be controlled. Now that she was cured, why did everyone have to go on taking it from her?

Tonia saw me looking at her in fury and insulted me. She took three swings at me without connecting. Lupita and my father were scared stiff when I tried to hit back. Lupita yelled, " Child of God, go downstairs. Get out, quick. She'll tear you to pieces." Someone pushed me out of the door and made me go home. I went, cursing my luck. I, who always ran from fights, was always in the middle of one.

I got to the Casa Grande and told Roberto what had happened. I knew what they did to me hurt him also. I went outside and sat on the steps in the little garden. It was after ten o'clock and everything was dark. What Yolanda had told me was true: "Hmm, Consuelo, when you're an orphan, everybody takes advantage of you. I was an orphan too. They all try to use you like a floor mop, and if you let them it's just too bad for you."

Everything this *señora* had warned me about had come true. Our father's love had been completely stolen from us. That was why he behaved so differently in Lupita's house. There he joked, chatted with the neighbors, ate late and let the lights stay on until eleven or twelve at night. At noon, when he had his meal, he ordered sodas for everybody, and when he left, he let my half-sisters run after him so he could give them money for the movies. He called Lupita by a nickname and seemed delighted with all of this.

Whenever I was unhappy, I would look up into the sky at night and search for something, something that I thirsted for with all my love. There was one star I looked at particularly because one time my aunt had told me that my mother was watching over me from heaven and that every night she took the form of a star. Even though I was a big girl then, I partly believed it and passed it on to Marta. Now I began to talk to that star in a whisper, begging it to give me strength, and, if it were really she, to stop what was going on. Why didn't she make my father see what he was doing to us?

After a time my father came back to the Casa Grande, why I don't know. He just came back one afternoon, with his box on his shoulder, put it under the bed, and went out again without saying anything. Later, Tonia also came back to live with us. She rarely got attacks any more but was very nervous.

In March, 1949, my father said to Tonia and me, "What do you intend to study? Are you going to be loafers all your lives, or what? I'll make whatever sacrifices I can to pay for your courses. So, see in which school and what it is you want to study." These words were unexpected, but I was very pleased and quit my shoe job.

I thought about what a serious thing a career was. I did want very much to study. Vera, a neighbor, was talking to Antonia and me one afternoon and told us the Instituto María del Lago, where she was taking a commercial course, was very good and not expensive. A "commercial course!" I thought she must be studying a very important career. Antonia, with her arms crossed, listened, smiling. "Well, I'll tell my *papá*. Let's see if he wants to," she said. Tonia told my *papá* and he agreed.

Antonia took the course that my father liked, dressmaking and dress design. I thought, "What a bore to be at a machine all day long, and then there are people who are such nuisances—'this pleat isn't right, and that button!'" I told my father, "I like literature and books better." He agreed, and I entered classes in shorthand, typing, Spanish, filing, commercial documents, bookkeeping, correspondence, and arithmetic.

There in the Instituto I began to guess that I wasn't such an insignificant person after all. There I could express my dreams to my classmates without being afraid that they would turn their backs or make fun of me. I worked hard the first year and took to heart the precepts we typed in class exercises, "Perseverance wins," or, "Choose the right path and you will triumph."

In the second year, I began to change. I made friends with a group of eight girls and played hooky with them. I no longer studied and wanted only to have fun. We were so incorrigible, the teacher took points off our grades. The teacher warned me and I felt grateful for her interest, but, unfortunately, I was influenced by those girls. I should say, though, that this was the only time in my life that I was really happy and so I have no regrets.

While I was going to school, I forgot my troubles. All I thought about was having work later, having clothes, continuing my studies, and fixing up my house nicely, as I had always dreamed about. "I would like our next-door neighbor to move," I thought, "and my father to take that room. I would help him have the wall between knocked down and that room would be used as a living room, with a fireplace, a nice day-bed suite, the floor waxed and the walls fixed up. Then we would have a place to entertain our friends. The same with the kitchen—the two in one, with a nice gas stove, knives and forks, curtains, and some big flower pots with green plants all the way to the front door. The bedroom would have its window on the street. And if thieves wanted to come in? Well, we would have bars put over the window. There would be a record player and nice lamps. I would help my *papá* pay for the labor and everything."

My ideal was to see my family united and happy. I dreamed of helping my brothers and sisters and of bringing them consolation so that they would not feel the way I did. Whenever my father made Roberto cry, everything within me rebelled and shouted: "No! It isn't fair." But I always remained silent. My heart ached seeing my brother in a corner of the kitchen with his head lowered, the tears rolling down his cheeks. Then I would say, "Don't mind *papá*, he's angry." Or I would motion to my brothers to go out into the courtyard so as not to hear my father any more.

My father's words were destructive to everyone, but Roberto was the one who felt them most deeply. Manuel preferred to become cynical. He remained silent while my father scolded him, but after a few minutes he would raise his head and go out into the courtyard, whistling. Finally, he began to turn his back on my father and leave immediately. Roberto remained rooted to the spot and cried.

I believe that this is what gave rise to my desire to help my brothers and my sister. I wanted to be (what a dreamer I was!) the one who guided and counseled them. For Manuel, I dreamed up the career of lawyer or teacher. For Roberto, I wanted the career of an architect or engineer. By that time my father would not work so much. I dreamed of winning the lottery so that I could buy him a farm and chickens and have nice upholstered furniture. At night he would sit in his easy chair in front of the fireplace, with his robe and slippers on, surrounded by all of his children (four) and he would think or say to us, "These are my children, my creation. I educated them!" I lived in hopes that all these things would come about some day.

What a bitter disappointment for me when the years passed and I only saw my family grow apart. I always came up against the inflexibility of my father, who was like a hard rock. I wanted to hear him say with pride, "These are my children!" But I heard only, "Ungrateful wretches, that's what you are. You'll never be able to raise your heads." Nevertheless, I kept on hoping that some day I would introduce harmony into my family. This was my ideal, my golden dream, my illusion. Afterwards, when I began to rebel against my father, I dreamed of studying to show him that I was good for something. I did not even know for what, but I had to prove that I could do something.

When I graduated from the Instituto, the same thing happened that had happened in the sixth grade. It is true that my father had bought me everything I had needed for school and had given me money for tuition. But he didn't show up at my graduation ceremony, nor at the Mass held in the Cathedral. What a deep emotion I felt to be in the Basilica singing Schubert's "Ave Maria" with the other graduates. I can't explain why I felt so strongly when the organ began to play, with our voices coming in, softly at first, then rising to carry our prayer to the feet of the Virgin, where it deposited our faith and our love.

We were all dressed in the regulation colors—black toga and mortarboard, white shoes, gloves, and cape. Black stood for responsibility, white for purity. The principal spoke to us over the microphone, telling us that we were leaving the school, healthy girls, which quality we should preserve until the day the Lord would send us the man who would make us happy. "You are leaving this world to go into another one in which you will have to fight every step of the way. You are going to get to know new faces, new characters, but do not forget that you must continue being upright, honest and pure." These were some of the words I managed to hear; I was all the way in the back.

Finally it was over and the notes of the organ gradually faded away until all was silent. My *padrinos* of graduation, *Señora* Cristina, who lived in the Casa Grande, and Dr. Ramón, my father's doctor, met me outside the church with a bouquet of flowers. I had begged my father to be there with my godparents, but he had said as always, "I can't just drop my work. I can't go."

I struggled to understand my father. How many times, looking at him from behind his back, I would think of all that he had suffered, of his noble heart, of his absolute sense of responsibility. His back gave me the impression of a conquered man, a tired man, a father who inspired much love and admiration. But when I saw his cold eyes and his hard glance and heard his dry words, he seemed to me like an adversary who never gave one the opportunity of demonstrating friendship or love. He was like a person who had been given the task of raising some little animals. He fed them and gave them clothing and a home, but without affection, without realizing that animals also think and feel. If he had not been so hard he would have been an ideal father.

One month after my graduation, in January, 1951, I began to work as a typist for *Señor* Santiago Parra and his wife, Juana. They paid me a hundred *pesos* a month and treated me very nicely. I knew they had a high opinion of me because of the many times they took me to the movies and invited me to dinner.

I was just sixteen when I went to their house for the first time. It made a deep impression upon me, especially the parlor, for without ever having been in such a nice one before, it was exactly the kind I had so often dreamed of. It made me feel important to be there, and at the same time, ill at ease. Somehow, I felt my father's eyes upon me and could hear him saying, "Fool! Why do you go pushing yourself where you don't belong!" I stood there, squeezing my folder and my purse in my sweaty hands, until Juana made me sit down.

Seeing me so disturbed, *Señor* Parra said, "Would you like a drink?"

"*Caramba!*" I thought. "Are they going to drink? What will they say at home if I come back drunk?" I must confess that I didn't know it was the custom among the middle class to drink aperitifs before dinner. In the *vecindad*, to drink meant to get drunk. I was frightened but I took the vermouth they offered. It was the first time in my life I had tasted it, and as I lifted the glass with my new friends, in a house far better than mine, I felt very pleased and flattered.

When dinner was ready, we went to the dining room. The table was set very nicely, with a cloth and knives and forks. I was still carrying my folder and purse (I was afraid to set it down in the wrong place) when I sat at my place, worrying about how I would eat with a fork. At home, we ate with a spoon or with a *tortilla*, but here was *Señor* Parra using a fork. Somehow I managed to eat the rice and fish, although they both kept falling off the fork. But the salad! That was more of a torment! Never did a meal taste more bitter to me. When it was over, I was red and sweaty. To make matters worse, Juana and her husband did not take their eyes off me, as though they wanted to see my embarrassment. To show his sympathy, *Señor* Santiago patted my head, but that upset me even more. I had the idea that only animals were caressed that way. So I jerked away my head, thinking to myself, "Does he think I am a cat?" It was a relief to get back to the office.

At first, *Señor* Santiago was polite and respectful, but after a while, he tried to make love to me. He openly proposed, saying he was ready to leave Juana and marry me. Of course, I did not accept. I made him understand I wasn't just a cheap girl.

Unfortunately, at this time my brother Roberto was put in jail. The next day, I went to work early and locked myself in the office to cry. How to help him? I didn't even know what to do for him. Besides, a lot of money would be needed. "Oh, Lord, help me!"

I opened the door and saw *Licenciado* Hernández, the lawyer who had his office across the hall. He asked what was wrong. At that moment embarrassment didn't matter and, after all, I planned to pay him back, so I asked him for help. When *Licenciado* Hernández said, "Come, come, don't worry. Let's see what we can do." I felt my feet touching earth again.

I asked *Señor* Santiago for the day off and went with the *licenciado* to the Penitentiary, feeling like a little girl following someone who gives out candy. It was too late for visitors, but I went back later alone and saw Roberto and his friend Hermilio. They were without shoes and all ragged. I got scared; I was used to seeing my brother in bad shape, but not like that. The other prisoners had beaten them up and had taken their things. I wanted to cry but I thought, "If I cry, he'll cry too."

Roberto said, "Look, sister. Get me out of here. I swear I'll behave from now on." Roberto signed the papers I had brought, and I left. He was calmer, but I felt as if my heart would break to see him there among so many dirty, tough-looking men.

I went to the courts for his record and the *licenciado* arranged the paper for bail that same day. Later, at home, I told my father how much money was needed to get Roberto out, and his answer was, "I won't give one single *centavo* for that rat. He was just looking for trouble. Let him rot in jail. I don't want to hear another word about it."

I spent the whole night in a sea of confusion and tears, wondering how to get the money. I would sell or pawn my clothes, or borrow from a loan shark, no matter how high the interest was. I didn't want to have to ask my boss for a loan, since he was trying to get hold of me. When the time limit on the bail was almost up and I still didn't have the money, I cried very much.

Señor Santiago kept watching me and finally asked what the matter was. Crying, I told him, and he got mad at my *papá.* "What's wrong with your father? He should be the one taking care of the matter. What business is it of yours to be going around among that gang of ruffians and criminals, up and down the stairs, exposing yourself to insults? I want to have a talk with your father."

"Don't start in on my father, *Señor* Santiago. He knows what he is doing. After all, we are grown up now and there is no reason why we should bother him." *Señor* Santiago smiled and held out two hundred *pesos* to me. It would be deducted from my pay, but even then I hesitated. Thinking of Roberto, I had no choice but to lower my head and take it.

After putting up the bail, Roberto was free. But what all this cost me! My face burned with shame on leaving the Penitentiary. When anyone from the *vecindad* turned around to look at me, I had to lower my eyes. Everybody knew about it and I avoided people. I thought Roberto really would behave himself after that, but I was mistaken. He was supposed to go to the Penitentiary each week to sign in, but after the first few times he stopped. If I urged him to go, I would get slapped in the face.

My brother was locked up again a year later for not complying with the parole rules and once more I was the one who had to get him out. This time a girl at the office introduced me to *Licenciado* Marroquín and he helped me. Roberto was in the Penitentiary about eight months, during which time my father didn't want to know anything about him, not even hear his name, and did not go to see him. Roberto always asked for my father and would hang his head and say, "It is good that he doesn't come to a place like this. It would soil him."

Manuel visited Roberto only once, but Marta, my aunt and I went every week, bringing what we could. I went to church almost every day to pray for him and to light candles.

When my brother was released, the *licenciado* wouldn't accept payment, not even the present I wanted to give him, nor had he ever hinted at anything improper. He always behaved correctly with me, for which I am infinitely grateful. Roberto continued to be nasty to me. But now, when he wanted to hit me, I would threaten to have him locked up again and that stopped him.

Señor Santiago began to arrive at the office in bad humor, threw papers at me and if I made a mistake reprimanded me harshly. One time, to my shame he said, "I am going to wait for you to get married. Then it will be easier for me to have you—to have your body, which is what I want." When I went to their house for dinner, he would rub my foot or wait until his wife went into the kitchen to stroke my head and ask me for a kiss. I still owed the money for the bail, but later I quit working for him, without telling his wife anything. I remained friendly with her for many years and *Señor Santiago* kept waiting until he got tired.

After that I went to work for *Licenciado* Hernández. It was then I discovered he had helped me because he liked me. One afternoon while he was dictating, he said, "Your mouth is like a plum, a juicy plum. Like a delicious fruit I feel like biting. And your slant eyes make me want to close them." I remained silent. I felt flattered but on the other hand his words reminded me of my brothers who when I was little made me cry by calling me "tea flower," "slant eyes," "piggy-bank eyes," "Chink eyes," "crack eyes," "Chinkie," "cat eyes." I didn't like such nicknames because I had once seen a very thin, ugly Chinese, whose eyes were so narrow they were almost hidden. Besides, Irela and her cousin, who really had Chinese blood, got mad when they were called that. So it must be something bad, I thought. I left *Licenciado* Hernández after only two weeks because I got sick.

When I began to work again it was for an accountant, *Señor* García. His office was in a tall building, the first elevator building I had ever been in. My only co-worker was Jaime Castro, a short young man, who hardly came up to my ear. He had very thick eyebrows, prominent eyes, small mouth with straight lips and a very sharp nose. His hair was black and shiny with brilliantine, his fingers were thick and stubby. In his tight-fitting jacket, he looked like one of those little dwarfed figures they put on cakes. But what a good friend he was at work!

Jaime was the assistant accountant and I just a secretary and he would get me out of any kind of jam. When I didn't know how to do the work and made mistakes, my excuse was, "I don't know, *Señor* García. Jaime told me to do it that way." Jaime would just turn around to me and smile, and for the moment, I was saved.

He invited me to the movies, to have coffee, to see American football, to Chapultepec Park, to the Sixteenth of September parade. He made a regular thing of taking me to a different place every week. It was through him that I got to know the city's parks, the swimming pools and bullfights. He brought me candy, flowers and little presents of no consequence, except that they made me realize he was thinking of me.

In short, he won me over and I began to feel a friendly affection toward him. He would tell me his love problems and I told him mine. When he invited me to the movies, I expected him to make love to me, but he didn't do anything and I came to believe he was different from the others. I was delighted because I could go out whenever I wanted to without being afraid of getting involved with him. I felt sympathy for him and nothing more.

I knew Jaime drank because of an unhappy love affair. His drinking was the only bad thing about him but that didn't matter to me then. I tried to give him advice about it. I didn't get to love him until later. He taught me the real meaning of the word.

We were very good friends but he never invited me to dance, which was still my greatest pleasure. When I danced it was as if I took flight. I felt as though I had no feet and my tiredness melted away. The music was irresistible. The notes of the *danzón* penetrated my soul. Note by note it would begin to work its way inside me until without realizing it, I would find myself dancing, flying, almost. The music entered me sweet as the perfumed water one bathes in. The *señoras* would stand around watching, condemning the style of dancing. "*Qué!* They have no shame any more. Imagine if I did things like that in my time!" But none of this mattered to me. This was how I escaped from the happenings of the day.

When Jaime and I came to love each other he forbade me to dance. I wouldn't go out to dance when he came to call on me, until after he had left. In spite of my dancing and my family troubles, Jaime was nice to me and to everyone in my family. A day didn't pass but that he brought toys, cakes, or dolls to my nieces and nephews. He never failed to give my sister-in-law Paula money on Sunday so that he could eat at my house. On Paula's Saint's Day he brought her a bouquet of flowers and presents for all of us.

He won over my family, except my father, who didn't like him because he drank. He had said to Jaime, "I will never give my consent to your marriage and will fight to the end to separate you." Whenever

Jaime tried to chat with him or give him a present, my father would answer only yes or no and never accepted the gift. Jaime tried to win his affection but did not succeed.

On my father's Saint's Day, Jaime bought him a cake and gave my sister-in-law money to make chocolate. But instead of being pleased, my father pushed the cake aside and refused to have supper. I was embarrassed because I was always treated very well when I went to Jaime's house. His *mamá* seated me at the head of the table and served me before anyone else. My *papacito* would insult Jaime in every way he knew how until I was afraid Jaime would no longer love me. But he always accepted my excuses and, kissing me on the forehead, would say, "Yes, *mi vida,* I understand."

One Christmas, my father put me through the worst shame of all. Jaime and I had given Paula money to make the traditional supper, a salad and two other dishes. Jaime had brought the bottles of soda and the poinsetta flowers, and Paula had arranged the table and the room very nicely. But the same thing happened. My father arrived at about ten o'clock and didn't even say hello as he came in. I greeted him with a smile, full of fear. "*Papacito,* we've been waiting for you to have supper."

"I don't want anything. Get to bed! Come on, get all this stuff away from here." He immediately shut the doors of the room. He threw the tablecloth on one of the beds and the flowers landed on one of the chairs.

"At least let me take the table out into the kitchen to have supper."

"You're taking nothing out of here. The table doesn't leave this room. Everybody to bed. Turn that light out!" Paula went to bed with the children.

I went out to the courtyard with Jaime. A dance was going on. I didn't know what to say to him. He pulled out a cigarette and lighted it. "Don't worry about it, Skinny. Maybe somebody made him mad and that's why he is acting like this."

I said nothing. I leaned on his chest and began to cry. After staying with me half an hour, Jaime said good-bye. I let him go, feeling very sad. "He's not going to love me any more. He's going to change toward me," I thought.

I wasn't wrong. He began to criticize my father and order me about. He wanted me to obey him instead of my *papá* and, of course, I wouldn't. Jaime acted as though we were married and began to show his true colors. He drank more than before and would come to see me, completely drunk. Sometimes he would whistle for me at three or four o'clock in the morning and if I didn't appear, he would bang on the door. I began to be annoyed with him and kept trying to make him stop drinking.

Then, one day I realized I had been too innocent in going through with our engagement. A girl named Adelaida had come to work in our office long after I had. Everyone in the office knew that Jaime and I were going to be married, so I don't believe this girl could not have known. One afternoon, I came back from lunch early and sat down in Señor García's armchair in his private office. I heard voices in the next office and looked through the little telephone window. There I saw Jaime kissing Adelaida and stroking her hair. He was about to say something when he saw me. He remained dumb.

I stood there thinking, "Am I seeing right? Who knows if he knew her before me?" I felt bitter, defeated, and furious with myself for having believed in him. "Great idiot! But didn't you see all the attention he pays her? Didn't you see how she seeks him out for any little thing?" I was burning with jealousy and I felt an infinite hatred for him. He tried to explain but my heart was broken. I cried on the bus all the way home.

When I arrived home, I wanted to burst into tears again, but a very dear little voice, dearer than Jaime's, stopped me. Mariquita, my little niece, said to me, "Auntie, Auntie, take us to the merry-go-round. I have my five-*centavo* piece." When I saw her, the bitterness dissolved into sweetness because of the great love I had for that child. "Yes, *madre*. Put your little sweater on and put on Alanes' also."

Their pleasure completely washed away the deception that I had suffered that afternoon. Once we were at the poor little fair and I saw how happy my little niece and nephew were, I was happy too. The pleasant dizziness of the merry-go-round, the up and down motion of the horses and the children in my arms, made me laugh out loud. My little niece was my adoration. It was as if she were my own child— Jaime was even jealous when he saw how much we loved each other. He would ask me if I preferred my niece to him, and I always said yes, I preferred her.

I didn't want Jaime to come to my house any more, but he was jealous and distrustful and came around to see whether I was going with somebody else. Since I was still in love with him, I let him come.

I really needed his moral support because my father was bothering me about my health.

I had become terribly thin and had a cough. He had always worried about me becoming tubercular and took me to his friend, Dr. Santoyo, who wasn't really a medical doctor but a curer of some sort. Dr. Santoyo agreed that I looked tubercular and prescribed two injections a day, one in the vein and one intramuscularly. Later, he added a third one, subcutaneously. He also gave me tonics, pills, transfusions and serums. I had a strong taste of iodine in my mouth and my body ached from so many punctures.

Sometimes I didn't go for my daily injections and my father would get angry, scolding me cruelly. He threatened to put me in the hospital where Elena had been. "I'll put you there and then you'll see. Imbecile! Like dumb animals that don't understand! The only place you'll go from there is to the cremation furnace." Even in Jaime's presence, my father, with his scornful look, would say, "With that tubercular dog cough you have, you're going to end up in the morgue." I listened to all this with my head bowed and didn't dare talk back. How completely without compassion my father was! As for Dr. Santoyo, he had arranged for me to enter the hospital and told us that he had a bed ready. I cried desperately.

Jaime's mother heard about what was going on and took me to her doctor. He took an x ray and said I didn't have the slightest trace of being sick. My ex-employers, Juana and Señor Santiago, also took me to a specialist, who had me under observation all afternoon. My sputum, blood, pulse, lungs, everything, was examined. I had more proof to show that Dr. Santoyo was wrong. Screwing up my courage, I showed my father the doctors' reports. Far from believing me, he and Dr. Santoyo were angry because I had gone to someone else. My "treatment" continued against my will.

I didn't understand my father. Things couldn't continue that way. One afternoon, I went to visit Santitos and told her what he was doing to me. "Why, why, why? Why is my father like this?" I asked. She hunched her old shoulders and puffed on a cigarette and said, "Someone must be 'working' on him. I think someone is bewitching him."

"*Ay*, Santitos! Do you think so? If I only knew who it might be!"

That was when I went to the telepathist with her. He told me my father was not bewitched, but that it was his nature to be like that, and I should not worry about him. He didn't help me with my problem at all, but he saw something in the cards about myself that gave me a fright. He said I had a strong will and could become someone very important, or, if I was not careful, I could fall very low. He told me to come often for advice, for he could keep me from falling. I left him three *pesos* and went home with Santitos, feeling foolish. I didn't believe he was a good diviner but nevertheless I remembered for years what he said about me.

Things got worse at home. My dishes and spoons were kept apart and the children were forbidden to come near me. I can't begin to explain how I felt when my sister-in-law pulled them away from me by their arm or hair. Paula gave Mariquita terrible spankings for disobeying the new orders. I couldn't mix in because when Manuel had first brought his wife home, my father had said, "The day I find out that any of you has been disrespectful to Paula, I'll break your necks." She never bothered us and, indeed, I thought my sister-in-law was very nice.

The time Manuel beat Paula without pity, Marta and I and Paula's mother, Cuquita, mixed in and tried to defend her. Marta was living with us again, with her babies, because she had left Crispín for the third time. I was in the kitchen and didn't see when the fight began. Paula was lying on the bedroom floor, crying and insulting him, and he was kicking her in the belly. He seemed crazy and didn't care where the blows fell. I felt a tremendous desperation and screamed for him to stop. I got the children out first and left them crying in the courtyard. Marta and Cuquita were pulling at Manuel's clothes, but he continued to hit Paula. Her abdomen was big with child, and that was precisely where he kept kicking her, there in her womb, her beautiful womb.

I don't know who it was who forced the knife out of my brother's hand, but, thank God, he didn't get to use it. In desperation, I broke a clay jug over his head, fearful that he would turn on me, but he didn't even notice it. I remembered how they knocked out men in the movies and I put my palms together and brought them down hard on the back of his neck, once, twice, four times! But that barbarian didn't stop until he finally got tired.

I defended my sister-in-law more than once, so I couldn't understand why Paula told something to Manuel which made him hit Marta and me. All I know is that something woke me up suddenly one morning and I heard Manuel saying "Get up, you! Do you think you've got servants or what? Just lying around all the time!"

Paying no attention, I spit on the floor. I was still half asleep when I felt that my eye was swelling up. I rubbed it and sat up. I saw my brother sitting on the other bed, swearing at me. The cardboard horse that Jaime and I had bought for the children was lying on the floor, where it had landed after hitting my eye. I said nothing, but spit again.

Manuel shouted at me, "Stop spitting! You are not the one who has to clean up." But I was stubborn and spit again and at that Manuel leaped from his bed and hit me.

"Why are you hitting me? Who do you think you are? Imbecile, idiot, stupid!" He kept hitting me. Then my sister Marta jumped up and hit Manuel.

But how could we two women get the better of a tough guy who was used to street fighting? I was terrified when Manuel kicked my sister on the floor. I tried to help her, but couldn't. If I managed to get a blow in, I got three or four back. I tried to run out even in my underwear, to call Yolanda. I had one foot in the courtyard when I was pushed so hard I rolled to the next room.

When Manuel finally stopped hitting us, Marta and I were black and blue all over; she was bleeding, my face was bruised and I had a black eye. But Manuel had also got some scratches and kicks. Marta cried a lot. I told her to get dressed, that we were going to leave the house, that I was going to get money. I was sure Jaime would not refuse to help me. I telephoned him and he came immediately in a taxi. He took us for breakfast, then to Lupita's house, saying I should stay there until Manuel moved out. I argued against this because I thought if Paula left the house, the children would suffer. I knew my brother wouldn't take care of his children. He didn't even on Christmas Day; I was the one who bought them their toys.

We told my father what had happened and he said Manuel was the one who should leave. When we got back, Paula had already left, taking the children. Marta and I lived there alone. But Paula dressed up my Mariquita and sent her once a week to see us. To be sure, this caused gossip. People whispered that the little girl was mine. As a matter of fact, I really did feel as though she were part of me.

I found a temporary job addressing envelopes for a Bacardi rum firm. But we had no one to take care of the house because Marta by now had gone back to live with Crispín. Only my father, Roberto and I lived at home. One afternoon a girl, Claudia, came looking for work. She said she had just arrived from Zacatecas without a *centavo*. I felt sorry for her and gave her the job. That night when I told my father, he didn't want her, but I said I would pay her and, in spite of my father, she stayed.

A number of months went by when my father told me he was going to bring Paula back to the house because she was very sick. I was alarmed, but since he always exaggerated, I didn't believe it when he said she was like a corpse. She had been very fat at the time she left our house. I warned Claudia that there would be a little more work, but said I would help. The clothes would be sent out to be washed and it didn't matter if she couldn't finish the housework. The children were to be looked after first. She agreed.

When my father brought Paula, I was almost struck dumb to see her. What my father had said was true, she was unrecognizable, just skin and bones. She kept on her feet only because of her great love for her children. I pulled myself together and greeted her, smiling. "Hello, Paula, come on in and lie down."

When she lay down, I went into the kitchen to cry. I loved Paula very much, much more than my sister. Now she looked so ill, I couldn't believe it was she. However, here were the three children and the new baby to prove it. When Mariquita saw me, she ran to hug me, and Alanes, too. Paula, in a very faint voice, said, "Give my little girl some milk. She's hungry. I haven't any to give her." I heated the milk and gave it to the baby in a soda bottle. She was beautiful; her eyes were enormous and she was very fat, like the other three, who had grown big and filled out with life and color.

Claudia took care of the children while I was at work. Things had been going well and I was satisfied with her. When I got back, I would fix the food. Once a week I would clean the house, washing everything —floor, tables, chairs, the stove—and finish up exhausted. The baby was just seven months old and I had to give her her bottle early in the morning and change her diaper.

The house was very crowded now. Paula, the baby at her side, slept with Manuel and the three children crosswise on one of the beds. Roberto slept on the floor in the kitchen, and I in my bed. Later, Manuel made his old "bed" on the floor in front of the wardrobe because "the damned brats don't let a man sleep." At night, sometimes one of the children would wet the bed and Paula would pull his hair or pinch him and make him cry. Rather than witness that, I took the three children into my bed. I didn't get much sleep but I didn't complain.

In the mornings, it was difficult too, for I had to pick my way quietly among the piles of clothing, benches, chairs and get dressed while the others slept. Manuel's sleeping form usually blocked the wardrobe door and I bumped him when I tried to get my clothes.

"What the hell are you doing, you damned brat?" or, "I'll break your snout if you wake me up again," he would say.

"Let's see if your man enough!" I would answer. "What a fine fellow and he doesn't give a *centavo* into the house!" And a quarrel would continue until everyone was awake and the children crying. I would escape with a bang of the front door and, with a smile on my face and usually nothing but coffee in my stomach, I would be off to work.

This situation didn't last long, because Paula died soon after. When she died, I almost died. I would rather it had been me. I wished it with all my soul and shouted that they take my life and leave hers. I screamed for her not to die. Only He knew why He did it.

The night she was dying, we took the children to another house after she had blessed them. Paula looked like a corpse already, but that tiny flame that gives us our thirst for life made me keep hoping she wouldn't die. Dr. Ramón came to give her a plasma transfusion. Dr. Valdés was taking care of her also. But she died. It was the most terrible blow of my life. It was as if suddenly a hand made of wax was pressing on my brain. The color of the sunlight changed to a whitishness, like that of the bones I had seen in the graveyard. I don't even know what I felt when she expired. I just cried. I cried so much my eyes ached.

The day we buried Paula I got another awful blow. When we came home from the cemetery, I asked Roberto to spread out some sacks for me, so I could lie down. I had no strength at all, I didn't even feel like talking. Claudia sat down to eat with my father and my half-sister Marielena before serving my brother. I watched them eating together. It made me mad to see Claudia sitting there with my father. I became suspicious that there was something going on between them. I couldn't take it when my father shouted at Roberto, "You, loafer! Take the knife and get to work and scrape the floor and wash it."

I don't know where I got the strength but I said to Roberto, "Why should you do it? It seems to me that's what we pay this girl for. It's her job to do it."

I didn't finish speaking before my father, with one leap, was right on top of me, shouting with real fury, "And who are you, you miserable creature? You're not worth a five-*centavo* piece! Just look at yourself!"

That night he made me sleep in the bed in which Paula had died. Perhaps he thought this was a punishment. Once the light was out, I began to cry, not from the pain in my body now, but because I felt that my heart had been hurt.

After this, I had to swallow the presence of Claudia. She wasn't the one who had to do the work, but I was. When I called her attention to the fact that she hadn't brought water, or something else, she would complain to my father and I had to take humiliation and ill treatment. I couldn't order Claudia to do anything. Again, I felt like nothing in the house.

But I remained in charge of the four children. My father said Manuel should support the children while Roberto and I help with the household expenses. My job for Bacardi came to an end just at that time, but I didn't have to worry yet about paying rent or light. Later, Manuel said that what he earned wasn't enough and I had to look for work so we could cover expenses.

In the meantime, I was happy with my little nephews and nieces, taking care of them, bathing them, and once in a while spanking them for misbehaving. They began to fatten up. I tried to feed them the best I could—raw sliced tomato with salt in the mornings, and milk during the day. I kept them clean, and the house too, and I was a little fatter myself. I wanted to keep these little children from suffering. The ideals and dreams I had had for my own family now centered on them.

My father began to show more favoritism to Claudia. My father gave her money or authorized her to get things on credit. Almost every day, she showed me new clothes she had bought. Whenever she asked for an advance he gave it to her, but when I asked for a *peso* or two to look for a job he would refuse. I saw that I was losing ground in my rights as the unmarried daughter. Marta had her home with the father of her children, Antonia and Marielena lived with their mother, I had come to know the run of the house and now that Paula was dead, I wanted to be the woman of the house. I saw danger in Claudia.

My father told me one night he was thinking of marrying her. I said he could do as he pleased but that he should recognize my rights and give me my proper place in the house. I fought to make my father see I wasn't mad at his wanting to marry her but rather because of the way he treated me. He criticized and belittled me; he said I was conceited and arrogant, that I was trying to get out of my class. He told me to beat it because he was fed up with me. His words became harsher and harsher. One night he told me, "You look like your mother's drunken race and you are as foolish as you look."

"My mother is dead, *papá*, what harm is she doing you? Say anything you like to me but not to her." His words hurt more because Claudia was there. And how I hated that woman!

The next day I went to my aunt's and told her what my father had said. I cried and beat my forehead, cursing my bad luck. Again I began asking, "Tell me the truth, Auntie, am I not his daughter?" My aunt was very angry with my father and said she was going to take back my mother's photo which hung next to one of my father on our wall.

"My sister isn't going to be laughed at by any wretch!" she said. We both went to my house to get the picture. When I saw my father's photo I said, "There's no reason for that picture to be here. I'll treat him the way he treats us." I pulled it out of the frame I had bought in installments and began to beat it on the floor while Claudia and my aunt watched in amazement.

I was yelling and crying and tearing the picture when Roberto came in. He was furious and hit me, but the thing that made me cry most was that my father, my saint, had fallen from his pedestal. And that night he punished me in a way I did not expect. I came home late and found him sitting with all our baby photos on his knee and tears rolling down his cheeks. He was smoking, which was unusual. He asked me, rather gently, why I had torn up his picture and I didn't know what to say. I cannot describe the terrible remorse I felt at that moment. I knelt at his feet, crying and begging his pardon. My *papacito* didn't answer or move; he just held the photographs in his hand and the tears kept falling.

But my rebellion continued and I told Claudia we didn't need her any more. When my father came home and didn't find her there he chased me out and sent Roberto to bring her back. "If that girl doesn't come back, you'll be sorry, both of you, because I'll rent this place and throw you out on the street." Claudia came back and naturally after that did what she pleased. I spent all day at my aunt's house, coming home only when my father was there.

That's when I thought of Delila, Paula's sister. She had left her husband, who was a drunkard, and needed a home for herself and her son. "She is of the same blood as the children, she is their aunt. How can she not take good care of them?" I said to my father. I kept insisting that Claudia was not a good worker and that the children were being neglected. Manuel had disappeared and was not contributing any money for them. My father was convinced and went to fetch Delila, although he still kept Claudia.

How could I have known when I said to my father, "Let Delila come, *papá*," that I would grow to hate her! The few times I had had the opportunity of seeing her, I took her for a sweet, long-suffering girl who needed help. But now I know that she used that pose as a mask behind which to study the person she intended to attack. She thus gained an advantage which she used without scruple. She was like a snake who lay in the grass to spy on the fat victim she intended to destroy. She was astute and tricky and all that was evil.

When Delila moved in she behaved very well at first. She left her son Geofredo with her mother, so that he would not be in the way. We would talk and go to the movies. But this began to change little by little, or rather, she didn't change but my father kept getting more difficult with me. I couldn't touch anything any more. He would accuse me of taking things to my aunt and treated me like a thief. I couldn't explain why my father hated me more than ever.

My father was also annoyed with Jaime, who was becoming unbearable even to me. His drinking became almost continuous. At night, Roberto would have to get up to take him home or put him in a cab, but thirty minutes later he would be back again, banging on the door. Rather than console me for what he saw was happening at home, he would get angry, insult me, shake me by the shoulders and say that I was annoyed with him because there was someone else. One time, completely drunk, Jaime smashed my picture against the door frame. Another time he tried to cut his veins and gave me a terrible scare. I couldn't break with him because whenever I tried, he would make an attempt on his life. Besides, his mother cried and begged me not to be cruel to him.

One night I thought I should make him face things; the time limit my father had set was soon going to be up. "Three years," my father had said when I introduced Jaime. If we lasted that long, we could get married. When I told him that I was thinking about the time limit being almost up, he said, "Look, Skinny, I had the money saved up for us to get married, but because you got mad, I spent it with my friends."

I felt as though the sky had fallen in. I had clung to the illusion that we would be married. His *mamá* had assured me we would.

"You and my son will marry in August. We will make a lovely *fiesta* for you. I'll pick out a dress with lots of lace and a long veil." She would say how proud she was and how understanding my father would be.

Her words had made me go off into a thousand rosy dreams, like when I was fifteen. To honor my father was my greatest ambition; to enter on my father's arm, in my white dress, and to go up to the altar with him, where the one who was going to give me his name would be waiting for me; to have the bridesmaids all around as I danced the waltz and to see the pleasure my father would feel when the daughter whom he had treated the worst and for whom he had the most contempt, had honored him. After the wedding, I would have my house, all furnished, and every week my family would come to have dinner with us. I had no intention of being disobedient to my husband in anything. I could stand next to him and hold my head high. Through all the trouble with Jaime I still had cherished this dream. But with his money gone there was no hope left.

But Jaime wasn't my only problem. One morning Delila was preparing breakfast and my little nephew, Alanes, was sitting in the doorway trying to lace his shoe. Delila gave him a slap and told him to go to the store for something. The child said, "Right away, Aunt, I'm lacing my shoe." Delila began to scream at him and hit him on the head with a spoon.

"Why do you hit him?" I said. "Don't be unreasonable. The child can't do two things at once."

That was enough to bring Delila over to me shouting, "What business is it of yours? I'm breaking my back here, and I can do what I want with them. Don't stick your nose in where you don't belong."

After looking at her for a minute, I smiled and said, "Ah, poor thing. How hard she works. Don't kill yourself like that or you'll die on me any minute. And as far as your being able to do what you want with them, that's out around here. First you ask my permission."

"And who do you think you are, the Queen of Sheba or what? You're nothing in this house—your father has said so."

I got mad and shouted; "The reason you're here, idiot, is because I asked my father to let you come, not because he wanted you here."

"That means nothing to me. I am here because your father wants me. I can throw you out without lifting a finger. Let's see who goes first, you or me."

"A woman like you can go to bed with anybody."

She tried to jump on me and hit me. I got up to defend myself bu the children started to cry and so nothing happened. I calmed them; after all, there was no reason for frightening them.

I decided I was placing too much importance on that bitch. I went to my aunt's house. I stayed there most of the day and didn't get home to talk to my father before Delila did. As I walked into the house, my father slammed the door shut. In a very grim voice, he said, "Why did you answer Delila back that way? What did she do to you? Why did you try to hit her?" I started to explain. "Lies, lies, always lying. Faker, scum. You are just like the other sons-of-bitches, you're on the same road. That's the way you're headed and you'll never amount to anything else. You're from the same miserable blood your mother came from, all drunks, all—"

I didn't let him go. I stood up to him. My tears dried as if by magic, and I said, "Don't you talk about my mother! Don't even mention her name in front of this creature. What does she want from you? She's dead now. Neither she nor my uncles ever come knocking at your door. They may be poor, but they never ask you for anything."

Then Delila spoke up: "She is mad because she wants her aunt to come to work here, so she can take things out of here later."

I walked over to her and yelled, "My aunt asks you for the same thing the breeze asked Juárez," and at the same time I tried to slap her. My father caught my arm and pushed me and I ran to my friend's house to have a good cry.

Delila kept her word. Day by day it became more of an inferno for me to live in that house. Every night when I came home to sleep, I found my clothes out of place or the things in my drawer upside down. My niece told me that Delila's son searched through my things in the mornings. One time there was some money missing. I complained to my father.

"*Papá*, tell that woman to correct her son. He is always going through my things. Let him learn respect for other people's property."

My father was in bed already, but he sat up and said with his usual loud, gruff voice, "If you don't want anybody to touch your things, get them out of here. That way nobody can take anything." He slammed a chair to one side and said, "Get out of here. Beat it!"

I picked up my coat. "Yes, I'm leaving, and thanks for your hospitality," and I went out.

Everyone was asleep at my aunt's house when I arrived, and there was a strong smell of alcohol. My aunt and uncle were in the bed and some visitors were lying on the floor. Holding back my tears, I told my aunt I was going to sleep there. She was so drunk, she hardly understood me. I got into the narrow bed as best I could and lay down with them, covering myself with my coat.

I thought and thought of how I could escape from there. I loved my aunt for her sweetness and goodness but I hated to live in such squalor. My aunt was getting childish and lived like a happy girl, the friend of everyone, without distinguishing between good and bad. Her tiny figure, her white hair, her happy laugh, reminded me of a doll, deteriorated from misuse. She lived in a reduced world; her games were washing and ironing clothes, and drinking with my uncle and their friends. With all her virtues, she liked to talk a lot and her gossip and vulgar expressions made my head spin.

The people they knew were different from those I was used to. It was all very well that they treated me with respect, lots of respect, but the odor of alcohol, the dampness, the bedbugs, the cramped quarters, the people who lived in that *vecindad* . . . In the rainy season my aunt's little room, which was reached by going down a few steps, was often flooded. The courtyard where the water taps were, became a sea of mud. To keep a job I had to be well groomed and I couldn't be that here. How could I live in this place? I kept thinking until my head ached. I found no solution.

To put the finishing touch to my state, Jaime arrived at dawn, very drunk and shouting, "If you don't come out, I'll kick on the door."

All the neighbors must have been aware of what was going on. I had no choice but to go out. "Jaime, you're dead drunk again! Haven't you any pity on me? Please let us sleep." He just mumbled incoherently and staggered. He said he could fight six or seven men—to let him at my father or my brother. He had had many battles with various men that same night, in all of which he had come out victorious, and the glory was all for me. I stopped crying when he said this. But the next moment I hated him when he said, "You should see how much you look like Bélica. But *she* obeys me, *she* does what I want. For you I am nothing but a toy, a puppet. But not for her—she loves me! Bélica, Bélica."

The worst of it was that I still expected pity and consolation from Jaime. I saw in him a tiny ray of hope, of light, to lead me away from what was blinding me and dulling my mind. But instead of loving words he had only glassy eyes which seemed to see me from a great distance.

The more I asked for peace, even for one night, the more calamities fell upon me. I was getting it from both sides daily. From my father with his insults and at my aunt's, from the ugly surroundings, the poverty, the lack of facilities, not being able to get away from Jaime, not having a job, feeling hungry all the time. All this had me in such a state of nerves that anything made me cry.

I sought advice from the priest. "There is nothing else you can do but become independent. If you have some relative, go and live with him. Leave your father; get away from him." My aunt said the same: "Come over here, my daughter. You'll have food here, even if it's only beans and hard *tortillas*. The day we have, we eat, and the day we don't, we don't. We can manage. Stop torturing yourself now. Leave your father."

One night I went with my aunt to watch a dance at the Casa Grande. How my father found out I was there, I don't know, but he sent my brother for me. I refused to go. "What does he want me for? To throw me out?" Then my father came out and made Roberto pull me into the house. Face to face with my father, I stood up to him, ready for anything. He said, "What a spectacle you are making of yourself, you fool!" He said it was a fine life I was leading, going to dances and from one man to another. "Do you want to end up on the streets?"

When he said that, I exploded with rage. Before, I had always lowered my head at his words, but not since he had thrown me out of the house for that woman. I answered him, clenching my fists, "If I go out on the streets, it will be your fault. All I do is follow the example you have given me. First, that Claudia, and now this woman, the likes of whom you can find on any street corner." He slapped me, but I didn't feel the blows. "I won't shut up. Hit me all you want. I won't shut up." Then Roberto slapped me.

I screamed at them, "Hit me, hit me all you want, but you'll never wipe out the hate I have. I am your daughter, but you'll get tired of *her* and afterwards no one will even remember who she was. I warn you that if anything happens to me, it will be your fault and your fault alone." I was out of my mind with anger. I felt the blood in my brain and saw sparks. I thought my head would burst. My poor father was frightened and tried to embrace me, but I screamed, "Don't touch me. I tell you, don't touch me. Get away from me."

"Drop your eyes," he said. "Don't you dare look at me like that!"

"I don't have to, because my conscience is clean."

Out in the courtyard again. I kept crying, thinking of one thing after another without being able to find a solution. I looked up at the brightest stars and begged Elena and my mother to make my father understand. I sat down on the pavement and my hand touched a razor blade. That was the solution—to open the veins in my arms and feet. Imagine the look on my father's face when he leaves for work and finds me lying outside his door bleeding!

"He'll be sorry." I cried even harder to think of Jaime. He would see that I didn't just try to scare people the way he did. I began to scrape the veins on my wrists but it hurt. "It will get infected," I thought. Then I laughed at myself. "It will get infected!" But either my skin was very tough or the razor blade was no good, or, what is closer to the truth, I didn't have the courage; I succeeded in making only a small cut, which was very painful. I threw away the blade and went to my aunt's house.

When I thought of my sister and my brothers, I became bitter, for not one of them would or could help me. Of the three, Manuel had the hardest heart. He was never there when he was needed and even if he were, nothing concerned him. He reminded me of a person walking backwards in darkness, without setting foot upon solid ground. He walked and walked and got nowhere. He just moved his legs to give people the impression he was doing something. His gaze was fixed upon little stars shining in the firmament. He tried to catch them and when he managed to get one, he would sit down there in the infinite emptiness and play with it until the dazzling light lost its power. Then he would leave the dead star floating in the air, and go irresistibly after another.

He never looked to either side or downward, because if he did, he would see the dark abyss beneath him. He was in dread of falling; if he ever reached the ground, he would feel how rugged and hard is the road where people walk. So he looked upward to the heavens, not to implore, but to make loud excuses when he fell. "I didn't see . . . I didn't know."

Maybe he was afraid of being judged or smashed down, or of finding that he had no salvation. Maybe that was why he had two or three personalities and many faces. He tried to show that he had an invincible worldly quality, but it was a lie. He was only superficial and cynical. He had a spark of generosity and appreciation in him, perhaps because he had known his mother's and Paula's love, but why wasn't he more human? He knew the damage he did, but under no circumstance would he say, "Yes, I did it."

Why did he show such fury when he was in a fight and yet turn his back when he had to face problems that came up? He claimed he loved Paula very much. Then why didn't he marry her? When a Latin really wants to capture some illusion, whether out of vanity or caprice, the first thing he will do is get married. He managed to be a winner in card playing, why then, when his father gave him the opportunity of setting up a shoe shop, didn't he come out on top? If he studied up on gambling, why didn't he take the same trouble to find out the value of a nail, for example? Why?

And why did he always have to be shirking responsibilities? He closed his eyes to everything. Any idea of unity or aid from him was impossible. When I was in trouble he said to me, "The day you need help, don't count on me. If I happen to see you someday in a cabaret, just assume that I'm not your brother, that you don't even know me." In this egotism, he was unable to feel anything deeply, even being a father. His life was completely free and he defended his liberty before everything. With Manuel, liberty had become an abominable vice.

I tried to find refuge at my sister Marta's. She, who had a home, said to me, "No, why do you come to my house? No, not here." She said this to me, who so many times had fought with Crispín and his family because they mistreated her. When I saw her without shoes or money, I gave them to her, depriving myself. I was willing to take blows to defend her, I always listened to her troubles. And now that I needed her most, she said that to me. I choked back my tears and all I said was, "Look, Marta, pray to God that you always have your husband and your home and that you never have to go from house to house like me. Pray to God!"

Marta had always been my father's and Roberto's favorite, but never did she help or console anyone, with the exception of that morning Manuel hit us both. It was the first time I felt a spark of consideration from her. She had always been unsisterly, even to her brothers. She lacked a sense of spiritual obligation; she never gave anything unless she also received. To me, she was a false type of woman. But the thing I liked least about her and which I found unpardonable, was her lack of concern for the future of her children.

Roberto was the best of the three. He would say, "I'm sorry for you, sister. I'm a man and can go any place, but what can you do?" He was generous, sympathetic and truly sincere, but he had no money and no real home either. And what a child! He was violent and still had temper tantrums. He imagined he was a Samson who could demolish whole battalions. Compared with Manuel, he was pure emotion, although the emotional circle in which he whirled about was infantile.

Even though Roberto was a man, he walked along the highway of life like a child of eight or nine, in knee pants, short-sleeved shirt and heavy boots. He was a frightened child whose intelligence had been sidetracked by the broken road. His way was full of accidents and he had fallen countless times, leaving him deeply scarred. He walked with his right hand stretched out, trying to reach something . . . the shadowy form of a woman which floated before him. He wept and cried out, calling to that thing to stop. Occasionally it disappeared and that was when Roberto threw himself to the ground in a tantrum.

He kicked the stones, beat them and threw them away because they seemed to be mocking him. He would get angry and say, "Who are these to make fun of me! I'll show them who I am!" He didn't realize that he would get hurt colliding against the rocks. When his tantrum passed, he regretted having smashed himself so stubbornly. Now he would think, "They were only looking at me."

In contrast to Manuel, Roberto had a fixed goal . . . to find the security he needed. When he has finally found it, the sobbing will end and he will smile as he looks back over the whole course he covered. Then, with "it," he will take a new road. Roberto was a good boy, so long as he had someone to pay attention to his problems, to listen to his complaints, join in his pleasures and give him advice about how to dress. In spite of everything, he had a docility, a sensitivity of feeling that was foreign to Manuel.

The hardest, bitterest, saddest time of Roberto's life was when he was in jail. I know of many people who come out brutalized and hardened and filled with hatred. Not my brother. He always kept alive that tiny flame of hope and he never fell into vice. He still realized he had a family and preserved a feeling of love toward others. He was capable of taking off his own clothes to cover someone who had none, saying, "No, poor thing, cover him up." But Manuel! That one would probably think, "It's none of my business. That's what he gets for being a dumb jerk."

Roberto looked at things with passion and tried to find his ideal.
To him, no one in the world should sin. He was shocked by the
things he saw, not like Manuel, who in that respect was more worldly.
To Roberto, many things were sanctified and holy. No one better lay
a hand on his saints, because that turned him into a devil.

If that happened, or if Roberto was neglected, his irrational emotions were unleashed. Many times, when he "stood in the corner"
and cried out his repentance, if no one came to comfort him, all that
pain turned into rage, or fury, or envy. Then he would be carried
away by desperation and would try to get consolation at any price.
Roberto needed someone to guide him and give him moral strength,
someone to say, "If you do this, 'el coco' will get you; if you do that,
the witch will come." Left to himself, something bad was certain to
happen to him.

The thing that made me saddest about my brothers and sister was
that they did not wish to get out of the situation in which they lived.
They were satisfied to have poor clothes and to spend their time fighting. To me, the low roof which covered us was insecure, for tomorrow
the pillar supporting it could fall. But they didn't think of tomorrow.
They all lived in the present.

And even if they tried to change, I don't believe they could. None
of them, perhaps myself included although I meant to try, seemed to
have the right qualities of character. For example, if someone gave
Manuel a common stone, he would hold it in his hand and look at it
eagerly. In a few seconds, it would begin to shine and he would see
that it was made of silver, then of gold, then of the most precious
things imaginable, until the glitter died.

Roberto would hold the same stone and would murmur, "Mmmm.
What is this good for?" But he wouldn't know the answer.

Marta would hold it in her hand for just a moment, and without a
thought, would throw it carelessly away.

I, Consuelo, would look at it, wonderingly. "What might this be?
Is it, could it be, what I have been looking for?"

But my father would take the stone and set it on the ground. He
would look for another and put it on top of the first one, than another
and another, until no matter how long it took, he had finally turned it
into a house.

Much as I dreaded to, I finally had to move to my aunt's house.
There was no way to avoid it. It turned out that I lived there on the

Street of the Bakers for about six months. The atmosphere in that *vecindad* was one of complete poverty. The people lived almost like animals. God had given them life, but they had none of the essentials of living except daily bread, and sometimes not that. Most of the women and children had to work to support themselves because so many of the fathers were drunk and irresponsible. The younger children played out in the dirt completely naked, and the older ones got odd jobs to earn a few *centavos*. A very few went to school for a year or two. Mothers frequently had to pawn the radio, the iron, the bed-clothing (if the family owned such articles), a dress, a pair of shoes, in order to pay the rent or buy enough beans to feed their large families.

The fathers being indifferent toward their wives and children, spent their money on drink or on mistresses who might even live right there in the same *vecindad*. If a wife complained, she was likely to be beaten or driven out of the home, because it was her duty to protect her husband from embarrassment in his love affairs. The men spent most of their free time in saloons, and at night the wives might have to hunt them up and half carry them home.

At my aunt's house we ate only two meals a day, like everyone else in the *vecindad*. I would get up in the morning, pick up my "bed" from the floor, sweep or straighten up the room a little. Then I would bring a basin of water from the faucet in the courtyard, so that I could wash myself in the room. This settlement had no door or fence and if I washed outside, the way the other tenants did, people in the street could see me. I didn't have enough money to go to the public baths. While I was doing all this, my aunt, "my little old lady" as I always called her, would go to the market to get things for the first meal, while my uncle Ignacio either stayed in bed a little longer or got up and went for his morning *pulque*.

I would sit down in the large chair, the only one my aunt had, to a meal of black coffee or tea, leftover rice or beans and, at times, *tortilla* fried with cheese and chile. My aunt insisted on giving me the chair to show that she and my uncle were glad to have me staying in their home. She took good care of it and had had it for many years. Their meal was the same as mine, but they drank *pulque* instead of coffee. They ate a fiery sauce, and also strips of green chile fried with onions in oil. They told me I ought to eat what they did because it would build up my blood and improve my appetite. But since I wasn't used to it, I refused. My uncle would say I wasn't a Mexican, that I would soon be a blueblood. He was always joking.

After the meal, Ignacio would get water to wet his hair, wash himself, and straighten his mustache. Then he would cross himself and make his offering of alfalfa to San Martín Caballero, so that many people would buy the newspapers—*La Prensa, Las Ultimas Noticias, El Este*—which he sold to earn the pittance he brought home to my aunt. My aunt would go to wash clothes for others, or to work in the kitchen of a lunch stand called Lonchería Morelos, opposite the Morelos movie theatre. When she worked as a kitchen helper, she was gone from eight o'clock in the morning until eight or nine at night and would bring home a few leftover crumbs for me. When she was taking in washing, she would wash at the tubs in the courtyard from eleven in the morning until about three or four o'clock in the afternoon, rest for a while, then continue until she was finished at about seven in the evening.

She almost never ate until my uncle Ignacio came home, bringing her a few *pesos* to buy the food. Supper consisted of noodle soup if he gave her only two *pesos*; when he gave her four or five *pesos,* she would buy a little bread and milk for me, and I would also eat the soup. All I would usually have to drink was black coffee; they had their beans and, of course, their *pulque.* They might go without food but never without *pulque.*

My uncle had another woman, and my aunt often fought with him about her. When they were a little drunk, my aunt would say to him, "I'm not going to kill you this time, Shorty, just because I don't want to be scared by your dead body!" I was terrified the first few times they quarreled. Almost in tears, I screamed at them not to fight and when they saw I was frightened, they calmed down.

Later, when I understood them better, their quarrels made me laugh. Although they drank *pulque* with their evening meal and then *chinchól* (a drink made of alcohol, the fruit of the hawthorn tree and of some other plant), and might be quite intoxicated, they never harmed each other. The same thing went on night after night until about eleven o'clock, when they got tired or passed out from the alcohol. Then I would turn back the bed, and they would go to sleep.

In my father's house nothing of this sort had ever happened. I never saw my father drink with anybody. Dinner was at a regular hour and there was everything on the table—milk, bread, butter, and eggs or some dish one of us might have a taste for, chicken heads fried in oil, salad, refried beans covered with grated cheese, or toasted *tortillas*. Compared to my aunt's place, our house was prosperous and peaceful, at least until that devil Delila came along.

At "my little old lady's," many of their friends would arrive while we were eating supper. They would sit in the threshold or wherever they could find a place and wait for my uncle to tell them jokes and funny stories about his life, and for my aunt to offer them a *taco*. I don't know how they understood each other, for some would be talking about one thing and the rest about something else. By the time supper was over my head would be spinning and I would be nauseated from the cigarette smoke, the smell of *chinchól* or *pulque*, and the awful hubbub they raised.

Late in the evening, I would get my "bed" ready. I would lay a piece of mat and some cardboard on the cement floor and cover them with a sheet or an old quilt. They gave me a pillow and another quilt, somewhat better, and an old coat of my aunt's to cover myself with. Later on, I slept in their bed and they slept on the floor because I was thin-blooded and suffered terribly from the cold. Sometimes I felt bad about taking their bed, but they wanted me to and it didn't seem to bother them at all. On the contrary, they really seemed to love me like a daughter.

Once my aunt set me to grinding the chile for the *mole* sauce she was going to make for my uncle's Saint's Day. I tried, but couldn't. My aunt said, "*Ay*, child, what are you going to do when you are married? What if you get a husband who is very demanding, like my first one? I had to get up at three in the morning to grind five *cuartillos* of corn to make *tortillas* for his breakfast. And when at first I couldn't do it, he would beat me to make me learn."

My aunt made my uncle's birthday a family affair. She didn't invite the neighbor ladies because I had been nagging her not to. I finally made her realize they weren't good neighbors; whenever they needed food or assistance, my aunt would help them out, but when we needed help of some kind, they refused. They borrowed things that they never returned. So the only ones at the meal were my sister Marta, my brother Roberto, and two very close friends of my uncle. For this modest *fiesta* my aunt managed to buy a carton of beer and some *pulque*.

In my aunt's house I learned more about the religious festivals.

When Lent began, on Dolorous Friday, she covered the table that held the Virgin of Sorrow, first with a white cloth, then with a layer of purple India paper. On either side of the image she put three flowerpots with sprouted wheat, then flowers, and, most important, a candle. At night she prayed to the Virgin with great devotion. My uncle took good care of the altar. He would get very angry if someone thoughtlessly left a pencil or anything on it.

During Lent we abstained from meat on Fridays and the Holy Days —Holy Thursday, Good Friday, and the Saturday of Glory. On Wednesday and Thursday my aunt cleaned the room, and all the special foods were prepared beforehand. On Holy Thursday, if my aunt had the ingredients, she made *romeritos* (a stew made of prickly pears), *charales* (tiny fish) and potatoes in chile gravy or *pipián* (a cucumber-like squash).

On Good Friday we did no chores. She didn't even light the fire; we ate the food cold. That day we went to church at eight in the morning and remained there to witness the "Three Falls" of Our Lord Jesus Christ. At this time my aunt said, "Look, child, how beautifully they present the sufferings of Our Lord. See how well He bore all that, and we are able to bear so little." She meant that I should not be so angry and rebellious with my father. I saw I was at fault and promised not to behave that way any more.

My aunt was devoted to the Lord of Chalma and liked to tell me about the pilgrimages she made year after year. I was the only one in the family who had never, never gone to Chalma. My aunt would say, "This year you are going with me, child, and you will see how nice, how pretty, the Sanctuary is. But you musn't try to turn back or the Lord will get angry and punish you." With that she only made me less eager to go, but I liked to look at the relics and ribbons and tidbits she always brought home from Chalma.

In May, when Mother's Day came, I had a job and I bought a present for my aunt. On her part, she lit a candle for my grandmother and my mother, and placed their pictures on the table, with flowers next to them. We wanted to go to the cemetery that day, but since we didn't have any money left and I had to work, we didn't go. I had noticed that on the Day of the Dead, my aunt always put out a large offering of food for my dead mother. At home, my father never put more than a candle and a glass of water.

On Father's Day, June 15, my aunt advised me to go see my father, but the visit turned out to be a bitter disappointment. Delila was there and my father hardly spoke to me. This made me angry, and I left the house without even saying good-bye. At that time I still visited my father because I wanted him to acknowledge that he had a daughter. My aunt usually told me not to go. "Why go only to have him make you cry?" My uncle very seldom said anything, but they both were angry with that witch, Delila, and all her family.

After I got a job, our situation improved a little; we had money to buy food and were getting caught up on the rent. But all this time I suffered because I really didn't like to live there. If I neglected the housework, my uncle would scold me and say I seemed to be a doll on a shelf only good for display (well, he used other words). He wouldn't say these things when my aunt was within earshot. If she heard him, my aunt would say, "Don't be bothering her, you damn tub; leave her alone or you and I are going to have things out." I was really in the wrong, however, because I hardly knew how to do anything.

One day my uncle told her to have me wash the clothes. I thought she would joke about it, but, sad to say, she gave me the black soap, the lye, the bucket, and the scrub board, and said, "Get going, lazy, and get the clothes clean, because if you don't, I'll make you do it over." This order displeased me, not because I was unwilling to work, but because everyone, both inside the settlement and outside in the street, would see me.

While I was squatting on the ground, washing the clothes, I realized the neighbor girls were tossing jibes at me. "Oh, you're washing already!" Leonora said to another girl. "It's high time, sister!" Another one said, "The thing is that I'm not living in a rich house. My father cut me off." I said nothing. I knew they wouldn't pay any attention to me and besides I already felt low and to answer them would have meant lowering myself further.

At the end of June, I got sick. I had become very thin and my nerves were bad. Instead of asking for a few days off from work as my aunt suggested, I just stayed home and lost the job. The fast began again for us because it was impossible to live well on what my uncle made. Some days I ate only lunch, and they had little but their *pulque* or *chinchól* at night. I ate their hot sauce but never the *pulque*, even though they said it would strengthen my lungs and cure my bile trouble. When my stomach hurt after an emotional upset, my aunt made me absinthe or camomile tea.

I suffered all the more because I wasn't used to this kind of care when I was sick. In my father's house he would bring the doctor home and they'd put me to bed and give me medicines. But in this place people treated illnesses lightly. Even when people would be seriously injured in an accident, it wouldn't occur to them to call a doctor. Everyone, including the family of the injured one, would stand around casually chatting about it. And no one would remember the incident the next day.

My cold and fever turned into bronchopneumonia; I had a pain in my lungs and couldn't breathe. My aunt didn't know what was wrong with me, but she tried to cure me with a water bath and alcohol rub and on my head she placed two leaves of a plant they call "The Shameless One." The water bath consisted of emptying hot water into a basin and adding ashes; then I kept my feet in it until it got cool. After the alcohol rub she covered me up until I started to sweat; my aunt explained that this way the body threw off all the sickness. Unbelievable as it may seem, my temperature went down, although the respiratory pain remained. Then I sent for my friend, Angélica, to come and give me a shot of penicillin. I got enough relief from that to be able to get up and go to a doctor who cured me. My aunt pawned my coat for the money and my father didn't find out a thing.

During the months I lived with my aunt, Jaime kept coming there. They never dared chase him out even though I begged them to. Jaime knew how to win their affection and confidence and he took advantage of them. He had complete liberty to enter their house at any hour, in whatever condition he might be and with any friends he wished. There were many times when he arrived drunk at dawn and I had to stretch out on the cement with only my coat to cover me so that he could sleep off his drunkenness on the bed.

The truth is that my aunt was becoming annoyed with me because I had no job and no money. I noticed how she served my breakfast, with a sour, serious expression, not the way she used to at the beginning. But I was hungry. I looked for work everywhere. Angélica helped me with bus fare and encouraging words. I thought that it would be best to leave Mexico City. But how? With what money? I didn't have the fare, nor the price of a suitcase.

My uncle began to scold me harshly, saying words he had never used before. In the mornings, seeing me put on make-up, he would say, "You are no different from the dummies in the shop windows, just standing there with paint on. Get organized, bring in some money, I don't care how. The thing is we need it—anything at all. You have to bring money into the house." At other times he would say, "The day you get married, what are you going to give your husband to eat if you're no good for anything? Is he going to want you just for bed? Let's get going. You've got to get moving in life. It doesn't matter where the money comes from—you can see your aunt needs it. I can't help her much."

Just for bed! He spoke to me now as if to a woman who had already taken that path. His words made me leave the house thinking of doing the worst. The worst to me was to give myself to a man for money. But I couldn't—the shame held me back, and I took refuge in the church and cried. Unfortunately, I began to lose this shame little by little.

If my aunt had known about it, she wouldn't have forgiven him. She, however, grumbled among the neighbors that I didn't help her at all, that I didn't give her even one *centavo*, that her bed was wearing out. While I was washing clothes the neighbor kids told me that my aunt was complaining a lot about me. But what could I do? I almost always looked for work through the ads in the newspaper, but when I arrived the vacancy was filled. Or the men, seeing how depressed I looked, made dishonest proposals. "If you want, there is no need for you to work. You are just a young girl. Well, I can't offer you much, but if you want—" On two occasions I left slamming the door. Go back to my job with *Señor* García? Impossible! Jaime worked there.

When Jaime came, how angry and ashamed I would feel to be seen eating in the big chair or on a bench. He was proud of his family and their nice house and the way all of them sat around the table to eat and talk. He said his family was not on the same level as mine. I was angry with my aunt and uncle because they didn't see that he looked down at them.

He thought he was stronger than I in that house, and one night he tried to prove it. He arrived drunk at about eight-thirty. I was on the bed sewing, the little radio he had given my uncle and aunt was playing, and my aunt was sitting in the doorway between the small room and the kitchen. When I looked up I saw Jaime staggering, holding on to the door frame, shirt open, tie on one side, his pants down around his hips and fastened with a *Pachuco* belt. *Qué bárbaro!* To think I had hopes for him!

Suddenly he pulled the sleeve of my dress and scratched my arm. I got up faster than I thought, pushing him, and he fell into a chair. I was very angry. I swore at him, "Kept *Pachuco,* what do you think, you miserable thing! If you think I am one of your women from the cabaret, you go and fuck yourself." My aunt got scared and said, "Calm down, woman. Calm down, Jaime. Better go."

Then I turned on my aunt and uncle. "You are the ones to blame. How many times did I tell you not to let that drunk in here. Let him beat it or I'll call the police." Jaime looked at me with that scornful, glassy look and made some reference to his radio. I disconnected it with one yank and gave it a push. "Go and fuck yourself. Don't think that you are going to be able to buy me with this. Now beat it with your idiocies." My uncle managed to catch the radio a few centimeters from the floor. Jaime began to cry, but his tears did not affect me any longer. I was standing with my fists clenched. My uncle got him out and started him on his way.

After he was gone, I began to tremble. I didn't know how to smoke, but I grabbed a cigarette anyway. My aunt had never seen me like that and was silent. My uncle came back smiling, "*Qué bárbaro!* Poor little runt, this time he saw the devil, all right." My aunt said to me, "*Ay,* what is this? I never heard you say a dirty word before. This is the first time. If you broke his radio, how would you pay for it?"

"What do I care about his radio, Aunt. Let him take it. I don't want him to have any excuse to come here. And please don't let him in any more; don't let him in any more!"

One evening when I came back from job hunting, Jaime was waiting for me as I got off the bus.

"Consuelo, please, *mi vida,* I won't keep you long. I know that I don't mean anything to you. I am nothing, but I love you. Please, just a couple of minutes." Hearing his words, I felt as though a covering of cardboard had dropped away from around my heart, allowing my old love to pass through me. I agreed to walk with him for a few blocks.

He was talking about repentance, about his mother, about his love for me, when I noticed that we were getting far away. We had come to an empty lot. There was no light in that neighborhood, and the lights of the passing cars barely reached us. I told him I wanted to go back. I got a terrible scare when I saw his face change suddenly. He grabbed me by the arm. I was afraid, but as always, appeared calm and secure. "Let's go, Jaime. I want to go home. You don't have to take me. I'll go alone."

But he didn't let me go. His words came out, little by little. They sounded different, very hollow, very thick. "Do you think I am going to leave you here, eh? How innocent you are. I brought you here for you to decide. Either you be mine or—"

Jaime pulled out a stiletto. It was very close to my stomach. All it needed was one little push and it would have gone into me. I felt my sight get hazy. I didn't answer for a few seconds. I just squeezed my purse and inwardly begged my mother to help, and the Virgin of Guadalupe, too. The worst of it was that he was in complete possession of his senses, so I couldn't fight with him. I could already feel the chill of the point in my stomach.

Without moving, but trembling inside, and wishing I could bolt and run, I said, "Come on! If you are going to kill me, why don't you do it? You know you will be doing me a favor. I ask you to do it, as I would ask for alms. You know nobody needs me, and so it doesn't matter to me if I die here or someplace else. You would do something that the rest would thank you for. You would be getting rid of the proud one, the cynic, the disrespectful one, the vain woman you say I am. I have no feelings, so do it." There was a silence . . . I felt as if I were going to fall.

Finally Jaime lowered the weapon and began to cry. I drew a deep breath. I heard his sobs, like those of a child. He threw down the weapon and embraced me. "Forgive me, *mi vida*. It's that you drive me crazy, you are so indifferent. But I love you, I love you." His words kept getting louder and louder until he shouted. "I don't care if they see me cry. I love you, I love you." I took advantage of the moment. "Let's go, *mi vida*, forget all this. After all, I love you, too. Why should we make each other suffer like this? Let's go, *negrito*. I promise that I won't be so harsh with you any more. I love you, *mi vida*."

We went back to my aunt's house. I was more dead than alive. I felt as though my legs were made of rubber, and I began to sweat and tremble. My stomach ached dreadfully. "What's wrong with you?" the people who were there asked. I couldn't say anything in front of them. My aunt gave me some camomile tea and that was the end of it. I did not see Jaime again until two weeks later when he showed up drunk, raving about Rebeca, Bélica, Estela, Yolanda, Adelaida, and I don't know how many others.

About this time I got to know Mario better. He was now the one who took charge of me, saying, "I haven't much to offer you, only these two hands that will work for you. I have no profession, but I promise that I will do everything possible so we won't lack anything. Even if we eat only a pot of beans at least you'll get away from all of this." Mario, who worked near my aunt's, had already proposed to me on two or three occasions. But I still had the hope of getting out of the city and making another life for myself without tears, without humiliations, and with a will to live, even to study.

I made one more try to enter a convent or some religious order. "I wasn't born to be outside. I want peace. I want tranquillity." That is what my thoughts were. "But money, money, a thousand *pesos*, a thousand—" They had told me the amount of money necessary to enter a convent was a thousand *pesos*. I never confirmed this but I did ask a nun what I had to do to get in.

"If you have your parent's consent—"

"I have no *mamá*."

"Well, if your father agrees, you can get in."

"What else do I need?"

"To be a legitimate child."

This cut off cold my desire to enter. My father had never married my mother, either by church or by civil law.

I found a job, but it proved to be temporary. I saw Mario the day I was fired and he promised he would talk to his father and get me a job. I didn't want to give my aunt the bad news that day and, besides, I wasn't really welcome with my uncle, so I decided to go and live with Santitos. My aunt regretted it very much and was also a little angry.

After I moved to Santitos' house, I found work at the CTM union, the Confederation of Mexican Workers. Irma, an ex-classmate of mine, helped me get the job. I began to feel good and I never would have gone back to my aunt's house if it hadn't been for the fact that I worked until eight-thirty or nine at night. After work, I went to a dance hall with Irma for an hour or so and didn't get home until about 10:00 P.M. The section where Santitos lived had no electricity or water, or pavement, and scared me at those hours. It was near the canal where there were holdups. When I finally got home it was because I had said all the prayers I ever knew, with my heart in my mouth and my eyes bulging, trying to see in the dark.

A girl at the union accepted another job and her boss had me work for him at more pay. But my bad luck hounded me. Irma got jealous and began to intrigue behind my back. I couldn't take more trouble, so I left that job and moved back to my aunt's.

I was coming around to deciding to stay at Mario's house. What irony! I, who had promised to be as humble as a saint, to follow the example of St. Francis of Assisi, who had so ardently desired to have the purity of a nun and the dedication of a priest, would go with this man to have peace. Little by little I had changed. What was happening hurt me deep inside but I never showed my feelings. I tried to act cynical. What difference did it make? I closed my eyes to everything and decided I could do it. After all, if my father didn't care, it certainly didn't matter to others.

One afternoon, Mario and I came back from the movies and went to his house. He said, "Stay, don't go." If he only knew the whirlwind that went through my mind at that moment in spite of all the deciding I had been doing. If I stayed, it meant I was his. But what was the point of going home? For them to throw me out? For my father to ask me what I came for? I couldn't stand it at my aunt's any longer. I had no job. I had hoped others would open their doors to me, but they hadn't.

"Be it as God wills!" I closed my eyes to everything at that moment. Nothing interested me any more but getting out of that world that was smothering me. I wanted to stop the stabbing pains in my eyes and the daily humiliations, to put an end to my hunger, to get rid of Jaime.

"All right," I said and felt my head whirl. Mario was very pleased, of course, and told his mother. She accepted but I could see that she didn't like me. That night, she had me sleep with her, and Mario slept with his father, *Señor* Reyes. The next day, even the sun seemed different and the streets prettier. How calm everything was in that house. Mario's mother insisted on renting a room on the next block for him. I went there only to do the household chores after he had left for work. His mother wanted to keep us apart, she said, until after we married. Mario was impatient, but I was happy with the arrangement.

Then one morning when I came in with the bread, I heard Mario and his mother quarreling. She was shouting and accusing him of wanting her to support him and his girl friend. "Don't tell lies, *mamá*. I give you money for her," he answered. I acted as though I hadn't heard but when he went to work and his mother left for the market, I threw all my clothes into a paper bag and went to my aunt's house. I wasn't afraid to look for a job again and support myself. But it killed me to go back to my aunt's house.

I was sitting in my aunt's chair having a cup of black coffee when Mario arrived. He was terribly pale and when he saw me, he began to cry. He blamed his mother for everything and embraced me and said I must never stop loving him. (I had to lie to him about that.) He refused to go home and moved into the shoemaker's shop next door to my aunt, selling his clothes and other things to get money for the rent and food. He had only one suit left.

I had been telling him that I didn't like the neighborhood, that it was doing me harm and that I wanted to leave it. I managed to convince him that we had to move out of Mexico City. That was when he confessed to me that *Señor* Reyes was not his real father. His father was in the *Sindicato* of the Department of Communications and could get Mario a transfer to some other city. By then I didn't believe anything. But his father did come through with a transfer to a job in Monterrey.

All the neighbors promptly knew I was going to leave. The afternoon we said good-bye they were at my aunt's house. My aunt had told me, "Give them something, daughter, so they'll remember you." I thought this strange, but I complied. They were only humble gifts, a glass to one, an old skirt to another, but they received them with pleasure. When I had given four or five gifts my aunt said, "With these things you won't forget her, will you?" They thanked me and left, asking me to write them often. My aunt was crying.

Poor Mario! He took me to Monterrey, hoping to find true love. He was looking for a love so abstract, that it could not be touched or understood or explained in words. He thought he would find this love in me. But love is something both people must feel, a beautiful light that falls from above upon man and woman. The light fell upon Mario, but not upon me. I still loved Jaime and there was no room in my heart to love Mario. I was using him as a life rope to help me get out of the deep well into which I had fallen. I planned that once he took me to Monterrey, I would remake my life alone.

Marta

In CRISPÍN'S HOUSE, MY MOTHER-IN-LAW GAVE THE ORDERS. THE CHIL-
dren paid no attention to my father-in-law. Crispín was very mean
to him, and acted like his equal. Once he scolded his father for
coming home drunk, as though the father were the son and the son
the father!

My mother-in-law pampered Crispín, who was the youngest. He
was the type of man who was always taking sides and who didn't
like to be left behind in a discussion. He quarreled a lot with his
older brother Ángel and when his mother intervened, Crispín would
say foul things to her.

This brother, Ángel, was married by church and civil law, to a
woman named Natalia. They separated and got together a few
times and being so Catholic, they really carried the cross. Ángel got
a job in Acapulco and took her there to live. His work kept him
away from home a lot, and once, when he came home early, he found
her in bed with another man, a fruit vendor. He beat them both, although to my way of thinking, he was to blame for leaving his wife
alone. Ángel spent three days in jail, and then he brought Natalia
back to Mexico City.

My mother-in-law wanted Ángel to kick Natalia out, but he kept
her for revenge. At night, I could hear her crying and begging to be
allowed to go home. Then came a slap or a blow and more howls.
This went on for fifteen days, night after night. Crispín, too, let her
have it. He was a great admirer of the fair sex, but when he heard of
a woman betraying a man, he wanted to wipe her off the map.

During the day, Natalia was not allowed out alone, not even to the

[287]

bathhouse. When she went to see her mother, they accompanied her. She was just like a prisoner. I asked her why she didn't leave, once and for all, and she said they had threatened to take away her son, her only child. She and Ángel are still together and have two more children.

Crispín's eldest brother, Valentín, also had trouble with his wife. At sixteen, when the family still lived in Puebla, he had married a woman much older than himself. They were married by both laws and had two children, but that didn't mean a thing because when they came to Mexico City she took up with another man. She finally went off with him leaving her children with Valentín, which was unusual, because most women who go off with another man leave their children with their own parents. So Valentín took the children to his mother-in-law and got a divorce.

Crispín's family never liked me because I didn't know how to do a thing. I helped my mother-in-law very little. She was one of those exaggeratedly clean housekeepers who changed the bedsheets every eight days and was always scrubbing and dusting.

I found it hard to attend Crispín properly. He was very fussy about his clothes and his meals. When I washed his pants, my hands blistered and my mother-in-law had to finish the job. No matter how hard I tried, I couldn't wash and iron his shirts the way she did. No wonder she was annoyed with me! But I tried and it is not true that I spent all my time in the street, as she said.

Crispín wanted to continue living with his mother, but I couldn't stand it. After two weeks, we set up a place of our own. We had one small room and a kitchen, in a *vecindad* of about fifteen families. Crispín bought a bed and his mother gave us a table and two chairs and some pots and pans.

At first I liked it. I admit our life was disorderly. I realize I was useless and not fit to be a housewife. I kept the house as best I could; it was not perfect but at least it was not too dirty.

I didn't become pregnant for about nine months and Crispín was angry about the delay. He would follow me to the toilet to see if I was taking douches. Then he took me to a woman doctor to check whether I had taken anything to keep from having a child. After that he suspected the doctor of having made me sterile! But the very next month I became pregnant with Concepción.

For three months I felt nauseated and kept vomiting. I couldn't take anything but liquids. Everything bothered me—my breasts, my belly, the baby moving . . . until I got used to it. I thought Crispín would be pleased about the pregnancy, but it was then that he showed me what he was really like. Do you know what kind of a man he turned out to be? One of those who like to have a wife and children, but without being responsible for them! While I was pregnant, he began to go out with other girls, and I learned that he had a child with another woman.

Now that I had a husband, I had a presentiment that I should not trust my girl friends. I noticed that Irela and Ema would talk to Crispín about their problems and ask him for advice. I was waiting for Ema to do me dirty but my bullet missed its mark because it turned out to be Irela. She was my best friend and already married and I just didn't expect her to fool around with Crispín.

Crispín had always chased women. He was without morals. One day he invited Irela for a soda, then to the movies, then to the fair. He was out enjoying himself, while I was shut up with my mother-in-law. I noticed how he changed even before I knew about Irela, because a woman can sense these things. He'd come home and dress up. If I didn't have a clean shirt for him, he'd bawl me out right in front of his mother. I tried to have one always ready for him. No sooner did he take off his dirty shirt when I'd have the water full of suds to wash it.

When he went out, he never said anything to me, but to his mother he'd say, "*Mamacita*, I'll be right back." He'd come home at midnight and instead of using his key, he'd make me get up and unlock the door for him. I really think he began to hate me. He'd get mad and say I was incapable and that only his parents knew how to take care of him. He didn't drink, but he hit me anyway, like a drunkard, over insignificant things. I couldn't find any way to please him.

Crispín had forbidden me to go home, but I would rather die than not see my father, so I went secretly almost every day. My husband didn't like the way my *papá* helped me with money and food. Crispín gave me only twenty-five *pesos* a week and for a woman who was beginning to run a house and who didn't know where to buy things, it wasn't nearly enough. So my *papá* would give me fifteen or thirty *pesos* in cash and would send milk, sugar and other things. But Crispín didn't care whether I had enough or not and he wanted me to cut myself off completely from my family.

It was during one of my visits home that Antonia told me Crispín was fooling around with Irela. I didn't want to believe it, but one day, as I was leaving my mother-in-law's to buy kerosene, I surprised the two of them. I was passing through the alley when I saw Crispín making signals to Irela about what time to meet her. Irela saw me and realized that I knew what was going on. I just kept walking.

The next day Crispín took me to the movies. As we were going home, we saw Irela and Ema talking together. They caught sight of us and began to laugh. Crispín said, cynically, "Are they laughing with you or at you?" That made me very angry and I said to myself, "I'm going to get hold of that bitch, Irela."

When I went for bread, I met her in the entrance of the Casa Grande. Right away I said, "Listen, Irela, what are you trying to do, fooling around with Crispín?"

Instead of keeping quiet, or denying it, the way any married woman would, she said nervously, "It's Crispín's fault. He insisted on taking me to the movies and I had to go so that my husband wouldn't come home and find him there."

"Do you expect me to believe that?" I asked. "And what were you and Ema laughing at?"

Then she had the nerve to say, "Well, it was very funny because Crispín had asked me to go to the movies with him, and when I couldn't go he took you."

I began to shout, without caring who heard. "Watch out, Irela. All you do is fool around with married men. I don't intend to make a fool of myself every time Crispín goes after some skirt, but I'm giving you warning. If you don't leave him alone, there'll be trouble!"

Then I noticed a silver slave bracelet on her arm. It was one my brother had given me. Crispín had taken it and then said he had lost it. So that was what he did with my bracelet! I ripped it off her and ran to look for that cynical bastard husband of mine. I told him to marry Irela and let me have my baby in peace. I also told my mother-in-law so that if we did separate she wouldn't blame me. But Crispín denied everything, and his family believed him. We didn't separate that time and things went back to normal.

When my sister Antonia first told me about Crispín's wanderings, she had advised me to pray to the *Santa Muerte* at midnight for nine nights, with Crispín's picture and a candle made of suet in front of me. She promised that before the ninth night, my husband would forget all about the other woman. I bought the *novena* prayer from a man who sold these things in the *vecindad* and memorized it. It went like this:

> Jesus Christ, Triumphant, who triumphed on the Cross! I want you to intervene, Father, and bring Crispín to me so that I can overcome him. In the name of the Lord, if he is like a fierce animal, make him as gentle as a lamb. Make him as mild as the *romero* flower. He ate bread and gave of it to me, he drank water and gave of it to me. Now, Lord, I want all the things he promised me. With Your infinite power, bring him to my feet, beaten and tied, to fulfill his promises. For You, Lord, all things are possible and I beg you insistently, to concede this to me, promising to be your most faithful follower for the rest of my life."

I learned the prayer, but never used it. If he came back to me it would have to be because he wanted to. I didn't want him by force.

The majority of women I knew prayed at noon to the soul of Juan Mincro, with a votive candle and a glass of water behind a door, knocking three times with each Our Father. San Antonio is also very good for bringing back husbands or lovers. Julia, my aunt's neighbor, who knew about these things, said that the saint loved his child very much and if you covered the picture of the child with a ribbon, the saint quickly fulfilled what you asked, so that he might see the child again. It is even more effective if you cover the saint with a piece of clothing owned by the wanderer.

San Benito also brought back husbands, but he did it by beating them while they were with the other woman. I was afraid to pray to this saint. In all probability it would turn out worse for me because Crispín would come back angry!

My mistake was that I never made my husband jealous. I couldn't be like other women, Irela, for example, who was completely without shame. The great respect I had for my father was like a wall, separating me and the decent life from a life of sin. Besides, in that neighborhood it was impossible to meet a good man. It is rare to find one who is responsible and who dedicates himself to his wife and children. The one who doesn't stand on the street corner all day, goes to dances or gets drunk. What could I hope for from one of them, except to have more children? I couldn't get anything else out of them!

In spite of the fact I am too short and not pretty, there was no lack of men after me. It made no difference to them that I had a husband. When Crispín and I set up our first apartment, one of our neighbors, *Señor* Ruperto, let us connect our wire to his electricity. That was nice of him, no? But then he spoke to me and wanted to collect for it in his own way. I told Crispín not to take electricity from him any more . . . that it would be better to use candlelight.

The truth is, I was not interested in having other men. If I couldn't get along with one, wouldn't it be worse with two? But Crispín kept bringing home his friends and there was always one who propositioned me.

Once we went to a baptismal party with some of Crispín's friends from the carpentry shop. They began to drink and one of them asked me to dance. I didn't want to, although Crispín was dancing with another girl. But my husband was one of those men who have the terrible habit of making their wife dance with anyone who asks, and so I had to dance. This fellow held me closer and closer and put his face next to mine. He pulled me over to a dark corner, and tried to kiss me, but I left him standing alone, because my mother-in-law was on the other side of the courtyard, watching.

Then the *compadre* of my sister-in-law asked me to dance. He was just my height and good-looking, with curly hair, blue eyes and light skin. He kept looking at me, and asked me my name. I've always been pretty forward, so I told him.

"Marta! What a lovely name," he said. "You are the girl of my dreams." His wife was at the party, but it didn't matter. He took me to the darkest corner and danced cheek to cheek. He told me how nice I was and asked for us to meet somewhere. You see what traitors men are? He was like the cat who, with the rat in the house, went out looking for meat.

He kept talking: "I like you. Why don't we live together? We'd get along swell. You are my ideal woman." I tried to joke it off, but he really wanted to make an arrangement with me. I began to see that there were lots of opportunities if I wanted them and if my in-laws didn't find out. But I thought better of it and refused to dance with him again. With Crispín right there that fellow followed me about like a dog all evening!

Crispín's family and friends continued to spy on me. His mother said I was never in the house and that I had too many friends. The sister-in-law who didn't say I was lazy said I was dirty. No sooner did I do something or go somewhere, when Crispín knew. They caused a lot of trouble for me.

Once my brother Roberto visited me. He was sitting on the bed when my sister-in-law Sofía came in to ask about my health, for I was ill. She left right away, and Roberto did too. Sofía must have told Crispín because he came home in a rage, saying, "How is it you get angry when my nephews climb on the bed, but you let your brother lie down whenever he wants to?"

Just think of that! Sofía had told him that Roberto was eating and sleeping there, which was not true. Crispín shouted that he had set up the apartment for his family, not for mine, and he wasn't going to be supporting my relatives.

I was angry and said, "If the house is for your family, let them come and live here instead of me." That was when he punched me hard for the first time.

I didn't go to see my father until the swelling went down. My brother hardly ever came to see me after that. He must have understood. I was really afraid of Crispín. Just to see him angry made me tremble. If I had raised a hand to him it would have been worse. When I was three months pregnant, I tried to hit him back and he socked me. I couldn't stand that life any longer, so one day I told him I was going to the toilet (the toilets were outside in the courtyard) and, instead, I went home.

Crispín sent his sister Sofía to tell me that he was going to change and would I come back. My father urged me to go back and beg my husband's pardon. That was always hard for me to do; I went back, but I didn't apologize. It is true I had raised a hand to him but it was to defend myself. After that he was even worse. He kept fighting on one pretext or another. He would turn up the radio so that no one could hear when he beat me. Once he gave me such a kick in the small of my back that I almost aborted. So I left him again. I went to Lupita's on Rosario Street, where my father and Consuelo were living. Manuel and Paula were in the Casa Grande at the time.

I never told my father or brothers that Crispín beat me. They noticed it all right, but didn't do anything because it would have been worse for me. My father only said that I could go home to live any time I wanted to. It wouldn't have cost me a thing to tell them, but I couldn't take such a serious responsibility because when two men start to fight here, nothing in the world can stop them. Roberto and Manuel went mad when they fought, and I was afraid of the consequences. If it were just a question of fists, I wouldn't worry, but if they shifted to knives, then what? And what for! To go on the same way anyhow?

I was sixteen when my daughter was born. My father was with me at the sanatorium and I held on to his legs when I had bad pains. He paid for everything and Crispín didn't even know what it cost. Nor did he ask. Crispín had wanted a boy but I could see he was pleased to have a daughter. He came every day to the sanatorium, to Lupita's house, and then to the Casa Grande, on the pretext of seeing the baby. But I no longer had any affection for him. I hated him when I found myself with the responsibility of caring for the child. I pinched him for any little thing; he didn't dare hit me in my father's house.

All the time he came to see me, he never gave me a single *centavo*. My father paid for my clothes, my food, and for all the baby's expenses. Crispín would talk to my father and apologize to him for the way things were. My father would ask him why it was so difficult for us to live together and Crispín would blame me and say the fights were all my fault, that I was a very difficult person, that I never took care of him, that I was never at home. Imagine that! With my sister-in-law and everybody spying on me I couldn't misbehave if I wanted to!

My mother-in-law came to see the baby and finally asked me to go and live with them. I accepted, but didn't stay more than three weeks, because of Crispín's niece. This little girl, Lidia, was the daughter of Crispín's dead sister, who had gone with a man who later abandoned her. I don't know how she died, but the result was another child without a father or mother.

I was ironing one day when Lidia began to embrace Concepción and shower her with kisses in an exaggerated way. She was holding the baby too tightly and her overaffectionate manner infuriated me. I kept telling her to leave the baby alone. Talk to her, talk to the wall! My father-in-law, who was a tailor, was working at home but he wouldn't interfere and told me not to be so touchy. He didn't reprimand Lidia when she said, "If you don't want me to hold the baby, shove her back where she came from."

I was so angry, I packed my things and started to go. My father-in-law blocked my way and said, "You're not leaving this house until my old lady gets back from the market."

"Who are you to tell me what to do?" I asked, adding a few sharp words for good measure.

"I'm your father, you ungrateful, common woman. And you are a disgrace!"

The other daughter-in-law, Natalia, was there and she said, "Run, Martita, because when she comes it will be worse."

And so it was. When my mother-in-law came she threw me out. I had packed only my clothes, but she made me take my dishes and my bed. She said I wasn't fit to be the wife of their son and Concepción probably wasn't even his child! I ran out of her house.

That night, Crispín came to look for me at my aunt Guadalupe's house. He was angry and threw a fit. He accused me of having cursed his mother. I told him what Lidia said, but he wouldn't believe me and hit me. That's the way he always was. I didn't see him for a month after that, but then he began to whistle for me outside our door.

I kept saying I didn't love Crispín any more and my father didn't compel me to go back to live with him. But my husband was not easy to put off. When I wasn't near him, I didn't have physical desires, but when he kept insisting and tempting me, I reacted strongly. Unwillingly, I began to go to hotels with him. But he wasn't satisfied and complained that he couldn't make use of me because I was always scowling and sullen and like a stick of wood.

He was one of those low types who wanted the worst of women. If we were alone in the house, for just a minute, that was what he wanted; if we went out, it was to go to a hotel. He just had me to relieve himself. I was useful to him because I was clean and he didn't run the risk of getting a disease. But I didn't satisfy him because he was exaggerated. He was always kissing and caressing me. That was all he thought of. He would have liked me to be one of those extreme women who undressed and moved a lot and was expert in every way. He wanted it two or three times a night, but I felt that I couldn't stand so much. With my resentment and his desires, we couldn't do much together.

When Concepción was a year old, I had to wean her because I was pregnant with Violeta. It didn't bother Crispín at all that I was pregnant again, as though it were the most natural thing in the world. He didn't care what my father or anyone else said. He considered himself my husband with the right to get me pregnant at any time. He said we should live together again for the sake of the babies and the neighbors. I accepted, not because I wanted to, but because of necessity and convenience. I was having difficulties with my brothers and sister . . . I wanted to get away from my family.

Roberto, my brother, was making my life bitter, because of his drinking and stealing. When I was small, though I was afraid of being caught using a compact or a pair of earrings he had stolen, I never interfered with what he did and didn't betray him to my father. Later, when he brought home pieces of bronze and iron, aluminum pipes and other things from the factory where he worked, I thought he would be caught and I told my father. But nothing stopped Roberto. He would file the pipes and sell the pieces in the Tepito Market. Sometimes he brought home tires, hub caps . . . he grabbed whatever he could. A woman from the Casa Grande came to complain that a tank of cooking gas had been stolen from her roof; another accused my brother of taking her turkeys. My brother had a bad reputation around here and I was getting tired of defending him.

Then there was a fight with Manuel. The trouble began between Paula and Consuelo, who had always been a bit difficult. My sister-in-law made a complaint to Manuel and he threw Domingo's hobby horse at Consuelo, hitting her in the head and making her cry. She began to insult him and he hit her again. I felt I had to stand up for my sister, so I went into action.

It was like a man-to-man fight; I kicked and scratched and hit him with whatever I could find; Consuelo was frightened and told us to stop before the neighbors called the police. I got him down on the bed and grabbed his balls and squeezed tight. He couldn't do a thing to me because of the pain. He begged me to let go and told Paula to make me stop, but I wouldn't. He was the one who gave up first.

The neighbors who had crowded around our door watching the fight criticized him for hitting his younger sisters. Paula began to get her things together because she thought my father would come and raise hell. She knew he would stand up for his daughters rather than his daughter-in-law. Sure enough, my *papá* came and slapped Manuel twice and told him to get out seeing that he couldn't get along with his sisters. He and Paula went to live with her mother and sister Delila. Consuelo and Roberto remained in the Casa Grande and I went back to my husband.

Crispín set up our second home on the Street of the Carpenters, next door to his sister. When it was time for Violeta to be born, he took me to the Maternity Division of Social Security. I suffered more pain with Violeta than with Concepción, for in the Social Security they did not give any anesthetic. They let me suffer all the pain one is meant to suffer.

I left the hospital like an unmarried mother because Crispín was asleep drunk in his mother's house. No one remembered that I had to leave the hospital after five days, and so, without money, or a coat, I took the baby and boarded a bus. Luckily, the hospital gave me a basket with baby clothes for Christmas, so I had something to dress the baby in. All the neighborhood shops with phones were closed for the holiday, and I couldn't telephone to send a message to my father or to my mother-in-law. Perhaps my husband's family didn't come because I gave birth to another girl. Before I went into the hospital they had said, as a joke I thought, that if it wasn't a boy they would not even come to see the baby. Crispín had always preferred boys, and was nicer to his nephews than to his own daughters.

Crispín and I began to have difficulties all over again, partly because of my sister-in-law and partly because he had taken up with a woman again. He didn't hit me as much in that house because he knew Sofía would hear us. He hit me only when we were alone, but this time I'd hit him right back, for the sake of my daughters. Why should I let him kill me? They would be the ones to suffer.

When I asked him for money to buy the children clothes, he told me to wait. We always had to wait and finally I said I would have to go to work to provide them the things they needed. He went and told his mother he was going to leave me and she said, "All right, son. Your home is here." She didn't intervene in my favor, but left me to my fate. Later, she even went to my father to tell him not to take me in.

I said I wouldn't leave the house, so Crispín took out his things. He left me only the bed and clothes closet which didn't belong to us. He took the electric-light bulb and the cord and he left me in the dark, with the two babies. He went away and didn't even know whether his children had enough to eat.

The next day, Roberto went with me to the Police Station to accuse Crispín. Crispín and his father were summoned and they said it was not Crispín's fault, that he had gotten me an apartment but that I was the one who left. It was a lie, but the court officials said they could not force Crispín to do anything because we were not married.

I could get no help from the law. Violeta was just three months old when I returned to my father's house.

By that time, my sister-in-law Paula had died, and her sister Delila had moved in to take care of Manuel's children. Delila was only two years older than I, and she was already bearing my father's child! I had known her before, when she lived with her mother, Cuquita, and a bunch of relatives in a "Lost City" on Piedad Street, near the Tepito Market. Paula would take me there to visit. Their room was filthy and crowded, dirty dishes everywhere, the beds unmade, garbage on the floor, children running around, and the full chamber pot in plain view while they were eating. They lived like pigs!

When Paula lived in the Casa Grande, our room was always filled with her relatives. Crispín and I once came in the middle of the day and found them all eating in the courtyard. They had plenty of food but didn't invite us to eat. I couldn't have eaten anyway, because Cuquita's husband, who worked in the slaughterhouse, had brought tripe and heart for Paula to cook. That is what they always ate, tripe and heart. And Cuquita was so ugly that one look at her face and a person didn't even want to enter the same room. She ran us all out, just with her face! That sainted *señora* was always giving Consuelo and me dirty looks and calling us lazy daughters-of-a-whore behind our backs because she thought we let her daughter Paula do all the work in the house.

When we were girls, I would often see Delila at dances. She liked to dress up and dance even more than I did. She danced so much that her legs gave way under her and she became pregnant with a child that died at birth. She married the father of her child, by church and civil law, and went to live in a room near her mother-in-law. They had another boy named Geofredo, but by that time her husband was drinking and running around with other women. He turned out to be a thief with a police record. He didn't give her any money so she went out to work. And would you believe it? While she was working, he would take other women into her very bed! And her mother-in-law knew about it. That woman was a regular go-between for her son! I learned about it from a friend who was their neighbor.

One day Delila came home and found all her furniture and things gone. Luis, her husband, had emptied the room, leaving her to the four winds. She accused him in court and got into a bad fight with her mother-in-law, who attacked her with a scissors. Delila wasn't the kind to just stand there and let herself get beaten up; she threw everything she could lay her hands on. It was a real battle!

She was living with her mother when she accepted my *papá's* offer to go and live in the Casa Grande. Her husband came after her but she threatened to call the police if he bothered her any more and because of his record he didn't. But I heard that she met him in the market now and then and I wondered whether she was giving my father a cat for a hare by cheating on him. Lupita had told me that my *papá* couldn't have children any more . . . that Marielena was his last child. So I would have given a lot to know whether or not my *papá* was able to beget a child with Delila, or whether it was really Luis' baby. But I never told my *papá* any of the gossip, because, you know, doubt does more harm than disappointment.

So when I returned home, I found Delila was my father's mistress, because though she didn't want to admit it, that was what she really was. My *papá* was still free . . . he wasn't tied down by any law, only by his own sentiments. If he had been different, he would have abandoned us a long time ago. But there he was, taking care of everybody, Consuelo, Delila and her son, Manuel's four children, me and my two babies, Antonia and her little girl, Lupita and Marielena.

Manuel had gone to the United States and Delila was mad at him for taking along her brother Faustino. According to her, Manuel and his friend Alberto came to her house in the middle of the night and talked Faustino into going. She said, "My poor little brother! They dragged him off and now he has to search garbage pails for something to eat." They had a hard time in Mexicali before they got across the border and there were days when they didn't eat.

But once they were in the United States they were well off and even sent money home. It must be nice there! I imagine it is a country so civilized that even the people are different. Here, if there isn't something in it for a person, no one will do you a favor. Or if someone does, when you least expect it, he demands repayment. Here, people have too much self-interest. Of course, there are good people too, but in Mexico one does not progress. We have freedom to do and undo as we please and we don't exactly die of hunger, but it is like being in a stagnant pond . . . there is no way out, one cannot get ahead. From what I have seen in the movies and newspapers, it is not that way up north.

It has been one of my dreams to go to live in the United States, even if in a very humble little house. But because of my children I would be a little afraid, for I have heard that juvenile delinquency is a bit more advanced there and that the youth lacks respect for their elders. Instead of the parents shouting at the children, the children shout at the parents. And there, women can go out with any man and the husband doesn't think it is bad. Here it is impossible for a woman to have a friendship with another man because her husband would beat her. And some say that the *gringos* want to come here and govern us, that the laws of the United States are stronger than our own laws. But I say it wouldn't be reasonable to expect the little one to eat the big one or the younger son to have more power than the older one, isn't that true?

Anyway, when Manuel and Faustino began sending money home, Delila stopped complaining about my brother. That's the way Delila was, like her mother, very changeable and two-faced. If she was sore at someone, she'd take it out on the first person who came along. One minute she might talk to you very nicely, the next thing you knew, she would turn her back on you and chew you up alive.

From the start, Delila was angry because my father was helping me. She was envious of everything he gave to his children or to Lupita. Consuelo had warned me that Delila intended to drive us out. Delila sounded like a saint when she said she'd take care of her dead sister's children so long as God gave her life, but according to Consuelo, she was just using the children to accomplish her evil purpose. Consuelo was already living with my aunt Guadalupe, and Roberto was only God knew where. Neither of them could stand the sight of Delila.

When Paula died, my sister had made the mistake of bringing a girl, Claudia, into the house to help with the work. Later, Consuelo wanted to throw her out because my father began to give her presents and it looked as though he might make her his mistress. Claudia was still there when Delila came, but with both Consuelo and Delila jealous of her, the girl couldn't stand it and left when her month was up.

Then Consuelo and Delila went after each other. Delila became pregnant and Consuelo hated her more than ever. My sister slept in the same room, and so she knew that my father was getting into Delila's bed when the lights were out. She was beside herself with jealousy and anger and acted very badly. When she came home from work and saw Delila there, she would slam the door hard, so that everyone would notice.

She looked for trouble, right? and was expert in saying *indirectas* very directly. She would say to Mariquita, Manuel's oldest girl, "Ay, how dirty everything is here!" or, "There is never anything to swallow in this house any more." She suspected that Delila gave all the leftovers to her mother and complained that there was never anything for her to eat. If a slip or a pair of her panties was missing, she would calmly take one of Delila's. That was her way of saying that Delila was stealing her clothes.

My father was very hurt by Consuelo's nasty behavior and she even made him cry. They told me that once she yelled at him across the courtyard in front of the neighbors: "What kind of a father are you that you always take up with women!"

One evening, when my father was eating supper, my sister came in, slammed the door, and asked him for money for shoes. He couldn't give her anything that day because he had a lot of expenses to pay. He said, "What are you working for? What do you do with your money anyway?"

Instead of answering his questions, she began to argue. "You don't have money for your daughter, but you spend plenty on other women."

He got angry and said, "I tried to educate my daughters so they could take care of themselves!"

Then she screamed at him. "Not every woman gets the kind of things you give Delila. You should acknowledge the children of your first wife before those of whatever tramp you take up with."

"Shut your trap, you miserable girl! Get out of here and don't come back. I don't want to see you here again!"

"All right, I'm getting out," she said. "But before I go I have one more thing to do." That's when she took down my father's picture and threw it on the floor and danced on it, right before his eyes, yelling, "Cursed is the hour that I spent money on this!"

Since then my father can hardly look at her. When they told me what she did, I got angry with my sister too. She had no right to meddle in his affairs. If he was happy with that woman, what right did his daughter have to judge him? Later, Cosuelo said she was sick in the head, but I don't think so. Whatever she did, she did consciously. She had always been touchy and her outbursts were caused by pure anger.

In contrast, I have always had the luck to make friends easily and I got along well with both Claudia and Delila. I figured it was none of my business if my father got into Delila's bed, although I was ashamed to hear his intimacies. I couldn't see anything because it was always so dark, but I could hear them talk. Once, when I couldn't sleep, I heard him say he was going to get her another room because here he couldn't do what he wanted freely. Later, I heard him go back to his own bed on the floor.

When Delila and I had a quarrel, it was usually over the children. Delila spoiled her son Geofredo and let him do what he pleased. She was harder on Manuel's children, hitting and cursing them when they got her angry, but also giving them too much liberty . . . out of pure disorderliness. Once, Manuel's oldest boy, whom we called Skinny, was hitting Concepción. Delila and her mother were eating in the kitchen and didn't pay any attention when I asked her to correct the boy.

Then Skinny pulled my little girl's braids and made her cry, and I said, "Let her be, you damned brat!" That got Delila's attention and she said angrily, "Don't you dare call him names! If you don't like it here, go tell your husband to set up a place of your own! Why do you stay here anyway?"

I said, "Because this is my father's house, not yours. You're a fool if you think I'm going to let you scold me. Why don't you yell at the children when they need it, not at me!" I was very angry. "And if you are so interested in me, go look for a house for me yourself."

With that, I took my pillow and blanket and clothes and went to my aunt's house. In the evening, just as I was spreading my bedding on the floor, my *papá* appeared.

"Pick up your things and come home," he said. "Don't pay any attention to Delila, I'm the one who gives orders in my house."

"Yes, *papá*," and I went back with him. Delila and I didn't quarrel again for a long time, although she continued to begrudge every *centavo* my father gave me. He gave me money for food but often, at night, my *papá* told me to sit down and eat with him or he would send out for *pozole* or some cheese that I liked. That would get Delila even angrier. She would say, "Why can't she eat beans like the rest of us?" To me, she sometimes would say, "Your father gives you money for food, but here I am feeding you," or, "Do you expect us to believe that the father of your children is not also giving you expense money? You are quite astute, aren't you?"

Difficult as she was, Delila took care of my babies, while I went back to my job in the ice-cream factory. I worked from nine o'clock in the morning until nine at night for only four *pesos* a day. I really did it to get out of the house. My boss would send me out to buy meat for her dinner and that is how I met Felipe, the butcher, once again.

I had known Felipe before I became Crispín's *novia*. All of the girls of my gang would hang around the butcher shop because Felipe was so good-looking and nice. Once, he locked me in the refrigerator with him and wouldn't let me out until I let him kiss me. Right off, he asked me to be his *novia* and to go away with him. He said he would send his older brother to ask my *papá* for me. Although I liked him a lot, even more than Crispín, I said no, because I was so young.

Felipe recognized me right away and we talked. Then one day, a boy brought me a note from him asking me to call at such and such an hour. I did and he invited me to meet him at the Frontón between eight and nine that evening. It cost me a lot of work to get out of the house that night but I went because I liked him. He respected me and didn't give me the line about going to a hotel. We saw each other two or three times a week, until one night he didn't show up.

I felt hurt and bawled him out on the telephone, hanging up before he had a chance to explain. When I called back to say I was sorry, he hung up on me. I missed him very much so I apologized to him. Then he told me what the father of my children never told me: he didn't want me to work, he would support me and my children, his ideal was to live with me and to set up an apartment. He didn't ask me to run off with him or to go from one hotel to another. And he thought it wouldn't be right to make love in front of the children. He was just the opposite of Crispín.

Felipe had a car and we would drive to a different part of the city so as not to be seen. When I went with him during the day I took my children with me. I told him that if he thought I would abandon them for him, he was mistaken, but he said that he'd never expect such a thing.

Somehow my *papá* found out I was seeing someone, so I asked him what he thought. He said I was mistaken if I expected any man

to accept the responsibility of my children and that I should not think
of putting another in their father's place, because they would surely
suffer.

I was afraid, very much afraid, of becoming pregnant again, but
because I really loved Felipe, I went with him to a hotel. I was not
sure he wouldn't just "do me the favor" and then leave me with the
"profits." Lots of men only make a fool of a woman and don't care
what happens to her. That's why everyone respected my *papá*. He had
a great sense of responsibility, which they say he got from his father.
Neither of them abandoned their children.

I became pregnant so easily, my friends always said I wouldn't even
make a good prostitute. But Felipe and I were together only twice,
and I had nothing to worry about. After the second time, Felipe began
to give me seven *pesos* a day for expenses, so that I wouldn't have to
work or go back to Crispín. I didn't want to see Crispín any more. I
liked Felipe's way of doing it . . . quickly and without wasting
time . . . much better than Crispín's excesses. If Crispín had left me
then, instead of later, I would be living with Felipe now. By that time,
Felipe was my god!

It wasn't that he gave me what Crispín didn't, but rather that he
made me want to live happily again. For a long time I had been depressed; I didn't go out, avoided my friends and no longer cared what
I looked like. At night I would cry, and call for my mother . . . my
thoughts were of death. Felipe changed all that. He needed me and
gave me back my interest in life.

He had been deceived by another woman and was tired of fooling
around. He wanted to settle down and be a good father to my children. But I was still distrustful, and because of my fears, everything
went wrong. Instead of breaking with Crispín forever, I didn't tell him
the truth and let him in when he came around to the Casa Grande
every two weeks.

It was not that I cared for Crispín any more. I really began to hate
him, because if it hadn't been for him I might have been happy with
Felipe. Whenever Crispín and I were together we would fight. He had
heard from his spies that I was seeing a butcher, but I denied it.
I could hold my head high. I was sure no one knew which butcher
it was because we were careful not to be seen. But I lost Felipe anyway, for one day Crispín and I were coming along the Street of the
Potters, fighting as usual. I didn't think that Felipe would be in the

butcher shop at that hour, but when we turned the corner, there he was and we walked right by him.

I felt my legs buckle. I was so ashamed that I knew I could never again look him in the face. He would surely think that I was the kind to go with two men at the same time, and that I was giving his money to my husband. I knew what men were like when they saw that a woman was deceiving them. That's why I didn't ever speak to him again. I gave him no explanation and preferred not to see him, rather than have him say I was no good.

He had treated me so well and that was the way I paid him back! I couldn't lift my head; it was my love and shame that made me withdraw from him. Losing him was the most painful thing that has happened to me, the thing I regret most . . . and it was Crispín's fault.

How could I tell Crispín that the affection I once felt for him had turned to loathing? He began to come around for me again, but I avoided him. I got a job in a skirt factory for forty *pesos* a week, but I couldn't get along on that so I looked for another. Consuelo was working in an accountant's office and once she sent my aunt to tell them she was sick. My aunt, who was always looking out for me, asked if they had any work for me and so I got a job there for fifty *pesos* a week, answering the telephone.

I had to get the bus on the corner across the street from the butcher shop, and I saw Felipe every day. I wanted to embrace him and speak to him but my shame stopped me. When our eyes met, I saw that he still cared for me, but I'd get on the bus just the same. I had gone with him only two or three months but I couldn't get him out of my mind.

Crispín kept going after me. The moment he'd start to move toward me, I prayed to the saints that he wouldn't touch me.

"All you ever think of is intercourse," I would say.

"And who did you go to bed with that you don't?" he would answer.

He aroused me, but I could usually control myself. When I did go to a hotel with him and he pawed me in his gross manner, I would imagine I was with Felipe. With him I would have done it in any position he wanted. I would even have taken off all my clothes! But with Crispín I refused because he made me feel like an alley cat.

Crispín was always suspicious of my boss when I worked. When I had the job in the office, he would say, "Only you and that ac-

countant know what happens on those couches," or, "God knows
how many times you've gone to bed with that lawyer." He'd say, "You
certainly don't have any difficulty finding jobs. I suppose you want me
to believe that you and *Señor* Miguel don't have your fun in the store-
room?" And when I worked in a shop: "Why shouldn't you speak well
of *Señor* Santos? After all, he pays you for your favors, doesn't he?"
It got so I couldn't work because he was always marrying me off
to the bosses. The truth is, that on every job the boss or the employees
did go after me. Here, there is no respect for the woman who works.

While I worked I had money to buy clothes for the girls and myself,
and we looked more presentable. I used lipstick again and had a
permanent wave. I wore a sweater or a coat instead of a shawl and
my shoes were never torn. I felt like a queen compared to the way
I was dressed when I lived with Crispín. I met my mother-in-law in
the market and she looked surprised at my neatness. I could see she
thought I was running around with someone. She and my sisters-in-
law had considered me a slob and they hardly ever went out with
me. But then I had only three cotton dresses, even when I was pregnant, and I had to keep my sandals together with string. Crispín
wanted me to satisfy him sexually but he never gave me money to buy
clothes or lipstick. All he would say was that he had no money. My
papá helped me by sending an apron to keep my dresses clean, and
empty flour bags for the babies' diapers.

Crispín would sometimes meet me after work and take me home.
One day he didn't come as he had promised, and so I went home
alone. The next evening he bawled me out for not waiting. He knew
he hadn't come for me, but he scolded me all the way home on the
bus. I kept quiet, for fear that he would hit me. No matter what he
said, I kept my mouth shut.

"I'm talking to you," he said. But I didn't answer. When we got off
the bus, it looked as though he was going to start something on the
street. I said to myself, "If he hits me, I'm going to hit him back."

When we reached the school, across the street from the Casa
Grande, he slapped me and then I really showed my claws. I was
carrying my lunch plate and jar and dropped them, along with my
purse. My coat fell in the mud. I yelled, "Don't hit me, you miserable
wretch!" And I scratched and hit him so fast, he was taken by surprise. I didn't expect that of myself either!

He socked me with his fist, and instead of warding off his blows and crying, the way I usually did, I kicked and let loose with everything I had stored up in me. We beat each other up and cursed, while people gathered around to watch. I didn't even feel ashamed and hoped for someone I knew to come to my defense. But I fought it out alone and from that day, he never again raised a hand to me.

The deeply painful thing about it was that I was pregnant with our third child, Trinidad. When I had told Crispín about it, he said he would take care of me and the children and stop his wanderings. The day after our fight, he told Manuel he didn't want me to work and would give me an allowance until he could set up an apartment. The first week, he came to see me every day and gave me twenty-five *pesos*, so I quit my job. The next week, he gave me only twenty *pesos* and didn't come to the house. By the third week, he had disappeared. I didn't see him until the following Tuesday, when he came and offered me fifteen *pesos*. I threw them in his face and said I didn't take alms. That was when he told me he didn't think the child was his! I don't know what he based it on, but anyway he used that as a pretext not to give me money any more. Consuelo found a job for me taking messages in a lawyer's office, so I went back to work.

I had been living in the Casa Grande, but there was an argument with Delila and I moved to my aunt Guadalupe's again, this time staying until just before Trini was born. Their place was poor and tiny, with hardly room to turn around; Concepción and Violeta had to eat sitting on the doorstep and the three of us slept on sacks on the floor. My aunt would invite me to sleep in the bed with her and Ignacio, but the bed was so narrow, how could I?

The *vecindad* was full of bedbugs, mice and other vermin, and the two outside toilets were filthy, but I was happy. I got along well with my aunt and practically ran the place, so I was well off. But my father didn't like it there and that made me sad. When he came to see me he would arrive scolding and was impatient to leave.

The major annoyance for me was that my aunt always had many visitors. If it wasn't a *compadre*, it would be a few *comadres* who dropped in for a *taco* to eat with their beer or *chinchól*. I couldn't stand seeing all those drunken faces, and some of them were downright disgusting. I was angry because one of them stole a watch and some *centavos* from me.

Things were always disappearing in that *vecindad;* nothing was safe. That's why my uncle had a watchdog and people never left their rooms unguarded. When something was stolen, the victim would go to a seer to find out who had taken it, but I didn't go because it would have led only to arguments.

Everyone there used vulgar language, even my uncle, who was usually amiable. If he came home and found my aunt too tipsy to prepare his supper, he would start insulting her mother and calling her "bitch" and "daughter-of-a-whore." But they really loved each other a lot, especially after he gave up seeing his other woman, Cuca. He had had six women besides my aunt, but he always said they meant nothing, that they were just talk, and that it was my aunt who had all the keys to his house and was the boss of his *centavos*.

My uncle was respectful and correct with me, and was fond of my daughters. He would tell me about my mother, with whom he sometimes went out to sell, and how jealous Guadalupe would get when he was mistaken for my *mamá's* husband. When Ignacio was drunk he would make advances to me, but I never led him on, and he didn't insist. If he ever complained about my children yelling, or my brother coming in drunk, my aunt would defend us. The only one my uncle really fought with was Consuelo, who would come and try to be the boss.

Both Ignacio and Guadalupe were very short, gray and wrinkled, though not yet old. My uncle often said that youth had nothing to do with the number of years you have lived. What counted was how much you suffered in your life. He would say, "Do you know the age of a gray hair? No? Every gray hair has its story . . . its destiny and its end. They come from the knocks in life, from your failures, the many people you've seen die." He called my aunt "the-young-person-who-looks-old" and believed that she had aged because of all the sacrifices she had to make for her family.

My aunt had an unbelievably hard life. When she was thirteen, she was raped by a man of thirty-two. Because she had been deflowered and "wasn't worth anything any more," her father beat her hard and made her go through a church marriage. Her mother-in-law hated her, so her husband beat her and took her from one aunt to another until her son was born.

Then her husband went into the army and she never saw him again. She and the baby had no place to stay and almost died of hunger; they swelled up for lack of food. She walked all the way back to

Guanajuato, and nearly drowned trying to cross a flooded river. A teamster pulled her out by her braids, otherwise she wouldn't be alive today.

In Guanajuato, Guadalupe learned that her brother Pablo had been killed while defending a friend and that her sainted father had died of anger and grief. Her mother had gone with the rest of the children to Mexico City to seek her fortune selling hot coffee on street corners. Guadalupe's aunt Catarina was in the capital and had advised her mother to go. So my little aunt went to look for them, carrying her child in her shawl and begging food along the way. When she arrived, she looked like a beggar and her mother didn't even recognize her.

Guadalupe's brothers were all ill with typhus and she caught it too. Bernardo died, but the others recovered. José and Alfredo worked in a bakery, Lucio got a job in a *pulquería,* and my aunt and my *mamá* sold cake and spiked coffee at a little stand on a street corner. Putting alcohol in the coffee was a legal offense; my aunt went to jail three times because her mother couldn't pay the fine. Guadalupe was afraid they would send her to the Penitentiary next, so she worked as a servant, and later, in a *tortillería* as a *tortilla* maker.

My aunt had always complained that my grandma had favored my *mamá,* who was the youngest girl. She said, "I worked to support my little mother, but she was very hard on me, may she rest in peace! My little son and I would cry because she didn't bring our lunch to the *tortillería.* She would forget all about us, but she never failed to bring a *taco* to your *mamá,* Lenore. I asked my aunt Catarina, 'Ay, Auntie, am I not my mother's daughter? Why does she love only Lenore?' My aunt would say that I had bad luck and that I must resign myself to it."

When Guadalupe's son was five years old, her mother-in-law came and took him away. She told Guadalupe that the boy's father had come to a bad end in the Revolution . . . he had been chopped up with *machetes* and dumped into a river. My aunt prayed to God to forgive her husband and she vowed to the Virgin of Guadalupe never to re-marry. She let her mother-in-law take her son because she was having a hard time feeding him. But they turned the boy against her and taught him to be a drunkard. At eight, he was already being given *tequila* punch and he got the habit. When Guadalupe brought him a piece of cake or fruit, they shut the door in her face. He finally died of drink while still quite young and she lost him forever.

My aunt got the habit of drinking when they tried to cure her of malaria. She had gone to Veracruz as a servant and had come back sick. They gave her sugar cane and *jícama* roots; they put a mouse on her neck to startle her; they gave her green alcohol and strong coffee, then *pulque* with ground *pirú;* for seven months they tried this and that, usually with alcohol, until finally a woman cured her with nopal leaves, chile and honey.

Then a man just did my aunt "the favor" and left her, even before her son Salvador was born. When she met Ignacio, he wanted to marry her and accept her son as his own. She liked Ignacio, but refused to marry him. Ignacio's father wanted her to have a church wedding, too, because in those days they were more strict. Now people just get together in the doorway and they think themselves married. My uncle says that God, the Father, ran things then, not God, the Son. Ignacio's father was the law and he educated his son to have a conscience. Ignacio could never raise a hand to my aunt because his father was there with a stick to defend her.

But my aunt stubbornly refused to be married. She said, "I vowed never to marry because I suffered too much as a wife. If Ignacio wants to live with me like this, very well. God will find the way to pardon me." And that's the way it was.

Ignacio had been a news vendor since 1922. Before that he made good money as a varnisher in a furniture shop but he said he "left his lungs" in that place and took the first other job God offered. He and Salvador went out selling papers together, in rain or shine, and gave the little they earned to my aunt. My uncle always said he would do all right in the newspaper business if only he sold all his papers. But there were no returns allowed, and he would lose his profits because of the rains, which was the scourge of the vendors. God! all the hiking he did to earn a few *pesos!* My poor uncle will probably die walking the streets, holding on to his papers.

Ignacio was good to Salvador, but my cousin began to drink and became quarrelsome. Things got worse when Salvador married because his wife took their child and ran off with another man. Salvador hit the bottle even more and was drunk all the time.

I was only five or six years old when my cousin died. Tipsy as usual, he was standing in front of a beer parlor on the Street of the Tinsmiths, when along came his wife's lover, Carlos. As soon as Carlos saw him, he said, "This is the way I wanted to find you, son-of-your-smutty-mother!" And with that, he took out an ice pick and stuck it into Salvador's belly.

Salvador held his wound with both hands and started to run. At that time, he and my aunt and uncle were living half a block away with Prudencia, my uncle Alfredo's first wife. But instead of going there, my cousin went the other way, to the Casa Grande, with Carlos running after him. At the gate, Carlos turned back and my cousin ran into our courtyard.

We were just finishing supper when he shouted, "Uncle Jesús, let me in!" My *papá* opened the door, but thought Salvador was drunk.

"Are you here again? I told you before that I won't let drunks in here. I don't want any bad examples for the girls."

Salvador fell in the doorway and my *papá* saw that he was full of blood. He was stretched out on the kitchen floor, with his feet across the doorsill. My father unbuttoned his pants and saw the wound.

We were very frightened and I began to cry. My *papá* sent me to get Roberto, who was eating supper at his friend's house. Roberto went for my aunt Guadalupe and Ignacio, who came running with Prudencia and her son. Someone sent for the Red Cross ambulance. The cut was very deep and my cousin's intestines were coming out; my *papá* said he didn't think he would last long.

The ambulance took him away. He died while they were operating on him. My poor aunt! It was the work of God that she didn't go crazy, because she gave out tremendous screams. The old bastard who was her boss in the café wouldn't give her permission to take that day off and she had to look for someone to stay with her dead son.

Then that Prudencia, who had always been envious and mean, said the wake could not be held in her room, though it was the only home Salvador had known. My poor little aunt told me that Prudencia had never liked Salvador, in fact, that no one had liked him and that even his grandmother would chase him off. When Guadalupe had gone begging Prudencia to let them stay in a corner of her room, she was told, "My house is yours, but there is no room for your son."

They moved in with Prudencia anyway and had to suffer her snubs and abuse. Sometimes she would lock herself in with her children and wouldn't open the door even if it were raining. Guadalupe, Ignacio and Salvador would cover themselves with newspaper and stand huddled in the entranceway of the *vecindad* until she decided to let them in. That's why my aunt says it is awful to live off some-one else and that she must have been born under an unlucky star because she suffered all her life.

When Salvador was killed, my aunt had to plead with Prudencia for permission to put the coffin and candles in the courtyard. So the wake was held outdoors. Years later, when Prudencia's son went crazy and was put in the insane asylum, my aunt Guadalupe said, "Yes, we pay for everything we do in this life. God is slow but he doesn't forget."

Of all the women I know, my aunt Guadalupe was the one I most admired. She was the kind of woman who knew how to suffer! I wish I had her courage to go on, to never let trouble conquer and to be resigned to whatever happens. True, she complained a lot about money and was always worrying about paying the rent, but she was so resourceful that no matter how little she had, she managed to cook enough for everyone there. She would buy fifty *centavos* worth of pork, twenty *centavos* of bruised tomatoes, a few *centavos* of oil, dried up onions and garlic and make a casserole full!

She said no one ever gave her anything or helped her out, and that she had to open her own path in the world. Even though she had a mother, no one showed her the way. Perhaps that is why she was never able to give me worth-while advice or to be a true mother to me. She was so lacking in moral judgment herself!

As for helping her, only Manuel could be accused of never giving her a thing or not visiting. Roberto and Consuelo came often and would give her a few *pesos* whenever they were working. All the time I lived with her, I gave her money for food, so that my children would eat well. Every day I would buy one quart of milk from the CEIMSA, the government store, until they passed the rule that for every quart, we had to buy one egg. That made it difficult, because some days I had enough for the milk, but not for the egg. And who needed so many eggs, anyway? They did it just to bother people!

I got along well with everyone in that *vecindad*—with Julia and her husband Guillermo; Maclovio and his wife; Yolanda and her husband Rafael; Ana, the janitress; *Don* Quintero; and all the others. Many of them had known me since I was a baby. Yolanda and I would wash laundry at the tubs together, and go to the market. I don't know how she stood the life she led with Rafael. He was all right for the first few years, but when his mother died he took to the bottle and stopped giving Yolanda money. All she got from him was hunger, blows and babies. She was a factory, producing one child after another. There were seven ragged ones already, and another on the way.

Yolanda's mother, Julia, wanted to give her lemon ice with red wine to chill her matrix so that she wouldn't conceive again, but Yolanda wouldn't hear of it. I, too, was tired of bringing babies into the world, but I refused my aunt's offer to cure me with water that had been boiled with a gold ring and a piece of bull's horn. Who knows why I was afraid to be cured?

Nor have I ever tried to produce a miscarriage, although I know many remedies . . . strong orégano tea, vinegar, cinnamon tea, douches of permanganate. Women here make many sacrifices to have miscarriages, but for those with tough matrixes, only "a cleaning" works. For that, the midwives want 150 *pesos*, so few women do it. Medicines and operations are so expensive that we have to place our faith in herbs and household remedies.

In my aunt's *vecindad* there was no lack of gossip. Everyone noticed who had more and who had less, especially in clothing and food. If someone bought something new there was a lot of envy and suspicion. "I wonder how he did it?" was what the neighbors would say. Anyone in that place who owned a bed, a mattress and a wardrobe was a "somebody." When I lived there, Ana was considered on "top" because she was the janitress and both her daughters were working. She also sold *pulque* on the side, and all her grandchildren helped her with some piecework. Now Julia and Guillermo are on "top" because they have a television set.

Life should have been sad in that *vecindad* because everyone was so poor. The men drank and the wives had to feed large families on less than five *pesos*. If a woman bought a new rag of a dress, she would have to hide when the man came to collect the installments. But in spite of that, the people would laugh and joke. The very tragedies which some suffered, gave others something to laugh about. The men were always making love and rolling around with women. If it wasn't some husband sleeping with a neighbor's wife, it would be some wife running around with a neighbor's husband.

No sooner do men know that a woman has made a misstep, when they come offering her the world. The first thing they do here is to offer to set up an apartment or to take you elsewhere to live. But I had suffered such cruel disillusionment I didn't believe any of them. They would take me all right and then leave me in the middle of the road! In my aunt's *vecindad* several men went after me, Rafael, Maclovio, *Don* Chucho and *Don* Quintero, but I rejected them all.

Of the bunch, the nicest was *Don* Quintero, with whom I had an innocent friendship. He was a shoemaker and we became friends when I gave him a pair of my daughter's shoes to repair. He was about forty-two years old, had grown children, and called my girls "daughters." He was separated from his wife and lived alone. Naturally, he did suggest a few times that we get together. He would say, "Don't be stupid, Shorty. If you're not happy with your husband, why stay with him?"

I felt attracted to *Don* Quintero because he told me he was not potent any more and that we could go to bed like brother and sister. I wanted a man who couldn't have children and who wouldn't be making use of me every moment. But I treated it as a joke and nothing serious developed between us.

It was Yolanda who told me that Soledad, Ana's daughter, was angry because she thought I had an understanding with *Don* Quintero, who was her lover. Soledad went around calling me "hot pants" and "the slippery one" until all the neighbors thought I was going to bed with him. There was so much gossip, it got to Crispín. He went to *Don* Quintero and accused him of being the father of the child I was expecting. Think of it! He thought *that* man, who couldn't even do it any more, was the father of Trinidad! My husband was always doubting the paternity of his daughters, even when he was the only one I went to bed with. And still I stuck to him!

That year, I went to Chalma for the first time. All my life, I had wanted to go with my aunt and would cry when my father wouldn't allow me. He would say, "Go? What for? It's pure foolishness! They don't know anything about God and just go to get drunk. And they'd probably leave you there." When I married, it was Crispín who wouldn't let me go.

So when my aunt told me she was going with Mati, my uncle's niece, I decided to take my two daughters and go along. We had twenty-five *pesos* among us, two blankets, two quilts, extra clothing for the children, a clay jar, powdered coffee, sugar, and other food. We had to carry the children and two large packs.

It began to rain as we were standing in line for the Chalma bus and I bought Concepción a plastic raincape for two *pesos*. She and Violeta both had the measles and were completely covered with red spots . . . that was why I didn't want them to get wet. It was still raining when we got off the bus at Santiago that night, and my aunt took us to the courtyard of the municipal building where a lot of people were stretched out for the night. We spread our bedding and saved a place for my aunt's goddaughter and *comadre*, who were coming on a late bus.

The courtyard looked like a sheep pen with valises, packs and people everywhere. Soldiers were on guard to see that the pilgrims were not robbed, but even then some bundles disappeared. All night, gangs of boys and girls made noise and people kept arriving or leaving, getting up or lying down. Before we went to sleep, we women had hot coffee spiked with alcohol.

At three in the morning, my aunt woke us to leave for the pilgrimage. "Let's go," she said, and we all got up and packed. My aunt's *comadre* Luz had come with her husband and daughter, so there were eight of us when we started out. It was still dark and the only light we could see were the kerosene lamps of little food stands here and there on the road. We stopped at one for coffee, and learned that we had lost our way in the dark and had to go back to find the right road. As we walked up and down the hills, through the woods and over large rocks, I felt happy. I loved being on the move and seeing the little Indian women selling coffee, *tortillas*, chickpeas, cheese and butter to the stream of pilgrims passing by.

We walked all night and the next morning, until we arrived at Ocuila. I couldn't walk any more so we rented a little shed for twenty-five *centavos* per person and rested until the next day. I had to hire a *burro* for three *pesos* to carry our packs, because by that time both children wanted to be carried all the time. I was so tired, I wanted to go back, but all the women said, "You must not turn back, because the road will become very difficult and you will never arrive." I don't know whether that was the truth or just a belief, right? but I kept on until we arrived at the *ahuehuete* tree.

Because it was our first time there, my children and I had to look for a godmother to give us each a crown of flowers so that we might dance before the tree. We gave a *peso* to two old Indians to play for us on their violin and guitar. As we danced, I felt all my fatigue drop away . . . then we placed our flower crowns on the cross. My aunt told me to bathe the children in the spring because the water was miraculous and cured many illnesses. The girls were burning with fever . . . even their eyes had measle spots. I was afraid to put them in the cold water. I said, "*Ay!* these girls are going to die on me here." They were hot and sweating from the road, but my aunt dipped them in the water. I thought we would be burying them in *petates* right there, but no, the spring didn't hurt them at all.

From there to Chalma was a short walk, only about two hours. We passed the enchanted rocks and arrived at Chalmita, where my aunt's godmother lived. She received us well and let us cook there without charge, before we went to the shrine. All along the decline to the Church, the road is lined with stalls and shops, so that wherever we looked we saw roofs of tin or wood. There were dancers who blew on the *chirimía* as they went along, making a sad kind of music. The penitents on their knees, blindfolded and wearing crowns of thorns, others with cactus leaves on their chests and backs to fulfill vows, bands of musicians playing . . . seeing so many of the faithful who had come to venerate the Lord, I was filled with feeling and began to cry. Pilgrimages and churches have always made me cry and there, at Chalma, almost all those who reached the Church door were crying.

The Lord of Chalma was very miraculous and very punishing. I prayed for my father and all of us to be saved. I asked Him to send me a good job, but He never did, and I prayed that if Crispín was not for me, then for my sake and for my daughters' to take him away from me forever.

The trip back was boring. The children cried and I was tired and desperate to get home. We sold the clay jar on the way because by then we didn't have enough *centavos* for food. I think I had only five *pesos* left. I couldn't walk any more, so I spent two *pesos* for seats for my aunt and myself on a truck from Ocuila to Santiago, where we waited in line for a bus. Mati and the others had remained in Chalma to drink *pulque*, and were no longer with us. The bus fare was three *pesos* each and I didn't have enough money to pay, so I sold an extra pair of shoes I had taken with me. Just think, they gave me only four *pesos* for them and the shoes were almost new! But what else was there for me to do? I couldn't leave my aunt there, could I? So I bought two tickets and we arrived in Mexico City without a single *centavo*.

I would like to go to Chalma at least once a year, because it is a good thing to see the *Señor* and to pray, no? Especially since I hardly

go near a church any more. I cannot go to Sunday Mass and confess
the way I did when I was a girl because I am living in sin. I pray an
Our Father or an Ave Maria to myself at home, or when I get very
desperate I go to the Villa to ask the Virgin for help. After I give
birth, I go to thank the Virgin.

I may not be very Catholic, but neither am I a Mason or a free-
thinker. I send my daughters to Catechism in the Casa Grande every
Tuesday to prepare them for their first communion. After that, if
they want to stick close to the Church it will be because of themselves,
not because of me. I am satisfied to have my pictures of the Virgin
of Guadalupe and the Virgin of the Sacred Heart and to pray at home.
Besides, I never did like to confess my sins to a priest, who is a sinner
like myself. Many say that the priests bother women at confession
and deceive them just like other men. When I was eleven years old,
I confessed that I took money from the house and had a *novio*, and
the priest gave me a whole rosary of penances. After my first communion, I never again confessed.

My prayers were always the same: I asked the Lord that if Crispín
were not the one for me, it would be better to take him away once and
for all, or if he *was* meant for me, then to please improve him so that
we might live a normal life without so many ups and downs, for
the sake of the children. But the Lord heard my first prayer better
than the second.

My other prayer was always that my father should never be taken
from us. When his end comes, I don't want to be alive. When the wall
falls, all the bricks fall with it. Then, none of us will be able to get
up. If we cannot rise now that my father is alive, it will be impossible
later. Like my brother, Roberto. If he cannot marry and lift his
head now, how will he later?

When I think of how close death is to us, and that only God
knows which of us will wake up the next morning, I say why don't
we do everything possible to make life happy for others? For example,
my aunt is not going to last much longer on this earth and I would
like to do something for her, but all by good intentions turn out bad
because the very thought that I too may cease to exist from one
moment to the other, prevents me from doing anything.

As my pregnancy developed, my legs swelled and my teeth hurt.
Here, as soon as we have a toothache, out comes the tooth, so I had

two molars pulled. My clothes didn't fit and I had no money to buy a larger dress. I forced myself to ask Crispín for money, but he refused on the grounds that he was not responsible for the child. His words hurt. He said, "No! Why should I give you money if you just go around like a whore, opening your legs for anybody."

I became discouraged. To avoid Crispín and other people, after work I would take my daughters to the movies, or to the market, or window shopping. I never went out without my children. They were always at my side, otherwise I felt something was missing. Their father, on the other hand, never liked to take them anywhere and scolded them if they turned their heads. And he almost never bought them anything. The saddest part of my life was not to be able to buy my girls the nice things in the windows, or shoes and medicine when they were needed. Moments like those hurt me, and I would become angry with Crispín and call him a louse in the presence of my children. Then Concepción would say, imitating my aunt Guadalupe, "May all the money that Crispín earns turn to water and salt." She didn't even call him *papá!* This saddened me, for after all, he was their father. If that was her attitude toward him then, what would it be when she grew up?

Crispín came now and then and whistled for me. Sometimes he would apologize for not giving me money, saying he earned very little and was afraid my family would be more against him if he gave me only small sums. He advised me to go to a hospital to give birth (though he didn't offer to pay) and made me feel ashamed because I couldn't afford it. *He* belonged to Social Security but refused to give me the credentials I needed to enter the Maternity Hospital. Two months before Trini was born he disappeared and I didn't see him again until she was about a half year old.

When my time drew near, my father told me to quit my job and move to the Casa Grande. Delila no longer lived there because she was pregnant again and was ashamed of the neighbors and my brothers and sisters. My father set up an apartment for her on the Street of the Lost Child and since, by that time, she had won him completely, he lived there too. That was his main house, where he ate, slept and had his clothes washed. Lupita, Antonia and her children, and Marielena, were living in the house my *papá* had built in the El Dorado Colony. They took care of his animals and he gave them expense money every day, so they had no reason to complain.

My father didn't usually stick his nose into my affairs, but still he wanted to know who was going to take care of me when the baby came. I planned to have a midwife, but I told him a doctor would deliver the baby, hoping he wouldn't see through my lie. I thought my father would have more confidence in a doctor and would not insist on staying to see that things were done right. I didn't want him around because he gets very nervous and besides I was ashamed in his presence.

The pains began while my *papá* was having supper. I didn't say anything to him and sat on the edge of the bed, hoping he would go home without noticing anything. He finally left when my pains were becoming bad. My *comadre* Angélica Rivera, who lived just across the courtyard, came and she and Roberto got busy, fixing the bed, preparing the alcohol, boiling the water and staying up all night with me. Violeta woke up and started to cry. I was afraid to pick her up, so she ran behind me holding onto my skirts as I walked up and down. At about six in the morning, Roberto went for the *señora* who was my midwife. I had a worse time with Trini than with the other two, and the midwife gave me an injection because I was so weak. My heart went out to my poor little daughter, because even before she was born, her father did not recognize her. And that is why I think I loved her more than my other two.

Part I I I

Manuel

THE TRIP TO THE BORDER WAS ROUGH, MY COMPADRES BOUGHT BUS tickets to Guadalajara and from there we hitched rides to Mexicali, because we were running out of money. The first thing Alberto said when we got out on the highway was, "Ay, *compadre*, I'm hungry already."

"Me too, *compadre*, but we have to stretch the *centavos*, so, just let's hang on for now, eh?" We got short hitches on trucks, and helped load and unload along the way. After one wild ride, we had to walk a stretch past Mazatlán. There was nothing but long, steep hills and big drops, without a house in sight. The sun was strong; the asphalt was so hot it smoked. We hadn't eaten and were without water. We were in bad shape, especially Faustino. Ever since he had been burned in the restaurant, Faustino was sort of half-paralyzed and couldn't move easily. Besides, the soles of his shoes were made of automobile tires, and were burning his feet. We all began to see spots before our eyes.

We got a slow lift, sitting on the blade of a bulldozer, then, in desperation, we stopped a bus and had to give the driver almost all the cash we had. That day and the next, the only thing we ate was watermelon. Along the road, we saw lots of boys and men on foot, heading for the border, and in the railroad yard at Hermosillo, where we spent the night, there were hundreds more, stretched out, hungry and covered with dust, just like us.

I was so hungry, I didn't know where my stomach was any more, so I exchanged my windbreaker for twelve *pesos* and an old cotton jacket. We ate two rolls and a banana each, because food was so expensive. The next morning, we bought some more bread and hopped a freight train. Unfortunately, the boxcar we picked was loaded with ice. There we were, like three trembling penitents, standing on ice in that cold coffin, until we had a chance to get into another boxcar, where we stretched out and fell asleep as though it were a Pullman. We were so tired we slept the whole night through, missing our stop at Santa Ana.

We took another train back to Santa Ana, but it was going too fast for Faustino to jump, so we missed that stop again and went to Benjamin Hill. It was two or three in the morning when we got off, and was it cold! We asked the watchman for permission to sleep in the train yard. He pointed to a pile of bricks and said we could lie down behind it. We spread out newspapers and tried to sleep, but all we could do was shiver and shake. I thought up the idea of two of us getting on top of the third to warm him up for a while. We took turns and kept from freezing, but we didn't get any sleep.

Out on the highway again, we couldn't get a lift. Then a truck loaded with goats stopped. "Climb on, boys, but each of you stand in a different corner so the floor doesn't break." The truck was divided into two stories, the top one for the little goats, the bottom one for the big goats. So away we went in the truck with those damned goats.

The heat was fierce and the stink of the goats got so bad, I couldn't bear it. Every time the truck slowed down, the goats slid back and I had to keep pushing them forward. So I went up front to talk with my *compadres* and the weight of all three of us, plus a bad bump on the road, broke the crosspiece on which the second-story support rested, and all the little goats spilled in with the big goats.

The driver blamed us and I was afraid he would kick us off and leave us in that red-hot desert, where we would die for sure. So, without a word, we fixed the floor and kept pushing those god-damned goats back as we rode along. A big goat died and the driver said, "Throw it the hell over on the side of the road." So we grabbed the goat and threw it away.

"Ay, *compadre*," I say, "what a shame to throw away so much meat. Poor goat! It would have been delicious!"

Further on, the driver stopped at a water hole. "Let's go, boys. Take the goats down to water them . . . and keep a sharp eye on them, eh? Because they can get away from us." We washed ourselves first, then took down the goats, one by one. Their flanks were sunken, they were sweating and panting from the heat, and without anything to eat . . . those poor goats were in the same shape we were.

We took down a great big ram with curled horns. He staggered and shook and acted drunk until he had some water. Then he looked us over carefully and began to walk off, with me right behind him. I tried to head him off, but he broke into a trot. The other boys went after him too, but he ran faster. I made a dive for him but only buried myself in the sand. The damned goat had us all chasing him, with the driver yelling for us not to let him get away. Well, we lost him and then it got too dark to look. Only God knew where that goat went.

The owner said, "I don't move from this spot until that goat is caught. It was the best one I had. How can I just leave him? Tomorrow morning we'll catch him." He made us pinch the teats of the female goats so they would bleat. Off in the distance we could hear the ram answer. "Watch out, boys," the owner says, "because the bastard will come back during the night." So there we were, on the watch.

I said to Alberto, "Listen, *compadre*, this business with the goat is very thrilling, but, brother, go see if you can get a little coffee." We got together three *pesos* and sent him off to look for a house or a store. We built a fire and, sure enough, Alberto came back with coffee and a clay pot to boil it in.

While we sat around waiting for the coffee, the driver told us all about the United States . . . that the grape crop was the best to pick . . . that only the first tomato picking was good . . . from the last two pickings you can barely make enough for "*el borde*." El borde was what you pay for meals. After our coffee, we all dropped off to sleep.

At dawn, the driver woke us up. "All right, let's go for the goat, boys." Well, we chased that damned goat up and down the hills all morning. The owner was mad as hell and wanted to shoot the animal rather than leave him there. But at last we took off. A little before Río Colorado, where the trip was going to end, I said to my friends, "Boys, how about taking a goat with us?" No sooner were the words out of my mouth when they jumped on one of the goats. Alberto grabbed her around the neck and choked her, and Faustino banged her on the head until she was dead. So I told the driver that another goat had died and could we take it with us when we got off. We got down at a place where we could barbecue the animal.

The sun was too strong for me and I sat under a bush in the shade while the boys began to hack away at the goat with some pieces of tin.

They pulled out the guts and made a fire. The smell of the burned goat, the blood and the skin mixed with sand, and my *compadres* eating the meat almost raw, with the blood running down their chins, nauseated me. After all that goat stink, I couldn't eat a thing.

I was weak and dizzy and couldn't stand up. As I lay there in the shade, feeling faint and tired, I heard their voices far away. My eyelids felt like lead and all I wanted to do was sleep. I heard one of them say, "Don't let him sleep. If he sleeps, he'll die." They made me get up and walk. My head felt a little clearer and we kept walking toward the village.

I said, "Look, Alberto, you're proud and don't want to ask for a handout, but we're starving to death. We have one *peso* left and we must get something to eat with it." At the next house, I asked if we could work for a meal. The *señora* looked us up and down and went inside. I thought we wouldn't get a thing, but she came out with a pot of soup and a pile of *tortillas*. We sure ate fast. Our arms were going up and down like in a card game, the way we were shoving those *tortillas* into our faces. I began to sweat and sweat and then my dizziness went away.

We got to Mexicali, on the border, the next day. We didn't have a *centavo* and didn't know a soul, so we figured we'd sneak across the border right away, to look for work. We crossed the way the gamblers and border bums did, through a sewage ditch and under the fence. We thought if we worked even for a few hours we could get enough money for food and then they could throw us back over to this side.

We walked for two days, sleeping in ditches under a cover of grass. Our only food was oranges picked green from the trees. Alberto advised us to jump a train to get deeper into the country. Well, we went running alongside a train and Alberto and I grabbed the ladder and got on. Faustino, poor guy, was trying to run but couldn't make it. Alberto looked at me and I looked at him and, well, we both had to get off. What else could we do? We all went back sadly to the "dipo" and crawled through a broken window and went to sleep.

During the night Faustino disappeared. We thought he had gone to the Immigration Office, to turn himself in. We were both sore at him and were sorry we had brought him along with us. Then he came back and told us he had gone to a church to pray. Imagine! And all the time we were talking bad of him! It made me feel emotional, like crying, you know what I mean?

The very next day we were picked up by a station wagon. When the *Inmigrate* Officer stepped out of the wagon I was impressed. Right away I thought of the movies. "Now he's going to pull his gun and give us the works." But all he did was put us in the wagon and drive off to round up a bunch of Mexicans riding the freight train. The jail was crowded and suffocating and they didn't give us a thing to eat. One of the officials kicked a Mexican in the rear, real hard, and it made me mad. Later, they sent us back to Mexicali in a bus.

We were tired and hungry, but we went to look for a job in one of the bakeries. There was no work. We looked in such awful shape, the *maestro* took out three *pesos* to give us. "Take this, boys. Drink a cup of coffee to my health." I felt humiliated, as though we were beggars or something.

"Look, *maestro*," I said, "we came to ask for work, not charity. I thank you from the heart, but we don't want a handout." I guess he caught on and saw the sadness we felt, because he said we could work it off the next day.

Well, we went to one of those "sudden death" lunchrooms and had some *tacos*. Then one of the bakers came along and gave Faustino a job baking French bread. As soon as we were alone, Alberto said, "You know what, *campadre*? Let's go to a cabaret and look at the whores."

"*Chihuahua*, what are you giving me? Here we are, starving to death, and you want to see the whores. Once a bastard, always a bastard."

"Sure, but let's see if there isn't something in it for us. Let's get hold of some little whore and get her to pass her *centavos* over to us . . . I'm going nuts from hunger." So we went to the cabaret but there was a minimum charge and the women were awful. We went back to the lunchroom and asked the lady if we could sit there until morning because we had no money.

"But how awful, boys. Why didn't you say so?" And she goes into the kitchen and comes out with *tortillas* and beans and wouldn't let us pay.

We were half frozen and exhausted when Faustino came back at 7:30 A.M. It turned out he had gone to sleep in the bakery because it was nice and warm there.

Lots of men like us were living in an abandoned customs house, so that's where we headed for. Right off, we met Joaquín, a boy from the Casa Grande, and he and my *compadres* decided to build a little shelter in the yard. I went to sleep in a corner while they looked for empty cardboard boxes and wood. They nailed the cardboard to a wood frame and soon had a three-walled house, with a roof and a floor. The south side was left open so we could stick out our feet when we slept. We collected rags to sleep on and used Joaquín's blanket to cover all of us.

The very day they made the house, I found a job working two shifts in a bakery, at twenty *pesos* a shift. I went home happy and said, "*Compadres,* you can stop worrying. I have money now . . . I'll be the husband and you can do the cooking." They had already made a hearth of bricks and a sheet of metal and had some tin cans to cook in. From then on we had enough food.

Our little house became famous, because of our carryings on. We were known as "the boys of the little house." In the evenings, when all the *braceros* were sad, I would begin to dance and sing and kid around to pick up their spirits. I really should have been an actor because I liked to entertain people with jokes and stories. Well, after making the men happier, when I had them jumping and horsing around, I would sit down and watch them. And that's the way the time went. For a month and a half we spent the days working at different jobs, and the evenings clowning. We lived by God's will, as we say here.

Meanwhile, we tried to get into the United States legally. We went to the Center every day and finally got all the papers filled out. The next step was to show up at the U.S. Customs House. We got in line in front of the office and waited.

There were people from all ends of the Republic, all dirty, in rags, and starving. Most of the men were so weak that the strong Mexicali sun made them walk like drunkards. I saw one or two just fall over dead, poor things. Really, they seemed like souls in anguish. It was a sad thing, all right, a sad thing to see. Everybody was anxious to get through; I understood their desperation because I felt the same way.

Then the squeezing and pushing began. I told Alberto, "Stay in line . . . just stay in line." Faustino and Joaquín were not with us because they had drawn higher numbers and had to wait. In a way, I was glad to be rid of Faustino. We had to do everything for him. For a long time he couldn't work because his feet were in bandages. We always shared our money with him, we had to get his number, to scrape up the money for his photographs . . . everything. He didn't make a move to do things for himself. And when he worked, he sent his money home to his family. That made us sore. On the other hand, maybe he did right and we were the ones who were wrong to forget our children.

The shoving got worse. I was standing between two big guys, much taller than I, and when I was being smothered and felt walled in, I grabbed the two of them around their necks and pulled myself up. They told me to get down. "What do you mean, get down?" I said. "If I let go now, they'll kill me." Then Alberto got careless and they threw him out of the line. There were so many people there, I lost sight of him.

The Immigration Office was at the head of a flight of stairs. Well, these guys began going up the stairs with me hanging from them; otherwise I wouldn't have made it. As we were moving along, a poor fellow screamed in an awful way and everyone turned around to look. The boy had been squeezed against the handrail and had broken his ribs. There he was, almost across the border and they broke his ribs!

When I reached the office, I got nervous. We were all convinced that the Immigration Officer knew who was lying and who wasn't and that he recognized each man who had been through there. I suddenly realized that my hands were not dirty and calloused . . . I had forgotten to smear them with earth. I tried to remember how you harvest corn and when you plant, but I couldn't think at all. *Caray!* I shook all through the questioning. What a nightmare!

Then, "Thank God and the Holy Mother!" I said to myself, "I think they are going to let me in." I went past a wire, into the Center, where they examined us. They took the first x-rays of my life there. Finally, I found myself sitting on a cot, waiting to be called for a job.

To think that I was in the United States! It was quite a sensation . . . the emotion of the unknown . . . too exciting for me. I thought, "Thank God they let me in. At least I won't have to go back a failure and have all my friends make fun of me."

I had no idea what had happened to Alberto. What a jerk! I hated to go on alone. I figured I wouldn't take a job until he came. I had permission to stay three days, so I waited. The men were friendly and gave each other advice, and the time passed.

The next morning we heard a bell and a line started forming. I didn't know what it was for, but I got in line too. I mean, when a line starts forming, I get in it. After breakfast, they began to call people for jobs. I kept looking for Alberto, hoping he'd come soon. Sure enough, he was in the first car that arrived. *Uy*, the joy came back to my heart. "Come on, *compadre*. They are picking men."

We were chosen, with sixty others, to go to a farm in Catlin,

California. We lined up and marched out very proud, like soldiers. Our fingerprints were taken, and distinguishing marks, and we were given our passports. A Greyhound bus was waiting and off we went.

We drove all day and through the night and I thought, "Uy, how pretty the United States is." When we got out at a restaurant all the North American men and women stared at us, in a special kind of way, which made me feel inhibited. We were pretty dirty, but we were really not to blame. We couldn't speak a word of English, so we all went straight to the washrooms and back to the bus.

It was dark when we arrived at the camp. The manager, Mr. Greenhouse, was waiting for us. He didn't speak much Spanish, but he could say, "Welcome, boys. This is where you are going to live. And try to behave yourselves."

They took us to a wooden house with rows of bunks along the walls. I grabbed one of the bottom beds and Alberto took one, three bunks up, near the roof. The room was small, three by five meters, and there were sixteen of us there. It was very dirty and hot, and at night we couldn't sleep because of the mosquitoes and flies.

I must confess I was disappointed when I saw the place. I had expected rooms, not well furnished or anything like that, but more like a hotel . . . at least made of brick . . . a house with beds. And so many different natures should not be thrown together in one room. Such things shouldn't be done.

We began to clean up the place and got the other boys to help. We washed the room down with hoses and cut the grass around the house. We did our best and left the room a lot cleaner than we found it.

From the first day, sadness got hold of me. Before that, I had no time to think of my troubles, of what made me leave home. But now it came back to me again and again. I couldn't believe that Graciela, who had loved me so much, could have hurt me so cruelly. I felt bitter and scarred. I thought about my children and wrote a letter to my father. I told him they were paying us ninety cents an hour and that I worked eight to ten hours a day from Monday to Saturday. I also wrote a letter to Alberto's house.

From the first day, the priest was very nice. He came to the camp just to speak to us. "I'll be expecting you in church tomorrow. I am going to make a special Mass in your honor." Man! After hearing something like that, you feel more human. At least, that's how I took it. But on Sunday, some of the boys said, "I'm not going." Others were going to play cards instead.

I began to tell them a few truths. "Don't be such ingrates. The *padre* comes with all his heart and good will, to invite you to a special Mass and you leave him flat. Good people don't act like that. If you were invited to get drunk you would be off like a shot. Man, what is one hour of your life going to cost you? Even if what you are saying about the priests is true, that they are just like anyone else and sometimes even worse, it has nothing to do with it. Let's say you are not going to see the *padre*; you are going to pray to God."

Well, only one in the cabin stayed back, and he did it because he was an Evangelist. I told him, "Look, you are making a mistake. To me, all religions are alike, as long as you worship and respect the Lord, and have faith deep in your heart. I respect everybody's belief, although I am a Catholic."

Actually, by that time I had already read the Bible and was beginning to lose my faith in the saints and in Catholicism. In Mexicali, a *bracero* who was an Evangelist had given me a copy of the New Testament. Before he left for the United States, he had said, "Manuel, I know your religion forbids you to read this, but in case you might want to someday, I'm leaving my Bible with you."

I had always had an enormous curiosity about the Bible, but had been afraid to read it for fear of being excommunicated. When I was about fourteen, I read the Old Testament because of my passion for history. I don't know how I got hold of it, for my father would never permit it in the house. A friend of mine had told me it was all right to read the Old Testament, but that I shouldn't, under any circumstances, read the New Testament.

One afternoon in Mexicali, I had nothing to read, so I began to leaf through the Bible. The terms and parables were difficult for my intellect, but I tried to go to the roots, to translate it, right? And in the Bible, there are no half measures; something is either all good or all evil. It was really strong stuff.

As I read, I was overcome with fear, not because it was different from what I had been taught, but because I realized that reading the Scriptures and the Commandments and learning the laws myself, I would be like a graduate lawyer, like an advocate who knew the punishment for every offense. I wouldn't need to place my faith in lawyers and secretaries when I myself would be capable of speaking directly to the President! The go-betweens, the saints, were only idols of stone or plaster, made by the hand of man, so why should I pray to them? I realized that because of the saints, we had as many gods as the Aztecs; the only difference was that we modernized the images! For me, there was only one God, and God was Love.

Well, I began analyzing things, right? Jesus said, "Like this fig tree, by their fruits you shall know them." In the Mexican penitentiaries, out of one hundred prisoners, ninety-nine are Catholics! And if my friends who were thieves could light a candle to a little saint before going out to rob, if prostitutes kept a saint in their rooms, and burned sanctified candles and prayed for more clients, if there were such perversions within Catholicism, well, can that be the true religion?

And the priests! I was disillusioned about them, too, for they did not carry out God's law. I knew a priest who drank and played poker right in church. And by coincidence, priests always seemed to have a sister and a couple of nephews living in their house. After reading about the humble life of Jesus, I asked, "Does the Pope sleep on the floor? Does he live the life of the Nazarene, begging alms, going without food, suffering rain and cold, to go out and preach love for one's neighbors?"

No, the Pope lived in portentous opulence and was fantastically wealthy, because the churches all over the world sent him the money they collected. Why, just the money collected on one Sunday at the Basilica of Guadalupe here, would support me and my family all our lives! Then, in what kind of poverty does the Pope live? And where is his charity if there is so much misery in Rome itself?

In Mexicali, two missionaries had come from California to build a mission among the *braceros*. They invited those of us who were hungry to eat . . . it was not just the food they gave us . . . the thing I noticed was the love they had, the compassion and sincerity. Being from Tepito, I could tell when a person was lying or being a hypocrite. I swear that those men came with good hearts, and gave spontaneously, as though it didn't cost them any effort.

Then I began to think about the Evangelists, the Adventists, the Anglicans I knew. Well, I never had seen one of them stretched out drunk in the street, they never carried knives, or smoked, took drugs or cursed. Their homes had everything they needed; their children were well dressed and well fed, and they treated their wives the way human beings should be treated. They lived healthful, peaceful lives. But under Catholicism, people lived like, well, the way I did.

I didn't lose my faith . . . I remained a Catholic, because I didn't feel strong enough to obey the Commandments and to carry out the strict rules of the Evangelists. I would no longer be able to enjoy smoking, or gambling, or fornicating, and well, I was absolutely incapable of living up to the laws of God. *Carajo!* it seems that the nicest things in the world we owe to the Devil! I felt I was not born to be a martyr. I still had a way to go to tame my spirit.

Finally, Monday came. Very early in the morning we heard the trucks arriving, and then the call for breakfast. The food they gave us the first two days was better than what they gave us afterwards. In the morning it was bread, oatmeal, eggs and coffee with canned milk. For lunch, we took three sandwiches along with us, and beans. In the evening, when we got back, it was *tortillas*, liver and potatoes, Mexican style, and soup. It was good . . . at first.

After breakfast, on my way to the truck, I passed the kitchen and saw a great pile of dirty dishes. Tony, the dishwater, was mad, and was cursing. I said, "It's a lot of work, isn't it, *maestro?* I've worked as a dishwasher too, so I know. That sure is a mountain of plates you have there." Then I got into the truck with Alberto and went off to work.

On the way, a boy from Michoacán said, "Don't work too fast. Take your time. If you don't, they will get used to us doing a lot and the day we don't feel like working and slow down, they will fire us." When we got there, we grabbed cans and began to pick green tomatoes.

I started out real lively. Reach out, bend over, there I go, pum, pum, picking tomatoes. Everybody was moving along even. After a while, I stopped to rest, then I moved along sitting down, trying not to lag behind, because they watched you. The two men next to me, what dopes, those two! They looked like windmills, they were picking so fast!

Well, you have to get used to the fields. *Qué bárbaro!* Oh, it was hard, hard, hard. When the can was filled, we lifted it to our shoulders and, jumping the furrows, would go to empty it into the crates. *Madre Santísima!* How my back hurt! Well, anyway, at least I knew that in the evening we would rest.

That night, after supper, the head man in the kitchen called me. "Hey, boy, would you like to work in the restaurant? Do you know how to wash dishes?"

"Man, but of course. Everybody knows how to wash dishes." So they put me to work in the kitchen. My job was to serve the oatmeal and coffee and prepare the box lunches. The work I was paid nine hours for didn't take more than three. Imagine, just because I had said something to Tony that morning! Alberto said, "What luck! Who knows what saint you pray to. Me, I'm going to beat my brains out in the field. Why don't you see if you can get me in with you?"

Later, I managed to work on other jobs between meals. A Filipino came around every once in a while and offered us a dollar an hour to work in his fields. We were not supposed to do this, but we hadn't come there to spend the time sleeping. We grabbed extra jobs whenever we could.

When we got our first check, Alberto said, "Let's go to the dance hall."

"Nothing doing," I said, "I won't go, brother. It's going to be a matter of spending money. Then it'll be 'Let's have a beer.' And the next thing you know we'll be without a cent. No, I won't go." To make a long story short, we went—in Tony's car. Tony was a Mexican but born in the United States—a *"pocho,"* not really Mexican and not really American. The girls at the dancehall were also Mexican-Americans. They wore elegant dresses and we thought they wouldn't want to dance with us.

But Tony introduced me to Inez, a friend of his girl friend, and I danced with her all evening. She was pretty and spoke Spanish. It seemed strange that she spoke to me right away and let me dance with her. Before the evening was over she said, "Why don't you come to my house tomorrow to talk? I'd love to hear about Mexico. Come at seven."

Well, that night I dreamed of little pink elephants. I really felt happy again. The next morning I worked with lots of will and served the whole camp. In the afternoon, the Filipino came and took me to pick pomegranates. I worked for five hours and made $6.25. Then in the evening, I went to see Inez.

I was a little embarrassed about going into her house. She lived alone with her two kids, who were sleeping in one of the bedrooms. She had been married, but I didn't know what had happened to her husband. Well, I went in and we talked and had coffee. Later, she turned on some music and we began to dance. She kept looking at me and we kissed. And then, well, that night we made love, right off the bat. I said to myself, "Now, that's more like it." I had got myself a girl friend.

The following evening I was sound asleep in my bunk, when I heard a knocking on the window. It was Inez. She had come to camp looking for me. "I felt like having you sing me a song," she said. So I got into her car, and off we went. I had learned to drive on Tony's car, and it sure felt good to drive her around all night, singing and kissing.

She caused a lot more commotion one day by driving me right into the middle of the camp, just when everyone was coming out of the dining room. The men watched her leave and then the comments started. "How do you like that? Look at that guy! He finally caught himself one with shoes." All of them kept kidding me.

Inez was pretty, all right, but I didn't fall in love with her. After what happened with Graciela, I didn't want love mixed into my life ever again. To me love meant suffering. Love was what killed me, it left me scarred. When I felt myself going for a girl, I immediately remembered all the errors and wounds of my affair with Graciela. But I didn't regret it because that was the only true love I ever had, the only real passion I have felt. Graciela helped me live and feel great emotion at an early age, and I am grateful to her for life! But how much it cost me!

In the United States, I noticed that marriage was different. I liked the independence and the blind faith the husband and wife had for each other. I think it exists because it is based on a strong moral principle. The more sweetly they treat each other, the better they behave. There, they don't like lies. When they say "No" they mean "No." Even if you kneel and beg, it is still "No."

In Mexico, it is not that way. Right off the bat, I can say that fidelity of the husband for the wife does not exist here. It is exactly nil. Out of one hundred friends of mine, one hundred are unfaithful to their wives. They are always on the hunt for new emotions, they are just not satisfied with one woman, you know what I mean? The wives are more faithful . . . I would say that out of a hundred about twenty-five are absolutely faithful. The rest, whew! they run the gamut.

Several of the men in the camp began to get sick because of the bad food. They complained to Greenhouse and he said that anyone who didn't like it could pick up his things and consider his contract terminated. Immediately they got scared and kept quiet. Then two hundred *braceros* in a nearby town got food poisoning, and everybody began to protest again. Greenhouse decided to send people away, one by one.

There weren't many men around, so they sent me out to pick. It was the third tomato picking by then, and we didn't earn much any more because it was piecework. I didn't like the work and it didn't pay. My *compadre* Alberto was in the hospital for an emergency gall-bladder operation. I wanted to be with him when they operated, no matter what. I thought, "They might kill him and I wouldn't even know about it."

I felt a throbbing in my side, and it really hurt a little, so I pretended to be sick in the appendix. I went to the manager and he took me to the hospital. I wanted to be there two days, just until Alberto's operation would be over. They put an ice pack on my stomach and when I said I felt better, they telephoned the manager to come and take me back to camp.

But I wanted to get back to the hospital, so I began to act sick again. "*Ay, ay,* my appendix." They took me off to the hospital and this time I was put to bed, next to a North American. I figured they would put on another ice pack and send me home the next day. I lay in bed very calmly, trying to talk to the North American through my English book. He was very nice and even invited me to visit him when we both got out. He was the first and only North American to do that and I wish I could have gone.

Then I saw them come in with a rolling table. They made me get on it and rolled me down the hall, with me whistling and the nurses saying, "How brave! How brave!" They spoke English and I had no idea what they were trying to explain or where they were taking me. Well, they stuck me in the operating room. "Move onto the table." I figured they were probably going to take an x-ray. It was not going to be just an ice pack this time.

The doctor came in, wearing a mask, then the anesthetist and two nurses. But me, I wasn't nervous. I thought they were going to give me an examination. They tied down my hands. It wasn't until then that I began to get excited. I said to myself, "Well, well, what's going on? What are they going to do to me?" They tied my feet and covered my eyes with pieces of cotton. I began to holler, "No, no, I don't want to be operated. Nothing hurts me any more. No!"

But nobody there understood Spanish and I couldn't speak English. They put a mask on my face and began to pour on the ether. I kept shouting, "Please, please. Nothing is wrong with me. I don't want to be operated, please." I felt as though I was smothering. "I'm dying . . . my heart, my heart . . ." Then I thought, "They are going to kill me for sure." My heart was jumping, palpitating.

I don't think there is a worse horror than to have to keep still when you can't breathe. I desperately tried to free myself and couldn't. Ever since they did that to me I have been afraid of being buried, of being held down, unable to move. Now I know that Hell means the grave, and I am so afraid of burial and the Infinite that I feel like crying when I think it's going to be like that.

I was sure they were trying to kill me there in the hospital. But why? "For money?" I thought. "But what is money to these people? With such a luxurious hospital, what is a thousand dollars to them?" Then I said to myself, "You see? Why did you put yourself in their hands? Why did you trust them? Why did you come here?" I tried not to breathe, so I wouldn't be put to sleep.

I heard a humming, and I felt I was falling, falling, at a terrific rate. I saw a light, like a headlight being driven away fast, at supersonic speed. Then, in the middle of that well, of that abyss into which I was falling, I saw my wife standing . . . my dead wife, looking me full in the face with an expression of anger in her eyes. I called, "Paula, wait for me. Wait, old girl." She turned away and walked down the abyss. I wanted to fall but I was floating in the air, with my hands and feet out. My daughter Mariquita appeared . . . she was saying, "*Papá.*"

"Have you died, too, daughter?" I asked. In the middle of all this, I heard the anesthetist say, "Now, doctor?" I said, "Not yet! I'm still not asleep. Don't put the knife in yet. Please!" Then I didn't know anything any more.

Little by little I started coming to. I tried to get up and heard Alberto say, "Be quiet, *compadre*. You will hurt yourself."

"Is that you, Alberto? Is it you? Listen, don't let them operate on you. Run, *compadre!* Leave me here and go, because they'll screw you up." Something was burning me and I tried to pull down my pants. It was my bandage, and then I knew they had operated on me. The nurse gave me an injection and I fell asleep.

The next day I kept saying, "I want my *compadre*. Take me to Alberto." He had been operated on and was saying the same thing in his room. "I want my *compadre*, Manuel," I found out the number of his ward and got out of bed. Supporting myself against the wall, little by little, I went toward his room.

He was in bad shape. They had his stomach open and a tube coming out so it would drain. I saw the hole and said, "Why are they leaving it open? Something is liable to get in and you'll die." *Madre Santísima!*

I really thought he'd die on me. What would I tell his aunt . . . his children? But Alberto wasn't worried.

"Go back now. Nothing is going to happen to me." Just then, the nurses came with a cart and bawled me out for getting out of bed.

Actually, everyone was very nice to us. The nurses taught me more English words and corrected my pronunciation. I was jumping around, getting in and out of bed, as if nothing had happened. But when the doctor came and took off the bandage to remove the stitches, I took one look at the gash they had made and didn't feel like moving any more. I couldn't even walk after that.

I spent seventeen days in that hospital. The insurance company took care of everything . . . a very pretty room, luxurious beds with radios in the headboard . . . telephone in the room . . . everything that was out of our reach in Mexico. It didn't cost us a single penny.

I really felt like somebody in California! Everybody treated me well, both in the hospital and on the job. I like the life there, even though I found its form too abstract, too mechanical, in the sense that the people were like precision machines. They have a day, an hour, a fixed schedule set up for everything. It must be a good method because they have lots of comforts. But the government charges them a tax for food, for shoes, for absolutely everything. If our government tried that tax business here, I believe it might even cause a revolution. A person doesn't like to have what's his taken from him.

The *braceros* I knew, all agreed on one thing, that the United States was "*a toda madre.*" That means it's the best. Every once in a while someone complained . . . like Alberto said the Texans were lousy sons-of-bitches because they treated Mexicans like dogs. And we looked badly upon the discrimination against the Negroes. We had always thought of American justice as being very strict and fair . . . we didn't think that money or influence counted there like it did here. But when they put a Negro on the electric chair for rape, and let whites go for the same thing, well, we began to realize that American justice was elastic too.

But we all noticed that even the workers who were not so well off, had their car and refrigerator. When it came to equality and standard of living, well, they'd lynch me for saying this, but I believe that the United States is practically communistic . . . within capitalism, that is. At least it was in California, because I even heard a worker shout at his boss, and the boss just shut up. The workers there are protected in lots of ways. Here in Mexico, the bosses are tyrants.

Thinking of Mexico's system of life, I am very disappointed. It is just that when I was living in the United States, I could see that people were glad when a friend got ahead, you know what I mean? "Congratulations, man, it's great that things are going good with you." Everybody would congratulate him if he bought a new car or a house or something. But in Mexico, when a friend of mine, with a lot of sacrifice and hard work and skimping on food, finally managed to buy a new delivery truck, what happened? He parked it in front of his house and when he came out all the paint was scratched off. If that isn't pure envy, what is it?

Instead of trying to raise a person's morale, our motto here is, "If I am a worm, I'm going to make the next fellow feel like a louse." Yes, here you always have to feel you are above. I have felt this way myself, that's why I say it. I guess I'm a Mexican, all right. Even if you live on the bottom level, you have to feel higher up. I've seen it among the trash pickers; there's rank even among thieves. They start arguing, "You so-and-so, all you steal is old shoes. But me, when I rob, I rob good stuff." So the other one says, "You! Turpentine is all you drink. At least, I knock off my 96-proof pure alcohol, which is more than you ever do." That's the way things are here.

It is not that we hate anyone who has had better fortune. I don't feel hatred against a rich man any longer than it takes for three drags on a cigarette. It would be bad for me to get too wrapped up in thinking about that, because then I would feel less than what I am. And I would at least like to be what I am. That's why I don't want to analyze things too carefully. Maybe it's a case of running away or of not looking at the reality of my condition. Anyway, when one of my class hates another person, it is almost always for reasons of sentiment. I can't ever remember it being for economic reasons. Whenever you hate the world, it is practically always because of something a woman has done to you, or because a friend has betrayed you. The women are the ones who go most against the rich, possibly because women feel privations more than men, don't you think?

The thing is, there is no equality here. Everything is disproportionate. The rich are very rich, and the poor are infamously poor. There are women with babies in their arms and a few more hanging on their skirts, going from door to door to beg for food. There are plenty like my uncle Ignacio, who give their women three *pesos* a day for expenses, and others who don't know where the next meal is coming from, with nobody to give a thought to them. If the rich people knew how the poor managed to exist, it would seem like a miracle to them.

Look, when a rich man throws an orgy, one of those *fiestas* or receptions those millionaires in Lomas make, in one night they spend enough to support a whole orphan asylum for a month. If they would come down off their pedestals to share the lives of their countrymen and see their misery, I believe that out of their own pockets they would install electricity, sewage, and do something to help. If I were rich, I would ease the pain of the poor, at least some of those closest to me, and let them have a few necessities. But who knows? Maybe if I were a rich guy sailing in my boat or traveling in airplanes, I wouldn't remember any more, eh? The poor stick to the poor . . . they know their place . . . and the rich, well, they go to the Hilton. The day I dare go to the Hilton Hotel, I'll know there has been another revolution!

I don't know about political things . . . the first time I voted was in the last election . . . but I don't think there is much hope there. We can't have any kind of social welfare for the working people, because it would be used only to make the leaders rich. The men in the government always end up rich and the poor are just as badly off. I have never belonged to a union, but my friends who do say they can be fired at any time without indemnification, because the union leaders and the bosses make agreements among themselves. Yes, we have a long way to go down here. I tell you, progress is a difficult thing.

Alberto was discharged from the hospital first. As soon as he got back to camp, Greenhouse took him to the bus station, to send him home. Alberto managed to give him the slip and went to live with his woman, Shirley. When I got out, I had a little trouble getting away from the camp manager, but I hid in a ditch until I got a lift to Shirley's house.

Greenhouse reported us to Immigration and we had to lay low for a couple of days. Shirley fixed a bed for me on the floor and Alberto slept with her. Later, we worked in a grape camp, and twenty days after my operation, I took a job as a swamper, loading heavy crates. The work was hard and I got sick. I wrote to my father to send me some money so I could go home. But he answered that as my money had arrived, he kept investing it in materials to build a house in the El Dorado Colony. He didn't have a single *centavo* to send me.

So I had to keep on working to save money to go back. I picked cotton, but I saw it was a job in which I wasn't going to get very far. Besides, my hands swelled up from the cotton and got real nasty looking. Finally, I said to Alberto, "Look we have stuck together up to now, but I can see you are in love with that woman, so if you want to stay, just tell me. I'm leaving."

So he tells me, "No, *compadre*, I can't leave now because my clothes are at the cleaners."

The next day I took a bus to Mexicali. I had been away nine months and was really anxious to see my children, my father and my friends. In Mexicali, I couldn't get a train or a bus out of the city. It was so crowded, there wasn't even a hotel room anywhere. It was dangerous for me to walk the streets with about two thousand *pesos* in my pocket, carrying my carton of clothes. The bodies of returning *braceros* who had been murdered and robbed, were often found on the streets of Mexicali. This time, I was afraid all right.

I decided to take an airplane to Guadalajara. It was very expensive, right? It cost over five hundred *pesos*, but it took only nine hours, instead of fifty-two hours by bus and I saved a lot of time. All I wanted was to get back. In Guadalajara, I took a first-class bus to Mexico City.

I arrived at about six in the morning, on the twentieth of November, the anniversary of the Mexican Revolution. I remember because there was a parade that day. When I got to the Casa Grande the gates had just been opened and a few women were going for milk. The janitor, *Don* Nicho, was sweeping near the west gate where I entered.

"How goes it, Manuelito," he asked. "Where have you been, you tramp?"

"Well, I went as a *bracero*, Señor Nicho."

"Ah! Crazy one, so the fever hit you too?"

"Well yes, I went to see what it was like."

I was glad to be back, right? I walked through the courtyard and stood in front of our door, my heart jumping inside me. I didn't have a key . . . my father was the only one who ever had the key to the door . . . so I whistled my usual whistle. Sounds of feet came from inside the house and voices saying, "My *papá*, my *papá*."

My father opened the door . . . he was in his underwear. I could see an expression of joy on his face, but as soon as he saw me he tried to hide it, swallowing his emotion and becoming serious.

"So you finally came back."

"Yes, I'm back, *papá*."

I think he wanted to embrace me, I also had a great desire to give him a hug, but since he restrained himself, I did too . . . there was the same old barrier between us, no?

I wept to see my children again. They were dancing around, grabbing me by the waist and hanging from my legs, laughing and shouting, "What did you bring me? What did you bring?"

I felt bad to have to tell them that the toys I had bought for them, and a watch for Delila, were still in the Customs House in Mexicali. I had forgotten to remove the price tags and the wrappings from the gifts, so those characters at Customs wanted to charge me a luxury tax that was more than the articles had cost. When I wouldn't pay up, one of the guys offered to buy the things for practically nothing. I got so sore I kicked my presents to pieces, right in front of the officials. I wasn't going to let those bastards have my stuff! I explained what had happened and gave each of my kids a *peso* to spend.

Before going off to work, my father said, "Son, do you have any money around?" I took out my wallet, meaning to give him half of what I had, but he kept saying, "Come on, come on," and one bill after another came out. I gave him all but two hundred *pesos*.

It was after he left that I noticed a little bundle moving on my father's bed. My mother-in-law, who had been sleeping on the floor, got up and came over to me.

"That's your sister," she said.

"What do you mean, my sister?" I felt as though I had been hit over the head and was dizzy from the blow. I stood there like a jerk and said, "*Ay, chirrión,* don't tell me my *papá* has been out fooling around." I was so mixed up I couldn't make a quick deduction.

Delila took me out of my confusion by saying, "This is the reason why your brother and sisters are angry with me."

Then I understood. Boy! So my *papá* had conquered her! Imagine, the chief had made Delila! My admiration for him grew. I wondered how he did it, because he was old enough to be her father. I don't believe she loved him then. Now, yes, because she sees that he gives her everything she needs. He is a man easy to love because of his straight behavior. At that time, she must have thought, "Well, my sister left me in charge of her children . . . after all, they are my nephews, and if I have to be with them, I might as well sacrifice myself all the way. Rather than take care of them for nothing, I'll marry Manuel's *papá*. That way I'll kill two birds with one stone."

Underneath, I was a little angry, but I controlled myself and said, "That's great! You did very well, sister-in-law. And don't pay attention to my brother and sisters. Send the crazy bastards to the devil . . . it's no business of theirs. You did right, both of you."

In the afternoon, I went out to look for my friends. I felt good walking through the streets of my *colonia* again. I had lived here all my life and it was my whole world. Every street had a meaning for me: the Street of the Plumbers, where I was born and where I had still enjoyed my mother's caresses; the Street of the Bakers, where the Three Kings had brought me my first toys and made my childhood golden; Tenochtitlán Street always reminded me of the song, "Lost Love," which a neighbor happened to be singing while my mother was carried out in her coffin; the streets where each of my relatives, friends and *novias* lived. These streets were my school of suffering, where I learned what was dangerous and what was safe, when to be sincere and when to dissimulate.

Outside my *colonia*, I felt I was no longer in Mexico. I felt like a fish out of water, especially if I went to the rich sections, like Lomas or Polanco, where people looked at me with suspicion. I wouldn't even dare walk there at night because they'd think I was a thief, the way I dressed. People with money can't stand seeing anyone hard up; right away they think he's out to steal. And where there is money, there is right, so the only thing to do is to stay away from those places.

Yes, I was happy to be back, but after having been to the United States, everything looked very poor and dirty to me. I realized what poverty we lived in, and when I saw the market, with oranges and tomatoes piled on newspapers on the ground, I felt so sad, I wanted to go right back to the U.S.A. The truth of the matter is, and this is not *malinchismo* or giving preference to the foreigner, I would have liked to have been born in the United States or in some European country, like England . . . not Italy, with its romanticism and scenery and all that . . . but in a nation with a more advanced culture.

I had returned with a thousand illusions, because in the United States I had learned to enjoy working. I wanted to fix up the house, to see that my children ate well, eggs every day and milk . . . I had the reputation of being a hard worker, and I had come back with the intention of keeping it up. But from the first night I felt disillusioned because my father let me sleep on a burlap bag on the kitchen floor, the way I had always done. I had expected different treatment, right?

Because, like I said, I came back different. I thought he'd say, "No, son, don't sleep on the floor. Sleep on the bed, with your children." But no! When I lay down on the floor, he didn't say a word!

For a while I spent time with my family. Consuelo and Roberto had both left home because of Delila. No one knew where Roberto had disappeared to, but Consuelo was living with my aunt Guadalupe. Whenever I saw my sister, she cursed Delila and made her out to be one point lower than a cockroach, so she could step on her. She had hated Delila from the start because Delila had taken away her position in the house. And although Delila had offered her the olive branch of peace, my sister threw it back in her face as though it had thorns a meter long.

The truth is, my sister was selfish. She was always looking out for herself. Ever since she got that bug about completing her studies, she felt set apart, as though she had nothing in common with us any more. Just because she had acquired a little learning, she became rebellious at home and no longer bowed down to paternal law. She claimed my father had no right to throw her out of the house because he was legally responsible for her. She was demanding a kind of legal justice from her own father, as though she were dealing with the government! But how could she do that? He was our father and had power over us!

Consuelo used her troubles with Delila and my father as an excuse to run off to Monterrey with some chap. It seems that ever since excuses were invented, there have been no wrongdoers. The thing is, my sister lacked moral courage. Why, I knew a woman who was kicked out of her house by her father when she was only fourteen and she didn't use that as an excuse to run off with the first guy she met. She went to work and is a virgin to this day.

Consuelo had always said she loved my children, but she never bothered to wash a piece of clothing for them, or to prepare their food. It's one thing to say you love them, and another to prove it, like Delila. It's true that after my wife died, Consuelo had good intentions and felt brave and humble enough to take care of them, but she couldn't stick it out for more than two weeks. If she was such a good aunt why didn't she give my father money for my children? She bought them candy and presents, but if she gave them clothing or things like that she'd come and ask me to pay her back. What I mean is, Delila didn't have money or education but every day she worked for my children and that impressed me more.

I felt sorry for my sister Marta because the fact is she was really of no account, for she was even poorer than the rest of us. She had left Crispín again and had come home with her three little daughters. She wasn't the person to open her heart to anyone and she seemed happy enough because she still had her father, but deep down I knew she was suffering. She thought the world had ended for her. She must have felt condemned to live alone the rest of her life, because no man would accept her with three children.

The truth was that the lives of my brother and sisters, and especially of my father, have always been a mystery to me. I never understood how my father managed, and frankly I don't want to. He had always provided us with enough food . . . he took care of so many people on so little money. I cross myself when I think about it, not that I believe my father did anything wrong . . . he has absolutely no use for a crook . . . but since he bought all the food for the restaurant, he probably charged them a little more and kept fifty *centavos* or a *peso* on every purchase. It's also possible that dealing in the market for so many years, they gave him fruit, coffee, meat and things because he was a good customer. Otherwise how could he manage with a wage of only eleven *pesos* a day?

If my father kept back a *peso* or two when buying supplies, I don't hold it against him. On the contrary, I feel I'm the guilty one, and my brother and sisters, because he did it for our sake. Every day that passed, my father grew more in my esteem, not because he helped me with my children, but because you really have to be quite a man to keep things together like he had.

Meanwhile, I got a job again at the glass place. One Monday I came in late and my boss decided to punish me by docking me for a week. "O.K.," I said, "big deal," and I got up and left. To kill time, I went to the Tepito Market, which is also known as the Thieves' Market.

I met Joaquín, the friend who had lived in our cardboard house in Mexicali. He was a peddler now, a dealer in second-hand goods, and he was carrying a pair of gabardine pants on his shoulder. He told me that I was an idiot to work on a job when I could be making more money selling stuff in the market. I thought it was risky, today you make something, tomorrow nothing, and maybe I wouldn't be good at it.

Actually, ever since my mother had taken me to the market, I liked the atmosphere there. It was picturesque, very colorful, like the rural markets where buyers and sellers know each other, tell jokes, dicker and bargain. There is nothing impersonal here, like in Sears, Roebuck and the Palacio de Hierro, where the clerks don't dare chat with the customers. There, they only tell you the price and do things mechanically, and the joker is that the prices are fixed, right? The customers don't have a chance to defend themselves; they can't even make an offer like we do in the markets, if the price doesn't suit us.

The market place has always been generous, very bountiful, to the peddlers. In the old days, famous peddlers like "the Bear," "*el Contola*," "*la Gringa*," and "the Evil One," made as much as five hundred to two thousand *pesos* a day. Now they own nice houses and even cars. I had some idea of what it was like to work in the market, because I used to watch my mother and my uncles and other peddlers hawk their wares. I knew the old-style method of buying and selling.

So when Joaquín told me to try to sell the trousers for at least fifteen *pesos*, while he was buying up more stuff, I agreed. I noticed a boy on the other side of the street, staring at the pants. I thought, "So you like the trousers, eh?" and crossed the street.

"Go on, pal," I said, "I'll give it to you cheap." I wasn't embarrassed at all. I took to selling right away. It was easy.

"Well, yes, but I have no money. I'm selling too." He takes out a watch, a luxury-type Haste, very nice. He wanted 125 *pesos* for it.

"How many jewels?"

"Fifteen, I think," he says.

I opened the watch and it was twenty-one jewels. "No," I say to him. "It's fifteen jewels, pal, and you're asking too much for it."

Meanwhile, Joaquín came over with three other "coyotes"—dealers —and surrounded us while I was bargaining. They just watched, no one butts in while someone is bargaining.

"Look," I say to the boy, "let's make a deal. You like the pants, it's exactly your size, it fits you perfectly." I held it up to his waist. "I want fifty *pesos* for the pants. I'll give it to you, plus twenty-five *pesos*, for your watch. How about it?"

"No, nothing doing, there's nothing in it for me. I want more for the watch."

"*Ay*, brother, I don't work here . . . I only want the watch for myself." I say, "Let's see if any of these bastards here offer you more."

Anyway, to make a long story short, I gave him forty *pesos* and the

pants, so the watch came to fifty-five *pesos*. I offered Joaquín his fifteen
pesos for the pants.

"No," he says, "don't be a crook, pal! Only fifteen *pesos* and you took
in a great sale." Then he laughed, and said, "O.K. Say no more. It's
your debut here in the market. Beginner's luck."

Well, one of the "coyotes" wanted to buy the watch. I thought I'd
ask seventy-five *pesos* for it and make a fast twenty *pesos* profit. But
before I opened my mouth, Joaquín says, "Two hundred."

"No," says the "coyote." "Son-of-a-bitch! Don't push your luck. The
stinking watch just cost you fifty-five . . . I'll give you a "century" and
you'll make forty-five on it, no?"

I was ready to sell, but my partner, Joaquín, said, "What? Moron!
Hold your horses." So I wait with my little watch, see? and we walk
away.

He comes along behind us and says, "So as not to be frigging around,
I'll give you a hundred twenty-five, yes or no?" I held out for 175.
"Don't be a bastard. God's truth, I want it for myself, I don't wanna
make a deal with it. Don't be like that, you son-of-a-bitch."

Well, he gave me 170 for the watch. I made 115 *pesos* on it. There
in a minute, in a few seconds, I made more than I made in a week of
hard work at the shop. "What am I working like an idiot over there
for?" I said to myself. Then and there I decided to quit my job and
dedicate myself to trade in the market.

I liked selling . . . I liked the freedom. I had time for myself and no
one bossed me around. Up to that time I had been blind, and couldn't
see further than my nose. Like other laborers, I knew only one thing,
working on a job! Even when it doesn't pay off, a worker doesn't try
another road or look for other horizons, but goes on doing the same
thing. My father was like that, until he began raising animals . . . that's
when he started getting ahead. I'm going to see to it that my sons
aren't workers. If they can't be professionals, I'll put them into some
business. That's the only way they can earn money without being
dependent on others.

For a couple of years now I've been working at the Tepito and
Baratillo markets. I deal in second-hand stuff, clothes, shoes, gold, silver,
watches, furniture, anything that comes along. In a way you take a
chance in this kind of work, but it's never been really bad for me. On
the worst day I make at least twelve *pesos*, enough for food.

The only time I lost in the market was when I bought a thing called a mimeograph. I didn't even know what the gadget was for, but, well, I was real impressed with the word, see? "Mimeograph," I thought; "with a name like that it must be worth something."

The character who was selling it spotted me for a moron. He made a fool out of me, one of the many times it happened. He says to me, "See this little machine? I want only two hundred *pesos* for it."

"Holy shit!" says I, "so it's really worth something! But that's a lot of money. I'll give you fifty." We argued the pros and cons and I started to back out. I was getting a presentiment. "Maybe this damn thing doesn't even work and I'm talking my head off. The truth is I don't even know what that pile of crap is good for."

"O.K.," the guy says, "over here with the fifty."

There go my fifty *pesos*. The first customer offered thirty, the next was willing to give me twenty-five. And that's how it went until after fifteen days of lugging around my famous mimeograph, they were offering me ten. I finally abandoned it in the market administration office. But usually I make good money in the market . . . more than I had on any job.

I figure this way: if I start working right now on a job, where I make the legal minimum wage of twelve *pesos* a day, I could never raise my living standard. Out of the twelve, I'd have to give at least six to my children, and a man can't live on six. I couldn't pay rent, eat three meals outside the house, buy shoes or clothes or anything on six *pesos*. Suppose one of my kids gets sick and I need to buy medicine for one hundred *pesos* . . . any good medicine costs at least that . . . I'd have to borrow the money and pay it back at fifty *centavos* a day. At that rate it would take over six months to pay for the medicine and most likely in that time someone else would get sick. It's just a vicious circle and there is no way for a working man to get ahead.

In my business, all I need is capital. With five hundred or a thousand *pesos*, I'd make out all right, the least I would earn would be a hundred *pesos* a day. There are lots of low, crude characters mixed up in it, but they have money in their pockets.

The fact is, I have a horror of being poor. I get depressed when I haven't got five *centavos* in my pocket. Whew! Do my nerves get on edge! That's when I feel poor, really poor. When I see someone who looks hungry, I am absolutely horrified. It makes me want to cry because I remember the days when I was that way, when I cried tears of blood because I didn't have money to feed my wife and kids, or to pay for a doctor. I really cannot stand that life any more. I am not back at peace until I start hustling to get some money in my pocket again. That's why I let my father take care of my children for me, so that I won't have the responsibility.

The way I figure, if I'm going to die anyway, I ought to treat myself well while I am alive, right? How do I know what will happen to me in the next world? If I have ten *pesos* in my pocket, and feel like having a sweet, I'll buy it, even if my other expenses are not taken care of. So that I won't be left with just my desires, eh? I hate to deny myself little things.

I have often asked myself, what is worth more at the end of one's life, the things one has accumulated or the satisfactions one has experienced? I believe that human experience is worth more, no? And although I have worked all my life, now, when I want to go somewhere, I go in a taxi. I never travel in a bus.

If I go into a restaurant, I don't order beans. I order a fried steak or a couple of eggs. If I want to sit down, I sit; if I don't feel like getting up in the morning, I sleep. Yes, the best heritage I can leave my children is to teach them how to live. I don't want them to be fools ... I swear by my mother, I won't let them become ordinary workers.

But it wasn't all easy going at the market. The market administration sometimes asks traders for their credentials, to force us to join a union, see? The market superintendent is in cahoots with all of them. Imagine, to sell second-hand clothing in the Thieves' Market they ask you for a Social Welfare card, a Department of Health card, a union card, your police record! I have no cards and I've had a lot of arguments about it. I resent it, it makes me rebellious, you know what I mean? There I have my merchandise spread out on the floor and the guards come and want to take it away, so I argue with them, see?

Like once, I had just finished fighting for a spot one Saturday, because every morning when the doors are opened, we have to run to get a good spot. There are no permanent places for the peddlers, the one who gets there first, gets the spot. It's like those cowboy pictures, when they open the market doors, we all race in like horses. I had just had a violent argument over my spot when the guard comes over and squats down to take the cloth with my merchandise on it.

"You can pick up this at the office," he says. "You don't belong to any organization and you don't have any card."

"Look, you, leave my stuff alone or I'll knock the shit out of you,"

I say. "The market wasn't built for you sons-of-bitches or for the organizations."

"Go talk it over with the superintendent," he tells me.

"No," I say, "he's just here to collect money for the government. The Constitution says that nobody can prevent another person from working honestly. Why should he count for more than the Constitution? You touch my things and I swear I'll kick the stuffings out of you."

We use strong language here at the market. That's the way they understand each other, you know what I mean? The one who hollers the loudest is the one who is feared the most.

Once I had to do something that disgusted me. I had to kick a guy. In the market, we are all *braveros*, tough guys, and whenever I was making a deal this *bravero*, "Whitey," would come over and stick his nose in and would get the merchandise away from me. He tried to lord it over me and when I asked him not to butt in, he answered with dirty language. I tried to avoid a fight and held back, I always kept holding back. Finally, one day I was closing a deal and had the goods in my hands, when this guy "Whitey" took out the money and paid. He said, "Let's have the goods."

"What do you mean? I'm the one making this deal. Who the hell told you to pay for it? Give it to you? I'll give you shit!"

"Give it to me or I'll take it!" says he.

"I'd just like to see you." And then, wham! I let him have one right between the eyes. He dropped. He got up and I caught him against the wall and kept hitting him. I knocked off his eyebrow with one punch. He tried to kick me and that made me blind mad. When he was on the ground, I kicked him and his ribs made a funny sound.

"Poor guy," I said to myself, but there was the whole bunch from the market around us and I had to finish him off. Otherwise they'd think I was a jackass and they'd keep starting up with me. Even though it was repulsive to me, I kept kicking him, not trying to kill him, of course, but catching him in the side or on the rear end. I didn't even aim at his face, it was already covered with blood. Finally, he said, "Enough, enough." I didn't give him his money back and he never tried anything with me again.

Since I've been working at Tepito, some people have a poor opinion of me. They think that everything in the market is stolen goods. But that's a lie, yes, a lie. The truth is that only about 50 percent of the stuff sold is crooked. But it's only little stuff . . . the handful of tools, the dust mask or rubber boots that the workers rob from the factories, or a bicycle someone stole on the fly. If it's a radio, it's the kind that's practically falling apart. Like everywhere else in the world, the real good "hot" merchandise, the fine radios and machinery, is bought up by the big capitalists. Nobody around Tepito has the money to buy good stuff.

When I know something is stolen, I usually don't buy it. In my type of work you have to be somewhat of a psychologist, to know whom you're buying from. I can always spot a crook, a cop, a dope addict, a prostitute or an innocent.

The majority of my friends in the market are reformed crooks. They practically have a language of their own, called "*caló*," which I understand very well. When a thief wants to sell you something, he says, "Hey, *ñero*, you wanna buy the swag? Hey, ya c'n have the junk cheap, ya c'n have the crap almost f'r nuddin'."

"How much do you want for these things?"

"Ain't got no time, wanna make a fast deal, slip me a "*sura*.""

A "*sura*" means twenty-five *pesos;* a "*niche*" means fifty; a "*cabeza*" is a hundred, and a "*grande*" is a thousand. Some of the expressions are now used by upper-class boys. It's become sort of a fashion.

Ten years ago there was more "hot" merchandise in the markets because the police were not so active. Now they consider the place a gold mine and are on permanent duty. Even on their day off they come to the market to see whom they can screw. It's a business with them. They know that just by putting one of my buddies in the patrol car, they can make themselves twenty, thirty, or fifty *pesos*. We all feel obligated to give the police money whenever they ask for it.

In my opinion, the Mexican police system is the best system of organized gangsters in the world. It is a disaster, a filthy thing. I might as well come right out with it, the justice here in Mexico turns my stomach. Why? Because justice is for the one who has the money. When a rich man gets killed, the police don't let grass grow under their feet, because there is money around. But how many poor guys are found drowned in the canal, stabbed in the back, or lying in the gutter in a dark street, and the police never, but never, solve the crime. And there are people who do two or three years in jail, because they have no one to stand up for them, or because they don't have fifty *pesos* for a payoff.

Most of the police start out wanting to straighten out the world. They start out wanting to be upright and not accept a single *centavo*. But once they are given the pistol and the shield and have the power and they see that wherever they turn they are offered money . . . well, it's a kind of epidemic that hits them. One of the generals of the Revolution once said that the official did not exist who could stand up under a fifty-thousand-*peso* broadside. And that's about the size of it. They take a bribe once, then twice, and after that it becomes a habit, a racket.

Suppose you are robbed of thirty thousand *pesos* and you go to the Police Department. They register the complaint, but before you leave, someone gets a good-sized tip out of you to "hasten" the investigation. When you pay them off they get active.

They start by questioning their "goats," their stool pigeons, about which buyer might have the stolen money or goods. The buyers don't operate in the markets; they live here today, there tomorrow. The police go to the house of the likely buyer and try to force it out of him. If he doesn't give it up willingly, he is taken to the station for a "heating." Sooner or later the police get the money or the goods, but when you come back to ask about it, they don't give it to you. They get more money out of you for the "investigation." You go back and forth to the Police Department, but your stolen goods don't appear.

The police agents have their own buyers of stolen goods, who they sell your stuff to after they find it. Some policemen come personally to the market to sell "hot" articles. I have bought things from them, because it is safe, since they represent Justice, no?

Two or three times I bought "hot" things from crooks. It was risky, but if things were bad with me financially I'd think over the possibilities of getting into a jam and take a chance. But most of the stuff I bought was not worth much.

I wasn't lucky all the time, even when I was acting within the law. One time I bought a radio chassis; it worked but it had no case. I bought it from a fellow peddler for fifty-five *pesos* and since we don't cheat each other, I didn't even test it. I left the market and this pal grabs me, this cop, whom we call "the Bird." He's a guy who isn't good enough even to be a cop. He is very fat and always has one cuff of his pants higher than the other. His coat is so greasy you could scrape it with a knife. He isn't wearing a disguise either, he is just a character, a dirty *rastrero*. He grew up in the market but since he became a cop he gives himself all kinds of airs.

"Let's see the bill of sale," he says.

"Look," I say, "it has no bill of sale because it's just a chassis."

"Get in, you bastard," he says. He had three crooks in his patrol car already.

I tried to talk my way out of it but he took it badly. "So you're giving me lip in the bargain," he says.

"No, but you want to bleed me and I'm not even out of line."

We drove off and I heard the crooks bargaining with him. He wanted five hundred *pesos* from the first one and two hundred from the second one. We made several stops so the crooks could collect the money. He let those two go. To the last one, "the Bird" said, "Okay, kid. It's a long time since you signed in . . . a long time since I picked a flower in your garden. Let's get up to date, what do you say?"

This guy says, "No, boss. I've been in bad shape . . . really bad off . . . I haven't been out to work at all."

"Yes," says the cop, "you look like you're dragging your ass. Well, if you're that bad off, get out and get me twenty-five *pesos*."

And there I am listening to all this. When all the business was finished we drove to the Precinct and entered through the basement. "The Bird" then says, "You know what the story is? Two hundred *pesos*."

"Well, what do you know!" I say. "Justice is progressing! You let the guy who is really a crook go for twenty-five *pesos* and for this dumb jerk who is trying to earn a living, the rap is two hundred. You are going to screw me, no matter what. No, I haven't even got that kind of money."

Well, we talked and talked and I had an answer for everything. Finally, he said if I didn't kick in with some loose change he would book me on suspicion. I offered him fifty *pesos*, all I had on me.

"All right, all right, let's have it and get the hell out of here."

Once I was really caught red-handed by the police and it cost me plenty. I didn't know what I was getting into that time. I had a partner by the name of "the Bull," and we had money in our pockets then. What with the merchandise and cash, "the Bull" and I had about ten thousand *pesos*. We were on the corner, one day, selling old clothes. I was yelling: "Buy old clothes cheap . . . pick up something . . . take something home . . . right over here . . ."

There I was, shouting my head off, when Macario, the janitor's son, comes over. He was an old friend of mine and had married a girl of the Casa Grande and now had a son. He looked real beat, his clothes all patched, flat broke, because he hadn't worked for a long time. We had worked together in the leather factory and I always knew him for an honest person.

"Manuel," he says, "damn it, lend me something for today's food, will you?" He was with two other friends. "Lend me five *pesos*, brother, can you?"

"Sure, Macario." I thought, "What can this poor devil do with five *pesos*? Five *pesos*, so easy to get and so easy to spend . . ."

"Look, Macario, take ten *pesos*. God has been good, maybe tomorrow I'll need you."

"Thanks a lot, brother," he says. "Damn it, Manuel, I can't seem to get work. In the tannery it's very scarce." He started to leave, then he said, "Look, Manuel, I almost forgot the main thing I came for. Do you see the guy in the red cap?"

So I turn and look at the guy with him. "Well?"

"Look," says Macario, "his wife and the wife of another guy were going to set up a dressmaking shop, but since this fellow drinks and got drunk for fifteen days straight, his partner made off with the machines and five thousand *pesos* in cash. The only thing left was a batch of cloth they had bought to make aprons. They want to sell it."

When it's a matter of business, I get suspicious right away. I trusted Macario but, you know, just in case, I went through the usual routine of asking questions.

"No, Manuel, hell! after you doing me a favor do you think I'm going to saddle you with something hot? This boy is honest. He works in the tannery with me and I guarantee he is honest."

I talked it over with my partner and we decided to buy the cloth at one *peso* a meter. There were 1,800 meters and I had to go to pick it up.

When I got to the *vecindad* I found that the guy had gone out for a drink. His mother was there, an old, respectable white-haired lady. There was the cloth, brand-new and all tied up in steel strips. I chatted with the lady for a while, then I came out with it.

"Look, lady, talking straight now," I say to her, "aren't . . . maybe . . . isn't this stuff hot? You know, if something's wrong, the cops come screwing around and then we end up working for those bastards. Look, I really don't want to get into trouble, lady, sincerely."

She got red in the face and bawled me out good. She said, "*Señor*, if you have any suspicions you just better not buy it. We are poor but honest here! I'll guarantee that, I'll swear that before anyone. All of you in the market are suspicious. The lion thinks everyone is like himself." She really let me have it.

"O.K., lady, don't get mad. If they're hot, I'd buy them anyhow. But you have to tell me where they're from, because if they're from around here, how can I sell them here? The owner is bound to show up. I'd go to Toluca or to Pachuca to sell them. I'm not asking because it frightens me. Nothing frightens me. The dead don't frighten me." I was thinking that if she told me it's hot, I wouldn't touch the stuff. I just wanted to get the truth out of her. But she just bawled me out, and I was convinced it was really straight, see? So I bought it.

Well, there we were selling the cloth. "Come on and buy it at one-fifty a meter. Cloth for sale, cheap!" A man comes up and buys six hundred meters. "Oh, son-of-a-bitch," I say, "three hundred *pesos* in one damned swoop. We're going to make money here." I started shouting, "Cloth here, two *pesos* a meter!" It sold quickly. It got so I couldn't measure so many meters at the same time. That morning we sold over a thousand meters!

In the afternoon again we spread our canvas on the ground and sold some more, tranquilly. Macario had come to help us sell, but he was timid.

"Shout, Macario, go on, you son-of-a-bitch," I said, "don't be afraid. I suppose you're ashamed . . . be ashamed of stealing, not of selling, brother. Look, business is fun, it's more fun than working. Yell a little." That's what I told him. It was a good market, at its height. All the ladies were out buying their little chiles and tomatoes. By six in the afternoon I had 1,800 *pesos* in my pocket.

At that time I was eating at a certain café, where I was a friend of Gilberto and Carolina, the owners. As soon as I turned the corner to go to the café, a man embraces me. "Now we're really screwed!" I thought. I tell you I can smell them! I can smell a cop, I can pick them out with my nose. I had never seen that agent, but right away I knew.

He asked about the cloth, all right. He held me close to him and we kept walking toward the patrol car. The cops had been waiting for me at the café all day, but Carolina hadn't sent anyone to warn me because the police would have followed. I didn't think the cloth was hot, and I still don't. But the cops have a special way of working here.

Well, when we got to the car, this character wasn't embracing me any more. He clutched me by the belt. He really was not a bad sort, for a cop.

He said, "Well, if it's not what we're looking for, please excuse me, but in our line of work we make lots of mistakes."

I was surprised. The cops are always so arbitrary and here was such a decent bastard! "What stuff is he smoking?" I wondered. He got me into the car and I kept explaining how I got into the cloth deal.

"*Ay*, Manuelito," he says—he was already calling me Manuelito— "it's going to be damned messy, because the creditor wants the cloth or three thousand *pesos*, and we want two thousand."

"*Ay*, no," I say, "no, then there's no way out and I'm screwed."

"No," he says, "it's not worth it, Manuel. Think of the consequences. You'll get a prison record and then . . . just for a few *pesos* that you could dig up somewhere."

"But it's five thousand *pesos* you want! That's all! In my whole stinking life I never saw five thousand *pesos*." Well, there we go, off to the Police Station. On the way, they picked up a few other friends, some pickpockets. They took their money and let them go. My cop friend kept talking.

"Think of the consequences. Money comes and money goes but, well, you're in real trouble. The creditor is powerful and he wants the cloth."

"Look," I say, "take me to the creditor, the owner of the cloth, and let's see if I can convince him to let me pay it off little by little. I'll give you guys something too. You don't work for free."

"We can't make deals like that," says he.

Then I thought of Abram, my father's *compadre*, who worked in the Police Station. I began to talk about him to the cops, hoping it would do some good. I was terrified because never in my life had I been in a jail. They said I would have to go in for a while. When we got there, the guard asked me if I had any dough. I had 1,800 *pesos* in my pocket but I wasn't going to give it to those bastards.

"Look," says the guard, "inside they're going too shake you down and take everything you've got."

"Sure, sure, but I haven't a thing, not a thing." I was well dressed, see? I had on my gabardine pants, a good shirt and a windbreaker. Well, they opened the door of the cage and inside I went, scared to death. There was a bunch of evil-looking characters there, the worst collection of faces I had ever seen. "*Madre Santísima!*" I thought, "how am I going to take care of these bastards? Let's see if I can impress them . . ."

I came in, angry, real angry. Inside I was shaking but I looked mean. They had to think I was real wild. I see this guy sitting on the floor, and wham! I give him a kick in the pants.

"Move over, son-of-a-bitch!"

"Hey, you bastard . . . what . . ."

"Shut up!" I give him another kick. "Shut your trap, you bastard. Didn't you hear me . . . move over." He moved over and the others made room for me. I was saying, "Cowards! Fags! Stoolies!" *Pas!* I punched the wall, and kicked, see? I punched the door. I looked furious.

"Hey, what's eating you?" one of the guys asked.

"What the hell do you care? Am I asking you? Bastard!"

"Cool off. Maybe I can help you, give you advice, see? I'm an old guest here. I know all their tricks."

I kept acting real angry. I take out a cigarette and light it, and I notice another guy who looked even meaner than I. I saw I was getting on his nerves, so I said to him, "Hey, friend, you want to smoke? Have a cigarette." I passed them around. The ice was broken, and I felt safer.

Then a guy comes over, a powerful-looking fellow, and says, "Hey, friend. Why did they bring you here?"

"Look," I say, cranking myself up, putting it on thick, because they have their class distinctions too. "I had fifty sewing-machine heads, I had liquifiers, television sets, radios, everything . . . And that son-of-a-bitch, the one who sold them to me, turned me in. They just took everything, brother, and I'm out a hundred thousand *pesos*." I had to give myself class because they have more respect for you that way.

I noticed a guy there, lying face up, with his legs spread, like a compass. His balls were all swollen from the beatings the cops had given him. Every little while he'd say, "Please, boys, face down." Then ten minutes later, "Turn me over again, please." Face up or face down, he couldn't bear it. His face was all split and he had marks from the pistol butt they hit him with. Really heartbreaking, that poor guy.

Then one guy said, "You know, I was in 'The Well' for two weeks, pal." That's a prison called El Pozito, the little well. All you have to do is say El Pozito to the pickpockets around here and they cry. You know what they do there? They tie their hands behind their back, tie up their feet, and say, "Was it you or wasn't it?" and wham! a punch in the stomach, but hard, to knock out your breath. Then they throw them into a well of filthy water, full of horse urine, and when they're half drowned, half dead, they take them out and do it again.

This guy who said he was in "The Well," went on: "That's how they kept me there. For ten days I didn't eat or drink a thing. The bastards didn't even give me water! You know why? I buy stolen cattle, pigs, any kind of animal they bring me. But why should I give these bastards money? They've screwed me plenty already. Why should I? They'll have to work to get me to talk! But I won't! I won't talk! I've been here fifteen days and every night those god-damned bastards take me out."

You know, I admired that guy. He really wears pants! He had that Mexican courage that I think doesn't exist any more. I was there fifteen minutes when they came to take him out. Just as the door closed, we could hear them hitting him. He came back looking yellow. "Not a frigging thing, pal," he said, "and they'll kill me but they'll get nothing from me." And the poor boy with the swollen testicles, they dragged him out like a dog. Imagine the state he was in and they still took him out and beat him.

All this time I was wondering when my turn would come. When I heard my name I was really scared. But there was my friend Abram talking for me. I finally offered the cop a thousand *pesos* to let me go, otherwise I'd get myself a lawyer. Well, that got him, I had him checked. Because if he didn't take the thousand, it would go to the lawyer. So he said, "O.K., just because of Abram and all that. Let's go and get the money." I had the money in my pocket but they didn't know, see?

So he drove me to the café, and I asked Gilberto to lend me five hundred *pesos*. I dropped my roll behind the counter, so he could see it, and right away he took the five hundred from his pocket and gave it to the cop. He was to get the rest the next day.

"O.K., Manuelito, let's go." He was real friendly. He even took me out for some *tacos* before he locked me up for the night. I spent the night in jail, listening to all the pickpockets tell of their adventures. I really enjoyed being there with them.

Well, I kept going to Gilberto's café. It was practically my home. I ate all my meals there, and sometimes I slept on the floor at night. My *papá* moved Delila and my kids to a room on the Street of the Lost Child. Meanwhile, he bought a lot on the edge of the city and began to build another house. A week or two would pass without me going to see my children, and that bothered me a lot, although I hid it even from myself. I don't know why, but when I don't see them every day, little by little my love for them quiets down, gets paralyzed, and I avoid thinking of them. I have asked myself why I am that way with my children, but the truth is, I am afraid to analyze it. I am afraid to answer my own question, because I feel I will hate myself if I do.

I didn't attend my children the way I should because I was trying to live the kind of life I couldn't really afford. I was like a trapped beast, looking for a way out for myself alone. I felt like a heel. I couldn't sleep at night. I always thought of my children just as I sat down to eat, and then the food didn't go down easily any more. It is paradoxical, but I didn't go to see them as a kind of punishment to myself. And when my father or Consuelo came to the café and shouted insults at me in front of my friends, I felt more justified. I felt I had paid for my behavior with my humiliation.

Gilberto and his wife Carolina were my closet friends. He was a first-class printer and a union member, and she ran the café. I tried to get him to work in Tepito, but he preferred his wage of fifty *pesos* a day, Social Security and a pension later.

It was Gilberto who introduced me to the horse races and to *jai-alai* and *frontón*, which were my ruination. I even gambled on boxing matches and cockfights. Yes, the vice of gambling took hold of me more than ever. Card playing was small stuff, compared to this. I always had the hope of hitting the jackpot, which would pay three, four, five thousand *pesos*. I dreamed of the satisfaction it would give me if I could say, "Look, *papá*, take this. Take the whole lump." Because, *por Dios*, I didn't want the money for myself. I swear if I had ever hit the jackpot, I would have given it all to my father and my children. I don't love money!

One day, Gilberto took me to the race track and it was my misfortune to buy a lucky ticket for ten *pesos*. The bet paid off 786 *pesos* and right away I said, "What am I wasting my time working for, when I can make a killing here?" From that moment to this, I loved the horses. I learned to read the racing forms and studied up on weights, times, mounts, distances, and all that. I knew so much, I became scientific about it. Maybe that was my undoing. I should have stuck to hunches and dreams, like Gilberto did.

I lost a lot of money there at the Hipódromo. I was doing well at Tepito, sometimes earning at least one hundred *pesos* a day, but all of it, all of it, went on the horses. Once, I arrived with 1,200 *pesos* in my pocket and left with only thirty *centavos* for the bus. That day I didn't even eat . . . I'd rather bet than eat . . . and at night I bought my supper on credit at the café. I won only twice . . . a mere 1,300 *pesos* in all. It is unbelievable, but sometimes my losses amounted to a thousand *pesos* a month, if not more. The money I should have used as capital in the market, went down the drain. I could have been well off if I hadn't had the bug of gambling.

Don't think I bet for fun! For me, it was a business, a job . . . the fastest way I had of really getting ahead. I was always full of hope. When I lost all the money I had on me and couldn't place any more bets, I felt my body collapse. I'd go into a cold sweat. I reproached myself for being a fool . . . for having picked the wrong number . . . for not following Gilberto's hunch . . . for misinterpreting a dream . . . for my bad luck. A thousand and one times, I advised myself to quit, but no sooner did I make a good business deal, when I ran to the race track with my money. The next morning, I went to the market without a *centavo*, to look for a friend with capital who would go into partnership with me for the day.

And to make matters worse, a partner of mine went off with about five thousand *pesos*' worth of goods, leaving me to pay the creditors. I still owe about 1,200 *pesos* on that deal.

My *compadre* Alberto had stayed in the United States for another season, until Immigration grabbed him and threw him out. I saw a good deal of him when he came back, but we were not so close any more. At first he spoke to me like he always did, but then I noticed that he was drawing further and further away. There was a certain coldness in his tone, see? A certain something. This went on for about three years. Then one day, he showed up with his aunt at Gilberto's café, dead drunk.

I was baking bread for Carolina that morning, and refused to have a drink with him. He sat down and kept staring at me while I worked. He moved his head from side to side, sadly, with his eye on me. "What's eating this guy?" I wondered. He raised his glass and said to his aunt: "*Salud,* to the best and most treacherous of friends." Then he looked at me, see?

He did it a second time and I couldn't ignore it. So I went over to him and said, "Listen, *compadre,* there was never any crap between us. Why do you say that to me?"

"Look," he says, "if it weren't for my children, I swear I would have killed you by now, *compadre.*"

"Wait a minute," I say. "What's on your mind, *cabrón?* Are you crazy?"

"Isn't it true that you sang on the buttocks of my woman?"

"Who told you that?" I was furious. I felt a volcano boiling inside me.

"Juanita, my wife, told me. Isn't it true that you got into her when you found her in the cabaret?"

I began to understand what it was all about. A short time after I got back from the United States, I met a friend who said, "Say, *Chino,* whose woman is working at El Casino, yours or Alberto's?"

I didn't like to hear that because El Casino was a cheap cabaret in the neighborhood, a real dive. So I say to the guy, "Well, my *compadre* was a chaser, he had lots of women. Who knows which of the bunch you are talking about, brother."

"Maybe so," he says, "but listen, this one knows you and she let on that she has children with Alberto."

"Go on, you're not trying to tell me it's his wife. He's legally married to her. It couldn't be Juanita!" Suddenly, a feeling hit me. I had a feeling it was Juanita, but I acted as though it didn't mean a thing, so as not to make my *compadre* look bad.

That evening I went to El Casino, to have a look around. As it is dark in those places, I couldn't see a thing at first. I had to take a leak and on my way to the toilet I passed a woman in a clinch with some guy. When I came out, I saw her face and sure enough it was Alberto's wife. I felt horrible, as bad as if she were my own wife. So I grabbed her, using rough language.

"What is this!" I say, and I pulled her away, see? "What the frigging hell are you doing here? You whore!"

She pulled away, saying I had no right to interfere, that she wasn't doing anything . . .

"Not anything? Slut! What do you mean I have no right! You're getting out of here this minute or I'll drag you out."

"It's that the baby was sick and Alberto didn't send me money. Was I going to let my baby die? I had to . . . that's why I did it."

"You're lying through your teeth, *señora*. Only five days ago I myself wrote Alberto's check for fifty-five dollars and sent it to you . . . I, personally."

Then she began to cry and I came to my senses. After all, she wasn't *my* wife.

So I calmed down and told her, "Look, *señora*, there's no reason for you to work here. If you need money, if Alberto doesn't send enough, I can let you have some until he comes back. I'm going to start work soon. When Alberto comes, he can pay me."

I paid the bartender twenty *pesos* to let her leave, and another ten to the cop at the door, and I sent her home, feeling I had done right by my *compadre*.

So when Alberto accused me I felt very bad.

"Look, *compadre*," I said, "I don't like gossip. Let's not beat around the bush. Get up and let's go to your house."

We took a taxi and got there fast. Alberto and his wife were janitors in an apartment building and we went through the courtyard to their room in the back. Juanita was surprised to see me, and looked uneasy. Then we had it out with her.

"No," she says, "I don't understand how Alberto could have taken it like that. I told him you had offered to lend me money to live on, not to sleep with you."

Alberto just stood there glaring at her. Then he clouted her a couple. I let him, because she deserved it, pulling that stuff. He might have killed me, or I him . . . and for what? So I let him slug her a few. But when he kept on beating her, I tried to stop him. He was like crazy . . . as if in a fit, yelling, "Slut! Slut!" That was all he could say. Finally I got him to bed.

He comes round to see me now, but it is not the same between us. Knowing me a lifetime and us caring about each other the way we did, well, he should never have doubted me. It wounded me. I didn't show it, but at bottom, it made me feel cheated. It even had something to do with lessening my faith in religion.

But I really admire my *compadre*. He has a will of iron. When he makes up his mind to do something, he does it. He drives a taxi, his sons are going to school, he has his little television set . . . a gas stove . . . and is even talking about building a house. His big dream is to drive one of those huge sightseeing buses, and I don't have the slightest doubt that he will.

He has always advised me to settle down and stop living according to my whim. He says I'm more intelligent than he, and can be even more successful. I don't know where he gets his will and perseverance . . . maybe because he can't read there is nothing to distract his mind. Maybe it helps him focus more clearly on practical things, right?

Well, I was a widower and still in my twenties. I was really a free man. I got up at noon, spent the afternoon and evening at the market, on the streets, at the racetrack, or some other place where I could gamble. I had plenty of friends, but I felt lonely for a woman. Three times I went to whore houses, but left without doing anything. I can't stand those women.

Then I met María, Carolina's goddaughter, at the café. She was just a kid of seventeen when I first saw her. Her mother had been killed by her stepfather a few years before, and she had lived from pillar to post with her grandmother and her three kid brothers and a sister. They used to sleep in a stall in the old market, before it was torn down. When I met her, they all slept on a little balcony in Carolina's and Gilberto's room.

I recognized Maria's faults from the beginning. She was sloppy and lazy. But she was a well-built girl, pretty and young. The thing was, I had a very strong desire for her. I thought, "With patience, with tenderness, she'll change. She had a miserable life, but little by little, I'll make her change."

It was not that I loved María, for I didn't. My capacity for love had been killed. I knew this because when I saw Graciela in the street every once in a while, I didn't even have a slight stir of feeling for her. No, my motive in going after María was strictly convenience.

So I invited María to go to Chalma with me and a friend. I had intended to fulfill my wife's vow to walk on her knees from the *Cruz del Perdón* to the Sanctuary of the "Little Saint," but when they gave María permission to go, I forgot about the vow.

All the way there, I kept trying to make her, you know what I mean? and in the bus she had already given in . . . she said she would. When the pilgrimage on foot began, we spent our first night together. We slept on a *petate* out in a field, but it turned out to be very upsetting.

Imagine, the moment arrived . . . she was already beginning to have regrets . . . and I couldn't do a thing. I couldn't get a reaction. She resisted just a tiny bit and I got nervous and couldn't . . . I just couldn't. I got a terrible attack of nerves. I acted like I was sore at her, to cover up. We slept on the same mat for three days, but that is as far as it went.

From that time on, I've had a whole string of upsets like that. I kept going after it, and when I had it all set up, I couldn't again. All I had was a horrible pain in my testicles and I spent the night in rage and disappointment. I had always been virile, but since my wife died I haven't been the same. I think the moral depression I felt, piled up on me.

I thought, "Well, who knows? Maybe God didn't want her touched by me." Then another boy began to go after her and before I knew it they were *novios*. I wasn't going to let that rascal beat me out! After all, I had slept next to her. I knew her body, so how could I let him get her?

So I began asking her to marry me. I promised to work hard and give her everything and all that. I reminded her that I had behaved respectfully. "See," I said, "that's what a person gets for behaving decent. That's something you don't even appreciate. I could have had you but I held back, because I had promised to respect you."

So, you know what she said?

She said, "Why did you promise? Because you couldn't! When it got right down to it, you couldn't do a thing."

I got so mad, I slapped her. "Now you throw it up to me that I held back? Is that what I get for being honorable?" And I slapped her again. Naturally, my male pride didn't let me admit what really had happened.

After that, we didn't speak to each other. Another woman began to go for me. She was living with a man and I didn't want her, but she kept after me, until finally, when I least expected it, I had to give in.

Then, suddenly, one day María comes over to me and says

"Manuel, you kept asking me to marry you, didn't you? Well, let's do it right now." I was completely surprised, but I took her to a hotel before she changed her mind. What had happened was that she was jealous of this other woman and wanted to show that she could take me away.

It was obvious right away that María was inexperienced. She was a virgin and completely passive. She let herself be taken and that was that. Because of my state of nerves, I had to work hard and even then just barely made it. After that, María went back to sleep on her balcony and I slept at the café. We kept living that way for several months.

I hoped that María would change. But she was always passive, the same desperate way all the time. I don't want to sound depraved, but from my experience, a woman should reach a certain point of excitement. Well, I tried . . . I prepared her, but she wouldn't react. Sometimes even while I talked to her and worked on her, she fell asleep! That would freeze up a person, no?

I scolded her about it. "Look, María, why do I always have to be the one to take the initiative? Why can't you be the one to ask? It's the normal thing in a marriage. How come it has never occurred to you?" Ay, poor me! I thought it was because she didn't love me, but she said all along that she wouldn't live with me if she didn't.

She didn't complain about my impotence, though. I wasn't always that way and besides I could disguise it. But it tortured me! Sometimes I blamed it on my brain, which was never at rest. Even when I was in the act, I wasn't really in it. I was always thinking, or listening to music inside my head. My mind wandered from one thing to another, entirely unconnected. I felt terrific throbbings and heavy feelings; sometimes I'd think so much my head felt it would burst open. There were times when the world stopped for me and I had no desire to do anything. The street, the noise, the movement, people . . . were all dead for me . . . the flowers had no color.

When I was with María I would forget my worries a little. I tried talking to her about the serious things in life but she got bored. I was not very cultured, but at least I liked to read, to cultivate myself a bit. But do you know what interested her? Comic books, love stories, gossip . . . she talked plenty with other people about things like that, but when I discussed things with her, she only answered "Yes" or "No."

Then her sloppiness bothered me. "Fix yourself up, please, María," I'd say. "Try to be a little cleaner. You go around looking like disappointment itself, as though you had no illusions left." She showed no interest in life. I wondered if something was wrong with her.

I was thinking of leaving María when she became pregnant. I had no intention of abandoning her now, or of giving her a hard life. She wanted us to be married by civil law (someone had told her that a child born out of wedlock develops donkey's ears and walks in the shadow of the cross all his life). But I wouldn't marry her because it would be a kind of treachery toward my children and my dead wife. The children I would have with her would have all the rights before the law, and my four kids would lose theirs automatically.

It was at about this time that my *papá* told me to take back my children. "I'm fed up," he said. "I'm sick and tired of your kids. You've got to get them out of here. I can't stand them any more."

So I brought them to the Casa Grande, where Marta and her children were living. Marta agreed to take care of them if I gave her expense money. Well, on the third day, when I went to give her the money in the evening, I found my kids abandoned, without having eaten all day. My sister had gone off with a man, her kids and all! She left without a word and my poor children looked like hungry orphans when I got there.

That's when I brought María to live with me in the Casa Grande. I thought she would be of use to fix the children's food, if nothing else. My father said I could have the room if I paid the rent. When he found out about María, all he said was, "So, you've taken on another responsibility. It'll be just like the other one."

I started out with lots of illusions about setting up a home at last. Then my father insisted on sending the furniture to Acapulco, where Marta was living with her man. Consuelo came to pick out stuff, then Delila, and soon we were left in an empty room, just the four walls and us.

When Consuelo came by and saw us sleeping on cardboard on the floor, she said, "Listen, brother, I am not using my big bed at Lupita's. Why don't you pay me fifty *pesos* for it and go over and get it."

"But, sister," I said, "my *papá* sleeps on it when he goes to see Lupita. How can I take it away?"

"I don't care," she says. "The bed is mine. After all, I paid for it. I'd rather have your children sleep on it."

So I paid her and went and got the bed. María and I slept on it and I put the mattress on the floor for the children. When María gave birth to my little girl, Lolita, the baby slept with us on the bed. When Consuelo saw this arrangement, she began to make a fuss.

"What's the idea? I gave you the bed for the children, not so that . . ."

I got mad right away, because she was always implying that I mistreated my children. Why, I had slept on the floor all my life! And Roberto and I had been much worse off, because we didn't have a mattress or sheets like my children did.

"Consuelo, you didn't give me the bed, you sold it to me. I give the orders in my house . . . I . . . me . . . not you. Don't come here ordering us around. As soon as I have money, I'll buy another bed."

Well, that one kept bothering me about the bed. Finally, I said, "Look, don't get a hemorrhage about it. Give me back the fifty *pesos* and beat it, with the bed." But she didn't have the money, so the bickering went on. Once, she even waited outside the movies for me, and started an argument when I came out.

"You're nuts," I said, and I left her screaming on the corner. I guess I made her mad, because the next day she came to the house, gave María the fifty *pesos*, and took away the bed.

Then I made a lucky deal in the market and came home with a bedroom set.

"What pretty furniture," María said. I thought the furniture would animate her, but she was still as indifferent and careless as ever. Wherever I ran my finger, there was dust, fingerprints, filth.

"For the love of God, woman, what do you do all day?" I said to her. "Take a rag with a little oil and polish the furniture. Try to keep the house clean."

Two weeks later, the wardrobe door was broken. I really got mad and called her everything in the book. First she blamed my brother, then my youngest son. I couldn't get the truth out of that woman. All I could do was talk.

"What's the use of getting things, if you let them go to the dogs? You like to live in dirt, okay, let's live in shit. We'll see who gets tired of it first. We don't have much, but at least you don't go hungry. That's a boon you have to thank God and me for. Lots of women would be happy just to have a man to lean on; everybody is more considerate to you, just because you are living with a man.

"Possibly you consider me too old. Maybe you feel cheated because I don't come home stinking drunk and kick you awake in the middle of the night. Maybe you feel bored, María? What do you want? I don't want to crucify you. I crucified one woman, one woman died at my side, and I swear I'd rather leave you than sacrifice you. I don't want a slave for a wife, I want a companion. Study something, go to work, be active . . ."

She just listened to me. When I asked a question, she said "Yes" or "No." I don't want to throw all the blame on her, but if she hadn't been that way, my life would now be radically different.

Then her family began to move in on me. That was something terrific! I have lived under the poorest possible conditions, but my wife's family really shocked me. What happened was that her aunt and grandmother were put out of their room for not paying the rent. One of the aunt's sons came and asked for permission to sleep there one night. So he stayed.

Then one day his mother, Elpidia, came with her other kid burning up with fever. A strong wind was blowing outside and the *señora* kept saying, "Where am I going to stay? Imagine, the child is sick and me having to go looking for somewhere to stay." Well, she didn't have to draw me a diagram, so I said she could stay until the kid got well.

María had a cousin, Luisa, who was living with her second husband. The kids from her first husband were living with them. This case is in a class by itself! The stepfather violated her little girl, a child of eleven, and got her pregnant. The mother tried to act like she didn't know what was going on, but she knew all right and continued to live with him. Now that is one thing that is not accepted in my environment, no matter how low it is. The stepfather with his stepdaughter! Never!

Well, Luisa came to our house with the girl, who was in a bad way. The child looked like a pullet, the innocent, nothing but skin and bones. I took her to a doctor and he said she had a frightful case of malnutrition and bronchopneumonia. He didn't know she was also pregnant! I paid for the doctor and the medicine, and they stayed at our place, seeing the poor kid was so sick.

Then the grandmother came with María's brothers, supposedly to visit the sick kids, and wham! they stayed too. Now there was Elpidia and her two sons, Luisa and her daughter, the grandmother, my wife's three brothers, and later, her sister, and another daughter of Luisa's, my four children, María, Lolita and I. Eighteen of us living in one room! Later, my brother Roberto had no place to stay, so he and his woman moved in too.

Disgust, disgust, disgust, is what I felt on entering my home each day. They were spread all over the floor, day and night. They were messy, dirty people, and the house really stank. The grandmother was the best of the lot. She tried to keep herself clean, but the aunt, Elpidia, was the most shameless of all. She would sit in the corner of the kitchen, delousing her children, pulling out the bugs. As far as I could see, she never even washed her hands. She would offer me food, but how could I eat? Just to see her hands made me sick to my stomach.

María's little sister always had snot down to her chin. The toilet smelled and they didn't even bother to close the door when they went. The kids were always screaming, especially in the morning when I liked to sleep. What a racket! It was like all hell let loose. It got to the point where my nerves were getting sick.

My father came by every day, as always. He never said a thing, but I could see he didn't like all those people being there. My first reaction was to run them out, but my other self kept saying, "Poor things, they have no place to go. Today it's them, tomorrow it's me. How can I chase them out?"

I said to María, "*Ay*, old girl. It's not that they are a burden, but I'm paying all the expenses and my money is running out . . . the little capital I had to work with. Tell them, please, to see what they can do for themselves."

"No," she says. "How can I tell them to go? You tell them!"

"But it's your family. Don't run them out, but break it to them, find a way. It's not fair, especially now because I am in a *tanda* and these people are costing me thirty *pesos* a day here." My friends in the market organized *tandas*, so we can have money to operate with. Every week, about ten of us each buys a ticket for fifty *pesos* and we take turns getting the five hundred *pesos* in a lump sum. So there I was, paying in fifty *pesos* a week and supporting all those people!

But María never told her family a thing. The truth is, she was happy with them there. She never looked happier. I got more and more nervous, but I didn't tell them anything either. My money ran out completely. It got so I asked my father to take back my children because for a long time María was using the expense money to feed her family and gave my kids only black coffee and bread. My poor kids! María and her family gave them a rough time.

I had absolutely nothing. I had to sell the bedroom set, and take María and Lolita to eat at the café on credit. The first one to leave was María's grandmother, because she was the most considerate. She realized something serious was going on with me, and she took María's sister and brothers with her. I didn't chase out the others, but they left one by one, because I had nothing more to give them. It was really a triumph to get rid of that aunt! They had been with us for two months, I was flat broke and deeply in debt by the time they left.

My life has been a tangle of inexplicable emotions. I seem to be one of those morbid persons who enjoy torturing themselves. I curse myself with all the power of my soul. I swear there have been times when I have cried at night, alone in the café. My life has been so sterile, so useless, so unhappy, that, *por Dios,* sometimes I wish I could die. I am the kind of guy who leaves nothing behind, no trace of themselves in the world, like a worm dragging itself across the earth. I bring no good to anybody; a bad son, a bad husband, a bad father, bad everything.

Looking back over my life, I see that it was based on a chain of errors. I have treated it frivolously. I have been content to vegetate, to survive in a gray twilight, without effort and without glory. I waited for a stroke of luck . . . for a million *pesos,* so I could help my father, my children, my friends in need. I couldn't do things on a big scale, so I did nothing at all.

But now I feel a little more self-confident and more reasonable. I would be proud to set up a modest home, to educate my children, to save my money. I would like to leave something behind me, so that when I die everyone will remember me with affection.

It sounds laughable, but if I could find the appropriate words, I would like to write poetry someday. I have always tried to see beauty, even among all the evils I have experienced, so that I wouldn't be completely disillusioned by life. I would like to sing the poetry of life . . . great emotions, sublime love, to express the lowest passions in the most beautiful way. Men who can write of these things make the world more habitable; they raise life to a different level.

I know if I am to be constructive I shall have to fight against myself. More than anything, I must win in the fight against myself!

Roberto

It was on a night in December, 1952, that I went to jail in Veracruz. You see, I happened to be in a whore house, passing the time, having myself a little fun. I have always been a lone wolf and there isn't a place I won't go to. I had been there quite a while, drinking in the company of a lady. We were at the bar when I saw a guy named "Chicken" Galván come in. So what? . . . just another one of the local boys, as far as I was concerned. I found out later that he was the son of a high state official and went around accompanied by armed police, which was why he was so arrogant. He would insult and humiliate anybody he wanted to. It was easy for him to talk rough, because he had protection.

It happened that he came over to the bar and stood behind me. I was drinking and turned around. He stood there looking at me, so I looked at him, very natural, right? I didn't say a thing to him and he didn't say anything to me. We just looked at each other.

Well, that's how the *pique* began, as we say in Mexico. But I wouldn't take it from the very beginning. They played a *danzón*, which is the music I like best, and I asked the girl to dance. "Sure, why not?" After all, she was with me, wasn't she? Along about the middle of the number, this boy walked up to me and said, "Step aside, I'm going to dance."

"O.K., but right now I'm dancing with her," I said. "Wait until the number is over."

"What do you mean, 'Wait!' In the first place, don't call me '*tu*.' And in the second place, I am going to dance, because I feel like dancing."

"Look, I call you '*tu*' because that's the way you talked to me, and, secondly, you are not going to dance with her because even though she is a prostitute, I am not going to let her go, just like that, and that's all there is to it." I respect any woman who is with me and I see that she is respected, I don't care what her social status is.

Well, then the fun started. He let me have one with his right that still hurts every time I think of it, and down I go. That did it! There was no way of getting out of the argument now, was there? Because, if there is anything I've got, it is that I never run away from a fight. I got up, and two or three of his cops came over and wanted to grab hold of me. What this guy had fixed up was that once the argument got serious, down to fists, the cops would step in, grab his enemy and he would begin to slug him to his heart's content. But he said, "No. Leave him be! I can take care of this bastard all by myself."

The police stepped aside. And so we mixed it up, but rough. I once used to box and he was not much of a boxer, so, frankly, I was getting the better of him. All of a sudden, he pulled a gun and threatened me. I don't scare when I see a weapon. Instead of getting scared and backing off, I go absolutely blind mad and try to beat them to a pulp.

He said, "Today you die, you son-of-a-whore."

"Let's see about it. Anybody can pull a pistol . . . that's easy . . . but it's something else again to shoot it . . . you've got to have guts."

"You'll see right away," he says.

Then I pulled my knife and wounded him. I can't say it was a mortal wound, but I did wound him. I stuck him three times, twice in his body and once in the hand.

So a big fuss was kicked up and the cops arrested me. They said, "Now, wait and see, son-of-a-whore, now you are going to die." And to be honest, that's what I expected. I was sure they would kill me. Others who had just dared raise their voices to him had been given terrible beatings. And I, I had wounded him! This being the case, I shot the works. I figured I was done for.

The cops were saying, "You'll see, son-of-your-damned-mother, you'll see . . . you're going to die."

"O.K., but before I die, one or two of you goes before me." They began to cock their guns, but what saved me, and I thank God for it, was that one of the three cops said, "No, let's take Galván to the doctor and then we'll know what to do with him . . . if not, we might be going out on a limb, and it isn't worth it."

"So, I'm not worth the trouble, you son-of-a-whore," I said. "Just try it and you'll see . . ."

Well, they took me to the municipal jail, there in Veracruz. I had fallen in, like a stone in a well. I was feeling pretty low. My family didn't know I was there. What would it have cost me to send a letter, right? But how was I going to break the bad news? Several days went by and I felt worse than depressed, worse than sad . . . I was desperate.

I had only one idea in mind, and that was to get out no matter what it cost me, no matter how. But I had to think of the best way of doing it, not to miss. To get to the courtroom, you had to leave the jail, so I asked for a hearing. I got it and the date was set.

I had sold my shoes to buy food, because I couldn't eat what they gave us. Even pigs would have thrown it back in their faces and told them a few things to boot, if they could talk. So I was wearing wooden clogs with wide rubber bands across the middle to hold them on. I practiced getting them off quickly, without bending down, because it would have been impossible to run with clogs. I kept practicing until finally the day came. I didn't have it all figured out, but I had made up my mind to escape.

I went to court, accompanied by an armed cop, walking between him and the wall. We turned left, through the corridors which led out to the street, where there were soldiers on guard. The cop started to ask me questions but I really didn't pay much attention. I was concentrating on the street, on which way to run, on how many people were around, and such things. The cop was saying, "Don't worry about it. You'll be getting out soon." With those words, I'm off like a shot, throwing away my clogs, I don't know how. When the moment came, I forgot all about what I had practiced.

I took off, barefooted, and ran like the devil was after me. I got away with a good head start. Then, I heard the sound of the 7-millimeter Mauser being cocked, a very special sound for me ever since I had been in the army. The bystanders and clerks were shouting, "Let him have it. Don't be a fool. Kill him. Shoot at his legs." I didn't turn around because if I had and saw that he was aiming at me, I would have gotten scared.

I was risking my life to get away and with God's help I was going to make it. I was running like a bullet, with him and various others after me. The people would pull away to one side when they saw me coming. When I got to the outskirts they began shooting. It sounded like the sixteenth of September, for all the shooting that cut loose. *Qué bárbaro!* the way the bullets were hitting alongside of me . . . or in front of me, at my feet . . . just like in the movies. A whole swarm of people were after me, even civilians, who just wanted to give their trigger finger a good time.

Instead of heading for the hills, I started toward a coffee plantation that was closer. But, first I had to pass through a group of houses, where there were all kinds of watchmen and guards. I ran right into the wolf's jaws, without realizing it. I was more than tired by now . . . really, really exhausted. I had run more than a kilometer and had given all I had. My lungs and my temples felt like they were going to burst, my eyes were popping out of my head. I really had no more strength to go on running. But, even so, I still had hopes that I could get away. I had a tremendous lead; I must have been two or three blocks ahead of all of them.

I had to pass through the patio of a private house around which there was a hedge. But hidden in the bushes were wires, which I ran against. I hit the ground and could barely get up again. I pulled myself together and jumped over into another yard. There were dogs there and even they chased me!

I turned a corner to get to the street and ran right into a guy sitting there. By then I wasn't really running any more, kind of walking with long strides, but I thought I was still running.

He said, "What's going on? What are you running for? Stop!"

"None of your business," I said to him. "What did I do to you? Do I owe you anything, or what? Leave me alone." But no, he wanted me to stop and pulled out a knife and grabbed hold of me.

I said to him, "What did I ever do to you? Let go of me please. Look, you might get hit with a bullet."

"No," he said, "now we'll see why you are running." But we didn't stop . . . we kept running, with him hanging on to my jacket. I dropped to the ground, to see if that would make him let go. He went down with me, still holding on, so I stood up again fast, giving him the knee in the testicles. He threw the knife, but I managed to dodge and it went through my clothes.

Then, bang! some shots again. I started to run and that guy stopped me. But I was dead, by then . . . really finished . . . I didn't even have strength to talk. The others got there—that cop; those jokers, the officials and the clerks; and all the civilians and a mob of people. Somebody grabbed me by the arm on the right and somebody else on the left. I fainted for a moment and they held me up. The cop had his gun in his hand and was coming toward me with the idea of putting a bullet into my chest. But the ones who were holding me up said, "O.K., now, you bastard, this man is all in. He's all beat up, why hit him any more? We've got him, so don't hit him now."

For the moment that cop didn't hit me. We walked to a taxi that had joined the chase . . . rather they carried me, as I couldn't even walk any more. The cop was real sore. I don't blame him because if I had managed to get away, he would have had to take my place, you see. It seems like that was the law there. The policeman is responsible for whatever happens to the person under his custody.

But there was no reason for him to hit me. As we went up the steps to the jail, he kept hitting me with his gun in the little bone at the bottom of the spine where it is terribly painful. He was hitting me and saying, "Up you go, *desgraciado.* If you got away from me, I'd be in your place now, wouldn't I?" And every word was another jab with the gun. It hurt so much I could hardly stand it. After we got there, the officials said, "*Ay, negrito!* You can run like a rabbit. How would it have been if you'd gotten away on us, eh? Put him back in again."

Wham! they gave me a kick in the behind and then that cop started to beat me. He opened my head, beating me with his gun. I still have the scar.

"What kind of a lousy bastard are you, anyway?" I said. "I can't even walk under my own power, and still you hit me. Have a heart!" Everybody around recognized that he wasn't doing the right thing. They were saying, "That's enough. Leave him alone. You've got him now."

Back in jail, the other prisoners began asking questions: "How did they catch you? Why didn't you run this way . . . or that way?" They gave me all kinds of advice as to what route I should have taken, but it was too late. My companions in misfortune respected me a lot more, now, you know what I mean? Most of them were in there for more than just one killing. One guy, Eduardo, had eighteen to his name, and bragged about it. He would say, "*Ay,* what tramps! I killed eighteen and look at me. I don't even mind jail. I'm resting." After a couple of years he'd get out, paying money, of course.

You cannot imagine the things that happened to me in that jail, and the remorse I felt. Physically I was dead, and morally I was buried. But I don't want to make myself tragic; thanks to God, I always get back on my feet and throw out a laugh. Why shouldn't I laugh? Life is a comedy and the world is the theatre and we are all actors.

I don't know how they found out about me at home. I had sent a confidential letter to Marta, telling her that I was working in the Veracruz jail as a messenger and that they shouldn't worry about me. I couldn't tell her I was a prisoner, could I? I asked her not to tell my father, but on the sixth of January, the Day of the Three Kings, he was there.

When I heard them shout out my name, I thought it was a letter from Marta. In such places a letter is a big event, so I was happy. It was too impossible to imagine that my father would come, even if he knew, because his obligations and his job wouldn't permit it. I thought the day my father came, the sun would black out or the moon would fall. I was afraid to have him find out, but at the same time I felt sorry for myself and prayed. "God, I know I'm a first-class bum and deserve what I'm getting, but have a little pity and make my trouble easier for me to take, because really, I'm like a stone in a well, here."

Up there, little Jesus must have been listening, because, as I said, there was my *papá. Ay!* to see me! I felt like I had come to heaven, but, of course, I was also afraid that the jail would come down on my head. Well, we greeted each other and—this hurt me—my father cried. He held his breath a moment and threw his head back as if he was gasping for air, and his voice broke when he started to talk. As for me, frankly, the tears came to my eyes. I couldn't help it. Well, that's about as far as it went.

I guess my father came to see if I was still alive or if he could settle this affair of mine. I said, "Don't worry about me. After all, it won't be more than a year when they throw me out of jail." What advice can a son give his father when he's locked up?

Then my father began to bawl me out. "See, you see what happens when you don't behave like I say? This will keep on happening to you and you are going to fail in life, so long as you don't behave like decent people, as the Lord orders." Simple words, but containing a great truth. I had nothing to say and didn't even look my father in the face. I have never looked him in the face and least of all that time. As a general thing, my father saw me with my eyes to the ground.

Well, he left me fifty *pesos* to get a lawyer, but I didn't trust lawyers and invested the money in a bed . . . two saw horses and a plank . . . which I bought right there in jail. I had been sleeping on the bare ground, with nothing to cover me. We were a hundred-odd guys in the gallery and when one of them went to the toilet, he'd step on my foot or my face while I was sleeping. With a bed, I was "up on top." It was harder than a rock, but they didn't step on me any more.

My father visited once again, with Consuelo and my half-sister Marielena. Later, I received a letter in which my *papá* told me he had to have his appendix out and that the doctor was doubtful that he would come through it all right. He let me know he forgave me everything, that I should make over my life and behave better. After that, I didn't receive a letter for two months, so you can imagine what gloomy thoughts I had.

"God, give me a sign, something to let me know how my father came out. If it was Thy will to call him to accounts, do Thy will, but at least don't keep me in ignorance. I beg You from the depths of my heart, leave him with me, even if for only another year. I'll go further . . . if it's possible, take me, who least deserves to live, and not my father. He still has people who need him, so I prefer to die in his place." That's the way I was for two months. No letter . . . no letter. The mailman came every day, but nothing, nothing, nothing. *Ay!* Sincerely, it was a living death. I had died a thousand times before, but that time I was nearly dead for real.

I went to Mass every week in jail. Even there, when I knelt before the altar and made the sign of the cross, I felt the same spiritual peace I got only in church. I was transported, if not to another world, at least away from the vileness and deceits of this world. And when I spoke to God, I felt he was listening. I can't explain it, but I never felt that way anywhere else. It was my only comfort in prison.

One of the prisoners was an Evangelist and he dared to insult the priest and the nuns, and tried to teach us his doctrines. He was always reading the Bible and knew more than we did. He criticized confession and Mass and when he asked us what we meant by being a Catholic, we couldn't answer him. I'm really not versed in Catholicism, but first I want to understand my own religion before I learn about another, no?

One day, the Brother, which was what we called the Evangelist, said to me, "Come here, Otelo." That was my nickname there. "What do you think, Otelo? Isn't it true that the priests are earthly sinners like the rest of us? And aren't nuns women, after all, who also have desires to lie with a man?"

"I can't answer that, Brother," I said, "but what I can say is, why don't you go fuck your smutty mother and leave my religion alone?" Now this Evangelist was a real fighting cock and when I mentioned his mother he immediately reached for his knife. I was working in the carpentry shop at that time, so I had a sharp knife, too. All the other prisoners were Catholics and were on my side, but the officials broke it up and made me mop the courtyard and the "Brother" clean the toilets.

My thoughts were very sad ones, because I was planning to escape. Either I got out or they would kill me! But before I died, I wanted to confess and leave this world satisfied in that sense. So I went to one of the little priests and asked him to show me how to confess, because I had never done it before. I told him all my sins, including the one about being in love with my sister. I told him all the thefts I could remember and as a penitence, he said when I got out of jail I should give back whatever I had robbed, or at least tell them it was I who had done it. And I had to pray three *Padres Nuestros, El Credo,* and *Yo Pecador,* and a few Ave Maria's.

I cried a lot while I prayed, and afterward felt so calm and content that I didn't think of escaping any more. I resigned myself to waiting for my hearing and sentence. They had told me that the boy I had knifed was in bad shape. Then I heard he had died . . . later, that he hadn't, and that he was living it up, as usual.

I took my first communion, right there in jail, at the age of twenty-one. They gave us each a candle, a cup of chocolate and bread, and after that I got into bed for the rest of the day. I didn't want anyone to disturb me because I felt such a tranquillity, so at peace with myself, that I didn't want to move.

As a reward for my first communion, I guess, I received a visit from my brother, and another lecture. Manuel came all the way from Mexico City, to bawl me out. "Look, brother," I said, "I know I deserve everything you are saying, but consider the punishment I am getting here. You are older and I respect you, but please don't bawl me out, please." And tears came to his eyes, too. My brother is more noble than I; as a matter of fact I cannot call myself anything like noble, because I have been a bum. And the bad thing about it is that I realize it and torture myself about it all the time.

Well, then Manuel said, "Do you know who came with me?"

"No, who?"

"Graciela, the one who was my girl."

"Let's see! Bring her in." And so he brought her to the gate. She had very pretty eyes and wavy hair. And her voice was sweet.

"Hello, Roberto, how are you? What bad luck, eh?"

"Well, don't worry about me, please."

And then they went away.

Well, I was working with Paolo, the carpenter. He had all his tools right there in the jail and I helped him, not because I got a *centavo* out of him, but because he would give me some of the food he prepared. Then, some time in July, I was playing cards with a companion in misery and went to bed late. During the night, I got up and went to the toilet, stepping on one, then the other. I was urinating when I saw something glitter on the outside of the bowl, down at the bottom. Standing nearby was the Cock, the tough guy of the jail, who had already been a prisoner for ten years and still had a couple of hundred to go.

"What's the gag?" I asked.

"Shut up, you son-of-a-whore, or you die," and he pulled his knife on me.

"Don't be a bastard, you can't scare me like that. What's it all about?"

"Shut up, Otelo! This is how we get out."

They had a pretty deep hole dug, deep enough for a fellow to get into. The glitter I had seen was a candle to light up down below.

"We're going to get out through here to the other side of the jail wall."

"Do you think you'll make it?"

"Just you help me stand them all off, and you'll see how we get out." He passed me his knife and pulled out another for himself. A guy called the Cover came out. He was a homosexual and was the one who had begun the hole. In the course of the digging, there were a number who helped . . . one digging, another collecting the dirt, another taking it out. We made mattresses and pillows out of it and covered it up so no one could see.

The gallery was washed every month and the bedding was taken out and deloused. There sure were bedbugs there! The "mayor" would come in with a bar and poke at the walls and the floor to see if there had been any digging. The day before it was our turn to wash the gallery, we went around with our hearts in our throats. We dug until five in the morning, because they woke us up at seven. By then, the majority of the prisoners in the gallery realized what was going on.

That morning, before seven, we sentenced each other to death by agreeing that anybody seen talking to a guard should be killed. What a day that was, with everybody looking this way and that. In the evening, we lined up to go back to the galleries and for some reason, we were left outside. We thought they had found out. My heart was beating like mad and the Cock was ready to kill the first guard who came near. But we had been delayed because they were fixing the lights in our gallery.

When they let us in, we immediately began to dig. We got below the wall and to the other side. The Cover was the first one to go through. *Huy!* we were all jubilant. The Cock said, "Watch it, Otelo, these guys will panic and everybody will want to go at the same time. This has to be done calmly so that no one gets wise." It was a hard job to calm them down, because each one wanted to be first.

There I was, saying, "O.K., go ahead. Next. Next." Then I said, "Nothing doing. You're not going to leave me behind. It's my turn now." We entered the hole, head first, face down, and arms forward, to be able to pass under the wall. I got in all right, but went with my arms down and got stuck midway. There I was, struggling, when I felt someone grab my foot. "*Ay*, dear God, they've found us out!" But no, it was a comrade who put his head against my feet and pushed up. I never knew who it was, but if it hadn't been for him, I would not have gotten out, nor would he.

On the other side, we were faced with a gigantic door. We fumbled with the lock, until an expert lockpicker among us opened it. We had agreed that we would walk out as if nothing was happening. But a lot of good it did. As soon as the door was open, it was as though they'd heard the starting bugle at the race track. They went out like a bunch of horses, and I wasn't far behind. The bombardment began when I was only two blocks away. What a racket they raised, shooting and blowing whistles. Then a bullet went by me. I said, "Now run, *compadres*, otherwise we're done for."

One prisoner shouted, "*Ay*, they've given it to me! They got me," and he fell. Me, the hero, I go back. It wasn't my intention to be a hero, but I went back to pick him up. "No, Otelo. Keep going. Don't be a jerk! I can't go any more." The bullet hit him in the back and that boy died in my arms. "Well, may you rest in peace and forgive me," and I took off again. The prisoner in front of me fell. I turned a corner and Moisés, the prison barber, grabbed me and put his scissors against my throat. "Wait up, Moisés," and I held his hand.

"*Ay,* Otelo. A bit more and I would have killed you. I thought you were a cop."

"No, *compadre,* let's get going."

We ran through the night, past the railroad tracks and to the mountains. That was our salvation. Up we went, with police and guards all over the place, and lights going from one side to another. We ran into a briar patch, *ay,* my God! did we get full of thorns! We had to get out on hands and knees, clearing a path with a stick. When we were through and way ahead, we stopped to pull the thorns out of one another.

We walked through the whole state of Veracruz, for several days and nights. It was the rainy season and there was a downpour, of the kind that only happens around there, really torrential. We gathered sugar-cane leaves to make raincoats, but they were of no use at all. So we curled up back to back, shivering with cold.

We kept from starving by eating fruit along the road. There were lots of mango trees, and bananas, *guayaba,* oranges, lemons, *malta,* all kinds of fruit. Moisés had four or five *pesos* on him and in the first town we hit, we bought a drink. After that, we walked day and night.

At the entrance of one town, we stopped to make ourselves some *huaraches* out of a strip of rubber tire. Our feet were swollen and bleeding, and were the part of us that had suffered most. I was sitting with my back to the town, and Moisés was facing it, so that he could see who was leaving and I could see who was coming in.

We were cutting the thongs when all at once Moisés said, "This is it, boy. Don't move or turn, but be ready for anything." He passed me his scissors and he held his razor, on guard, see? "It looks like they got us. Here come the police."

Out of the corner of my eye I could see two cops and two armed civilians coming. They passed right by, saying, "Good afternoon, *señores.*" We answered, "Good afternoon, *señores.*" "*Adiós . . . adiós.*" We lost sight of them around a curve in the road. A few minutes later, I heard the sound of a carbine being cocked.

"Be careful," I said. "They are going to ambush us. We'd better get out of here." As we started, we heard the first shot. But the shots weren't meant for us. The men were just target shooting at a tree. *Ay!*

How were we to know? My heart went back to its normal place, because, to tell the truth, I was really scared.

We walked all the way to Oaxaca, where Moisés had a friend whom he had once worked for. We found him shucking corn on a machine and he gave both of us jobs . . . and, what I liked more, plenty of food. I had shucked corn before, but there I learned to plant pineapple. I was soon planting eight hundred to a thousand plants a day and they paid nine *pesos* per thousand plants.

I meant to stay until I had enough money to go back to Mexico City, but it didn't work out like that, because of the heat and the mosquitoes. Those damned mosquitoes gave me such a beating that I had to surrender. I was like a cobblestone street, with bites all over my body. I just worked two weeks and then I said to myself, "It's time for you to go to Mexico City now, Roberto."

To do that, I went back to Veracruz. Well, when you drink you meet all kinds of people. Your tongue loosens with the ones you should least speak to. I was drinking with a boy I didn't know and we began to talk about our exploits. Since I was as much of an adventurer as he, and without money, he invited me to help him on a little job he was planning. He had studied the house and knew where the money was, and how to get in, and everything. All I had to do was follow instructions . . . he did the stealing, I was the lookout.

He got thirty thousand *pesos* in cash, some watches, some rings and a pistol. We divided it on the beach . . . my share was 14,700 . . . and then we each went our way. I heard later that they caught him and were looking for me because he sang to the police. I boarded a freighter which took me to Guatemala.

We arrived in Chetumal, on the border, and right off, I got a job on a coffee plantation. I worked during the day, and in the evenings I invited everyone I knew to go with me to the cabarets. For a month I went to bordellos and cabarets, treating half the world to drinks and women. And even though I always went to cabarets of the lowest category, I spent over a thousand *pesos* in one night. The women would charge fifty, one hundred, seventy-five *pesos*, and I treated everybody.

That was the way all my money went . . . well, not *my* money but the money I took from others. I've left thousands in places like that. I give you my word as a man and as a bum, that there have been some years in which I've thrown away fifteen or twenty thousand *pesos*.

When I was down to my last five thousand *pesos*, I took a boat back to Veracruz. I had my doubts about that old boat and, as a matter of fact, it sank a short time ago and there were several deaths. From Veracruz to Mexico City, the easiest way is by train. Although I was a magnate with plenty of money in my pocket, I went my usual way for only fifty *centavos.*

What I always do is buy a thirty-*centavo* ticket for the first-class bus to the train station. Then, I buy a platform ticket for twenty *centavos,* so that I can get in where the trains are. I board the train and mix with the passengers. Once the train starts, I know they will check the tickets, so I go to the door of the coach and get between the cars and climb up to the roof.

To avoid suffering from the cold I go along the roofs until I get to the locomotive, which has a warm ventilator on top. It is safe and no one bothers you. Ask the man who knows, right? But sometimes I travel underneath the freight trains. They have rods down below, especially made for tramps, if you know what I mean. With a board across the rods, you can travel comfortably. That was how I went back that time.

I arrived in Mexico City at about seven in the morning and spent the whole day in the house waiting for my *papá.* Manuel and my sisters kept asking me questions, but I didn't tell them anything until my father came home. He walked in, looking very serious.

"I'm back, *papá.*"

"When did you come?"

"Just today."

"How did you go free?"

"Well, they found out it wasn't my fault." I told a lie, see, because I was never able to talk frankly to my father. "They decided it wasn't my fault and they let me go."

"Let's see if you go to work now. You're a grown-up man and you have to work seriously, not just a month or two and then rest for three."

Unfortunately, that's the way I have been. I worked at a job until I had some money in my pocket, and then I quit. That time, I didn't even begin to look for work until I had spent my five thousand *pesos* with my friends. Then I went back to glass cutting, in a place that made fancy candelabras.

We did all the work by hand, cutting the crystal, shaping it and polishing. I was good enough to be a *maestro,* but I never wanted to be anything but a worker, so as not to be over people or to have responsibility. I just wanted to do what I was told and to have a definite salary per week, and that would be the end of it. One of the good things about being a humble worker is having a clear conscience, being able to eat and sleep in tranquillity, with no one and nothing to bother you and no reason to reproach yourself for your behavior. And perhaps, because one is humble, one doesn't get ambitious and covetous. One is satisfied with the hope that some day, through honest and productive labor, one can get out of the hole one is in.

It might have been possible to have started my own business and to improve economically, but by the time I got around to thinking of it, fine candelabra work had declined and the things were being mass produced. Besides, I lost my job because I got into a fight.

I was pretty drunk the day of the fight because it was the New Year. I don't care for alcoholic drinks; whatever I drink, I don't like, but there I am, hoisting them. Don't ask! I have drunk everything. Well, from time immemorial, there has been a feud between the boys of the Casa Grande and the guys from the Street of the Bakers. When the fight broke out, three of them ganged up on me. I was putting up a good struggle when somebody slugged me from behind, one of the worst blows I'd ever gotten. I fell and got kicked in the ribs and legs. No matter how much I tried, I couldn't defend myself.

What made me madder than anything was that my whole gang saw what was going on, and left me there to die. It is not an obligation, but lots of times I have mixed into fights to defend them. But not those guys! I was beaten up so badly in front of the boys and girls of the *vecindad*, that I couldn't get over the shame of it. And by guys who were not known to be fighters!

Those boys were terribly worried, as they knew I always took revenge. Why, once I looked for a guy six months because he punched me when I was too drunk to fight back. He hid and sent his wife and mother-in-law to see where I was before he would step out of the house. He missed more than one day of work because I was waiting for him on the street corner. I had almost forgotten about him, when I met him at a saint's day *fiesta*. When José saw me, he hugged the wall, trying to hide in a corner. Later he told me, "Ay, *Negrito*, when I saw you come in, I tell you man-to-man, they shrank up on me!"

He swore that if he had known who I was, he never would have dared punch me. To show me how sorry he was, he offered me a

Johnson lighter his wife had given him on his Saint's Day. Then his wife and her whole family, people I have known since I was a kid, came and talked to me, and the upshot of it was that we were soon drinking beer with our arms around each other.

But it didn't work out that way with the boys from the Street of the Bakers. After they had beaten me up, I didn't drink anything but Alka-Seltzers and went to bed for a week to recover my strength so I could call them to account. Well, I did, and one of them got cut with my knife. It was an accident, because it really didn't call for anything as drastic as that. It was just a scratch, but it was more the fuss he made. His whole family came at me and called the police.

Never in my life have I turned my back to an enemy but since I had had experience with the police, I took it on the lam. I thought, "Fights are also won by running." That time I ended up in Texas, where I spent a few weeks.

By the time I learned that Antonia, my great love, was living with Francisco and had two kids with him, I didn't care any more. My feeling for her had calmed down, though when I saw her at the Casa Grande once in a while, it still gave me great pleasure. Francisco was a no-good character who ran around with other women and who didn't even give her daily expense money. My sister deserved something better.

But what hurt my soul and heart was to learn that Consuelo had taken a misstep and had left home. I had four sisters and not one of them has given me the joy and honor of seeing her married in a white dress. It is true that my father threw Consuelo out of the house, but my sister was intelligent enough to know that, as a woman, she should never have used that as an excuse to go off with . . . what's-his-name. She wasn't the only one my father had thrown out, because he did it to me, and especially to Manuel. But being a woman, she should have borne more and spoken to my father in a nice way, more like to a friend than to a father, and I believe he would have listened to her. So she had no right to blame him for what happened to her.

That was another search for me . . . I looked for Consuelo and Mario everywhere. I even went to the airport where they said he worked. God be blessed that I didn't find him, because I would have dragged him from the airport to my father's house, to account for his actions. Later, when it was all over, Consuelo told me she didn't love him but had gone out of desperation. "*Ay*, brother," she said, "without doubt I treated the poor skinny little thing badly. I put on my dramatics for him all the time, and I realize I was unjust to him."

Really, my sister is very honest, because she admits her faults, though a bit late. Think of it! I didn't know about that drunk, Jaime, being her *novio*, until after she went with Mario, who was the better of the two. He even left a good job and all his things, because of my sister. I believe if they had continued together, they would have amounted to something.

Marta had had a fight with Consuelo and had gone off to Acapulco with a man, Baltasar, who, you might say, was my new brother-in-law. I didn't know about this until my return home, when we received a letter from her. As soon as my father knew Marta's address, he sent me to Acapulco with some of her things. That time I went as a paying passenger because I carried a large tub full of dishes and clothing. I left on the night bus and arrived there in the morning.

With the tub in a cart, I started up the hill to the street where my sister lived. There she was, coming down, carrying her market basket. I was about to whistle, but no sooner did I take a deep breath when I noticed that she was pregnant. All the air went out of me and I just stood there. But I was so glad to see my little sister again that nothing else mattered.

"Sis, how are you?"

"My little brother! What a miracle! When did you come?"

We greeted each other and she took me home to meet Baltasar.

Frankly, he looked lousy to me. He resembled the many people I have had to fight with. He didn't look exactly fierce, but rather aggressive and ready for any contingency that might come up between us. He was barefoot and his shirt was open to show his chest. He had a small gold earring in one ear lobe, which must have caused him a lot of trouble with Mexican men. He explained that he wore it because of a vow he had made to the Virgin.

Baltasar's shack had a dirt floor, a tin roof and walls loosely made of boards. The kitchen was smaller than a closet and the kerosene stove was very dirty. Everything really looked very poor.

Well, I asked Baltasar for an accounting and he explained that he had known my sister in Mexico City, where he worked in a bakery, and that he knew about her daughters when he asked her to go with him to Acapulco. He had told Marta to write to my father but she wouldn't until a month had passed, because she was afraid we, her brothers, would go after Baltasar with knives.

"No," I said, "you have nothing to worry about. I am not a knifer, but any brother would get angry at this, don't you think?"

When I heard Baltasar was a butcher, I thought to myself, "Ah, you bastard, I did well to bring my knife." I hadn't come looking for a fight, but I was armed and ready to measure him with the same stick he measured me. He was peaceful and so I was, too. He told me about his family . . . a big family, with two mothers and two fathers, but he didn't have much to do with them. He said, "I don't want to bother my people. After all, they give me nothing and I have nothing to give them."

My sister and her children seemed calm and content there with Baltasar. Though he drank, Marta was sure of daily expense money because he sent her to collect his pay, and every day he brought home meat from the slaughterhouse. Marta took care of the money and it was something new for me to see a Mexican asking his wife for bus fare, or for *centavos* for a smoke or a drink. But at the same time, I realized it was a good thing.

Above all, I had to admit that Baltasar had shown nobility in accepting Marta with three children, though I believed I was capable of doing the same thing. It would have been absolutely nothing for me to support a wife and children in the style he did. I was not afraid of women or of marriage, but I didn't feel like tying myself down.

My family kept telling me I ought to get married, but I knew that I was a first-class avoider of obligations and that I wouldn't make a woman happy. I wasn't enough of a beast to make a woman live with me, nor had I met a woman worthy of marrying. If I had been a heel, I could have had the use of two or three young ladies, but I never did anything to them, or even with my *novias*. I've been only with prostitutes, also with two or three married women who were separated from their husbands. They satisfied my sexual desires. I've never had any children, not that I know about, because I picked only sterile women.

I've been a mean sort of fellow, but when it came to love, I've always been a man. Like we say here, I've always been able to give them a good hard screw, although they would sometimes wear me out. I'm an ugly fellow, but women preferred me. I've made two or three girls unhappy, but I preferred to wound them with a disappointment than to be hurting them all their lives. I don't like to hurt anybody in these matters because I couldn't take it when it was done to me.

If there was one thing I hated, it was for *novios* to be deceiving each other. Look at the contradiction! I was a first-class liar and when it came to doing the wrong thing there was no one who could beat me. I've been a bad egg, a hopeless case, and nothing good had come out of me. Well, that was not altogether true because if I had been 100 percent bad, why, man alive, it would have been better for them to shoot me. That type of person simply does not deserve to live. Yet, when it came to love, I just couldn't bear to deceive or to be deceived. And love was the thing where lies and deceit were most used.

Well, Baltasar and I got along very well together. He called me "*tu*" right off, and that made me feel more relaxed with him. He devoted himself to showing me around Acapulco. I accompanied him to the slaughterhouse, to the movies and to the *cantinas*. In fact, he made me go wherever he went.

One evening, I wanted a beer. "But let's go where we can dance or where there is a *sinfonola,* because I don't like a place that resembles a morgue."

"Well," he said, "then let's go to the 'zone' where my sister works."

"Your sister? And just what is your sister?" The "zone" was where all the prostitutes were, and I was full of curiosity about this. How was it possible that . . . ?

"Come, you'll see. Calm down, we're almost there. Marta knows that I have a sister working here. Luisa is one of the finest whores around, but I don't see her often."

Well, we arrived and Luisa looked just right for that place. That is, her body was not very deformed, let us say. She sat with us and we drank many beers. I had to pay for it all, including the extra charge Luisa made for her company. Baltasar bawled her out for charging to drink with her brother and brother-in-law. So she said, "No, brother, you should understand that this is my business . . . if you don't want me to work in a place like this, then pay to get me out!" Anyway, I handed over the money and we left.

I didn't remain in Acapulco more than three days on my first visit because I felt uncomfortable eating off them. Besides, I was working in a factory at home and I wanted to get back before I lost my job. So I said good-bye and went to Mexico City.

It was the best factory job I had ever had and I really liked it. They paid me twelve *pesos* a day for eight hours of work and gave us three days vacation a year. There were about four hundred men working there and we were all forced to join the CTM. I had never been in a union before and I must say that it was a terrific mockery. I was never called to a single meeting and I didn't even know where the headquarters were. They didn't bother to tell us that, but they never forgot to deduct our five *pesos* dues every month.

And politics is another gigantic farce, because millions of *pesos* are dancing around in it . . . millions for this public work and millions for that, but it is only a front to hide the millions which go into the pockets of the bureaucrats. I don't understand politics, but all this business of campaigns and elections is such a farce that I don't know why the people of Mexico are accepting it. Here the elections are not free because they know beforehand who is going to be the President.

I don't claim to know much about freedom, except that I have been free all my life and have done what I always felt like doing. But when I was working in the factory I was no longer free because they forced me to register to vote, and they sent around circulars telling us we must vote for the government party. The vote is secret but they threatened us with a three-day no-work punishment if we didn't vote their way. For me this is no longer the principle of free elections. It is anti-constitutional, but that is nothing to be surprised at any more. Frankly, I don't care which candidate gets in, because either one of them will rob the people.

The year I worked in the factory I was in only three fights. The environment we live in demands fighting. I don't want to leave here unless I am carried out on their shoulders. That's the way heroes and corpses go out.

The first fight was over a poker game between me and three boys from the Street of the Tinsmiths. All of us were half drunk, especially Roberto, because liquor had a strong effect on me. I felt great about that fight. I knocked down one after another, until they stopped. The four of us remained good pals. That's the way it used to be here, but now these rules have degenerated.

In the second fight, I was attacked by a gang one night while I was walking with a friend, Miguel, near the market. Miguel ran away and left me to be beaten up by five fellows. I had been drinking and couldn't defend myself well. They cut my head and raised my eye to the size of a tomato. My lip was hanging down because of a cut that took six stitches. I hadn't looked for that fight, but I got a bawling out from my father and from Manuel anyway.

The third fight was the worst. I didn't go looking for that fight either, but they forced me. I was having a friendly discussion about a boxing match with a couple of fellows. Three cops came along and told us to move on.

I said, "Can't a fellow have a chat on the street without anybody stopping him? This is a free country."

"No, it's not a free country," says this wise guy. "Move on, you bums, and make it snappy."

"All right, don't push me, I can walk."

Then they tried to put the bite on me for twenty-five *pesos*, and I didn't give it to them, see? I had twenty-nine *pesos* on me, and I gave them to a friend of mine.

"Here," I said, "please take this money because it seems these gentlemen want to rob me."

"Shut up!" and bang! one of the cops hit me with his stick, one of those billies made of hard rubber. When they hit you, you don't bleed but they almost knock you out. All the bleeding is inside. I got sore, really mad, and took a swing at him. Then they began clubbing me and punching me, clubbing and punching, back and forth, like a ball. They also kicked me, until everybody thought they had killed me. They injured my ribs and my head, and gave me such an awful kick that they wrenched my knee. And then they broke my leg bone.

By that time, the neighbors had notified my family, and Consuelo and Manuel came out and argued with the cops. All the while, the fellows and neighbors shouted to the cops to leave me alone, but none of them mixed in, not one of them. Two or three times my friends have disappointed me. When I see one of them in trouble, even if he had turned his back on me before, I go all out to help him. But they only looked on. Oh, well . . .

The cops didn't arrest me, they just left me there on the ground. My brother and sister took me in a cab to the station house to file a complaint, but nothing happened to those cops. So you can see what I think of justice here. Hand them a *peso* and you get justice.

It took me a long time to recover from that beating. The wind was taken out of me and I have really tried to avoid trouble and fights since then. Many people judge a man by the way he fights. They see him pull a pistol or a knife and they say, "Ah! there's a man for you. He doesn't back down for anything or anybody." I don't judge a man like that. The real man is the one who faces up to life with integrity, the one who faces reality without retreating. I judge a man by his deeds. If he can face up to life and to his obligations, then for me he is a man; in a word, a real man is a man like my father.

And to my way of thinking, a man who only produces children without accepting the obligations that go with them, doesn't deserve to live. That god-damned son-of-a-whore Crispín is that type. He has forgotten all about his daughters and sends them a present only once a year. It's better for him not to come to the house, because the day he does, I don't know which of us will come out alive.

I'm sorry to have to say it, but my brother has shown a lack of responsibility in this respect, though he did his best to get ahead and to provide his children with at least the necessities of life. My father has set him a good example, so I don't understand why Manuel neglected his children. It seems to me that my brother's life has been a pity and a failure. He had more education than I, and more intelligence even than Consuelo. And he had fame as a storyteller . . . . a party without him was no fun . . . but, in spite of all this, he wasted many years of his life. I haven't done much for my family either, though I'm ready to give every drop of my blood for Consuelo, Marta, Manuel, my father, and for my nephews and nieces.

My family is uppermost in my mind. My biggest ambition in life is to improve their economic situation, if I can do it honestly. I've never been concerned with having a better life for myself, but only for them. It has been my greatest desire that we should be united. But when my mother died, our castle crumbled, its foundations fell and sank into the ground.

When Manuel's wife died, Delila came to take care of the children. My father seemed very happy with her and she and I got along better than I did with my other stepmother, Elena. There is a monument to Delila here in my heart for her noble work in taking care of my nieces and nephews. None of us, not even Manuel, the father of these children, did as much. I esteemed and loved her for it, and that is why I regretted what happened between us. I didn't want to hit her, but she made me do it. And I believe she did it intentionally.

One evening, I was having a beer with my friend Daniel, when my nephew Domingo came crying. "What happened, son?" I asked. Geofredo, Delila's son, had knocked him down. This had happened many times and I had never said anything, though it always made me angry. I went to make a complaint to Delila, and then I gave my nephew some advice. "Don't be a fool, son. I have already told you not to give in to anyone."

"Yes," said Delila, "go on, tell him to grab a knife and stick it into Geofredo's guts. You are always teaching him to fight and to give it to the other fellow."

It was true I had taught my nephews something about personal defense, but only with the hands, with clean fists, the way any man must learn. This time I told Domingo not to speak to Geofredo or to play with him. Delila was listening and finally she said, "I've had enough of your frigging around. What's bothering you? Let's come out with it . . . are you fighting me because I am with your father?"

"Listen, Delila, why bring up things that have nothing to do with the case? We were talking about the kids."

She went on. "Well, if you don't like me being with your father, why don't you give him what I give him!" Those were very strong words for me and I warned her, "You'd better shut up or it will go badly for you."

"It won't go badly for me! Who do you think you are? For me, you are only a pitiful jerk!"

That's when I punched her and she jumped on me. She was quite a fighter and I had to give her four or five punches. I held back because, first, she was a woman, and second, she was pregnant, and third, she was my father's wife. She scratched my face and hands and I had to grab her. At one time, she fell and pulled me down on top of her. I would have fallen on her stomach but I stopped in time, kneeling over her and holding her hands. The children ran to the café to call Manuel.

When he arrived I had calmed down a bit, but then Delila told him I had come in drunk on marijuana and that I had pulled her by the hair into the courtyard and had locked her out. That was a big lie because I had pulled her out by her hands. Manuel didn't ask me for my side of the story but began to bawl me out and insult me. That hurt because I was only trying to defend his children, and he should have been a little less righteous.

I didn't wait for my father to come home. I went to Ramón's to get some money and took off for Acapulco.

Marta and Baltasar had invited me to come back to visit them, though I don't think they expected me so soon. Again, I noticed that

Baltasar took me wherever he went. "Come on, let's go," he always said when he had to go out. It seemed quite natural to me and I went along in good faith. It wasn't until much later that I realized my brother-in-law was jealous of me and didn't trust me with my own sister.

This time I looked for a job. Baltasar kept saying he would speak to this one and to that one, but I don't believe he ever did. I might have gotten a truck-driver's job, if I had had a driver's license. I still don't have a license, because of my history. I'll have to save up five hundred *pesos* to buy back my prison record and destroy it, before I can apply for a license. Here, with money you can do anything!

If I had a driver's license, I could laugh at the world. Ever since I learned how to drive, I felt I wanted something more out of life. I wanted to do anything that involved cars, like the automobile business, or a parking lot, or being a chauffeur. If I could go to a training school, I would study to be a first-class auto mechanic.

I almost got hooked up with a girl there in Acapulco. Rather, she was a married woman, married in church and all, and with a child, and a husband, but she was so young and pretty, that I liked her right away. She was very friendly and one day I asked her, in a joke, whether she would like to go to Mexico City with me. She said yes, anytime I was ready, just like that! And we weren't even *novios* yet! Although she opened the way, I never dared to make love to her, because, first, my sister was around, and second, this girl was married in church. If she had been married only by civil law, well, it would have been different.

Baltasar offered me another sister of his. He said, "She is as dark as you but she really is a pretty chick. You saw how Luisa was? Well, this one is younger and even better. Arrange your driver's license and settle down in Acapulco. It's not necessary to marry here. If you don't want my sister, I'll get Melania for you!" I never did go to see his sister, but as a joke, I sometimes called Baltasar my twice-brother-in-law.

I never thought Baltasar was a bad fellow, but he had lived as much as I, and between two sharp adventurers, there is little trust. My sister Marta would always be an impassable wall between us. You can imagine how I felt when he told me he had had thirty women, some of them the mothers of his children. And sure enough, we met one of his ex-wives in the street. She stopped him and said, "Listen, half-pint, how about getting me some fresh tripe?" And we passed a couple of his kids playing in the street.

He said Marta knew all this and accepted it, but from that time on I didn't like Baltasar. I didn't trust him. He might do to Marta what he did to all those other women. I never said anything to him or to my sister, because I might have put my foot into it.

I stayed on for a few days, or perhaps it was a few weeks, but Mexico City had a powerful hold on me, and I wanted to go back. I missed my neighborhood, in spite of the fact that it had deteriorated and become more corrupt. But I still felt like somebody there and had the people's respect, which I had bought with my fists. And because my mother had died there, I had a special feeling for the place. I, too, will die there some day, perhaps tomorrow, for I will never abandon it.

So after a while I said to Marta, "Do you know what, sister? I'm going home."

"What are you going back for?" she said. "You fought with Delila and don't expect my *papá* to receive you well. You know how he is."

"Well, yes, sis, from the moment I first punched her I've regretted it. But what do you want? The thing is done and there is no help for it. I'm going only to look around. I'll come back soon, I promise you by God."

She tried to discourage me, but when the travel bug entered me I got stubborn. There wasn't a person who could stop me. Marta was used to my character and to my desperate ways, so she loaned me a *peso* to get out to the highway, where I hitched a ride to the capital.

I arrived without a *centavo*, so I went to Ramón's. I never go to Ramón for money unless I'm down and out and desperate, because he doesn't just do you a favor, you have to work for it. That man always had the advantage over people like me, those of us who have lifted things. He was vengeful that way and used us. He had thousands of *pesos*, which I helped him get, but when I come to him for a loan he says he can't spare any. But if I would like to earn some . . . he usually had a soft job for me, like delivering a "hot" scale or picking up a "crooked" radio . . . or stealing something he had a customer for. All I usually asked for was a loan of twenty *pesos,* but the favor he wanted might have landed me in jail!

When I got back from Acapulco, Ramón's son, who followed in his father's path, said, "Listen, Roberto, I need some car-radio antennas, because a customer wants a few."

I thought it over and said, "Well, I must have some money, so lend me a bicycle to ride over to Lomas and I'll see how many I can find." It was an easy job, but I had bad luck with the very first one I tried to pull off a car. It wouldn't come loose and I pulled this way and that; before it came off I had lost a slice of flesh from my finger.

"Cursed luck of mine! To spill blood for kid stuff like this!" I was angry with myself. I rode back quickly, delivered the antenna and received ten lousy *pesos* for it.

My finger was wrapped in a piece of newspaper I had picked up in the street, but the cut continued to bleed. I went to my aunt, who washed it with boiled water and peroxide, and bandaged it. I was staying with her, for my father was still angry with me and didn't want me to set foot in his house. He had told my brother that what I had done to Delila was unpardonable and that he never wanted to see me again. My father was my world, and when they told me what he said, my world fell.

The next day, on June 25, 1958, a girl named Antonia (not my half-sister) came to visit my aunt. I had known this Antonia for years. She had lived with her mother and brothers in the worst "Lost City" in the neighborhood. As a matter of fact, I didn't remember until later that I had never liked this girl's manner. She was one of those who stood on the street corner talking to the boys in a loud, familiar way. It certainly never occurred to me then that she would ever become my woman.

It was early in the morning when Antonia arrived, and her hair was still uncombed and her dress dirty. I have never liked a sloppy woman, but something about her, I don't know exactly what, attracted me. Apart from physical desire, the thing I liked was her attentiveness. My aunt introduced us, and, right off, Antonia told me she had good hands for curing and that in no time she would have my finger fixed up.

So there she was curing me, holding my hand in hers, and asking me if I had a wife. Then she began to complain of her husband. "He leads me a dog's life," she said.

"But why?" It was the first time I had heard a woman complain like that.

"Ah, but it is because we live with my mother-in-law and everything I do is bad. He doesn't give me more than two or three *pesos* a day and demands good meals. I'm fed up. I guess I'll have to leave him."

Qué caray! She kept on that way, and the idea immediately occurred to me that I might be this girl's rescuing angel. I thought, "Poor girl! She suffers so much with that so-and-so and his family." My aunt backed up her story. And she wasn't bad-looking either, though a bit fat. That afternoon, Antonia sent me some *tamales* she had made . . . then she was asking my aunt how I liked my hamburgers and, sure enough, the next noon, there were hamburgers waiting for me.

Believe me, after that it was not so much selfish desire as compassion, that I felt for her. My feeling had turned into something nobler, for I wanted to help her. Since she had already left her husband and was living with her mother, I planned to propose that I give her daily expense money, in exchange for her taking care of me . . . with the understanding that we would marry if we got along well. Once I had made my decision, I went on a big drinking spree to celebrate with my friends.

Antonia didn't mind seeing me drunk, and even asked me to treat her to a beer. We sat at a table with her friends and I hugged and kissed her, right there in front of everyone. She agreed to go to the movies with me the next day.

I had to do another little favor for Ramón to get money for my date, but when I met Antonia, she said, "No, I don't like the movies. Better let us take a bus and get off somewhere." I was a bit slow, although I did suspect something. I realized what her goal was . . . that she was acceding to me in a nice way, right?

Well, we ended up in a hotel and I spent the most marvelous night of my life. No sooner were we alone, when she threw herself on the bed and pulled me with her. "Let's get to work," she said. I undressed her and, well, we enjoyed ourselves.

I took her to live at my aunt Guadalupe's house. We slept on a mat on the floor and were well off because all I had to do was pay for our own food. Antonia didn't go out at all the first few days, but I had lost my factory job and had to hurry each morning to look for small piecework jobs at the glass shops. When I couldn't earn any money that way, I usually counted on making ten or fifteen *pesos* by helping Manuel sell at the market. But there were days when I could give Antonia only two or three *pesos* for food. I would tell her I had eaten when I really hadn't, so that she would have enough.

The very first morning Antonia and I went out of the house together, there was her ex-husband, Cándido, across the street, talking to a couple of his cronies. He must have known what he was up to and I'm sure it cost him plenty for their help because the people who lived in the *vecindad* opposite my aunt's were all crooks, the flower of the underworld, some of whom I had seen in the Penitentiary. I expected trouble with Cándido, especially if he turned out to be a man with hair on his chest, because I had taken away his woman. I always carried a knife in my belt, and kept the lower part of my shirt unbuttoned so that I could grab the weapon quickly if Cándido and his friends ganged up on me. I was careful to stay sober, but that was easy because since I had Antonia I had no desire to drink or steal or fight. I wanted only to be left alone.

When I saw Cándido watching us, my blood went to my feet. I thought, "Now some throats are going to be cut." But that time he just looked at us and went on talking to his companions. The next few days I borrowed money so that Antonia and I could sleep at hotels in other neighborhoods, but seven *pesos* a day for a room was a lot and we had to go back to my aunt's.

We had other difficulties in that *vecindad*. There was a neighbor, a tigress by the name of Julia, who would insult me whenever she saw me because once when I was drunk, I had taken one of her husband's bicycles and had lost it. She would yell, "Yes, look at the crooked bastard! He should be ashamed not to pay for Guillermo's bicycle, the stinking son of his fucking mother!" And to Antonia, she was even worse. "Ay, there goes the horny beggar. The slut doesn't mind whom she sleeps with, any man will do!"

If Julia had not been a woman, of course I could have shut her up. But she was my aunt's *comadre* and one-time sister-in-law, and so Antonia and I would just keep walking without paying attention to her. Later, I told Guillermo privately that any time he wanted me to, I could go out and get him a better bicycle than the one I lost. The only hitch was, he would have to change the numbers and arrange the papers so it would all look legal. Guillermo and I got along well together, but his wife was a hellion who made my life miserable.

Cándido kept on hanging around across the street. It seemed he didn't have balls enough to speak to me or face me alone. He always had two or three of those thieving "rabbits" with him. Once, Antonia and I were walking arm in arm near the railroad tracks, when he came along with two of his "rabbits" and told Antonia he wanted to speak to her. The other two, whom I knew, were a bit drunk. One of them shouted, "Wait, *Negro*, just let us give that lousy whore what she deserves. She is a slut and a filthy bitch. She took you in, you pimp, and we'll give it to you, too."

When I heard the way they spoke, I insulted their mothers in language they could understand. "You sons-of-bitches! Just form a line so I can take you on one by one. Don't gang up on me because I've got enough for all of you!"

I was ready to fight but Antonia got between us and wouldn't let me. Then I told her to speak to Cándido for the last time, to see what he had to say. She went off with him and I waited on the corner, with my back to the wall, so they couldn't attack me from the sides or from behind. She didn't return and I got tired of waiting so I went to the market and helped Manuel sell a pile of used shirts he had bought from a laundry.

That night, Antonia didn't come home, but went to her mother's house. I refused to go after her, not because I was afraid but because I understood that, after all, the girl had her husband and I didn't have the right to interfere in her life. It was the first time we had separated. I tried not to see her again but she came looking for me and even cried. When I saw that, I said, "Good!" and I took her back. My father and Delila had moved out of the Casa Grande and only Manuel and his new wife, María, were living there, so I spoke to my father and he finally agreed to let me live there too, with Antonia.

In those days, in spite of difficulties with my wife, I was very happy. After having gone through so many calamities, it was a beautiful and pleasurable thing for me to be in love. When you get to love someone and it is returned, man! it is great, something sublime. I looked at everything differently, even the most insignificant details took on another aspect. Love is really life itself, that is, you feel as though you have reached the true goal of life. Love signifies God, goodness, understanding. Understanding for the other person helps spiritually and sometimes even materially. *Vaya!* That was what happened to me. But I had illusions, then, that Antonia would get to love me as much as I loved her, or more.

I worked with more gusto and my friends were surprised when I turned down their invitations to drink. From work, I went home and didn't go out again. I spent the evenings making plans with Antonia. First, I would get a steady job, then a room of our own, and a bed and, little by little, the things we needed. If all went well, we would have a

civil marriage and, later, a church wedding. Think of it! I was planning to have her marry in a white dress!

At first, Antonia behaved very well. She stayed at home all day
and didn't complain of a thing. Manuel and María slept on a mattress
on the floor on one side of the room and we slept on burlap bags on
the other side. Manuel accepted my wife all right, though I don't
believe he really got to know her. Antonia and María were friendly
and went everywhere together. I didn't like that at all. A married
woman should not go out with a companion; for good or bad, I wanted
my wife to be alone.

But one morning she went out alone without my permission and
didn't return until late that night. She had told María she was going
to a *fiesta* at a friend's house. I was indignant and hurt because she
hadn't even mentioned it to me. Right away I suspected the worst.
When she got back, I had to punish her. I hit her hard with my belt
and told her to take her things and get out.

"I don't like this kind of life," I said. "You want to enjoy yourself
in your own way, to be free. You want a husband but you don't want
to be tied down to a home and to a man. You just use me as a screen.
You are making a fool of me before everyone, so it is better for you to
go free. Take your things and get out."

She cried and had a temper tantrum and said she didn't want to
continue with me anyway because I was too jealous.

"Look, Antonia, it is true that I am jealous, so why don't you help
me get over it? Instead, you give me more reason for jealousy. Even
when we are in the street together, you keep turning your head from
one side to the other. Do you notice how bad that makes me feel? I
love you with all my soul. I don't just love you, I idolize you. Never
in my life has a woman penetrated my heart so deeply. That's why,
please, try to avoid doing these things."

But she didn't want to listen and put her things into a flour sack
and left. I didn't see her for a long time and I began to drink again.
When I was good and drunk, I would go to visit my mother-in-law,
to find out if they had any news of Antonia, for she had disappeared.
I looked for her everywhere, day and night. I asked about her, but no
one could tell me a thing.

One day, I met her with Cándido at the entrance to her mother's
vecindad. We had a few sharp words and then I said, "Antonia, tell
me the truth. Are you going with this bastard again?"

"Yes," she said, and moved closer to him. *Ay!* it is painful to recall! She was on his side and it gave me such a terrible feeling, not of anger but of grief. I realized I would be acting the fool if I fought for her, so I went in to speak to her mother, who tried to comfort me. My mother-in-law had always favored me. She was a fine woman whom Antonia didn't know enough to esteem. I think Antonia went wrong because her mother had to go out to work and couldn't watch over her properly.

After that, I went to see my mother-in-law every evening. If Antonia was at home, we would talk and quarrel about our problems. I still considered her my wife and once in a while I would take her to a hotel for some "chocolate."

My sister Consuelo had her own little apartment then, with a kitchen and bath. She had bought a wardrobe and a sofa and with all that it seemed to me she was high aristocracy. She kept telling me to come with Antonia to live with her. She thought we could start over again together that way. Antonia was willing but I didn't like the idea.

"Look, sister," I said, "not with you. With your character I know that one day it will turn out bad for us. You better live in peace and let me set up a home of my own for Antonia when I can, so that I will feel like a man. I want a place where I am the boss, where I can say what I please, and where only my chewing can be heard!"

But Consuelo kept urging me. "Don't be a fool, brother. I am offering you a real opportunity. Take advantage of it. You won't be living off me, because once you get a job you will have to help me pay the rent. You'll see. Antonia will be very satisfied because I go out to work and you will too, and she'll have the house to herself."

One evening, I found Antonia embroidering a pair of pillowcases, which she said were for me. On one was written, "I love you," and on the other, "For you, my love."

"*Ay, caramba!* For me? That's wonderful."

She said she had broken with Cándido, and wanted to live with me again.

"Yes, Roberto," she said. "I have thought it over. I want a man who will set up a home for me alone, where I can say what I please and where no one interferes in my life."

"But, Antonia, that is what I am trying to do. Just give me a chance to find a job and you will see. It won't have luxuries or riches, but it will be a home for you, where we will get along as best we can."

It was then that I spoke to Consuelo about moving in with her. "Yes, of course, brother," she said, and we did, although I still expected that one day the Sánchez in her would go to my sister's head and she would get fed up with us.

For a few months, everything was fine. But I wasn't working much and my sister was paying all the rent and lending me money for our daily expenses. From the start, I had wanted Antonia and me to sleep on the floor so my sister could have the bed, but she wouldn't hear of it. Some nights she slept on the little sofa and let us have the bed, but other nights, when she felt she needed a good rest, I had to sleep on the sofa and she slept with my wife.

I had to scold Antonia for not being cleaner, for leaving dirty clothes soaking in the tub, for yelling at my nieces and nephews. Then she began to go out without permission and when I hit her for it, my sister came and *huy!* the world fell down on my head! Both women let me have it.

The next day, when I came home from my new job in a warehouse, Antonia was gone. Again, I went out to look for her. Sometimes at ten or eleven o'clock at night I would begin to make the rounds. More than once, I stood on street corners until three in the morning to catch her. My mother-in-law didn't know where she was any more than I did and went to a spiritualist to try to bring her back. Antonia's mother was very angry and swore that if Antonia didn't go back to me she would disown her.

I got drunk almost every night and was beaten up twice by gangs who took advantage of my condition. I heard that Antonia was living with Cándido and in my grief and rage I hunted him, with my knife in my belt. I wanted to meet the bastard in a man-to-man fight, once and for all. But he kept out of my way, for I could never find him.

Then, one day, from the bus, I saw the two of them walking together. I saw her smile at him and, I don't know what happened to me, but at that moment, I let her go. "From here on, for me Antonia is dead," I said to myself. I got so drunk that just remembering it makes me feel drunk again. I got hold of hundreds of *pesos* and spent them all. My pain was too great and everything went in one big drunk.

I realized that Antonia wasn't worth a cumin seed. She had no feeling, no heart, not a spark of nobility. Nothing mattered to her, not even herself. I saw the kind of person she was almost from the start, but I overlooked it because I loved her. It took me six months and a couple of other girls to get me over that hurt!

When it comes to love, I don't understand my own actions. In the land of Cupid, there isn't a person who can control his impulses. One can impose one's will in the world of sinners and have command over the whole universe, but not over one's heart. The things that happen, have to happen, because they are predestined. They are already written somewhere up above and even though there are seers and prophets in the world I don't believe they or anyone else can know what will happen tomorrow. We cannot determine when we will be born or when we will die. It is all arranged beforehand. That's why I say I believe in destiny. Early or late, that which must happen, will happen. That's the way the world is.

Consuelo

In MONTERREY I REALLY GAVE MYSELF, BODY AND SOUL, TO MARIO, OR rather, body only, for I didn't love him. You might even say I hated him. I treated him badly and looked upon him as I would an enemy, in spite of the fact that he was good to me. All the time we were on the train, I was tortured by the thought that once we arrived and were alone in a room, many kilometers from my house, with nobody I knew around, I would have to be his. He had made me promise. I behaved coldly to him after that and could only think that this time I had no way out.

We moved into a boarding house the very first day. I was afraid of the night coming, when we would have to go to sleep. He had waited for this moment for a long time. In his *mamá's* house it hadn't been possible, because she had separated us immediately. At my aunt's, there was even less possibility, because the room was too small for him to try anything.

I managed to put him off the first two nights. By the third night, he couldn't take it any more. He began very lovingly, *"Mi vida,* finally we are going to be husband and wife." I felt my stomach turn with fear, and said, "Oh, stop bothering me!"

But he continued his attack. He caressed my shoulders and my hair. He kissed my face and spoke sweet words to me. I was sweating, thinking of the moment when I would have to give myself. I was wishing someone would come and save me. I threw his hands off me and told him to leave me alone. He reminded me that I had given my word. My conscience bothered me and without saying anything, I let him kiss and embrace me.

But when I was finally his, it was too much for me. I didn't hold back and pushed him off, giving him a kick in the chest at the same time. He groaned and caught his breath. Then he started to speak to me, calmly, and little by little, won me over again. I regretted having treated him the way I had and asked his pardon. He kissed my forehead and turned away from me. I remained looking at his white young back and black, wavy hair. I thought the struggle for that night was over and I went to sleep.

But toward morning he began to caress me again. I awoke in desperation and fought with him but again he broke my resistance with loving words. Mario consummated his act. He tried to hurt me as little as possible but I couldn't stand it. I wanted it to be over that instant, that whatever had to happen should happen and that I be left in peace. Finally, Mario was left almost in a faint, sweating, the poor thing. I turned around with my back to him and burst into tears.

"But, Skinny, what did you think marriage was? Don't be silly. I love you, Consuelo, believe me. I'll never leave you. Don't cry, don't cry."

But I paid no attention to him. I was thinking, "That's it! Now I'm ruined forever. Now I am no longer a *señorita* and all on account of that daughter-of-a——, Delila. But my father is to blame. Because of her, my father threw me out of the house . . . "If you only knew what you have done, Father! You are the one responsible for what happens to me from now on!" I continued to cry bitterly. I imagined my *papá* saw me crying and suffered also. He begged my pardon. But there was nothing to be done any more. Mario consoled me but I wanted to push him away. Finally, I took refuge in his arms and fell asleep like that.

The next day I didn't want to look him in the face. When he came home from work, he embraced me and didn't mention what had happened the night before. I knew exactly what his intentions were and I rejected him. He didn't achieve his purpose that night. We really had contact only a few times, he and I. I always refused. When he came close to me, asking that I stroke his head, that I say a sweet word to him without coldness, it would drive me crazy. My nerves would explode. I would push him away and belittle him. At the beginning, he gave in to me but afterwards we had real fights on that score.

His desperation reached such a pitch one night that he went wild. He destroyed everything he could lay his hands on. He tore his clothes and the blankets. He threw a glass of water in my face, all because I told him I didn't love him. It frightened me to hear him curse the love he had for me, curse the moment he had met me. We had no lights, only the oil lamp that was rolling around on the floor from the blow Mario had given it. Taking advantage of the darkness, I put on my dress and slipped around the corners of the room, holding on to the walls. Mario kept on cursing and I was terribly afraid until I found the door and ran away, barefoot as I was.

I stumbled more than once and trying to get under a barbed-wire fence, I hurt my back and tore my dress. I was trembling for fear Mario would follow and beat me. I was losing my breath and was scared by the darkness that was so different from that of Mexico City. I sat down in the doorway of a house, feeling lost. Not knowing anybody, without clothes, where could I go at this hour of the night? I pulled my hair and rubbed my feet, trying to get the thistle spines out of them. When I stopped crying, I heard heavy breathing, felt something tickling my legs. I jumped to my feet, imagining that it was a scorpion. I shook myself and felt things fall. I was frightened.

I approached the window of a house and whispered, "Señora, señorita, please be kind and take me in. My husband is drunk and I am afraid he'll hit me." Thank God, a woman's voice answered. It was the woman who had offered to cook and wash for us on the day we arrived. She let me sleep there. The next day she asked me if I was going back to Mario, and I told her no, I intended to work. Then Brígida really opened her house to me. After Mario left for work, I went to get my clothes.

I didn't have one single *centavo*, just a pair of earrings which I sold to get money for the bus and a newspaper. I answered an ad for a stenographer and was interviewed by Señor Pacheco's wife. She tested me and gave me the job. I began to work that same morning. It was an office-supply shop and I was in charge of answering correspondence and keeping the accounts in order. I earned only 125 *pesos* per month, but took the job until I could find something better.

At noon, Clemente, the mechanic who fixed the typewriters, and I had time out for eating. I had not eaten since the night before and my stomach felt like it was stuck to my backbone. I didn't have any money so I looked into some windows close by and went back to the office. The doors weren't open yet and I stood in the doorway with my arms pressed across my noisy stomach. The first one to arrive was

Clemente. He must have guessed that I had not eaten because he insisted that I have a drink with him.

He took me to some friends of his who ran a restaurant near by. He said something to the waitress and in a few minutes Priciliana brought me fish broth and a shrimp cocktail. I was terribly embarrassed but my hunger was stronger than my will to refuse such a delicious dish. I worried all through the meal because if Mario or one of his mailmen friends had passed by at that moment it wouldn't have gone well with me.

I expected Clemente to make some insinuation to me, but, thank God, he didn't. From then on we had a sincere friendship. I don't believe I will ever meet a young man like him again. He helped only for the desire to help, expecting nothing in return.

A short time later, a Chinese came in and watched me work. The next day he offered me the job of cashier at his café. The job paid twelve *pesos* a day and included three meals. I worked from eight in the morning to eight at night with no time off—not like in *Señor* Pacheco's office. The work was very simple: keep an account of the merchandise used, note down the money spent, and check the register.

A waitress there told me that now that I was a *señora*, I wouldn't be able to live without a husband. She said the day I least expected it, I would give myself to another man, not because I loved him but because the body demanded it. These words really made me afraid. If it was a choice between giving myself to somebody I didn't even know and continuing with Mario, I'd better to go back to him and be out of danger.

It hadn't been difficult for Mario to find me because he was working at the post office. He had taken me to meet the superintendent of the office and the others there, and I had been well received. So even if I wanted to hide, it wouldn't have been possible, as all the letter carriers knew me. When I was working for *Señor* Pacheco, Mario came to see me three times. "Think it over carefully, Consuelo. You've got to come back to me. We are all alone here. You need me and I need you. By the way, don't you want anything?"

I was arrogant, all right, that time. I said, "I certainly do not need you. I can take care of myself. And don't expect me to come back to you." But after he left, I felt sentimental about him. When I didn't see him, he grew more important.

He came for me every night at the Café Frontera. I had rented a little wooden shack for fifty *pesos* a month. It didn't have a single piece of furniture and I slept on the floor. The only light I had, came from Brígida's house, which was opposite mine. But at the café I didn't know what it was to be hungry any more. And I had a good friend in Brígida. I felt as if she were a close relative, like an aunt.

Everybody told me I should go back to Mario. I resisted, until one night when I worked later than I was supposed to and fell exhausted onto my "bed" on the floor. A terrible pain in the ribs on my left side woke me. I began to cry. I wanted to straighten up, but the pain got worse. I doubled over and my breath came short; my left leg became paralyzed. I wanted to shout but I couldn't. I didn't even have a candle. There was a lovely moon outside and I looked at it through the window thinking that at home my father and sister and everybody were in bed, sleeping calmly, without a worry, and with their stomachs full.

I cried a long time, bearing the pain. When, little by little, I was able to move my leg again, I remembered Mario. If he had been there, he would have taken me to the doctor or prepared some tea. At least, in his company, I wouldn't feel afraid. The next day I met Mario and told him that I would go back to him after all. I quit my job and Brígida loaned us a cot and a blanket and gave me permission to cook on her stove.

It was strange, but little by little I felt stronger. Now I had something to occupy my thoughts, not love, because I didn't love Mario and didn't really want him, but a sense of duty. I found it hard to feign an enormous love I was far from feeling and my indifference and coldness toward him continued. Mario said I had a refined type of cruelty because when he was suffering one of his rages . . . they might be called attacks . . . I did nothing to quiet him. He would lock the door and not let me out and would desperately smash everything against the walls, tear his clothing, cry, shout, go half crazy. I would stand motionless, like a stone, showing neither my fear nor my anger, with my eyes fixed on some point in the room.

He said I enjoyed seeing him angry and desperate, but inside me I felt only horror and fear that he would turn on me. I wanted to run but was like a trapped dog, trapped by my cowardice and fear. I wanted to cry and say those beautiful words, "pardon me," but I was paralyzed.

Mario had often begged me to try to calm him when he had these attacks of nerves. "With just one caress, you can quiet me. Please, Consuelo, please. When you see me angry, speak to me, insult my mother, punch me if you will, but don't just stand there. Have you no heart?"

To my shame, I would just watch him rage, until he grabbed his head in his hands and fell sobbing on the bed. A day didn't pass without a fight and the few things I kept buying soon lay smashed on the floor. The neighbors would get scared and knock on the door, asking, "Did he hit you?" But I would always come out and calmly say, "No, he never hits me. It's his nerves."

The truth of the matter was that I was the nervous one. I couldn't find any way out. I wasn't satisfied with anything. If he would say "Let's go to the Zócalo, a little relaxation for you," my answer would be, "To the Zócalo? What a big time you're going to give me!" If he said, "Let's go to the movies," "To the movies? Not me. You know I don't care for them. Go with your friends!" He let all this go by. He bored me and I regretted having gone back to him. But when he said he would leave if I was not satisfied, I promised never to be nasty to him again.

During that time, the only reason I didn't take my own life was because I didn't want to fail Him. But in what a fever of anxiousness I begged Him to take me! In the afternoons or at night before Mario came home, I would stretch out, face up, on my poor bed. The bed consisted of a small spring on a frame, with a mattress made of a blanket spread over a pile of cardboard and old clothes. A bolster I had made, completed the bedding. The room was lighted by a candle. Looking up at the ceiling, crying bittersweet tears that came from deep inside me, I would ask Him, beg Him, to take me.

My body belonged to Mario, but how hard it was for me! Never in my life did I desire to belong to a man, not even once. I had never thought of it! And now I died every time he came home, happy from his work, to embrace me. I was afraid of it. "Why are they so base? Better take my life, Lord. I don't want this life. I wasn't born for it." These were not mere words. It was my being itself, all my feelings, everything that was in me that was asking Him to grant me this miracle. Always waiting, waiting for it to happen. You might say I was already dead.

Mario made every effort to see me happy, contented. What a bad thing it is not to know how to pretend! I remained in a stupor until the moment he would arrive. "Little Skinny one, where are you, *mi vida?* I'm home. What's wrong? Why are you crying? Come on, let's eat out, or let's go to the Zócalo. Don't be sad." He loved me so much he didn't realize that minutes earlier I had been asking to die, to escape this life.

I really got to love him, when the letter from his mother arrived, advising him to leave me. "That woman is not good for you. She is older than you and very tricky. Leave her. Find a sweetheart there and bring her home. I'll send you the money." I felt as though I were being stoned, each word leaving a bruise. Continuing the letter, I read at the end, "Your son has no shoes any more. Send me money for them and don't squander it on that woman." I turned and looked at him. "So, he has a son." I hid my face and cried.

In reality, I didn't know a thing about Mario. The love that I had begun to feel for him collapsed. He explained to me about the boy. "Look, *mi vida*, there are things I haven't told you, because of my honor as a man, but Camilia—" Then he told me about the life he had led with that woman. Mario's mother had had them married by force when she discovered he had gotten Camilia pregnant. But it had been the girl's fault, because she had gone after him. He hadn't ever even liked her, because she was too forward. His mother had called the police and they had dragged him to court in his underwear. From there, they went to the church—the police, Camilia's parents and Mario's mother—to marry the couple. A short time later, after his sixteenth birthday, he suffered his first deception when he found his wife in a dance hall with one of his friends. The second time he caught her in their house with a soldier; the third, he saw her coming out of a hotel with another man. After that, he left her.

I accepted his explanation, but the only thing I could think of was that we could never be married. There wasn't even the slightest possibility. And knowing he had a child prevented me from coming close to him. I felt like a thief. I kept on living but I got no pleasure out of anything. Life had no color. To be alive without living was an ugly thing. I was useless, a person in a faint who moved about but who no longer felt anything.

How horrible it was at night, when he would overcome me and I had to give myself to him against my will. There is nothing more terrible than to surrender yourself, to be just an instrument. But Mario said to me, "No, *mi vida*. I don't do it out of desire alone. There are lots of women who can satisfy me better than you. No, don't think

that way, *mi vida*. I do it because I want a child, your child. Can't you
imagine it? A little girl just like you? How happy I would be, if you
gave me a child!"

A child was the last thing I wanted. I would say, "A child? The
child I have must have her father's name. You gave that to the other
one. If I had a child with you, it would have to take second place and
my child must be first."

He kept on trying to convince me that it would be something sublime if I gave him a child. One afternoon, filled with anger, I cursed
the day I should have a child. He had never hit me, but that day he
did. He kept slapping me. I didn't even protest, because I understood
that he was right.

Luck continued against me. One morning the votive light tipped over
and the house burned, not all of it, just a part. But we were left with
only two shirts and two pairs of pants of Mario's and three or four
dresses of mine. I just looked at the burned things. Mario lit a cigarette
and smoked. He said, "Aren't you going to cry?"

"Why should I? It's over and done with." And so, back to life without interest.

It is painful to remember certain things—things which make you
feel bad even when you keep quiet about them. Yes, I was going to
be a mother, though I didn't know it then because I didn't notice any
of the symptoms. I felt fine until the month of January. I had no nausea
or stopping of menstruation. That is why Mario did not believe me
when I told him my back hurt.

"I wonder if we are going to have a baby?" I said. But he had lost
confidence in me. He looked at me coldly and said, "The post-office
building will fall down before you are a mother. I believe that the day
you are pregnant you will die." I just twisted my mouth and that is
the way things were left.

But that night, like on other nights, I wouldn't let Mario sleep with
me. I told him to sleep on the floor as he had been doing. We had a
fight and he went into a fury. He was weeping with rage and insulting
me, comparing me with his wife whom he placed above me.

"Yes, Camilia is superior to you. She could give me a son, but you
can't even do that. You aren't good for anything!" I felt terribly
ashamed and humiliated at that moment, lying there half naked next
to him, only to be insulted. I covered my head to shut out his shouts:
"Camilia, Camilia! Come, I need you. Only you know how to cure me!"

He cried as he hit me in the face with a magazine. He seemed to be drunk on his anger. I saw him grab his razor and thought he meant to use it on me, but he held out his arm to cut his own veins. Somehow, I managed to make him drop the blade. I got him to bed. All that night, I had a terrible pain in my abdomen. He went to work early the next morning without believing my complaints.

I woke to the shout of "Consuelo, the north wind is carrying away your clothes." Very sleepy, I got up and ran toward the wires to take down the wash. The cement was slippery and I fell and fainted. When I woke up in the maternity ward two days later, Mario was at the side of my bed, crying. When I saw him like that, what love I felt for him! He asked me to forgive him and said that he despised himself for not having believed me. I smiled. He hadn't abandoned me and I felt happy to have him next to me. He came to see me every day during the five days I was there. He didn't want to let my father know. But I felt bad, really sick and broken. Thanks to Brígida, I managed to send a telegram: "Papá, need money. Am in hospital."

One afternoon, the cry of a newborn baby awakened me. In a little while a stretcher came by, carrying a woman who had given birth. It wasn't until then that I felt the sadness of not seeing my child next to me. How beautiful it would have been to have a baby at my side. When I left there, it made me sad to see children playing in the street. I was like that for a long while, thinking every time, "My baby would be six months old now," or older, according to the amount of time that had passed. As time went by, I resigned myself and tried to wipe out what had happened.

At home I waited for an answer from my father. I was worried, for none came. It wasn't possible that he hated me that much. One afternoon, I was lying on my bed of rags in the room which measured six by six feet, with its thin walls and ceiling made of black compressed cardboard held up by six narrow beams joined with nails and bottle tops. The walls were supported by three horizontal beams, one of which served as a shelf for my saints. My clothes were hanging from some nails in the boards; my shoes were in a wooden box.

There I was, in that little room, alone. Mario had gone to work at the post office. I hurt all over. My hip and legs felt as if I had been beaten with clubs. My hand felt numb, my face swollen and my teeth as if they were crumbling. And I was deaf. All I could hear was a buzzing in my ears.

Then my pain began to disappear. My body was free, as if I suddenly became divided in two. One part floated and the other remained in bed. "Finally," I murmured and felt a smile on my lips. I felt so light, as I had never felt before, and saw Him there, there on the ceiling. There was a luminous cross in a strange shade of green, with a little flame in the center. It seemed as though it were incorporating me into it. I didn't feel my painful body any more. I was a kind of veil that, little by little, rose in the air.

What I felt was so beautiful I cannot find the exact words to describe it. I can only say that with a zigzag I entered nothingness. This was what I had been waiting for all my life. My happiness had no bounds, it is impossible to explain the degree of joy I reached. It lasted several minutes. Far away I heard the voice of a neighbor's child, "Consuelo, Consuelo, someone is looking for you. I think it's your *papá*." It didn't disappear until then. I would have liked to remain that way forever. When I came to, I felt a sharp pain in the abdomen and I embraced my father.

We both cried and after calming down, he said to me, "Is this what you went to school for? Is this why you became a shorthand stenographer? Just look at this dump of a room you have!"

I felt myself getting angry. Up to then, nobody had said anything like that to me about my house, where I was the boss and where I could move my few things from one side to another without being afraid of anyone, where María or Brígida or any other girl could talk to me without being embarrassed, where there was nobody to tell me I wasn't different from the pigs. I had gotten to love my little house. "I am happy here, *papá*. Mario is very good. He doesn't give me more because he can't. But he is good."

My father wanted me to go to Mexico City with him and he brought another doctor, who said I could travel. I thought it over. Mario was married to another, by church and civil law, and could not get a divorce. He had a son to support. Besides, Mario had begun again to insult me and to set his wife above me. "You can't even compare with her! Her skin is very white and yours is dark. She gave me a child. That's a woman!" Mario had said this to me when I refused to be his.

That is why I agreed to go with my *papá*. Mario stayed in Monterrey. I told him, "As soon as you arrange your transfer, I'll be waiting for you. I'll never let you down, you know that." I returned to Mexico City by bus. My father wanted to take me to the Casa Grande, which meant facing Delila again. I didn't want to have anything to do with her, so he took me to my aunt's house. Mario began sending me letters right away. I still keep them for consolation—those words of tenderness and love.

Fifteen or twenty days later, Mario came to my aunt's house. I was well by then. My father paid for my whole treatment, which included four transfusions, serums and injections. Mario said that he would pay back everything but I was already thinking that we should separate. I couldn't give myself to him any more. When I would not go to Monterrey with him, he moved back to his mother's house.

I know now that when I refused Mario, I lost the chance of my life to have a home and a family of my own. He was good to me from the start, he spoke up for me, defended me, gave me all he earned, consulted me in everything. But in my cursed pride and senselessness, I did not know how to value those things.

At my aunt's, the battle started again, except that it was worse now because my uncle didn't hold back foul words when he scolded me. The neighbors felt sorry for me but gossiped even worse than before. I had come back defeated.

I began to look for a job. From my friends, I learned that Jaime had gone up in the world and was still unmarried. He made a very good salary, but that meant nothing to me. I got a job working for *Señor* Ruiz in a used-car lot. He was very nice but I couldn't stand the snickers and vulgarities of the mechanics and the manager when they got together in the office to play cards. All day at the office I had to put up a fight to make the men respect me. I stayed on because I couldn't get another job. One good thing that resulted from this job was that I met *Señor* Ruiz's aunt, who later befriended me when I needed help.

Meanwhile, there had been some changes in my family. My father had built a little house on a lot he had bought way out in El Dorado Colony. He had won two thousand *pesos* in the National Lottery and that was how he happened to have money to buy the land. He sold some of his pigs to get money to start building the house. It was the first property my father had ever owned and he was the only one among our friends and relatives who had achieved such a thing. But the house was not for us. Lupita and my half-sisters, Antonia and Marielena, were living there and taking care of my father's animals.

Tonia had two children but she did not live with Francisco, their father, because he had not been willing or able to set up a house for her. My father had supported her and the children ever since she had become Francisco's common-law wife.

Marta now had three little daughters and had left her husband, Crispín, for good. When she moved back to the Casa Grande, our room was very crowded. Manuel and his four children were there, Roberto, my father, Delila and her son, and Marta with her three children. My father decided to move with Delila to a room on the Street of the Lost Child and to leave Marta in charge of the place in the Casa Grande.

Marta was depressed and I tried to encourage her. I would say, "Don't be foolish, sister. You are right to leave Crispín. If he doesn't meet his obligations, what do you want him for? Look, you are young, there is still time, but if you keep on having babies, you will be ruined. Study something, like dressmaking . . . it will only take a few months and then you could work without leaving the house. There is a training school around here, go see how much the registration fee is and let me know. I will pay for it. My aunt will take care of the girls while you are in school. Go, and let me know. There is still time."

Marta kept quiet while I sat on the bed trying to convince her. She was on a bench near the door, with her eyes down, looking very pretty. But she was like a living statue. I wanted a glance, a gesture, something to let me know that my words had struck home. I wanted to see her smile, with zest for life, the way she had been with her gang when she was younger. I remember her straight white teeth and the dimples when she laughed, and how she walked with her arms entwined with her friends. But now there was no response to my concern for her. She was like an Oriental statue that breathed.

I tried to get her a job that would take her out of that environment. I wanted to show her that places existed where she would be treated decently and where she might find some responsible young man who would help her solve her family problem and educate her daughters. I absolutely refused for a long time to accept the fact that my sister belonged to the low cultural level of her surroundings.

But she was far from understanding the healthiness of my intentions. She twisted everything, and, it hurts me to say so, she considered me a whore or a crazy girl who got everything with her body. I didn't even know until later that my sister, my dear little sister, thought of me in that way. When I was working, I did my best to take care of my appearance, to paint my lips and my nails, and to have my hair set once in a while. By being well groomed I was fighting to maintain my position and to keep people from humiliating me and lording it over me. But I didn't dress up to please men! My sister couldn't understand that. To her . . . I can laugh at it now . . . taking care of my appearance meant only that I was a loose woman.

I didn't have the remotest idea then, that she preferred harsh criticism to my kind words, that she used personal slovenliness to protect her "morals," severe clothing to preserve her religion, and economy of words to maintain the respect of her children. And she did all these things to keep the love and favoritism of my father. I speculated about her and tried to understand her, but couldn't. I always ended up saying, "Oh, the poor thing, she never knew her mother."

Marta paid no attention to my suggestion and agreed to look after Manuel's children, although I know she didn't love them. I moved in to help her. My father came every day at about seven o'clock to check on us and to leave Marta her daily expense money. With Manuel, Roberto and me working, it began well enough, but then Manuel refused to contribute and Roberto stayed away a lot. I could not eat the fried meat and food made with lard my sister served at home and, to escape her arguments, I ate dinner in cheap restaurants. That used up almost all the money I earned, so I, too, stopped contributing to the house.

Marta didn't need my help, although it made her angry when I didn't give her anything. I noticed, and, yes, it hurt me, that every day my father brought her soap, sugar, coffee, rice, tomatoes, oil, chocolate and so on, in addition to the ten *pesos* expense money. Then he gave her money for the movies three or four times a week, and shoes and clothing for the children or whatever she needed. She enjoyed his favor and all the liberty she wanted. Every day she took the children to one of the markets, or downtown to look in the store windows, and if she wanted something extra, she asked Roberto for money, for he was working in a factory then. On Sundays, she went with my aunt and uncle to the Villa or to a park to eat *tacos plazeros* and drink *pulque.* Once in a while, I caught sight of Crispín around the Casa Grande. So I asked myself why I should help her. She had my father and brother on her side, she could go out whenever she wished, she could have relations with her husband, and didn't have to worry about anything. And she had her children. I had only my work . . . and very little peace at home.

As the days passed, Marta and I had more differences. She had the bad habit of letting Trinidad, the youngest girl, go about without pants. Naturally, the child did her necessities on the floor or wherever she pleased. I kept telling Marta to put pants on Trini and to teach her where to go. Unhappily, my sister only became angry and would say that I thought I was high-class or a *"pocha,"* imitating the way of others. One day, I lost my temper when Trini moved her bowels on the floor near the stove where Marta was cooking. My sister kept on working, then picked up the baby and washed her at the sink.

I couldn't contain myself. "Why don't you teach her to sit on the chamber pot? This way you are making a pig out of her!"

"If you're so fussy, move out! You don't give a *centavo* into the house and yet you are so delicate. Why don't you move to Lomas with the rich?"

That was my sister's answer, no matter what I said. I tried to teach her to cover the garbage can and the cooked food, to protect them from rats, to keep the dirty laundry in a carton under the bed, instead of piled under the sink, to keep food away from the heat of the sun and the stove, so that it would not spoil, but she refused to learn. When I described *Señor* Santiago's house or the way one of my friends lived, she would take offense and say I was looking down at the poor. She made fun of me to her friends and complained daily to my father, who always backed her up.

Marta didn't like taking care of all the children and found a job in a paper-cup factory. She didn't tell me she was going to work; on the first day, she left at seven in the morning and didn't come back until seven at night. I stayed home with the children but worried all day about my sister, not knowing where she was.

I refused to take on the job of looking after the kids. I continued to work and my father hired a woman, who had two little ones of her own, to move in and take care of things. The house was noisier and more crowded than ever. Every night I had to take medicine for my nerves. Sitting on the edge of my bed, I would look around the dim room. The electricity had been cut off again and the candle barely lighted up the table and the children's pale little faces over their coffee mugs, or my sister, her hair uncombed, her apron dirty and half falling, shouting at Concepción to clean up after Trini. "Hurry, you damned brat, clean your sister, if you know what is good for you!" It drove me out of my mind to see my sad-eyed niece leave her bread and coffee to wipe up the diarrhoeic mess on the floor.

Right after supper, everyone would go to bed. Marta in the big bed with her daughters; Mariquita, Conchita and I on my little bed; Alanes and Domingo and Roberto doubled over with cold on the floor; and now, the maid and her children, also on the floor. Night after night, this was the sad picture before my eyes. I tried to make it better, but by that time, I was almost afraid to speak up. They blamed me for everything, even if the stove wick was slow in lighting. Not only Marta and my father, but even Roberto said that I was the one who had brought the apple of discord into the house. They wanted me to move out but I wouldn't give up trying to get them to live better. Besides, I was afraid to live alone. People would wonder about me and think the worst, and men would take advantage of my position.

To make matters worse, Mario, and later Jaime, drunk as always, came looking for me. One night, as I was leaving my aunt's house, I saw Jaime coming toward the Casa Grande. I ran back to our court-yard. He saw me and ran, too, but, thank God, I got to our room before he did and locked myself in. Day after day, Jaime hung around, until I spoke to him and agreed to go out with him. He said he still loved me and wanted to marry me. I didn't believe him, but took everything passively to avoid trouble, especially when he was drunk. Frankly, I was tired of my home and had not been eating well. He took me to restaurants and to the movies and gave me presents and as a result, I was able to save up some money.

Meanwhile, my brother Roberto advised me to use my money to buy a record player, saying I could make back more than it would cost by renting it out for dances and *fiestas*. And if I ever needed money, I could sell it or pawn it. I loved music and thought how nice it would be to have records of my own. One day, I was ill in bed, when Roberto came and said, "Sis, just think, I met a fellow who wants to sell a very good record player for four hundred *pesos*."

"Really?" I must confess that I didn't trust Roberto, but he was my brother and I loved him. I always thought he was the one who had suffered most because we lost our mother. I wanted to show that I had confidence in him, that I believed in his goodness, and that someone, at least, had faith in his character. In short, I gave him the money. He said he would be right back with the record player.

While I waited, my aunt came to be paid for washing my laundry. I told her what I had done and she got angry, saying I shouldn't have given him a *centavo*, that I was tempting him, that I was a fool.

"But, Auntie, he is my brother. How is it possible that he would . . ."

Later, when I went crying to her because Roberto had not returned, my aunt and uncle scolded me some more. I told Angélica, my friend, and she, too, said, "*Qué barbaridad!* How could you be so foolish? Why did you hand over so much money?"

"But he is my brother!" I cried, not because of the money, but because he had betrayed my confidence. I found him drinking beer with a friend in a café near the Casa Grande. I was afraid to ask him for the money because I might embarrass him or hurt his feelings and make him angry.

"What happened?" was all I said.

"Nothing," was all he answered.

I thought it would be better to have my aunt and uncle with me when I asked for the money, so I went to get them. By the time we returned to the café, my brother was gone. He didn't come home for three days and I had plenty of time to cry. When I next saw him, I didn't ask for an explanation, but said only, "You will pay it back, little by little." Yes, he gave me ten or fifteen *pesos* every week, until he had paid about half of it.

He never apologized for what he did. He just explained that the record player wasn't good and that he intended to give me back the money . . . he still had it in his pocket when I saw him in the café . . . but then some of his friends came along and he invited them all out to drink. "But I'll pay you back, sister, don't worry."

I had such hopes that my brother would change! I thought that with advice and more support, with study . . . if only he would finish primary school! If only he would try! When I saw the reality of things it frightened me. I didn't want to believe that he would never change.

The next blow came only two days after I got up from my sickbed, as thin as a toothpick. Marta and I were already asleep when *Señora* Luz, who sold *tacos* in the gateway of the Casa Grande, banged on the door and said the police were beating up Roberto. How terrible it is to be awakened that way! We jumped out of bed. Marta slept in her dress but I had to put on my old blue bathrobe, trembling and full of fear because I well knew what the police were capable of doing. I got the fright of my life to see Roberto stretched out on the ground with two policemen standing over him beating him barbarously. Their blows had made him vomit. He was bleeding from the nose and yelling curses at them, which only made them beat him harder.

I shouted, "No, Roberto, no, little brother, shut up, for you are making it worse."

"Let him alone," Marta said to the police. "Don't be mean. Can't you see he's drunk?"

"Well, tell the bastard to be quiet or else . . ." and they kept beating him with their clubs. My God, I felt so helpless! I turned desperately, looking for help, screaming, "They are killing him! Stop them!"

Three of Roberto's friends tried to interfere; the crowd that had gathered also threatened to join in, but the policemen took out their guns and chased them away. When they saw that my brother couldn't move any more, they ran. Marta and I were crying. People advised us to take Roberto to the Police Station to accuse the two policemen, so Marta went to get Trinidad, who was still nursing, and I got my coat. I took fifty *pesos* I had hidden away and went to look for a taxi. An ambulance arrived to take my brother and two of his friends who went along as witnesses, to the Police Station.

When we arrived, Roberto was in the infirmary, crying and complaining of terrible pains in his head, stomach and legs. He kept shouting insults at the police, making matters worse. I held my hand over his mouth . . . The doctor sent him to the hospital, and just as the ambulance was leaving, Manuel arrived, full of indignation at what had happened. He accompanied Roberto, while Marta and I stayed to try to get justice. Justice! We stayed there until five o'clock in the morning, accomplishing nothing and only wasting our time.

I was in despair. I had gotten nowhere with Marta, had spent my few *centavos* on Roberto, my father took the children back to Delila . . . I felt I would get ill if I didn't escape his mean looks and hard words, his daily threats to throw me and Roberto into the street. I couldn't stand it any more and decided to move.

My boss's aunt, Señora Andrea, had an empty bedroom that she rented to me after I had told her my situation, with certain reservations, of course. She lived almost at the opposite edge of the city and I thought I could flee from those who were troubling me.

But Jaime found me there. At first he behaved himself and I began to depend on him. Then another blow! "I don't want anybody in my house to know I am seeing you. My mother forbade it. If my father finds out, there will be a big fight. But if you want, I'll set up a house for you." Instead of marriage, Jaime was now offering to make me his mistress.

I received such offers from several men, some from whom I least expected it. A friend of the family, a man I had always considered like an uncle, said to me, "If you want to, you can work; if not, you don't have to. I'll set you up a house." After that it was my brother-in-law: "If you want, I'll set up a house for you somewhere else, in Veracruz or Guadalajara." I stopped talking to him, too. Then Elida's husband, whom I thought of as a friend, proposed to "take care of me."

My mind became bewildered. "My God," I asked myself, "do I represent only an instrument of pleasure?" I wanted to get away from all evil and like a curse it followed me. I began to be afraid of everyone. Then one night, Jaime came, drunk and yelling, insulting me and kicking on *Señora* Andrea's door. Waking up and hearing his scandalous noise in that respectable house came as a shock, and I fainted.

At that time I didn't eat properly, sometimes because of not having money, or because I wasn't hungry or had to catch the bus. The daily rages at my job had also undermined my health. I was as thin as when they called me "tubercular." I began to lose control of my nerves. I had crying fits and became dull. My way of speaking was like that of an idiot or a drunkard. I don't have to say I made innumerable mistakes at work.

I began to have many vivid dreams. One of my dreams, or rather nightmares, started with me on a beach. I swam until I came to an island, where I noticed a small cave. I went to see what it was like inside, when suddenly the earth moved under my feet. I fell into a whirlpool. I struggled with all my strength to come to the surface, but the water of that whirlpool sucked me under. I thought I would die. I fell and fell. When I reached the bottom, the whirlpool threw me into a kind of room made of earth, divided into two areas by a platform. At one side was a wooden ladder of the sort the Indians sell. The water ran along one side of the room but did not come into it. My clothing was torn to shreds. My hair was dry, but it was very long and straggly. My feet were covered with the earth of the floor. The curious thing is that there was a lighted electric-light bulb hanging from one of the beams which supported the platform. I began to climb the ladder. Suddenly a man appeared. I could see his clothing but not his face; he was dressed like a pirate. He pulled a cord, and dirt began to fall on me, tons of sandy, whitish dirt. I continued climbing, and to my surprise, on the platform there was another lake of blue water. But then, without knowing how I got there, I was in a sailboat. Some men in it had saved me, but I kept telling them to let me go. They did not want to.

The little boat capsized. I fell back into the whirlpool and was swallowed up again in the water and sand. I fought, I struggled with all my strength and escaped again to the cave. The water of the whirlpool covered me completely except for my head, which was covered with an oilcloth cap. The water was a very dark green. A board came floating toward me and I started toward it. When I reached it, somebody gave me a hand and pulled me up on the plank. I couldn't see the person's face, just the arm which reached out to help me. I lay exhausted on the board, but still inside the whirlpool. I no longer had the strength to swim, but lay there face down on the board, which kept spinning around and around.

My condition became worse. One night on the way home, I fainted and fell on the highway. I don't know how long I remained there until I got up and went home. *Señora* Andrea thought I was drunk and gave me lots of advice. I finally fell into bed. I was afraid of the dark, of people, of the noise of the cars. I couldn't work any more.

My father moved me to Lupita's house. I don't remember anything about the first two days. I just remember that I looked at everybody and talked, I don't know about what. Then, suddenly, I wouldn't recognize them. Things looked enormous and seemed as though they were going to fall on top of me. Voices sounded strange and far away. A very strong pain in my head didn't leave me in peace. At night they would put alcohol on my head. Everything looked far away, the furniture so small and so far from me. Faces, when they laughed, almost made me faint—I couldn't tell exactly who they were. I knew Lupita was there, I guessed it, something told me she was helping me. When I began to get better, I couldn't talk right and stuttered a lot.

The first time I went out alone to go to the doctor's office, I remained standing in the street. I had forgotten the place. Suddenly everything had changed. I began to tremble and cry. A woman came and asked me if she could help me get there.

"Get there? Where?" I asked.

"To your house, of course."

"My house?" I couldn't remember it. After a while, I pulled myself together and went into his office and told Dr. Ramón about it. He said I ought not to go out alone. My father came for me. When I arrived home, my bed looked so small it seemed impossible I could fit into it. I looked at it from very high up. I fell into it and went to sleep, I don't know for how long.

Out of the emptiness within me, I tried to solve my problems. I felt alone, hearing the jibes of others when I tried to raise myself up. I felt submerged and whirling in a spiral of events, of scenes dancing by, of things I could not understand. I thought people were full of hate and deprecation, wanting to hurt me, to see me go under. I didn't know why things happened and there was no one to help me. I came to conclusions without understanding the situation but I had no way to correct my errors. I felt fear, I didn't know of what, except that I was certain it was not fear of death, which had always seemed inviting to me. I trembled and my hands perspired when I went out into the street. Whenever I saw a lot of people, I wanted to run. When I crossed the streets, I felt like throwing myself in the path of a car. I was very ill; only my faith in God kept me going. Somehow I got better.

One night I had a wonderful dream in color. It gave me courage. I was inside a very nice house, a boarding house for students. But first it was a sort of sidewalk café, something like a boulevard where people on an excursion go on their way to swim. In that two-story café, the tables were behind me and the roof was of straw. From the roof to the railing on which I was leaning, were woven some very pretty strands of grass, with tiny heart-shaped leaves. I stood looking down at the place where, a short distance from the tree, the pool began, with its border of small stones and its clear blue water. Suddenly from somewhere there appeared several pairs of lovers, who walked along the corridor leading to the pool, arm in arm, the boys turning to look at the girls very lovingly. I watched them from above and smiled. Somebody came up to me and at once I moved away from the railing.

When I went down to where the swimming pool was, it disappeared and in its place I found myself sitting on a kind of red counter next to a bookcase which was against a brown wall. The books were an intense brown. Next to this bookstand and back a bit, was the window. A little lower was my bed, a very small one. Again there appeared several young men and girls—I don't know where they came from. I watched them in astonishment from where I was, holding a book in my hands. They laughed and talked loudly.

Their clothes caught my eye—red trousers and yellow shirts. The boys would turn to look at their girl friends, pulling them by their hands. They jumped over my bed and disappeared through the window. One of the boys, the last one, asked me to jump out with him. "Come on, let's go," he said to me with a laugh. They were all quite gay. Even I, so exhausted, felt very happy. When they all disappeared, there was silence in my room. I turned to look at the walls, and what magnificent colors I saw! A pistachio green, a ruby red, a beautiful yellow. I closed my book and set it down on the red counter. I discovered that I had long hair done up in curls; I also had on red slacks.

I went to the window and saw the young people again and a dark green hedge at some distance from the house. The grass was yellow-green. The young people were blonds, very well groomed. They kept running about and jumping over the hedge. The last one insisted that I jump too. "Come on, come on, hurry!" But from the window I shook my head no.

When they disappeared, I felt an uncontrollable desire to follow and jumped out the window. I was about halfway across the boulevard when I turned back to look at the house. It was white, such a pretty white that I felt sorry I had left it. But something told me that I could not return there, so I kept on running to try to catch up with the others. I could no longer see them. I could only hear their laughter. I tried to climb the hedge, and managed to get to the top but there I remained fast. When I woke up I was caught lying crosswise on that hedge, face down, looking at the green color of the grass and at that white, white house with its red roof.

Slowly, I lost my timidity and regained my strength. The deep circles of my spiral began to diminish and become clearer, until little by little, I emerged from it. I felt alive again, like a new Consuelo. My body felt full, not incomplete as before. I felt the strength I had when I was in school. I knew I was something once more, someone who could do things, who was worth more "than a peanut," as my father used to say. I began to learn the true face of life.

Down deep, I felt a strong hurt and anger, but it was better that these were not aroused for I was capable of taking terrible vengeance against those who had damaged me. I really did not wish to harm anyone, least of all my father, and I would rather quietly suffer the pain that slept inside me. It was enough that I could again look with defiance at anyone who insulted or humiliated me. I felt I could assert myself and reject what did me harm. It was enough that I could face the world without fear.

I have always aspired to reach "something," something different from what I had known, something outside of my surroundings, perhaps even outside of my possibilities. I was not resigned to remain in one spot, the place where I had my beginnings, whether it was where I lived or where I worked. To limit myself to one job, one field of study, one activity, had no appeal. I did not want to follow any one route laid down for me by past generations. I opposed the word "destiny," which I heard on all sides. "He who was born to be a pot, doesn't leave the kitchen." How many times have I heard this from my father, my aunt, friends and neighbors! At wakes or after accidents people liked to say, "It was his destiny!" and they would be satisfied. But I wasn't. I was afraid to say it aloud, for the others would have squelched me. They would have said I was opposing the course of life, and who did I think I was to do that? My family, especially, would have said that I, who was the weakest and most foolish, was the most rebellious. They would not have understood me, so I never said my thoughts aloud. But inside me I would think of what had happened and would try to find the explanation. Never in my life did I believe it was "destiny."

"Nothing can be done about it," they would say. "Don't oppose the will of God." I couldn't accept that and even entered a struggle with the Church and Divine precepts. More, I began to analyze the personality of my God, against whom I had never rebelled. I thought about it and studied it from corner to corner. I noticed that some people did not give in to destiny, but fought it with an unbreakable will. I knew a Spaniard who started a furniture store which failed after a few months. He didn't give up, but borrowed money and began again. He had to start over about five times, but he finally achieved what he wanted. Then I realized it wasn't destiny, but will power, that had made him succeed.

Among our neighbors, there were some who progressed and moved up in the world. Raúl became an accountant, another worked in the movies, another set up a business. None of these young men had followed the gang, loafing in the street in dirty clothes, speaking un-grammatically and using vile language. They were serious and learned to dress with good taste, always resisting the criticism of the others. Resisting, rejecting, not giving in to the majority—that was their secret. I didn't know what they were against, but they always seemed to be against something. They would say, "What? it has to be this way! Not on your life!" or, "No, man! you're a stupid jerk if you think I'll do what you want me to!"

I would think of these things sitting on a bench outside the door or leaning against the wall. People would say I was too pensive, I was "in the clouds," dreaming with my eyes open. But I was watching. I saw that one needed a strong character to resist the others. One had to be indifferent to a handsome face, or a nice pair of pants or to the most popular boys. If one of these condescended to choose a girl who was younger or not as well dressed as he, she would feel flattered to be selected and would consider it a kind of triumph. At a dance, if one of these "superior" boys chose me, I would accept and then leave him standing there in the middle of the dance floor while the music was still playing. That was severe punishment for anyone. I did it to avenge myself for his cocky attitude.

I realized it was necessary not to offend others and many times I had to condescend to laugh at the jokes of my sister's friends, even when I didn't understand them. I never took the attitude of Rufelia, for example, who would get angry and say, "We are not equals, you idiot, for you to joke with me." Naturally, that only earned for her the antipathy of everyone. It was very, very difficult to find exactly the right approach to resist in that environment. If I was too severe, I would be isolated, if too accessible, the others would take over.

My aspirations were different from those of the people in the circle in which I lived. Even before I studied stenography, I dreamed of studying languages. Why? Who knows? While I was a typist, I looked forward to becoming a stewardess in an airline. I didn't get anywhere, but I wasn't disillusioned. Sleeping in my brain, with quiet desperation, was the desire to get hold of money. I needed money to live on a different level, to become a member of another circle, to be of some worth, to have a better life.

And why did I want to have money and a better life? Not because I was interested in material things but because I thought if I could pass through the wall that closed me in, then, little by little, I could get my four nieces and nephews out too. The money would be to hire a lawyer to make me their guardian, to defend them from the others, to send them to school, to form the kind of family I did not succeed in forming with my brothers and sister. I didn't want history to repeat itself; they must not become another Manuel, Roberto, Consuelo or Marta! I wanted to give the children everything they asked for and to see that they were well brought up, with a career, so that they could face life without fear or shame and advance with firm steps. I wanted them to love me.

I also hoped that if I could get out of my circle, my brother Roberto might escape and rise to the surface where he could breathe freely and move without fear. And when I was older and well established, I could show my face with courage, knowing that I had not made a misery of my life and that my family, too, was worth something.

Those were the motors that impelled me out of the lethargy brought on by my illness and by circumstance. I didn't see it so clearly then. I just directed my steps along the road that I liked, simply because I liked it, without needing any other explanation. I always had the hope that it could lead me to that "something," not even troubling to look ahead to notice if there was a branch of a tree that might fall and knock me out.

When I felt strong enough, I looked for work and found a job in an office; the pay was little and the hours were long. While I lived with Lupita or in the Casa Grande, I didn't have to pay rent, I had no children, no husband, not even a *novio*. I was free to do what I wanted. I would have liked to go to secondary school at night, but I was too tired and it would have taken years to graduate. For months I went from my home to my work, from my work to my home, and nothing more. Again, I felt myself sinking into the sea of family troubles. "Roberto is drunk and fighting"; "Mariquita's eyes are infected and Manuel pays no attention"; "Marta is seeing Crispín again"; "Aunt Guadalupe needs *thirty* pesos for last month's rent."

I had to get away from my family and I looked for a furnished room. It took me two weeks to find one I could afford. Nowhere would they accept a single girl and finally I had to say I was a student from a different state to rent a little room for 190 *pesos* a month in a *señora's* apartment on Dr. Manzanares Street.

The *señora* had other roomers and one of them, Beatriz, became my friend. She was nice and I liked her, although the landlady warned me that she had a bad character. Beatriz would wake me in the mornings and we would eat breakfast together in the kitchen. "We are both alone, sister," she once said, "so we need each other." Sometimes she and I would sit in the sun on a bench outside the front door of the house. Felipe, the mailman, would stop and chat and make us laugh, or Alejandro, Beatriz's *novio,* would join us. The landlady didn't like this and would later insult us. "Only street women sit in the doorway like that, looking for clients. Please stay in your rooms from now on." But our rooms were dark and cold and we paid no attention to the old hag.

But one thing led to another and she began to make trouble for us, throwing away our food or anything we left out of place, flooding the kitchen floor when we wanted to eat, or strewing garbage about. She wanted to raise my rent because I took a bath three times a week and kept my light on after ten o'clock. She forbade us to boil milk or meat or beans, for they consumed too much gas; she examined the pots on the stove to see that we obeyed.

I was getting fed up with the *señora*. I had noticed that her apartment was not registered as a rooming house, nor were there tax receipts on her wall. I figured her income from the tenants was about a thousand *pesos* a month. When I was two weeks behind in the rent and asked her to wait because I didn't have the money, she became annoyed. The next day, the kitchen floor was flooded, with garbage floating in the water.

I was very angry and went to her room and knocked. "*Señora*, who the devil do you think you are! Do you believe that because I am quiet I will stand any abuse?"

"If you don't like it, you can move out."

"I will leave when I please and not before I complain to the government about your secret business here. I suppose you have paid your taxes? Where are your tax receipts then? You overcharge us for this partitioned cave and have the nerve to call us loose women. Who knows what class of insect you are! For all I know, you have a prison record."

That woman didn't say a word. She just stood there all in one piece. Perhaps what I said was true. Anyway she didn't bother us again. I was relieved, for I didn't want to move and leave Beatriz, although I was beginning to dislike her way of life. Alejandro was her lover and paid her rent and everything but she made a fool out of him by going around with other men. I was getting tired of their quarrels.

Then, five months after I had moved in, I heard Jaime's familiar whistle. I don't know how he learned my address (probably through my aunt) but once, at three o'clock in the morning, he rang every bell in the apartment house and got into the courtyard where he yelled my name and insults and curses for all to hear. He began to follow me home from work and spy on me. He would walk behind me without saying a word, nearly driving me out of my mind. I got into the habit of looking back every time I went out. I felt my nerves going and knew I would have to move.

I answered an ad in the newspaper and was lucky enough to find a nice room for two hundred *pesos*, in a house rented by a Cuban family. How I liked it there! It was clean, had plenty of hot water, a lovely bathroom, a parlor and a telephone. I liked my roommate, Nancy, and Emita and her husband, Lucy and Raúl, their children, and all their Cuban friends and tenants who had come to Mexico to escape Batista. Here I found true hospitality and good manners, gaiety, parties, and companionship. They invited me to play cards and joked and teased without tiring. The men flirted outrageously and tried to make love, but a few sharp words stopped them. I was happy there and would have remained forever.

But the economic situation of the family became worse. Money stopped coming from Cuba, the husband had no job, Lucy had trouble with her *novio*, some of the roomers moved out. Emita decided to transfer the house to a new tenant, who would pay her a few thousand *pesos* for it. Nancy went to live with her married brother, who was a lawyer, but I couldn't find another place quickly and had to stay on with the new family, whom I did not like as well. After looking for a room, one day I returned to find my bed and clothing in the middle of the parlor because it had occurred to the landlord to paint my room before I left. I was coming down with bronchitis and had to spend the next few days sleeping in the parlor.

I found a room on Sonora Street in an apartment in a nice building. The rent was high, 250 *pesos*, but the neighborhood was the nicest I had ever lived in. My new landlady, Juanita, lived alone with a servant and I was the only roomer. She gave me permission to use her record player and television set (I had bought myself a little radio by this time), and to bring Mariquita or another one of my nieces and nephews to spend Sunday with me. On that day, I washed my hair, bathed, and rested.

Up to a certain point, Juanita was a good landlady, although at times she frightened me. She insulted her servant very harshly, laughed in an uncontrolled manner and told me a lot of lies about herself. She said she was from an aristocratic family but she used some of the worst language I had ever heard. I didn't care about her private life but it annoyed me when she told me that her husband was a doctor who came home only twice a week. In between, she sometimes had long visits from her "uncle" or some other male "relative."

I paid no attention to her goings on, but she tried to influence me to take the same path. She wanted to introduce me to her visitors, saying, "Come on, Consuelo, don't be a fool. You are so young. Who is there to stop you? I've had three husbands and I know that all men are the same cheats. You have to learn how to take advantage of them. Life is for those who know how to live! Tell me, what's stopping you?"

"No, Juanita. I couldn't, even though I wanted to. I would like to be able to do such things without worrying, but my conscience would bother me."

"Conscience! None of that now! The Church talks about conscience because it suits them, but in reality, what is it? Tell me, who in this world is not human? Live while you can, before you are too old. Put aside your scruples. What good are they, except to make fools of us. There are many men who are not happy at home and if they find a woman who knows how to satisfy them, naturally they will be generous to her. Because it is a need, something mechanical that the body asks for, so why not take advantage of opportunities."

"Yes, but . . ."

"But nothing! Stop this foolishness. Life isn't such that you can consider everything. Man! Do what I say and in the end you will find someone who will marry you and give you a nice home. Why not?"

Juanita showed me her watch and bracelets and rings. "See this diamond ring? One of my *novios* gave it to me. I pawn it whenever I need money. See how pretty it is?"

I felt a kind of admiration and respect for Juanita. She seemed so mature, so sure of herself. She had everything, a beautiful apartment, a servant, all the money she wanted. Beside her, I felt insignificant. I felt she was probably right. I was killing myself to earn a few miserable *pesos*. But still I looked down at her and couldn't think of leading her life. I wasn't born for that. I thought, "Better to do it my way and hold my head high. It is true she has many things, but must she also not feel shame? No, if I want a dress, I'll buy it. If I have no money, I'll wait. I couldn't use anything I had paid for with my body. And if my brothers or the children should find out? No, a thousand times no! You may have a lot now, Juanita, but someday you will repent."

Carmelita, a girl who worked in my office, was living in the same world as Juanita. She was very pretty and for a while I liked her. She also spoke to me frankly. "Don't be a jerk! Get all the money you can out of men. All you have to do is put on a sad face and right away they will give you something. Take Honorato, for example, do you believe

I go with that fat slob because I like him? No, man! I've had better ones than that!"

"Yes? And why do you accept him then?"

"Man! How can you be such a jerk? Because I get money out of him, of course. He comes around saying, '*Ay, mamacita!*' Do you think I don't make him pay for it? Don't think I am not worth anything. I say, 'Come on, *papacito*, anything you want.' But later I gather in the wool."

"But he is married."

"Married, but not castrated. Who tells his old woman not to know how to watch him? Listen, I'll introduce you to León. The old goat has lots of *pesos*."

I laughed at what she said, and I let her teach me how to put on make-up. She had nice clothes, though they were not so expensive as Juanita's. I kept going out with Carmela, although my boss and others warned me not to. I liked the way she laughed and joked with everyone, especially the men, and I envied her when she rode off in their beautiful cars. She invited me to go with her, but I never accepted. The truth is, I felt inferior to her, and to everyone else. When I saw their luxurious cars and good clothes, I did not feel up to them. In spite of everything, ever since I was a girl, I didn't know how to take advantage of others. I knew nothing about evil, hypocrisy, astuteness, and I wanted to learn. I wanted to get out of the fog I lived in.

Meanwhile, I kept looking for a better job and finally, with much work and many letters of recommendation, I got a job in a government office. I worked from 8:30 A.M. to 2:30 P.M. for 540 *pesos* a month. Many times I had to work after hours without pay "to have a good record," my chief told me. I enrolled in an English course in the evening and, at last, began to study a foreign language. What is more, I applied for an apartment in a government housing project for civil service employees. I had a good chance to get one because my friend's *novio* worked in the housing department and promised to put in a good word for me. I was coming closer and closer to building a new life for me and, God willing, for my "children," my dear little nieces and nephews.

My chief cause of worry was still my family, but the emotion and anxiety I felt before, had lessened. Away from them, I realized they formed a united circle, or rather, a net, in which they were enmeshed together. I was the only one out of it. Being near them only made me feel more alone. It had always been like that, but I hadn't had the courage to face it. I knew I should not mix into their lives, that I should struggle for myself alone.

Had I lived only for myself, I would have gone away. But my love for my family, that strong Mexican love, was like a powerful coiled spring pulling me back, pulling me under. I wanted to advance, but it wouldn't let me. They didn't understand that I wanted to clear a path for them. The terrible thing about me was that I felt obliged to extend my hand to them, not because they were beggars . . . not at all! They were braver than I, to face life, to face hunger, humiliation, bad treatment, day after day. They faced it and I couldn't. I was too cowardly.

How I wanted to pack my things and go far away! I dreamed of going to the border, to California. Perhaps I would marry a *gringo*, who would be more understanding than Mexican men. My character was too dry . . . I couldn't be sweet or submissive enough to please the men here. The *macho* Mexican, in his pride and vanity, considered women inferior and enjoyed humiliating them. Only *he* is right and only *his* feelings count. In a discussion, he is not interested in learning the truth, but only in outtalking the others. If a man in a Nash is overtaken by a Chrysler, he will speed to pass it, to show that he is superior, after all. A woman cannot walk alone, without some virile man asserting his "rights" over her. All the men I knew, my father, my brothers, my *novios* and my fellow employees, believed it was their place to give the orders and to be obeyed.

I could never get along with a dominating, imperious man. I didn't like crushing authority, I didn't want to feel inferior. I even fought my father on that score. A thing was not right just because he said it! Men were stronger physically (but not morally), and behind all their "superiority" was force! That was why I had no confidence in Latin men and could never, never, get along with them. I wanted to be independent, to make my own way, to find the right environment.

I made brave dreams for myself, but when I went to the Casa Grande and saw the situation there, I faltered. It would be cowardly to abandon those four motherless children. Delila had a quarrel with my father and sent the children back to Marta. Again, every evening, instead of studying English, I went to the Casa Grande to give them their supper and put them to bed.

I will never forgive my father and that woman of his for the way they used those defenseless children for their own purposes, first, as a pretext to marry, and then, to threaten each other. To be sure, Manuel was a bad parent, but why hadn't my father obliged him from the start to take care of his own children? My *papá* did nothing more than complain and scold, with the same words: "How could he be such a lazy bastard? It is unbelievable! He sleeps till noon, while I break my back working. I don't know what to do with that tramp. He doesn't even work for himself!"

It hurt my heart to think that the children did not have a better tomorrow to look forward to. Were they condemned to have no home, to receive blows from this one and that, to lack clothing, toys, even a bed? It enraged me to see Manuel regularly "forget" to leave money for their food. He and María lived in Gilberto's café and didn't even trouble to visit the kids. My protests were like a cry in the desert; I felt the hot flames of the sun burning me and those four little trees.

I decided that if force were used, Manuel would take his obligations more seriously. One night, I told my father I would speak to the lawyer, *Señor* Marroquín, who had helped get Roberto out of jail. My father hesitated, but agreed. Before I knew it, I was in the Social Service Department, accusing my brother of irresponsibility. He ignored the first two summonses, but I sent a policeman to the café with the third. Manuel turned pale when he was handed that summons and he showed up at the office the next day.

I had brought the four children to the Social Service office in the morning, though I wasn't at all certain Manuel would come. I went in and out of the front entrance to look for him. At about ten o'clock, I spied him standing at the foot of the stairs. I confess I was afraid to face him, but because he might have left without going in, I went to him and said, "My *papá* is waiting for you inside."

Manuel looked at me with anger and hatred. "What are you up to? What are those snakes bothering me for?" Unwillingly, and muttering to himself, he went into the office. I followed, my heart in my mouth.

He was amazed to see his children.

"What are they doing here?"

Alanes hid behind me. Mariquita said, "Don't worry, *papá*. They won't do anything to you. My aunt only wants you to buy us shoes and clothes and give us money for food." I stood on the other side of the desk, well away from my brother. The social worker, *Señorita* Olga, said, "Are you the father of these children?"

"Yes, *señorita*, at your service."

"Young man, your father has accused you of neglecting your children. They are flesh of your flesh and blood of your blood and yet you do not support them. What is it, don't you love them?" She lectured him for a long time. All through it, Manuel listened coldly, his arms crossed,

now and then giving her answers. "Yes, I love them. No, naturally not
. . . No, I don't want anything bad to happen to them . . ."

When *Señorita* Olga was through, Manuel said, "Look, miss, my
children were not abandoned. They were well off with their grandfather. It is not true that they are hit or mistreated. My sister has always
exaggerated. If you give a child a little slap, she calls it a beating.
That's completely false! Delila is a saint. I wish all women were like
her. My children lack nothing. My sister wants them to live like Ameri-
cans. I don't earn enough for that. It is not that I don't want to
support my children, it is that I don't have a regular income."

It made me angry to hear his excuses. "What a barbarian! Is it living
like an American to eat three times a day? to sleep in a bed and have
a coat to cover you? You earn enough to play cards and the horses
and dominoes and to bet on boxers! If you spent that money on the
home, the children would have what they need."

Then Manuel made the mistake of putting out his hand and asking
me for money. He said, "Go on, give me. I don't want advice. What I
want is money to buy them things. If it hurts you to see them without,
then hand over some money."

Then and there, while his hand was still outstretched, the social
worker accused him of refusing to support his children and said they
would be sent to an orphan asylum and he to jail if he did not leave
fifteen *pesos* a day for them at the office. My brother swallowed hard
but had to sign the papers. I also signed and agreed to collect the
money from the office once a week and turn it over to whomever was
taking care of the children.

I don't know how Manuel felt when he left. It must have been a mixture of anger, shame and a wish to beat me. The children and I were
afraid to leave the office though they were already talking excitedly
about the things they wanted to buy. As it turned out, my brother never
went to the office to leave money, but he did give expense money into
the house after that, and he or María went to the Casa Grande to see
the children every day.

One morning, on Ash Wednesday, I arrived before the children left
for school. Conchita, Manuel's youngest girl, came over to tell me that
Marta had bathed them in cold water. It was very cold that day and
naturally it made me angry, although I said nothing for fear of a quarrel. I told Concha not to worry, but to put on her sweater. Marta was
in the kitchen and without further ado, she began to scream at me.

"And what business is it of yours, you daughter-of-a-whore!" She called me a rotting slut, a public whore, and things I cannot repeat. Then she wanted to hit me and, not being a saint, I defended myself. I didn't want to fight but she was out of her mind, kicking and scratching and yelling insults. I still cannot explain why my sister has always hated me so. In the presence of the children, she said I slept with a different man every night. I couldn't stand it and went crying to Roberto's factory to tell him, then to my aunt, and then to my father, who scolded my sister and told her to leave her children with Delila and go to work. Marta got angry and that very night she disappeared with the girls. We believed she had gone back to Crispín, the father of her children.

Manuel and María moved intc the Casa Grande to take care of the four children. For a while everything was fine. Then that witch, Delila, moved into the new house my father had built for her. She took everything out of the Casa Grande and left Manuel without so much as a chair, a dish, or a stove. She took Marta's things, too, and would have taken the flooring as well, if she could. For no reason at all, she tore up my Stenography Certificate and my school papers. Seeing that Manuel had nothing, and always thinking of his children, I told him to go to Lupita's house for my little bed. I also had a big bed there which I would let him have for the children to sleep on. I had sold the mattress to my half-sister, Antonia, so he would have to buy another. I needed money at the time and offered to sell him both beds for only a hundred *pesos*. I considered that just. *Caramba!* He was older than I, and a man, so I thought he should pay me something. Well, he gave me fifty-five *pesos* and forgot about the rest. That's the way it remained . . . well, he was my brother.

The thing that infuriated me was that he didn't buy a mattress and made the children sleep on filthy hemp bags spread over the bedsprings. He and his wife slept in the little bed, on a mattress, and well covered with a blanket. But those poor little things had only a piece of an old quilt over them and they froze all night. Only my brother, who had no soul, could not see the injustice of it.

Mariquita developed bronchitis and was hoarse for three weeks, until I took her to the Children's Hospital. Her father didn't even want to pay for her medicine! One evening, I found little Concha lying on a pile of rags on the floor, burning with fever. María and Manuel hadn't noticed she was sick! María's relatives began to move in and the room became a madhouse. I felt I couldn't let a day pass without going to see what new calamity was happening to the kids. I pestered Manuel to buy a mattress for their bed. He told me to mind my own business and if I loved them so much, to take them and support them.

"Yes, I'll take your children but I'll see that you go to jail first!" I shouted back. "And you know now that I do what I say."

I began to take the children to my room at Juanita's house for four or five days at a time. How I wanted to keep them with me always! I felt they were truly mine. I wished I had a home of my own where they could run and play freely, where they would hear only loving words and would live the way children should. Slowly my wish became a need to do this for them.

Meanwhile, we heard from Marta in Acapulco. She was expecting her fourth child—and I didn't even have one! My *papá* went to see her and returned saying she lived in a place unfit for animals. Who knows whether he wasn't exaggerating. But frankly, I didn't want to hear about my sister. I was much more interested in finding a home for me and the children, yes, and for my brother Roberto.

Roberto had a woman now, his wife, Antonia. He had no house, no job, no clothes, but yes, he had a woman! They were like two little children, sleeping through life. He kept the poor thing, first at my aunt's, and then in the Casa Grande. But my *papá* was angry with Roberto for having hit Delila and one day he chased my brother out. "You cannot stay here!" he said. "You have mud on you and yet you expect to be given a prize!"

We were all embarrassed and angry because he said this in the presence of Antonia, who began to cry. Without a word to my father, Roberto said, "Grab your blanket, old girl, and let's go."

I begged my father to let them stay until they found another place. Thank God, he agreed. My poor brother began to think of setting up a room of his own, although he still had no job. Partly because of him and partly because I, too, wanted a home of my own, I proposed that we share an apartment together. I couldn't do it alone, but with their help ... I had learned to live on a budget and knew the value of money. Every two weeks, on payday, I set aside half the rent, paid ten or fifteen *pesos* on the money I had borrowed to buy clothes, put aside twenty *pesos* for bus fares and snacks, and laid up a week's supply of food. If I had anything left, I would get little things, very insignificant things, for my aunt or for the children. More often, I was short of money before payday and had to go without one or two meals.

I had to convince Roberto that it would be a good thing to live together. "Man! It will be a help to you. I know someone who can get you a job on the railroad or on a Coca-Cola truck and then you can pay half the rent and expense money. Antonia can cook and clean for us and will be happy all day in her own house." He finally agreed and we found a little two-room apartment with a kitchen and a bathroom, in a modest building not far from the Casa Grande.

I was enchanted with it; Roberto and Antonia thought it was a palace! It had windows through which the sun poured all day, a wood-burning water heater in the bathroom, running water, and tiled floors. The rooms were tiny even without furniture, but so much the better, since we had none. The rent was 240 *pesos* a month. We left eighty-five *pesos* as a deposit and went to look for a cosigner for the contract. My father flatly refused. Antonia and Roberto knew no one who would be accepted, and I finally had to ask the supervisor of my office to do it. I sent Antonia back two or three times to leave more money as a deposit and to be certain the landlady would hold it for us. Roberto became annoyed at all the delays and fuss. "So much bother for a damned apartment," he kept saying. He had no idea what it meant to have a home and to pay rent and I think he lost interest, or became frightened. Anyway, he told me he didn't want it any more and I could keep it for myself. I tried to get my deposit back but couldn't, so there I was, stuck with it.

When I moved my things over in a taxi, all I had were my clothes, a radio and an ironing board. I had warned Manuel that if he didn't give me the rest of the money for the beds, for a down payment on a new one, I would take back my little bed. He paid no attention to me, and the day I moved, I went to the Casa Grande and took my bed, leaving them the mattress. Naturally, he and María were angry, but how could I sleep on the floor? Later, Manuel was heartless enough to take the big bed for himself and put the children on the floor, where they had no protection from the rats. I counted nine large holes in the flooring, and my brother did nothing to close them up! He bought a good mattress for the bed, and let the children sleep on a straw *petate*!

Well, I fought him on that because I had told him when I sold it to him that the big bed was for the children. He said he had paid for it and could do what he pleased with it. He refused to speak to me even when I chased after him in the street. That decided it! I went straight to the Casa Grande, left the money with María, and took away the bed in a taxi. Roberto wanted me to give it to him, but *chihuahua!* after all the things he had done to me I wouldn't give it unless he paid for it. I finally sold it to a neighbor for one hundred pesos.

I had been well off in Juanita's house and gave up many comforts when I changed. I didn't have enough money to have the electricity connected, so I used candles the first month. No wardrobe for my clothing, no stove, no way to iron. It took one hour to get to work and I had no time for breakfast. I had to use my food money for other things and for days I ate only coffee and bread. Luckily for me, at ten-thirty every morning, all the girls in my office chipped in to buy candy and cookies and soft drinks.

I worked extra hours to earn money to fix up the house, but Christmas came around and I still had no furniture. One evening, I went to pay Juanita some money I owed her and I confided my troubles to her. I told her I wanted money to be able to bring my nieces and nephews into my home, once and for all, but it would take forever to save enough from what I earned. "I shall have to borrow money at interest."

"*Ay*, Consuelo, what a shame! Why don't you try out in the 'Amateur Hour' on television? You can sing! You can dance! If you win, you will have a pile of money, and contracts for jobs as well!"

All I could think of was, "I must have money. I must have money." I wasn't looking well. I had lost weight and was pale. Every few weeks I had a cold or bronchitis or stomach trouble. But the thought of winning money gave me strength, and one day I went to the offices of the *televicentro*. I passed the test for singers and dancers and was accepted for the final tryouts. One of the judges thought I was better "material" for dancing than for singing, and instead of putting me on the "Amateur Hour," they gave me a scholarship to study dancing at the School of Fine Arts! They would pay all the expenses and after six months, if I did well, I would be launched as a dancer in the theatre or movies or in a night club so that I could pay them back. I said yes to everything, without thinking, and there were more appoint-ments, telephone calls and interviews. In April, I entered the school of modern dance.

I worked at my government job until 2:30 P.M. every day, and had classes at the dancing school from four to eight or nine o'clock every evening. I was on a scholarship but had to take out another loan to buy dance slippers, a leotard, and extra fares. I worked furiously at the exercises and the steps, to catch up with the others in the class-

It took an amazing amount of energy and left me sweating profusely. All those previous months of not eating well had undermined my body. I was still eating on the run ... some days I had nothing but Coca-Colas and sweets until supper time at ten o'clock at night. By then, Roberto and Antonia were living with me, and to save a few *pesos*, I waited until I went home to eat what my sister-in-law had prepared. Never in my life had I worked so hard! I had to budget my time and my money, every minute and every *centavo* counted.

After two months of this, I began to have bad headaches every day. I couldn't get up in the morning and all day I was too tired to work. I lost weight and felt that my spirit and my health were going. I didn't see how I could possibly continue to study dancing. It looked as though I had to face another defeat, another disillusionment. What was I to do with the volcano of hope that had been aroused in me, the hope to become something, the hope not to die without leaving a mark behind me?

So when one of the young men in the dance class asked me if I would like to be a movie extra during the vacation, I accepted. Through him, I got a job at the Churubusco Studios. I was very happy, and a bit afraid, to be there among the stars and important people of the movie industry. Never in my life had I dreamed of acting before a camera, and *zas!* there I was, on location. I acted as naturally as I could and they seemed to be satisfied, for they kept me on a whole week. I earned 190 *pesos*, including meals, for those seven exciting days.

As I was hanging about the employment office, hoping for another assignment, this character, a minor actor, came over and told me to get into the car, for he was taking me on location. I believed him and got in.

"What kind of work are you looking for?"

"I? Well, I like to sing. But I am only an amateur."

"That's nothing, one must begin somewhere. We all must start at the bottom to get to the top. Look at me! I'm not ashamed to admit I started with nothing, and now look where I am. Have you seen my last film?"

"No, I don't go to the movies often. What did you say your name was?"

While we were speaking, *Señor* Ángel Montero drove his big car out of the studios onto a tree-lined highway. He was handsome and well dressed and ... an actor! He showed me some of his recent photos and promised to autograph one for me. He spoke of his roles, of the famous stars he knew; he said that he was starting a booking agency and was looking for talent. He needed a young woman to sing with a trio. He asked me to sing. When the song was over, he looked impressed.

"Man! I admit I didn't expect you to be that good! I think you will do. All you need is some coaching to get more expression into it. I'll get the singer, Sarita, to coach you. She's a good friend of mine and won't refuse. I'll take you there right now."

"*Señor* Ángel, excuse me, but aren't we going on location?"

"What a girl! Don't you trust me? I don't know how others have treated you, but I am a gentleman."

"No, no! I didn't mean that . . . I would like to meet *Señora* Sarita. I was simply curious . . . just asking, that's all."

"That's better. Look, the truth is, I like you. If you only knew how many women . . . how many opportunities I have! I don't look for them, they run after me. For example, do you know the actress Martita? Well . . ."

While he spoke, I thought, "Naturally, knowing all the artists, he wouldn't bother with me." We had been driving for quite a while. It had begun to rain. He kept talking about his women friends and about himself. I began to get apprehensive.

"Where is Sarita's house? I didn't know it would be so far."

"Man! I told you it is near. Don't you trust me? You make me feel like a barbarian!"

"Excuse me, *Señor* Ángel, but I'm anxious to meet her."

He looked angry and I felt ashamed of myself. Suddenly, he turned into a driveway and there before my eyes, through the heavy rain, I saw the word "Motel."

"*Señor* Ángel, I am not going in there! You said we would go on location, that's why I went with you."

"Sh! Stop making a racket. I don't like that kind of clowning. I'll take you on location, but right now I'm tired."

He stopped the car in front of one of the bungalows and got out to open my door. I was nervous and worried. I felt a lump in my throat and wanted to cry but couldn't because of fear or shame. I wouldn't get out. It was raining hard and he was getting very wet. He pulled me out of the car and held my arm so tight it hurt.

"I don't want to go in. Let me alone!" How humiliated I felt!

"I'm not asking your permission. Don't be absurd. What a fool! It will only take a moment. How many girls would like to be in your place. They would feel honored! So why not you? Do you think you are a goddess? You should thank me!"

I sat on the bed. He laughed mockingly, locked the door, and unbuttoned his shirt.

"Kiss me!"

"No. I don't want to. Let me alone! You'll have to do it by force. Let me go, you're hurting me."

"Oh, shut up! Why are you making such a tango of it? I suppose you are a virgin? Come on, girl, take things easily. This is the most natural thing in the world. What are you afraid of? You are an enchanting little witch, but I'm not used to begging. If I can do it with Sarita and Martita, why not with you, eh?"

Four months later I found out I was pregnant. I didn't suspect it because my menstruation had not stopped. I had never seen *Señor* Ángel again, and when I called the studios or at the *televicentro,* where he had appeared, they told me he was away on location. I finally found a doctor who was willing to do the delicate operation and I sold my new clothes closet to pay the expenses. I was very ill after it and missed two weeks of work.

Thus, to my sorrow, was my first, bitter encounter with that infamous, cursed Mexican *machismo.* I, like an infinite number of other Mexican women, was part of that cruel game, in which the domineering male wins. "Shall I knock you down or let you free?" There is nothing generous, noble or worthy in it, for there is a price to being let free. It is a barbarous act of egotism and advantage, adorned with persuasive words.

After my illness, I was too nervous to work in an office any more. I was in debt and three months behind in the rent. My father refused to help me and there was no one else to ask. I needed money desperately. I went back to the Studios to see if I could become a permanent extra. I met a girl who had made three thousand *pesos* as an extra in just one movie. She said I must become a member of the *Sindicato* and sent me to *Señor* Pissaro, a union official who might help me.

He said to me, "So, once you put your shoes before a camera, you want to do it again, eh?"

"Yes, *Señor* Pissaro. It is that I need the money."

"Ah? And you don't have membership papers? Can you leave the city to go on location?"

"Yes, sir."

"Good! Are you married?"

"Mmmm . . . well . . ." I looked at his face.

"Man! I'm only asking to see if you are really free to be sent out. You have nothing to worry about. I will arrange your papers and everything. Be here on Monday."

This time, I realized what I was doing. *Señor* Pissaro was not bad-looking. He must be worth something to become an official. He was in a position to help me. If he wanted something from me, I would be willing . . . especially when we were out of the city on location, or at least after I got to know him better. I fixed my nails and hair and got my best dress out of the pawnshop where Roberto had taken it when he needed some quick money. It wouldn't hurt to look attractive!

But I hadn't expected *Señor* Pissaro to take me to a motel that very day, and to force himself on me like *Señor* Ángel! Is it that I really looked like an easy woman? But I tried to fight him off! Then when I couldn't, I turned into a stone. I controlled myself in an incredible way and didn't respond. He was desperate and forced me down with his knee.

"Please, *Señor* Pissaro, don't treat me like this!"

"What do you want? To let you go, so that later you can mock me? Above all I am a man, and you are trying to demean my manhood! Why don't you fulfill your duty as a woman? Don't be ridiculous! You help me and I will help you."

He got what he wanted. But when I asked him about going on location, he said, "If I go, you go. I don't know whether they will send me. Call me tomorrow at this number."

I called and he wasn't there; I went to the *Sindicato* offices and could never find him. Finally, I admitted to myself that I had been taken in. I didn't let myself think about it, but closed my mind to all feeling. A short time later, I went to live in the apartment of an American student who had come to Mexico for his vacation. He introduced me to some of his friends.

Caray! So many things have happened to me since then. I don't know where I get the strength! What can I do to stop punishing myself? Was it bad luck or bad faith that was my undoing? Not a day goes by when I do not have some filthy proposition, nor a powerful reason to accept it. But now nothing matters to me, not morality, nor principles, nor my love for my family. I try to quiet the pain and anxiety I feel in my breast and look with indifference on the four children I have loved so much. It wasn't right for me to expend all my moral and physical strength to offer them a better life, only to fall in a faint.

I have no job any more and that gives me a powerful defense. Now, when I see my aunt sick or upset, I can say, "I am not working. I cannot help you." When Roberto needs a lawyer or has to pay a fine, I can say, "I have no money. Don't come to me." And the same with the children, for whom I had once held out so many hopes. I must break the chain that drags me down and injures me, thought it costs me five years of my life and all my noble sentiments. I will live half blind, like the rest of the people, and so will adapt to reality.

But though I try to disengage myself, I cannot fail to see what is happening to my family. Oh, God! They are destroying themselves, little by little. They are using themselves up, disappearing slowly, like my uncles, my mother, my grandmother, Elena, Paula . . . they have all gone and left me too soon. Now my aunt Guadalupe is like a light going out, a wax candle at the foot of the altar; Marta is but twenty-four years old and looks over thirty; each year, I think this will be Roberto's last, for his life is agitated and he fears nothing. To him the edge of a sharp knife is the same as a piece of velvet. Manuel? yes, he will live, but at whose cost? How many more times will he test the love of his children by denying them food? It is horrible to think that he will survive his own children! Paula! how could you have let yourself die so easily? How could you have abandoned your adorable children, knowing what was in store for them?

Marta

THE REASON I WENT BACK TO CRISPÍN . . . WELL, NOW, HOW WAS IT? The thing was, after all that time, his mother was asking to see the girls, Concepción and Violeta. Trini was just one and a half years old and Crispín had never asked about her or made her a single *fiesta*. I took the two older girls to see their grandmother in December. Crispín and I talked things over, though there was really no need to discuss, because he knew very well he was to blame for Trini.

Well, it was a long time since we had spoken and we kept looking at each other, you know what I mean? So he said, "All right, then, so what?"

"Well, so what?" I said. "Concepción needs shoes and clothes because she hasn't any. And Violeta, too." I really didn't have anything else to say to him.

"We'll buy them on Saturday," he says.

"All right, fine."

"Your *papá* is with Delila, isn't he?"

"No, I don't know." I think my cheeks got red, because then he said, "Well, you don't have to be ashamed."

"I don't have anything to be ashamed of. Is it a shame to live with a woman?"

"No, don't get embarrassed."

And that was as far as we talked. He said he would wait for me at the Social Security building on Saturday, and I went home with the girls.

Saturday came and we went and bought Concepción a pair of shoes, and Violeta, too. I didn't mention Trini at all. The only thing he said to me was that I was too proud. I told him it wasn't pride, but shame, that after what he had done, he shouldn't even have spoken to me again.

"What did I do?" he says, as if he expected me to overlook everything and go back to him without mentioning Trini. It seemed he was willing to recognize her as his daughter, as though she was just going to be born starting from that moment. Imagine, he hadn't left me until I was seven months pregnant; that was when he tried to make out that she wasn't his daughter. If a man knows his wife is going to have a baby and it is not his, right away he would say, "Okay, where did you get it, because I am sure it isn't mine."

But Crispín didn't do that. He didn't leave me until two months before Trini was born. He wasn't ashamed to go around with me all that time. If it was like he said, he would have left me from the first minute, don't you think? I really don't know what was the matter. His mother and sister had a big influence over him and told him I was going around with other men. And I wasn't going with anyone at that time. Wherever anyone saw me, I was alone or with the girls, so I have nothing to reproach myself with on that score.

When we were through buying, I said good-bye and started to leave.

"You're going? Just like that?" said Crispín.

"What do you expect? What do you want?" I said. Then I got mad. "Do you expect me to pay you back? What do you want me to pay with, my body?" I talked like that ever since the time I had tangled with him on the street, when we beat each other. You might say that was the day I freed myself from him. From then on, I said what I had to say with strong words. Lots of times I would even tell him that he should be ashamed not to support his little girls and all that, things I couldn't say before because I was afraid to go too far.

"Don't be like that, Marta," he said.

"Why not? That's what you always wanted, isn't it? I knew just what to expect from you, that you would have to get something in exchange for what you give your daughters."

"No," he says, "it's not that . . . I don't know how to explain it."

"If you were fed up with me, why do you want to go back to the same thing?"

"I never said I was fed up."

"The proof is that you left and didn't even say a word."

He kept quiet and we walked on, until we came to the door of a hotel.

"Come on," he says.

"No!" I say.

"Don't make a fuss."

"I'll make one if I feel like, even if you bust me in the mouth." Then I said all of a sudden, "Sure, you have to receive some kind of payment, don't you?" So I up and go in. After being without a man for so long, I went into that hotel with him.

Why did I do it? Because I felt like? Because of desire? Not exactly. There were several men around who hadn't just proposed taking me to a hotel, but who had offered to set up a home for me. Nevertheless, I didn't because I knew perfectly well ever since Trini was a year old that if I went with a man I would become pregnant again. I have always gotten pregnant after the girls were a year old and that was precisely why I held myself back.

But I really couldn't say that Crispín forced me into that hotel, not in a certain sense. You might say I had my next baby for two pairs of shoes. He knew when he bought them that I had no other way to repay him. I fell in, because I said to myself, "This man is not going to change."

So we had this interview in the hotel. As far as whether I enjoyed it . . . well, I didn't because I did it with anger. The second time we went to the hotel . . . the thing was, we went again to buy clothes for Concepción but, as a matter of fact, we didn't buy anything because we went straight to the hotel. That time I made him mad because I got away from him. I began to see that I was being a fool; all at once it made me mad to see that we were going to do the same thing all over again. We were in bed and he was just on the point of making use of me when I got mad and got out of bed.

"Where are you going?"

"I'm leaving."

"Why are you leaving?"

"Because I feel like it."

"You just try to go out and you'll see what will happen."

"You won't do anything to me. Not you or twenty like you will stop me. You're not dealing with the same dupe as before."

This had happened other times in hotels, but I never got past the door because he would catch me and slap me around. He must have figured I would be afraid to go this time. He was still lying there when I left. I was nervous in the street, wondering when he would catch up with me and start a fight.

That was in December. In January, I waited for my menstruation and it didn't come. I didn't even have time to tell Crispín I was pregnant because when he came on the sixth of January, the Day of the Kings, to give Concepción and Violeta their toys, he was angry with me and wouldn't come in. Then, that evening I saw him in the street as the girls and I were going to visit Lupita. When he saw us, he crossed the street to avoid me, but Concepción yelled, "Look, there goes Crispín," and he came back.

"Where are you going?" he says to me.

"To Lupita's."

"Ah, you are going to see your lover there."

"What lover?" I was fed up with his suspiciousness and to change the subject I told him about the circus in the El Dorado Colony. He gave me five *pesos* to take the girls.

"What about me?" I asked, and he gave me another five *pesos*. Then he said to Concepción, "I'll come for you on Saturday, daughter, to buy you candy."

The week went by without me seeing him. On Saturday morning, my friend Raquelle came in and said, "How do you like that! There's Crispín standing in the doorway of his house and that Eustakia is walking up and down in front."

"Yes?" I say, "I've got a yen to see them together."

"Okay, then let's go."

This Eustakia had gotten mixed up with Raquelle's *novio* and came out of it pregnant. Then she took up with Crispín and told him he was the father of her child. So Raquelle and I were both sore at the girl.

We walked by Crispín's house but nothing was happening and we kept going around the block. The next thing I knew, I saw Crispín in the distance, walking with his arm around another woman, who turned out to be an old friend of his family. She was married and had children and I had often seen her in Crispín's house. I had always thought there was something queer about her, but how was I to know she and Crispín . . . I was such a kid then, anyone could make a sucker out of me.

"Just look at that snake," I said to Raquelle. "Here I am expecting to see him with one woman and I find him with another. And look who it is! It's Amelia."

Crispín went into the Social Security building and Amelia sat down on the steps to wait for him. Just to be mean, I up and very calmly sit next to her, just like that. I don't know what saint she commended herself to, but at that moment a man she was acquainted with rode by on a bicycle and she went over to talk to him, acting like she didn't know what was happening.

I figured Crispín would come soon, so I hid in the corner beauty parlor, which was run by Nicha, a friend of mine. When Nicha saw me she said, "What do you say? What are you up to?"

"You'd be surprised," I say. "My old man . . . my ex-old man, is running around with that bitch there and I just want to see them together."

"Really? Are you that thick-skinned toward the louse?"

"Why not? We haven't been together since I-don't-know-when and I want to catch him with one of his women. But I have no way of making demands on him or of accusing him."

I saw Crispín coming. Amelia had crossed the street and had passed the beauty parlor, where I was watching from behind the curtains. He was following her. Just as he came by the shop, I sent out Concepción to greet him.

"*Papá*, give me a *quinto!*"

Crispín turned around, very surprised. I came out carrying Trini. He was saying to Concepción, "Saturday, I'll come and take you on Saturday." He was real nervous and kept looking toward Amelia, who had turned around to watch. Then I said, "Come, daughter. Can't you see you're not wanted here. Come on, why are you making a pest of yourself? You are interfering with your *papá*."

And instead of him asking, "What makes you say that?" because after all we were beginning a reconciliation, what he came out with was, "You and I have nothing to say to each other."

It made me furious to see him turn toward that woman with a frantic expression on his face. He must have been saying to himself, "Now I've given away the show!"

I said, "You are right. We don't have anything to say to each other, so don't get the idea that I am going to fight. That's where you are making a big mistake. Come on, daughter, let's go."

I was still calm. Then all at once he came out with it.

"If you want me to support you, why do you go whoring around?"

"Look, I don't go whoring around. I didn't get my children on the street. You know very well who gave them to me."

We were in front of the machine shop and there were plenty of people listening. I kept on talking.

"It's too bad about the skirt you got hold of. Maybe you were right to change me, but not for such a woman. You like the kind who already has some sucker hooked so that you have no obligation. You are a man who likes to take advantage. A real man doesn't do what you did."

"You shouldn't talk, because you've got your pimp."

"I don't have one, but I'm going to find myself one just to break your jaw." I called him bastard and a bunch of foul names. I was plenty vulgar to him. "And don't bother me again. That's all I ask. Just don't bother me again."

That was one of the biggest fights we ever had. I had once warned him that I would stick with him until I saw with my own eyes that he was going with someone else. Other people would tell me he was going with girls, and I would try to forget what they said. But what I saw with my own eyes, I could never forget. "So watch out that I don't see you," I had told him. "For if I do, don't count on me from that time on."

I should have been able to develop a shell and be like other women who do not pay attention to what their husbands do outside the house, especially since mine was trying to get me back. But when I saw him making a fool of me by taking up with that old woman, I couldn't contain myself. I preferred to renounce everything again. I could never accept the idea of him being able to have another woman and me at the same time. No! It would be better for him to abandon me, or me to leave him, once and for all. So I up and got on the bus, and I haven't spoken to him since.

In February, on the thirteenth, I had my big fight with Consuelo. Delila had gotten tired of taking care of Manuel's children, so I had charge of all four of them, in addition to my three. Roberto was working in the factory and had been giving me money toward expenses, but after a while he stopped. He just didn't want to any more and there was no way of forcing him. The only one who helped me was my *papá*. He gave me ten *pesos* daily besides bringing me coffee, sugar and oil. When the children were brought to the Casa Grande, Manuel agreed to give me ten *pesos* a day for their food. His new wife, María, came over once in a while to help me with his kids.

I had warned Manuel that the day he didn't leave me expense

money, I wouldn't have anything to give his children. I said it without raising my voice but it didn't do any good. Twice, he didn't give me money and I had to send the children to Gilberto's café to look for him. I gave them their breakfast early and then said to Mariquita, the oldest one, "Go on, go to your father and tell him that you haven't had breakfast yet because he didn't bring me money."

I had to step lively to feed all those kids and send them off to school. I brought Roberto his dinner at the factory at twelve o'clock sharp and the children had to eat at twelve-thirty to get back to school. And I always sent them to school bathed, or at least washed.

So this day it got to be time to go to school. I said to Mariquita, "Now, I'm late. I am going to let you bathe them. But don't bathe them with cold water, daughter." Well, she bathed them all with cold water . . . Alanes, Domingo, Conchita and Concepción. I managed to bathe Violeta and Trini and was hurrying the older ones off to school when Consuelo came in.

Well, right off Consuelo saw Concepción come over with a pencil and a notebook of Domingo's. So Consuelo began to scold her, saying, "I told you not to be taking things that belong to your cousins."

Consuelo and my oldest daughter had had a few quarrels because Concepción did not want to lend her toys to Alanes and Domingo, who destroyed everything. She was very careful with her things and, naturally, she didn't want the boys to smash them. That made Consuelo mad. She had always favored Manuel's children, especially Mariquita, and rare was the day she gave anything to mine.

So I up and say, "It seems like you don't understand your aunt, Concepción. Apparently you like to be scolded."

"Yes, from now on I'm going to be as mean about your cousin's things as you are about yours," went on Consuelo. That made me mad and I threw the pencil to her.

"Here's your stinking pencil. Is that what you are fighting about?"

We had been half sore at each other for some time anyway, because Consuelo was butting into my obligations too much. I was the one who had those kids day in and day out, and she came only in the evenings to make their supper and to boss everyone around.

Just think! Manuel usually gave me the food money the night before, so that I had it for the next day. When I gave the kids supper, I served them coffee with milk and bread and what was left over from dinner. That was what everyone I knew ate for supper. But not

Consuelo! No, Consuelo, the presumptuous one, would go and buy eggs for them, just as if I had plenty of money. Ever since she went to school and worked in offices, she became so high-class she looked down on the way we did things. *La Presumida* kept insisting that we didn't eat right . . . she even bought herself a knife and fork . . . and when she went out to buy food, she would come back with things like cornflakes and canned soup and tomato juice. She would spend all the house money on things we didn't need. Why should I buy a can of peas when with the same money I can get each of my children a slice of meat? I knew how to stretch the money so we could all eat well, but she didn't understand.

There were times when she left me with not over two *pesos*. Imagine having to face the day with two *pesos!* She did this to me four times, but I didn't say a word, I would just receive my money from my *papá*, without complaining to him about her, and would use the money to feed all of us. I didn't fight with my sister, but we weren't getting along well.

After I threw the pencil, Conchita complained to my sister that I had bathed her in cold water. That made Consuelo angry. She turned to me and said, "If you had any shame you wouldn't even show your face."

"Shame? What have I got to be ashamed about?"

"Sure. Even though my *papá* is supporting you, even though Manuel buys you your clothes and puts food in your mouth, you aren't able to take care of his children properly. It is obvious they are not your childen. Manuel is supporting you and you do this to his kids!"

"Supporting me? He is not that good-hearted. If he barely gives enough for his children, he won't be giving to others." Would you believe it? She said that to me, and it wasn't only Conchita who was bathed that way, but all of them. My sister kept it up, too.

"Your children are being supported, and you still have the nerve to be touchy."

"Yes," I said, "but you are not the one who is supporting me. When did I ever ask you for anything?"

"Oh," she says, "then give me back all the clothes I gave you."

"What clothes?" I had a few clothes then, but they were made out of dress lengths my *papá* brought me, or were ones I bought myself on payments. Consuelo had given me a little jumper and robe that didn't fit her. Her boss's wife had given her a bunch of clothes, but that was all she had passed on to me, because they were of no use to her. She kept telling me that she was the one who had been clothing me and it was a lie. If she ever gave me anything, it was old stuff that didn't fit her any more.

So I up and open the wardrobe. "Go ahead, take out your dresses. If you think I have clothes of yours here, take them out." It made me mad because she said that all I did was whore around, opening my legs so that they could give me kids. "If it comes to whores, who knows who is a bigger one! All my children are from the same father. So far you haven't been a procuress for me, have you?"

It made me mad to hear her talk that way, especially because she went to live with Jaime after breaking up with Mario. Yes, she was stupid enough to go back to Jaime after losing her piece, as we say here, and of course it didn't work because all he did was take revenge on her for the times she had humiliated him. I don't know how it was that she didn't become pregnant . . . she says she didn't let him use her once, but I don't see how that is possible since they slept in the same bed. She got sick with anger and finally left Jaime. But later she began to paint herself up again and have nice clothes and manicures and who knows how she got them. She worked but spent all her money on rent and food and things for her new apartment. Naturally, what she earned wouldn't cover those expenses.

I reminded her of all that. "Just because you have no children, doesn't prove a thing! Who knows how you get rid of them."

I pulled out the jumper and ripped it. It had been too big for me and I had paid to remodel it, so I had the right to tear it.

"Here is your dress!"

"Miserable one!" That was her favorite word "Miserable fool! Don't tear my dress. Don't tear it!" When she saw it torn apart, she started for the wardrobe, to rip my clothes. "Now, you'll see," she yelled.

So I stepped in and tangled with her. We really fought, scratching and tearing each other's clothes. I didn't realize it until later. For the moment, I was so mad I couldn't see anything. María, who was pregnant then, came in and separated us. The children saw the whole thing and didn't make it to school that day. I didn't even notice when Consuelo left.

My *papá* arrived at about three-thirty. I took one look at him and said to myself, "Mmmm . . . this is it. The bomb went off already."

"What happened?" he says. "Consuelo came around crying and saying you called her a lot of dirty things and tore her clothes."

Imagine, my sister went to bother my father at the café and fill him with a lot of lies. So there I was, letting him scold me, keeping my mouth shut. That's the way my father is, he just bawls you out without knowing the way it happened.

"You have children and you still don't know how to act. You all refuse to understand. Not one of the four of you behaves like a brother or sister."

"But, *papá,* it wasn't my fault. I can't help it if she got mad because I bathed the kids in cold water." That's all I said, though it made me very angry to be blamed for everything.

Consuelo had started it by saying I just let them all give me babies. That was always a sore point with my sister and was at the bottom of it. I don't know whether it was jealousy or what . . . she had always been envious and angry, like my great-aunt Catarina . . . but the fact of the matter is that she didn't like the idea that my father was helping me. I think that was the reason why she couldn't take it and blew up.

The rest of my family was the same and I felt resentful. Manuel, too, judged the way I lived. One day we were talking about María and he had said, "That she-goat only likes to go walking in the street. I told her that when she gets tired of staying in the house, she should go out for a little while. I'm not the type to keep my woman in a cave like a rabbit, only to make babies. I don't want her to be like you, just buried by four walls and never dressing up and going out."

"If I don't go out, it is because I have plenty to do in the house. What business do I have in the street? I don't see that it will advance me any."

I don't know whether he meant to call me a rabbit or what, but indirectly he did and it made me mad. Who was he to talk? At least I took care of the children I made! He never loved his children enough to be close to them. The trick of having children is not just to bring them into the world, but to feed them and send them to school and give them the attention they need. What use is it to bring them up like animals?

And his wife was worse. María had told my friend Herlinda's daughter that we were crazy if we expected her to take care of Manuel's kids. She couldn't stand them and she didn't intend to kill herself working for them, that they were his kids, not hers, so let him do it himself. Naturally, if he doesn't feel anything for them, how can you expect her to? There isn't anyone who can feel for kids like their own father or mother. Manuel never acted like a father because he wasn't obliged to. He knew that even if he didn't work or give expense money, he could always count on eating and having a place to sleep in my father's house. If my father had made us work when we were small, if he had said, "If you don't work, you don't eat," we all would have been different.

Anyway, I was sick and tired of being criticized and blamed for everything, especially when I was not the only guilty one. My *papá* stayed on for a while, to scold me. So I up and began to do things around the house. To begin with, I had a lot of dirty clothes. I sorted out my things from those of my nieces and nephews. My father watched me closely. He must have been suspicious, for he said, "What are you going to do with the clothes?"

"I'm going to wash them," I answered.

That was when he told me he was going to give me half of the lot in the El Dorado Colony and build me a room, even if only out of boards, so that none of my brother's or sisters would mix into my affairs again. He said he would arrange the papers and build the room and move me there very soon. I said nothing and he left.

As soon as he was gone, I found a flour sack and put in it a blanket, a sheet, three dresses each for me and the girls and a bunch of rags for Trini's diapers. I gave all the kids their supper and told Mariquita to bring María. I sent Concepción to see if my friend Herlindita would buy my new watch for eighty *pesos*.

I hated to sell the watch because it was only one week old. The week before, I had received four hundred *pesos* from a *tanda* I had joined with ten other neighbors, and I used the money to buy myself a watch and a jacket. I took a trip to Puebla with Angélica Rivera and my girls, and I still had fifty *pesos* left.

When María arrived, I told her I was leaving.

"Where to?" she asked.

"I don't know where, but I'm going. Everybody here has something to say about what I do. I'm like a holy-water fount, everybody sticks his hand in."

"But what will you do? Better don't go," she said.

"No, I'm not staying here."

Roberto came in, but he was mad at me, too, and didn't even ask me where we were going or anything. Herlinda didn't have the money to buy my watch, so I picked up the girls and the sack and went across the courtyard to say good-bye to my *comadre* Angélica.

"Better don't go," she said.

"But I can't stay. You see how things are here."

While we were talking, along came my aunt Guadalupe. She had come to scold me about something, but I was fed up by then and said, "No, stop pestering me. I'm sick and tired of everything." I had never spoken like that to her before.

She just looked at me. "Come on, come on, or I'll think you really meant it."

"Listen," I said, "stop bothering me. You'd think I was your daughter or something."

I picked up my sack and took a bus to the central depot. There, the night bus to Acapulco was the only one taking passengers, so I bought a ticket and got on with my three girls.

I was so scared when I got on that bus, I must have looked as though I had robbed someone. My ticket was for seat No. 13, but I sat in the one behind it. The man who had the ticket for No. 12 got on just as the bus was leaving.

"This is my seat," he said.

I was so nervous and depressed that one seat or another was the same to me. When I had first boarded the bus, there was a boy, he couldn't have been over sixteen, sitting in front of me across the aisle. Right away he asked me where I was going and if I knew anyone in Acapulco.

"No, nobody."

"Me, either," he says. "I'm running away from my father and going to look for my godmother. My father is a government agent."

Then he offered me some chocolates and talked some more. I didn't feel like talking to anyone. I wanted to be absolutely alone.

"If you like, I'll take one of the girls in my seat so you won't be so crowded." But the girls didn't want to go. I said, "Thanks, all the same."

That was when Baltasar got on, and I had to move to seat No. 13. He sat behind me, so I didn't see his face or talk to him or anything. This boy across the aisle kept talking to me.

"I had a girl friend who gave me a ring." Then he shows me a couple of pawn tickets. One was for fifteen hundred *pesos* for a ring. He said he had plenty of money, but I didn't pay much attention to him. When the bus stopped, he invited me for a cup of coffee, I didn't accept and stayed in my seat with the three kids on my lap. Because of that boy, I later had a big argument with Baltasar. He kept throwing it up to me that we were *novios* and that I had gotten on the bus with him. He even thought the kid was the father of my child!

Baltasar and I didn't talk at all during the trip, except once when he said, "Pass me one of your girls. The inspector is coming through and he will make you buy another ticket."

"Another ticket!" I said. "I'll be ruined!" So I handed him Violeta for the rest of the journey.

I sat with the other two, crying nearly all the way. I think it was the saddest day of my life. If it hadn't been for the children, I would have done away with myself. It was not the first time I had had such thoughts; in fact, once I bought some rat poison, a package of The Last Supper, and had already mixed it with water, when my father came to look for me on the roof and stopped me. I was little then, still in school, and he had scolded me, I don't remember why, and all of a sudden I felt alone and fed up with my life. I really gave my father a scare. If he hadn't noticed that I got out of bed and went to the roof, who knows what would have happened?

Later, with Crispín, at times I would just see my situation and would feel desperate. I was in the same despair on the way to Acapulco. I felt that for me everything was finished. Life was a lie and all doors were closed. It is a bitter thing to have your brothers and sisters throw up to you what you are, and to be blamed unjustly. I never liked them to interfere with me or my children, especially the children. I would light up like a rocket, because I saw the way Roberto and Consuelo would take Manuel's kids here and there and do things for them only when it occurred to them. They just pulled those kids apart and upset them. I never permitted that with my children and so my brothers and sister say I am very touchy and cannot be spoken to.

It's true that my character is the worst in the family. I am very rancorous; I *never* forget and I stop speaking to the person who does a thing to me. If he is in the wrong, I hate him all the more. Delila always says that Manuel and I were the best because we get even with others by shutting up. They soon forget their anger, but not I.

I wish I were like other women, like my aunt and my stepmothers,

who took their sufferings with resignation. They never complained of
their lot or thought of throwing themselves into a life of perdition. But
some of us are not prepared to bear up under great trouble, and we act
crazy. Like me, for example. I took my children and up and left,
without knowing what would happen to us. Not until we were on the
bus, did I think, "And now what? Where am I going? What shall I do?
I haven't enough money . . ."

Toward the end of the trip, Baltasar leaned forward and asked me
if I had relatives in Acapulco.

"No, I'm going to look for work."

Then he says, "If you are interested, I have an aunt who runs a
restaurant. I can get a job for you there right away. You won't have
any problem about food for the children there."

I thought it over. I could do something there, even if washing
dishes. So I said, "I'll see. What I want is work."

"I'll talk to my cousin when we get there."

Finally, the bus arrived in Acapulco and we got off. Then this boy
says to me, "Look, there's a hotel. You can put up there if you want."

Baltasar was standing beside us. He said, "Are you still coming with
me or not?"

So there I was between the two of them, asking myself which one I
should go with. I figured the kid had money on him but wherever
we went people would say I was his sweetheart. And maybe he stole
the pawn tickets or the money and I would be blamed. Baltasar didn't
look too good either. His shirt and cotton pants were dirty and
wrinkled (he told me later he had been drinking for two days
straight), and he was wearing the cheapest kind of moccasins. His
shirt was unbuttoned all the way down, showing his fat belly. I didn't
like the looks of the gold earring he had in his right ear. With that,
and his curly hair and gold teeth and eyes that popped like a frog's,
he looked, like Manuel says, a bit exotic. But he was older than the boy
and gave me more confidence.

"Well," I said to Baltasar, "let's go see your cousin." I didn't want
to hurt the kid's feelings and to let him know I wasn't showing favoritism, I said to him, "Come on, let's all have a cup of coffee meanwhile.
What do you say?"

So the kid says, "All right. I'll catch up with you. I want to buy
some cigarettes." He left and I never saw him again.

Well, Baltasar took me to his cousin's lunch counter and ordered coffee. He had his problems, too, as he was adventuring at that time. He explained his situation. He did trucking around Acapulco but had no place to live. He slept in the truck and ate on the road. He was wondering where to put me up. It was not that he had no family there, for he had a mother and stepfather, a father and stepmother, and I don't know how many half-brothers and half-sisters and aunts, uncles and cousins. But he wasn't on good terms with most of them, and didn't like to ask favors.

His uncle Pancho came by and they whispered together. Then Baltasar said, "Come on, let's go to my uncle's house. He is a good person and you will be fine there." And off I went, like a cow to the slaughter.

"Well," I thought, "if I see something wrong, I can always scream, can't I?"

We rested up in Pancho's house and then Baltasar took us to the beach to see La Quebrada and the Malecón and the wharves. I found out later that he sold his radio to his cousin for eighty *pesos* to have money to spend on us. I still didn't see things clearly or know what Baltasar was like. I was upset and not really at peace, but there I was, smiling and laughing. I was just saying over and over to myself, "Thank God, we arrived all right." That was about as far as I could think.

In the evening, I was very suspicious because Baltasar said his boss wanted him to leave for Acapona for a few days. He told me not to worry about anything, that his uncle would not molest me. Before he left, he brought me meat and lard and corn dough for *tortillas*, and gave me twenty *pesos*.

"Take this until I get back. If you need anything, tell my uncle."

Pancho loaned me a cot. I put the girls to sleep on the floor on one side of the cot, and Pancho slept on the floor on the other side. He turned out to be a very nice man and never bothered me. I found out later that he had asked Baltasar whether he could have me, but was told no, that Baltasar was thinking of me for himself. When Baltasar came back, he slept on the floor near the girls and still didn't bring up the subject of my going to bed with him.

I kept saying to myself that he was going to expect something from me in return. "If the father of my children demands payment from me, then another man would be even more justified." I felt uneasy every night, between those two men. I figured if it wasn't one, it would be the other who would jump on me. I couldn't sleep. In all that heat, I didn't take off my clothes. I would lie there, sweating and starting at every little noise, expecting one of them to get into my bed.

But Baltasar was a man like no other. For eighteen days he gave me expense money without touching me. I told him I needed work and didn't want to be a burden on him, that I felt bad letting him support me.

"If you like," he said, "I'll set up a fruit stand for you, or a tomato stand. After that, if you still want to leave, it will be all right."

When he came back from his trips, he would take us swimming or to the movies, and, at night, would sleep on the floor beside my cot, always keeping his distance. We would talk in the dark, and that's when I told him about my family and learned about his life.

He was born in Acapulco, but had moved to many towns and cities with his parents, who struggled to make a living. Wherever they went, his mother would set up a little food stand in a park, and he and his father would sell newspapers. Baltasar worked from the time he could remember, first, taking care of his younger brothers and sisters, then, when he was seven, selling papers, hauling water, catching fish, making sandals, and anything his parents wanted him to do. They sent him to school four times, but he didn't last more than a week or two each time, because he would be thrown out for fighting or using bad language.

When Baltasar was thirteen, he found out that his father was really his stepfather. He said deep in his heart he knew it all the time because his father was very mean, and treated him worse than the other children. His stepfather beat Baltasar for any little thing, for playing instead of working, for not turning over all his earnings, for asking for food . . . He got a beating for breakfast, one for lunch, and one for supper.

In Puerto México, they sold newspapers to the passengers on the night trains and while they waited for the trains, the stepfather would play pool or go into a *cantina*, leaving Baltasar outside the door, to sleep on the pavement like a dog. He would be sent to deliver papers to houses on the other side of the woods or the cemetery, and the little fellow would be afraid of the animals, the ghosts and the dark. Once he had to walk five kilometers to deliver a paper and as he crossed a bridge, he saw a man without a head, standing on the other side. Baltasar was afraid, but he couldn't go back because he was more afraid of his stepfather, so he ran past the headless man, delivered the paper, and ran all the way home.

Baltasar was beaten so much that strangers took pity on him. One time, in Cuernavaca, some men bought him a ticket to send him back to his relatives in Acapulco, but his stepfather saw him on the bus and pulled him off. After that, he punished Baltasar by not giving him food. His mother had to steal *tortillas* for him, as though he were a stranger in the house.

When he was nine, Baltasar was apprenticed to a butcher in the mornings, and to a baker in the evenings, so he learned two trades at once. They paid him with a piece of meat and some bread, and he wasn't hungry any more. Then Baltasar got sick and when his parents went back to Cuernavaca, they left him with his mother's sister until he was well enough to travel. That's when he lost his affection for his mother, because she abandoned him to his aunt. His aunt was the kind who wanted only to put money into her purse and never take out any. Out of pure self-interest, she kept Baltasar there to work for her son in the slaughterhouse. He worked all day long, washing and drying cows' intestines and stomachs and carrying the waste to the garbage dump. Then all he got to eat was one *taco*. They beat him if he said he was hungry, or if he cried or wanted to go to his mother. His mother sent money for the bus ticket, but his aunt put it in her own purse.

Later, Baltasar had a fight with his stepfather, who tried to hit his mother with a hammer while she was drunk and couldn't defend herself. So they threw Baltasar out of the house and that's when he struck out for himself. When he was twelve, he got a job in the slaughterhouse for fifty *centavos* a day. They also gave him tripe, which he cleaned and dried and ate when he had no money. He slept on the beach or on hotel steps with other boys. They would catch fish and cook it on the beach and stretch out for the night, covered with newspaper. He would wash his own shirt and pants, spread them out on a hot stone, and bathe in the ocean while they were drying. It was a sad life. He felt like an orphan because he had no one to cook for him or take care of him.

Baltasar didn't see his real father until he was sixteen. His father was a fisherman who lived in a different village. He was a good man and received his son well, but Baltasar didn't go to see him and his stepmother and half-brothers again for several years. Baltasar had lots of women, but not one knew how to make a home for him. He said they didn't understand him . . . all he asked of a woman was that she be for him alone, that she wash and cook for him at the proper hour, and when he came home drunk, to take off his shoes, put him to bed and forget about it.

The first night Baltasar and I slept together, it seemed to have been all arranged beforehand. His uncle didn't sleep there that night, why, I didn't know. I suppose it was already too much for Baltasar. I was expecting it by then. Anyway, there I was on the cot and he on the floor. It was very dark.

"Marta, I want to talk to you," he says.

"What is it?"

"No, come over here."

When I heard that, I thought to myself, "Hmmm, this is what he wanted. This was what he was waiting for." So I said, "No, I can hear you fine from here," making out that I didn't know what was happening.

"No," he says. "Look, I'm tired of going back and forth. If you want to live with me, I can't offer you much, but at least you won't go without food."

I said no, that I had to go, that I had to wait . . . that I couldn't. I knew I was pregnant. How could I tell him that there was still another child coming, in addition to the three girls. No!

"Tell me the reason. Is your husband coming?" He thought Crispín and I had separated only for a short time. I kept saying no and no and no.

"Look," he said. "Stay and if you see that I don't suit you, tell me, and if you don't suit me, I'll tell you. It will be like putting me to a test because I don't know how I'll be with a woman. I haven't been with a woman for a long time."

"Whew, this fixes me!" I thought. "Being a long time without a woman, he is going to want it all the more." I was just about to tell him I was pregnant, when he said, "Why? Because of the baby that's coming?"

"Yes, that's why." I have always been very, very honest with him, like I never was with Crispín.

"Well, then, what you have to do is not leave until the baby is born properly. He is innocent . . . children are not to blame for anything. I myself was the same. My true father only inseminated my mother. He knew nothing of me . . . it was a different man who took on the obligation of bringing me up, and I want to repay that, even through another person. I'm not jealous about your past. What is behind is not important, it is what is ahead that interests me."

By that time, I had gotten out of bed and was moving closer to him. "Be quiet or you'll wake the little girl," I said. I got under his blanket. "You are like the rest, looking for payment for everything."

"No, don't accuse me of that. What I want is to live with you."

"Even if I didn't want to, I'd still have to pay you back, wouldn't I?"

"No, don't take it like that. That's not the way it is."

"I can't take it any other way." When he embraced me, I felt myself getting mad. I tried to stop him but he said, "No, whatever has to happen, let happen, once and for all." To make a long story short, it happened.

Then I cried. I said, "I didn't think you were like that. I was going to pay you back for everything some day. I wasn't going to take it for nothing. I don't want you to think I came for that reason . . . to earn money with my body. Now I'm carrying a child inside me and I am afraid it will come out mixed with other blood. If I knew this was going to happen, I would have left the first day."

But from then on, Baltasar wouldn't let me go. He wouldn't let me work. He had all the more reason to give me money and to bring me meat. After that, we started looking for another room.

Life in Acapulco was very peaceful. I really had miraculous luck to have met Baltasar at all, especially since he had almost missed the bus that time. Little by little, I began to care for him. As the saying goes, "Husbands and children are loved for their actions." Baltasar was good and generous and though he shouted at the girls, he did it to keep them from getting bad habits. He would light the stove and help with the cooking. If I couldn't go out, he wasn't ashamed to take the basket and go to the market, or to carry a child. From the start, he gave me his money and an account of what he spent. These were things Crispín never did. I don't know why, but the men I know in Mexico City do not treat their women this way.

With Baltasar, I was no longer sad. I had more courage because I saw that at least I received more respect from people. Before, I led the disagreeable life of an unmarried mother, with even my own brothers and sisters calling me a whore and marrying me off to any man that came along. And as for Baltasar, he didn't bother me too much. He wasn't like Crispín, who wanted it every day and in different positions. No, Baltasar didn't clown around. He was normal. But if I didn't want to, he would say, "If you don't give it to me, I can find a pair of buttocks anywhere." Sometimes I would refuse, but usually I did it, whether I wanted to or not.

I may not have loved Baltasar the way I loved Crispín, but we got along better in every way. It could be because I wasn't afraid . . . because I knew how to defend myself. I had more freedom and could do and say what I pleased and take anything I wanted. I could turn the house upside down and no one said a thing about it.

And I wasn't afraid to speak frankly to Baltasar. I had such self-confidence that I sometimes came out with strong things. I'd say, "You are already old, so what can you expect? The day you no longer please me, I'll leave you," or, "I won't die of grief if you go off with someone else." He told me he had loved me from the first moment he saw me, but I said bluntly, it hadn't been that way with me, except when I fell in love with Crispín. Why should I tell Baltasar I loved him if I didn't? Because I didn't beat around the bush with him, he said I was cruel, that I had an iron breast and a heart of stone.

It is true that I had liked Crispín from the very first time he spoke to me. What had impressed me most was his appearance and his good manners. He was thin and short and had nice features. His ears were as small and fine as those of a mouse, and his eyes were light brown. Right away I could see he wasn't a roughneck like the other boys in the neighborhood. I could tell by the way he spoke that he was not so common. He had a better vocabulary and didn't use dirty words with girls. His work clothes were always clean and on Sundays his shirt and gabardine pants were well ironed. He didn't dress like a *Pachuco* or keep his hair long like Tarzan, and, at that time, he didn't drink or smoke or mix much with his gang. He was a steady worker and altogether a better class of man. I felt lucky that he liked me.

Baltasar was just the opposite. The truth is, he was very coarse. He knew only vulgar language and even in the street or on a bus talked about intimate things in a loud voice, without caring who heard. I would feel embarrassed and that's why I didn't like to go out with him. And the way he ate! He made so much noise with his mouth that I could not sit at the table with him, especially when there were others present.

I was always correcting him: "Shut your mouth, man," "Lower your voice," "Button up your shirt, haven't you any shame?" But he would say, "What business is it of others? I feel better this way," or, "No, Martita, I'm too old to learn." That was his excuse when he corrected the children for eating noisily. "I can't change because I'm on my way down. But I can teach them good habits because they are young and on their way up."

And his famous earring! When we got on a bus, people looked and began to whisper to each other. It bothered me and I told him that he might as well put one on the other ear, since he looked like a pansy anyway. I don't care if he did make a vow to wear it! What kind of a vow is it that made him act like a clown?

Baltasar kept saying, "Write home. Write to them. Your father and brother will be worried." But for two and a half months I felt so hurt by my *papá*, I just wouldn't. I would say, "I haven't anybody to write to." But Baltasar bothered me so much, that I finally wrote. My father answered right away. The next time, he didn't send a letter but came himself.

Baltasar was still asleep because he worked in the market from four to six in the morning, and again in the slaughterhouse in the evening. I knew it was my *papá* as soon as I heard his knock. He came with my half-sister Marielena. Baltasar took them to the market and to the beach and they left on the night bus.

My *papá* would never miss a day's work, unless he was so sick he couldn't walk. If my father wasn't there to open the café, it was never opened in time. That's why his boss valued him and kept him for so many years. He trusted my father with money and everything and I had always believed my *papá* was the manager. It wasn't until recently that I found his union card and learned that he was listed as only a helper. And all the times I had boasted to my friends that my *papá* had an important job!

Then Roberto came, bringing some of my things. He was serious with Baltasar at first, asking his intentions and things like that. Baltasar told him he loved me, and the girls, too. He said, "If I love the tree, I have to love the roots, too, no?"

Roberto was satisfied and that was all there was to it. But from the start, Baltasar didn't like the way Roberto put his arm around my shoulder or held my hand when we walked. My brother and I had a secret language which we used together and I noticed that it annoyed

Baltasar. He told me to quit and I said we always did that in Mexico City. "Well," he said, "you are in Acapulco now. Here if we see a brother and sister behaving that way, we take it badly. I don't like it."

He told me he had been "burned" once, by a brother and sister act. One of his women introduced him to her "brother," who turned out to be her lover. He knew very well Roberto was my brother, because of my father, eh? but he was scarred once, and couldn't forget it.

Just think, when the baby was born, Baltasar had to help the midwife. I had a hard time. The baby's head came out all right, but it was choking, because I didn't have the strength to labor any more. Baltasar didn't know what to do, but he pinched me hard on the shoulder tendons at the base of the neck. He said later he did it because he knew it would relax my lower muscles and let the baby come out. It hurt a lot and I screamed and the baby was born. For a while, Baltasar was angry because he thought the baby looked like my brother.

Baltasar tied the umbilical cord and cleaned the baby and buried the afterbirth. He did everything, and looked after the other children, too. The next day, Roberto and Marielena came . . . my father had sent them to help me . . . but they went to the beach instead and spent the whole day bathing. Baltasar was annoyed and wanted them to go home. Before they left, he told them he planned to marry me in church. Roberto became serious and asked him to think it over carefully, and Marielena said the same, because marriage was complicated and one had to learn all the Church rules. Baltasar said, how could he, if he barely knew how to read? "Look, Marielena," he said. "I know I'm Catholic because I go to church. I commend myself to a saint, but more than that, no. I barely know even how to make the sign of the cross!"

"Uuuuh, then you won't be able to get married," she says. Marielena was the most Catholic person in our family and she knew all about these things. She discouraged him, but he said, "God will say what we should do to get married. Meanwhile, we'll marry by civil law so that I can adopt these children and make them my legitimate property. I want the 'bill of sale,' so that son-of-a-bitch Crispín can't take them away. Señor Jesús told us Crispín was looking for Concepción and when the poor kid heard that she got scared and started to cry."

Baltasar wasn't jealous of my past and didn't reproach me, but he was afraid Crispín might go after me again, on the pretext of seeing Concepción. He would say, "I'll bet you even prefer him and want to

see him on the side, eh? I don't understand you. You say you didn't
live with him and here you are with four of his children! What is he,
your pimp or something? If he comes here, I'll meet him with a knife
and split the bastard in two. And why is Roberto against me marrying
you? Does he want you for himself or something? What business is it
of his?"

I would get angry and tell him he was crazy. We would quarrel a lot
because I didn't let him push me around, but usually he was nice
Even when he was drunk, he would come home in a good mood. He
only hit me twice, there in Acapulco.

The first time, before the baby was born, it was because of his two
cursed brothers. They had come to visit him for the first time in two
years. I heated supper for them and served them on a table outside
the house. They talked and talked among themselves, about old times,
about some of the women Baltasar had had, and other things that
didn't interest me. They didn't call me or invite me to sit down, so I
thought I would mind my own business and stay inside. When they
left, I was in bed, pretending to be asleep. I heard Baltasar apologize
for me, but he didn't say anything to me that night.

The next day, he came home drunk and began. "You old she-goat!
When my brothers come, see that you attend them the way you should.
You went off and left us like dogs. Is that the way I treated your father
when he came? Or your brother?" Then he hit me twice with his
strap. It made me angry but he was drunk and I was afraid he might
really get rough. I only cried and began to get my things together.

"You're a fool if you think I'm going to stand for this," I said. "If I
left the father of my children because of his blows, why should I take
them from you, who isn't even my husband?" I told him off, but that
was all that happened. A little later, he took me to the movies to calm
me down.

The second time he hit me, he was also drunk. He had bought a
hog, legally and all, and they had agreed to let him pay for it after he
slaughtered it. But the meat was confiscated by the Courthouse because Baltasar hadn't taken out a slaughter permit. He came home and
said, "Imagine, they took the hog and charged a fine."

"Well," I said, "next, they will be taking you!" That's the way he
was, not responsible for his acts and then complaining about what
others did to him. He went down the hill again, to do some errands,

and didn't come back. The clock struck four, five, eight, and he didn't appear.

"They must have put him in jail, with the hog. That's where he is for sure."

This happened after my son, Jesusito, was born. I remember very well, because I had already made the chocolate for his baptism. That evening, the baby and Trini were asleep. Concepción was in Mexico City visiting her grandmother, so I said to Violeta, "*Ay*, daughter, Baltasar might be in jail and we don't even know. Let's go down and look."

First, I went to the pool parlor, then to the *cantinas*. I said, "Look under the doors, daughter, and see if your *papá* is there." I turned and saw Baltasar coming out of a *cantina* across the street. It made me furious to think I was worrying about him being in jail when he was out having a good time. He had his arm around a girl. "Ah, the cursed fellow will pay for this!" I told Violeta. I followed them and saw the girl leave. Then Baltasar took some money out of his pocket and gave it to a friend. A car stopped and they both got in and drove off, in the direction of the red zone.

"The twice-condemned one! He'll see!" I went straight home and started to pack my things. I had saved up one hundred *pesos* and planned to leave before he got back. "So, in addition to drinking, he goes around with other women. The bastard!"

He came back, saying, "*Ay*, old girl, now I really am good and drunk. Be nice and take off my shoes for me, won't you?"

"You son-of-a-bitch, of what interest is it to me that you are drunk?"

"*Uy!* the old she-goat is very angry, eh? When have you spoken like that to me!"

Then he up and punched me. He noticed my packed valise and cut it with his knife. I thought he would knife me next, so I kept my peace. We were angry for only one or two days. After that, he didn't know what to do for me. He took me to the movies and bought me this and that and even protected me from drafts. He thought my anger would cool, but he was crazy to believe he could buy me that way. Since that argument, I lost a lot of my respect for him. Before that, I had never used bad words in his presence and I wasn't as vulgar with him as I am now. He thinks I am real depraved, the way I talk, but if one doesn't speak up, one is left behind. Like Paula with Manuel. When Manuel was carrying on with that other woman, Paula kept quiet, so as not to make a big thing of it. Manuel didn't even notice that she was suffering, but how could he believe that she didn't know what was going on? No, when a man makes a woman suffer, she should speak right up, so God will hear her. If I am uncouth with Baltasar, it is because he made me this way.

I was well off in Acapulco, but my *papá* wanted me and the children back, so I kept telling Baltasar I had to go home. He didn't want to leave Acapulco. He said, "I'm not used to it there. Here we have meat every day, and bread, not just *tortillas*. When I am short of money, I can go fishing with my friends, or play dominoes and win thirty or forty *pesos*. Here we always have enough money for the movies. How can I go to the capital without money, to live like a dog?"

I was stubborn and kept nagging. My *papá* wrote that we could live in his house in the El Dorado Colony because Lupita was leaving him and moving out. That crazy Marielena kept saying her mother was living in sin with my father and that if he wouldn't marry her the priest said she would have to separate from him. Maybe that was why Lupita finally left, but I believe it was because she couldn't stand to see how Delila had won over my father. He almost never went to see Lupita and when he did, it was to take care of his pigeons and pigs.

So my *papá* said we could live there as soon as Lupita moved, and he would give us a pig to begin with, so that Baltasar could be a butcher and sell the meat among the neighbors. Baltasar thought it was a magnificent opportunity and set about raising money for the trip. He had to lie a little, but he did it to please me. He went to a friend who worked in the Department of Health and asked him for a letter saying he had to go to Mexico City for a hernia operation. He really did have a hernia because when he had his appendix taken out, the doctor told him. So he takes this letter to his companions at the slaughterhouse to see if they would take up a collection for him. Baltasar had only one hundred *pesos* at the time, and we couldn't very well go with only that, could we?

Well, his friends got together one hundred and fifty *pesos*. It wasn't enough and Baltasar went around as if he was in pain and it was an emergency. His friend from the Health Department came and told them his was a bad case, so they collected fifty *pesos* more. They said if he needed more after the operation, to let them know and they would send it.

We left in a hurry. Baltasar wanted to take the night bus, so that we would not have to spend money on food on the way, but there was a misunderstanding with the driver, who demanded eighty *pesos* just for taking our furniture. We waited in the station until one of the drivers agreed to take it for seventy. Baltasar loaded the bed and chiffonier and other things on the roof of the bus, and bought us tickets for another forty-six *pesos*. There were more expenditures later for food for the children, for a jacket for Baltasar, and for a truck to take everything to the Casa Grande, so the trip was costly, right?

Lupita was still in my father's house, so we moved in with Manuel and María. Roberto and his Antonia were there at the time, and my cousin David, his mother, wife and four kids. The place looked like a barracks with all those people stretched out on the floor at night. They slept with the candle burning on the altar and Baltasar began to complain to me that in such a setup he couldn't even calm his desire. In Acapulco, at least we could send out the children during the day and enjoy ourselves alone. He wasn't voracious and took care not to overdo it, but even so, he missed my caresses. Thank God, my cousin moved out with his family as soon as he could find a room of his own. Later, Antonia deserted poor Roberto and he went to live with my high-class sister, Consuelo. He lost his job and kept getting into fights. His only consolation was the bottle.

So there we were, sharing No. 64 with Manuel, María and their little baby girl, Lolita. Manuel's four other children were staying with my *papá* and Delila, in the little house he was still building in the Ixmiquilpan Colony. Delila had had another baby, and people were still gossiping about it, saying she got it with someone's help, that it wasn't my father's. This business of doubting who is the father is bad, as I know from bitter experience. Who could know better than the mother, who is the father of her child? For my part, I am willing to take the mother's word for it.

Well, we began to have trouble right away. We were supposed to pay the rent one month, and Manuel the next month, but after we moved in, the landlord told us Manuel owed for five months and if it wasn't paid up, my father would lose the room. To get off to a good start with Manuel, Baltasar offered to pawn his new radio and pay five months rent in advance, so that we would have a place to live. So Manuel took the radio and gave the landlord 165 *pesos*, three months back rent, and only God knows what he did with the rest of the money. He said that was all he received but Baltasar didn't believe him because the radio was worth five hundred *pesos*. At first, I defended my brother, but when Manuel took the pawn ticket and sold it, I sided with Baltasar.

By that time, Manuel and Baltasar were *compadres* because it had occurred to me to ask my brother to be godfather at my son's confirmation. So there was Baltasar having to behave respectfully to him, while trying to get justice. He would say, "With all due respect, *compadrito*, stop screwing around and give me back my radio." But no matter how he said it or what he did, he never saw that radio or the money again. Manuel promised to pay it out little by little, but before he paid even one *centavo* he decided that the radio must have been a stolen one, so why should Baltasar worry about it.

Baltasar looked for work in the slaughterhouse, but he had no city license and they wouldn't take him. He tried the bakeries but he needed money to buy a place in the union. My father got him a job at a key factory, but Baltasar quit because he said the union was run by the boss and was good for nothing. When he was sick for three days they deducted from his pay, and anyway, they paid only twelve-fifty *pesos* a day.

At other factories, they laid down too many conditions . . . they wanted to know who his family was, how long he had been in the capital, if he had a certificate from primary school, a letter saying why he left his last job, a letter of recommendation. He explained that he was a stranger here and couldn't get a letter from anyone, but they didn't understand. They said, "A letter or a bond. A letter or a bond."

Baltasar was beginning to hate the Mexicans. He said they were dogs and selfish, that *Acapulqueños* give work to anyone who asks because if he didn't need it he wouldn't be asking, that Mexicans were all thieves, that if there was stealing in Acapulco, it was always someone from the capital who did it. He was ready to go back to his homeland.

My uncle Ignacio wanted him to sell newspapers, but how could we live on such a pittance? Finally, Manuel offered to show Baltasar how to be a "coyote" in the Tepito Market. Baltasar started by selling my table. He used the money to buy a pile of unwashed shirts from a laundry. When he sold those, he bought up other things. With both men working as peddlers, our room was cluttered with mirrors, broken toys, second-hand clothes, shoes, tools, and things like that. When they had nothing to sell, María and I had to hide our clothes because those two would grab anything to raise money for the day's expenses. Once Manuel took off Lolita's sweater and sold it to a customer, then and there!

We got along better for a while, because Baltasar gave me my ten *pesos* a day and we had enough to eat. He even paid the back bills to the Power Company so that the electricity could be turned on again. But when Manuel didn't pay for the next two months, the company cut us off again and Baltasar left it that way. He said we were better off with candles, because that way Manuel and María couldn't turn on the lights and wake us up when they came in late. They ate all their meals at Gilberto's café and stayed there every day with Lolita, until past midnight.

Baltasar needed capital, so when Roberto asked to borrow twenty-five *pesos* to go to Acapulco, Baltasar remembered the fellows at the slaughterhouse. He was crazy to think of sending my brother to collect money from them, but Roberto was going anyway, to dispose of something "hot," and it wouldn't cost us fare. Besides, Roberto told Baltasar that if he sold the stuff for a good price, he would get us another radio.

I didn't believe my brother. I was angry with him because he had pawned a ring that Antonia had borrowed from me, and wouldn't give it back. I had scraped together the money to buy that ring with so much sacrifice! If he wanted to steal, why didn't he take from the rich, not from us? But he said, "Little sister, don't upset yourself. I'll get you a better one some day."

Baltasar didn't listen to me, and borrowed twenty-five *pesos* from my father, to lend to my brother. Four days later Roberto came back from Acapulco with only fifty *pesos* for Baltasar. He said he had spent the rest of it on food, hotels and bus fare. We never found out how much the butchers had collected, but Baltasar believed that my brother had robbed him of more than half. He began to feel hatred for Roberto.

One day, they were both mixing punch for a party at my aunt Guadalupe's house, drinking as they went along. The more drunk they became, the more they spoke from their hearts and their rivalry came out. Baltasar told Roberto not to come to the Casa Grande any more, because he arrived like a big shot, pushing in the door as though he owned the place. Baltasar had paid three months rent and figured he was the boss there. He wouldn't let María's brothers come to sleep there any more because, he said, if either of those bastards got hold of one of my girls he would feel responsible.

Roberto said it was his father's house and, as my brother, he had the right to come and go as he pleased, and to eat and sleep there too, if he wished.

"Are you saying I am obliged to support you?"

"Yes," says Roberto, "so long as I want you to."

"Well then, you are charging me for your sister's affection. That means you are selling her!"

"Yes? And what are you? Didn't you come like a sharp one, to be supported and helped by my father? No one knows better than you how to get something for nothing. My father does more for you than for his own sons."

One word led to another, and they ended up insulting their mothers and taking out knives. My aunt got her fingers cut trying to separate the two of them. Baltasar then told me ho he was leaving for his homeland, with me or without me, because he didn't want to depend upon my family for anything. It took some time for me to cool him down. He said, "All right, I'll stay, but if your brother kills me, it will be your responsibility."

I stopped speaking to Roberto after that, and, for the first time, ordered him to keep out of my house because he came only to cause trouble. The truth is, no one wanted him around. He cried and got drunk but, thank God, he agreed to stay away, for the sake of the children.

At last, Lupita and Marielena left my father's house in El Dorado, and we moved in. It was a humble place, but it had a high wall around it and the courtyard was for us alone. It was clean and quiet and had two bedrooms, a real kitchen, and a window in every room. Water was brought each day by a truck, but we had electricity. In short, it was the nicest house either Baltasar or I had ever lived in. I said, as a joke, we ought to put up an antenna on the roof so the neighbors would think we had a television set and were real high-class.

I wanted Baltasar to know, at last, the warmth and affection of a home. He had never had that from any of his women. They were all sluts who drank and left him and the children for other men. His life saddened me and that's why I stuck it out with him. He was like a child who needed me. I, too, had never felt I had a home, even though I always had a place to sleep and enough to eat and wear. I saw my brothers and sisters but we were not united. We might have worked together, like others, to make a nice home for ourselves, but instead we each went our own way. I had never envied the rich, who were above me, because there were always those who were below me, but I did envy people who had good families and nice homes.

I wanted to show Baltasar I was not like those women he had known. True, we had simple quarrels and told each other off, but it was never worse than that. The only thing we quarreled about at first, was the baby, Chucho, as we called him. I said Baltasar loved the child too much and was doing him harm. When I spanked Chucho for wetting the bed or his pants, Baltasar would get angry. He wouldn't let me put pants on the boy after that. He would carry Chucho on his shoulders to the market, on the bus, and even to the park on Sundays, with the child dressed in no more than a shirt. When Chucho urinated on him, Baltasar would only laugh. If the baby cried for something, Baltasar would give it to him, even though it was something the girls were playing with. Though Chucho was only one year old, he seemed to know that when his *papá* was at home, I couldn't say, "Don't do this, don't touch that." Baltasar warned me that if he saw me spank Chucho, I would be given mine, and when he left the house, he would say, "Remember, let the boy do what he pleases."

I never spoiled my children that way. Baltasar says I am hard on them. I think that because of all the things that have happened to me and the anger I have felt, I am becoming neurasthenic. I don't have the patience to answer the children's questions, "*Mamá*, what is that? *Mamá*, where are we going?" I shut them up right away. I am becoming more like my *papá*. If I am reading the papers or the weekly story, I don't let them interrupt me. My poor little girls are becoming withdrawn, the way Consuelo used to be, because I don't hold them or embrace them any more.

When I became pregnant again, I was resigned to it. Baltasar deserved at least one child from me, I thought, especially since he had married me in court even before he knew another one was on the way. My family believed Chucho was his son and I had never set them straight because it would have been embarrassing to admit that Crispín had given me another child. So I had married Baltasar even though my *papá* told me not to, because he had no faith in stepfathers. I had heard what some stepfathers do to their stepdaughters, but that could never happen in my home so long as I was alive.

I thought Baltasar would be happy to have his own child, but he wasn't. He said the new baby would only rob love from little Chucho and make him *chipil,* ill of jealousy. Instead of Chucho getting ill, Baltasar did. At night, he would twist and turn and complain that his heart felt heavy and that he couldn't breathe. My aunt Guadalupe wanted to take him to the Temple of Light to be cured by the Spiritualist, but Baltasar preferred to go out and drink with his friends. That's when he changed for the worse, when he took up with his lousy friends and left me without expense money.

He would come home tipsy and we would quarrel. I'd say, "If you don't find happiness here in your home, if you find it with your miserable pals in the market, better leave me and go with them."

He complained that I had changed, that before, I would at least give him a hug or a kiss. And I would answer, "Yes, frankly I am losing my affection for you. If I have changed, it is your own doing."

"Well," he'd say, "in that case, the day I find another pair of buttocks, I won't stay here for anything."

"But until you get her and while you are wondering whether you want apples or pears, don't come bothering me. Screw the next one, because I'm not going to the dogs for you. When I met you I didn't go around the way I do now, badly fed, badly dressed and badly treated. What would it cost me to get another man to give me things? It's the easiest thing in the world to lead the gay life, to begin with one, then two, then with every man who came along. But I'm not like your other women who threw themselves away. While my father exists, I will never take the easy way. No, Baltasar, better pray to God that my father doesn't die."

I told him that even if I had a dozen children, I wouldn't cry if he left me, that no man was worth crying over, especially a drunkard. Men like that were better dead, because then everyone lived in peace. I would rather get a job sewing in a shop, even though I'd leave my lungs in a place like that and would earn a miserable eight or nine *pesos* a day. And I warned Baltasar, that if he stayed, he would have to work. "Don't think that I'm going to let you be a burden to my *papá.* Do you want to become like another son? It would be a thousand times better for you to leave."

We didn't have a single *centavo* in the house, and Baltasar had no money to work with, so we sold the pig my father had given us, before it was fully grown. If my father knew, he would be angry and would say we couldn't hold on to anything and were the kind who would never progress. I wanted to use fifty *pesos* of the money to go to Chalma with my aunt, but then I thought it would be better for Baltasar to work, so we stayed. After all, if we don't have some *centavos* when my time comes, who will deliver the baby?

So Baltasar took the money and started to work again. I don't know what happened, but he got himself a partner called the Pig, who took him to the cantinas and ended up carrying the money. I waited and waited for Baltasar to come home because I needed money for some medicine. My father didn't like the way I looked and had sent me to Dr. Ramón, who gave me a prescription for a tonic.

Baltasar had been coming home very late, or not at all. I warned him that it was dangerous for him to be out alone when he was drunk, but he thinks it's like in Acapulco. The other night a bunch of boys . . . all rebels without cause . . . chased him and he barely escaped. I told him that if anything happened to him, his relatives would come and blame me. They would come and chew me up alive because that's the way his race of people is. But he doesn't think of that. He says all I do is scold and get angry, that all I want is to keep him tied up at home.

Baltasar stayed away for two days. When he came in, I handed him the prescription. "Take this," I said, "and ask the Pig for money to buy it because the doctor told me it was urgent." He was surprised that I didn't yell at him and he tried to embrace me. All I said was, "Stop bothering me. Here I am, so happy with my daughters, and you come molesting me. Who told you to come? What devil brought you? The street is your home!"

"What? Can't I come to my home any more? I'm late because I had to deliver some merchandise."

He was always delivering merchandise, eh? Then I noticed some lipstick on his shirt. Up to then, according to him, all his sprees were with men and didn't include women. I wasn't born yesterday, so I never believed that, but here was evidence.

"Is that why this is on your shirt?" I asked.

"Oh, I couldn't help it because where I went there were rags with red paint." Later, he told my cousin David, who by then had moved in with us, that he had gone dancing with a woman on Tintero Street, because I wouldn't sleep with him any more and was always angry. And he had me almost believing it was red paint! It is not that I am jealous. I realize a man can never be satisfied with just one woman, but I cannot stand being made a fool of.

Well, I sent him for the medicine and he didn't come back until the next morning. He didn't bring the tonic and had even lost the prescription. He was a little drunk and had the face to tell me that the Pig had invited him to Tintero Street again. "I made it clear that I couldn't spend much, and we went around asking prices," Baltasar explained. Think of it, the Pig even helped him choose!

"Look," I said, very angrily. "You weren't my first man and you won't be my last. The thing that rubs me the wrong way is that you try to make me look stupid. Just tell me straight out that you are not coming home, so that I won't be expecting you." He knew that I would never go to look for him, the way I did in Acapulco. It is worse for me to run the risk of catching him with a woman. Suppose he sided with her against me? What a shame for me then! No, I don't look for him because I don't want to catch him in deceit.

I go to the Merced Market every day, to see my father's face. When things go bad for him and he is sad, I am sad. Right now, he is peaceful and content and I feel better. After all, he is all worked out and cannot stand as much as a young person any more. None of us can buy life and I have to consider the fact that he may die at any time. While my father lives, I have nothing to cry about. After that, yes, the world will end for me.

At first, I covered up for Baltasar, but now I tell my father everything. "Who would believe," I say, "that Baltasar would turn out to be such an ungrateful wretch? He doesn't pay rent, what more does he want you to do for him? He has completely washed his hands of his obligations. He knows you won't let me starve, so he doesn't give me money any more."

My *papá* is losing money on the house, because he could have rented it to someone for 250 *pesos* a month. That's why I said we should clean out the room in which the pigeons were, and rent it to my cousin David, so my *papá* would make some *centavos*. At least now he gets one hundred *pesos* a month, to help with all his expenses. None of us give him money, on the contrary, we take from him the little he has. When I see him at the market, he never lets me go without giving me five or ten *pesos*, and one for each of the children. He looks at their shoes and clothes and if he sees they need something, he buys it the next day. If they have a sore or a cold, he scolds me for neglecting them and gives me money for medicine, as though it was his obligation. If I don't want to take it, he says it is not hard for him to support three or four more, especially his own grandchildren. He is one man in a million! But it's not right for him to give so much to me. What do I have Baltasar for?

Now my time is drawing near and I am afraid. Like I say to Baltasar, "Look, what good is it for us to have a place to live in, if when the baby comes, there won't be a single *centavo* in our pocket. I have nothing prepared . . . no blanket, no sweater, no anything."

"Soon," he says, "just as soon as so-and-so comes, or such-and-such gives . . . You just wait."

It makes me desperate to see that he doesn't have confidence in himself and doesn't hustle. This business of waiting burns me up. What am I waiting for? I'm waiting for nothing, exactly nothing!

I have never been so afraid of a birth as of this one. Trini had been difficult, and if Baltasar hadn't helped me with Chucho, I think I wouldn't have made it. Now, like I tell Baltasar, I feel as though I am going to die, the way my mother did. I'm not worried about myself, but about my children. If it hadn't been for them, I would have wiped myself off the map long ago. But I know very well that they need me. Without me, they would be through, because no one would love all of them the way I do. They would be parceled out, Crispín would take Concepción, someone else Violeta, Trini elsewhere. Without the mother, everything falls apart.

Baltasar says, "Look, I am thirty-four and older than you and still I don't want to die."

"Yes," I say, "because you are more or less a man. You go out, you get drunk, you have diversion and forget your worries. But I am closed up in the house and trouble weighs me down more."

At night, when I cannot sleep, I begin to think. I say the thing that pains me most is that I broke up my home with Crispín. Lately, I even have dreams of his mother and sisters receiving me well. Perhaps, if I had waited a bit, Crispín and I might have gotten together again. I hurt myself and the children by joining up with Baltasar. I was used to being alone, so I should have remained that way. I tell Baltasar

I won't die of grief if he leaves me. But who knows? Once I see that I am alone again . . . who knows?

Maybe we should go back to Acapulco. Baltasar could work in the slaughterhouse and give me money and meat again. There he could not depend upon my father. He would know that if he didn't give me money, we wouldn't eat. There, after all, his only vice was drinking. He understands his own race of people and native land and would be confident once more. There, at least I won't have to see all the trouble and suffering and quarreling of my family. This is what makes me ill. Perhaps I will stop having bad dreams about me and the girls being cut up and quartered and Baltasar being shot. Here, when I lie down at night, I feel as though I will not rise any more in the morning. If I live through this next birth, maybe we should go back to Acapulco. I felt more peaceful there.

Epilogue

Jesús Sánchez

I AM A PERSON WHO BEARS GRUDGES AND I HAVE A LOT AGAINST THREE OF my children, Manuel, Roberto and Consuelo. My body is becoming half-paralyzed from being so angry with these children of mine. I am ashamed to talk about it. It is hard for a father to have such sons. They turned out bad because of bad surroundings, bad companions. Their friends are doing these boys no good. It is a shame that I cannot do anything about it. In spite of my advice, they go the other way instead of taking the straight path.

There is nothing better in this world than upright work. I am a poor and humble person but I try to do things the best way I can. They can't say their father came home drunk, or abandoned them. An uncle of theirs just died of drink. It seems they take after their uncle more than they do me. I don't understand it.

My sons haven't amounted to anything because they don't like to have anyone order them around. First, they want to be millionaires and then get a job. How can you expect to start from the top? We all have to work our way up from the bottom, isn't that so? But my sons, they want to do it the other way around. So everything they do is a failure.

They don't have any stamina for work. They haven't got common sense. They don't have the will power to get a job and stick to it, an honest job so that they can go out into the street looking decent and feeling proud of themselves. I'd be happy, it would give me the greatest satisfaction, if they could be like that.

The other day I said to Consuelo, I don't want you to be somebody you're not supposed to be or to forget what social class you belong to.

When people who've had a little bit of education suddenly start acting uppity, they get slapped down. Now take me as an example," I said to her. "I've always been a simple worker and I'll always be that way and nobody is going to slap me down. Even though you've gone to school a few years, that doesn't mean you should feel you've joined the upper classes. Take a look at yourself in the mirror and tell me what class you belong to, what your place is in society." It's all right for her to improve herself a little, but she shouldn't get swell-headed and look down on her own people, the class she belongs to. I told her the other night, "I'm your father, whether you like it or not. No matter how I go dressed or how poor I am, I'm your father and you can't get away from it."

I admit I've made some mistakes. I am no white dove but I've always taken care of them. There are a lot of men who get rid of their children when they take a woman. Do you know what it's like to have mother-less children on your hands? An orphan has everything against him, nobody wants him. And so what could I do? I've provided everything for them because I like to do things that way. I work like a slave and go on struggling the best I can, moving ahead, as everyone can see. Lots of times you can do more harm to your children by giving them their food and having the table spread for them all the time . . . they don't worry about doing anything for themselves.

I wanted them to go to school, to learn a trade. I didn't ask them to work so they would bring me money, to buy their own clothes or to feed themselves. I have taken care of them for over twenty years and they have never lacked for a plate of soup or a cup of coffee. Why should they have turned out bad? I don't understand.

A few years after Lenore's death, I met Elena over there in the *vecindad*. Like I said before, I must be lucky, because women fall for me. That's the way it's been. Why? I don't know. Now just think! Here was this woman, this girl, may she rest in peace, living right next door with her husband, a fellow who was going to be a priest. But he didn't give her anything to eat, and of course she came into our house because the children's grandma sold cake trimmings there, a basket a day, see? So she came into the house to buy and she saw how our house was, and she liked it. It all happened quickly. She had an argument with her husband; they weren't legally married.

You know, she was really a very pretty woman and hot as a furnace. She had a good shape, the girl was very well built and a fellow gets hot, he wants to have her, eh? Well, the thing was arranged in a wink of an eye and she came over to live in my house, since I was alone at the time, just with the kids.

When her husband called me, I thought my last moment had arrived. I never carry a weapon. So I said to him, "Now, look here . . . your wife came to my house to work as a servant. If you want, you can go in and get her. It's all right with me if you go and get her, if she wants to go back with you, but I know she doesn't." Just like that, face to face. Well, he didn't get mad, he didn't swear at me like a lot of them do, they pull a gun and kill you on the spot. But I took a great risk.

Twice he stopped me in the street; it was nighttime. I thought, "Here it is, now anything can happen." Because these people from Jalisco have the reputation of being killers. So anyhow, she moved her things out of his place, though she really had nothing. He was very stingy. It's good to be thrifty, but you shouldn't go too far. Too much of anything is harmful. Well, anyway, she came to live with me. And don't think she was scared, because she had quite a temper. She was very young, only fifteen, but when she decided to do something, she did it. And she wasn't afraid of him at all.

She took care of my children like she was their mother. She loved them and protected the girls when the boys tried to beat them. Consuelo and Roberto felt their mother's death more than the other two. Manuel played in the courtyard and forgot. He went to school but didn't show much aptitude, like his son Alanes now. He didn't want to study and was slow in school. Roberto and Marta were worse. The only one who learned was Consuelo. She was quiet and obedient and didn't have friends. She didn't give me trouble until later. But the boys couldn't look at Elena. They made life hard for her.

Today we have the same situation with María taking care of Manuel's four children. Of course, I am here to see that the children behave themselves and respect María. She doesn't do much for them, but at least she looks after them a little. That's how Elena was and one feels grateful. There is no way to repay them. How is it possible not to like and respect a person like that?

Elena lived with me for five years. I had no children with her. But there are some things I can't begin to understand. Why is it that when one meets a person who is good and useful, who helps so much, she has to get sick and die?

She was very Catholic and asked me to call a priest to marry us, so I did. I did it because she wanted me to, not because I believed her soul would burn in Purgatory. No, I don't believe that. And I'll say something else. When one is healthy, one doesn't think of even going to Mass, but when we are dying, we become cowardly toward God and the Church. That's when we confess and call a priest. It is fear of the unknown and repentance for all the bad we did in our life.

While Elena was ill, I didn't earn enough money in the restaurant to support my family so I began to sell birds and raise pigs. I met a woman in the market who had a large corral on the outskirts of the city, in Ixmiquilpan. I asked her to rent me a part of it. I bought some lumber and built a small pig sty. Then I bought some pigs for twenty-five *pesos* and sold them for one hundred. There in Ixmiquilpan they sell pigs very cheap, but I bought pigs of fine race and I made good *centavos* from them. From each pig I slaughtered, I got six to eight hundred *pesos*. I sold one pig for fifteen hundred *pesos*. The others charged ten *pesos* for a stud pig but I charged fifty *pesos* for my stud because it was a Chester White crossed with a Jersey, very white and pretty. That little pig earned good money for me, too, and left good litters there in Ixmiquilpan. Fifty *pesos* was a lot to charge, but it was because the pig cost me four hundred. He was four months old when I bought him and he grew nicely. I bathed and fed him every day. There was a pond of crystal-clear water right next to the sty and all I had to do was dip in the pail and throw water over the pigs. That's how I bathed them. For years, I would go daily to my pig sty to feed and bathe the pigs.

Then, one day I bought some National Lottery tickets and I won two thousand five hundred *pesos*. I was sitting here when Lupita's daughter came and said, "*Papá,* there is a man in the El Dorado Colony who wants to sell his lot with two rooms. He wants two thousand five hundred *pesos*."

"It's a lot of money." I said, "Take me there. If I'm going to make this deal, let's do it right now." I went and spoke to the man. I said, "Let me have it for two thousand *pesos*. I have no money." I asked him if he would take a pig as the balance.

He said, "Well, all right, let's see the pig."

Then he asked me how much I wanted for it. It was a stud pig, a cross of a Chester White with Jersey. I said, "Give me twelve hundred *pesos*."

He said, "No, too expensive. I'll give you eight hundred."

"He's yours," I said. With the 1,700 *pesos* I had left from my winnings, we closed the deal and the next day I went to the company that sold the lots. I signed the contract and that's how it was done, all straight, clean and legal.

A few days later I sold another pig, bought some building materials and began to work on the new house. Meanwhile, I kept going out to my pig sties every day at the other end of the city. Rain or shine, tired as I was, I would get on the bus practically asleep from exhaustion and not find a seat, I would ride that bus standing up, asleep on my feet. But you should see the house I built. Should I tell you its a palace? Well, for a man like me who has never had anything . . .

And in all that hard work, my sons never helped me.

Later I bought that lot in Ixmiquilpan Colony and began to build a little house there so I could have my pig farm. If only God would help me with another lottery prize! The house would be for my children. I'd like to divide up the lot in four.

Yes, I beat the boys hard, especially Roberto, because he began to take things from the house. If I work hard to buy this table, and I come home and its gone . . . who is not going to punish a thing like that? And twice they put me out of my house because of the boys. Once, because they made too much noise skating in the courtyard, and on Cuba Street for breaking a water pipe. Roberto was a daredevil and violent, like his mother.

I kept the girls in the house and watched over the boys, to see that they didn't catch anything and bring a disease into the house. When their grandmother or someone washed the laundry, I examined the boys' underwear. Once, when they were older, I found a piece of absorbent cotton in a corner and I made both boys pull down their pants so I could examine them. But they never caught any venereal disease. That is an important point about them. Being their father, I could never speak frankly to them, but I watched.

Well, I don't understand my sons. You can see that here they have a home which they can use to improve themselves, to learn a trade, to study. Why don't they do it? I improved my lot. I live better than I did thirty years ago. Why don't they? Because they don't have the will power, that's all. They like to be lazy. Tell me, what more could they ask for? Other boys would have been only too glad to have the big help I gave these two. I've spent my life working for them. I never failed in my duty as a father. I never shirked my responsibilities, never put them aside. No matter what it was, they could count on me, whether it's a doctor at midnight or at dawn, or money for this or money for that or to pay for medicine.

To tell you the truth, I don't know where I get this feeling of mine that makes me want to keep up with my responsibilities, to meet all my obligations. Here I was, a poor illiterate, a peasant, without any education—I could have left them for good when their mother died, right? But I didn't.

I already had Lupita and she'd had a girl or two. But she lived down there on Rosario Street and I didn't want to bring anybody to live at home so there wouldn't be any trouble with the kids. I gave that some thought. You see, you need someone at home who can take care of your clothes, do things for you, serve you a hot cup of coffee, things I didn't have at home because there was no one to do them. Grandma helped me a lot and she did take care of the children. But she got mad when Elena came. She had no reason to, because this girl did the work for all of us, not for me alone. However, one day my brothers-in-law told me Grandma had moved out of the house, that she was very sorry and one thing and another. I said to them, "What do you want me to do, really? You see how things are, you know the situation, and even though you say you are their uncles and like the children a lot, you haven't come even once to bring your nephews a mug of coffee. I go to work every day, I never miss a day, so I can't be working and taking care of the kids at the same time. I've got to find somebody, and you can get as sore about it as you like." I couldn't take them over to Lupita's. Half-brothers and half-sisters living with stepfathers and stepmothers almost never get along well together.

I love my sons and Consuelo but I can no longer treat them with affection. They have made me spend a lot of money uselessly. When Roberto was in the Penitentiary, it cost me 1,200 *pesos*. When he was in the army, he asked me to arrange his transfer to Mexico City. I spoke to a captain and it would have cost money so I didn't take another step. After all, Roberto had joined up voluntarily. He didn't want to work, so he joined the army! I don't know how much they paid him. Never did they tell me things. Never did they say, "*Papá*, I am going to make so much, here is some for you." Nothing! Never anything. I have sons, yet it is as though I didn't have them. But in spite of that and the fact that they are now men, I still watch over them. I scold them and let them know when they do something bad. I am always thinking of them and when I don't see them, I ask about them.

Manuel is the father of five children and he still doesn't want to open his eyes. To get him to do the slightest thing for them, it costs me too much effort and too many sermons. With the help I have given him all these years he should have his own house by now, or be able to rent another room for his children. He went into partnership with a fellow in the market and he claims his partner ran off with their money, leaving a debt of five thousand *pesos*. But I don't believe a word he says. It's bad for a person to be telling lies all the time. Even when they tell you the truth you don't believe them. They try to convince you that the next day they will turn over a new leaf. But they don't fool me any more. I'm their father and I know them.

Consuelo has made me suffer because of her strong character. She is a headstrong girl, like her mother. She was jealous of Antonia. You know that usually half-sisters or brothers don't get along well and they fight. Well, in our house there were no fights because I was right there in the middle of it. I had to bring Antonia to the Casa Grande because her mother worked at night and there were certain difficulties. Antonia grew up alone and was going to the dogs. I had to lock her in a room to keep her from going to dances and cabarets. I had never given her anything, absolutely nothing, but she sought me out and naturally I had to pay attention to the girl. I bought her a few clothes and things and, unfortunately, that bothered Consuelo and the others.

As much as I talk to Consuelo and give her advice, she doesn't listen. She doesn't give me a *centavo*. I don't want anything for myself. I want absolutely nothing from my children. Thank God, I am working for everybody. What I build is for them. If she gives me anything, it would be put aside to pay for a lot to build a house for them.

Imagine my heartache when Consuelo wired me from Monterrey a few years ago. I didn't have a *centavo* and had to borrow seven hundred *pesos*, a hundred here and a hundred there. I went and spent seven hundred *pesos* and there was no need to spend that money. Seven hundred *pesos* is a fortune. And then I left my work which I never do, even in vacation time.

I made a big mistake in not moving far away when I got together with Delila. You know, when the children are grown they get angry if the father marries again. I read the other day that a mother was beaten up by her two sons because she married a second time. And in Mexicali the sons killed their father when he married again, but in that case it was because of the inheritance. They must have been savages to do that, or very drunk! I should be grateful because even though I have not always conducted myself at the high level a father should, my sons have never answered back or mistreated me.

When Claudia worked for us, Consuelo said, "Get married, *papá*." Well, I got married and things changed. Her reaction was very different. It hurt me a lot. It is because my children don't realize that, rich or poor, we need each other's help. Only now are they beginning to learn what life is like, that alone one cannot do a thing. They think because today they are strong, they will need no help tomorrow. But two sticks burn better than one!

This Claudia was very light and pretty and plump. She was fifteen or eighteen and I was thinking of marrying her. But Delila was living there then and she was cleverer. When a person sets out to get something, if he has a little intelligence, he gets it. To tell the truth, there were two things involved for me. It wasn't just my sex life I was thinking about, but I needed someone for the children. Claudia wanted to stay with me but when she noticed that Delila already was big with child, she went away to her people.

I did a bad thing when I chased out Consuelo. She went off with that fellow out of anger, pure anger, but it wasn't I whom she punished, it was herself who was hurt. I said, "My little daughter, you stained your life forever."

I went to the boy's house and spoke to his mother. He said he would get a divorce and marry her. He promised a mountain of things but it was all a lie. He was one of those lazy fellows who didn't like to work or bring money home. That, and Consuelo's character and . . . nothing happened. Now my daughter must make her own way.

And just think of it, these three little girls of Marta! I worry about Marta a lot. Look what bad luck she's had. It was lack of experience and because she didn't want to listen to advice. I told her to go ahead and live with Crispín because she already had two little girls with him. She cried and didn't want to for some reason or other. I don't know why. But as her father, I couldn't tell her to get out with her kids and see how they would make out, could I? It's a question of luck. It's like a lottery, sometimes you win, sometimes you lose. The world is full of these things. There are thousands of cases like mine.

Will power and the tremendous love I have for my little grand-daughters is what is keeping me going, with the help of God. I rest only one day a year, May 1. There are always financial problems. You pay in one place and you owe in another. I'd like to leave a little house for each of my children when I die. With the building I'm now doing, I need lots of money. Why, man alive, with fifty or a hundred extra *pesos* I get, I can buy a load of sand and rocks and little by little finish that house I'm going to leave for my children, so they'll have a place to live. What father would struggle the way I do to build a house, a room, to leave to sons who have turned out to be bums?

I do not fail to recognize my mistakes and my suffering is because of the bad atmosphere my children lived in. What can I blame: My own bad luck? My lack of experience in life? The absence of a guide? I don't know but I don't stop. I keep on going like a *burro* with a load on his back. I established my home with much effort, much work. What wouldn't I give for my sons to do the same. I would live happier than a millionaire to see them working honorably and supporting themselves.

About religion, well, you see, I got this religion of mine from my parents and of course a man who studies, a man who is educated, has a different point of view concerning religion. And from the way I see things, I criticize the attitude of my people, Mexican Catholics, because they do a lot of foolish things. My way of being a Catholic is like this—I seldom go to church but I'm still a Catholic. I don't like to go out and shoot off firecrackers and bring flowers to the saints and things like that so everybody will know I'm a Catholic. I'm a Catholic in my own way and it suits me just fine. As for other religions, I think they're all right because people don't go and get themselves drunk and killing one another and all the things my fellow countrymen do, the crazy things they do in order to show they're Catholics. Not for me, I don't like it.

Like a priest said in church a short while ago, God doesn't want candles, he doesn't need all these things, what he wants are more good deeds. The rest of the stuff is unnecessary. So that's the way it is with these people. Leave me out, is what I say.

No, I don't believe our souls will suffer in Purgatory. Who has been there and returned to tell us? We need proof. I say this cup is round and white because I am looking at it. But who can tell us about his experiences in Purgatory? No, God has given no one permission to return. If there is a God, I'll know it soon enough when I die, and I'm sure to go.

People say witchcraft exists, but I've never seen it, perhaps because no woman has ever put a hex on me. It could be that I've just been lucky because they say a jealous woman will stop at nothing; yes, she's capable of murder and these things happen all the time.

I'm told there are people with special power in their eyes and the mother of a doctor, the one who operated on me, told me about a very curious case. Some people who lived in Toluca had a bird that sang, a very pretty thrush, and a woman came by and said, "Señora, sell me your thrush," she says, "I think it's a fine bird." So the other one says, "No, Señora, I'm not going to sell it, it's mine." She says, "I got it as a gift." So the woman says, "You better sell it to me because when I leave, the bird will die." Well, so the woman left and she'd scarcely gone when the bird dropped dead. So maybe there are people with a special power in their eyes.

I once went to Pachuca to see a woman because they told me some one had put a hex on me. One of these women who sell birds knows a curer over there, but all they do is take your money, you understand. There's no such thing as witchcraft, it's foolishness, not witchcraft, because any one who leaves his money there is a fool.

Now as for my problem, I couldn't get an erection, see? I was fine with Elena, but sometimes I couldn't get an erection with Lupita and with Lenore. But, of course, any time you abuse something it's harmful. You drink a lot of alcohol and you go under, you're dead in a few days, eh? Well, it's natural, if you abuse your sex life you can't help getting a bit weak. Now add to this the two hernia operations I've had. The doctor told me some delicate parts were cut, and this weakens a man and his member. My doctor, Santoyo, told me about a fellow who liked to screw a lot; he used to live right here, and was very young, but he loved to do it. Well, he told me he's given injections to him and to boys of fifteen and sixteen who were all petered out. They sure must have led a terrible life, those unlucky kids, and now what good are they? Like I say, I'm still in pretty good shape.

Once a homeopathic doctor told me women are more passionate than men. And that's why, when you are with a Mexican woman—I don't know anything about the others—the longer you are with her and the more you give her, the more she wants. You can't satisfy them, they're very hot. There are some women that have to have a man every day.

Well, as I said, I went to Pachuca, and the *curandera* told me to bring a turkey egg, and stuff like that, and she took something else and started to "cleanse" me and do various things. She charged me ten, fifteen *pesos* each visit. I went five or six times. But I didn't improve. The trouble I had was not the result of witchcraft; it was a case of sexual weakness.

I don't know how I got the idea it was witchcraft. Some women . . . well, you see, I think it was over there where I was working, and here in the *vecindad* too. And, well, you understand, it's a pretty mean trick to disappoint a woman when you're already in bed with her, you feel ashamed. A lot of them grab hold of you and give you a rough time, they give you a beating. Of course, no woman beat me. Why, I'd leave Mexico City if that happened!

I didn't go back to Pachuca because I saw it didn't do any good and my condition was the same. You see, the trouble is I need the kind of woman I can have complete confidence in, one who will kiss and fondle me. Of course, I've had a lot of wear and tear. I'm tired and in my sex life I've had several women. I'm not a boy of twenty, so I need some fondling. Just let a woman caress me and I do all right. I need a feeling of security, like in this room, if somebody interrupts, if I hear a noise or somebody speaking, then I'm through, I can't do a thing.

With Delila, we put the mattress on the floor, but I make sure all the kids are asleep because it would be setting a bad example for them. Very bad. Just on account of what they see, it's terrible living in these tenements here in Mexico City. Many women take off what they put on when they're menstruating and throw it over in a corner. And little boys and girls see it. So they go on learning, and after a while they know everything, because they've seen everything at home.

It's hard for a man to satisfy a Mexican woman. I've been told personally, "Oh, *querido*, you've quit on me and I'm not halfway through." Just like that, can you imagine. "Well, look, *mi vida*, I better get you a length of pipe because I'm finished now." That's the way Mexican women are. I've heard that some women who are happily married and always behave very well at home, go out once in a while and look around, discreetly, and find themselves a lover because their husbands don't satisfy them. I've run into several like that. A fellow can't satisfy them.

I take care of myself. Twice a week and like they say, the vulgar

way, you give them a couple of jabs. That's about all I do, because
I've never been very potent sexually. Even when I was younger I
didn't overdo it, understand? Once or twice at most, and I mean
once or twice a week, and not every day. You see I'm sort of puny, or
let's put it, I'm not very strong, and naturally on account of I didn't
eat very well when I was a child, I think I'm affected by it today, in
my sex life. I've practically stopped my sex life with Lupita a few years
ago. But with Delilia its different. Even though I'm old, she likes me
a lot, really. She's a hard-working girl who is worth her weight in gold,
believe me. An honest woman, hard-working. Yes, Lupita was also very
decent, she was, and honest. You never heard her say a bad word,
you never heard her say anything. Once she did get mad when she
found out about this thing with Delila, and I talked to her, see?
seriously: "There's no reason for you to make such a fuss," I said. "In
the first place, you've got board and lodging, which not everybody
has. I've had two daughters by you, all right, they're working now,
they can take care of themselves. So if you keep on nagging me about
this, you'll have to get out of here and you don't get any more expense
money from me. I'll turn this place over to one of the boys if you
don't want to stay here." She became very angry. She had been in bed
about two or three months with rheumatism. Of course, a fellow feels
guilty up to a certain point, but, well, I ask you, what would I do
with my four grandchildren, practically abandoned if it weren't for
Delila, who has been a mother to them, their second mother.

They all need shoes right now. My other two little ones need clothes,
money for a doctor, for medicine. Delila is pregnant again. If I had
money I would like to have her operated . . . to have her tubes tied
up . . . so that she cannot have more children. I spoke to her about
it although I don't have the money. I belong to Social Security but we
don't use their hospital or services; I lose a lot of time there, as much
as half a day. The baby cannot be born there because I am not married
to Delila. I would have to present a paper from the Civil Register to
get her in. That's why I say that one of these days I may marry
Delila . . . for the children. It is because the Maternity Hospital gives
good care.

I have to designate my beneficiary to my union, because when I die,
there will be a four-thousand-*peso* benefit. I am thinking of putting
down Marta's name for that. Delila will get the house and property
in Ixmilquilpan for the children. I have only to arrange all the papers.

If it weren't for Delila, what would I do? She had a hard life, worse than mine, because the poor thing received blows from the father of her son Geofredo. He was a drunkard and didn't want to work. Poor girl! With me she lives quietly, she lives well, and I hope things don't change. She is a woman who can work hard and who deserves help. When Manuel's children were small, she came to take care of them. She left for a month or two because she got sore at them. Actually, it was on account of Consuelo, and she became very, very angry. But Delila came back.

I think about these things and I know what's involved, but like I told you before, sometimes you do things just to get along, not for your own pleasure, not because of sex desire. I'm not twenty any more or twenty-five. Sure, I can still function a bit, but believe me the children also had something to do with this situation because if I didn't ask her to come here to this house, my grandchildren would have died of hunger—abandoned and dirty.

My son Manuel isn't a father, he's not worth anything, in my opinion he might just as well be dead. So I carry the whole burden, the responsibility for his kids and mine. When he went to the U.S.A., he sent me only $150. I've got to pay all the expenses and I've got to find a way, whether I'm tired or not, I have to go out and get money for these kids. One of them gets sick, you have to call the doctor. Another gets sick, you have to get the doctor. So what shall I do? Throw them out into the street? No, I can't do it.

The biggest mistake we Mexicans make is to marry so young, without money, without savings and even before we have a steady job. We marry and have a houseful of children before we know it, and then we're stuck and can't possibly get ahead. To tell the truth, we Mexicans lack preparation for life.

There are lots of cases of abandonment of children in Mexico. It happens all the time. The government should take a hand in the matter and put a stop to it. I wish we had laws in Mexico, in my country, like you have in the United States. We wouldn't have so many bums . . . all this rotten treatment of people, speaking frankly, all of this is bad for children, for people, for the whole country. All of this freedom is bad for people. They should close up 80 percent of the saloons, build more schools, close up 80 percent of these places that breed vice. There should be more control over youngsters, over youth, rich and poor alike. "O.K., tell me, how many children do you have?" "Well, four." "How old are they? Fifteen and up, right? What do your children do, who supports them, how do they spend their time, where do they work?" "Well, they're not working." "Why aren't they working? You make them go to work and if you don't, you'll get a week in jail to start with." No bribes, a week in jail, and when it happens the second time, then it'll take a year and you'd see how much more orderly everything would be and how the Mexican people would behave more decently if we had stricter laws, because the laws we have here in my country are very loose. The Mexican people are going under, because there's no leadership and no faith, and there's so much lousy corruption, as you can see.

If we ever got a really tough government here, and it called up everyone who had been a president and said, "You go to the Zócalo and pile up all the millions you've robbed from the people," why, there'd be enough to build another capital!

You have to live among our families to see what we suffer from and how it can be cured. They haven't made a thorough study of the problem. Those gentlemen who rule over us have expensive cars and many millions in the bank, but they don't see what's underneath where the poor people live. Why, they won't drive over to look from their cars. They stay down there in the center of town where all the fashionable stores are, but as for the sections where the poor live . . . they just don't know what a miserable life we lead. They disregard this great and deep problem which exists in Mexico today. They disregard the fact that right here in the capital there are lots of people who eat only one or two meals a day.

There is not enough money, not enough work and everything is so expensive; prices went up again today. The cost of living has gone up a great deal within a few days. For example, take a family with eight, or six mouths to feed. How are you going to support them on a wage of eleven *pesos* a day? True, they've raised the minimum wage a *peso* a day. What does a *peso* amount to if the stuff you buy has gone up three or four times? Well, that's the way it is. We need different rulers who can make a better study of Mexico's problem and do something for the people, for the worker and the peasant, because they are the ones who most need help. Take a worker in the capital for example, if he gets two hundred *pesos* on pay day, he'll throw away 150 or 180 in the saloon and take twenty *pesos* home. People don't know how to use the money they earn. Poor mothers, and the kids half naked! You see kids five and ten years old with tuberculosis.

What do you think is the reason? Lack of care by the parents in the home, lack of responsibility and lack of money. They spend more out on the street on foolish things than they do for what's needed at home. There are very few fathers who try to meet their obligations. A fellow who is halfway decent and tries to do what he's supposed to, he'll find some way to make out, one way or another, he'll bring some bread home to his family.

I've gone so far as to tell some people I'd like to see us have an American president here in Mexico. Then we'd see how Mexico would change and make progress. He'd pull in all the bums, all the tramps. "You don't like to work? Off you go to the Islas Marías for the rest of your life." None of this passing out a little money and this and the other and back they come. No sir, they stay right there. They're parasites.

Yes, there has been progress and some have benefited, thanks to the governments that have concerned themselves with the workers. But they never helped me! My situation is better because of my pigs and the lottery. I have been very lucky in the lottery. I won my first prize with No. 9878. I never forget the numbers that have given me prizes. With that money I bought the radio. With the same number I won again and I bought the bed. My biggest prize was five thousand *pesos*, which I won with No. 19228. With part of that money I built my house in El Dorado. And with the rest of the money, I bought the wall clock. The little I had, I used well and it helped me get ahead.

But in the thirty years I've been in Mexico City, the life of the poor people has changed very little, very little. Some of them call it a big change when, for example, they used to make one or one and a half *pesos* during the Calles period, which was very little, right? But then sugar and beans cost fifteen *centavos*. Now take beans; you make eleven *pesos* and beans cost from three to four *pesos*. That's a fact! So where is the improvement? Now, for example, you have things which cost twenty *pesos* yesterday and they've gone up to thirty-five. All right, so for one reason or another they reduce it two *pesos*. So you say something, and they tell you, "Why, no, sir, if it was thirty-five yesterday and it's thirty-three today, we've reduced the price." Reduced the price . . . with an increase of thirteen *pesos*! That's the way they reduce prices here today. So what's the advantage for the people, for the worker, for the peasant? None at all, the way I see it. On the contrary, every day they're squeezing us more. So what?

We need officials who study and take a look at what's going on in the home of a poor family and actually see the misery in which people are living, and how they're practically dying of hunger. Why don't they do it? Why do thousands and thousands of farm hands leave Mexico? Here you have a proof you can put your fingers on. Because there's no security here, because wages are terribly low, miserable wages which aren't enough to support any family. Naturally, people have to scout around for a job where they can make a little more and bring something home to their families.

The political gang won't let good men run. They've got these gangs here, like everywhere. When Alemán was running, as I found out—you always find out a lot of things, right?—a lot of propaganda money went to the people who sell narcotics, also to the bus owners, the bus monopoly. They told them, "If we win, we'll let you raise the fares five *centavos.*" He won and the fares went up.

And the trade-union leaders don't help either, everything right into their pockets. Take my union, one of those fellows owns one or two houses and sixteen taxicabs. There's nothing to hope for there. No, sir! I pay five *pesos* a month dues in my union. But there are lots of us, thousands. When somebody dies, we give another five *pesos* apiece for the family of the dead man, in addition to the five *pesos* every month. What do we get in return? Nothing! We haven't had a convention for years. All we get are dues slips. They deduct on payday. So if you owe for two slips, it's ten *pesos.* If somebody has kicked the bucket, another five *pesos.* So I tell the fellow, "Does this go to the dead man or to a live person?" He says, "A live person, of course, are you kidding?" Then I tell him, "Listen, I don't know what you're doing with my money that you keep deducting; we're making very little and everything is so dear nowadays, so the money doesn't go far. It looks like people are dying too often here." And that's the way it goes.

I do not see that the unions help the worker much. I see the *Sindicato* as a cave, a trap, to exploit the mass of workers. The leaders become rich with the workers' money and I ask myself why the government allows such a thing. Isn't it possible to arrange things in favor of the workers without having leaders? If the government could eliminate the unions and make special departments to work out matters between the workers and the bosses, all that money they collect every month from the workers' dues could be used to build schools, hospitals, and other things for the workers' children, instead of buying cars and homes for the leaders.

I am not an educated man but I see that before the workers were exploited in one way and now they are exploited in another way, and will go on being exploited. Naturally, Mexico has progressed, but the worker continues to be a worker and continues to be poor, and will be until he dies, because when he gets a raise of fifty *centavos*, food goes up one, two, five *pesos*. So the raise doesn't help the worker, it only hurts him because there is no effective control.

That's why I don't worry myself about anything but my work. I don't know potatoes about politics. I read one or two paragraphs in the newspapers, but I don't take it seriously. Nothing in the news is important to me. A few days ago I read something about the leftists. But I don't know what is the left or what is the right, or what is communism. I am interested in only one thing . . . to get money to cover my expenses and to see that my family is more or less well. The worker should only see that his family has what it needs, that there should be food at home. Politics is very complicated and let those who were born to it take care of it. If there is a third world war, the gentlemen who provoked it will go to the grave along with millions of others. I don't worry much about it.

I don't understand this business of communism. This communist commotion started in Russia, didn't it? They had a war there, they killed the czars and all of that. Lenin and that other fellow, Trotsky, killed a lot of people there. The other fellow died, or they threw him out, this fellow, what was his name? Stalin. They say they couldn't stand him any more and I think they bumped him off because he was getting ready for another slaughter, another purge in the army. He was quite a killer, this fellow was. How can they kill so many people, I ask you?

I would like to visit Russia, even for one month, to travel all over the country to personally see how the worker lives and to find out if socialism or communism benefits him. According to the newspapers, they are worse off than in Mexico, so I doubt that communism is good for the proletariat. But since I never go to Russia or anywhere else, how can I really know?

I suppose they also have a gang over there that runs the country, according to the papers, don't they? Here the PRI (*Partido Revolucionario Institucional*) runs everything, so if there's another candidate they stick a machine gun in his face. So who won? Well, the PRI candidate. That's all there is to it. Like now its López Mateos, and the

PRI says this and that and the other thing, he's the candidate, he's already president. It's a sure thing.

Things must be different in the U.S. Well, maybe it's better that we just have one gang running the country here, because it's got a pistol in each hand. Don't you know this story about two fellows who were playing cards and one had two aces and the other fellow asks him, "What do you have?" "Two aces. And you?" "Two pistols." So he says, "O.K., you win." And that's the way the PRI is here; it's got the pistols and anybody who objects, well, he gets run over by a car.

And as far as there being any protection for the rights of people who live in the country, the peasant keeps on eating beans out of an earthenware pot and hot peppers which he mashes on a stone slab, that's all the peasant eats, and he goes around half naked all his life. He doesn't make any progress, he doesn't get ahead. If the government happens to be a decent fellow, the gangs that control him won't let him do anything. Anytime there's a good man who wants to do something for the people, the other fellows won't let him.

There's nothing dirtier than politics. It's pretty rotten, and there's been a lot of bloodshed too, and who knows what else. How many people die so a man can get into power? Things are muddled up, not aboveboard, I'd say. Of course, the people have no education, they're ignorant, they're like a flock following wherever the shepherd leads them. He tells them, you go this way, and they go this way, you go that way, and they go that way. You should see how they act in the unions when there's a meeting. They tell them this, that and the other. All those in favor? Everybody votes in favor. They don't even know what they voted in favor of. The other month we got two dues slips. What for? Well, you voted in favor of it, didn't you? You see how it is? The people, the masses, follow any spellbinder who comes along; as a result, instead of things getting better for them, they are worse off. And if sometimes you want to talk to them, try to make them understand, reason with them and show them what they're going to vote for is against their interests, they won't even listen to you.

They listen to the follow who's on top, sitting behind the desk, even though he's not doing them any good, see? Then they applaud him. So how are you going to straighten things out. What can you do?

Now besides all of that, the Mexican people have no unity. They're not united, one pulls in one direction, the other in another and so on. If people would unite, in union there's strength, they say, then things would change. I know in other countries, if they don't like a president, they toss a nice little bomb and you have a different president. Not here. That's what they should do here, but they don't. A bit of cyanide, a heart attack, yes, there's what many of our presidents and governors and police chiefs need. Well, it's not nice to say so and admit it because they are my compatriots, eh? they're Mexicans, but like I told you a little while ago, the truth will always out.

I struggled and worked day and night to establish my home, a poor home, as you can see, but I have my happy moments with my grandchildren. It is first for God and then for my grandchildren that I'm on my feet, plugging away. When I'm downtown, I'm careful about traffic. At my age, it isn't myself I have to watch out for, but the kids. I won't be able to give them very much but at least they go on living and growing and I hope God will allow me to be with them until they can earn their own living.

I want to leave them a room, that's my ambition; to build that little house, one or two rooms or three so that each child will have a home and so they can live there together. But they don't want to help me. I asked God to give me the strength to keep struggling so I won't go under soon and maybe finish that little house. Just a modest place that they can't be thrown out of. I'll put a fence around it and no one will bother them. It will be a protection for them when I fall down and don't get up again.

OSCAR LEWIS was born in New York City in 1914 and grew up on a small farm in Upstate New York. He received his Ph.D. in anthropology from Columbia University in 1940; he taught at Brooklyn College and Washington University, and has been a professor of anthropology at the University of Illinois since 1948. He has also been the recipient of various distinguished fellowships and grants.

From his first visit to Mexico in 1943, Mexican peasants and city dwellers have been among his major interests. His book *Life in a Mexican Village: Tepoztlán Restudied* initiated a whole new trend in independent restudies in anthropology. In addition to *The Children of Sánchez*, his other studies of Mexican life include *Five Families, Pedro Martínez* and *A Death in the Sánchez Family*. He is also the author of *La Vida: A Puerto Rican Family in the Culture of Poverty—San Juan and New York* (available in Vintage Books), which received the National Book Award. A further study of Puerto Rican culture, *Six Women*, will be published early in 1970.

Oscar Lewis has published articles in anthropological and other journals, many of which have been collected in *Anthropological Essays* (1969).

Professor Lewis is now in Cuba on a research program to study family and community life.